Contents

This Work is Dedicated by all its Authors to the Memory of

JERZY WRÓBLEWSKI 1926–1990

Colleague, co-author and friend of us all, a scholar of unsurpassed rigor and analytical insight, he had great physical and moral courage, tested alike in time of war and in time of peace. Educated at the Jagiellonian University of Kraków, he took up his chair at Łódz as a very young man, and served his University devotedly as professor and as rector; in difficult political circumstances, he retained unimpeachable integrity as scholar and as citizen, and conducted himself as a faithful friend of liberty and academic freedom. His tragically early death came at the moment at which political change and the challenge of a new appointment had opened to him the opportunity to develop long-considered themes in moral and political philosophy as well as seeing into print an English edition of his leading work in jurisprudence. His family has lost a kind husband and father; his colleagues a dear friend whose austerity of manner served only to disguise but not conceal the warmth of his affection; and the international community of legal scholarship a distinguished and distinctive member. He is greatly missed among us.

Series Preface

The objective of the Dartmouth Series in Applied Legal Philosophy is to publish work which adopts a theoretical approach to the study of particular areas or aspects of law or deals with general theories of law in a way which focusses on issues of practical moral and political concern in specific legal contexts.

In recent years there has been an encouraging tendency for legal philosophers to utilize detailed knowledge of the substance and practicalities of law and a noteworthy development in the theoretical sophistication of much legal research. The series seeks to encourage these trends and to make available studies in law which are both genuinely philosophical in approach and at the same time based on appropriate legal knowledge and directed towards issues in the criticism and reform of actual laws and legal systems.

The series will include studies of all the main areas of law, presented in a manner which relates to the concerns of specialist legal academics and practitioners. Each book makes an original contribution to an area of legal study while being comprehensible to those engaged in a wide variety of disciplines. Their legal content is principally Anglo-American, but a wide-ranging comparative approach is encouraged and authors are drawn from a variety of jurisdictions.

TOM D. CAMPBELL
Series Editor
The Faculty of Law
The Australian National University

Preface and Acknowledgements

A group of scholars who subsequently called themselves 'The Comparative Statutory Interpretation Group' (and finally the 'Bielefelder Kreis') gathered together for the first time to discuss issues of interpretation in August 1983 at Helsinki during the IVR World Congress in Philosophy of Law and Social Philosophy. Their idea was to compare ideas about interpretation in law, and to see if some kind of comparative study would be possible and worthwhile. The initiative was taken by Robert Summers after some discussions in the Italian Alps during the summer of 1982 about problems of interpretation with Aleksander Peczenik and Enrico Pattaro. The group which came together in Helsinki did so purely on the basis of individual interest and commitment, and had no official standing of any sort.

Various meetings were organized to take place coincidentally with a variety of international congresses (Lund 1983, Bologna, 1984, and the IVR World Congress at Athens, 1985). In 1985, it became clear that more time was required for discussions dedicated solely to the project, so a special meeting was organized in Edinburgh in August 1986, with the support of the Centre for Criminology and the Social and Philosophical Study of Law of Edinburgh University. Thereafter, the Zentrum für interdisziplinäre Forschung of the University of Bielefeld was approached for, and generously granted, substantial support for some further special meetings, and those took place in March 1988, March 1989 and June 1990, interspersed with two briefer meetings in Tampere in August 1988 and in Edinburgh in August 1989 (the latter coinciding with the 1989 IVR Congress).

Over the years, our group ultimately came to include Professor Aulis Aarnio (University of Helsinki, Finland), Professor Robert Alexy, (University of Kiel, West Germany), Mr Zenon Bankowski (University of Edinburgh, United Kingdom), Professor Gunnar Bergholz (University of Lund, Sweden), Professor Ralf Dreier

(University of Göttingen, West Germany), Professor Christophe Grzegorczyk (University of Paris, France), Dr Massimo La Torre (University of Bologna, Italy), Professor D. Neil MacCormick (University of Edinburgh, United Kingdom), Professor Enrico Pattaro (University of Bologna, Italy), Professor Aleksander Peczenik (University of Lund, Sweden), Professor Robert Summers (Cornell University, USA), Professor Michele Taruffo (University of Pavia, Italy), Professor Michel Troper (University of Paris, France), Professor Jerzy Wróblewski (University of Łódz, Poland), and Dr Enrique Zuleta-Puceiro (Buenos Aires, Argentina). (On 29 May, 1990, Professor Jerzy Wróblewski died, only 10 days before the final meeting of the group.) The project's principal outside advisor has been Dr Geoffrey Marshall of the Faculty of Politics, University of Oxford (The Queen's College). Persons who earlier participated as members of the group but were unable to continue are Professor Jan Hellner (University of Stockholm, Sweden) and Professor Jean Louis Gardies (University of Nantes). All of the foregoing group members are scholars and theorists of jurisprudence. In addition, Michele Taruffo is a comparativist. Robert Summers served as Chairman of the project and D. Neil MacCormick as Vice Chairman.

The main method of operation from the beginning has been to develop a set of common questions which each member would answer for his own legal system and exchange with other group members prior to each discussion meeting. Quite substantial guidelines for answering the questions were also prepared and circulated. In the course of time, we revised our common questions and guidelines, and also, of course, revised the sets of answers each of us had prepared. During the annual roundtable discussion sessions, which usually lasted two to four days, we addressed the common questions and the answers each of us had prepared for our own system. The Chairman prepared minutes of each of these meetings and circulated them, along with agreed redrafts of the common questions, and revisions of the guide to answering the questions. The most important key to an understanding of project method, and of the contents of the chapters devoted to interpretation in each country (Chapters 3–11 below) is provided by the questions, which in their final form, are printed as an Appendix to this book. (The guide is available on request).

After the Zentrum für interdisziplinäre Forschung of the University of Bielefeld became a sponsor of the project, several interdisciplinary advisors met with us annually. For 1988, these were Professor Hubert Rottleuthner, Free University of Berlin, legal sociology; Professor K. Cramer, University of Göttingen, philosophy; Professor Jan Van Dunné, University of Rotterdam, comparative law. For 1989, the interdisciplinary advisors were Professor John Bell, University of Leeds, comparative law; Dr James Evans, University of Auckland, philosophy and law, and Dr Geoffrey Marshall, all of whom met with us at the Edinburgh 1989 meeting. For 1990, Dr Geoffrey Marshall again met with the group in Bielefeld. At other stages in our project, Professors Reed Dickerson and William Popkin of Indiana University, Rudolf Schlesinger, Emeritus Professor of Comparative Law at Cornell Law School, Professor Hans A. Linde of the University of Oregon (former Justice Linde), Professor Herbert Hausmaninger of the University of Vienna, Professor Bernard Rudden of the University of Oxford and Professor Dieter Grimm of the University of Bielefeld provided valuable advice.

On 12–13 October 1989, Robert Summers visited the Max Planck Institute for Comparative Law at Hamburg, West Germany, where he discussed the work of the project and received valuable advice from Professors Ulrich Drobnig, Hein Kötz, Kurt Siehr and Dr H. Puttfarken. Documents recording details of this visit were circulated to all members.

The authors and co-editors of this book wish to thank Mr Harry Dutton of the Cornell Law School for extensive administrative and secretarial assistance over several years. They also wish to thank Mrs Jylanda Diles and the Cornell Law School Secretarial Staff for heroic assistance in the final stages of preparing the manuscript for the publisher. They wish to thank Mr John Hasko, Associate Law Librarian, Cornell Law School for much valuable assistance as well. The co-editors wish to thank Dorothy Summers for much assistance in the preparation of the final manuscript. They are also grateful to John Moscati, Jr., Cornell Law School Class of 1992 and Elizabeth Anne Summers, Cornell Law School Class of 1991 for performing various chores on the manuscript.

Professor Summers is also grateful to the Cornell Law School and Dean Russell Osgood for research support relating to the project.

The project members owe a profound debt of gratitude to the Zentrum für interdisziplinäre Forschung of the University of Bielefeld, and in particular to Dr Gerhard Sprenger of the Zentrum, and also to Professor Dieter Grimm of the Board of Directors of the Zentrum. The Zentrum and Dr Sprenger provided support without which the project could not have been completed.

We dedicate this book to the memory of Professor Jerzy Wróblewski.

D.N.M.   R.S.S.

A Special Note by Neil MacCormick

I have a particular mandate from all the authors of the papers printed here to express our collective sense of indebtedness and of gratitude to Robert Summers. His was the original inspiration that set our project on its way; his was the vision, energy and enthusiasm that kept the project going when it might have drifted to a standstill. Our meetings were always fruitful and good-natured, even though they involved debates among powerful personalities with strong, and sometimes divergent, opinions on the issues considered. The excellent and cooperatively creative atmosphere which prevailed had one primary source, in the unfailingly courteous, cheerful and good-natured convenership of Robert Summers. He also kept splendidly accurate records of our deliberations, and after each meeting circulated remarkably speedily copious notes of matters agreed for consideration at subsequent meetings.

In these circumstances, it was my wish as his present co-editor that our names should appear in this book in inverse alphabetical order, to make it quite clear to which editor the primary credit was due for the book. Having been overruled on that, I append this note to the preface in order that the truth of the matter shall nevertheless be clear.

Neil MacCormick
Loch Awe Village, Argyll, Scotland, August 1990

1 Introduction

ROBERT S. SUMMERS, *Ithaca*

As lawyers and legal theorists, we have found it extraordinarily interesting to take part in the international project which has yielded the following set of essays about statutory interpretation as a major field of legal reasoning considered in comparative and jurisprudential perspective. We hope here to convey the same sense of excitement to you, the reader. The published justifications appearing in opinions of the higher courts in Western legal systems comprise what is perhaps the greatest repository of recorded practical reasoning known to humankind. We remind the reader also of the absolutely central importance of statute law in modern legal systems; and thus of the equal importance of statutory interpretation.

It is hard enough to keep track of interpretational norms and practices in any single contemporary system of law. Yet this book takes a bold step into what may be a wilder Maelstrom of confusion by exploring questions of interpretation comparatively and jurisprudentially across a wide range of legal systems. The authors represent nine disparate systems — common law, civil law and mixed, East and West European, North and South American. Yet, for all this, the authors have maintained a common purpose and (to a considerable extent) a common approach. They all agreed on some key points of method (see Chapter 2) and all asked themselves the same basic questions in the same order. (See the Appendix). Then at group meetings held more or less annually over seven years, each contributor subjected everyone else's answers to constructive criticism. The questions themselves were worked out and revised several times through a similar process of group deliberation and debate, and in the light of the emerging answers.

So nine of the chapters, Chapters 3–11, here are 'country-by-country chapters', each dealing with interpretation in a particular national jurisdiction or jurisdictions. But those nine chapters, distinctive in style and legal–philosophical tradition though each is, have a common structure – that provided by the common questions, and by the fact that each chapter is an ordered set of responses to those questions. The authors are both lawyers, familiar with the legal systems reported, and scholars of jurisprudence and legal philosophy, with special interest in the theory of legal reasoning.

In the upshot, then, what do these labours of many hands offer? Chapters 3–11, one on each of the nine different countries represented, provide information and insight into interpretational practices as revealed in the published opinions of the higher courts of those countries. Also, these nine country-specific chapters and the two more general chapters at the end – Chapter 12 on comparative analysis, and Chapter 13 on justificatory theory – are all organized and presented largely in terms of a common general framework. Of central interest in this framework is the set of concepts and terminology we have devised for identifying, individuating and describing a wide range of types of arguments recognized and deployed by the various national judiciaries as reasons for decision.*

While, as we will shortly see, the two more general chapters at the end of the book, Chapters 12 and 13, presuppose and to a considerable extent address comparative and jurisprudential questions posed by the materials in the country-specific chapters, it should be stressed that these two more general chapters by no means purport to address all materials of general interest in Chapters 3–11. This is especially true of those materials in the country-specific chapters on the general origins of interpretational issues within legal systems, statutory gaps and gap-filling, the role of constitutional law, the effect of statutory provisions prescribing interpretative method, and the nature of collisions between statutes and other norms and how they are resolved. Yet the materials we have not been able to address frontally in Chapters 12 and 13 are not only informative; they, along with all the other country-specific materials, comprise an addition to the present-day comparative law 'database', and may now be used by comparativists as well as by legal theorists and scholars interested in statutory

---

*A leading American scholar of our subject once observed: 'It would be hard to think of a field of law that needs clarifying more than that of statutory interpretation.' He went on to stress 'the difficulty and even impossibility of conversing sensibly on statutory intepretation without elaborate precautions to establish or stabilize terms, concepts, and premises.' R. Dickerson, *The Interpretation and Application of Statutes* p. 1 (1975).

interpretation and justificatory theory as such.

We now come to the general Chapters 12 and 13 at the end of the volume. These chapters for the most part select from materials in the country-by-country chapters and generalize from them or use them as points of departure for comparative and jurisprudential analysis. This is not to say that the factual basis for generalizations and analyses in these later chapters is always fully spelled out in the earlier country-by-country chapters. Part of the factual basis for Chapters 12 and 13 appears instead in formal and informal minutes of our numerous roundtable discussions held over the years.

In Chapter 12, we set forth 11 major types of arguments and advance our 'universalist' thesis that all systems in our study share these as a common core of good reasons for interpretative decisions; to the extent there are variations we also argue that these are rationally explicable by reference to differences of political systems, of institutional frameworks, of judicial roles in relation to the legislature and the executive, of general legal culture and of traditions with respect to the training and staffing of the judiciary. We believe that our 'common core' thesis could be important, for at least three reasons. It implies (along with the rational explicability of variations) a common rationality rooted in shared values, a topic we treat in detail in Chapter 13. It also implies the feasibility of constructing an ideal normative model (necessarily elaborate) for the justified interpretation of statutes generally, or perhaps a set of such models each with discrete ranges of application the totality of which covers the field, a topic we introduce and discuss briefly in Chapter 13. On a less theoretical plane, the common general conception of good reasons has positive implications for major contemporary experiments in the unification of diverse and highly developed national legal systems, as in the current case of the European Community.

In the course of developing the common core of good reasons thesis, Chapter 12 provides some systematic treatment of the types of interpretational argument shared in the various countries. The key questions raised, and to some extent addressed, include the following: How are particular instances of a general type of argument conceived and constructed? What material content do they require? How widely available are such materials? What are the sources of the justificatory force of this type of argument? What factors may operate to weaken the force of such an argument? How does this type of argument differ from other closely related types of argument? What is the relative general decisional role of the type of argument within the system? What, if any, role can the type of argument have as directly reinforcing any other types of argument? What is the relative force of the argument when in conflict with other arguments? Does the type of argument have any distinctive use or limits? For example, does it play a special 'second order' role in the resolution of 'first order' conflicts between arguments? Finally, what does the argument have in common with any of the other types of argument? Can the various arguments be illuminatingly grouped under more discrete unifying categories? We think all of the above questions interesting and important, and some of them are relatively new questions in our subject.

But comprehensive treatment of all of these questions in regard to each type of argument has not been at all possible. Indeed to give these types of arguments their just due in the foregoing terms would require, at the very least, a whole chapter devoted to each. Some of the arguments, for example, the argument from ordinary meaning and the argument from legislative intention, might each require a whole monograph. In our view, scholars have traditionally underestimated the demands of the subject.

Chapter 12 on comparative analysis also identifies significant variations in types of arguments and patterns of justification in the different systems. It reveals major differences in the structure, logic and style of the opinions in the higher courts. For example, the higher judiciaries in about half the countries follow a magisterial approach in which opposing arguments are usually not recognized at all in the published opinions, while the other half take an argumentative approach in which opposing arguments are answered, with the opinions including, at least implicitly, dialogues with counsel, or with other members of the court, or with lower court judges. Further, most countries adopt a deductive rather than a discursive justificatory model. In the European panorama, a finding of some importance is the emergence of a new and distinctive justificatory style overall that borrows from both of the traditional systems − common law and civil law.

In regard to all major differences between systems, we also suggest how they are at least consistent with the hypothesis that they are both explained by, and rationally grounded in, political, institutional, cultural and other factors specially operative in the systems. Thus, in our view, these differences are not necessarily inconsistent with the common rationality we discern. At the same time, the analysis reveals in concrete terms how the interpretational practices of the judges of the higher courts of different countries may *rationally* vary, depending on the nature of the institutional, political and cultural worlds that the judges inhabit.

It is also a finding of some importance that the differences we discern in justificatory structure, logic, style and substance seldom track the traditional common law−civil law divide.

The materials in both Chapter 12 and Chapter 13 also explain and analyse basic patterns of justification that appear in the opinions of the higher courts. In the simplest pattern, one form of argument dominates, and usually this is either what we call the argument from ordinary meaning or the argument from technical meaning. A more complex pattern is essentially cumulative, and it takes two basic forms. In the first, arguments are usually cumulated to reinforce the argument from ordinary meaning or the argument from technical meaning. In the second, there is no viable linguistic argument and various other arguments are cumulated in its place to clarify and specify an appropriate statutory meaning. An interesting question that arises here is how far the overall force of cumulative argumentation may exceed the sum of its parts, that is, exceed the overall force of instances of types of argument if they were merely added together individually.

In the most complex pattern of all, arguments in favour of the decision are cumulated, and opposing arguments are overtly canvassed and rejected, with reasons. Another question of great jurisprudential and practical interest that is considered in some detail in Chapters 12 and 13 is how far the 'weighing and balancing' metaphor, so popular in American legal literature, accounts for the resolution of conflicts between arguments. It is our view that this metaphor felicitously applies to only *one* of four modes of resolution discoverable in the opinions of most countries.

Chapter 13 is more theoretical than Chapter 12, and also rather less comparative, though it necessarily builds on Chapter 12 and therefore also on Chapters 3—11 (which, as we have said, provide nearly all of the material for comparative analysis in Chapter 12). In Chapter 13, we distinguish between the basic idea governing the construction of particular instances of a type of interpretational argument on the one hand, and the underlying values that give rise to its justificatory force on the other. The idea governing the construction of a type of argument can be analysed into the circumstantial conditions ('directives', to use the late Professor Wroblewski's term) that must be present if an argument of that type is to be available or applicable in the first place.

In Chapter 13 (and also to a degree in Chapter 12) the wide-ranging primacy of arguments from ordinary usage and from technical usage is analysed and discussed. Arguments from systematic harmony and unity of the overall statute book and of the law generally are given a major place (a rather larger one than is usually acknowledged by US and UK scholars, for instance). Arguments from purpose are also put in their place.

Chapter 13 classifies all 11 of the major types of argument in terms of four basic kinds: linguistic, systematic, teleological—evaluative and intentional. We believe the factors unifying the types of arguments falling into each category cast special light on the basic character of the types of arguments involved. Also, in the case of the various appeals to intention, distinctive light is cast by high-lighting the inherently 'transcategorical' nature of arguments from intention.

The chapter provides theoretical accounts of the various basic patterns of complex justification, especially judicial resort to the cumulation of instances of types of argument, and judicial invo-cation of various modes of settling conflicts between instances of argument types beyond 'weighing and balancing'. A tentative model is set forth of the interactions between basic categories of arguments: linguistic, systemic, teleological—evaluative and, finally, the intentional. Second level problems of choice between conflicting arguments are treated further, drawing on the various modes of resolution in addition to 'weighing and balancing' intro-duced in Chapter 12.

Chapters 12 and 13 address some evaluative issues. Several arise with respect to the types of interpretative argument: what are the standard criticisms of specific forms of argument, and when are they valid? For example, what precisely is it that motivates the common criticism that a proposed ordinary meaning argument is 'wooden', or 'excessively literal', or 'conclusory'? When is such a criticism valid? Why? Similar questions are raised about the mani-pulation of purpose and about abuses of other types of argument. Still other evaluative issues are treated, including ones that relate to the structure and style of justifications as a whole. For example, what might justify the magisterial approach so prominent in some countries?

These issues raise still broader evaluative questions: What would an ideal system of justificatory practices look like? How might one, in these terms, differentiate between a system that, overall, approximates to the ideal and one that falls short? Interpre-tational practices may be more advanced because free of false theories about the way language works, or more sophisticated about linguistic meaning and legislative intent, or more subtle in regard to contextual harmonization and coherence, or more analy-tical in regard to all types of argument, or more systematic and consistent with respect to the resolution of conflicts between competing arguments, or more realistic and candid about disclos-ing reasons for decision, or more careful in handling the various types of materials relevant to the construction of reasons, or more comprehensive in making available within opinions all resources necessary for a reader to make an independent judgement about the quality of the justification.

We are not able to treat many of the foregoing issues at all fully, but we believe we now see them rather more clearly than before. Indeed, we prefer to believe that one of the contributions of this book may be that it identifies many new and significant questions and thus, in a sense, redefines the subject. We are confident that our own project members, and still others, will soon carry matters beyond where we have had to leave them here.

2 On Method and Methodology

ZENON BANKOWSKI, *Edinburgh,*
D. NEIL MacCORMICK, *Edinburgh,*
ROBERT S. SUMMERS, *Ithaca,*
AND JERZY WRÓBLEWSKI, *Łódz*

If we were asked by what method the authors prepared the present work, there would be a very simple answer. Over seven years they met intermittently and developed a set of questions about interpretation in their own countries that they should all answer, and they then tried to answer in a common way the questions they had agreed upon, bearing in mind comparative points thrown into relief by awareness of the others' answers. Each was to do this with a view to producing a mainly descriptive account of the prevailing practice of statutory interpretation within one's own legal system (or set of related systems, as in the UK). The questions are listed in Appendix I below. (The group developed, as well, an elaborate set of guidelines for answering the questions.)

Many readers will neither wish nor need to know more about our method, and will not care about the methodological justifications that make our approach a sound one in our view. Such readers should forthwith proceed to the next chapter, pausing perhaps, to review the questions in the Appendix. Other readers, however, may be inclined to press further on methodological issues. They will want to know how the authors justify the whole project of asking just that set of questions, and giving just the kind of answers disclosed in Chapters 3–11 on interpretation in the countries represented in the project. Valuable criticisms of the whole project offered by, in particular, Professors Hubert Rottleuthner and Jan van Dunné at a Bielefeld meeting in 1988 made clear the need for an account at this deeper level and for some alterations in the questions (and guidelines). Professor John Bell and Dr James Evans and Dr Geoffrey Marshall subsequently added further points of no less importance for clarifying the authors' approach.

In response, a summary statement on method and approach has been worked out to the general satisfaction of all the participating authors. Each of Chapters 3–11, about interpretation in the various countries (structured as a set of answers to the common questions), should be considered as aiming to produce the following:

> a rational reconstruction of public authoritative practices of legal reasoning (or 'argumentation') in the operative interpretation of statutes in each of the several national legal systems, carried out with special regard to institutional, constitutional, and cultural background and to the doctrinal, comparative and international legal context of interpretational decisions.

An important addition, briefly treated at the end of this chapter, has been the adoption, so far as is possible without distortion or misrepresentation of materials discussed or described, of a common terminology and typology for use by authors.

Some have expressed concern lest our use of 'rational reconstruction' as the common name for our general method might mislead. This name should not be taken as suggesting in any way that the authors view themselves licensed by it to advance radically innovative theoretical schemes in lieu of faithful attention to the current actualities of interpretational practice, or to indulge in some deeply evaluative ideological critique of such practices. For good or ill no such licence is intended or claimed, far less exercised, by any author.

Over and above this caveat, our methodology requires expansion and elucidation. We shall provide this through an explanation (1) of our field of inquiry; (2) of our concept of 'operative interpretation'; (3) of our focus on interpretational practice in higher courts; (4) of the problem of 'facade legitimation' versus genuine justification; (5) of the specific method we call 'rational reconstruction'; (6) of the comparative aspect of our work; and (7) of the common typology and terminology, to the extent it has been possible to achieve either.

I   THE FIELD OF INQUIRY

Statutes as a distinct form of law are of greater importance than ever before in modern industrial countries. In countries with codified law, statute law has long been the dominant form of law; nowadays, even in common law countries such as Great Britain and the USA, statutes are the most important part of the law, certainly in quantitative and arguably even in qualitative terms. It is an interesting question, and one on which it is hoped the present essays cast light, how greatly and in what way (if at all) the presence or absence of an assumed background of common law has distinctive effects upon approaches to the interpretation and application of statute law. It may be that in the 'code' countries, the codes as interpreted form a background and context for more recent and specifically enacted law rather akin to the background and context which the common law furnishes where it is observed.

The topic of these essays is the interpretation of statutes in the several jurisdictions under review. This topic has long been a major branch of legal theory and presents a particularly rich and complex subject for investigation. This richness and complexity might have proved overwhelming if the project had been conceived as including any kind of full-scale study of constitutional interpretation. Particularly in the USA, constitutional interpretation has long been deemed a topic quite distinct from general statutory interpretation; this sharp differentiation of constitutional from general statutory interpretation is less marked in other jurisdictions, as can be gathered, for example, from the German and Polish chapters in the present book. In general, we seek to avoid discussion of constitutional interpretation as such.

That point apart, we take 'statutes' in a wide sense, so as to include also regulations issued by duly authorized executive organs, especially where, as in France, these constitute a source of law coordinate with parliamentary legislation. Statutes in the wider sense, or even in the narrow sense in which they comprise only the enactments of a supreme legislature, are in any event a highly visible, and readily available and accessible, form of written law; they thus provide one inviting field for comparative study. This field of study is eminently sufficient to allow a valuable comparative set of studies in the theory of legal interpretation. Indeed a further narrowing of the field has been found desirable, for interpretation is an omnipresent human activity and statutes are available for all to interpret in a huge variety of contexts and settings and for a great variety of possible purposes, both practical and speculative in nature. The necessary narrowing of focus is achieved here by concentrating attention on 'operative interpretation' of statutes, that is, interpretation by the higher courts, in the various countries considered.

II   INTERPRETATION BY COURTS: 'OPERATIVE INTERPRETATION'

One highly important task of law courts is to apply statutes to particular cases with a view to giving authoritative and binding decisions upon the matters in dispute or under trial. In performing this task, they must in every case form a view as to the proper meaning of the statutes which seem to them applicable in the case. Where this view is an articulate one, and especially where the Court gives some public expression of its articulated view as to the way in which the statute should be understood, it is proper to consider the Court's activity as one of 'interpretation'. In the decision-making process, the public statement of an interpretation is a part of the justification of its decision in the case: that the law to be applied is being applied according to its proper interpretation is a justification in law (even if not a complete justification) of the decision as an application of law.

Such judicial interpretation of legal norms in decision-making is what we mean by 'operative interpretation'. In so doing we adopt and follow a definition offered by Jerzy Wróblewski. As Wroblewski observes, 'interpretation is a very general term'. He identifies three main senses: 'interpretation' *sensu largissimo, sensu largo,* or *sensu stricto. Sensu largissimo,* it is used to cover all sorts of understanding of cultural objects. For example, we may interpret a set of large stones protruding from the ground, not as a bare geological phenomenon, but as a human artifact erected for some purpose of religious worship. We interpret them in the light of a presumed purpose, but not in the light of any supposition that their makers used them to convey some message to us. The term is used *sensu largo* whenever one speaks of the 'interpretation' of language or any other system of (intentional) communication, meaning no more than that the person who receives or intercepts a message is able to understand it as having a certain meaning. Every understanding of any linguistic message is an interpretation in the broad sense (*sensu largo*). A case might be where a car driver sees on the road a 'Keep Left' sign, interprets it as meaning that he/she must drive to the left side of the road, and does so.

Interpretation in its narrow sense (*sensu stricto*) is a sub-class of interpretation *sensu largo* and occurs where there are doubts in the understanding of a language when it is used, in a particular context, in an act of communication. Where one or more persons experience practical doubt or engage in dispute as to the meaning which ought to be ascribed to some particular communication, the choice of one or other possibility involves an act of interpretation *sensu stricto*. For example, if I say I will meet you at ten o'clock on Wednesday, you may experience doubt as to which Wednesday I mean (this Wednesday? next Wednesday?) and as to whether I mean ten in the morning or ten at night. However you resolve this doubt (and perhaps even if you do so by asking me for a clarification), you make an interpretative choice among possibilities which you view as conceivable but conflicting senses the message may bear for you. Such a choice among alternatives in a setting of real doubt or dispute is a case of interpretation *sensu stricto*.

Interpretation in this strict sense often occurs in law. A jurist preparing a commentary on some statute may find significant ambiguity in some of its provisions. The commentary should draw attention to these and should state a reasoned preference for one or other of the possible interpretations. Again, a legal adviser seeking to advise a client on, for example, the tax implications of some transaction or another may encounter doubt as to the meaning of the tax statute for this purpose. The giving of advice requires some resolution of this doubt. The citizen who receives a contractual offer through the post may notice an ambiguity and respond to the offer on the basis of the seemingly most reasonable interpretation in view. None of these instances of interpretation *sensu stricto*, however, is what we call 'operative interpretation'. That occurs only when there is an act of interpretation *sensu stricto* performed by a judicial or other tribunal for the purpose of making a binding legal decision in an actual trial or litigated controversy. That is, it takes place when a court or other legal tribunal has to determine the meaning of legal language in a way sufficiently precise to make a decision in the case and to provide a justification for the decision on the ground of the interpreted meaning of the provision in issue. Operative interpretation, then, occurs in the official application of law, and is determined by the requirements of justified decision making in concrete cases.

III   INTERPRETATION IN THE HIGHER COURTS: AUTHORITATIVE DOCTRINES

A further narrowing of focus here is the concentration by the essayists on operative interpretation as practised in the higher courts and tribunals of the several jurisdictions. (We construe 'higher courts' quite widely, to cover supreme administrative and constitutional tribunals as well as civil and criminal courts of the strictly and narrowly 'judicial' order; and, while we focus mainly on tribunals at the ultimate stage of appeal or review, we do not exclude other superior courts exercising intermediate appellate functions.) There are two principal reasons for the restriction of our inquiries to higher courts in this broad sense. First, as has been noted, the stating of an articulated interpretation is a part of the justificatory process, yet it is one which is itself susceptible to further justification. In the higher courts in the jurisdictions represented, the judges often have a duty not only to justify their decision by stating their interpretation of a disputed legal text, but also have a duty (or anyway make it their practice) to explain what in their view justifies their choice of an interpretation rather than one of the other possibilities which might be taken seriously, and which would yield a different practical result. This being so, the written opinions of higher courts or of individual judges within them are normally the best legal examples available of responsible agencies confronting, in a methodologically self-conscious fashion, the problems of justifying decisions on the interpretation of statutes. The highest courts deal with the most obstinately disputed (and in that sense hardest) cases as courts of last instance, either hearing appeals as of right, or exercising discretionary power to select and review such cases. Moreover the nature and pace of proceedings at such exalted levels is normally such as to secure that the court has been made aware of all reasonable possibilities in the way of rival interpretations and of grounds that can be proffered for these. Opportunities for fully and carefully articulated justifications are thus maximized. Even here, though, it turns out that there are variations from system to system; for example, as Chapter 7 makes clear, the Italian *Corte di Cassazione* has no power of selection of cases referred to it, and hence has a colossal case-load, with but little opportunity for extended deliberation compared with ultimate appellate tribunals whose case-load is in some way screened. (This point is discussed further in Chapter 12 below.)

Second, since what is in issue is always the question of correct or preferable interpretations, better as against worse among arguable possibilities, it is plain that interpretation is subject to normative or evaluative controls. There must be *good reasons* for preferring some interpretations to others. This can in part be itself a question of positive law. The interpretation of statutes is a process that may be governed *partly* by constitutional law, ordinary statute law, or case-law. The decisions of the higher courts may thus themselves constitute sources of authoritative guidance as to sound practice in interpretive decision making by all within the legal system. And even apart from this, the grounds given by the higher courts as justifications of their interpretive decisions are the most authoritative statements of interpretive reasoning to be found within the system. If the system as a whole is to be in the formal sense a rational system at all, there will have to be some constancy over time in the modes of reasoning accepted as sound and authoritative in respect of interpretational decisions. In so far as there are established criteria for saying that a decision interpreting a statute is correct or incorrect, or criteria showing one interpretation as preferable to another, these criteria will be authoritatively recognized in (if not indeed laid down by) the higher courts. There will, however, be important differences in the degree to which judicial usage and practice makes explicit the courts' own conception of proper interpretational practice. All courts are engaged in interpreting statutes authoritatively, and in deciding cases according to their interpretation of the law; but not all courts give detailed accounts or discussions of the methods they use in this interpretation, or prescribe for other tribunals within their system. In this, there is an obvious contrast in judicial practice as between, for example, France at one extreme and the USA or the UK at the other. Where the justificatory reasoning stated by judges is less explicit, greater reliance may necessarily be put on doctrinal discussions by academics of the underlying methodological principles imputable to the higher courts in their decision making.

Subject to such variance, this is then the sense in which the present essays seek to explicate interpretative practices. For obvious reasons it would be incorrect to suppose that interpretation itself can be explicated wholly as a matter of rule-following, for the interpretational 'rules' (or 'directives' or 'canons' or 'criteria') themselves, however authoritatively stated, must in turn require interpretation. Moreover the complex nature of justificatory reasoning in the interpretation of statutes is such that much of it cannot be law-governed in any very close way anyhow. This is perhaps most obvious with respect to the settling of conflicts between interpretative arguments. Each interpreter faces in the end the question: what are good or bad reasons for interpretations? A view on this question formulated by any particular interpreter for any given occasion might indeed be restated in the form of a rule or rules (formally speaking, all good reasons are restatable in the form of rules), but it is at best unlikely that a clear and generally acknowledged set of positive rules governing interpretation exhaustively and authoritatively could be formulated for any system of law nowadays.

So our notion of the authoritative character of the decisions and justifications given by higher courts has to be taken with all due caution. Indeed it may be that a shared style and a common approach to reasoning, rather than any set of authoritative pronouncements about norms of good reasoning, are what gives interpretational practice its special quality in any particular legal system. The relevant style and approach are perhaps at best only partly explicit and are to a considerable extent implicit in the arguments and decisions of the higher tribunals. As if to confirm this, the processes of legal and professional education always have special regard to an appreciation of the governing style and approach as revealed in the acts and pronouncements of the higher tribunals. To understand a legal system's 'official' interpretative approach, one must have a good knowledge of the style of argumentation of its higher tribunals — in particular the style articulated and approved in 'leading cases' dealing with interpretational problems. This is so even where the official approach is honoured in the breach as well as in the observance.

Some such leading cases exist in every system studied here, although the significance of leading cases as such may be much greater in some systems than in others. The concept of a 'leading case' is one defined and understood by lawyers, judges and treatise writers within the system (and poses no real sampling problem here). It is justified to concentrate (though not exclusively) on the justificatory reasoning of such courts in leading cases. Of course, in common law systems, leading cases have a different authoritative status than in Code systems. In the former, a precedent can be a truly recognized normative basis of decision, even within an area broadly covered by statute. But in the latter, the statutory provision is the only legally recognized normative basis of decision. This by no means entails, however, that lower courts fail to take account of the precedents of higher courts in Code systems.

IV   FAÇADE LEGITIMATION OR GENUINE JUSTIFICATION?

A critic of our project might argue that, in concentrating on the published written opinions of higher courts in leading cases, our project is addressing only what might be called 'façade legitimation' and that the project therefore fails to look behind the decisions to see what their real motives are and how they are arrived at. The critic might further argue that our concentration upon higher judicial and legislative formulations of what is right may have precious little to do with the way trial courts actually process the day-to-day administration of the law's business, or how the law affects lay people. On either or both grounds, one should seek a different perspective better geared to discovering the 'reality' of what goes into decision making.

We can respond to these criticisms in several ways. First, the 'façade' criticism presupposes a distinction between the psychological process of arriving at a decision and the justification of this decision by supporting arguments. Investigation of the former addresses empirical relations of cause and effect, whereas the latter is concerned with the relations of justificatory reasoning linking arguments as premises with interpretive decision, as conclusion. Although in many cases the actual psychological process of arriving at an interpretative decision mirrors the steps of justification, this is certainly not inevitable. Even so, the practice of stating justificatory reasons remains available for study independently of any findings or hypotheses about links to the psychological process of discovery.

Secondly, it is a mistake to suppose that, even in those cases where the psychological motivations diverge from the stated justification, the alleged 'façade' that results is itself somehow unreal. The alleged façade is in fact worthy of study itself, since at the very least it represents an effort at self-conscious public justification. Thus it enables us to understand what are regarded as satisfactory and publicly acknowledgeable grounds for decision making.

Thirdly, institutional controls on judicial decisions are based on a critical analysis of the justifications stated by judges for their decisions, not on their psychological heuristic. Courts of appeal (or of 'revision', 'review' or 'cassation' and so on) analyse the set of arguments offered in support of the lower tribunal's decision, and this appraisal is always a partial basis of, and in many systems the sole ground of, the upholding, quashing or revising of the decision under consideration. For this very reason, there are in some systems statutory provisions which define the required elements of a publicly justified decision, by indicating what must be stated in any legally sufficient and formally proper justification.

Finally, the 'official' style of justification as established in the practices and approaches of the higher courts has a social and legal significance independent of the question whether or not all lower tribunals always act in that style and spirit. For many jurisdictions, there is some evidence that the lower courts, which in fact discharge by far the greater part of the legal business of any country (doubtless including an abundance of cases which would be recognized as 'hard cases' if they were taken on to a higher level) follow quicker, more summary, and less well-articulated styles and methods of interpretation and decision making. Nevertheless the ideal of legality for which the system stands reveals itself more fully in the higher courts' practices, and thus is frequently itself taken as a basis for the critique of lower court practices.

Our project is concerned with justification as such, even if the social realities of court room work fail to measure up to the publicly acknowledged standards of justification. To look behind the judicial decision simply to psychological motivations; to look also at the way the body of citizens responds to authoritative legal determinations, to whether and how far legal officials themselves do, to whether the lower courts implement the higher courts' rulings, to whether even the judges of the higher courts do so; to look at the connections between this and façade legitimation are all interesting and important lines of inquiry. But they are not the only important questions, and they are not our questions. Our project is concerned with the authoritative public *justification* of interpretational decisions. This requires us to have particular regard to pronouncements and determinations of the higher courts. Since we are looking at the ultimate justificatory 'face' of the system we need not make any empirical assumptions about the rest of the system beyond one common to all legal science, namely that the system is, by and large, efficacious.

Constitutional and other institutional background can have effect on the way the highest courts approach interpretation of statutes. A written constitution may include provisions about some features of the rule of law that affect the way statutes are interpreted. Or a written constitution may assign the highest court the power to invalidate statutes, and the possibility of such invalidation may influence the way statutes are interpreted. Or the legal system may permit courts to engage in a large law-making role and, as a result, courts may tend to combine law making with interpretation whenever possible. These are only some of the major ways that constitutional or other institutional factors may influence interpretation. Obviously these factors vary from system to system, and it would be a mistake for our project to ignore their bearing. In each of the essays an attempt is made to provide an account of such constitutional or institutional variables. The same applies to the influence of prevailing legal culture. Thus statutes will be interpreted differently where, for example, the prevailing legal theory is formal and positivistic rather than substantive and instrumentalist. And traditions with respect to staffing the judiciary play a role.

V   'RATIONAL RECONSTRUCTION'

It is material now to repeat the statement given in the introductory section concerning the aims and objectives of the present essays as being:

> a rational reconstruction of public authoritative practices of legal reasoning (or 'argumentation') in the operative interpretation of statutes in each of the several national legal systems, carried out with special regard to institutional, constitutional, and cultural background and to the doctrinal, comparative and international legal context of interpretational decisions.

What remains to be elucidated is the relevant conception of 'rational reconstruction' as the governing methodology of the project. This has much in common with the traditional methods of legal dogmatics or scholarly legal writing.

By 'rational reconstruction' we mean the activity of explaining fragmentary and potentially conflicting data by reference to theoretical objects in the light of which the data are seen as relatively coherent, because presented as parts of a complex, well-ordered whole. In a wide sense, this can apply to the methods of the natural as well as the human sciences, but in the case of cultural objects, such as law, the object presented as a coherent whole is so presented on the assumption of some degree of internal rationality in the relevant human activity. Specifically, in the present case, the rational reconstruction of interpretational justification involves *presenting it as consisting in structured types of arguments which all belong within a coherent mode of justificatory reasoning* (see Chapter 13 below).

The traditional lawyerly, 'juristic' task of producing clear and systematic statements of practice and legal doctrine is sometimes misunderstood. The legal scholar is not a mere amanuensis to the true decision maker, legislator or judge, simply transcribing the rules and rulings issued by the decision maker. Neither is he or she a deluded empiricist who believes in the accuracy of the rules transcribed as though they were behavioural generalizations. Legal scholarship calls for the exercise of a disciplined and intelligent imagination in order to reconstruct the fragmentary material issued by decision makers into rational, coherent and systematic wholes. This systematizing activity certainly envisages the law as normative and not descriptive; that is, as providing grounds for appraisal of acts, events and states of affairs, and guides to action of various sorts. Nevertheless the jurist's work produces a statement of the law, not a prescription or programme of how he/she thinks people should behave or what he/she would wish the law to be. What it yields is a descriptive and explanatory account of a normative order envisaged as validly in force in some jurisdiction.

Why this is a reconstruction and not mere depiction or transcription is because of the episodic and fragmentary character of the information and materials with which the jurist works. Acts of the legislature, regulatory acts by other public authorities, decisions by courts and tribunals are all issued as occasion arises and policy or the accident of litigation require. They focus on particular topics of contemporary concern. They envisage the admixture of new materials into a supposedly diachronic and ongoing normative framework for the conduct of human affairs. They can be stated at almost any level of generality or particularity. Since many intelligences are engaged in the tasks of decision making, the probability of any perfect overall scheme being exhibited in the new material issued at any one time, far less over a particular period of time, is negligible. One sees tendencies towards chaos as well as tendencies towards system. For example, the reconstructing scholar or theorist often encounters half-formed interpretative arguments in judicial opinions, or the running together of two or more instances of quite different types of arguments, or the failure to draw cognate arguments together under a common head so that their joint thrust can be fully grasped, or the inarticulate and confused selection of one argument over another, and more.

Hence the task of producing a rationally coherent view of the system is one that calls for imaginative insight into the possibility of a principled and structured ordering of material which is potentially chaotic despite being itself, in each fragmentary part, the output of intrinsically rational activity. Normative order as order is not a natural datum of human society but a hard-won production of organizing intelligence. The task is by no means incomparable with that of a grammarian who seeks out the organizing principles of a language he/she speaks as a native speaker.

Certain value commitments are involved in such an enterprise. An essential presupposition is a belief in the possibility of practical reason, of rational order in human activity. Since one also has to be willing to exercise empathetic imagination in order to envisage the normative order described as making sense given some value position or positions, to that extent one's activity exhibits a commitment to understanding, that is to hermeneutic method. It does not, however, require a commitment to more substantive values for one can detachedly and disinterestedly seek to reconstruct a normative order whose substantive values one does not share, or even rejects. A contemporary scholar could, for example, produce an account of the Roman law of slavery, or that of the USA before 1861, without any commitment to the institution.

Thus the position of the lawyer-as-jurist or scholar, by contrast with that of the lawyer-as-advocate is a relatively detached and disinterested one. The former position is one which seeks to make sense of the law in a relatively abstract way as a coherent normative order. The latter, on the other hand, is that of someone with a case to win for a client with a concrete concern about the application of a particular law. The advocate has to make the best that can be made of the legal material available in favour of the client's case. The jurist or scholar has to strive to make the best reasonable sense that can be made of the law as a rationally coherent and generally applicable normative system, though certainly without disguising any irresoluble antinomies present in the system at any time. (The judge has a similar commitment to rationality, but is always also responsible for decisions in individual cases, and aspects of individualized justice may conflict with ideally coherent law.)

All that has been said so far applies to what might be called 'classical legal (or "juristic") method', the approach to the cognition and exposition of law which characterizes good lawyerly elucidations of the law both in concrete settings and in more abstract and academic ones. Enough has been said to show why such work is more properly deemed a rational reconstruction than a simple reportive depiction of the law. We owe to Hans Kelsen this view of classical legal method as essentially reconstructive.

The present essays share with classical legal method the aim of rational reconstruction of a body of normative and axiological materials. But they proceed at a more fundamental level of inquiry and of reconstruction than does a standard legal treatise on interpretation. The reason for this is that they are (to repeat) concerned with 'a rational reconstruction of public authoritative practices *of legal reasoning* (or "argumentation") in the operative interpretation of statutes . . .'.

The stress upon legal 'reasoning' or 'argumentation' is important. As was already said, standards of good interpretation could never be fully reduced to or reconstructed as some sort of posited or positive rules. Much justificatory reasoning in the interpretation of statutes is not law-governed in any very close way at all, nor could it be. The point is that operative interpretation is embedded in legal argumentation as a form of practical reasoning aimed at the justification of decisions in the law. Thus it can only be within the setting of some view about rational practical reasoning (or 'argumentation') and their legal application that one can produce a rational reconstruction of criteria of soundness or unsoundness in interpretative practice (on this, see particularly the closing section of Chapter 13). This reaches down to a fundamental level of theorizing which lies beyond the scope of classical legal method. Yet still what is involved is rational reconstruction. A practice of operative interpretation exists in a framework of legal justificatory reasoning. The task of the present essays is to reconstruct its rational character as a mode of practical reasoning. This aim is an appropriate one to the skills and experience of the present essayists, all of whom have contributed in one way or another to the theory of legal reasoning.

Rational reconstruction aims at a descriptive account of normative material. It is descriptive in the sense that it starts from and purports to remain faithful to the materials it reconstructs. As part of its descriptive aim, it purports to reveal an underlying structure to which one can relate the particular justificatory arguments apparent in judicial opinions. But the aim to produce a purely descriptive account can never be perfectly achieved; for rational reconstruction has also a normative element in so far as the rationally reconstructed underlying structure presupposes a model of good or acceptable justification for the decisions of rational beings. Any description of norms about reasoning has to start from some view of what can possibly constitute good or sound reasoning and this will be reflected in the descriptive account produced. Since the primary material is in any event somewhat episodic and gappy, the way in which it is shaped and filled out in the descriptive account will necessarily draw on, and reveal, background normative assumptions. These will further affect one's judgements of satisfactoriness or adequacy in any descriptive account.

It is a much discussed and highly ambiguous question how far such activities are or can be 'value neutral' or value free. We shall not explore this intellectual minefield here. At the very least, there are important limits on the kind and degree of value-commitment which the theorist can properly bring to bear on work of this kind. First, as a scholar, the theorist has to have a commitment to truth and objectivity in any attempt to describe activities and practices. This in turn requires an acknowledgement of the necessity for some observational and theoretical framework within which objectivity is possible; the commitment to a theoretical framework involves some evaluative stance justifying adoption of that framework as distinct from a different one. Secondly, in the present sphere, as a theorist of rational justification, the theorist necessarily has a commitment to some conception of rationality as a fundamental value in human discourse, both theoretical and practical, and some conception of the way in which a scheme or system of norms and values can inform material content of practical justifications.

Given this second element, one has the necessary framework within which to scrutinize and to understand the justificatory practices of the judges in a legal system. One can explain how the norms and values they uphold can for them constitute justifications of the decisions they give. One can reconstruct from the great assemblage of leading decisions in higher courts a sense of the forms of interpretative (and other) reasoning which constitute acceptable justifications within that system. Thus one can advance a mainly descriptive theory of the modes of justification and of interpretative reasoning which one understands as being in use within the system studied. Such a theory is mainly descriptive exactly because of the degree of detachment it permits (or even requires) from the governing values in use in the system described. To do the job of rational reconstruction well, one need not share the values which, for the active participants in the system, are its guiding values. Even if, for other purposes, one shares those value commitments, or holds some very similar value-commitments for one's own practical life, it is important not to confuse one's own sense of what is right *tout court* with one's sense of what is right within the system and for its purposes. Equally, if one rejects the system's values or some important subset of them, this does not disable one from a clear and objective reconstruction of it. In either case, one's own critique of the system can and should be kept distinct from one's reconstruction of it.

In terms of commitment, therefore, one has a necessary commitment to certain scholarly values and to a certain theoretical framework, as well as to a conception of the possibility of practical rationality in the implementation of norms and values. These commitments are essential to the work. But beyond that, a certain detachment is also essential. One must reconstruct the system in view in order to understand and explain it without regard to the question whether it itself expresses sound values or value-commitments. Good legal description is neither advocacy of the system nor critique of it. Our aim here is good description in this sense, not advocacy or critique.

This balance between commitment and detachment has been often discussed by legal and social theorists, and in many specialist terminologies, such as H.L.A. Hart's, concerning 'internal' and 'external' points of view, or in Hans Kelsen's differentiation of *Rechtsnorm* from *Rechtssatz*. It remains controversial how far this form of commitment to scholarly values coupled with detachment from substantive system-values is possible. We all believe it to be possible, but rather than argue the point more extensively in this chapter, we prefer to leave each of the individual chapters on interpretation in a particular system to critical judgement of their character as practical proofs of our efforts to realize the possibility.

One remark must be added. Nothing said above would enable one to deny the possibility that scholarly work, in enhancing general understanding of interpretational justifications in the system, may also make a contribution to a wider acceptance of the substantive values embedded in the system. This is possible no matter how 'detached' a scholar's work is. But this is almost always true of scholarly work in the humane disciplines, and nothing prevents the scholar from stepping back from interpretational materials and ultimately adopting a critical approach to the practice involved as well.

VI   THE COMPARATIVE ELEMENT

Chapters 3–11 deal with the interpretation of statutes, each being an essay in rational reconstruction of interpretative method in a given legal system, as outlined above. A further aspect of the work, deserving of separate mention, is its comparative element. Though each author (or authorial team) has dealt primarily with his/their own system, each has had the annual opportunity to do so during and with subsequent reflection upon several days of intensive roundtable discussion with all project members over a seven-year period. Each has prepared for these annual sessions by reading some of the work of the others.

Thus each has arrived at the final text of the essay here after an opportunity for comparative reflection, both at the level of an awareness of issues and approaches important in other systems and at the level of an improved insight into each other's approach to the issues of legal theory which structure one's own particular essay in rational reconstruction. One of the great virtues of a comparative approach in legal and jurisprudential studies is the heightened awareness it generates of one's own system, both in reminding one of its traditional and well understood strengths and weaknesses and yet also, all the more, in enabling one to notice and appreciate hitherto unnoticed features. Each author has in this sense profited from the comparative approach, because each has worked out the final account of domestic interpretational practice question-by-question with full opportunity to consider every other system-based answer to each particular question and, indeed, after critical discussion of each answer in its earlier drafts. Thus the questions have come to be used in a tradition-transcendent way, and each author has been able to profit much in rethinking one system in the light of its comparabilities with and differences from other systems.

Thus the whole of Chapters 3–11 is pervaded by comparativity of spirit. In the end, only one chapter, Chapter 12, explicitly offers a detailed comparative account of differences and similarities of approach. Although comparative questions were asked of and discussed by each author, it became clear that this material was best treated through the necessarily selective synthesis provided by the authors of Chapter 12, who drew not only on the methodology of rational reconstruction, but also on that branch of legal learning known as comparative law.

VII   COMMON TYPOLOGY AND TERMINOLOGY

One difficulty in pulling together some common theoretical understandings and in pursuing the comparative aspects of our work
relates to typologies and terminologies. We have a natural interest
in the types of problems and in the types of argument used to solve
interpretational issues. We also have such an interest in any rules or
principles or canons of interpretation used in resolving problems of
interpretation. It would be ideally convenient for reportorial and
comparative purposes if we were able to describe problems, arguments and rules or the like in a common terminology adapted to a
common typology. Indeed any such effort would be part and
parcel of our enterprise in rational reconstruction.

But there are three difficulties about this. First, that judicial
discussions of statutory interpretation, and judicial acknowledgement of types of problem, have differed as between the various
systems reviewed; hence our aim of reasonable descriptivity pre-
cludes any absolute identity of typology or terminology.
Secondly, the juristic discussion of statutory interpretation, and the
development of leading scholarly doctrines about it, have pro-
ceeded under the influence of a diversity of theoretical impulses in
politics and law, and even of philosophical and linguistic doctrines
(and the doctrinal discussions have in turn influenced and been
influenced by judicial practice in all its diversity). Thirdly, in the
aim to strike a balance between casting new light on practice in the
given jurisdiction and describing it in acceptably recognizable
terms, each author or authorial team has had to make their own
scholarly judgement, having regard to general theory and particular legal system. Not surprisingly, there is here no entire uniformity
of typology or terminology. To have insisted on this would have
been to purchase uniformity at the price of distortion.

Even so, we have been able to agree on some elements of
uniformity, arising out of our agreed common understanding of
the task. The interpretation of statutes is after all one instance of
the interpretation of written texts, and the texts in question are not
only all written in some natural language (German, French, Polish
and so on) but also in a special register or sub-language of the
natural language (that is, legal language − legal German, legal
French, legal Polish and so on). Further, statutes are uniformly
instances of legislation enacted by a legislature (or, sometimes, by
executive authorities) with a view to their forming a part of the
relevant legal system. Finally, the activity of enactment is commonly supposed to be an activity with some purpose or point, to
do with producing whatever good(s) it may be that laws bring
about.

It is a general truth about linguistic productions of all sorts, and hence of statutory texts also, that their intelligibility is context-dependent. We can understand texts as texts only if we presuppose or have regard to some context. In the case of statutes, we subdivide this into four facets of context. First, we may consider simply the linguistic context, that is, the context of a natural language, or one of its specialized sub-languages (German, or legal German, for example); secondly, we may consider the context of the social–legal structure, institution or practice to which the text distinctively belongs, namely, the systemic context of the legal system; third, we may consider how the purpose of the statute (in so far as it is discernible) leads to an evaluation of one interpretation as more apt than another, and how substantive reasoning emergent in the context favours one interpretation over another; finally, we may consider the evidence of the intention of the law giver. These points are all derivable from general semantics: the meaning of a text depends on its being read in context. The special point is the claim that, for the texts of statutes, the whole context in which any relevant text has meaning can be exhaustively subdivided into the linguistic, the systemic, the teleological–evaluative (or, more exactly if less intelligibly to the general reader, 'axiological') and the intentional element. Meaning is dependent on an understanding which takes account of the whole context, albeit that in given instances we may leave some facets inexplicit and unproblematized.

This general conception, for which the rest of us are indebted in some measure to Jerzy Wróblewski (though his preferred version of the terminology was 'semiotic', 'systemic' and 'functional' as against our 'linguistic', 'systemic', 'teleological–evaluative' and 'intentional', has great utility in generating a typology available to us all, and used by us all except where other reasons of fidelity to established local usage outweigh. For Wróblewski's semiotic theory enables us to consider characteristic problems of statutory interpretation as being, in origin, linguistic, systemic or teleological–evaluative (axiological) or 'transcategorical', the most important species of this being arguments of an intentional kind. Difficulties of interpretation may arise out of some problem of the words used in the text, or out of some problem of fitting the text in a given understanding coherently within an understanding of the legal system to which it belongs, or out of some problem about the purpose or value towards achievement of which one envisages the text as being directed, or out of some problem of taking due account of evidence of legislative intention. The same typology applies to interpretative arguments and to any rules, principles, canons or directives which are supposed to guide interpretation.

We may subdivide them into the types: linguistic, systemic, teleo-logical—evaluative and intentional.

These terms — linguistic, systemic, teleological—evaluative and transcategorical or intentional — have been adopted by common agreement for use in the present volume only in the sense explained here. We do not asume that all the phenomena con-sidered can be satisfactorily classified according to this typology. But we have generally applied it except where difficulties of the kind noted make it essential (for example, for fidelity to the system described) to use a different typology or terminology. We have also found that there may be some items which do not fit into a single category ranging over more than one of the types in question. Thus intentional argumentation is not merely a fourth basic category, as indicated above. For reasons worked out in Chapter 13, it turns out that the argument from the intention of the law-giver (which is also everywhere rather important) is also transcategorical in the sense that the *objects of intention* that figure in the basic category of argumentation include all of the objects — language usage, systemic context, and purpose and value — that figure in the other major categories of argumentation.

In sum, we have achieved a considerable degree of conceptual and terminological unity, not by way of some false consensus, but because we find ourselves able to agree to some extent on a common view about types of problem, types of argument and types of directive in statutory interpretation.

3 Statutory Interpretation in Argentina

ENRIQUE ZULETA-PUCEIRO, *Buenos Aires*

PRELIMINARY

Ruled by a constitution established in 1853, Argentina is a federal country, divided into 23 provincial states, a Federal Capital City and a national territory situated at the southern part of the country – Tierra del Fuego and the southern Atlantic islands. The provincial states have their own constitutional organization, based on the republican division of powers. They preserve the institutional powers and competencies not explicity granted to the federal state. They interpret and apply national regulations through a judicial hierarchy consisting of three levels.

From the point of view of judicial organization and practice, this is a complex system organized, on the one hand, under a constitution basically similar to the Philadelphia model but, on the other hand, with most of its ordinary legislation organized on the basis of a purely statutory system, strongly influenced by the European code models. From the comparative law point of view, one can speak of a peculiar and mixed form of legal and judicial organization with obvious consequences in the field of interpretative doctrine and practices.

The judicial branch is organically interrelated with the executive and legislative. The judicial power extends to every issue regulated by the constitution (CN, Art. 100). From the beginning of the Argentine constitutional organization, the Supreme Court (CSJN) has understood its function to be that of a concrete exercise of independent and active state power, one that guarantees the equilibrium of political power as a basis of the republican form of government (CSJN, *Fiscal c/Rios y Gomez*, 1 Fallos, 35–37 (1863).

This wide control over all the causes regulated by the constitution has not only a constitutional basis but also explicit legal support. An early statute of 1858, Law 128, organized the federal judiciary and established that the federal tribunals will decide according to the Constitution and the national statutes concordant with the constitution (Art. 3). Its primary goal is 'to reinforce the national constitution in all litigious matters, uniformly interpreting the laws and applying them according to the constitution and in no other way' (Art. 3). In 1862, another statute, Law 27, stated that 'one goal of the national judiciary is to support the constitution, avoiding, when deciding its cases, every statement from any other state power opposed to the Constitution' (Art. 3).

The basic organization of the judicial power starts from a national Supreme Court (CSJN), that shares constitutional interpretation and application with all the judges of the country, no matter their jurisdiction or level. The Court is not a special constitutional Court but the top of the judicial power, with a wide jurisdiction, dealing with all kind of matters, related not only to the constitution but to all the other federal matters. There is a diffuse, non-concentrated and non-specialized judicial review system, shared at the national or provincial level by any judge or tribunal. The Supreme Court traditionally had five members, until a recent and highly polemical reform that enlarged it to nine members.

According to the Argentine Constitution, the Supreme Court and the lower federal tribunals (Federal Judges at the first level and Federal Chambers at the second level) have jurisdiction ('knowledge and decision') on every case related to matters governed by the constitution and national (federal) statutes, except those matters regulated by the codes mentioned at Art. 67, inc 11 of the constitution (civil, penal, commercial, labour law), where the federal judiciary shares its jurisdiction with the provincial judicial powers. The federal jurisdiction also covers all cases regulated by international treaties, cases concerning foreign diplomats, maritime jurisdiction, disputes where the nation is a party, interprovincial disputes or cases between provinces and foreign countries or citizens. The Supreme Court always has appellate jurisdiction and only acts as an original tribunal in cases concerning foreign diplomats or conflicts where a province is a party. The Court acts as a constitutional tribunal and, in fact, through the extraordinary appeal of Law 48, as a sort of third instance tribunal.

As in the American model, in the Argentine system the constitutional jurisdiction is incidental, so that constitutional issues can be raised in the course of any type of judicial proceeding and at every level of judicial organization. Courts exercise much power to override statutes. Only the Supreme Court can give a last word to the compatibility of norms with the form and substance of the constitutional order. Constitutional review can be raised by the lower tribunal. Every citizen can raise a constitutional question before any Court at the federal level, based on a collision between a legislative, judicial or administrative decision and constitutional rights and guarantees.

The Supreme Court has a wide jurisdiction and activity, both on constitutional and general matters, including the interpretation of federal norms and acts, and the uniformity of judicial interpretation of legal and procedural norms. Nevertheless there is no uniformity or consistency in Argentine doctrine on legal interpretation. One can only establish, via rational reconstruction of interpretive judicial activity, certain principles, criteria or rules, as part of an implicit and inorganic doctrine of judicial interpretation. The abrupt institutional history of the country also reflects deep changes in judicial orientations.

As a peculiar feature, different from the American model, the Argentine Supreme Court has little control over its docket. So, every year it considers around 4 000 cases, taking into account those that are decided and those that are *in limine* refused. There is an evident overload of activity. In May 1988, the Court received 346 cases and decided 443. The accumulated number of unsolved cases as of that month was 3 583. In 1987, when the Executive Power submitted the first project for reform of the Supreme Court, there were 6 000 unsolved cases. The practical response of the Court was an acceleration of its activity and as a result of that, when the enlargement of the Court was decided in March 1990, there was a minimal number of unresolved cases. The acceleration of the Court's activity through the summary rejection of many cases was severely criticized. Now the Court refuses around 65 per cent and accepts around 25 per cent, while the rest are decided in other ways. There is a clear overcharge of work, and that explains most of the attempts to establish new mechanisms, as in the American experience of the *writ of certiorari* or in the European experience of different specialized courts. (For a general overview, see Morello, 1989.)

In general terms, Argentina's legal system and interpretative practices could be considered among the most significant examples of the gradual trend towards a certain convergence between common law and statutory-based systems. Starting from a comparatively old constitutional organization, basically shaped on the model of the American constitution, Argentina has gradually adapted this institutional set to an entirely different political and legal culture. This process has not been the result of natural evolution but the product of a deliberate political will.

The original design of this process of institutional reception was based on the assumption that democratic rule of law was a means to cancel a long period of civil conflicts and open an age of national state-building. The Anglo-Saxon sense of freedom and the American *ethos* of originality and experience of political citizenship were envisaged by the Argentine founders of the new constitutional order as means to enforce a basic commitment to limited government and rule of law.

The new Argentine constitution was adopted by a strong legal culture, deeply rooted in the hispanic tradition, but ideologically and politically oriented towards the private law codification movement, initiated by the French *Code* (enthusiastically supported by the liberal élites, triumphant in the Spanish and Latin American intellectual and political realm).

The Argentine constitution is rigid, defined as the supreme law of the country, prior to any other kind of enactments, and unchangeable by ordinary means. At all the levels of judicial organization judges must protect and preserve its primacy, declaring the unconstitutionality of the norms considered contrary to the letter or the spirit of the constitution.

The early Argentine debate on the value of American precedents shows clearly to what extent constitutional and, in general, legal interpretation was considered as a political task, fulfilled by political actors in a political process. In an early statement, the Supreme Court underlined that 'the ruling institutional system is not our personal creation. We founded it in action, after long years of fruitful experiences. It has been said that one of the great advantages of this reception and appropriation is to take into account this large body of American doctrinal experience and judicial practice, illustrating basic rules that we can and must use, especially in those fields where we haven't introduced peculiar solutions' (*Fallos*, 19–236).

The internal tension between complex and even contradictory elements, originating in different cultural and ideological backgrounds, must be considered as a basic standpoint for a rational reconstruction of authoritative doctrines about legal reasoning or justificatory argumentation in the operative interpretation of statutes. The periodic and permanent disruption of the Argentine political system must be understood not only as the result of purely political struggles between social forces in conflict but, to a great extent, as a reflex of the contradictions and blockages of the institutional system, as it seeks to process and assimilate demands of a changing society, ruled by legal models historically superseded.

Statutory interpretation offers a privileged point of view on these tensions, and the Argentine judicial doctrine offers great evidence — seldom recognized by legal philosophers — of the judicial power's awareness of the real nature of its decisive role. The theoretical understanding of these fragmentary materials, their reconstruction in terms of a systematic picture of the judicial interpretative experience, affords an account of the way a constitution can be transplanted to another society, basically inspired in the very different, and even antagonistic Spanish political culture, and throughout a period of legal development involving the reception of a further basic element: continental private law codification. The new cultural outcome must be understood in its own and non-transferable identity.

I GENERAL ORIGINS OF INTERPRETATIONAL ISSUES

Interpretational issues do not grow from sources very different from those in any other statutory-based legal system. As has been said, the early Argentine experience integrated a complex tradition, in which the ancient Spanish colonial law, valid even 20 years after the 1853 Constitution and until the time of adoption of the new private law codes, co-existed with the new imported legal traditions, represented by the American constitutional model and the French codes. Some scholars underline the idea that the Argentine legal system evolved out of the replacement of ancient customary law by new scientific ideas about systematization, codification and drafting, and out of the displacement of the original normative disorder by the coherent order of codes.

Nevertheless this idea must be discussed from a strictly historical point of view. In fact, Spanish and colonial law recognized a relatively high degree of stability, in an integrated and hierarchical relationship between different positive sources: the *Recopilación de Leyes de los Reynos de Indias*, the *Ordenamiento de Alcalá*, the *Fueros Municipales*, the *Fuero Real* and the *Partidas*. In addition, there was a complex regulation of public matters. A very casuistic judicial doctrine, inspired in the Spanish law tradition, evolved without significant conflicts.

The new Constitution of 1853 reshaped the entire structure of institutional power, redefining the scheme of legal sources. The idea of a systematic legal order, unique and complete, presided by statutory law and subsidiarily completed by other traditional sources as a result of a mechanism of normative habilitation, became central. The rule of law, considered by Arts 18 and 19 of the Constitution as a basic leading principle, established the premise that whatever is not prohibited is permitted.

This premise establishes a methodological basis for various aspects of problem-solving judicial activity, but it does not exclude the possibility of interpretational issues. On the contrary, this original cultural and technical clash is still a permanent source of interpretational issues. The judicial decision always presupposes an hermeneutic situation. It never operates at the abstract level of legal doctrine. The cognitive moment of judicial activity is essentially interpretative. The judge begins by seeking a preliminary understanding of facts and then tries to find a regulatory canon, able to provide a normative ground for decision and an interpersonally sufficient argumentative justification. Since the beginning this activity implies interpretation, *sensu largo* and *sensu stricto*. Every attempt to systematize the matter could start from the following distinctions.

1   *Linguistic sources* are the most obvious and recognized sources of interpretational issues. Argentine scholars have had a traditional academic interest in linguistic matters. Overgenerality, vagueness, ambiguity and a generalized usage of poorly defined terms are unavoidable features of the natural language used by legal norms. This open texture of legal language seems to be a primary source of interpretative issues, understood in the narrow sense (*sensu stricto*): issues that arise as a result of understanding problems of legal language within specific usage contexts.

The linguistic sources of interpretational issues have always been widely recognized by judicial doctrine. The Supreme Court has established that

> the first source for legal interpretation are the words used by legislative enactments. Those words must be understood as used in their right senses, that is in the every day life and common sense. The safest interpretative rule says that, if the statute uses different words, those words are not superfluous. They have been used with some purpose, either for enlarging, limiting or correcting concepts. The main task of the legal interpreter is to give plain effects to the original intent of the legislator. (*Enrique J. Piccardo* v. *Caja de Jubilaciones de la Marina Mercante Nacional* in *Fallos*, 200–176)

Interpretation means to go beyond the natural vagueness, fuzziness and open texture of language, seeking the real dimensions of the interpretative question: the conflict between the plain literal meaning and background considerations, the existence of technical insufficiencies, incompleteness, inconsistencies or incoherences, the conflict between what the norm says and what the norm means within a certain interpretative situation.

2   *Background considerations.* Besides the linguistic sources of interpreting issues, the judicial doctrine has widely recognized other sources of interpretative problems, specially dealing with the conflict between norms and generally established presumptions. The general trend to a less formalist approach to legal reasoning shows many examples of a tempered acceptance of generally accepted presumptions, mainly in the most changing legal fields (that is, economic law, liability, commercial law, welfare and tax law). The emphasis on some basic values gives rise to interpretational issues in traditionally non-conflictive legal fields. In that sense, the Supreme Court has established, as a general criterion, that 'legal interpretation is a matter of very special prudence. The understanding of legal terms must always avoid risks to individual rights. An excessively rigorous reasoning can threaten the real purpose of law' (*Fallos*, 303–578).

3   *Internal structure.* In Argentina, the lack of technical support of drafting activity is a major source of internal contradictions of statutes. The constant reform in important legal fields (that is, tax law, labour law, provisional law) also shows changes within the structure of the codes or compilations of norms. Quite often some parts of the codes contradict new regulations, not always adapted to the previous framework. Another good example is the partial Civil Code reform by Law 17.711, that introduced crucial legislative changes through strategic modifications of certain articles or even paragraphs of articles of the Civil Code, leaving the rest of the Code unchanged. It opened an important activity of tribunals, interpreting the extent of the reform and the important inconsistencies, incoherences and internal contradictions of the Civil Code. The reform was explicitly based on the creative and adaptive activity of judges, considered by the law-maker as a living part of the legal system. Sometimes, the internal inconsistency of statutes also reflects the conflictive process of political or corporatist bargaining underlying drafting activity.

4   *Relation between different statutes.* An important feature of the contemporary 'legislative flood' is, at least in code systems, the growing quantity and importance of complementary legislation, added to the original codes. The relationship between different statutes is often regulated by transitory or provisional regulations. This is only a partial and basic

response to an important source of interpretational issues.

5   *Contextual sources.* The original context of norms is not always considered to be the decisive interpretational standpoint. Nevertheless rapid social change makes arguable the received meaning of statutes. This is particularly evident in the case of very old codes, established almost a century ago. A good example could be the original reception of *ius soli* as a general criterion for the definition of nationality. This was quite clear for a country that, at the end of the nineteenth and in the early twentieth century, was importing millions of inhabitants from the European countries. What happens nowadays, when the country exports people? The *ius sanguini* criterion seems to be better, in order to protect the Argentine population living outside the country.

6   *Conflicts of values.* The discussion about the impact of value change on judicial decision-making processes has been especially important in recent times. The recent activistic trend of the Supreme Court on such issues as freedom of expression, family law or privacy has generated a judicial argumentation around the conflict between norms that are in principle undoubtedly clear but which, mainly because of the change in social values, have become obscure or arguable, demanding a special adaptation to new temporal circumstances. Clear examples are the evolutionary doctrines stated in such cases as CSJN, 'Ponzetti de Balbin', 112 El Derecho, 242; 'Campillay' 1986-C La Ley, 411; 'Bazterrica', 1986-D La Ley, 550 or 'Sejean', 121 El Derecho, 534. The change of socially predominant values is not the only source of conflicts. Quite often the interpretative conflict arises from some basic values, independently of its historical evolution. The conflicts between legal certainty and concrete justice of the case, national security and individual guarantees, private property and the general interest, economic freedom or private economic initiative and emergency needs are quite frequently significant sources of interpretative disputes.

7   *Change sources.* Social and economic change is — as has been previously said — a crucial dimension of Argentine legal and judicial experience. Instability is the normal condition and this rapid change of economic circumstances leads to a very special assessment of contextual change, mainly in economic matters. The changing conditions of economic stability or instability are often considered in order to establish the meaning or the extent of economic norms. The modification of the factual presuppositions of legislative enactments

has been considered, especially in recent times, reflecting an increasing awareness of the active social role of judicial interpretation.

Long periods of interruption of democratic rule have also been an almost permanent additional occasion for thinking about the legislative activity of courts. Depending, of course, on the subject matter of statutes, legal interpretation has developed an institutional function far beyond the originally established constitutional limits of the division of powers.

8   *General sources.* Some other sources come from the very nature of interpretational activity. The most obvious is the fact qualification (characterisation), which is always open to a judicial review by higher tribunals. Sometimes the difference between interpretation and gap-filling judicial activity is in this sense very problematic. The peculiar factual conditions may raise the question whether the norm is, in the end, the right one.

II   INTERPRETATION AND GAP-FILLING

The Argentine judicial doctrine has accepted the established distinction between interpretation and gap-filling of law. In some specific fields the distinction has an explicit legal support. That is the case of the Commercial Code, when it says: 'In those matters not specially regulated by this Code, the Civil Code will be applied' (Art. I) or 'In those matters where private conventions can derogate the law, the nature of acts authorizes the judge to find out if it is essential to the act to refer to customs, in order to give to the acts and facts their own meaning, according to the presumptive will of the parties' (Art. II). This is not of course a direct reference to the existence of gaps, but reveals an open conception of the legal order, and especially a conception of judicial activity as an active element of the system.

Argentine judges clearly distinguish between interpretation and gap-filling, following a theoretical discussion initiated by Carlos Cossio, denying the existence of legal gaps. His argument about the hermetic completeness or wholeness of legal order and about the closing function of the axiom 'what is not legally prohibited is legally permitted' gave a consistent support to the generally assumed idea that the lack of a norm means a formal permission to act and, at least from the judge's point of view, an open authorization to decide, taking into account the always changing case circumstances. Judicial activity, suggested Cossio, following a

Kelsenian approach, 'closes' the system, providing a permanent solution to the so-called 'gaps'.

In general, judicial doctrine has accepted this idea as a purely logical argument. Nevertheless tribunals established that this activity 'completes' the legal system, providing solutions to situations where there is an absence of any adequate legal provision where it is needed. Economic and technological regulations are fields where this picture of judicial activity has been quite clear. New fields of legal life mean new interpretative issues, giving rise to the existence of normative extrinsic gaps.

Besides the above, there is the ever-open possibility of gap issues arising from consequences of the established enactments: that is, from situations where the social, economic or legal consequences are manifestly unreasonable, disproportionate, uneconomic, unjust or opposed to what the law clearly intended to establish. Here again we can speak about gaps, starting from the assumed evaluative nature of judicial decision making.

There is discussion of the possibility of what has been called *intrinsic* gaps. These arise whenever in existing enactments there seem to be defects of regulation or important cases without solution. Some very detailed regulations in the field of administrative and economic law offer clear examples.

Starting from a very broad distinction between interpretation and gap-filling activities, the transformations of legislation produce permanent sources of gap-filling issues. A first source is the important body of new legislation that deliberately creates gaps through the extended use of 'general clauses'. A good example of the adaptative evolution of statutes to the changing social and economic circumstances is the 1968 Civil Code reform, introducing new principles and institutions, primarily related to clauses referring to 'good faith' (*bona fide*) or *equity*. Art. 17 introduces the possibility of using customary norms as criteria in judicial decision making, especially in those situations which are in principle not regulated by law, 'considering the case circumstances'.

Another good example is Art. 1069, setting forth the idea of equitable determination of civil liability, 'considering the situation of the debtor'. Arts 1036 and 3477 again speak about equitable solutions in cases of divorce, and the law of wills and estates. Arts 1198 and 954 introduce clauses which, using various textual formula, regulate the unexpected consequences resulting from the occurrence of facts different from those contemplated in the original contractual relationship.

Labour law provides additional examples of this legislative establishment of conditions or sources of gap-filling questions. Referring to statutory interpretation in this field, Statute n. 20.744

states that 'whenever a problem cannot be solved through the application of accepted contractual norms or analogy, it must be decided according to principles of social justice, general principles of law, equity, and good faith'. Administrative and constitutional law also provide examples, demonstrating important and crucial changes in the field of statutory gap-filling. In the field of judicial review of administrative activity, there has been an important doctrinal development of open concepts and clauses such as 'reasonableness', 'good faith', 'due process of law', used not only as general criteria but also as specific boundaries of the realm of judicial discretion.

The wide reception of a principled theory of law, with important effects on the theory of legislation and on the theory of statutory interpretation, offers a new source for gap-filling problems. In this sense, the Supreme Court has frequently spoken of 'inner justice' and 'reasonableness', even qualifying decisions as 'just solutions', 'equalizations of sentences and constitutional principles' or 'reasonable derivation of the principles of the constitutional State'. In a very well known recent judicial decision, the Supreme Court said: 'The constitutional norms are designed to endure, regulating the evolution of life in Argentina, and must work together with it in the discrete and reasonable interpretation of the original intent of the constitutional creators' (*Sejean, Juan B.* v. *Zaks de Sejean, Ana M.*, Nov. 27-986, opinion of Justice Petracchi).

The Court has established reasonableness as a flexible criterion of constitutional control *Hileret y Rodriguez* v. *Prov. de Tucumán* in *Fallos*, 98–20 and *Barros*, in *Fallos*, 301–151). This canon is related not only to the reasonableness of norms but to the judicial understanding of norms, within the context of the particular factual circumstances of a given case. Also the idea of 'due process of law' considered in both a substantial and a procedural sense has been widely applied as a general criterion in the field of judicial review of administrative activity.

As a result of accelerated economic crisis, the judicial doctrine has emphasized the creative role of judicial decision making, filling gaps and integrating the naturally open structure and texture of new fields of legal development. Recently, while derogating a centennial prohibition of new civil marriage after divorce, the Supreme Court underlined that

> Constitutional review may not be alien to historical and social changes. This is because the reality of each age either perfects the spirit of the institutions of each country or unveils new aspects which were not previously contemplated. Thus constitutionality may not be opposed to the average concept of a society which in a different era

has acted differently. This hermeneutic rule does not imply the destruction of the basis of a pre-established internal order, but instead the defense of the national constitution itself for whose peaceful rule it has been instituted. (*Costa, Héctor R. v. Municipalidad de la Capital y otros*, dissenting opinion by Justice Fayt, March 12-987)

Regarding the same topic, the Court further stated that 'It is acceptable neither that the judges should clearly acknowledge the transformations which take place in questions of property, nor that matters such as the indestructibility of marriage, which bear directly on nature and human conditions, the development of personality and human dignity, should escape their perception . . .' (*Sejean, Juan B. v. Zaks de Sejean, Ana M.*).

In other words, the principle is that judges must be aware of societal changes and of the always changing nature of values and fundamental legal principles. That is precisely the idea stated by the Supreme Court in the extract quoted above.

III   TYPES OF INTERPRETATIVE ARGUMENTS AND THEIR INTERACTION

Despite the important developments of Argentine judicial interpretative doctrine, it is hard to develop explicit typologies of arguments. Even if we take into account the importance of some theoretical insights, coming from the different currents of interpretation theory, most of them are mainly interested in a normative approach, devoted to definitions about what judges should do, instead of describing what they really do. Nevertheless a general empirical description of judicial practices reveals most of the arguments commonly recognized within the cultural background of the inherited theories about interpretation: that is, the exegetic movement, German-oriented positivistic legal dogmatics or sociological legal functionalism.

As in other legal cultures, Argentine tribunals use arguments that merely reproduce purely logical arguments applied to law. That is the case of arguments well known through traditional notation such as *a contrario, a fortiori, ab exemplo* and *ab absurdo*. Other arguments are within more complex dimensions of legal reasoning — normative logic and theory of argumentation. In this sense, Argentine tribunals very seldom enter into technical discussions, preferring to mention, without much discussion, legal arguments based on unwritten legal principles, like the idea of 'equitable reasoning' or *analogia iuris*. Those arguments presuppose a complementary role of other types of arguments (that is, analogical argument needs another argument, able to justify the rationality of analogical comparison; argument *a fortiori* asks for previous justificatory argumentation on a major and minor scale; systematic argument requires a previous argumentation, based on the idea of wholeness and completeness of the legal order). The most accepted idea among judges is that interpretation requires different and complementary argumentative strategies.

Both the European civil law tradition and the American constitutional law tradition have a strong influence on Argentine tribunals, so that most of the comparative law efforts at establishing a general typology could be useful for the purpose of reconstructing and systematizing Argentine practice. (For general typologies, besides the following national surveys in this book, see J. Wróblewski, 1985; G. Tarello, 1980; F. Ost and M. van der Kerchove, 1989; and, in general, F.J. Ezquiaga Ganuzas, 1987).

Following a traditional approach to the justificatory arguments, Argentine scholars and judges generally speak about 'methods' of interpretation (grammatical or literal, historic, logic, systematic and teleological), referring to the legal text, its historic context and its systemic context. This could be the basis of a generic typology, more or less descriptive of what interpretative argumentation is in judicial practices. In line with the continental legal systems, von Savigny's typology of the elements of legal interpretation, or of 'legal methods', has had a wide acceptance, being part of the common culture of judges, scholars and practitioners. It is quite an obvious matter to distinguish between a *grammatical* element in statutory interpretation (or, in other words, a 'grammatical method'), related to the explanation and understanding of ordinary legal language in its own terms; a *logical* element, referring to the logical relationship between different legal propositions; a *historical* element, referring primarily to the historical origins of the interpreted statute and its dynamic evolution and, finally, a *systematic* element, which refers to the internal connection of norms within a given legal order. In general it could be said that each element is equally considered part of the whole cognitive and evaluative process. In other terms, different interpretative arguments deal either with semantic and syntactic dimensions of the understanding process, or with the problems of systemic relationship between statutes and legal system, or with the evaluative assessment of consequences of a proposed understanding of the interpretative issue.

Nevertheless this rough approach raises some problems, correctly underlined by Ost and van der Kerchove. First, it is useful only as a description of methodological interpretational directives, leaving aside some types of arguments referring to the definition of interpretative activity or to functional argumentation. Second, it does not describe accurately some directives and types of arguments not principally addressed to the basic 'elements' or materials of interpretation. Instead, it focuses on second-level directives or arguments which resolve conflicts between first-level arguments.

For a more complete description of the judicial argumentative activity, it could be useful to adapt the following typology, partially based on an extensive usage of the very well known typologies about directives or forms of arguments defined by J. Wróblewski, F. Ost and M. van der Kerchove, G. Tarello, and Ezquiaga Ganuzas, all cited above.

1   Constitutive Arguments

1.1   *Competence Arguments*

These define the institutionally competent interpreters and the degree of validity of their interpretative activity. These definitions are based on the constitutional framework, that is, division of powers, theory of legislation, theory of jurisdiction and so on.

1.2   *Procedural Arguments*

These refer to principles defining the institutional basis of judicial decisions, like duty of motivation, right of defence, civil or penal procedural law or rules about evidence. Tribunals often develop the concrete meaning of these principles within the circumstances of the case.

1.3   *Arguments about the Object and Limits of Interpretation*

One can distinguish arguments about the field of interpretation, applying the rule 'in claris interpretatio cessat' or establishing the concrete meaning of 'obscurity', 'silence' or 'insufficiency' of law as concepts that legally define justice. Other arguments define the border between interpretation and gap-filling. Another type of argument is related to the very nature of interpretation. One may mention argumentation based on the opposition between 'words' and 'spirit' of the law, 'objective' and 'subjective' meaning or 'actual' and 'historical' context of application.

2 Methodological Arguments: First Level

2.1 *Linguistic*

2.1.1 Semantic arguments relate to the type of language used – ordinary, juridical or technical – and the rules that should be used in order to establish priority. At this point, one can quite often identify contradictory rules, depending on the factual circumstances of the case, the legal field or the type of norms under consideration.

2.1.2 Syntactic arguments are also very common, dealing with doubts generated by unclear usages of syntactical rules about punctuation, gender or verbal conjugation.

2.2 *Systemic*

Systemic arguments start from the premise that every norm is a part of a complex whole. Ost and van der Kerchove propose a basic distinction that reconstructs accurately Argentine practice, speaking about either an *extrinsic* systematicity, location of the rule among the general order of codes, special statutes, parts, titles, chapters, articles or paragraphs, or an *intrinsic* systematicity, related to the logical dependence of the norm on a more general order. Arguments about basic principles like coherence, conceptual economy, utility, non-redundancy or conciliatory interpretation can be qualified under this last type. Most of the arguments related to gap-filling problems can also be included here.

2.3 *Functional*

The field of functional argument covers more or less what has been traditionally considered under the topic of historical or teleological methods. This approach – proposed also by Ost and van der Kerchove – has an advantage over the artificiality of isolated consideration of particular arguments. Functional argumentation is oriented to establish the goals of a given statute. These arguments mix argumentation about the historic or social context of the statute and its presumptive subjective or objective intent. One can distinguish some subtypes of functional arguments.

2.3.1 Some arguments here relate to the material sources of legislation. In the case of the Argentine legal system, this is very frequent especially in civil matters, where official notes refer to the sources of each article of the Civic Code and integrate the official text of the Code. The official proceedings of the constitutional conventions or congressional debates are also quoted.

2.3.2   Some arguments relate to the historical origins of the legislation. These arguments have two main subtypes. Firstly, some take into account not only previous projects, legislative discussions and gradual modifications, but also original intent. In the Argentine judicial tradition this argumentation is mostly functional. (By contrast, the original intent of the law-maker is the actual intent.) Judges mainly use the argument to extend the field of a given norm and very seldom to restrict it. Secondly, some arguments of historical origin focus on the analysis of the context and origin of the norm. In this second sense, the argument may operate either to restrict or extend the original scope of the norm. In *Sejean* the Supreme Court said that 'this Court does not make historical judgements or declarations intended to be perennial. It only must do justice in concrete cases submitted to its consideration . . . it would be nonsense to ask for the grounds of secular debates . . .' (*Fallos*, 308–2290).

2.3.3   There are arguments based on the doctrinal sources of the norm, considered not only as a historical fact but as a useful explanation of the meaning of the norm. The official notes of the author of the Civil Code offer common standpoints for this type of argument.

2.3.4   Some arguments refer to the goals of legislation. Some expressions such as 'object', 'intent' or 'spirit' of the statute open up the large field of what is traditionally known as 'teleologic' interpretation.

3   Methodological Arguments: Second Level

This type of argument covers an important field of justificatory reasoning, dealing with procedural and preference criteria. The conflict between alternative arguments is solved with this special type of argument about arguments, broadly considered below in section VI.

In general, constitutive and methodological arguments are used in an integrated picture of operative interpretation. Argentine judicial doctrine has evolved from an initial starting-point, where the influences of the *Ecole de l'Exégèse* in private law and of the American doctrinal construction of 'original intent' were dominant, towards a more developed stage, where the relevant data and consequences of rival interpretations can be evaluated in order to decide which solution can best harmonize words, principles, context, purposes and possible external consequences of every alternative solution. Legal doctrine of tribunals, even at lower levels, offers a rich account of this wide picture of the interpretative task, not always understood by scholarship. The Supreme Court states that judicial decisions must avoid interpretational alternatives that could destroy harmony and coherence in law (*Peron*, April 26-983). In the same case, the Supreme Court said that the primary source of legal interpretation should be the words of the statute. Nevertheless judges must go beyond the literal meaning, searching for the intention of the law-maker and the spirit of the norm. All these exist in a way that guarantees harmony of the legal order and its adherence to constitutional principles.

In other cases, it has been underlined that 'the analysis of the original intent must be complemented by a broader view of the different parts of the legal order. Judges must go beyond the literal meaning of statutes and determine the juridical meaning of the statutes. As servants of law and justice, judges must consider, beyond words, the *ratio legis* and the spirit of the norms' (*Chammas, E.T. y otro v. Banco de Córdoba*, July 10-982).

Interpretation is considered as a search for the plain meaning of the statute. 'At the end, the primary goal of legal interpretation,' said the Court, 'is to give plain effects to the legislator's will' (*Fallos*, 200–176, among other decisions). The first constitutional treatise, Joaquín V. Gonzalez's *Manual de la Constitución Argentina*, underlines that 'The best method for studying our constitution is to seek its more positive sense. The constitution is an instrument of government made and adopted by the people with some practical purposes, such as to live and develop men as real persons in the world. Its mission is the culture of the individual and of mankind . . .' 'Thus we must try to search for the sense of obscure or doubtful clauses within the frame of the same constitution. Only if we do not arrive at a clear solution may we advance towards other explanatory dimensions, like the historical origins, the opinions and doctrines of the authors of the precedent judicial solutions' (p. 33).

'A just solution to a case,' stated the Supreme Court in *Carlos Jose Outon y otros*, (March 29-967) 'does not mean rigorously applying the words of the statute, excluding its spirit. The best method of legal interpretation is that which establishes the purposes of the enactment . . . The basic hermeneutical principle establishes that we must attend to the general context of statutes, to its informing purposes' (*Fallos*, 235–453, 260–171, 253–344, 261–36). 'Legal enactments must be understood in such a way that their purpose can be accomplished according to the principles of a discrete and reasonable interpretation' (267–219).

3.1   Literal Meaning

The tribunals seldom use lexical sources such as dictionaries, reference books, glossaries or other technical sources of vocabulary definitions. The dictionaries only operate as a first step in a wider argument. Literal meaning is not always the dictionary definition but a first-hand usage of the words, at the level of ordinary language in everyday situations. 'Literal meaning' is a very common expression for a primary standpoint that ought to be displaced by a more technical meaning or more or less linguistic conventions, the understanding of which could allow a better interpretation, in the light of the reasonable purpose of the statute.

3.2   Contextual Meaning

One can observe an extended usage of the term 'context'. It conceives of legal language as a systemic whole, where each expression can receive an additional sense, useful at the moment when a strict consideration of the naked meaning of the words is not enough in order to understand more complex situations. The idea of 'harmonization' of meaning seems to be linked to a conception of legal language as a highly structured reality, so its understanding is not an automatic outcome of the interpretative activity, but the result of a gradual hermeneutic strategy, that considers the role of the expression within the textual context, its coherence with other parts of the same statute and with the legal order considered as a whole.

3.3   Reasonableness

The judicial criterion of reasonableness is always problematic. An interpretative argument ought to be always reasonable and this reasonableness is not automatically coincident with the literal or contextual meaning of a given expression. The courts have frequent recourse to expressions such as 'inner justice', 'just solutions' (as opposed to purely formal solutions), 'equalization of sentences and constitutional principles', 'reasonable derivation of the principles of the constitutional State' or just simply 'reasonableness'.

3.4   Functional Creativity

There is a generalized picture of judicial activity as an open and flexible contribution to the integration of legal order. Beyond academic disputes about the nature of legal order, judges tend to see law as an open structure that must be integrated by means of their decisions. Functional creativity describes the active role of judicial interpretation, filling gaps, enlarging the original semantic field of established legal categories and solving new problems through an adaptation process of previous solutions. The principle is that judges must be aware of societal changes and of the always changing nature of values and fundamental legal principles. 'The reality of each era,' said Justice Fayt, dissenting in *Costa, H.R.* v. *Municipalidad de la Capital y otros*, (March 12-987) 'perfects the remaining spirit of the institutions or unveils new aspects not previously contemplated.'

IV   GAP-FILLING ARGUMENTS

In gap-filling, the types of arguments are the same as those previously described. Some of them are specially appropriate for the filling of gaps, focusing on the use of analogy. As is generally stated in comparative law, the use of analogy is restricted in the case of special regulations, exceptions to general rules and principles, and norms that limit individual rights. In the specific case of criminal law, the prohibition of analogy operates as a basic principle. The punitive function of law is restricted to undubious cases. That means an understanding of analogy as a potentially discretionary instrument of reasoning, involving risks to widely recognized individual guarantees.

V   MATERIALS OF INTERPRETATIVE AGUMENTATION

Starting from A. Peczenik's well-known distinction between materials to which judges (a) must refer, (b) may merely refer and (c) may not refer at all, one may draw a very general account of the materials normally necessary or merely admissible for the judicial operative interpretation. In Peczenik's view, 'must-sources' are mandatory materials that precede 'should-sources', merely admissible, which in turn precede 'may-sources'. 'Must-sources' provide stronger support for an authoritative decision than all the others. What is really important to consider is that a precise interpretation of these concepts varies from one legal system to another, from one time to another, from one special field of the legal matter to another.

The principle is, at least in the Argentine experience, that what is admissible is any justificatory argument that provides support for a decision according to the higher principles that govern the interpretative task. As has been previously said, the Argentine legal culture maintains an open sense of what legal argumentation and legal justification means. As a consequence, 'may-sources' provide a wide field of research. What really counts is the purpose of grounding the judicial decision-making process.

Thus judges incorporate materials coming from historical knowledge, prior or current interpretations of the same norm, legislative history, prior judicial interpretations, sociological observations, scholar's opinions and general legal doctrine. Even some ideological, political or ethical arguments may be used as 'may-sources', when there are not primary rules explicitly excluding them.

The Supreme Court has expressed this very wide view of argumentative sources, when it stated that 'A basic rule of legal interpretation requires giving full effect to legislative intent, taking all the precepts into account, so that the laws harmonize with the remaining judicial order and with the principles and guarantees of the national constitution. This purpose may not be ignored by the judges in view of possible technical imperfections in the implementation of such laws.' What really counts is the *ratio legis* (*Romero, Romualdo F. v. Banco Hipotecario Nacional*, March 12-987).

To a certain extent, predominant judicial doctrine assumes that the realm of law is broader than the mere field of legal norms. The judicial task is to establish the connection between law and particular legal enactments. Such is the meaning of the Supreme Court position when it stated:

> Above that which the law seems to say literally, it is inherent to interpretation to inquire into what these laws mean from a juridical point of view. That is to say, what these laws mean in connection with the other norms that are part of the general legal order of a country, so as to harmonize the laws, making them agree among themselves, and especially with the principles and guarantees of the national constitution. (*Gunther, Fernando R. v. Gobierno Nacional-Ejército Argentino*, 5–7–86)

A more detailed assessment of the current doctrine about material support of interpretative argumentation shows some peculiarities of the Argentine doctrine on this topic.

1   In Argentina there is no 'Brandeis Brief'. There is interpretive integration of historical references to the contextual origin of the statute but never as a self-evident argument. In most of the cases, this historical argumentation has a rather negative function, discarding alternative interpretations and

focusing the argument on what is intended to be the right one. The most prominent decisions of the Court have made a significant use of historical materials demonstrating how contextual changes justify new interpretations. Functionally oriented interpretative strategies are commonly based on historical considerations.

2   Records of legislative history are used very seldom and only when the legislative discussion is really relevant for establishing the right interpretation of a given statute. Nevertheless many of the statutes in force have been adopted without open discussion, owing to the extensive authoritarian experience of the country. The records of technical or advisory committees can be made available and are also used by doctrine, but never as a judicial argument. The history of the language and concepts actually adopted in the statute is not considered as relevant material.

3   Some prior or current interpretations by addressees of the law who are not judges are also considered. Some of them come from official organs such as the *Procuracion del Tesoro*, which acts as an advisory organ for the Executive Power in most of the disputable administrative questions. The opinions of the Procurator are binding for members of the corps of official lawyers. Some interpretations by administrative organs are also important as 'must' or 'should-materials', that is, the decisions of the Ministry of Labour on collective bargaining, the General Revenue Office for tax problems.

4   The language and purposes of other related statutes or other statutes superseded, modified or otherwise affected by the interpreted statute may be considered as argumentative material. This seems to be less important, despite the fact that constant legal change offers many examples of very imperfect drafting, with very frequent partial overlapping of norms. Arguments on *pari materia* are cautiously considered.

5   Comparative law materials are not very relevant. A relevant law of another legal system or an international treaty could only be considered as a 'must' or 'should-material' if it is a binding legal source. But as a material in justifying reasons it is not usually important.

6   Prior judicial interpretations or precedents are really 'must-sources', despite the fact that Argentina does not have a precedent-based system. Judicial decisions are decisive materials not because of their grounds but because of formal authority. A given judicial interpretation could hardly be maintained against a Supreme Court decision explicitly devoted to the matter under discussion. With the increasing

complexity of legal matters, precedents become more important than academic doctrine.

7   The teleological or normative nature of the form of life or other phenomena subject to the statute is always an important point of discussion. Regulative ideas as the 'objective legal truth' (referred to as the very nature of facts under discussion) are very important, according to the substantive approach of judicial doctrine. Some social or economic facts are really 'must-materials'. Inflation offers a good field for examples. Economic facts, measured through strictly economic instruments ought to be considered as reasons for argumentative task. Some technical opinions about biological facts are also almost mandatory sources of judicial opinions.

8   Opinions of law professors (legal doctrine) are important materials. Authors and, at least in some fields, specialized national congresses are sources of interpretations not binding but highly influential, especially in some evolving new fields or in the new developments of traditional fields, that is, constitutional and particularly administrative law. In general, academic materials receive very special treatment, sometimes as arguments about alternative interpretations and sometimes as authoritative arguments. Foreign doctrine is also considered, following an old tradition, inaugurated by the civil code.

VI   CONFLICTS BETWEEN ARGUMENTS

In the case of Argentine judicial practice, it is very difficult to establish the existence of explicit conflict-solving rules. The study of decisions shows to what extent a decision is always a more or less arbitral option between alternative or even opposite interpretations. The problem is the real nature and value of some principles invoked as preference criteria during the weighing activity of the judge. Argentine scholars have devoted scant attention to the empirical assessment of argumentative strategies and criteria. Judges have, on the contrary, a special sensitivity to the topic. As in other legal cultures, legal interpretation is perceived as a weighing process, where legislative intent, literal meaning, plain meaning, actual intention and reasonable sense are considered relevant criteria for establishing what the Argentine courts very often declare as the prudent and reasonable meaning of legal enactments.

It is impossible to identify a best or even a standard view of the way conflicts between different types of arguments must be solved. There are some legally established criteria. Art. 16 of the Civil Code, says that, 'if a civil question cannot be resolved either through words or through the spirit of the law, it must adhere to the principles of analogous statutes; if the question remains unresolved, general principles of law must be applied taking into consideration the circumstances of the case'. In an annotation to this article, D. Velez Sarfield, author of the Code, notes that this solution is based on Roman law tradition and ancient Spanish sources.

The first doctrine of statutory interpretation in civil law, following the *Ecole de l'Exégèse*, underscored the primacy of the literal meaning of words. This doctrine was strongly emphasized in most textbooks and legal scholarship. Legal education was organized following the models of explanatory commentaries, based on very strict definitions of the literal meaning according to the normal meaning of language.

Subsequent to the first stage of this doctrine, a more dynamic view of statutory interpretation began to emerge. This view was decisive in the 1968 Civil Code reform, which introduced principles of equity, good faith and other flexible and elastic criteria into the interpretation of statutes. The basic idea is that interpretation is an open process, where the literal terms of statutes must be read with a flexible view of legislative intent, understood not only as strictly 'original' but as actual and plain.

The courts have said that 'the civil code does not contain rules for the interpretation of contracts; notwithstanding this, the requirement of good faith is considered to be obligatory' (C. Nac. Civ. Sala F, in LL, 12–955, p. 99). Or 'good faith and loyalty' is a directive rule concerning interpretation and application of contracts (C. Civ. y Com. de La Plata en 'La Ley', 126–967, p. 759).

The Supreme Court has established that interpretation is an always necessary precursor of application. Within this process, 'it ought to give full effect to the legislative intent. It is a rule of hermeneutics to try to harmonize the statutes being interpreted with the rest of the legal order. In doubtful cases, the interpretation which makes this harmony truly possible must be preferred' (*C.S. Jauregui v. Obreros y Empleados del Plastico* (LL, 1984-D:809).

In an effort to establish criteria for problem-solving conflicts between different types of arguments, the Court has said that, starting from the first source – the words – judges must consider the intent of the law-makers, and all this must be integrated harmoniously into the rest of the legal order, under the principles and guarantees of the Constitution (*Peron*, April 29-983). In the same decision the Court stated that the first rule of statutory interpretation is to comply with the intention of the legislator and it cannot be circumvented by arguing about technicalities of legal writing. Judges must apply the rule exactly as it was conceived, without analysing its merits or the appropriateness of the original considerations. Thus legislative intent must be considered as complemented by the idea of totality, under an integral interpretation, including precedent.

A primary consideration must be given to legislative intent. This rule must be understood always in a 'positive and dynamic sense'. Present factual situations must be evaluated in the light of the supposed or presumed intent of the law-makers, with the sole purpose of obtaining a final and just solution to the case. In Argentina, the courts affirm the 'complementariness' of different criteria, such as the literal meaning, the legislative intention and the meaning which is both reasonable and in accord with the purpose of the law. The Supreme Court has said many times:

> It is the task of the interpreter to inquire into the true meaning and scope by means of a careful and thorough examination of its terms. Such examination must consider the true meaning of the precept and the will of the legislator, and whatever the nature of the norm, there is no better method of interpretation than that which supremely considers the purpose of that law. (*Ibarguren de Duarte, Juana* v. *Peron, Juan D.*)

It has also frequently been said that, in fact, the primacy of a literal interpretation is connected to the intention of the legislator. It has been stated that 'the main rule of interpretation of law is to give full credit to the legislative intent and the first source for determining such intent is to examine the very text of the law' (*Union Civica Radical de la Prov. de Buenos Aires* v. *Junat Electoral de la Pcia de Buenos Aires*, 22-9-86). This principle is in turn connected to the necessity of producing above all a reasonable interpretation, because 'a legal principle . . . must not be applied "ad literam", without a prior circumstantial formulation that leads to the true legal exegesis because, in default thereof, one runs the risk of arriving at an unreasonable conclusion' (*Basigaluz Saez, Laura E.* v. *Gobierno Nacional -Ministerio de Educación y Justicia-*, 30-9-86).

Starting from this basic doctrinal background, one can summarize the current judicial doctrine around the following standpoints.

1   Priority of a positive interpretation, in the sense of primacy of arguments that favour a recognition of the validity of the norm. The Supreme Court has said, 'The question of constitutional validity of a certain norm is a very delicate one. It never ought to be solved negatively in dubious cases. It is an accepted doctrine that in such cases, judges must uphold the

validity of the law. In judicial review, the court must be cautious, being jealous in the usage of its powers and respectful of the rest of state powers' (*Fallos*, 306–635).

2   Statutes ought to be interpreted in a progressive sense, especially in those matters where constitutional considerations are under analysis. This is so because 'the constitution is not a fixed set of dogmatic prescriptions', but, on the contrary, 'it is a vivid creation . . . capable of a provisional regulation of the common interest throughout successive stages of development' (*Fallos*, 178–19). This is the basis of a constant affirmation of the primacy of a progressive interpretation. It does not mean automatically a declaration of political activism of the courts, but an open recognition of law and judicial activity as an instrument of social improvement.

3   In deciding cases, judges ought to respect the 'legal and moral consciousness of society' (*Fallos*, 248–342), because judges 'ought to have legal and political sensitivity, especially whenever their analysis focuses on the foundations of the State' (*Fallos*, 247–654). In the last decades, the Supreme Court has evolved from an explicitly natural law-based conception about the moral grounds of interpretative reasoning towards a philosophically more eclectic and open approach, but always with the same basic interest in enrichment of strict positivistic views.

4   Interpretation should contribute to the stabilization of legal order. The Supreme Court has spoken about 'calculable stability of the relationship between government and the governed' (*Fallos*, 248–324). This principle is understandable in the Argentine context in view of the fact of institutional discontinuity. Recently the crucial decision in *Bazterrica* said that 'our country lives at a particular and historic moment. From different sources, there is a general contribution to the reconstruction of the legal order, trying to re-establish and to consolidate in the future the republican and democratic forms of coexistence. This purpose must guide every form of constitutional hermeneutics' (Bazterrica, Gustavo M., August 29-986). This argument has thrived in important cases about privacy. In *Balbin*, trying to fix a general criterion for solving the conflict between arguments favourable to privacy and arguments supporting a wider view of freedom of expression, the Court stated that law ought to be considered adequately to the social reality of every moment, in order to avoid the freezing of its norms and principles.

5   Interpretation ought to be historically dynamic. Regulating

the extension of free speech, the Court has recently said that the constitutional principle about freedom of expression ought to be considered 'beyond the naked literality'. It also said that the constitutional text ought to be read as an answer to its original circumstances. 'Thus, what is necessary is a conceptual extension, in order to feed the democratic decision-making process, because the interchange of ideas must be complemented by information about those facts related to society as a whole' (*Balbin*).

6   Conflicts ought to be considered in a relative way, especially conflicts between opposite principles regarding rightness. The precedent of *Balbin* is a fruitful source of criteria. Considering the tension between constitutionally-based fundamental rights, the higher tribunal said in a similar decision that 'the conflict between freedom of expression and privacy is not absolute, because the maximum of liberty ought to be complemented by the maximum of due care and prudence. This right should not be extended beyond the necessary harmony between the other constitutional rights, including moral integrity and personal honour' (*Campillay, J.C.* v. *'La Razon'*, *'Cronica' and 'Diario Popular'*, ED, 118:302). The general principle is that, whenever there is a conflict between legal values, 'judges must prefer those of higher hierarchy, regarding the great goals of constitutional organization' (*Costa*, LL, 1987-B:267).

7   Axiological reference. Another way of solving conflicts between conflicting arguments is the reference to the possible underlying conflict of values. There is a doctrine about conflict between social standards, and *Bazterrica* offers again a valuable source of evidence. There the Supreme Court decided against punishment of drug possession for personal usage, stating that private actions (in the sense of the expression used by Art. 19 of the Constitution) are not only those actions exempted from the authority of magistrates (constitutional words), but also those that, although known by others, do not affect their rights, morality or the public order of a given community.

8   Consequentialistic approach. There is also the need to consider consequences of alternative interpretations. In *Bazterrica*, the Court stated once more that it ought to distinguish between the private ethics of the individuals, exempted from judicial control, and collective ethics, where public goods or interests ought to be regarded. 'Public order and morality protect those goods, always envisaging intersubjective behaviour, that is, the actions that harm third

parties.' This doctrine starts from the idea that 'Art. 19 of the Constitution is the very basis of modern freedom, that is of the autonomy of mind and personal will, committed to the idea that good actions ought to be an outcome of personal beliefs. This ought to be considered as a primary ethical duty' (Justice Petracchi's opinion in *Bazterrica*). He added that 'We cannot punish every behaviour affecting individual morality. In such a case, the State would be reinforcing certain morality, right on the border of totalitarianism.'

9　Reinforcement of individual rights. As in most legal cultures, arguments referring to the primacy of social defence usually conflict with arguments for priority of a rights-based answer. In this sense the option for the second alternative is quite clear.

VII CONFLICTS BETWEEN SOURCES

In line with the continental legal structure, Argentina adheres clearly to the idea of the primacy of statutory law as a mandatory source. The above mentioned hierarchy, established by Art. 31 of the federal constitution, is developed by lower legislative sources. Art. 34, inc. 4 of the National Civil and Commercial Procedural Code says that, among the judge's duties, he must make his decisions, 'respecting the hierarchy of established norms and the principle of congruence'. Art. 163 of the same Code, speaking about requirements of final decisions, establishes that a judgement must contain 'the foundations and the application of the law'.

One of the oldest statutes in Argentina, Law 27 of 1862, establishes that federal justice must always act through application of the constitution and national statutes to case decisions. It may not apply other norms produced by provincial state powers which are opposed to the constitution. The primacy of the constitution excludes the possibility of a conflict between constitutional norms and norms belonging to the lower level of provincial law.

Law 48, that regulates the competence and jurisdiction of federal courts, also establishes a hierarchical order. It states that federal tribunals and judges must apply the constitution as the supreme law of the nation. Below the constitution, judges can apply congressional enactments, international treatises recognized by the Congress, the particular provincial statutes, the former national statutes, and the principles of 'derecho de gentes' (natural law of nations), Art. 21.

Judges can consider the decisions of other courts, even of a lower level. These precedents are not binding, except in the case of *plenary decisions*, which, as mentioned before, are binding at the level of the same judges of the same Court and at the level of lower tribunals. Precedents of the Supreme Court act as a sort of legal doctrine. Precedents are not legally binding, but their force arises from their *ratio legis* and the institutional supremacy of the constitution.

Customary law can be applied only in those cases in which the legal enactments explicity refer to it. This is also true regarding a variety of regulations and norms in the field of administrative law, internal bureaucratic regulations, technical enactments in the fields of economic law, urban planning law and so on. In the field of commercial law, Art. V of the Code establishes that 'commercial customers can serve as rules when determining the sense of commercial words or technical expressions and interpreting commercial acts or conventions'.

The problem-solving activity regarding conflicts of sources is considered as both an interpretative and gap-filling activity. The types of arguments and priority criteria previously analysed are clearly applicable to this topic. The empirical evidence about judicial doctrine also shows a substantive approach, despite some indisputable formal rules, more or less existing in every legal culture. These rules are increasingly important because of the rapid and profound social and economic changes. Partial reforms are normal and interpreters have the permanent problem of reconciling norms of different origins and hierarchical levels. This is the reason for the importance of such rules within a modern legal system. As Peczenik has pointed out, all priority rules allow exceptions based on weighing of the various reasons, mainly because the priority rules only have a procedural function. Judges use them while they search for good reasons to decide concrete cases. The basic rules are the following.

1   Hierarchical Rule

Higher rules prevail over lower rules (*lex superior derogat legem inferiorem*). This rule is independent of content. The principle raises several definitional and operative problems, especially in a federal country like Argentina where one can distinguish a federal order and a provincial order, each with its own legislative activity. Likewise one can distinguish between national (federal), provincial and municipal (local) statutes. National statutes are those enacted by the federal organs (legislative or administrative), exercising powers explicitly or implicitly delegated by provinces (CN Arts 28 and 104). Provincial statutes are enacted by provincial organs, exercising those powers not delegated to the Nation (CM Art. 104). Municipal statutes are those enacted by municipalities exercising powers recognized and guaranteed by the provinces.

Starting from this basic structure, one can distinguish the following hierarchical order:

(a) National statutes, prior to provincial statutes, as dictated 'as a consequence of the Constitution' (CN Art. 31), respectful of the constitutional distribution of powers between the federal and provincial orders. National statutes can be constitutional (related to constitutional matters) or ordinary and have the following internal basic hierarchy: (i) legislative statutes, dictated by the legislative power, following the constitutionally established forms and procedures; (ii) legislative statutes enacted by decree of the executive power (administrative acts with general effects); (iii) legislative statutes enacted by general resolutions of decentralized agencies or of administrative agencies hierarchically dependent on the executive power. During non-democratic governments, the decrees of the executive power (Decretos-leyes) are recognized with the same hierarchy of legislative acts.

(b) Provincial statutes, that can also be constitutional or ordinary, prior to municipal statutes, as far as adequate to provincial constitutions. The internal hierarchy is similar to the national one.

(c) Municipal statutes (also constitutional or ordinary), enacted by those municipalities with delegated powers to do so. The internal hierarchy is similar.

In the case of Argentina, the hierarchical principle is clearly insufficient to solve possible vertical conflicts and ought to be complemented by competence criteria. Besides the hierarchical position of the organs, a priority in the scale of sources presupposes material competence. All the conflicts between national and provincial statutes can be solved through a successive and integrated consideration of the principles of hierarchy and competence.

2 Chronological Rule

Posterior rules prevail over prior rules ('lex posterior derogat priori'). This rule is independent of content, and its application only depends on the empirical verification of a natural fact (the formal publication of the norm, prescribed by Art. 2 of the Civil Code). The complex and dynamic nature of legislative processes has moderated the prerequisite of publication, accepting many different forms of publication. The most important interpretative problems regarding this rule are referred to as derogation. As in other legal cultures, in Argentina derogation can be explicit or implicit. Most of the statutes explicitly derogate, generally at the end of the new statute. Sometimes this derogation simply establishes that 'all norms contradictory to the present norm are derogated'. The express prohibition of retroactive effects (Civil Code, Art. 3) is an important complementary principle.

3   Speciality Rule

Special norms prevail over general norms ('lex specialis derogat generali'). As this rule depends on the ruled matter, it is necessarily an interpretative activity. In Argentina, special legislation is not marginal or accidental. On the contrary, it is the most important quantitative and qualitative expression of legislative activity. Thus the judgement of speciality is always a relative and complex matter, mainly when there is a conflict with other conflict-solving rules. These basic rules are only a basic standpoint. Each one raises complex definitional and operative problems that are, in fact, a matter for judicial interpretation. The hierarchical rule can be applied only when the conflict is between sources situated at different levels of the legal order. The chronological rule can be applied with successive statutes. The speciality rule can be applied only when there is a different extension of the conflicting norms. The interpreter is always the key. In the case of antinomies (that is, conflict between contemporary norms at the same level and of equal extension), the interpretative activity is creative activity. Beyond widely recognized solving criteria, there always is the possibility of an interpretative discussion, every time that judges perceive the possible unreasonableness of a given solution.

The conflict between constitution and lower norms is quite clear in the Argentine system. The Supreme Court has the last word in constitutional review, but the control of constitutionality of norms belongs to the competence of every tribunal. The declaration of unconstitutionality is considered as the *ultima ratio* of the legal order and must always be the result of a concrete decision of a case. There is no abstract control of legitimacy.

VIII   INTERPRETATIVE PRESUMPTIONS

One of the most basic general presumptions, underlying all judicial interpretation, is the principle of unity and non-contradiction of the legal order, postulating the wholeness, hermetic completeness and integrity of the legal order. This idea about the legislator derives from the more ideological theory of the *bon législateur*. Tribunals also speak about the 'unity of constitutional order' and the 'unity of economic order'. Other basic presumptions are that the will of the legislator is never contradictory, superfluous or wrong. The law-maker cannot be contradictory or unjust. On the contrary, he is always accurate, his decision has been inspired by exhaustive information and has good and useful purposes.

In the Argentine system every kind of legislative enactment is presumed to be constitutionally right and reasonable. Unconstitutionality must be affirmatively proven and declared. There is a background presumption of non-arbitrary and ever-rational purposes and behaviour on the part of the law-makers.

In the Supreme Court judicial doctrine, this idea has often been understood as imposing a presumption of justice. In the well-known decision about the responsibility of the Military Juntas for the military repression during authoritarian rule, a dissenting opinion of the Court stated:

> It is not appropriate to affirm that every type of punishable behaviour must be based or founded on the law in its formal sense, leaving aside the decisions of the interpreter. In effect, the application of positive criminal law implies the necessity of deciding in favour of one or the other of its possible interpretations, and that such decisions may not be deduced from the legal texts. (Justice Petracchi in *Causa originariamente instruida por el Consejo Supremo de las Fuerzas Armadas en cumplimiento del Decreto 158/83 del Poder Ejecutivo Nacional*, December 30-986)

The general presumption of the rationality of the legislator is imposed even on possible imperfections of the norms interpreted. Its rationality, coherence and sense of justice is presumed. The Supreme Court also expressed this idea when it said:

> The understanding of the law must be practised taking into account the general context and the ends upon which they are based, adjusting that practice to a careful and thorough examination of the terms. This examination must consider the rationality of the precept and the will of the legislator, and this must not be avoided because of any possible technical imperfections of the legal instruments, which would frustrate the objectives of the norm. (*Ferrer, Roberto O.* v. *Gobierno Nacional (Ministerio de Defensa)*, November 25-986)

The presumption of unity and essential coherence of the legal order is also clearly expressed in several decisions saying that the statutes must be interpreted in such a way as to avoid giving them

a meaning that is opposed to other regulations (one thus destroy-
ing the other) and by adopting as true that which reconciles them
and leaves all of them in full force and effect (*Carranza Torres José
M. v. Provincia del Chaco*, September 30-986).

Judicial doctrine has established that, if there is no contrary
disposition, all presumptions are supposed to be *iure et de iure*
without any possible contrary evidence, especially whenever there
is a common interest or a moral rule to be preserved. Presumptions
will be *iuris tantum* (can be destroyed through contrary evidence) in
cases of interpreting a will or understanding attitudes (CN Civ. Sala
D 27/5/1963, LL, n.487; ED, 4, 726). The construction of presumptions in some legal fields where factual questions are central is very
important, that is, liability, transit accidents, insurance law. These
presumptions, elaborated from the basis of experience and not
established by law, can be considered as sources only if they are
founded in real and proven facts, and only when these presumptions, because of the number, weight, seriousness, and lack of
contradiction, produce a clear conviction, supported by evidence,
according to the nature of the process, and the rules of 'sana crítica'
(Nat. Civ. and Comm. Proc. Cod. Art. 163). ('Sana crítica' is a
standard that refers primarily to a judge's reasonable judgement of
the concrete circumstances of the case.)

IX   STYLE AND STRUCTURE OF OPINIONS

The style and structure of the Supreme Court decisions reflect not
only the highly doctrinal approach to the judicial function of the
tribunal, but also a deep awareness about the public role of its
decisions. Decisions are written to be known not only by the
parties, but also by the specialized and general public. In Argentina
there are two legal newspapers and some more weekly legal
magazines, that reproduce in full decisions and publish doctrinal
articles, bibliographical notes and professional news. The Supreme
Court publishes all its decisions, whatever the relevance in a special
collection (*Fallos*). Any decision of the lower tribunals and judges
may be published, depending on the editorial decision of the
newspapers and magazines, and a substantial part of the higher
tribunals' decisions is finally published — sometimes even with
comments by scholars.

This possibility of an almost universal knowledge about opinion
leads to very careful argumentation, foundation of arguments,
footnotes, and comparative and doctrinal references. This external
circumstance has influenced the structure and style of opinions and
decisions. The idea of not only objective but also public control of

the argumentation pervades the intellectual tasks of judges and courts. The presupposed addressees of the reasoning processes are the parties, lower courts and, especially, public opinion. Justices are deeply aware of the creative role of the Court and of the objective and general impact of their opinions on the general legal order. The opinion not only indicates the results of the conflict to the parties and the general public, but it is also an attempt to justify the decision.

Regarding the minimum content, opinions vary, depending on the level of the tribunal. There are no explicit rules about structure, but there is a minimum content specified by law. Art. 163 of the Nat. Civ. and Comm. Procedural Code says that the first instance definitive sentence must contain: (1) place and date; (2) name of the parties; (3) a brief account of the issues; (4) a separate consideration of every question considered in the case; (5) the grounds and the applicable law; (6) the express, positive and precise resolution, and its relation to the contentions of the parties, considering the facts and the law; (7) the term of the sentence; and (8) express decision about costs and honoraries.

Regarding the form, in general, every decision has four parts: firstly the 'visas' — 'vistos' — that summarize the content of the different steps of judicial proceedings, describing the factual situation and the problem under consideration; secondly, the 'considerandos', devoted to the tribunal's account of positions and arguments of the parties, the results of evidence production and also the norms that ought to be considered for a decision; thirdly, the 'resultandos' where the tribunal analyses the facts, the evidence, the reasons and motivations argued by the parties, and, after all that, the tribunal's own view about the case; and fourthly, the final decision, written in a very concise way and expressed in numbered paragraphs. Every decision means an exhaustive delimitation of relevant facts, a legal qualification, and explicit mention of the norms applied to the case, solving all the interpretative or integrative problems, and the foundations and grounding of the resolution. The opinion contains references to the law to support every step of the decisional process.

The decisions of the Supreme Court have a different structure, because of its activity at the final highest level. A brief section of 'vistos' only mentions the name of the parties and the nature of the issue. Then the 'considerandos' describes, in numbered paragraphs, the different positions and arguments of the parties. It identifies the arguments and questions, giving explicit arguments about them. The argumentation is always supported by doctrinal references about the Supreme Court's traditional doctrine on every point of the debate. In a final paragraph, the Court fixes its position, deciding the case. The decision is signed by the justices, with an express mention of dissents, that are also published. The general mode of decisions is very flexible. The weighing model is the most common, but an attempt is always made to establish a rightly reasoned conclusion.

Decisions usually contain substantive reasons, besides a formal consideration of applicable law. The former are the most important and there are now limits to explanation and illustration. Opinions also try to link the partial and final conclusions to established interpretative patterns, quoting extensively prior judicial doctrine of the Court. There is nothing like an official ideology of the Court. The majority opinion only decides a case, without any formally binding consequence in terms of generality. This could be, of course, the natural consequence of the institutional weight of a Supreme Court decision.

X   INTERPRETATION AND THE SPECIAL CHARACTER OF THE STATUTE

The special character of the statute has an evident influence upon interpretative argumentation. The most obvious examples come from the field of criminal law and, in general, norms that limit individual rights in different legal fields. In principle, restrictive norms ought to be interpreted restrictively. The basic rule, 'nulla poena sine lege', prohibits analogic interpretation and application of penal statutes and retroactivity of more severe legal norms. Crimes and punishments are strictly defined in a closed catalogue. The penal code is a solid institutional barrier against state discretionary powers.

In the field of civil legislation there is an open reception both of 'analogia legis', from another statute, and 'analogia iuris', from general principles. This is the doctrine stated by Art. 16 of the civil Code.

In the case of tax law there is an important literature and judicial doctrine of interpretation. The nature of tax issues explains important peculiarities. Art. 11 of law 11.683 states: 'In the interpretation of this statute purpose and economic meaning ought to be considered.'

Tax law doctrine distinguishes between interpretation and application of tax norms. Interpretation is understood as a theoretical and abstract task, mostly because there are some institutionally established organs for general interpretation, such as director of the DGI, under general request of taxpayers, professional associations or any other organization representing collective interests.

The result of interpretation is always a general declaration, beyond any specific issue. On the contrary, application is considered by tax law doctrine as a practical task, where the identification and interpretation of facts is a crucial dimension. Most of the authors share the idea that general interpretational principles are applicable to procedural problems, but not to the so-called 'substantive tax law', where a different theory and technique of interpretation should be applied (see, in general, J.M. Martin and G.F. Rodriguez Use, 1986).

In recent years, there has been an extended discussion about the regular character of tax norms. In former times the basic idea was that such norms are almost punitive, so that there is a need for restrictive interpretation. However today doctrine envisages tax norms as ordinary norms that can be interpreted by normal methods and techniques, applying extensive or restrictive criteria depending on the economic nature of the issues. This is also the view of the Model Code designed by the Organization of American States and the InterAmerican Development Bank, highly influential among experts. Courts have constructed a specific doctrine where traditional criteria are adapted to the special economic nature of interpreted facts and norms. This doctrine underlines the functional method and the 'economic meaning' method. Some authors (Jarach and Garcia Belsunce) even speak of an autonomy of tax law theory of interpretation; others (Martin and Rodriguez Use) prefer to speak of a special adaptation, aware of the special features of tax issues and matters. Some principles are specially developed by judicial doctrine, that is, the primacy of *intentio facti* over *intentio iuris*. However modern doctrine tends to relativize the extension of these distinctions, arguing for a more rigorous application of general interpretative principles, as a basis for legal certainty in tax and economic relations.

In the field of commercial law, an old doctrine was that it must be interpreted restrictively, following the classical 'exceptio est strictissimae interpretationis' (A. Algorta, 1880). However predominant doctrine tends to reject this. Article II of the Preliminary Title of the Commercial Code says that the interpretation of commercial norms ought to consider 'the nature of facts'. The statute itself can be interpreted either extensively or restrictively, depending on the nature of the issue. What the Commercial Code calls 'uses and customs of commerce' ought to be considered as integrating the norm and, if there is no solution, the interpreter can use analogy, general principles of commercial law and, finally, principles of civil law, considered as a subsidiary source. Special attention to the economic nature of issues is always required in such interpretative argumentation (see R.O. Fontanarrosa, 1969).

Beyond differences related to the content of statutes, another difference comes from the terms of the statute. In recent times the style of drafting has been changing according to the increasing complexity of some legal fields, that is, economic, administrative, welfare law. Rapid obsolescence, poorly drafted statutes, contradictory regulations or purely declarative norms are more the rule than the exception, and this has a natural impact on the practice of legal interpretation, despite the fact that doctrine tends to prefer a reaffirmation of the general character of interpretational argumentation, trying to guarantee legal certainty and predictability, in the face of discretionary interpretations.

XI   THE INSTITUTIONAL ROLE OF THE COURTS

As in the American model, in the Argentine system constitutional issues can be raised in the course of any type of judicial proceeding and at every level of judicial organization. Courts exercise much power to invalidate statutes as contrary to the constitution. Nevertheless this decentralized schema for issues of unconstitutionality is complemented by a highly centralized system of constitutional review, because only the Supreme Court can give the last word.

Every party can raise a constitutional question before any Court at the federal level. The Court can decide the question along with other questions posed by the case. A constitutional question can also be raised by appeal from a decision of a first instance court. Thus constitutional questions are considered apart from the fact situation that gave rise to it and apart from the central issue.

This institutional background gives to the courts a wide field for intervention, not only through the normal problem-solving activity, but also through its protective function in situations of special measures protecting individual and private rights, 'recursos de amparo'. A special interpretation of the principle of division of powers avoids the possibility of formal 'updating' activity by judges. The updating reform, extension or development of a statute is a matter of legislative activity, to be conducted by Congress or through the broad presidential legislative powers.

In the case of Argentina, one cannot speak of a political role of the judicial power, at least in the sense of a partisan role. The Supreme Court and the judicial power in general have not been very sensitive to the demands and pressures of political power. The degree of autonomy and independence of the courts is remarkable, and it can be said that, despite political turmoil and democratic breakdowns, the judicial power has had more continuity than might have been expected. The political power of the Supreme Court is very seldom positively exercised.

Only in very recent times, again under the influence of American ideas about the activist role of judicial review, have some very well known decisions expressed the idea of progressive judicial activity of a legislative kind. But the acceptance of creative powers of the judge has more to do with the possibility of everyday law application, searching for basic values, related to just solution of concrete cases, than with the more progressive idea of a legislative function of the Court. Some recent decisions may have changed this basic position. The most remarkable has been the invalidation of the prohibition of divorce after almost a century under the Civil Marriage Act. The decision was based on the argument that the Court can act subsidiary to the legislative power whenever there are political obstacles to social change. Over many decades, the doctrine of *political questions* protected the courts from conflicts with the political power. Every question belonging to the realm of what the courts defined as 'political' was outside the field of judicial decision and reserved to the authority of the political power. Recent changes in this doctrine, mainly after the recent restoration of democracy, seem to offer a new institutional landscape, in which the courts tend to exercise plainly their constitutional political role.

XII STATUTORY RULES FOR INTERPRETATION

As has been previously said, there are some express rules, mainly set forth in the substantive and procedural codes. The substantive codes (civil, commercial, penal, labour and welfare) are enacted by the federal Congress. All of them have norms related to interpretation, gap-filling, sources and application of law. Besides that, as Argentina is a federally organized country, procedural matters are within the competence of each of the 24 provincial jurisdictions.

Each code establishes specific rules for legal interpretation and for the regulation of conflicts of application. The problem is to determine the real value of these, beyond practical interest as guides for legal practitioners and judges. Little discussion has developed to determine if these rules are really legal norms in the sense of complete enactments, capable of being enforced.

In Argentina, many scholars have discussed the topic, thinking in general that rules regarding legal interpretation are not strict regulations but general descriptions about sources for legal interpretation or simply priority criteria. Thus these rules are not considered a unique element in the weighing process.

XIII   CONSTITUTIONAL PRINCIPLES AND VALUES

The cyclical changes in the political system directly impact on this topic. It is quite clear how the transition to democracy raised the question of democratic principles and values as basic presumptions of judicial work. The Court stated in the decisive *Bazterrica* case:

> Our nation is undergoing unusual historical and political times in which the various levels of creation and interpretation of norms are reconstructing the legal order with the purpose of restoring and securing for the future all democratic and republican forms of coexistence for all Argentinians, in such a way that said objective will lead the constitutional study of interpretation in all fields. (*Bazterriça, Gustavo M.*, August 29-986)

Interpreting the possible content of the ideas of 'democratic and republican forms of coexistence', Justice Petracchi has recently pointed out that the Argentine constitution does not recognize the principle of democratic sovereignty as the only background (*Preamble* and Art. 33 of the Constitution). Besides this principle, Arts 19 and 29 recognize the prior principle of the rule of law, giving supremacy to the law as a general and objective rule, over the subjective will of officials.

In some fields the courts make special appeal to constitutional principles. This is, again, the case in criminal law, where the principles of rule of law have a central importance. The principle of legality is complemented by some other complementary or derived principles, such as the prohibition of analogical application 'in malam partem', the principle of non-retroactiveness of penal laws or the principles related to the idea of judiciality. As a regulative idea, the rule of law is another central value, inspiring the whole interpretational practice.

Legality, division of powers, human dignity, liberty, freedom and equality of opportunities or inviolability of property, and enforcement of justice are also invoked as basic substantive values. Every administrative or judicial decision can be resisted via the argument that constitutional values and guarantees are infringed, and this may justify the 'reserve of a federal case' that opens up the possibility of being heard at the Supreme Court level.

There is a wide recognition of general constitutional principles, beyond any debate about their nature and origin. Some authors prefer to speak about judicial 'construction' of such principles. Others prefer to speak mainly about 'recognition' of these principles, and this brings in the ideological influences of justices. In *S. and D., C.G.* (6-11-80, *Fallos*, 302–1284) Justices Gabrielli and

Rossi, quoting Art. 16 of the Civil Code – related to general principles of law – underlined the original reference of the Code to its source (Art. 7 of the Code of Austria), explicitly stating 'the principles of natural law'. In the same decision, the Court stated that

> the exceptional peculiarities of this case invoke the power of the tribunal in its specific mission of protecting and strengthening constitutional principles . . . avoiding a mechanical and non-discriminatory application of the norm that affects human fundamental rights, ignoring the purpose of an objectively just solution of the concrete case, beyond the general purpose of guaranteeing justice declared by the preamble of the Constitution.

These are not purely occasional references to an ideological background. Over many periods of the Court, the influence of natural law theories has been remarkable. In other periods the strongly axiological orientation has been maintained, despite the fact of less ideological declarations. Justice is recognized as a founding value, and its mention in the preamble is commonly accepted as an operative clause. Every solution ought to be a reasoned and reasonable derivation of law, and that implies some basic principles: (1) submission of judges to the rule of law; (2) impartial exercise of judicial power; (3) respect for the will of the legislator cannot lead to evidently unjust solutions; (4) a deliberate and conscious separation from justice is incompatible with an adequate administration of justice; (5) objective or material truth ought to prevail over purely formal truth; (6) sentences must be reasonable, just and plainly adequate to constitutional principles. (See G.J. Bidart Campos, 1984).

Freedom is another basic value recognized by the courts as a constitutional principle that ought to be protected against any excess of the authority. The only restrictive circumstances recognized by the Constitution are the due penal process (CN Art. 18) and preventive arrest under *état de siège*. Even these powers have been subjected to judicial control for reasonableness.

According to the institutional and political experience of the country, property, political association, privacy and freedom of expression have been strongly underlined by judicial doctrine. The individualistic version of these basic rights has been recognized at all times, despite the ideological changes of the Supreme Court. The general approach has been harmonic integration of values, within a general framework of reasonableness and respect for individual autonomy (CN Art. 19).

XIV   INTERPRETATION AND JUDICIAL ORGANIZATION

The Argentine judicial power is structurally and functionally near to the American model. The Supreme Court is a unitary organ of five (recently nine) members without internal division of labour. Final judicial authority is thus highly concentrated. The members of the federal Judicial Power are selected in an open and even politicized process, proposed by the executive with the agreement of the Senate. Most of the provincial constitutions reproduce this system. So there is nothing like the European 'judicial career'. The autonomy of judges is based on this political selection process. In the European tradition, judges are usually 'career judges' who enter the judiciary at a very early age and are promoted to the higher courts largely on the basis of technical merits and seniority. Their professional training tends to develop, as Cappelletti rightly observes, skills in 'merely interpretative' rather than 'policy-orientated' decision-making (see M. Cappelletti, 1989).

In the case of Argentina, the more political origin of the judges explains the more policy-oriented approach to legal interpretation. Judges are aware of their political and creative function. The absence of something like the 'stare decisis' doctrine and the flexible understanding of precedents gives to the judicial function a more creative and less 'reproductive' role.

Another interesting feature is that, under the European influence, the Supreme Court has been until very recently obligated to hear all the appeals. That means an enormous amount of work, a very slow decision-making process and even a decreasing quality of decisions. Clerks, secretaries and advisors tend to have a significant role. All of this justifies the recent reform introducing a special form of *certiorari*, inspired by the American experience, allowing the Court, for the first time, to select the issues that are going to be solved. The sense of the reform is to reinforce the Supreme Court's *auctoritas*, undoubtedly affected by overload of issues, flood of irrelevant decisions, great charge of administrative duties and routine issues.

In Argentina, 'iura novit curia' is an extended and widely accepted principle. This means that the judicial activity does not rely solely upon adversarial arguments submitted by the parties and their lawyers. The judge 'knows the law' and has an unlimited power to qualify (characterize) facts and search for the right legal answers to the facts proposed by the parties. His capacity to assess evidence is also important, guided by the aforementioned principle of 'objective legal truth'.

XV INTERPRETATION AND LEGISLATION

As has been previously said, Argentina has no tradition of technical and professional drafting. Most of the statutes have origins in authoritarian regimes, without open discussions, and with the intervention of the different ministries. In democratic times, things are not very different. A project can be originated within the legislative power (more precisely within the advisory staffs of individual legislators, quite often influenced by interest groups, professional associations, unions or experts). It also can be originated at the executive power, and this alternative is perhaps the most frequent and important. Different ministries and executive commissions discuss and bargain over the proposed statute, and the final result often reflects this heterogeneous and 'conflictive' origin. The discussion within Congress does not always improve the text. On the contrary, it is a new step in a very complex bargaining process. Argentina has two legislative chambers and both can introduce partial reforms, affecting the structure and the internal coherence of the statute. As a final step, the Executive has a veto power that can modify the text.

The records of this complex decision-making process are complete for democratic statutes. That is, the proceedings of the Chamber of Deputies and the Senate are complete and generally accessible. But there is nothing like this for non-democratic times, which is one important explanation for the slight influence of *travaux préparatoires* on judicial interpretation and gap-filling activity.

XVI INTERPRETATION AND LEGAL CULTURE

As with most of the countries that belong to a complex legal culture, derived from several waves of legislative and doctrinal reception, Argentina has a dynamic interpretational approach. Some basic features must be underlined.

1   Two main aspects of legal culture coexist. One is derived from the continental codified systems and the other from the American tradition. This gives rise to a rather tense coexistence of interpretational approaches: one close to the exegetic movements, derived from the influence of European codifications, and the other from more functional and pragmatic approaches that start from the American influence. This also explains why the American doctrines about constitutional interpretation and judicial review have displaced

the influence of European doctrines, traditionally deriving from private law. Within this broad process of change, substantive approaches tend to displace formal views about interpretation and gap-filling activity.

2   Rapid social change and economic crisis must be considered as an outstanding factor of legal change. One can even distinguish between general stages in the development of interpretative judicial doctrine, related to the changing role of law in society. First, after national organization (1853–63) and until the beginning of this century the exegetical view was influential within a framework of liberal individualistic law, courts and society; second, between 1900 and the 1930s, the influence of scientific positivism was quite clear, especially in terms of systematic interpretation; third, after the 1930s and until the middle of the 1940s, interventionistic economic ideas were received within an intellectual framework that included Keynsianism. During this period, the judicial theory began to receive American realistic ideas and a more functional approach to interpretation; fourth, between 1945 and 1955, during the first Peronist government, natural law theories were influential in the Supreme Court doctrine, specially through the leading intellectual influence of the president, T.D. Casares. Functionalism and anti-formalism also had an important role in this stage; fifth, after 1955 and during part of the 1960s, realistic and functionalistic approaches continued to be important, but, between 1966 and 1983, institutional interruptions generated a complex doctrinal picture in which liberal economic individualism coexisted with realistic and natural law theories about interpretation; sixth, since 1983, there has been a great change in doctrinal influences, with significant reception of American doctrines about a very activistic role of the judiciary: this has been very clear in the Supreme Court interpretative doctrine.

3   Argentine legal culture is the result of a complex process of reception, where the original factors remain strong and active. The importance and prestige of French, Spanish and Italian civil and commercial law doctrine, Italian constitutional and administrative law doctrine, American constitutional and judicial doctrine are complemented by a rich set of theoretical trends, in which natural law, analytical philosophy and critical legal theories exert real influence on judicial doctrines about interpretation. In the light of interpretative doctrine, we deny the existence of any unique interpretive approach. What we see is a tension between

coexisting and even contradictory models. Political turmoil, institutional interruptions and economic crises are factors contributing to this complex and dynamic situation.

REFERENCES

Algorta, A. (1880), *Estudios sobre el Codigo de Comercio*, p. 9, Buenos Aires: Casavalle.

Campos Bidart, G.J. (1984), *La Corte Suprema. El tribunal de las garantias constitutionales*, pp. 62–63, Buenos Aires: Ediar.

Cappelletti, M. (1989), *The Judicial Process in Comparative Perspective*, p. 51, Oxford: Clarendon Press.

Ezquiaga Ganuzas, F.J. (1987), *La argumentación en la justicia constitucional española*, Oñati: HAAE-IVAP.

Fontanarrosa, R.O. (1969), *Derecho commercial argentino*, ch. III, Buenos Aires: V. P. de Zavalia.

Gonzalez, Joaquín V. *Manual de la Constitución Argentina*, p. 33.

Martin, J.M. and Rodriguez Use, G.F. (1986), *Derecho tributario general*, ch. II, Buenos Aires: Depalma.

Morello, A.M. (1989), *La Corte Suprema en accion*, ch. XII, Buenos Aires: Ed. Platense-Abeledo Perrot.

Ost, F. and van der Kerchove, M. (1989), *Entre la lettre et l'esprit. Les directives d'interprétation en droit*, pp. 34–75, Bruxelles: Bruylant.

Tarello, G. (1980), *L° Interpretazione della legge*, cap. VIII, Milano: Giuffre.

Wróblewski, J. (1985), *Constitución y teoría general de la interpretación jurídica*, pp. 27–33, Madrid: Civitas.

4 Statutory Interpretation in the Federal Republic of Germany

ROBERT ALEXY, *Kiel* AND RALF DREIER, *Göttingen**

PRELIMINARY

The legal system of the Federal Republic of Germany is a codified system, and it is a federal one. Briefly (at the time of writing – September, 1990) the federation consists, prior to German reunification, of eleven states (Länder) and the federal system (Bundesrepublik). The states have legislative power to the extent that the Federal Constitution, the Basic Law (Grundgesetz), does not vest it in the federal system. In fact the federal system is the centre of legislation. The federal legislative bodies consist of the Bundestag (Federal Parliament) and the Bundesrat (representative body of the states).

The judicial system is partly state, partly federal; it is vertically divided into a hierarchy of normally three instances, the two lower of which are state courts, whereas the highest court is a federal one. There are five of these highest federal courts, each of them of special jurisdiction. Traditionally the most eminent highest court is the Federal Court of Justice (Bundesgerichtshof) which hears civil and criminal cases. The other highest courts are the Federal Administrative Court (Bundesverwaltungsgericht), the Federal Labour Court (Bundesarbeitsgericht), the Federal Social Court (Bundessozialgericht) and the Federal Fiscal Court (Bundesfinanzgerichtshof). In addition to these five special highest courts there is

*A list of the abbreviations used appears at the end of this chapter.

73

the Federal Constitutional Court (Bundesverfassungsgericht), which has a special status. It decides only issues of constitutional law. This court plays a central role in the legal system. Although most of the states also have constitutional courts, these are less important.

In this chapter we will refer mainly to the jurisdiction of the Federal Constitutional Court (BVerfG) and of the Federal Court of Justice (BGH). On the structure, the procedure and the workload of these courts see below, section XV.

I   THE GENERAL ORIGINS OF INTERPRETATIONAL ISSUES

In our view, there are three main reasons for the existence of interpretational issues and doubts in the application of statutes. First of all, there is the openness of statutory law; secondly, the uncertainty of legal methodology; and thirdly, the divergence of ideas about rightness or justice. These three reasons are interrelated: If the openness of statutory law did not exist, the uncertainty of legal methodology and the divergence of ideas about rightness or justice would be of but little importance. If the uncertainty of legal methodology did not exist, the openness of statutory law and the divergence of ideas about rightness or justice would not generate any problems. And if it were not for this divergence of ideas, the openness of statutory law and the uncertainty of legal methodology would be of only slight significance.

1   The Openness of Statutory Law

So far as accounting for the openness of statutory law is concerned, it seems useful to distinguish between factors that (a) arise from the language of law, and (b) follow from the structure of the legal system. In addition, there are factors that explain (a) and (b).

Each piece of legislation and each application of the law confronts the *language of law*, and thus confronts problems of ambiguity, vagueness and evaluative openness.

1   A word is *ambiguous* when it has a different meaning in different contexts. An example is the term 'law'. The Federal Constitutional Court has declared: 'The Basic Law's usage of the term "law" is not uniform. The concept is used both in the formal and the material sense' (BVerfGE 1, 184 (189)).

2   A concept is *vague* when there are some subjects that

indubitably fall within its scope (positive candidates), some subjects that indubitably do not fall within its scope (negative candidates) and a third class of subjects that cannot be said to belong to one or the other with certainty (neutral candidates) (compare Koch and Rüßmann, 1982, 194 ff). Vagueness is the most important factor of openness in statutory law. The concept of 'violence' in s. 240 (1) Penal Code (StGB) which provides that intimidation shall be punished exemplifies this feature. The Federal Constitutional Court has stated: 'The concept of violence is not entirely unequivocal and thus needs to be interpreted' (BVerfGE 73, 206 (242)).

3   Examples of *evaluative openness* are the expressions 'good customs' ('gute Sitten') in ss. 138, 826 Civil Code (BGB), 'good faith' ('Treu und Glauben') in s. 242 BGB, 'reprehensible' ('verwerflich') in s. 240 (2) Penal Code, 'to be weighed justly' ('gerecht abzuwägen') in s. 1 (7) Federal Building Code (BauGB), and 'sensible reason' ('vernünftiger Grund') in s. 1 Act for Prevention of Cruelty to Animals (TierschutzG). Expressions like these denote concepts that have but little descriptive meaning over and above their evaluative component. It is the task of the judiciary to fill them with descriptive meaning to match as well as possible their evaluative component, a task likely to be performed differently by different judges.

The factors of openness in statutory law mentioned so far concern single norms. Further factors arise from the *structure of the legal system*. The basic structure of the German legal system is that of codified law. One can distinguish general factors from factors specific to codification.

1   The *general factors* may be classified in different ways. It is useful to distinguish between contradictions between norms and gaps in the law. *Contradictions between norms* can appear within one statute as well as between different statutes. In our legal system, with its elaborate constitutional adjudication, the most important contradictions appear between constitutional law and law of lower rank. The concept of *gap* is one of the most contested concepts in German legal methodology (compare, on the one hand, Larenz, 1983, pp. 357 ff; Canaris, 1983, and on the other hand, Koch and Rüßmann, 1982, 246 ff). There is, however, consensus that gaps exist and must be closed (BGHZ 6, 102 (105 f)).

2   The German legal system is characterized by *codifications*,

that is, by comprehensive bodies of legislation designed to regulate certain fields of the law thoroughly. This is true especially for civil law (compare the Civil Code of 1900 (BGB) and the Code of Civil Procedure of 1877 (ZPO)) and for criminal law (compare the Penal Code of 1871 (StGB) and the Code of Criminal Procedure of 1877 (StPO)). To a lesser degree it is also true for constitutional and administrative law (compare the Basic Law of 1949 (GG), the Administrative Procedure Act of 1976 (VwVfG) and the Code of Administrative Court Procedure of 1960 (VwGO)). Codifications like these cause *specific interpretive problems* because of three factors.

The first factors relate to problems of *consistency and coherence*. Such problems arise from the specific conceptual and systematic interconnectedness of code law. The coordination of the relationships between the legal institutions of ownership, possession and unjust enrichment in the Civil Code exemplifies such problems (compare ss. 985 ff, 812 ff, BGB).

Secondly, historical experience no less than conceptual considerations shows that the ideal of completeness connected with a major codification cannot ever be fully realized. *Incompleteness* manifests itself in conscious and unconscious gaps in the law. Famous examples are the lack of express provisions for *culpa in contrahendo* (Jhering), and for positive violation of a claim (positive Forderungsverletzung – Staub).

Thirdly, in contrast to most single norms, it is typical of great codifications that they are quite long-lasting. Social change gives rise to problems of *obsolescence in a codification*, which traditional German legal method tries to keep under control through the concept of the 'subsequent gap' in the law. Examples in which such gaps have become evident and been filled are the development of a general right of personality (allgemeines Persönlichkeitsrecht) and of the conveyance by way of security (Sicherungsübereignung). A borderline case is represented by the judicial elaboration of modern labour law from the Civil Code's provisions dealing with employment contracts.

The law may have an open quality in any or all of the respects explained; the extent of its openness depends essentially on the *quality of legislation*.

The *mass production* of statutes in today's legal systems carries with it the danger of undesired complexity, and it creates external inconsistencies and incoherences distinguishable from the internal inconsistencies and incoherences of great codifications. An instructive example in the German law is the poor arrangement of the civil and the public regulations dealing with protection of neighbours and the protection against intrusions. Carl Schmitt coined the phrase 'motorized legislator' to describe laws of this kind: 'The machine of legislation increased its speed unbelievably, and positivist legal science's commentaries and interpretation were hardly able to catch up with it' (Schmitt, 1973, p. 406).

In spite of the frequent employment of very special and detailed regulations, the modern legislator must have recourse to various *general clauses*. Often such clauses express a double predicament. General clauses are supposed to cure technical imperfections and to take the place of compromises in issues of substance which were never in fact resolved (see Hedemann, 1933; Dreier 1980, 863–86).

Modern legislation's main flaw is a lack of sound and thorough *doctrinal analysis* of its subject-matter. The legislator acts without waiting for legal science to clear a matter conceptually and systematically. The consequences of this are unending interpretative problems (see, for example, Bachof and Brohm, 1972, 193 ff).

2   Uncertainty in Legal Methodology

The openness of statutory law would pose no serious problems, if there was a juristic method that in each case led to one single answer. However there is no such method. First, both aims and rules of legal methodology are deeply controversial. Second, neither aims nor rules always yield a single answer.

As far as the *aim* of legal interpretation is concerned, there is a permanent competition between the subjective and the objective theory. According to the former view, interpretation must work from the actual intention of the historical legislator, while according to the latter it must work from the reasonable purpose of the statute.

Partly owing to this difference, partly for other reasons, there is no consensus as to the number and order of the canons of interpretation. The most important of these canons are those of semiotic, genetic, historical, systematical, comparative and teleological (consequential) interpretation. These will all be treated later.

Finally there is disagreement about the way these canons and other rules and forms of interpretation ought to be applied. This disagreement is basically about substantive *judgements of value*.

This leads to the third main explanation for the existence of interpretational issues and doubts: the divergence of ideas about rightness or justice.

3   Diverging Ideas about Rightness or Justice

Inevitably interpretation of law is concerned directly or indirectly with the question of what the law requires, prohibits or permits in a certain case. This question is normative or practical. All hard cases of interpretation are characterized by the fact that an answer cannot be found in the mere wording of a statute by applying the rules of logic and of legal methodology. On the contrary, value-judgements are necessary and these are themselves not derivable with certainty from the authoritative material. The ideas of rightness and justice cherished by the particular person interpreting the law inevitably enter the process. This does not mean that their ideas are merely personal moral convictions. Usually they consist of moral values immanent in the legal system. Such immanent moral values, however, are far from clear and determinate, and their bearing is essentially contested. Disputes about the right interpretation are therefore often disputes about the true conception of justice and its correct application.

Many decisions of the Federal Constitutional Court and of other courts show that adjudication in the German Federal Republic is guided by the thesis that the positive law implicitly claims to realize justice (BVerGE 3, 58; 3, 225; 6, 132; 6, 389; 23, 98; 34, 269; 54, 53; BGHZ 3, 94; 23, 175; BGHSt 2, 173; 2, 234; 3, 357).

II   GAPS

1   The Concept of Gaps

In German legal theory and judicial practice the distinction between interpretation and gap-filling is generally acknowledged, yet the very concept of gap is controversial. The most elementary and most widely accepted criterion to distinguish gap-filling from interpretation is the *possible meaning of the terms in which a norm is stated*. Decisions which remain within the lexical meaning of a norm's wording are regarded as interpretative, whereas those going beyond or against that meaning are classified as gap-filling (Canaris, 1983; Larenz, 1983, 351–419; Koch and Rüßmann, 1982; 246–57). Notwithstanding this broad consensus, almost all further details are unclear. Issues here include the precise definition of the concept of gap, the classification of gaps and the permissibility of gap-filling. Here we will discuss only the last issue.

2 Permissibility of Gap-filling

There are many cases in the German legal system in which gap-filling is permissible.

A classic case is the extension of s. 463 (2) Civil Code (BGB) by analogy. Section 463 (2) provides that the buyer of a thing is entitled to compensation if a defect in the thing has been maliciously concealed from him. But the Civil Code does not provide for the complementary case in which a merit of a thing is maliciously pretended. In 1907 the Reichsgericht extended the applicability of s. 463 (2) Civil Code to this case:

> If a buyer is entitled to relief because a quality promised to him is lacking and because a defect has been concealed from him out of malicious intention, one must conclude — since the purpose of the statute equally applies — that the law wants to entitle the buyer to compensation also in cases where qualities the seller has led the buyer to believe in at the signing of the contract with the intent to deceive him are lacking, even if this is not explicitly provided for in the statute. (RGZ 66, 335, 338); compare further RGZ 92, 295; 132, 76 (78))

In this case a gap had to be closed by extending the statute's scope. Its counterpart is the filling of a gap by limiting the statute's scope. A famous example is the reduction of the applicability of s. 181 Civil Code performed by the Federal Court of Justice (BGH) in 1971 (BGHZ 56, 97 (101 ff); compare Larenz, 1983, 375 ff). Section 181 of the Civil Code disqualifies an authorized agent from carrying out a legal transaction with himself in the name of the principal. The purpose of this statute is to protect a principal represented by an agent. The statute prevents the representative from enriching himself at the expense of the principal. In some cases, however, this protection is not necessary, as where the legal transaction is only to the principal's legal advantage:

> Here the wording of the regulation exceeds the actual purpose of protection. If the representative concludes a transaction-in-se which is only to the advantage of the represented person, this person's interests cannot be endangered; he or she does not need the protection intended by s. 181 Civil Code against a conflict of interests in the person of the agent. (BGHZ 59, 236 (240))

Just as there are gap-fillings to correct single statutes there are gap-fillings that amount to the introduction of new legal institutions. Again, examples are *culpa in contrahendo* (Jhering), positive violation of a claim (positive Forderungsverletzung — Staub) and conveyance in security (Sicherungsübereignung).

The power to fill gaps is not unlimited. A borderline case is the Federal Constitutional Court's so-called Soraya decision. The Court had to decide whether civil courts could grant compensation for non-material damage in extreme cases of violations of the general right of personality. A weekly magazine had published a false interview with Princess Soraya, the divorced wife of the former Persian shah. The interview was entirely of the journalists' own invention. In 1964, the Federal Court of Justice granted Princess Soraya compensation in the amount of 15 000 German marks. This contradicted the wording of s. 253 Civil Code, which allows compensation for non-material damage only in cases determined by the law. Princess Soraya's case certainly was not one of them.

The Federal Constitutional Court upheld the constitutionality of this formerly highly disputed practice of the civil courts. A central part of the decision reads:

> The law is not identical with the whole of the written statutes. Over and above the positive enactments of the state power there can be 'ein Mehr an Recht' (a surplus of law) which has its source in the constitutional legal order as a holistic unity of meaning, and which can operate as a corrective to the written law; to find it and to deliver it in decisions is the task of adjudication . . . The task of adjudication can demand especially that evaluative assumptions which are immanent in the constitutional legal order, but are not, or are only incompletely, expressed in the texts of the written statutes, be elucidated and realized in decisions by an act of evaluative cognition which, admittedly, does not lack volitional elements. In this, the judge must avoid arbitrariness; his decision must be based on rational argumentation. It must be understood that the written statute fails to fulfil its function of providing a just solution for a legal problem. The judicial decision then fills this gap according to the standards of practical reason and the 'community's well-founded general ideas of justice'. (BVerfGE 34, 269 (287))

Opinions are divided as to whether this decision was correct. Many authors think that the civil courts did not have power to read an unwritten exception into s. 253 Civil Code. According to them, the civil courts should not have been allowed to decide for themselves, but should rather have asked for a decision from the Federal Constitutional Court as to whether s. 253 Civil Code is constitutional at all (compare, for example, Koch and Rüßmann, 1982, p. 255). On account of this controversy, the case is a borderline case.

In later decisions, the court has been more reserved in its opinions on *contra legem* gap-filling, but it has generally maintained that such action is permissible (BVerfGE 35, 263 (278); 49, 304 (318 ff); 65, 182 (190 ff); 71, 354 (362 f)). One decision in which the court held a *contra legem* gap-filling to be impermissible is the so-called 'social-plan decision'. Social plans define workers' claims to compensation for the closing-down of places of work. The question was how such claims rank in case of bankruptcy. The Bankruptcy Act (Konkursordnung – KO) states a rank order, yet it does not say anything about claims established by social plans. The Grand Senate of the Federal Labour Court corrected the written rank order by granting priority to claims established by social plans among the claims against the bankrupt's estate. The Federal Constitutional Court decided that the Federal Labour Court had exceeded the limits of judicial development of law here (BVerfGE 65, 182 (191)). It argued that the bankruptcy-statute was conclusive, and that there was no gap to be filled. The realization of the principle of social state was said to be basically the legislator's rather than the judge's task. The Federal Labour Court had 'decided for social–*political* reasons': 'It has obviously exceeded the limits of creative adjudication which are drawn by the constitutional principle of the binding force of the statute law' (BVerfGE 65, 182 (194)).

Special limits on judicial law-making also obtain in the criminal law. Art. 103 (2) GG reads: 'A deed can only be punished if the punishability was statutorily determined before the deed was committed'. The Federal Constitutional Court found that

> the need for legal certainty excludes ... analogical or customary justifications of criminal sanctions. Here, 'analogy' must not be understood in the narrower, technical sense; rather, each application is excluded which exceeds the content of a statutory norm of sanction. ... The possible meaning of the wording of a statute marks the outer limit of admissible judicial interpretation ... this meaning of the wording is to be determined from the citizen's point of view. (BVerfGE 71, 108 (115))

Apart from the criminal law, there are special limits on judicial development of the law arising from the principle of statutory authorization (Gesetzesvorbehalt), where the state wishes to interfere with basic rights. One example is the Federal Constitutional Court's decision concerning the withdrawal of the right to defend someone in court. A trial lawyer, suspected of complicity in the crime the accused allegedly had committed, was excluded from the defence. The Federal Court of Justice thought this legal. It admitted that there was no explicit provision for the exclusion, but held that the exclusion resulted from the meaning and purpose of a number of statutes in the Code of Criminal Procedure and the Federal Lawyer Code (Bundesrechtsanwaltsordnung).

The Federal Constitutional Court declared this to be impermissible: the verdict interfered with a basic right, namely the freedom to choose a profession. Such an interference required specific authorization by statute. The principle of statutory authorization did not allow the interference merely by reference to the meaning and purpose of statutes which, according to their wording, regulated something else:

> The Federal Court of Justice has misinterpreted the constitutional limits drawn by Art. 12 (1) GG under the aspect of the principle of the rule of law (Rechtsstaatsprinzip) with regard to judicial development of the law at least where a rule is established which considerably restricts a lawyer's performance as defending counsel. (BVerfGE 34, 293 (301 f))

III   TYPES OF GENERAL JUSTIFYING ARGUMENTS IN THE INTERPRETATION OF STATUTES

In practice as well as in the theory of statutory interpretation in Germany the following types of justifying arguments are generally accepted.

1   Arguments from the Canons of Interpretation

The canons of interpretation are the most important means of interpretation in Germany. The theory and practice of interpretation according to the canons has been greatly influenced by the writings of C.F. v. Savigny (v. Savigny, 1802/3 and 1840). There are different classifications of the canons, but the following summary may be considered representative (see Alexy, 1989, 234–44).

1.1   *The Semiotic Interpretation*

The semiotic interpretation – in Germany usually called 'Wortlaut', 'philologische' or 'grammatische Auslegung' – requires an investigation into the semantic content and the syntactic structure of a norm. Traditional German methodology identifies 'logical interpretation' as a canon separate from the semiotic. The function of logical interpretation is to ascertain a norm's conceptual structures.

Modern methodology treats this topic partly within the scope of semiotic and systematic interpretation, and partly within the scope of dogmatic argumentation. Legal practice and literature in Germany deal with the following problems by reference to the semiotic canon.

1   *Technical and colloquial terminology.* The first category of a *technical language* is that of legal language itself; to it one may add the technical languages of neighbouring sciences. Which technical terminology is decisive depends upon the respective field of law and is determined with due consideration of all criteria of interpretation. There is often an assumption that technical legal terminology takes priority. Arguments advanced against this are sometimes based on the principle of democracy. In judicial opinions examples of varying priorities can be found.

     The strictest standards obtain in criminal law. Art. 103 (2) GG and s. (1) Penal Code provide that 'a deed can only be punished if the punishability was statutorily determined before the deed was committed'. In this the Federal Constitutional Court finds support for its postulate of strict regard for *colloquial literal meaning* in criminal law:

> If, as shown, Art. 103 (2) GG demands recognizability and foreseeability of the impending punishment for the addressee of the norm, this can only mean that this meaning is to be determined from the citizens' point of view. (BVerfGE 71, 108 (115))

An orientation towards ordinary language is likewise obligatory whenever encroachment by the state on basic rights is in issue. Thus the Federal Constitutional Court has interpreted the expression 'searching [of a dwelling]' in Art. 13 (2) GG according to its colloquial understanding:

> Characteristic of the concept of searching is the deliberate and purpose-oriented searching by state organs for persons or things, or to find out facts, to discover something the inhabitant of the dwelling is not willing to reveal or hand over. (BVerfGE 51, 67 (106 f))

A hitherto widespread, more narrow and specifically juristic usage of the word, according to which a search by a bailiff was not a search in the sense of Art. 13 (2) GG, was rejected.

     On the other hand, the Court, deviating from the colloquial, and referring to a traditionally constitutional word usage, interpreted the concept of dwelling in Art. 13 (1) GG: 'The dwelling is inviolable' to include the business premises of dry cleaners. This interpretation, however, did not lead to a restriction but to an extension of the constitutional protection:

> Only the wide interpretation satisfies the principle according to which in cases of doubt that interpretation must be chosen which most strongly unfolds the juridical force of the basic right-norm. (BVerfGE 32, 54 (71))

On account of this and for other reasons in this case, it held that 'the wording of Art. 13 (1) GG cannot in this case be decisive' (BVerfGE 32, 54 (72)).

2   Since semantic rules can change over time, a distinction may arise between a norm's literal meaning at the *time of enactment* and its literal meaning at the *time of interpretation*. Which of these is decisive depends upon whether a subjective or an objective theory of the aim of interpretation is assumed. Particularly strong examples are afforded by value concepts (for example, in the law of sexual offences) that depend on value-judgements which have changed since the norm was first enacted. With respect to those concepts, there is a broad consensus that the literal meaning at the time of interpretation is decisive.

A problem has also arisen as to whether a descriptive term like 'weapon', if used in a norm of the Penal Code, has to be interpreted according to the time of its enactment or according to the time of interpretation. The Federal Court of Justice had to decide whether the use of hydrochloric acid as a means of attack was the use of a weapon in the sense of the Penal Code (BGHSt 1, 1 (3)). The Court held that, according to the usage current at the time of the enactment of the Penal Code, that is, in 1871, only mechanical means of attack counted as weapons. Since then, however, usage has changed. Today chemical means of attack could also be considered as weapons. Hence the court classed hydrochloric acid as a weapon.

3   The most important problem of semiotic interpretation is the problem of *recognizing the limits of the meaning* of a word. In contemporary German literature on method it is a widely held view that, when vague concepts are in issue, one ought to distinguish between spheres of positive certainty, of negative certainty and of possible doubt, and accordingly should classify the candidates for subsumption under a concept into positive, negative, and neutral candidates

(compare Koch and Rüßmann, 1982, 195 ff, and, critically, Neumann, 1979, 73 ff). The problem of literal meaning could be easily solved within the frame of this model if the borders between these spheres were clear. One could then distinguish precisely between a *necessary* and a *possible* literal meaning (border of the possible literal meaning (Alexy, 1989, p. 289)). Legal practice shows that this leads to a lot of problems. In the decision whether blockading a road by sitting on it (Sitzblockade) amounts to 'violence', four of the eight judges of the First Panel of the Federal Constitutional Court were of the opinion that the concept of violence was not clear. The border drawn by the literal meaning allowed for merely psychical coercion to be classed as violence (BVerfGE 73, 206 (243)). The four other judges did not agree: 'The language usage connects with the concept of violence against a certain person the idea of remarkable power at work; the concept of violence must not be extended so far that it could no longer be seen to accord with this usage' (BVerfGE 73, 206 (245)).

The example shows that the concept of literal meaning is far from simple. Indeed speakers of the same language have differing opinions about the literal meaning of a word. The question is how a third person should react to this difference. The best answer is that one must ask whether the proposed wider literal meaning is worth considering in the light of commonly held linguistic conventions. If so, it falls into the realm of possible doubt.

1.2 The Genetic Interpretation

This requires an investigation into the meaning of legal terms as intended by the historical legislator and/or into the purposes he pursued by enacting the statute. The latter is a special version of teleological interpretation, namely subjective–teleological interpretation. On this, see below.

Genetic interpretation investigates the legislator's actual intention. The problems connected with this concept are not, however, systematically and uniformly dealt with in legal practice. They are contested in the literature. A pragmatic approach is predominant. First of all it is assumed that there is a legislator's intention. Secondly, one tries to find out what that is.

1   As an example of genetic argumentation the following passage from BVerfGE 51, 97 (108 f), concerning the concept of searching in Art. 13 (2) GG, may be quoted:

On this the deputy Zinn (SPD) as a member submitting a report to the Committee on Principles remarked that for paragraph 1 sentence 2 it was doubtful whether the envisaged version was sufficient; searchings did not only occur within the frame of criminal law, but were also carried out by various other authorities. Therefore, he suggested, instead of using the phrase 'by the organs designated by the laws concerning the criminal proceedings', to make sentence 2 very general: 'by the organs designated by the law' (Committee on Principles, 5th session on the 29th of September 1948, shorthand minutes, p. 35). This general version was finally accepted by the Committee on Principles (23rd session on the 19th of November 1948, shorthand minutes, p. 18 and following.). On the Parliamentary Council's and its committees' following deliberations this version was neither changed nor was the question further discussed (compare v. Doemming–Füßlein–Matz, JöR n.F., vol. 1, ibid.).

This genesis clearly implies that the Parliamentary Council had in mind not only the searching common in criminal prosecution, but, as is shown by the change of the draft from the special to the general version, it also wanted to provide for the other cases of searching in Art. 13 (2) GG. This subjective intention of the maker of the constitution has been lucidly expressed in the version of Art. 13 (2) GG. An editorial mistake is to be excluded. (BVerfGE 51, 97 (108 f)).

Please note that this text is merely part of the court's argumentation concerning the intention of the maker of the constitution.

2   Genetic interpretation faces at least three types of problems. First there is the problem of identifying the *subject of the intention*. In view of the complexity of modern legislature processes, one must ask whose intention is in issue. Possible subjects are, for example, the parliament, the majority in parliament, its deputies present during debates on the measure, single deputies, parliamentary committees, the government and the ministerial bureaucracy. The answer must turn on those constitutional norms that assign legislative competence. Art. 77 (1) sentence 1 GG provides for federal laws: 'The federal laws are passed by the Bundestag.' Consequently the Bundestag as such is the subject whose intent must be considered. Other subjects' intentions are relevant only in so far as they can be ascribed to the Bundestag or allow for a conclusion as to its intent.

A second set of problems arises as to the permissible *sources of cognition* in determining intention. For instance, sources of cognition can be parliamentary minutes, committee minutes, commission minutes, official justifications and commentary statements in the media. In general, everything may be taken into account. The more official a commentary statement and the closer its relation to the parliamentary plenum, the greater is its weight. Of the greatest weight is an intention expressed clearly and unanimously by all participants in the plenum.

A third problem consists in defining the concept of *intention* and how this bears upon the legislator's factual and hypothetical intention. If a factual intention is not discernible, only recourse to hypothetical intention remains. But then the line between finding the intention of the historical legislator and the legislator's reasonable purpose starts to crumble.

1.3   The Historical Interpretation

Historical interpretation requires an investigation into the history of the relevant concepts, doctrines and institutions, as distinguished from legislative intention. The distinction between this canon and the canon of genetic interpretation is widely acknowledged. Some authors, however, regard the latter as a part of historical interpretation.

An example of historical interpretation is provided by the herein repeatedly quoted, and indeed paradigmatic, decision of the Federal Constitutional Court concerning inviolability of the dwelling. The court relied on the development of the law itself through Art. 140 Frankfurt Reichs-Constitution of 1848/49, Art. 6 Prussian Constitution of 1848/50, and Art. 115 Weimar Reichs-Constitution of 1919. The court added references to former decisions and former scholarly opinions on these constitutions (BVerfGE 32, 54 (69)). Within the frame of such a historical interpretation, historical knowledge of the conditions the statute was designed to remedy often plays an important part.

1.4   The Comparative Interpretation

Comparative interpretation is based on comparable norms and institutions of comparable legal systems. The decision quoted below also gives an example of this kind of consideration:

A look at foreign regulations shows that in the same or nearly the same version of the text of the statute the wide interpretation of the concept of dwelling predominates (compare, for example, for Switzerland BGE 81 I, 119 ff.; for Austria the Constitutional Court's decisions

of November 22nd, 1932, Nr. 1486, March 14th, 1949, Nr. 1747, July
2nd, 1955, Nr. 2867, and December 16th, 1965, Nr. 5182, as well as
Ermacora, Handbuch der Grundfreiheiten und der Menschenrechte,
1963, 241; for Italy: Encyclopedia del Diritto XIII (1964), 859 ff; and
Faso, La Libertà di Domicilio, 1968, 34 ff; for the USA the Dissenting
Opinion of Justice Frankfurter in the case of Davis v. United States of
June 10th, 1946 – 328 US 582, 596 f – and See v. City of Seattle of
June 5th, 1967 – 387 US 541). (BVerfGE 32, 54 (70))

1.5   Systematic Interpretation

This consists of an investigation into the relations between the
norm to be applied and other norms of the same legal system. It is
oriented towards consistency and coherence of the legal system as
a whole. There is accordingly an intrinsic relation between systematic interpretation and legal dogmatics. The above-mentioned
decision once again provides an example. The court employs a
systematic argument when interpreting Art. 13 GG (inviolability
of dwelling) with respect to Art. 12 GG (freedom of profession):

> The wide interpretation . . . fits sensibly with the principles the Federal
> Constitutional Court has developed for the interpretation of the basic
> right of the freedom of profession. If in that case professional work is
> seen as an essential element of the development of personality, and if
> it is therefore granted, within the frame of the single human being's
> individual conduct of life, an especially high rank (BVerfGE 7, 377
> (397); 13, 97, (104 f)), it is coherent to guarantee a correspondingly
> efficient protection of the spatial range in which the work is primarily
> conducted . . . (BVerfGE 32, 54 (71))

1.6   Teleological Interpretation

There are two versions of this canon, the subjective–teleological
and the objective–teleological.

1.6.1   Subjective–teleological interpretation requires an investigation into the actual intention of the legislator. In this form, it is a
variation of genetic interpretation, treated above.

1.6.2   Objective–teleological interpretation requires an investigation into the reasonable goals and/or the social functions of the
norm. The application of this canon presupposes identification of
reasonable goals or functions of norms. In Germany, this problem
is commonly expressed by the formula 'Sinn und Zweck des
Gesetzes' (sense and purpose of the statute). This formula is very
often used in legal practice. In the literature it is highly controversial. Its critics argue that it gives too much freedom to the

interpreter to read his own beliefs about right and reason into the norm. We shall discuss these problems in connection with the goals of interpretation (see below, section VI).

2 Special Types of Legal Arguments

Among arguments from *analogy* it is common to make a distinction between 'Gesetzesanalogie' and 'Rechtsanalogie'. *Gesetzesanalogie* means the application of a single similar rule. *Rechtsanalogie* means the application of several similar rules or of a principle supporting these rules. cf. s. 1 of the first draft of the BGB:

> In cases for which the law contains no rules, those rules are to be applied analogically which apply to legally similar cases. In default of such rules, the case should be decided according to principles embodied in the spirit of the legal system.

This norm was deleted in the course of legislation (by the second commission), because no special legal authorization for analogical reasoning was thought necessary (see Larenz, 1983, pp. 365 ff, and below, section XII).

The argument of *reduction* limits the scope of a norm the literal meaning of which is considered too broad. The court adds an unwritten exception. Usually a reduction is justified by the purpose (*ratio legis*) of the norm (teleological reduction). Reduction could be understood as a special case of the principle 'cessante ratione legis cessat lex ipsa' (Gratian). A well-known example already mentioned of this type of argument is provided by s. 181 BGB, which reads:

> An agent may not without leave enter into a legal transaction in the name of his principal with himself in his own name, or as an agent of a third party, unless the legal transaction consists exclusively in the fulfilment of an obligation.

This norm was further reduced teleologically by adding the clause: 'unless the legal transaction is only to the advantage of the principal' (BGHZ 59, 236 (240 f); compare further Larenz, 1983, 375 ff; Brandenburg, 1983).

Finally there is an open set of *special argument-types*. The most important are the *argumenta e contrario, a fortiori, a minore ad maius, a maiore ad minus, ad absurdum.*

3   Arguments from Precedents

In Germany precedents are not binding as in the common law systems. Yet precedents play an outstanding role in the practice of justifying judicial decisions. The importance of this role is underscored by the fact that a lawyer neglecting precedents of higher courts may be liable for damages to his client (BGH NJW 1983, 1665).

A legal basis for the large practical role of precedents of higher courts can be found in the power of these courts to protect the unity of the legal system and to improve the law; see Art. 95 (3) GG, ss. 136–138 General Court Act – Gerichtsverfassungsgesetz (GVG), ss. 11, 12 VwGO, s. 45 (2) Code of Labour Court Procedure – Arbeitsgerichtsgesetz (ArbGG), s. 43 Code of Social Court Procedure – Sozialgerichtsgesetz (SGG), s. 11 (4) Code of Fiscal Court Procedure – Finanzgerichtsordnung (FGO).

Although there are different theories in the literature, it is generally acknowledged that precedents have considerable impact on legal argumentation. But there is no consensus on how to explain that impact and the kind and strength of the binding force of precedents (see Kriele, 1976, 243 ff; Alexy, 1989, 274 ff; Koch and Rüßmann, 1982, 184 ff; Bydlinski, 1985, 149–55).

4   'Legal Dogmatic' Arguments

Legal dogmatic arguments are based on doctrinal or dogmatic theories. These are juristic theories about the law of a certain legal system. Usually they are prepared and presented by legal scholars in treatises and other writings. The main feature of such writings is that they strive to make the law as consistent and coherent as possible (see Dreier, 1981, chap. 3). The import of arguments based on legal dogmatics depends, first, on the correctness and, second, on their actual acceptance (*communis opinio doctorum*, herrschende Meinung, leading opinion – see Zimmermann, 1983).

5   Ethical Arguments

Ethical arguments (arguments from justice) are of considerable significance in German legal practice. In principle, their relevance is widely recognized. However there is a debate as to their weight in relation to arguments based on authority (see Alexy, 1989, 284 ff).

6 Empirical Arguments

Empirical arguments can appear in the context of almost all previously mentioned arguments. They are significant especially with respect to the teleological or consequential reasoning (see BVerfGE 7, 377 (413 ff); Philippi, 1971).

IV TYPES OF GAP-FILLING ARGUMENTS

All types of interpretive arguments may be employed in gap-filling. There is only one exception. The semiotic argument can merely serve to identify a gap, not to fill it. Of course there are some types of argument which are of specific importance for gap-filling. The most prominent among these are analogy, reduction and ethical arguments. See above, section III and below, section XIII.

V THE MATERIALS OF INTERPRETATIONAL AND GAP-FILLING ARGUMENTS

1 Types of Arguments and Types of Material

Legal arguments may be scrutinized from two points of view. The first focuses on the types of arguments, the second on the materials used in arguments. In Germany, the first perspective prevails to such a degree that it is not even common to make a distinction between types of arguments and types of materials. Thus, in dealing with the types of arguments in part III, we have already mentioned nearly all types of materials explicitly or implicitly.

2 Must-, Should-, May-, and May Not-Materials

The concept of 'must-material' can be interpreted in two ways. In a wider sense, it includes all materials necessary to resolve a concrete case correctly in a given legal system. In hard cases this may embrace almost everything. In a narrower sense, it includes only materials which, if applicable, must be considered in any case.

'Must-materials' in the narrower sense are, for example (1) texts expressing enacted norms of any kind; (2) facts, like long-standing customs based on conviction of their rightness, forming customary law; (3) documents and declarations of intention establishing private legal arrangements by acts-in-the-law. Completion of this list would require a theory of the formal sources of law which we cannot elaborate here.

'Should-' and 'may-materials', are materials which are neither 'must-materials' in the narrower sense nor 'may not-materials', as defined below. Although there is no rigid distinction between 'should'- and 'may-materials', a rough delimitation is possible. 'Should-materials' ought to be considered in any case, if they are applicable. To neglect them would amount to a mistake. By contrast, 'may-materials' can, if applicable, be employed in any case. Not to consider them is not always a mistake. To consider them is sometimes superfluous; sometimes it improves the decision.

In the German legal system there are three kinds of 'should-materials': precedents, generally accepted legal dogmatic opinions, and documents concerning the intention of the law-maker. All other materials, which are neither 'must-materials' nor 'may not-materials' are merely 'may-materials'. The great variety of things this class comprises is evidenced by what has been said about types of argument in section III.

'May not-materials' are all materials that must not be considered either on substantive or formal grounds. Everything incompatible with the principles and rules of the German legal system in regard to its content is excluded on substantive grounds. For example, principles of apartheid or one-party government may not be invoked. Excluded, on formal grounds, are those arguments the consideration of which would violate the judge's duty to comply with statute and law as well as his obligation to judicial neutrality.

VI   PRIORITIES AMONG CONFLICTING ARGUMENTS

1   The Priority Problem

Arguments of the different types described in section III can favour different results in the same case. The resolution of such a conflict requires a priority ordering between argument-types. A priority order may have either a strict or a prima facie character. It has a strict character if an argument of a certain type overrides one, some, or all arguments of other types in all cases or in a certain class of cases. It has a prima facie character if it establishes a burden of proof or of argument for opponents in all or in a certain class of cases. If in a case of conflict there is neither a strict nor a prima facie priority order, ordering must be *ad hoc*.

In German legal practice, there is no complete priority ordering, neither strict nor prima facie, embracing all types of arguments, and there is no strict priority ordering for any argument in all cases. In theory as well as in practice the priority problem is dealt with mainly with respect to the canons of interpretation.

2 Subjective and Objective Theories of Interpretation

Traditionally the problem of priority among the canons of interpretation is discussed in the context of theories about the goals of interpretation. There were and are two main views on this topic: a subjective and an objective one. According to the *subjective* theory, the aim of interpretation consists in finding out the historical legislator's actual intention. With the *objective* theory, the aim is to find the law's reasonable meaning. It is a controversial matter which aim is preferable and how the relationship between the two aims is to be determined (compare Larenz, 1983, 301 ff; Koch and Rüßmann, 1982, 176 ff). The answer depends, on the one hand, on legal–philosophical and constitutional considerations and, on the other hand, the extent to which one may talk about something like the historical legislator's intention and the law's reasonable purpose. The subjective theory involves giving priority to semiotic and genetic arguments, that is, to the wording of the statute and the intention of the historical legislator. The objective theory opens up the possibility of giving priority to objective–teleological arguments and to other arguments based on rationality in general.

3 Legal Practice in General

In Germany, the *practice* of legal interpretation reveals many facets. In easy cases, a judge is usually content with arguing from the wording of the statute and the legislator's intention. In hard cases, the objective–teleological argument gains importance. The decision to be made may or may not be covered by the statute's wording. If the wording does cover the decision, then the objective–teleological argument is ordinarily decisive. Where the wording cannot be stretched so far, *contra legem* decisions, supported by objective–teleological arguments, do occur but have to be regarded as exceptions. They are considered admissible only if the objective–teleological arguments, alone or together with other arguments, are of such importance that they justify a deviation from the wording of the statute and the historical legislator's intention. Under the Basic Law, the objective–teleological arguments are to a wide extent supported by constitutional principles.

An example was mentioned above in section II, namely the granting of compensation for non-material damages through violation of the general right of personality by the Federal Court of Justice (BGHZ 26, 349; 35, 363; 39, 124), which the Federal Constitutional Court (BVerfGE 34, 269) declared constitutional despite its being explicitly excluded by the Civil Code (ss. 249, 253, 847 BGB). Further examples of decisions against the wording may be found in section II. Once again it should be noted that the constitutionality of *contra legem* decisions is highly contested in the literature (see, for example, Müller, 1985).

The *Federal Constitutional Court* has made statements pertaining to the question at issue here in several decisions. Its answers may be summarized thus: while the starting-point of any interpretation is the wording, this is not controlling in all cases:

> The judge does not, however, have to stop at the wording of a norm. His being bound by the law (Art. 20 (3), Art. 97 (1) GG) does not mean being bound to its letter with the coercion to interpret literally, but being bound to sense and purpose of the law. The interpretation is the method and way by which the judge inquires into the content of a statute, considering its placement within the whole legal order, without being restricted by the formal wording. (BVerfGE 35, 263 (278 f))

The court also assigns a certain preponderance to the reasonable sense of a statute over the actual intention of its maker:

> Decisive for the interpretation of a legal prescription is the legislator's objectivated intention expressed in it, as it follows from the wording of the statute and the context of meaning into which it is placed. Not controlling, on the other hand, are the subjective ideas of organs taking part in the legislation, or of individual members about the meaning of the norm. The genetic history of a provision is of importance for its interpretation only when it supports the correctness of an interpretation found in accordance with the principles mentioned or removes doubts that cannot be got rid of in the said way. (BVerfGE 1, 299 (312))

> In interpreting statutes . . . one must not proceed from the legislator's subjective intention, but, in accordance with the Federal Constitutional Court's established adjudication, . . . from the law's objective intention. (BVerfGE 33, 265 (294))

> The law may well be wiser than the fathers of the law. (BVerfGE 36, 342 (362))

4   Strict Priority of the Wording

The foregoing quotations include statements of a very unspecific kind. One must differentiate with regard to special fields of the law and special groups of cases. In some of them we find a *strict* priority of the wording.

In criminal law, arguments based on the wording of the norm to be applied have strict priority. This follows from Art. 103 (2) GG and s. 1 Penal Code, which – as mentioned – require that 'a deed can only be punished if the punishability was statutorily determined before the deed was committed'. This means for the penal law: 'The possible literal meaning of the norm marks the extreme limit of permissible judicial interpretation' (BVerfGE 71, 108 (115)).

The Federal Constitutional Court has stated reasons for the strict priority of semiotic arguments in criminal law: the 'recognizability and foreseeability of the impending punishment for the addressee of the norm' (BVerfGE 71, 108 (115)). From this there follows, for this branch of law, another priority rule: arguments based on colloquial meaning take priority over arguments which refer to technical terminology (BVerfGE 71, 108 (115); 73, 206 (235 f)).

Furthermore a strict priority of the wording obtains where the state wishes to interfere with individual rights of freedom outside the realm of penal law. In section II above we cited the case involving a counsel for the defence suspected of complicity in his client's crime who was claiming freedom to pursue his profession. The Federal Constitutional Court held his exclusion from the defence to be unlawful since it was not explicitly provided for: 'These strict demands concerning clearness, certainty and completeness of the law are obligations resulting from the rule of law' (BVerfGE 34, 293 (302)). It is of special interest here to note that the court acknowledged that its own decision was dissatisfying: 'The Federal Constitutional Court realizes that this result uncovers a very dissatisfying state of law, which does not meet in any respect the requirements of a well-ordered practice of criminal law' (BVerfGE 34, 293 (302)). In contradistinction to the Soraya case, however, it does consider a correction by a court to be impermissible, this being the legislator's task: 'The legislator will therefore have to regulate the preconditions for the exclusion of counsel for the defence in the near future' (BVerfGE 34, 293 (306)).

A decision of the Federal Court of Administration of 1965 also illustrates the priority of wording where the state wishes to restrict individual rights of freedom: 'The court of appeal [Berufungsgericht] rightly declined the extension of this legal term in a way that a formerly free profession was subjected to certain restrictions' (BVerwGE 22, 32 (37)). The adaptation of the law to new conditions is explicitly left to the legislator.

Strict priority of wording also pertains to prescriptions of time limits. The Federal Constitutional Court points out that

> prescriptions of time limit as formal rules . . ., as jus strictum, serve exclusively legal certainty. Time limits have to be instantly, unambiguously and clearly recognizable. They cannot be found by expansive and perhaps even surprising interpretation of meaning and context of the regulations. (BVerfGE 4, 31 (37))

The foregoing list of *strict* priorities of wording could be elaborated and completed. This shall not be done here. Generally, in the German legal system, wording takes strict priority only if there is a special reason for it. We have stated three such reasons: the principle of 'nulla poena sine lege', the protection of individual rights of freedom, and legal certainty as a primary goal.

5   *Prima Facie* Priority of the Wording

Wherever wording does not take strict priority, it has a prima facie priority. This follows from the fact that the judge is bound by the statute. The wording expresses the statute. Thus, if it merely had the same rank as other arguments, talk of a statute's binding force would be meaningless. There is no general formula by which to decide when the prima facie priority of the wording may be outweighed. The Federal Constitutional Court states that

> the limits which have to be drawn to a creative adjudication in view of the indispensable constitutional principle that the judiciary is bound by the laws cannot be summarized in a formula that is valid for all fields of the law and for all the legal relations created or ruled by them. (BVerfGE 34, 269 (288))

Yet a range of criteria may be gathered from case-law. In *Soraya* the Federal Constitutional Court invoked the following arguments in favour of a decision against the wording: (1) the age of the norm; (2) its contested character right from the beginning; (3) the development of the law in other Western countries; (4) changed ideas about the law among the population; (5) the constitutional system of values; (6) a broad consensus in legal science; (7) the unacceptability of having to wait for the legislator; and (8) the fitting into the legal system (BVerfGE 34, 269 (288 ff)). On the other hand, the following arguments were raised against a *contra legem* decision in the social-plan decision: (1) the vagueness of the relevant constitutional principle; (2) the political character of the reasons supporting the decision; (3) the lack of a general legal consensus; and (4) the lack of a dogmatic consensus (BVerfGE 65, 182 (193 ff)). In another decision, the court emphasized that a *contra legem* decision would violate not only the wording but also legal systematic considerations (BVerfGE 49, 304 (322)).

6 *Prima Facie* Priority of other Arguments Based on Authority

Arguments which refer to the wording are arguments supported by the legislator's authority. Further arguments referring to an authority are arguments based on (a) the historical legislator's intention, (b) precedents, and (c) dogmatic consensus.

According to the general statements of the Federal Constitutional Court cited above, arguments which refer to the *historical legislator's intention* play only a supplementary and subordinate role. This is not quite in accord with the general, or even the Court's own, practice. In adjudication one may discern a prima facie priority of genetic arguments over arguments not based on authority, though not over semiotic arguments. Especially with more recent norms, the historical legislator's intention – if clearly determinable – is often thought sufficient for solving a problem of interpretation.

As we saw, *precedents* – apart from the peculiarities of the Constitutional Court – do not have the status of a formal source of law. Precedents do, however, play an outstanding role in justifying judicial decisions (see above, section III). This is expressed in that whoever wishes to depart from a precedent carries the burden of argument (Alexy, 1989, p. 278). This burden of argument does not prevent a line of decisions from being changed only because the citizens trusted in its continuance: 'This would result in the courts' being bound to a certain jurisdiction once established, even if it could not really be kept up on account of new insights or a change in social, political or economic conditions' (BVerfGE 18, 224 (240 f)).

Finally, the special weight of a consensus in *legal dogmatics* must be noted. Whoever argues against the ruling opinion carries the burden of argument (Zimmermann, 1983).

7 Priority Relations between Rightness Reasons

Within the class of rightness reasons, one may also discover priority relations.*

Rightness reasons deriving from the constitution or other valid law take priority over those that are not so grounded. This distinction is obvious in the Federal Constitutional Court's jurisdiction. In *Soraya, contra legem* adjudication is, among other things, considered constitutional since it is based on 'values immanent in the constitution' (BVerfGE 34, 269 (287)). By contrast, in the social-plan decision *contra legem* adjudication is thought unconstitutional since it is based 'on social–*political* reasons' (BVerfGE 65, 182 (194)). In another decision the court declared a decision of the Federal Labour Court constitutional because it is not based on that court's own values but on the legislator's evaluations (BVerfGE 38, 386 (396)).

The priority relation just mentioned rests on the general idea that authoritativeness takes prima facie priority over mere rightness. Apart from this, one may discern two further general relations of priority.

1   The first is the relation between formal and substantive reasons. An example of a formal reason is a reason which refers to legal certainty. A substantive reason is concerned with the soundness of a decision with respect to its content. In our legal system there is no general priority relation between formal and substantive reasons. This in turn is the result of both a formal and a substantive interpretation of the rule of law (Rechtsstaatsprinzip):

> The principle of legal certainty and the principle of justice in individual cases have the status of constitutional principles; legal certainty and justice are both essential components of the rule of law [Rechtsstaatsprinzip], one of the leading ideas of the Basic Law. (BVerfGE 7, 194 (196))

2   A second general priority relation seems to exist between individual rights and collective goals. In several decisions the Federal Constitutional Court talks about a 'basic' or 'general presumption of liberty'. Thus in a decision of 1964 we read:

> The principle of rule of law – especially if seen in connection

---

*Rightness reasons bring moral values and norms into play. They are non-consequentialist.

with the general presumption of liberty in favour of the citizen,
. . . demands that the individual be protected from unnecessary
interference by the public authorities . . . The more elementary
the expressions of human liberty that are disturbed by the
legal interference, the more carefully the reasons for the
interference have to be weighed against the citizen's basic
claim to liberty. (BVerfGE 17, 306 (314))

It is very much contested in the literature whether such
passages can be interpreted in the sense of a prima facie
priority of individual rights over collective goals and even
more so, whether this priority relation is at all recommend-
able (Alexy, 1986, 517 f).

VII CONFLICTS OF NORMS

Conflicts between norms are either conflicts of rules or collisions of
principles. This distinction is based on the structural difference
between rules and principles (Dworkin, 1978, 22 ff). *Principles* are
commands to optimize and, as such, they are norms commanding
that something be realized to the highest degree actually and
legally possible. The legal possibilities are determined essentially
in relation to opposed principles and this in turn implies that
conflicting principles can and indeed must be balanced. This
balancing is the form of law application characteristic of principles.
In contradistinction, *rules* are norms that, given satisfaction of
specific conditions, definitively command, forbid, permit or
empower. Hence they may be characterized as 'definitive commands'. The form of law application characteristic of rules is
subsumption rather than balancing (Alexy, 1985, 75 ff).

1 Conflicts of Rules

Conflicts of rules are resolved *either* by altering one of the conflicting rules by adding an exception clause *or* by invalidating one of
the conflicting rules. In regard to the latter, the following rules of
priority are generally recognized:

1   The rule of posteriority: 'lex posterior derogat legi priori'.
2   The rule of speciality: 'lex specialis derogat legi generali'.
3   The rule of superiority: 'lex superior derogat legi inferiori'.

A special case of the superiority rule is Art. 31 Basic Law:
'Federal law overrides the law of the Federal States.'

Special problems of superiority arise concerning the relations between the law of the European Community and the law of the Federal Republic. The law of the European Community is 'part of the legal system valid in the Federal Republic of Germany and its courts have to consider, interpret, and apply it' (BVerfGE 73, 339 (367)). In case of collision, it takes priority over the national law (BVerfGE 73, 339 (375)). There is, however, a limit to this priority. It is not allowed to

> give up the identity of the constitution of the Federal Republic of Germany by damaging its basic order or the structures which consti-tute it . . . An unrenounceable essential of the constitution's basic order are the legal principles on which the basic rights of the Basic Law are grounded. (BVerfGE 73, 339 (375 f))

This means that European Community law does not take priority if it infringes upon constitutional law which refers to the 'essential content of the basic rights recognized by the Basic Law' (BVerfGE 73, 339 (376)).

The practical consequences of this restriction are of little import-ance. In 1986, the Federal Constitutional Court declared:

> As long as the European Communities, in particular the Communities' Court's adjudication, generally guarantee an effective protection of the basic rights against the communities' authorities which is, on the whole, adequate to the protection of the basic rights demanded by the Basic Law, and which grants the basic rights' essential content, the Federal Constitutional Court will not exercise its jurisdiction concern-ing the applicability of community law, which is regarded as the legal basis for the decisions of German courts and authorities within the territory of the Federal Republic of Germany, and consequently will not review this law with regard to the standards of the Basic Law's basic rights any longer. (BVerfGE 73, 339 (387))

In spite of this holding, the restriction of priority of the Euro-pean Community law remains of importance for the character and structure of the German legal system. The 'as long as' proviso shows that fundamental legal principles of the legal system, especially the basic rights, must not be surrendered to the law of the European Community. Of course, their protection is partially transferred to EC bodies, in particular to the European Court of Law in Luxembourg (BVerfGE 75, 223 (233 ff)).

Concerning the relation between national and international law, Art. 25 Basic Law states: 'The general rules of international law are part of the federal law. They take priority over the statutes and immediately create rights and obligations for the inhabitants of the Federal Republic of Germany.' This rule grants priority to the general rules of the law of nations over the ordinary rules belonging to the legal system of the Federal Republic of Germany. There is some dispute as far as the relationship with constitutional law is concerned (Maunz and Dürig, 1983, Art. 25, no. 22 ff). According to the Federal Constitutional Court, the general rules of international law take priority only over ordinary law but not over constitutional law (BVerfGE 6, 309 (363); 37, 371 (378 f)).

Concerning the relation between statutory and customary law it is generally agreed that the latter has force to derogate from the former (Dreier, 1986, col. 1059–63).

Constitutional law takes priority over law below the constitution. According to the Federal Constitutional Court, in cases of statutory vagueness the superiority of the constitution entails the following rule of interpretation: 'If a norm allows several interpretations, but only one which leads to a constitutional result, that interpretation is obligatory which is in accordance with the Basic Law' (BVerfGE 49, 148 (157)). While the legislator's intent must be respected as far as possible, it may also be suppressed:

> (It cannot) be decisive whether an interpretation exceeding the constitutional constraints would have satisfied the legislator's subjective intent more fully. Yet in such a case it is necessary to retain, within the limits drawn by the constitution, as much as possible of what the legislator intended. (BVerfGE 49, 148 (157))

2 Collisions of Legal Principles

Collisions or 'tensions' between different principles are resolved by weighing them and working out concrete priority relations for individual cases or specific types of cases. The conditions under which the one principle, for example, that of the greatest possible protection of privacy, takes priority over another, for example, that of the greatest possible freedom of the press, form the operative facts of a rule which expresses the legal consequence of the overriding principle, for example the prohibition of certain violations of privacy by the press. The general process of weighing and transforming colliding principles into rules, especially within the established jurisdiction of the Federal Constitutional Court, may be summarized in two general rules:

> (1) The higher the degree of non-realization or infringement of the one principle, the greater must be the importance of the realization of the other principle. (Alexy, 1986, p. 146)

(2) The conditions under which the one principle precedes the other establish the operative facts of a rule that expresses the legal consequences of the preceding principle. (Alexy, 1986, p. 84)

One example involving the collision of principles is the Federal Constitutional Court's 'Lebach sentence'. The court had to decide whether a TV station could broadcast a documentary film about a criminal case that happened years ago, in which one of the convicts was identified and thus his resocialization endangered. The court stated that

there was a collision between the general right to personality granted in Art. 2 (1) in connection with Art. 1 (1) Basic Law and the broadcasting station's right of freedom of coverage granted by Art. 5 (1) second sentence Basic Law. (BVerfGE 35, 202 (219))

This conflict was resolved by weighing:

The weighing has to consider the intensity of the interference with the personal realm brought about by such a programme on the one hand . . .; on the other hand the concrete interest such a programme could satisfy must be judged; one has to decide whether this interest can also be satisfied without or with a less drastic interference with the protection of the personality. (BVerfGE 35, 202 (226))

The court concluded that, under the conditions of the Lebach case, the protection of the right to personality is more important than the station's right of freedom of coverage. These conditions establish the operative facts of a rule which expresses the legal consequences of the principle of the protection of personality in the Lebach case: 'A rebroadcast of a TV-feature on a major crime no longer covered by an acute interest in information, is not permitted at least when it jeopardizes the convict's resocialization' (BVerfGE 35, 202, (237)).

VIII   PRESUMPTIONS GUIDING INTERPRETATION

In Germany general presumptions designed to guide interpretation are not a special and independent subject of methodological research. However these are presumptions. They are dealt with in discussions of different types of arguments, in discussions of the priorities among conflicting arguments and in discussions of principles, particularly constitutional principles. For further explanation see sections III, VI, XIII and XIV. Here we mention three very general presumptions. In the German Federal Republic the legislator is presumed (1) to choose his terminology carefully; (2) to strive to omit contradictions; and (3) to refrain from producing absurd results.

IX   THE STYLE OF LEGAL DECISIONS

1   The minimal content of a judicial decision is statutorily defined in the Federal Republic of Germany. In s. 313 (1) Code of Civil Procedure (ZPO) we find that:

> The decision has to contain
> 1 the designation of the parties, their legal representatives and the attorneys of record;
> 2 the designation of the court and the names of the judges who took part in the decision;
> 3 the day on which the trial was brought to an end;
> 4 the operative provisions of the decision;
> 5 the facts;
> 6 the reasons on which the decision is based.

Similar listings are contained in s. 117 (2) VwGO, s. 105 (2) FGO and s. 136 (1) SGG. Section 60 (4), first sentence, ArbGG explicitly distinguishes between the facts and the reasons on which the decision is based. Section 94 (2) Patent Act (PatG) requires that certain decisions be substantiated. Supplementarily the act refers to an analogical application of the rules contained in the Code of Civil Procedure (s. 99 (1) Patent Act). The Code of Criminal Procedure (StPO) contains a specific rule which meets the special needs of criminal law. To illustrate, s. 267 (1) Code of Criminal Procedure provides:

> If the accused is convicted, the reasons for the decision have to contain the facts conceived as proven, in which the legal features of the crime have been found. As far as proof is gathered from other facts, those have to be named as well. For details, there may be reference to pictures which are part of the documents in the case. Compare further s. 260 (2)–(5); s. 267 (2)–(6); s. 268 (1); s. 275 (3) StPO.

2   In the juristic practice of the Federal Republic of Germany two styles of reasoning have to be distinguished: the *style of expert reasoning* and the *style of justifying a decision*. Expert reasoning starts with a question, for example, whether the action has merit. This question must be answered by discussing all alternatives. At the end there has to be a suggestion for a decision. The purpose of this style of reasoning is to

make a decision possible or easier for legally trained colleagues. In contrast, in the 'justifying' style we find at the
beginning of the decision not a question but an answer, for
example, that the action has merit. In what follows, this
answer is substantiated.

3   In justifying a decision the judge more or less follows the
model of the juristic syllogism. The norm under which the
case must be subsumed is always quoted. The norm is not,
however, quoted in its exact wording. This is assumed to be
known. Section 260 (5), first sentence, Code of Criminal
Procedure (StPO) reads: 'After the operative provisions of
the decision the norms which have been applied must be
cited according to section, paragraph, number, letter, and
with the name of the law.'

That the subsumption of the facts under a norm is the
basis for the substantiation of the decision does not mean
that this substantiation consists only of a major premise (the
norm), a minor premise (the description of the facts) and a
conclusion (the judgement). Such a simple solution is usually
excluded, since a variety of norms have to be applied to
solve a case. This often creates very complex deductive
structures. More important is another point. A *purely*
deductive substantiation, however complex it may be, is
possible only if there is no argument between the parties on
three points: (1) which norms have to be applied? (2) How
do they have to be interpreted? (3) On which facts does the
decision turn? If there is no argument on these three points,
ordinarily no legal action need occur. Yet, if an action is
brought, a court must decide it. This means that the court
will have to answer at least one of these questions, and the
answer in turn must be integrated into the deductive scheme
(Alexy, 1989, 221 ff), despite the fact that it exceeds it.
Arguments of this kind can be labelled 'discursive' to differentiate them from the basic deductive structure of an opinion.

4   In German courts, discursive argumentation is quite
common. The types of arguments and materials mentioned
in sections III and V are frequently referred to. One can
detect a tendency in the lower courts, all of which carry a
heavy workload, to take into account more precedents and
legal commentaries than do the higher courts. A clear
distinction emerges in the temporal dimension. The Reichsgericht's opinions (1879–1945) were generally shorter than
those of the Federal Court of Justice (since 1950).

5   Within the framework of discursive argumentation weigh-

ing is of special importance. Weighing, however, cannot be called a 'style of reasoning' in its own right. The weighings are integrated into the main deductive scheme. They occur, for instance, when a question of interpreting a certain statute arises. After interpreting the statute, the judge subsumes the facts under the norm thus interpreted. The practice of the Federal Constitutional Court frequently deviates from this procedure, when, as in the Lebach decision (BVerfGE 35, 202 (219)), it states a collision of principles to be resolved directly by weighing.

6   Courts generally try to answer only those questions which must be answered to solve the case. But higher courts tend to give *general answers* which far exceed the case. This is true especially of the Federal Constitutional Court. In this way, the courts play a major role in the development of legal dogmatics. It is also typical for the higher courts that they often – if only selectively – consult or at least discuss writings of legal scholars.

7   *Dissenting opinions* only appear in constitutional adjudication (s. 30 (2) BVerfGG). All other courts issue one opinion.

8   Higher courts select their most important decisions for publication in 'official' reports or digests. But there are other collections of decisions. Many decisions are published in academic journals. For the lower courts, this is the only mode of publication. A decision is published if a judge or lawyer sends it to an editor who accepts it. Legal database systems have become increasingly important as media of publication.

9   As far as the *announcement* of a decision is concerned one must distinguish between its operative provisions and its substantiation. In principle, the announcement of the result is public (s. 173 (1) GVG). But service to the parties may be substituted for public announcement (compare s. 116 (2) VwGO). In special cases, such as the protection of privacy (s. 171 b (2) GVG) or a threat to the national security (s. 172 Nr. 1 GVG), public announcement may not occur. For different courts, different rules govern the way reasons on which a decision is based are announced. According to s. 311 (3), ZPO reasons are supposed to be announced if this is 'considered appropriate'. The reasons can be read out in full or summarized. Section 60 (2) ArbGG provides that the main content of the opinion be announced if the parties are present. Section 116 VwGO does not contain an explicit rule on the announcement of opinions. Section 268 (1) StPO says that the verdict is announced by reading out the

operative provisions and pointing out the reasons. An opinion may be fully read out or summarized.

10   *Direct addressees* of an opinion are the persons involved in the trial, such as, in civil procedure, the parties and their lawyers and, in criminal procedure, the accused and his lawyer, as well as the public prosecutor. There are many indirect addressees. With decisions subject to review by higher courts, these are very important addressees. The opinions of the highest courts are especially scrutinized by the legal academics. Generally speaking, any person and any institution who is a relevant critic in the eyes of the courts can also be regarded as an indirect addressee of the decision.

11   Many *functions* of the decision's substantiation are discussed (compare, for instance, Luhmann, 1969; Brüggemann, 1971, 109 ff). On two of them there is general agreement: the respect for the rights of those involved and constitutional controllability. By giving an opinion, the court takes seriously the participant to whose disadvantage it decides. It tries to convince that party that the decision was right. This is the main subjective function of the substantiation. Its main objective function is the protection of constitutional control which is supposed to secure that the decision is legally correct. The substantiation is a necessary condition for the rational review of a decision by higher courts, colleagues, academics, and by the public.

X   INTERPRETATION IN THE LIGHT OF THE CHARACTER OF THE STATUTE

In principle, the same forms and rules of interpretation are applied in all fields of law. In some respects, however, there are important differences from one branch of law to another. The sources of these differences lie not so much in legal methodology as in substantive and formal legal principles which often have the character of constitutional principles. Perhaps the most striking differences are to be observed in criminal law. The principle 'nulla poena sine lege', laid down in Art. 103 (2) GG and s. 1 Penal Code, excludes gap-filling by analogy where this would be disadvantageous for the defendant. It demands strict priority of arguments based on the wording of the statute (see above, sections II 2, VI 4). Such priority also holds if the state wishes to interfere with basic rights. This is also of particular importance in tax law.

Several special rules apply to the interpretation of the constitution. Of greatest importance is the question of how closely the

Federal Constitutional Court should control the legislature, the executive and the judiciary. This court has developed a complex system of rules which takes account of a great variety of situations.

In principle, the nature of a statute's addressees does not affect the way courts interpret statutes. But courts tend to favour ordinary meaning where statutes are addressed directly to lay persons.

Concerning the age of a statute, the following maxim holds: the older a statute, the weaker the binding force of its wording and of the actual will of the historical legislator (BVerfGE 34, 269 (288)). This maxim corresponds to a second one: the older the statute, the greater the impact of recent precedents interpreting it.

Naturally interpretation depends on the structure of the statute. The more general and vague its terms are, the greater is the freedom of interpretation. This holds especially for general clauses. The more specific and precise a statute, the greater its binding force. It must be added that there can be a considerable degree of freedom in interpretation even in cases of rather recent and quite precisely formulated statutes. If statutes contain inconsistencies, the judges will try to eliminate them by way of interpretation.

XI   THE ROLE OF COURTS

1   In Germany courts play quite an important role. This role is based on the constitution and is widely accepted socially. This large role of the judiciary has been vigorously criticized, mainly in the light of the separation of powers and of democracy. One of its main critics has been Ernst Forsthoff. His thesis is that a transformation from the constitutional to the judicial state has taken place (Forsthoff, 1959, p. 59; 1971, 126 ff). In the last decade this criticism has sharpened the courts' awareness of the problem. A fundamental change, however, is not yet in sight.

2   The Federal Constitutional Court has power to invalidate all kinds of statutes as contrary to the Constitution (Art. 93 (1) Nr. 2; Art. 100 (1) GG). It has often made use of this power. Even on politically highly contested questions, it has decided against the majority in parliament. Examples are the decisions concerning abortion (BVerfGE 39, 1), the reformation of the university system (BVerfGE 35, 79) and the protection of confidential personal data (BVerfGE 65, 1).

For the protection of the constitutions of the Federal States, there are either constitutional courts of the states or protection has been transferred to the Federal Constitutional

Court in accordance with Art. 99 Basic Law.

So far as concerns judicial review of laws by other courts, one has to distinguish between formal and merely material laws (Gesetze im formellen und im materiellen Sinn). A formal law is a law enacted by a parliament – that is, either by the federal parliament (Bundestag) or by one of the parliaments of the 16 states (Landesparlamente). Merely material laws are norms not enacted by a parliament, for example administrative regulations, by-laws and customary law. Formal laws, which have been enacted later than the Basic Law in 1949 and which are contrary to the Basic Law, may be invalidated only by the Federal Constitutional Court. If another court considers a formal law to be important for its decision and considers this formal law to be contrary to the Basic Law, this court must suspend the trial and appeal to the Federal Constitutional Court (Art. 100 (1), first sentence, GG). The purpose of this provision is to guarantee that not just any judge may set aside the legislator's will.

All courts other than constitutional courts have the power to refuse to apply statutes enacted prior to the Basic Law in 1949, if these statutes are not compatible with it. An exception is made in cases where the post-1949 legislature has integrated the old rule into its intention (BVerfGE 2, 124 (128 ff); 70, 126 (129 f)). Then only the Federal Constitutional Court has power to declare the old rule unconstitutional as contrary to the Basic Law. This approach protects the legislature's intention against judicial disregard.

Today, 40 years after the Basic Law came into force, it is more important to note that all courts have power to refuse to apply law which has not been enacted by a parliament, that is, which does not have the character of a formal law, if that law is contrary to constitutional law.

A special procedure obtains for the review of by-laws and regulations of the states by higher administrative courts (s. 47 VwGO). Beside this, there are national and supranational procedures to resolve conflicts between national, European Community and international law.

3   Courts also play an important role in interpretation and in gap-filling. The reasons have been explained in section I. The competence to fill gaps or even to take *contra legem* decisions which is granted to the courts has been discussed in section II.

4   Finally we must mention the comprehensive control that administrative courts exercise over administrative bodies

and their work. The executive is controlled by courts even where the law allows for discretionary judgement. The court considers whether there might have been mistakes in the weighing of reasons for exercising discretion (Alexy, 1986, 701 ff). Courts also exercise close control where administrative planning, for example in the building sector, is concerned. There is a dispute in the literature as to whether these controls are too extensive.

XII CONSTITUTIONAL OR STATUTORY PRESCRIPTIONS ON INTERPRETATION

1   In Germany there are hardly any constitutional or statutory texts which prescribe specifically how statutes are to be interpreted or gaps to be filled. Statutory prescriptions on interpretation and gap-filling may be found in older codifications, for example in ss. 46–58 of the 'Introduction to the Prussian General Law of the Land' from 1794, and in ss. 6 and 7 of the Austrian ABGB of 1811. The first draft of the BGB contained a rule in section 1 about gap-filling by analogy and the application of principles which resulted from the 'spirit of the legal system'. This rule was eliminated in the second reading, with the following argument:

> The majority reckoned that no legal permission was necessary for the use of analogy, especially because analogy and interpretation were so closely connected and there were no regulations concerning interpretation in the Civil Code either. (Achilles/Gebhard/Spahn (eds), Minutes of the Commission for the Second Reading of the draft of the Civil Code, vol. 1, Berlin 1897, p. 2)

In other codifications, no prescriptions on interpretation or gap-filling can be found either. An exception is the prohibition of analogy in s. 1 Penal Code (StGB) and in Art. 103 (2) Basic Law (GG), cited above.

More recent administrative laws, in their preambles or introductory sections, often contain general formulations of goals which should be taken into account within the framework of teleological interpretation (compare s. 1 Federal Building Code (BauGB)). But general formulations of goals cannot be regarded as prescribing specifically how statutes are supposed to be interpreted or gaps to be filled.

2   Section 1 of the Swiss Civil Code (ZGB) (originating from Eugen Huber and oriented towards ideas of the Free Law

Movement) is widely, if contestedly, conceived of as expressing a general maxim:

> The statutory law finds application in all legal questions on which it contains a regulation, according to its wording and interpretation. If no regulation can be taken from statutory law, the judge shall decide in accordance with customary law, and if that is also missing, according to a rule he would make as legislator. In doing so, he follows approved doctrine and tradition

3   To sum up, we may say that, apart from the prohibition of analogy in criminal law, there are no statutory prescriptions concerning interpretation of statutes in Germany. In private law, however, there exist prescriptions on interpreting, for example, declarations of intention (s. 133 BGB), contracts (s. 157 BGB) and wills (ss. 2066, 2084 BGB).

XIII   CONSTITUTIONAL LAW AND INTERPRETATION

1   In Germany the interpretation of statutes is basically and thoroughly influenced by constitutional law.

Although the Basic Law (GG) does not formulate rules for interpretation, it contains *constitutional principles* that bind the judge. Such principles are especially enshrined in the provisions about basic rights and about the aims and structure of the state. The most important ones are the principles of human dignity, freedom, equality (Art. 1–3 GG), the rule of law (Rechtsstaat), democracy, and the social state (Art. 20, 28 (1) GG).

These principles are not merely programmatic prescriptions without legally binding force, but law of the highest rank, and this law constrains the judge directly. This is stated explicitly in respect to principles concerning basic rights (for example, human dignity, freedom and equality). Art. 1 (3) GG says: 'The following basic rights bind legislation, executive and judicial jurisdiction as immediately valid law.'

The binding force of, for example, principles concerning the aim and the structure of the state (rule of law, democracy and social state) results from the normative character and the superiority of the constitution: 'The Basic Law, being the highest law within the state, is not only the yardstick for the validity of legal norms . . .; their contents as well must be interpreted in accord with the Basic Law' (BVerfGE 51, 304 (323)).

The principle on which the courts have hitherto been most hesitant to act is the *principle of social state*. Its realization is mainly the task of the legislator:

> If Art. 20 (1) GG expresses that the Federal Republic be a social federal state, it follows only that the state has the obligation to take care of the balance of social contrasts and thus of a just social order; this aim it will first of all try to reach by means of legislation. (BVerfGE 22, 180 (204))

Ordinarily the indeterminacy of the principle of social state excludes its direct application by the courts:

> The Basic Law's principle of social state, because of its width and indeterminacy, does not normally contain straightforward commands which could be turned into ordinary law by the courts without a statutory base. It is less accessible to judicial determination of contents than the basic rights. (BVerfGE 65, 182 (193))

Yet the principle of the social state is not without importance for adjudication. It does not have to be exclusively realized by legislation but only 'first of all' by it. Its direct application by courts is only 'normally' excluded. It is merely less suitable to judicial concretization than the basic rights. In some decisions, the principle of social state plays the role of a substantial *ratio decidendi*. An example is a decision by the Federal Administrative Court (BVerwG) concerning the move by a Spanish employee's widowed grandmother to Germany. The Spanish employee, resident of the Federal Republic for about ten years, was married to a Spanish citizen who also worked here, and they had three children to raise. The responsible authority had refused to issue a residence permit to the grandmother. The court found this to be a faulty discretionary decision on the following grounds: 'Restriction of discretion follows in any event from the obligation of the Federal Republic of Germany to take care of foreign employees, an obligation resulting from the principle of social state (Art. 20 (1), 28 (1) GG)' (BVerwGE 42, 148 (157)). Basically discretion was wide: 'It may be restricted, however, when the need for care can be satisfied by means of a rather light burden for the public in comparison with the urgency of the need' (BVerwGE 42, 148 (157)). It is widely agreed that the principle of social state may be applied in this way. Divergences exist as to how extensively this should be done. For cases in which the Federal Constitutional Court applied the principle to justify or to limit individual legal positions, see BVerfGE 21, 245 (251); 33, 303 (331 ff); 45, 376 (385 ff).

The immediate validity of the constitutional principles exposes the judge to a *twofold tension*.

The first tension obtains between constitutional and statutory law. This can be traced to the constitutional principles themselves. These are partly procedural or formal, and partly substantive or material. The rule of law through its requirement of legal certainty (Rechtssicherheit) and the principle of democracy demand that judges be bound by statute. Correspondingly, Art. 97 (1) GG provides: 'Judges are independent and subject only to the laws.' These are procedural principles. Material principles, in particular those concerning basic rights and the principle of social state, must also be employed as criteria of justice in the interpretation of ordinary law. This is expressed in constitutional law by the fact that Art. 20 (3) GG not only binds the judge to statutes but to 'statutes and the law' (BVerfGE 34, 269 (286 f); Dreier, 1985, 353 ff).

To this tension between law below the constitution and constitutional law are to be added tensions among the constitutional principles themselves, such as the tension between freedom and equality or between the rule of law and the principle of social state (BVerfGE 5, 82 (206)).

2   The foregoing remarks have far-reaching consequences for the interpretation of statutory law.

Every judicial interpretation of statutory law must have regard to constitutional principles. The Federal Constitutional Court has expressed this in one of its most important decisions, the Lüth decision, as follows:

> It is . . . correct that the Basic Law, which does not purport to be a value-neutral order, has established an objective order of values in its part dealing with basic rights. . . . This system of values, which finds its centre in the human personality freely unfolding itself within the social community, and in human dignity, must hold as a basic constitutional decision in all fields of the law; legislation, administration, and judicial jurisdiction derive guidance and impulses from it. Of course, it thus also influences the civil law; no prescription of the civil law may contradict it, each has to be interpreted in its spirit. (BVerfGE 7, 198 (205))

This theory of the radiation of the constitutional principles over all fields of law has been attacked in the literature.

Authors like Forsthoff criticize the direct judicial recourse to constitutional principles with ironic pungency (Forsthoff, 1971, 139 ff). This critique, however, has not had striking success. There is general agreement that constitutional demands have to be complied with in the interpretation of statutory law. But how far this has to happen and the role of the Federal Constitutional Court here are controversial (Schlaich, 1985, 145 ff). Many jurists, rightly, believe that a differentiating solution is necessary (Wahl, 1984, p. 409).

The Federal Constitutional Court has stated: 'In the interpretation and application of ordinary law, esp. of general clauses, the courts have to take account of the Basic Law's standards of value' (BVerfGE 18, 85, (92)). But the Federal Constitutional Court restricts its competence to that of judging 'whether the courts' contested decisions are based on a generally wrong view of the meaning of the basic rights . . ., or whether the result of the interpretation itself violates the basic rights asserted' (BVerfGE 30, 173 (188)). The limits of judicial control are not drawn in 'rigid and constant' terms. They depend upon the 'intensity of the infringement of the basic right': 'In cases of the highest intensity of infringement [the Federal Constitutional Court] is by all means allowed to replace the evaluation made by the civil courts with its own evaluation' (BVerfGE 42, 143 (149)).

For adjudication, this has the consequence that, in many cases in which colliding constitutional principles are relevant, a *weighing* of such principles becomes necessary for the application of statutory law:

> The solution of this conflict must begin with the assumption that according to the constitution's intention both constitutional values are essential components of the free and democratic order of the Basic Law, so that neither of them can claim a basic predominance. (BVerfGE 35, 202, (225))

> That is why a 'weighing of goods' becomes necessary: The right to express one's opinion freely has to retreat if another's interest worth defending and of higher order were injured by the act of expressing one's opinion. Whether there are such predominant interests of others must be found out by taking account of all circumstances of the case. (BVerfGE 7, 198 (210 f))

These formulations show that, according to the Federal Constitutional Court, the constitutional principles to be taken into account in statutory interpretation do not have the status of rules to be applied in an all-or-nothing fashion, but are principles in the technical sense, that is, they entail obligations to optimize (Alexy, 1986, 75 ff); see above, section III.

3   Constitutional principles may be controlling in all situations of the *application of law*. The spectrum reaches from the interpretation of vague concepts (BVerfGE 59, 336 (349 ff)), to the filling of gaps (BVerfGE 3, 225 (237 ff)), to decisions *contra legem* (BVerfGE 34, 269 (287 ff)).

4   Generally the validity, especially of the six constitutional principles mentioned above, means that leading principles of modern legal and social ethics are incorporated into the law of the German Federal Republic as principles of positive law. This implies that the German Federal Republic's positive law is explicitly open to moral argumentation (justice). The judge in the German Federal Republic, on account of his function, has to treat *moral questions as legal questions* within the frame of interpretation and adjudication. Thus he confronts a tension between authoritativeness and rightness (justice) of the law.

5   There are many examples of the way constitutional principles have changed the content of statutes. Especially instructive are: the equalization of the sexes (BVerfGE 3, 225; 10, 59; 52, 369), the general right of personality (BVerfGE 34, 269), the right of pardon (BVerfGE 45, 187) and the right of demonstration (BVerfGE 69, 315).

XIV   INTERPRETATION AND PRINCIPLES OF LAW

When general principles or values in interpretation or gap-filling are used in Germany they are commonly traced back to the constitution. The basic constitutional principles and values were expounded in section XIII, where we also explained how these principles and values are applied in the justificatory practice of the courts.

XV   THE CHARACTER OF THE HIGHER COURTS IN THE FEDERAL REPUBLIC OF GERMANY

In the Federal Republic of Germany there are five independent special jurisdictions besides the constitutional jurisdiction: the general, that is, civil and criminal jurisdiction, the administrative jurisdiction, the jurisdiction of the fiscal courts, the social jurisdiction and the jurisdiction in labour matters. Each special jurisdiction is exercised by the courts of the states. Only at the highest level are five federal courts installed (Art. 95 (1) GG). Some special regulations concerning patent jurisdiction and disciplinary jurisdiction of the Federation (Art. 96 GG) may be disregarded here. We will limit our discussion to the Federal Court of Justice (BGH), which is the highest court of general jurisdiction, and the Federal Constitutional Court (BVerfG).

1   The Federal Court of Justice (BGH)

At present the Federal Court of Justice consists of 11 panels of civil jurisdiction and five panels of criminal jurisdiction, apart from a few special panels. Each panel comprises five regular judges. In 1987 this court heard 4 297 civil cases and 3 711 criminal cases.

The judges of the Federal Court of Justice are appointed by the Federal Minister of Justice and by a board for the appointment of judges (Art. 95 (2) GG). This board consists of the Ministers of Justice of the states and as many members of the Federal Parliament (Bundestag); the Federal Minister of Justice has power to reject the candidate appointed by the board. A representative body of the judges, the Presidential Council, has a right to be consulted. At the minister's request, the Federal President pronounces the formal appointment (Art. 60 (1) GG).

There are complex regulations about the role of the Federal Court of Justice. Its most important role is to hear appeals (Revision) from decisions by the higher courts of the States. The Federal Court of Justice is in principle bound to the account of the facts in the lower court. It hears only legal, not factual questions.

2   The Federal Constitutional Court (BVerfG)

The Federal Constitutional Court consists of two panels, each comprising eight judges. One half of the judges are elected by the Bundestag, the other half by the Bundesrat. In both cases a candidate needs two-thirds of the votes. This regulation has been chosen to guarantee the influence of different political parties. In practice, it has led to an apportionment of the offices of the judges among the big political parties. All judges must be qualified to hold judicial office. A judge's term of office is 12 years. A second election is not possible.

The Federal Constitutional Court hears a broad variety of

subject-matters. In 1988 the court decided 3 702 cases, 3 613 of which were constitutional complaints of citizens. More than three-quarters of the latter were heard by divisions of the panels – so-called 'chambers' (Kammern), which consist of three judges each. The court decides, for example, conflicts between the highest federal organs and between the federal states and the Federal Republic, and decides cases in which the constitutionality of legal norms is contested. Of special importance is its competence to hear complaints of citizens alleging that a measure of the state violates basic rights. Its extensive competence is one main reason for the central role the Federal Constitutional Court plays in the German legal system. Another reason is that its decisions bind all constitutional organs, all courts and all administrative authorities. In some special cases, the decisions even acquire the force of legal norms.

XVI   THE LEGISLATURE: STRUCTURE AND PROCEDURES

In the Federal Republic of Germany a statute enacted by parliament is either a federal statute or a statute enacted by one of the eleven states. According to the constitution, the legislative power is in principle a power of the states. The Federal Republic has legislative power only where it is conferred by the constitution (Art. 77 (1) GG). However the broad federal legislative powers mean that most of the important subject-matter is regulated by federal legislation.

Federal statutes are passed by the Federal Parliament, the Bundestag. The states participate in federal legislation by way of the Bundesrat, which consists of members of the Federal states' governments. In principle, the Bundesrat has only the right to raise an objection against a statute passed by the Bundestag. This objection in turn may be rejected by the Bundestag. But, in a great number of cases, the constitution requires assent of the Bundesrat. Thus the states do have considerable influence on federal legislation.

The members of the Bundestag are elected according to principles of proportional representation, as slightly modified by elements of majority voting. This has the effect that, besides two big political parties, at least one smaller party has always been represented in parliament. Consequently all federal governments have hitherto been coalition governments. This, together with the fact that the opposition frequently has the majority in the Bundesrat, explains in part why legislation in Germany often has the character of a compromise.

Bills may be introduced by the federal government, by members of the Bundestag or by the Bundesrat. In practice, bills of the federal government prevail. They are prepared in a highly professional manner by the ministerial bureaucracy which, as a rule, furnishes extensive explanations and reasons. The substantial legislative work of the parliament is mainly done by parliamentary committees. In order to pass a statute, at least three readings in parliament are necessary. The whole process is documented and the records are generally available to the judiciary. They can be and are used by the courts for purposes of interpretation, as described above (see sections III, V and VI).

There is a tendency in Germany's legislature to confirm and codify judge-made law. Corrections of judge-made law are rare, but they do occur. On account of the structure of the legislative process, compromises abound. In many cases the results are general clauses which must be implemented by the courts. These often pose serious problems of interpretation.

XVII   FEATURES OF LEGAL CULTURE

1   In general, the German legal culture is substantive and value-oriented to a significant degree. Its basic values are, as has been repeatedly noted in this chapter, defined by the constitution. However the German legal culture also is to a high degree characterized by the systematizing achievements of writings of legal dogmatics, and in this sense it has a pervasive formal feature. Both aspects have partly conflicting, partly complementary influence on statutory interpretation and gap-filling. Moreover there is, in practice as well as in theory, a fundamental conflict between two conceptions of legal argumentation which may be termed 'constitutionalist' and 'legalist'. Constitutionalism emphasizes the value content of the constitution and intends to realize it through the judiciary, in cases of doubt even against the legislature. Legalism emphasizes parliamentary sovereignty and restrains the extent of judicial power. In terms of legal theory, this conflict is manifest in the dichotomies of rule vs. value or principle and of subsumption vs. weighing (see Alexy, 1987, 405 ff; Dreier, 1988, 87 ff; Mahrenholz and Böckenförde, Dissenting Opinion in BVerfGE 69, 1 (57 ff)).

2   The German legal methodology includes generally acknowledged rules, principles and forms of statutory interpretation and gap-filling. In this respect it is relatively unified, but in

other respects there are deep controversies between different methodological positions. One of these controversies, constitutionalism vs. legalism, has just been mentioned. Others exist, for example between analytical, hermeneutical and critical schools of legal thinking. Within these schools, conflicting political ideologies and attitudes between conservative, libertarian, liberal or left-wing lawyers and legal scholars overlap with methodological differences. An instructive survey of the history of legal methodology in Germany may be found in Larenz, 1983, Part One.

3   German judges are highly influenced by academic writings and legal dogmatics. In particular, higher courts take account of and refer to scholarly writings. Yet the academic spirit permeates the opinions of all courts. This shows the vast extent to which the German legal culture is an expert culture. This in turn is the result of a long, uniform and comprehensive legal education obligatory for all German jurists; it comprises four to five years at a law school and two and a half years of preparatory service in the main branches of law, and it aims – with the second state examination – at the qualification to hold judicial office. Lay judges play a minor role within the judiciary.

4   As indicated above, the German jurist who has passed the second state examination is qualified to be a judge. This qualification includes the capability to take up any legal profession. Specializations within the judiciary are to be found in the various jurisdictions (see above, Preliminary and section XV). Lawyers are basically competent to work in every field of law. Of course within the bar there is informal specialization. Formal specialization is acknowledged only for tax law, labour law, social law, administrative law and patent law.

ABBREVIATIONS

ABGB	Allgemeines Bürgerliches Gesetzbuch (Austrian General Civil Code)
ArbGG	Arbeitsgerichtsgesetz (German Code of Labour Court Procedure)
BauGB	Baugesetzbuch (German Federal Building Code)
BGB	Bürgerliches Gesetzbuch (German Civil Code)
BGH	Bundesgerichtshof (German Federal Court of Justice)
BGHSt	Entscheidungen des Bundesgerichtshofes in Strafsachen (Decisions of the German Federal Court of Justice in Criminal Cases)

BGHZ	Entscheidungen des Bundesgerichtshofes in Zivilsachen (Decisions of the German Federal Court of Justice in Civil Cases)
BVerfG	Bundesverfassungsgericht (German Federal Constitutional Court)
BverfGE	Entscheidungen des Bundesverfassungsgerichts (Decisions of the German Federal Constitutional Court)
BVerfGG	Bundesverfassungsgerichtsgesetz (German Code of Constitutional Court Procedure)
BVerwG	Bundesverwaltungsgericht (German Federal Administrative Court)
FGO	Finanzgerichtsordnung (German Code of Fiscal Court Procedure)
GG	Grundgesetz (German Basic Law)
GVG	Gerichtverfassungsgesetz (German General Court Act)
JöR n.F.	Jahrbüch für öffentliches Recht, neue Folge
JZ	Juristenzeitung
KO	Konkursordnung (German Bankruptcy Act)
NJW	Neue Juristische Wochenschrift
NVwZ	Neue Zeitschrift für Verwaltungsrecht
PatG	Patentgesetz (German Patent Act)
RGZ	Entscheidungen des Reichsgerichts in Zivilsachen (Decisions of the Supreme Court of the German Reich in Civil Cases)
SGG	Sozialgerichtsgesetz (German Code of Social Procedure)
StGB	Strafgesetzbuch (German Penal Code)
StPO	Strafprozeßordnung (German Code of Criminal Procedure)
TierschutzG	Tierschutzgesetz (German Act for Prevention of Cruelty to Animals)
VVDStRL	Veröffentlichungen der Vereinigung der Deutschen Staatsrechtslehrer
VwGO	Verwaltungsgerichtsordnung (German Code of Administrative Court Procedure)
VwVfG	Verwaltungsverfahrensgesetz (German Administration Procedure Act)
ZGB	Zivilgesetzbuch (Swiss Civil Code)
ZPO	Zivilprozeßordnung (German Code of Civil Procedure)

REFERENCES

Alexy, Robert (1985), *Theorie der Grundrechte*, Baden-Baden: Nomos.
Alexy, Robert (1986), 'Ermessensfehler', in *JZ*, 1986, pp. 701–16.
Alexy, Robert (1987), 'Rechtssystem und praktische Vernunft', in *Rechtstheorie* 18, pp. 405–19
Alexy, Robert (1989), *A Theory of Legal Argumentation*, Oxford: Clarendon Press (translation of *Theorie der juristischen Argumentation*, 1978).
Bachof, Otto and Brohm, Winfried (1972), 'Die Dogmatik des Verwaltungsrechts vor den Gegenwartsaufgaben der Verwaltung', in *VVDStRL* 30, 193, ff.
Brandenburg, Hans-Friedrich (1983), *Die teleologische Reduktion*, Göttingen: Schwartz.
Brüggemann, Jürgen (1971), *Die richterliche Begründungspflicht*, Berlin: Duncker und Humblot.
Bydlinski, Franz (1982), *Juristische Methodenlehre und Rechtsbegriff*, Wien/New York: Springer.

Bydlinski, Franz (1985) 'Hauptpositionen zum Richterrecht', in *JZ*, 1985, pp. 149–55.

Canaris, Claus-Wilhelm (1983), *Die Feststellung von Lücken im Gesetz*, 2nd edn., Berlin: Duncker und Humblot.

von Doemming, Klaus-Berto, Füßlein, Rudolf Werner and Matz, Werner (1951), 'Entstehungsgeschichte der Artikel des Grundgesetzes', in *JöR n.F.*, **1**.

Dreier, Ralf (1980), 'Generalklausel', in *Staatslexikon der Görres-Gesellschaft*, **2**, pp. 863–86, Freiburg/Basel/Wien: Herder.

Dreier, Ralf (1981), *Recht-Moral-Ideologie*, Frankfurt/M.: Suhrkamp.

Dreier, Ralf (1985), 'Der Rechtsstaat im Spannungsverhältnis zwischen Gesetz und Recht', in *JZ*, 1985, pp. 353–9.

Dreier, Ralf (1986), 'Gewohnheitsrecht', in *Staatslexikon der Görres-Gesellschaft*, **2**, 7th edn., pp. 1059–63, Freiburg/Basel/Wien: Herder.

Dreier, Ralf (1988), 'Konstitutionalismus und Legalismus – Zwei Arten juristischen Denkens im demokratischen Verfassungsstaat', in *Rechtsstaat und Menschenwürde, Festschrift für Werner Maihofer*, 87–107, Frankfurt/M.: Klostermann.

Dworkin, Ronald (1978), *Taking Rights Seriously*, 2nd edn., London: Duckworth.

Fikentscher, Wolfgang (1975), *Methoden des Rechts in vergleichender Darstellung*, 4 vols, Tübingen: Mohr.

Forsthoff, Ernst (1959), 'Die Umbildung des Verfassungsgesetzes', in *Festschrift für Carl Schmitt*, pp. 35–62, Berlin: Duncker und Humblot.

Forsthoff, Ernst (1971), *Der Staat der Industriegesellschaft*, 2nd edn., Munich: Beck.

Hedemann, Justus Wilhelm (1933), *Die Flucht in die Generaklauseln*, Tübingen: Mohr.

Koch, Hans-Joachim and Rüßmann, Helmut (1982), *Juristische Begründungslehre*, Munich: Beck.

Kriele, Martin (1976), *Theorie der Rechtsgewinnung*, 2nd edn., Berlin: Duncker und Humblot.

Larenz, Karl (1983), *Methodenlehre der Rechtswissenschaft*, 5th edn., Berlin/Heidelberg/New York/Tokyo: Springer.

Luhmann, Niklas (1969), *Legitimation durch Verfahren*, Neuwied, Berlin: Luchterhand.

Maunz, Theodor, Dürig, Günter et al. (1983), *Grundgesetz Kommentar*, 5th edn., Munich: Beck.

Müller, Friedrich (1985), *Richterrecht*, Berlin: Duncker und Humblot.

Müller, Friedrich (1989), *Juristische Methodik*, 3rd edn., Berlin: Duncker und Humblot.

Neumann, Ulfrid (1979), *Rechtsontologie und juristische Argumentation*, Heidelberg/Hamburg: R. v. Decker.

Neumann, Ulfrid (1986), *Juristische Argumentationslehre*, Darmstadt: Wissenschaftliche Buchgesellschaft.

Pawlowski, Hans-Martin (1981), *Methodenlehre für Juristen* Heidelberg/Karlsruhe: F. C. Müller

Philippi, Klaus Jürgen (1971), *Tatsachenfeststellungen des Bundesverfassungsgerichts*, Köln/Berlin: Heymann.

von Savigny, Friedrich Carl (1802/3), *Juristische Methodenlehre* (lecture, recorded and elaborated by J. Grimm, first published by G. Wesenberg, 1951, Stuttgart: K. F. Koehler).

von Savigny, Friedrich Carl (1840), *System des heutigen Römischen Rechts*, **I**, Berlin: Veit.

Schlaich, Klaus (1985), *Das Bundesverfassungsgericht*, Munich: Beck.

Schmitt, Carl (1973), 'Die Lage der europäischen Rechtswissenschaft', in Schmitt, Carl (ed.), *Verfassungsrechtliche Aufsätze aus den Jahren 1924–1954*, 2nd edn., pp. 386–429, Berlin: Duncker und Humblot.

Wahl, Rainer (1984), 'Der Vorrang der Verfassung und die Selbständigkeit des

Gesetzesrechts', in *NVwZ*, 1984, pp. 409.

Zimmermann, Rita (1983), *Die Relevanz der herrschenden Meinung für die Anwendung, Fortbildung und wissenschaftliche Erforschung des Rechts*, Berlin: Duncker und Humblot.

Zippelius, Reinhold (1985), *Einführung in die juristische Methodenlehre*, 4th edn., Munich: Beck.

5 Statutory Interpretation in Finland

AULIS AARNIO, *Helsinki**

PRELIMINARY

1   The Nature of the Legal Order of Finland

Finland is a statutory law system, but the law has not been codified in the proper sense of the term (cf. the 'Code Civil' of France or the BGB of Germany). An 'Act of Parliament' is adopted when parliament approves a Government Bill for the act and the President of the Republic signs the law into force. The act enters into force (at the earliest) after it has been published in the Statutes of Finland. Most acts contain a provision specifying the date of entry into force.

According to the Constitution, the President of the Republic has the power to issue decrees on the implementation of acts. The Council of State has the power, in certain cases specified by law, to issue statutes ('decisions of the Council of State') that are to be followed as legal norms. Furthermore either a statute or a decree may empower a lower authority, such as a county government or a

*The author would like to express his special appreciation to his colleagues, Professor Hannu Tapani Klami and Judicial Secretary Jukka Kemppinen, Licentiate in Laws. Both have read all of the chapter and made many valuable comments. In addition, Professor Klami prepared a memorandum on the tenth topic. The final version of this topic was drafted on the basis of this memorandum.

I would also like to express my warm thanks to Olavi Heinonen, Chief Justice of the Supreme Court of Finland. He has also reviewed the chapter and was instrumental in ensuring that it corresponds to the prevailing practice in Finland.

The chapter has been translated from Finnish by Matti Joutsen. He deserves special thanks for a skilful translation that has remained faithful to the author's thoughts.

municipal council, to enact by-laws binding the administrative sector in question or by-laws binding a local area. Statutes enacted in this manner are official sources of law. An example is municipal by-laws.

2   The Organization of the Judiciary

2.1

The constitution of Finland is based on a tripartite division of powers (Constitution Act, Art. 2). Parliament and the President of the Republic exercise the legislative function, the Council of State and its subsidiary administrative structure exercise the administrative function and independent courts exercise the judicial function. The independent courts consist of two separate branches, the general courts and the administrative courts. Each of these two court organizations has three levels.

The general courts are divided into the lower courts of general jurisdiction — the district courts and the city courts, the seven courts of appeal and the Supreme Court. The district courts, which operate in rural areas and in some urban areas, are chaired by a professional judge or by junior lawyers undergoing court training. In addition to the judicially trained chairman, the district courts have a lay board of at least seven laymen. The members of the lay board are selected for a four-year term by the municipal council, generally on political grounds. In both questions of law and questions of fact, the position of the lay board becomes the decision of the court if the lay board is unanimous. Otherwise the issue is determined by the chairman. It is very rare for the lay board unanimously to vote against the chairman and in this way decide the case. So-called non-contentious civil cases, such as the probating of a will, are decided by the chairman without the lay board.

Most towns and cities have a city court. The members of the city court are generally judicially trained judges although, primarily in small towns, laymen also may serve as members of the city court. The city court generally functions in divisions of three members each. Each division is chaired by a judicially trained judge.

2.2

Each court of appeal has a president and ordinary or extraordinary justices, as well as senior secretaries to prepare the cases for decision. All of these are judicially trained. The court of appeal is the first appellate level for decisions of the lower courts. In addition, the court of appeal hears appeals against decisions of the executor in chief (the county government and the city administrative court). The court of appeal is the court of first instance in cases involving treason or high treason, and in certain cases involving charges for an offence committed in office.

Most appeals are decided by the court of appeal as the final authority. This is due to the provisions limiting the right of appeal. The reform of these provisions in 1980 has considerably increased the efficiency of the system. Except where the court of appeal has considered the case in the first instance, a decision of the court of appeal can be appealed to the Supreme Court only if the latter grants leave to appeal.

Leave to appeal can be granted in three cases: (1) if the hearing of the appeal is important for other similar cases, or if the decision of the Supreme Court would be important in order to secure uniformity of legal practice; (2) if there are special grounds for granting leave to appeal because of a procedural or other error that has been made in the case; or (3) if there are other important grounds for granting leave to appeal. Land and water rights cases can be taken to the Supreme Court without leave to appeal.

As a result of the amendment of the law on the right of appeal, the position of the Supreme Court in guiding legal practice has strengthened, since it deals solely with matters that are important for legal practice and for due process. The granting of leave to appeal can be illustrated by the following figures. During 1989, the Supreme Court received a total of 2 630 applications for leave of appeal; of these 275 (12 per cent) were accepted. The lowest rate of acceptance (5 per cent) was for insurance cases. The figures show that more than eight cases out of ten in which leave to appeal is sought from the Supreme Court are left to stand on the basis of the decision of the court of appeal.

The amendment referred to above has made it possible to avoid the large backlog of cases that has weakened due process up to the 1980s. For example during 1979, the Supreme Court decided a total of 3 200 cases, but at the end of the year almost 6 000 cases were still waiting for a decision. At present there is no backlog, which has also improved the quality of the decisions and speeded up the hearing of the cases.

The Supreme Court has a president and at least 21 justices. The work of this court is usually carried out in divisions of five members, each chaired by the senior justice present. If the proposed decision is at odds with an earlier decision of the Supreme Court on a similar case, the case can be decided by a so-called enlarged division (11 members) or by a plenary session (so-called change of practice: 'Prakisveränderung').

Precedents are not legally binding in Finland, either horizontally or vertically, even though the Supreme Court, owing to its standing orders, may not go against an earlier precedent except on the basis of so-called qualified procedure. In cases where the law was ambiguous, lower court judges deciding against precedent are not guilty of misconduct in office (Supreme Court decisions 1935 II 158, 1938 II 589, 1945 II 30 and 1957 II 8; see, however, an unpublished Supreme Court decision, 2649/19 October 1966, in which the opposite position was adopted with a vote of three to two).

In particular since the reform of the system of leaves of appeal in 1980, an attempt has been made to strengthen the role of the Supreme Court as a court of precedent. The intention is for decisions of the Supreme Court to be as binding as possible on lower courts. The head-note of a decision (a short description of the legal issue decided in the case) is taken to be an essential component of the guiding effect of the decision. In practice, the writing of the head-note requires the formulation of the legal norm(s) applied in the decision. We may speak of 'head-note norms' which, after the publication of the case, remain in force as independent legal guides. However no system of sanctions in the proper sense has been adopted in cases where a lower court has deviated from a precedent.

The decisions of the Supreme Court are published both in separate annual reports and in the 'FINLEX' data bank. The data bank provides the possibility of obtaining up-to-date information on decisions through a terminal. The data bank is regularly used by judges, lawyers and legal scholars.

The Supreme Court has adopted a relatively conservative approach to the publication of decisions. The bulk of the decisions are not published, and can be read only in the archives of the Supreme Court. The published decisions are divided into two categories: (1) 'reports' which deal with decisions made in plenary session as well as the decisions that the Supreme Court deems of particular significance, and (2) 'notes' which deal with the other decisions that are published. The decision regarding publication is made by the division that decided the case in question.

2.3

In administrative cases, a citizen who finds that the decision of an authority violates his or her right may appeal the decision as high as the Supreme Administrative Court, unless the law stipulates another avenue of appeal, such as to a Ministry, the Supreme Court of Office, the Rector of the University of Helsinki (for certain cases involving the University) or another authority. Decisions of senior administrative authorities, such as national boards, are subject to appeal either to the Council of State (in cases involving an appointment) or to the Supreme Administrative Court (in all other cases).

The first level of appeal for most decisions of lower administrative authorities is the county administrative court which, in administrative law matters, corresponds to the court of appeal. The county administrative court, for example, deals with all appeals in taxation cases. The normal channel of appeal from decisions of the county administrative court goes to the Supreme Administrative Court (see Supreme Administrative Court, 1976).

Restrictive provisions similar to those that apply to appeals to the Supreme Court do not apply to appeals to the Supreme Administrative Court. However many acts prohibit appeals to the Supreme Administrative Court on the issues covered by the statute, thus easing its docket of cases. The Supreme Administrative Court hears about 6 500 appeals each year, over 40 per cent of which deal with taxation.

The Supreme Administrative Court has a president and at least 13 justices. The cases are presented for decision by judicial secretaries and senior secretaries. Special experts may, on the basis of certain special provisions, participate in the hearing of a case as extraordinary members.

The competence of the Supreme Administrative Court is limited to questions of law. If the appeal concerns an issue that primarily requires consideration of questions of expediency (policy), the Supreme Administrative Court must transfer the case to the Council of State for decision. In practice, about one per cent of the appeals made to the Supreme Administrative Court are transferred to the Council of State. The decisions of the Supreme Administrative Court are published in accordance with the same principles as the decisions of the Supreme Court. However, in respect of the Supreme Administrative Court, there has not been the same discussion of the binding effect of decisions as there has been in respect to the Supreme Court. The decisions of the Supreme Administrative Court are not legally binding, although in many cases they have a binding effect as a practical matter.

2.4

The High Court of Impeachment deals, on the basis of Art. 59 of the Constitution Act, with charges raised against a member of the Council of State, a justice of the Supreme Court or the Supreme Administrative Court, or the Chancellor of Justice for an offence in office. The president of the High Court of Impeachment is the president of the Supreme Court, and the members are the presidents of the Supreme Administrative Court and of three courts of appeal, a professor elected by the Faculty of Law of the University of Helsinki, and six persons elected by parliament. During the entire period the Constitution Act has been in force (some 70 years), the High Court of Impeachment has been convened only three times.

2.5

Finland does not have a separate constitutional court that would consider the constitutionality of an act of parliament or interpret the constitution. Responsibility for the constitutionality of acts is held not only by the President of the Republic but also by the Constitutional Committee of Parliament, which exercises advance control of constitutionality during the legislative process (Hidén, 1974, p. 377). If a legislative bill marks a break with the constitution, a special, qualified legislative procedure must be followed. In the absence of a specific provision to the contrary, not even the Supreme Court or the Supreme Administrative Court have been deemed to have the right to interpret the constitutionality of acts of parliament. However the law states that the general courts and administrative authorities are responsible for deciding whether or not decrees and other lower regulations are compatible with acts of parliament.

I   THE GENERAL ORIGINS OF INTERPRETATIONAL ISSUES

1   Introductory Remarks

Interpretation in the broad sense of the term (*sensu largo*) refers to the meaning of a linguistic expression. In the following, however, interpretation will be understood as addressing the meaning of a specific text; in other words, we choose between two or more alternative meanings (interpretation *sensu stricto*). Any text may be the *subject* of interpretation. The term 'statutory interpretation' refers to the specification of the meaning of statutory texts or other legal texts that have an official nature. The reverse image of interpretation is *qualification*, the legal characterization of facts. A factual state of affairs is 'placed' under the scope of a text. In legal science (legal dogmatics), interpretation is normally at issue, while in the decision making of courts characterization is also often at issue. However the difference is not major, since every characterization requires interpretation, and interpretation cannot be carried out without charting what factual states of affairs a text covers. For this reason, interpretation and characterization can be understood as different facets of the same process — the clarification of the content of a legal norm.

In the judicial process, characterization is inexorably bound to the *weighing of evidence*. For this reason, the Finnish debate has distinguished between issues of law (the contents of a norm or of a legal text) and issues of fact (the weighing of evidence). In the following, issues of interpretation connected with the weighing of evidence will not be dealt with separately. However in practice the weighing of evidence is tied to the clarification of the contents of legal provisions. It is not possible to eliminate completely the role of knowledge of the legal system when we consider what *legally relevant* things have taken place. Knowledge of legal norms affects the weighing of evidence, and vice versa. For example, the concept of 'fraud' is a legal category, the scope of which depends on interpretation. This fact may affect what the court deems to have been demonstrated on the basis of the evidence.

2   General Origins of Interpretational Issues

Legal consideration may concern a question of law, a question of fact or the way in which these two questions are combined (traditionally, subsumption). Interpretational issues will be examined in our response solely from the point of view of *legal issues*. The consideration of facts and the consideration of issues of policy in administration fall outside the scope of this presentation.

A judicial decision may be either a so-called *routine decision* or a *hard case*. A routine decision is involved when the decision does not require any significant interpretation and there is no ambiguity concerning the facts. This is the case, for example, when a traffic warden writes out a summary penal order (a 'ticket') for the driver of a car that has been parked illegally. Significant interpretational issues concerning statutes thus arise only in hard cases. There may be four types of interpretatively hard cases: a provision (a text) *is ambiguous* or vague; there is *no provision* that would apply to the case (a gap); two provisions with *different* content apply to the *same* case (a conflict); or the same issue is dealt with in the same way in several different provisions (*overregulation*). In the following, the focus will be on ambiguous provisions (texts).

Firstly, a legal provision may be *quantitatively* subject to discretion. If the criteria are exact, there is no need for discretion. The benefit of a pension or of social welfare is tied to income levels and the decision-making situation corresponds to that involved in routine decisions. When considering a criminal sentence, a judge may move within the framework of a penal scale, and sentencing practice may vary from time to time and even from place to place. Also, here, it is not a question of interpretation in the strict sense, as the provision itself does not require clarification.

However a provision may be *qualitatively* open to discretion. *Syntactical ambiguity* as the source of ambiguity is rare, but in principle possible. For example, one qualification for a position may be 'a higher academic degree or a lower academic degree and practical experience'. In this connection, the words 'or' and 'and' are syntactically ambiguous. *Semantic ambiguity*, however, is a considerably more important source of ambiguity.

In some cases, the possible *interpretational alternatives* (the semantic alternatives) can be clarified linguistically, but it may remain unclear which is the best or right alternative. This can be called *true ambiguity*. For example, a legal act must be done 'in writing'. This provision may refer to a document, to a signed document, to a document signed by all or only by some of the parties to the legal act, to a document that is signed and certified by impartial witnesses who are present at the same time, and so on. It is up to the interpreter to choose between these alternative contents.

Weak and open expressions lead both in principle and in practice to a number of ambiguities ('special circumstances' and 'the circumstances of the case'). So-called 'resource and goal' statutes can also be considered open provisions. Such statutes provide an authority with certain resources or with a certain goal, without, however, providing clear guidance on how the resources are to be allocated or guided, or how one could or should attempt to reach the goal.

The criteria for the application of *general clauses* (flexible legal provisions) are, by nature, open. In addition, they generally require, either openly or tacitly, the weighing of values. A provision may refer to 'equity', 'manifest inequity', 'unearned benefit' and so on. The interpretation of, for example, the social grounds for an abortion require, in turn, a weighing of values.

Many central norms of private law and criminal law in Finland continue to be out of date. Small vestiges of the oldest codification of laws in Europe are still in force in Finland and the 1734 Code of Sweden–Finland has long since become antiquated. To a large extent, judicial decision making has had to rely on general legal principles and analogy. Because of the age of the statutes, their *travaux préparatoires* often cannot be used, which weakens general adherence to authentic interpretation. Over time, moreover, legal concepts have been redefined. For this reason, at first legal science and later on the courts have had a major role in creating law.

The development of society has also raised some totally new problems and these have been reflected in the interpretation of laws. The emancipatory interest of women has forced the courts to interpret, for example, many norms on matrimonial property in a manner favourable to the weaker partner, often the wife.

Also ecological problems and the protection of the environment have raised *value conflicts*. Environmental values and economic values often clash, as in the protection of the forests and waterways. Almost without exception, the values that have prevailed have been economic.

The most recent feature in the development is the rapid increase in general clauses (see Pöyhönen, 1988, p. 162). The judicial machinery must time and again consider the relative weight of *predictability* as opposed to *equity in the individual case*. Overemphasis on predictability (for example adherence to the maxim, 'pacta sunt servanda') leads to a rigid attitude, while an emphasis on equity in the individual case leads to a decrease in predictability, and thus also to a decrease in formal due process in society. Balancing these two values against each other will be one of the major problems in adjudication in Finland during the decade to come.

II   GAPS AND THEIR ORIGINS

1   General Remarks

In Finland there is an established distinction between *a statutory gap* and a *gap in law*. In the former, the gap is such that it cannot be decided on the basis of the statute, when appropriately (although expansively) interpreted. In the latter, the gap cannot be resolved on the basis of either statutes or traditional law, and may be 'empty of law' if the intention is that it remain outside legal regulation (see especially Brusiin, 1938 and Takki, 1985).

In practice, the question of gaps is focused on gaps in law. Such a gap can be either *manifest* or *hidden*. The distinction suggests the apparent nature of the gap. In practice, a hidden gap is more common than a manifest gap: generally, the gap cannot be seen until after interpretation. A gap may be *deliberate*: the legislator has intentionally left an issue unregulated. An example of this is the concept of 'futile attempt' in criminal law, a concept which has not yet been specified. An *unconscious* gap can be *original*, in which case it was in the law already when drafted, but its existence had not been noted. A *subsequent* gap arises as the result of technical or social development: a new and therefore unregulated situation arises in society. Examples of this are so-called 'hacker offences' involving computers. Also changes in values in society may give rise to so-called subsequent gaps, for example in the reformulation of ecological values.

A statutory gap reflects a defect in the legal system itself. We know that the norm on which the decision in the case can be based is not to be found in the law. Thus a statutory gap is distinct from an *interpretational* gap, where we cannot say for certain what provision would be applicable to the case at hand. An interpretational gap is thus linked to the difficulties of subsumption.

A distinction is made in Finland between interpretation and gap-filling, even though this is not apparent in the justification given for judgements. For this reason there is no clear difference between expansive interpretation and analogical reasoning or free gap-filling required when confronted with a gap. More generally, the use of *analogy* always requires a weighing of values, given the concept of similarity in itself. Thus, gap-filling is *preceded* by normal interpretational operations. The filling of the gap itself takes place either through analogy or through so-called free gap-filling.

When analogy is used, a norm is applied to the case which, even according to expansive interpretation, would not be applicable. In so-called free gap-filling, on the other hand, the judge fills the gap with due consideration to all the circumstances of the case. It is not a question of an 'inter legem' or 'secundum legem' situation, but of a 'praeter legem' situation, the continuation or replacement of the work of the legislator. Especially during the earlier periods, the Supreme Court of Finland was of the view that, in this, the decision was not based on any general rule, for no attempt was even made to formulate such a rule as the basis for the judgement. Before the present Product Liability Act came into effect, this pattern of thinking was followed in holding that manufacturers were liable for their products in cases where the product had caused injury (Supreme Court decision 1955, II 31).

In Finland, for example, there is no statutory provision on *unjust enrichment*. The legal regulations on this matter are thus based solely on the practice of the Supreme Court, on the 'praeter legem'.

III   THE TYPES OF INTERPRETATIVE ARGUMENT

1   General Remarks

From the Finnish point of view, the terms (type of) 'argument' (Question 3) as well as 'material' (Question 5) need to be clarified.

In the following, 'argument' means the same as either a substantive or an authoritative *reason*. In this regard, one also speaks in Finland about the *sources of law*. These are reasons that must, should, or may be used as reasons in justifying interpretation. The sources of law *sensu stricto* cover only the authoritative reasons, whereas the sources of law *sensu largo* include substantive as well as authoritative reasons. The present terminology in Finland is inclined to accept the latter meaning. Every reason that is a 'source' for a well-justified decision is a source of law.

Relevant texts and other information about the sources of law are typically materials of interpretation. In Finland one often speaks about the *sources of information* (see Aarnio, 1987, II.3.1.). With regard to this terminology, the documents of legislative drafts (*travaux préparatoires*) are a source of information that tells us something about the intent, terminology and purpose of the legislation (argument, source of law).

In adjudication as well as in legal dogmatics in Finland several types of arguments are either explicitly or implicitly recognized. The focus of the following presentation is on the types of arguments, not their order of priority. The types included in the enumerative list have been subsumed under the following headings: linguistic, systemic, teleological — evaluative and transcategorical.

2   Linguistic Arguments

2.1   *Semantic Arguments*

This type of argument refers to either the ordinary (non-technical) or the technical meaning of the statute.

1   There may be at least two kinds of ordinary or *literal meanings*, either an 'ordinary language' meaning, that is a meaning recognized in common everyday language, or a meaning defined in standard dictionaries (lexical meaning). Furthermore 'ordinary language' may mean standard everyday usage of the expression at issue or its usage in ordinary legal language. For the layman, 'personal property' means 'movables'. In legal language the expression has a wider connotation, and covers, for example, promissory notes. Ordinary legal language is formulated by the legal tradition over a lengthy period of time.

A literal meaning can change as a result of a change in semantic rules. For example, in the civil law of the early 1900s, the question was asked whether a contract could be made over the telephone. According to the literal meaning at that time, an agreement was possible if and only if both parties were present in person. When the telephone was brought into use, the literal meaning changed so that parties were said to be 'present' also in the case of a telephone conversation.

A literal meaning in the sense of a *technical meaning* may be defined in the statute at issue or outside such a statute, for example in engineering terminology. (An example taken from the Traffic Act: 'Motor-driven vehicles refer to motor-vehicles, tractors, motor-driven working machines and off-road vehicles.' Every subtype of motor-driven vehicles is defined later on in the Act.)

2   In some cases, the meaning of the statute can be clarified by reference to its 'contextual surroundings'. Linguistic expressions (words, sentences) are connected to other expressions in many ways. The more coherent the meanings, the more acceptable the interpretation that is based on them.

The context may be internal as well as external in regard to the statute. As far as the internal context is concerned, the word at stake is examined in the light of the title or subheadings of the statute, in connection with the other words in the sentence of the statute being interpreted, or together with the same expression as used elsewhere in the statute or act.

The external contextual meaning of a word refers to the same or analogous expressions in other statutes (for example, the word 'donation' in tax law, as compared to the same word in civil law). There are great difficulties in establishing the external contextual meaning in a normal case because of the variety of contexts (for example, taxation vs. inheritance).

2.2   Syntactical Arguments

In *grammatical* interpretation, the meaning of a word depends on syntax, that is, on the grammatical rules of a certain language. An example: (1) 'He lives in a house in Finland, which is beautiful' and (2) 'He lives in Finland in a house, which is beautiful.' Sometimes the punctuation or the place of conjunction vs. disjunction may change the way in which the text is to be read.

3 Systemic Arguments

'Systemic argument' in the following denotes the same as the reference to the properties of the system of legal norms (understood either as rules or as principles). Systemic argument thus goes beyond mere linguistic argument. In this regard, the intention and purpose of the statute as well as other reasons referring to the systemic framework of the legal order can be understood as systemic arguments.

3.1 *Intention or Purpose of the Statute*

Chapter 1, section 11 of the Code of Judicial Procedure requires the judge to examine carefully the genuine intention and purpose of the statute and make the decision on the basis of this purpose. A similar principle in Sweden functions in another way: the interpreter must be 'loyal' (faithful) to the legislator. Such a principle is considered to be an important element of democracy. Although the Finnish and Swedish legal systems are in many respects similar or even identical, the higher courts in Finland do not refer to the intention and purpose of the statute as often as is done in Sweden. Even so, this statement must be specified further.

The main reason for the difference mentioned above is to be found in history. Finland was affiliated with the Kingdom of Sweden for almost 700 years. In 1809, Finland became an autonomous Grand Duchy of the Russian Empire. The old Swedish laws remained in force in Finland; among these laws was the old Code of 1734. Both before and after the achievement of independence in 1917, the pace of legislative work was rather slow, and many of these old Swedish laws still retained their validity (see Klami, 1982). Because of their age, little attention was paid to the intention of the legislator (the historical will of the law-giver). Society during the twentieth century was quite different from that at the end of the seventeenth century when the Swedish Code was drafted. The old preliminary drafts of the Code, which were preserved only in part, were not published until the twentieth century. The principle of faithfulness has no role in such a case.

Later on, however, the same trend continued in Finland. One of the main reasons probably lies in the doctrine of the separation of powers, with the ensuing independence of the courts. Because the *travaux préparatoires* are not formally enacted, they do not have the same authoritative and binding force as statutes. Legislation has been thoroughly reformed during the past 20 years and many *travaux préparatoires* are thus quite new. Their argumentative force is therefore, for natural reasons, more significant than that of the old ones.

However there are several difficulties in the use of *travaux préparatoires*. Even when one refers or at least might refer to the intention of the legislator, important problems arise: (1) the identification of the *subject* of the paramount intention and purpose; (2) the identification of the *actual* intention and purpose; and (3) the *concept* of the purpose (intent). In addition the lapse of time brings more difficulties. Change in society and in values may make the original intention and purpose rather irrelevant.

The concept of the legislator is a simplification: a highly complicated interaction is interpreted as if it were the behaviour of an individual. The drafting of Finnish legislation begins with, for example, some preparatory work in a Ministry, and finds its culmination in the voting procedure in parliament and the endorsement of the statute by the President of the Republic.

There are no strict rules or principles for deciding whose actual intention should be chosen should there be disagreement or a failure by parliament to deal explicitly with a certain problem. Even so, the drafts preceding the bill or the written justification for the bill contain some information on intention. The following rough principles can be formulated:

- If parliament, in its official response to the government when passing a bill, or a Parliamentary Commission in its official opinion on a bill, has expressed an unambiguous intention in relation to the statute, and there are no counter-arguments, this intention can be accepted as the basis for interpretation.
- If parliament has not yet discussed the problem, or the intention of parliament is ambiguous, but the Government Bill has expressed an intent, this intention can be taken into account in the interpretation.
- The greater the 'distance' between parliament and the instance in question, the weaker the argumentative force of the intent.
- The more recent the statute, the more weight can be given to legislative intention in interpretation, and vice versa.

The interpretation of intention may involve problems that are similar to, and as difficult as, the interpretation of the statute itself. Ambiguity tends to diminish the argumentative weight of the intention.

In Finland one speaks of (1) the actual or *subjective* (historical) intention of the legislator and (2) the *objective* purpose of the statute ('ratio legis'). The subjective will and the problems connected with it have already been described above. In hard cases the courts sometimes explicitly refer to the objective purpose of the statute ('ratio legis', all things considered). This refers to a meaning that the statute has when all the pertinent circumstances are taken into account. One may also speak of 'the reasonable sense and purpose' of the statute.

3.2   Systemic Interpretation (Sensu Stricto)

Statutory interpretation in Finland is implicitly based on the assumption that, if semantic and structural interpretation fails, and if there is no clear intent of the legislator, the task of the interpreter is to determine the site of the norm within the system of norms – as it were, to catch the norm in the mesh of a norm net, and interpret accordingly.

In practice this means that the decision is based on the legal system or on the fundamental principles of the appropriate part of the legal system. This provides an answer in cases where there is a gap in the statutes or where the statutes are ambiguous to the extent that they, or other authoritative sources, do not provide an answer (see Question 4 regarding principles).

So-called conceptual jurisprudence ('Begriffsjurisprudenz') favoured deductive reasoning: norms and their interpretation were to be deduced from the system of legal concepts and principles. These concepts were defined partially on the basis of statutory material, but their essence included features of functional rationality. As late as just after the Second World War, there was a tendency in Finland to use this type of argumentation. Today the vestiges of conceptual thinking can scarcely be seen in Finnish court practice. However this does not mean that legal concepts as such have lost their significance in statutory interpretation. It is only the idea of deduction from concepts that is generally rejected.

3.3   Other Systemic Arguments

3.3.1   Customary law   If there is no statute applicable to the case, the judge must observe the 'custom of the land' if he finds this reasonable (Chapter 11, section 1 of the Code of Judicial Procedure). The Code thus prescribes two necessary qualifications for the application of local custom, later understood as *customary law*: (1) there is a statutory gap within the law, and (2) the custom itself is morally acceptable.

A custom is customary law if and only if (a) it standardizes a certain practice as would a statute, and (b) its territorial scope covers the entire country. Commercial usage is a classical example.

Customary law is seldom applied or even referred to in court practice, partly because of effective legislation. The social system is too complicated and dynamic to leave to customary law, with its slow processes.

3.3.2   Arguments from precedents   The term 'precedent' is equivocal. It may mean either the complex totality of the relevant facts of the case (that is, fact description; in Finnish, 'ennakkotapaus', or 'precedent case') or the precedential norms applied to the case ('ennakkopäätös' or 'precedent decision'). In the Finnish legal technical vocabulary, 'precedent' refers specifically to the decision, that is, the precedent norm ('ratio decidendi'). This precedental norm is usually written down in the so-called head-note of the precedent. In the head-note, the court briefly describes the relevant legal problem and the outline of its solution.

The term 'precedent' is normally used to refer to a decision of the Supreme Court or of the Supreme Administrative Court. However the situation is slowly changing. About 95 per cent of the decisions of the seven Courts of Appeal in Finland remain the final decisions in the case (see Preliminary). The Supreme Court tends to give guidelines only in important cases. The decisions of the Courts of Appeal therefore have a value as precedent in respect of the rest of the cases. In certain important types of cases (for example in housing and divorce cases) appeal to the Supreme Court is specifically excluded.

Two sets of concepts are used to refer to precedents. These relate to their *horizontal* and *vertical* binding nature, and to their *legal* and *factual* binding nature. The first pair of concepts deals with the problem of whether or not a court is bound to its earlier decisions and/or if the lower court is bound by decisions made by a superior court. The legal binding nature of a precedent is often but not always accompanied by some kind of sanction, whereas the factual binding nature of a precedent only means that precedents are in fact followed in court practice. There is, however, no clear-cut distinction here; the more binding a source of law is *felt* to be, the *stronger* arguments are needed to be in order to overrule it (Aarnio, 1987, II.4.6.).

Precedents have never been *legally* binding in Finland, either in the horizontal or in the vertical sense. If the Supreme Court wants to break with an earlier decision of its own, the internal regulations of the Supreme Court allow this to be done in two ways: either the case will be dealt with by an enlarged division (11 instead of the usual five justices) or – today quite rarely – in a plenary session (all 21 members of the Supreme Court). A normal division is thus bound to the earlier decisions of the Supreme Court.

A judge in a lower court cannot be punished if he or she departs from precedents, unless they constitute customary law. According to the Finnish view, this weak commitment to precedents guarantees the elasticity, creativity and dynamics of adjudication. However the judge has the burden of argumentation if he does not follow the decision norm in a precedent. Therefore the lower courts in practice very often solve the case precisely according to the precedents.

3.3.3   Comparative argument   In Nordic countries, and in particular in Sweden and Finland, there are many similar statutes, common legal traditions and legislative cooperation conditioned by similarities of society and culture. In certain fields of law, such as in family law and in the law of inheritance, even the statutory texts are nearly identical, since the Finnish legislator has often followed the Swedish one. Thus the intention of the Swedish legislator, Swedish precedents and doctrinal opinions are also widely used as arguments both in judicial practice and legal science.

Other comparative material is more problematic. There is legislation based on international conventions such as some elements of labour law based on ILO conventions, and legislation based on international agreements on promissory notes and cheques. Also, *inter alia*, the Bern Copyright Convention is in force in Finland as law. In spite of this, Finnish courts make very restrictive use of materials other than the drafts of these conventions. Court practice in other countries is not referred to. If a norm is based on an international treaty or convention that has been ratified by Finland, the ratification itself does not require the Finnish courts domestically to follow this norm (the so-called doctrine of dualism). In some cases Finnish statutes are based on the same principle as legislation in other European countries. A good example is provided by the basic principles of Finnish civil law. The large majority of these principles are quite close to those adopted in the German BGB.

3.3.4   Historical arguments   A statute may be properly interpreted only if it is placed in its historical context. The development of relevant concepts, dogmas and institutions provides the background for understanding the development of ideas. Often the historical argument is used to describe the social state of affairs that the legislator wanted to change.

3.3.5   Legal dogmatic argument   Until recent times Finnish adjudication has rarely included any public references to legal dogmatics. From the beginning of the 1980s, the situation has slowly changed.

In the more recent decisions there are both general references to the legal literature (the prevailing opinion) and references to specific research. However the references are often negative ones: 'AA, however, is of the opinion that . . .' This means, in other words, that the Supreme Court argues in support of a view that is the opposite of that presented in the literature.

Even so it should be emphasized that the legal literature is of considerable significance to the decision making of all courts at all levels. The standing orders of the Supreme Courts require the senior secretaries to review the *travaux préparatoires*, precedents and the legal literature. The legal literature is also widely used in the lower courts.

3.3.6   Special types of systemic argument   (a) Analogy. The term 'analogy' may refer either to a form of argument or to a kind of method (analogical inference). Here the term is used only in the former sense. In this regard, two different types of analogy should be noted (see Aarnio, 1987, II.3.4.).

- In *case analogy* one compares two or more cases (usually precedents) to one another in order to explain and understand the decision practice. Let us take three cases, A, B and C as examples. In A the decision norm is 'if F, then G1'; in B, it is 'if F, then G2'; and in C, it is 'if F, then G1'. This problem arises if there is a contradiction in court practice or if the court has returned to its original position. The answer depends on the similarities and non-similarities, respectively, found in the fact descriptions (F) of the cases. If the facts in A and C are sufficiently similar, analogical relations may prevail, and one cannot find any contradiction in the decisions. This is the situation with case analogy.
- In *rule analogy* the problem concerns the interpretation of a statute; let us say S1. The question is: what are the legal consequences in case F1, which is covered by statute S1? One knows that statute S2 prescribes 'if F2, then G1'. It is also clear what description F2 covers. Following the principle of rule analogy, one now analyses F1 and F2 in order to consider whether there are relevant similarities between them. If there are, statute S1 can be interpreted, 'if F1, then G2'.

(b) Other forms of argument such as 'e contrario', 'argumentum a fortiori' and *reduction* are also known in Finnish adjudication, although one seldom finds explicit references to these forms in court decisions.

4 Teleological and Evaluative Arguments

4.1 *Teleological Argument*

Most often the *objective* teleological argument states that the interpreter should take into account the reasonable goals or social consequences of the statute. 'Reasonable goal' in this connection means the same as a goal supported by as many relevant substantive and authoritative reasons as possible ('ratio legis').

However the proper consequentialist reasoning in Finnish court practice is as follows. Let us assume two possible interpretations for a statute, A and B. If there are no other sufficient arguments for the choice between A and B, the judge may consider the possible causal or systemic consequences of the two. The next step is to weigh and balance these consequences in order to ascertain the order of priority between them. On the basis of this choice the judge 'returns' to A and B, and makes a choice in favour of the alternative leading to the preferred consequences. This is thus a model of 'best possible consequences'.

4.2 *Empirical Argument*

Normally, empirical statements are components of consequentialist or historical argument. See the above.

4.3 *Evaluative Arguments*

Values and evaluation play an important part in legal decision making, for example:

1   There are no strict rules defining the order of priority between different arguments. Their hierarchy cannot therefore be value-neutral; however rules about priority also express certain values.
2   Special argument forms such as analogy (see below) include evaluative standpoints because, for example, the concept of similarity is value-laden.
3   Consequentialist argumentation also presupposes evaluations; consequence A is prior to B.
4   In some cases ethical or moral principles constitute the basis for the interpretational choice. This is always the case when

the subject matter is on the borderline between law and morality. An example in Finland is that a woman has the right to an abortion on social grounds. In interpreting the concept of 'social grounds', one cannot avoid taking a position on the value of human life, on the significance of the mother's welfare, and so on.

5   Certain basic values, such as the welfare state, may also play a role in interpretation. (See Questions 13 and 14.)

IV   TYPES OF GAP-FILLING ARGUMENT

The point of departure is that gap-filling is based on *analogy*. Of the different forms of analogy, rule analogy in particular is important. (See Question 3.) In some cases, however, the judge must *create* the applicable norm; this is the case, for example, when the judge considers restitution for unjust enrichment. This could be termed the development of law (in Germany, 'Richterrecht').

In the free creation of law, the judge may turn, for example, to the following arguments (see Takki, 1985):

1   Legal rules that are expressed in *precedents*, in which case the reasoning takes on the nature of case analogy.
2   Various types of *substantive* grounds, such as the weighing of interests and the consideration of consequences. The interests and the potential consequences may be general by nature (the smooth functioning of the system, arguments of procedural economy, the interests of society, the effects on the level of crime in Finland, and so on) or individual (the interests of the buyer vs. those of the seller, respect for the wishes of the testator, the need for social protection of the widow, and so on).
3   Opinions expressed in *legal science* (see section III).
4   *General legal principles.* Without taking a position on general legal principles from the theoretical point of view, the following types of principles can be mentioned as grounds for decision making that are used in practice.

(a) Principles that are part of the *basic ideological values* of the legal system, such as the principle of the rule of law, the principle of private ownership, moral principles underlying the concept of the family, and the presumption-like concept of the rational legislator.

(b) *Positive decision making principles*, that is, general legal principles that have been incorporated into, or are assumed by, the law in force. Examples of these are: (i) *Formally valid principles*, such as the basic rights manifested in the Constitution, the principle of equitable shares as manifested in the law of inheritance, the principle of the protection of the worker in labour law, and the principle of 'bona fides' in contract law. (ii) Legal *generalizations*, that is, general legal principles that have been produced through legal induction and heuristics. Examples are the principles of 'pacta sunt servanda' and of fidelity in contract law. These have not explicitly been incorporated in law, but they find certain institutional support in other, formally valid provisions. (iii) *Decision making principles*, examples of which are the principle of 'audiatur et altera pars', and the principle of legality in criminal law (see, for example, Frände, 1989).

5   Also (legal) principles that *lie outside the system* can appear as grounds for decision making. These are, in effect, moral principles that take on judicial relevance when they are used as grounds for a legal decision. The principle of equitable treatment must be taken into consideration also when it has not been stated in legislation or is not assumed as a general legal principle. In this, law and morality are interwoven. The decision maker's chain of reasoning is as follows: X is morally acceptable, and thus X is legally acceptable. This, however, is true only assuming that the moral principle in question has been accepted as a decision making principle with legal relevance. A moral principle does not prima facie have juridical relevance.

6   *Foreign legal rules* and precedents, subject to the conditions presented above (see section III).

7   Other *arguments from comparative law*, such as the structure of a foreign legal system or its fundamental principles.

8   *Arguments from the history of law*, for example the history of the birth of a provision, the historical development that led to the drafting of the law and the social facts or ideological factors that explain the development. In this respect, the history of law also produces material for decision making.

9   *Systemic arguments*, in other words grounds that refer to the structure of the legal system and the location of the case to be decided within this order. Various *conceptual arguments* can be included within this category, such as the argument that financial leasing involves of necessity three parties: the financial company, the party delivering the goods and the party receiving the goods, or that a last will and testament, since it is a juridical act premised on death, cannot be

enforced conceptually before the death of the testator and thus the beneficiary under the will does not have a right of action in respect of the juridical acts of the testator.

V   THE MATERIALS OF INTERPRETATIVE ARGUMENT

1   General Remarks

As was discussed in section III, an argument is normally called a source of law and the term 'material' is understood as roughly the same as a source of information. In the latter sense, 'material' means texts and other information used when putting forward an argument.

The Code of Judicial Procedure (Chapter 3, section 24) contains a statutory rule on *the writing of a decision*: 'Every verdict must be based on reasons and on a statute, not on arbitrary decision, and the main reasons as well as the relevant provisions of law must be clearly written down in it.' The statute thus speaks only of reasons (arguments) and law, which here is practically the equivalent of the statutes, not of the materials that give information about reasons.

Originally the term 'reasons' pertained to *evidence*, since the first part of the provision comes from the 1734 Code, and is still in force today as the so-called legal theory of evidence. The rule thus provides that the decision must be written down as a syllogism consisting of the duly established *facts* and the evidence admitted (for example, two witnesses), the *norms* applied, and the final decision norm (the conclusion).

However a widely held opinion in Finland interprets the term 'reasons' as referring to *legal arguments*. In respect of judicial practice, one may thus speak on the one hand of *reasons* (of the evidence and, for example, of the intent and purpose of the law) and, on the other hand, of *materials* (for example, of the *travaux préparatoires*). There are simply no rules or principles, either statutory or customary, that *oblige* the judge to refer to certain material. On the other hand, the legal theory of evidence was slowly but surely replaced by free evaluation of evidence (although this did not formally take place until 1948). In any case, it became rare to present any evidentiary reasoning whatsoever; only the established facts were presented.

Therefore the following classification is based on the priority of arguments. Theoretically, one can always turn the priority of arguments into the priority of material, but this theoretical 'rewriting' does not correspond to the prevailing court practice.

2   A Relative Classification of Arguments (Materials)

2.1   'Must-Arguments' (Materials)

Chapter 3, section 24 of the Code of Judicial Procedure only requires the judge to decide substantially *within the framework of the statute*. Thus the judge *must* use the statutory text. In other words, if necessary, the decision has to be supported by arguments that refer to the literal, plain or contextual meaning of the statute, although it is not necessary to mention the statute in the decision. However the dominant justification tradition has slowly changed. Practice today is more and more in accord with the literal interpretations of Chapter 3; thus the statute and its interpretation are usually mentioned in the justification for the decision.

If there is no statute, customary law is the decisive argument (Chapter 11, section 1 of the Code of Judicial Procedure; see section III, above). Even so it is only rarely that customary law is openly referred to in the justification for a decision.

The significance of 'must-arguments' lies in two consequences: (1) if the decision is not based on such an argument (the absence of a 'must-argument'), the superior level will return the case for a new trial. Previously the absence of justification was controlled only in criminal law cases. Today the Supreme Court may return all types of cases on the grounds of the absence of 'must-arguments'. At times, however, the Supreme Court will only remedy the justification, and at the same time criticize the erroneous argumentation of the lower court. (2) Overlooking a 'must-argument' may also lead to a sanction: the judge may, in principle, be found guilty of misconduct in office, in which case the primary sanction is a warning. This has relevance, for example, for the further development of the judge's career.

2.2   'Should-Arguments' (Materials)

Two arguments belong to this category: legislative history (the *travaux préparatoires*) and precedents. The 'should' property of the argument means that, if an argument of this category has not been used, the probability that the decision will be overturned by a higher instance is relatively high.

A formal reference to this kind of argument (or material) is quite unknown. One can say only on the basis of the final result whether or not sufficient attention has been paid to a 'should-argument'. The role of precedents has increased, in part at the expense of the role of the legislator. (See section XI.)

2.3 'May-Arguments' (Materials)

All other arguments belong to this third group. Furthermore, material that provides information about such an argument is, accordingly, may-material. (See section XI.)

2.4 'May-Not' Arguments'

Until now there has been no general discussion in Finland on what arguments (materials) may not be used in the justification of legal decisions. However one could say that anything which is, for instance, against fairness or equity or is *contra bonos mores* is also against sound legal justification. Hence references to clearly immoral norms, to principles of apartheid or to reasons that can be regarded as constituting a violent infringement of equality are prohibited. One can also find examples in Finnish legislation that clarify this: for example, there is a statutory prohibition against the sale of real estate on condition that the buyer marries a certain person. This is a condition *contra bonos mores.*

VI PRIORITIES AMONG CONFLICTING TYPES OF ARGUMENTS

1 A Historical Point of View

Finland was incorporated as a Grand Duchy into Russia and remained so from 1809 to 1917. Towards the end of this period, Czarist repression and the different attempts at Russification threatened Finland's legal autonomy. The question was above all on how laws binding on Finland were to be adopted, taking into consideration the fact that, since 1863, Finland had had her own Diet. This was reflected in a further question regarding the application of law: was a judge to bind himself to a law which, in his opinion, had been improperly adopted? Recourse was made to *legal argument*: the decrees of the Russian government were invalid and not to be obeyed if they violated statutory law that had been enacted in Finland.

Thus the strong legalist spirit found fruitful soil. The background theory for this spirit was taken from German conceptual legal thinking ('Begriffsjurisprudenz'), which was a widely accepted way of thinking at the beginning of this century. Legalism and constructivist thinking were thus the primary political tools against Czarist Russia, and the old, basically Swedish, statutory law was a national symbol.

Finland's declaration of independence in 1917 was soon followed by a civil war (1918), after which the pressure to create and effectively maintain 'law and order' was strong. Once again the victorious side of the civil war, the 'Whites', accepted legalism as a *political* tool. Legalism as a weapon in the fight for independence turned into the legalism of a young nation trying to stabilize social conditions and put down the 'rebels' among the defeated 'Reds', now backed by the revolutionary Soviet Union. All this continued until the end of the 1930s. The rapid social change that continued in the aftermath of the civil war (industrialization together with the ensuing cultural change) was interrupted by the Second World War.

In legal thinking and legal dogmatics, more pragmatic (realistic) tendencies as well as critical analytic thinking began to gain ground. Nevertheless legalism remained the basic ideology of the judiciary: the drafting of law sought to maximize the *formal* equality of people, the *predictability* of legal decisions and thus legal *certainty* in the formal sense (Helin, 1989, p. 145).

On the other hand, the main ideas of the old Scandinavian legal tradition remained silently present the entire time. This tradition not only emphasizes *formal* legal certainty but also, at the same time, the equity and reasonableness of adjudication. One often speaks about *substantial* legal certainty when referring to the connection between law and morality, legal norms and values. This tradition is at least 500 years old.

As early as the Middle Ages different 'Instructions for the Judge' were added to circulating manuscripts of Swedish law. At least since 1635 a collection originally formulated by the Lutheran religious reformer of Sweden, Olaus Petri (1542), has been printed at the beginning of the law book. This collection was, in effect, a general introduction aimed at judges. Since 1734, the instructions have been published as a permanent introductory part of the law book. In Finland this tradition continued also after the break in the Swedish–Finnish union (1809). Although the instructions do not have any binding force whatsoever, they represent traditional Swedish–Finnish legal ideology and its ideas about law and justice (see Aarnio, 1987, I.1.).

2 The Present Situation

The core of the old instructions consists in a reproach of arbitrariness, a feature which was typical of medieval adjudication. Naturally this idea was intertwined with contemporary political problems (the relationship between the King, the nobility and ordinary people). However these instructions also tell something about the optional way of applying statutes. In this regard, several principles (standards) have been formulated:

- Every decision must be *based on law*; at least it should not violate any statutes. (In Finland there are two national languages, Finnish and Swedish. Although both languages have two different words for law along the lines of 'lex' and 'ius', in older and even in present everyday language the words 'laki' (in Finnish) and 'lag' (in Swedish) refer to law in general, whether statutory or not.)
- The judge must, however, refrain from applying a statute if it is *not reasonable*.
- 'Reasonable' means the same as 'what is *best for the "common people"* '.
- A decision is 'best for the common people' if it fulfills their basic *societal interests*.
- A good judge always pays attention not only to the literal meaning of the statute but also to the *intent and purpose of the legislation*. A judge who decides against this intent also decides against the law.

In recent times judicial practice has slowly abandoned the strict legalist tendency and in a way resumed the old ideology expressed in the 'instructions for the judge'. The *general* intention of the higher courts in Finland is more and more to do justice to the reasonable sense of the statute in the light of all available 'must', 'should' and 'may' arguments. Nevertheless, in lower courts (the district courts and the city courts) and in the administrative courts, the legalist tendency is still quite strong. This means that in hard cases the proper argumentation often cannot be identified except on the level of the decisions of the Court of Appeal, the Supreme Court and the Supreme Administrative Court.

One may formulate a number of rules and principles giving guidance for the judge in interpretation. The following list is not exhaustive.

1   Rules of priority: (a) the meaning of the statute is the primary argument for every *decision*; Chapter 3, section 24 of the Code of Judicial Procedure also gives certain formal support to the legalist tendency.

(b) The priority argument in *interpreting* the statute is the reasonable sense of the statute in the light of its purpose (Chapter 11, section 1 of the Code of Judicial Procedure).

(c) Chapter 11, section 1 (second sentence): If there is no

statute, the judge must observe the custom of the land when deciding a case, provided that the custom is not inequitable. (See section III.)

2   Principles about the burden of proof. (a) linguistic priority standards: (i) A statute should not be interpreted so that any part of it remains meaningless. This is the principle of linguistic economy: no element in the statute is insignificant. (ii) The principle of consistency: if there are no counter-arguments, an expression should be given the same meaning at least within the statute, but also within the network of statutes referring to the same area. (iii) The priority of ordinary language: a term used in the statute should be interpreted in accordance with ordinary language, provided that there are no counter-arguments favouring another interpretation. This principle can be supplemented as follows:

- If there are no counter-arguments, 'ordinary language' means 'plain language', that is, the meaning given to the term in its everyday use.
- Every expression has a special linguistic context. The term should therefore always be interpreted in its proper context. The contextual meaning thus has priority over the other alternative meanings. Contextual interpretation always produces a 'legal' (plain) meaning for the term. Contextuality may be either internal or external. (See section III.)
- If there is no contextual or other plain meaning, one should adopt the lexical meaning.

(iv) If the statute contains a technical term, and no counter-instances exist, the technical sense of the technical term displaces the ordinary language regardless of whether it is defined in the statute itself or not.

(b) Other standards of priority: (i) If the *travaux préparatoires* are sufficiently unambiguous, and there are no counter-arguments, one may disregard the literal interpretation. In penal law cases this standard should be formulated even more carefully. Otherwise, this standard is in harmony with Chapter 11, section 1 of the Code of Judicial Procedure. (ii) Of several interpretations of a statute, all possible within ordinary language, and given the absence of any counter-arguments, priority should be given to the interpretation that corresponds to the *travaux préparatoires*. There must be special reasons for disregarding the *travaux préparatoires*. (iii)

If the *travaux préparatoires* of a new statute are sufficiently unambiguous, a precedent based on a repealed statute may no longer be used as an argument. (iv) If the *travaux préparatoires* are sufficiently unambiguous, and a later precedent conflicts with them, and there are no counter-arguments, the precedent prevails. (v) If the *travaux préparatoires* are sufficiently unambiguous and a substantive reason is in conflict with them, this reason is not a sufficient argument to overrule the *travaux préparatoires*. The overruling of the *travaux préparatoires* must be specially justified. (vi) If there are two non-identical precedents concerning the same case, and there are no counter-arguments, the later one must be used as an argument. (vii) If there is a precedent applicable to the case and a substantive reason conflicts with it, overruling the precedent should be especially justified.

In all of these standards, 'if there are no counter-arguments' means that the *travaux préparatoires* (and precedents) have only a prima facie priority as arguments. In the end, the interpretation has to be based on *all* (available) authoritative and substantive reasons, that is, 'all things considered'. In such and only in such a case interpretation corresponds to the 'reasonable sense and purpose' of the statute.

VII   THE CONFLICT OF STATUTES WITH OTHER LEGAL NORMS

Having heard experts on constitutional law, the Constitutional Committee of the Parliament of Finland decides whether or not a Bill conflicts with the Constitution. Not even the Supreme Court or the Supreme Administrative Court have been deemed to have the power to decide on the constitutionality of an act of parliament. This also means that the courts cannot – in a concrete case – refuse to apply a statute on the grounds that it is unconstitutional. Hence the court, where possible, must interpret the law in order to avoid any conflict between the statute and the Constitution (see Preliminary).

On the other hand, a statute with an unambiguous meaning overrides (already on the basis of Chapter 1, section 11 of the Judicial Code of Procedure) precedents and other legal material. This also applies to the relationship between a statute that has been given in the prescribed order and a general legal principle. The latter cannot set aside an unambiguous statute.

Because of the legalist tradition, the Supreme Court *interprets* statutes quite often on the basis of their wording and, in doing so, establishes how the wording should be understood. When such an interpretation reveals a range of possibilities, the statute is not in conflict with precedent and cannot be used to set aside the precedent. The precedent is understood as the proper interpretation of the statute, and in this way the Supreme Court can stay with its precedents in the manner outlined earlier, if there is no special cause to break with them. If there is such a departure, this signifies the creation of a new and, in principle, more correct interpretation of the wording of the statute.

The following are examples of the rules of priority *between* statutes.

1   'Lex superior derogat legi inferiori': an act which has been passed in accordance with constitutional procedure sets aside statutes on a lower level, such as decrees, decisions of Ministries or the regulations of local administrative authorities. However more specific provisions can be and in practice often are given by decree on the implementation of statutes that are on the level of acts of parliament.

2   'Lex posterior derogat legi priori': a statute given later and that deals with the same matter overrides an earlier statute, unless stipulated otherwise in the provisions on entry into force. On the other hand, Finland has adopted a prohibition against retroactive legislation, which means that the new statute cannot — barring some exceptions that benefit citizens — deal with rights that arose during the time of the previous statute.

The problem of retroactive legislation also appears in another manner. The possibilities that the Supreme Administrative Court has of changing its interpretations is restricted in practice by the long, five-year *period of appeal*. A change of interpretation in case X, which has been appealed to the Supreme Administrative Court, would raise the following problem: (1) would it be right that a great number of similar cases are left decided *in another way* (a decision that concerns a certain taxation year, such as 1989, would not come before the Supreme Administrative Court until several years later, and during the intervening period it is possible that a great number of decisions which accord with the prevailing practice have been made); or (2) should one allow a *retroactive decision* in all similar cases, which because of the mass nature of taxation, would lead to a huge backlog of cases? In practice, the threat of this latter option has forced the Supreme Administrative Court to be conservative when faced with the question of changing its policy.

3   'Lex specialis derogat legi generali': a special provision overrides a general provision. A special provision can both restrict and expand the scope of application of a general law.

4   The rule of 'lex posterior generalis non derogat legi priori speciali' is a specific application of rule no. 3: a later general provision does not override an earlier special provision unless this is specifically stipulated or this is the result of special circumstances.

VIII   PRESUMPTIONS GUIDING INTERPRETATION

The concept of 'presumption' fits poorly in this connection with the Finnish system. One generally speaks of presumptions in connection with evidence and the evidentiary law. Finnish law recognizes a number of so-called legal presumptions, such as the presumption of paternity in child law, and various presumptions on how a will should be construed when the text of the will itself is ambiguous or contains a gap. For these reasons, in the following the term 'presupposition' shall be used for 'presumptions'. In the application of law, 'presuppositions' refer to implicitly adopted background assumptions that remain unexpressed. Presuppositions can be roughly divided into two main categories: the assumption of the rational legislator and the assumption of the rational judge.

1   The concept of the rational legislator has not been written out in any statute, nor is there any written documentation on it. No reference is made to this concept in, for example, court practice. However, some indirect arguments can be made on behalf of the existence of this presupposition: (a) The doctrine of the tripartite division of powers specified in the Constitution of Finland emphasizes the independence of the legislative, judicial and executive powers from one another. This doctrine, when combined with the principle of democracy, presupposes that the legislator does not behave in an irrational manner. (b) The belief in the rational legislator is also reflected in Finnish legalism, which was mentioned above. (c) In particular during earlier years, Finnish courts have strictly adhered to the view that there is one and only one right solution to every individual case.

       The concept of the rational legislator in itself can be construed to imply (at least) the following in the Finnish conceptual framework: (a) The legislator seeks consistency in every legislative act; in other words, a tendency to avoid conflicts and redundancy is a part of rationality. At the same time, this means that the legislator is not assumed to seek an absurd result. Such presuppositions continue to be the basis for presupposing that the legal order is coherent which, in turn, makes so-called systemic interpretation possible. (b) The idea of the economy of legal language is closed connected with the demand for consistency: the statutes should not contain any unnecessary expressions. If interpretation concludes that a certain word has no meaning, there should be incontestable grounds for this. (c) The concept of the rational legislator also contains a presupposition of morality: the legislator is assumed to seek only results that are in harmony with the prevailing system of morality and values. We can also speak about the demand for justice as part of the rational drafting of legislation. (d) On the other hand, the prevailing mode of thinking in Finland does not accept the concept of the so-called hypothetical legislator. When interpreting the law, the courts do not start out from the view that the case is to be decided as if the legislator would decide it had the case been pending when the law was being drafted. Furthermore no reference is made in argumentation to what assessment the legislator would make of the case at the time of the interpretation; instead, the courts seek to establish the ratio of the law, in other words the intention of the law at the time of its application, all things considered.

2   One can at least cautiously argue that the Finnish court itself acts also on the basis of a certain presupposition of rationality. Court decision making is impartial consideration on the basis of the facts and the law, with justice as the goal. The presupposition of the rational court can be justified by referring to two factors. First, the duty of the Supreme Court is to ensure uniformity of application of the law throughout the country. Thus the Supreme Court, through its decisions, seeks to guide the decisions of the seven Courts of Appeal in the direction of uniformity. Second, the Supreme Court has also sought, during recent years, to increase further its position as a so-called court of precedent (see sections III and XV). The norms manifested in the decisions have the nature of general norms; they are precedents for future decisions. For this reason, the presupposition of rational decision making is further strengthened with the emphasis on precedents.

IX   THE STYLE OF STATUTORY INTERPRETATION

1   Background Factors

There is no legislation in Finland which would establish the minimum requirements for the justification (reasoning) given for decisions. The requirement that general courts justify their decisions is evident primarily in Chapter 3, section 24 of the Code of Judicial Procedure. Administrative adjudication, in turn, (that is, the decision making activity of administrative courts) is regulated by Chapter 3, section 24 of the Code of Judicial Procedure. The *type of justification*, however, has developed solely on the basis of practice.

Primarily because of the legalist tradition, the justification for decisions of the Supreme Court was very limited up to the 1970s. In particular during the 1950s and the 1960s, the decisions only described the facts and then noted how the case was to be decided. Even the legal provision on which the decision was based was not always expressly noted. The paucity of the justification applied both to issues of evidence and to issues of law. In the literature, decisions justified in this way were called 'we find that. . .' decisions, since the decisions simply stated that 'the Supreme Court finds the accused, N, guilty of . . . and therefore sentences N for . . .' (see Makkonen, 1959).

Since the beginning of the 1970s, first the Supreme Administrative Court and later on also the Supreme Court began to pay more attention to the justification given for decisions. The once typical 'we find that. . .' decisions have now almost entirely disappeared.

2   The Present Situation

At present, in such routine cases as many family law cases, the lower courts use special decision formulas which specify the plaintiff, the defendant, the claims, the response, the final decision in the case and the justification for the decision. The forms are useful in particular because of computerized data processing, and they speed up enforcement of the decisions.

In the superior courts, matters have not been standardized to this extent. Even so, the decisions of the courts of appeal and of the Supreme Court have been systematized to the extent that each decision has: (a) a head-note that sets out the legal rule and the statement of the facts in the case (with the claims of the plaintiff); (b) the response of the defendant and the facts, as well as (c) the part containing the decision (the provisions which the court has applied and the justification for the decision); (d) in addition, possible dissenting opinions are appended. (It should be noted that the court automatically sends the parties *sua sponte* only the decision itself. The file copy has to be ordered separately. If a party does not obtain a copy on his own, he will never know whether or not there had been a vote on the case.)

The decisions of administrative courts also include a head-note, which is necessary in order to ascertain what the case deals with, and the statement of the facts in the case (the parties, the relevant facts, possible interim measures and all the claims presented in the case). The part containing the decision contains not only the conclusions in themselves but also the justification that sets out the facts and the law applied.

The decisions of the superior courts, as noted, include a head-note that describes briefly the legal provisions applied in the case. In practice, it is precisely this head-note that is deemed to express the 'binding' part of the decision; this binding effect refers to its factual binding nature. However the head-note must often be interpreted; it must be given an exact meaning in the light of the facts in the case or the reasons given for the decision. For this reason it is impossible to distinguish sharply between what in the decision is binding and what is not.

The unvoiced background idea in the writing of judgements involves the idea of the judgement as a syllogism. The provision to be applied is the major premise of the syllogism, the facts constitute the minor premise and the conclusion expresses the judgement norm. However, in practice, the decisions are not written in the specific form of a syllogism, even though the structure of the decision reveals syllogistic thinking. To an increasing degree (since the beginning of the 1980s), the stated justifications for decisions are of the 'leg of the chair' or 'dialogue' type, and involve different levels of assessment. Even so a form of dialogue proper, with detailed arguments for and against, is still quite rare, with the exception, for instance, of the practice of the Labour Court in justifying its decisions (the Labour Court justices include not only professional judges but also representatives of the different interests).

Formal juridical arguments still have a prominent place in the justification for decisions. (This refers to the 'must-arguments', that is, mainly the text of the statute.) Yet, when reference is made to statutes, alternative interpretations are normally not presented, nor does the justification contain any references to the types of argument forms or interpretative principles. On the other hand, there is today − as is mentioned above − a tendency to add references to such authoritative arguments as *travaux préparatoires* and precedents as well as to all kinds of substantive arguments (see as an example Supreme Court decision 1989 II 87, which includes a many-sided justification of a dialogue type). However the Supreme Court typically does not include in this kind of written justification arguments speaking against the chosen interpretation alternative, but mainly arguments in favour of it.

The consideration of the case before the Supreme Court proceeds as follows. After the memorandum of a senior secretary has been presented to the justices (usually in a division), a draft decision, including a recital, is prepared. The draft decision and the documents in the case are circulated among the members, who each make their own notes for the final decision. After this, a proposal for the complete file copy of the decision is prepared by the senior secretary. This proposal forms the basis for the final decision making.

The final decision is made in a session of the division, where also the final justification and the wording of the head-note of the case are formulated. At the session a decision is finally made on whether or not the case shall be published in the annual report. According to the Supreme Court and the Supreme Administrative Court, unpublished cases have less value as precedents than do published cases.

In assessing the decisions of the two Supreme Courts, therefore, we must keep clearly in mind the distinction between the public (the publicized) justification and the justification that has actually affected the case (the factual justification). Only careful conclusions can be made on the basis of the public justification in respect of what the actual justification was when the case was decided. For this reason, the publicized justification can continue to be criticized in at least three respects.

1   On issues of fact, it is typical that the Supreme Court and the Supreme Administrative Court remain satisfied with a description of the facts, and issues of evidence are usually not justified to a sufficient extent. There is a particular lack of arguments speaking against the charges in criminal cases. Also acquittals are not justified. This latter fact can be considered a lack particularly because even an acquittal continues to cast a shadow on the character of the defendant. Since the media focus their attention on the charges and on convictions, the absence of justification for an acquittal is of significance to the personality of the defendant.

2   As has been noted, when appealing against a decision of the court of appeal, an application for leave to appeal must first be made to the Supreme Court. If leave to appeal is granted,

the Supreme Court will hear the case. However no justification is stated for a decision against granting leave to appeal, and so one who is external to the court remains uncertain about how relevant the justification of the court of appeal was in respect of the final result in the case. The absence of justification for decisions not to grant leave of appeal has been supported on the grounds that otherwise the Supreme Court would have to rule on the substance already at that stage. This, in turn, would go against the basic goal, which was to cut down on the backlog of cases.

3   The view that the one right decision exists for all legal problems even if it is not always possible to find this right decision has been widely accepted in the Finnish court system. The concept of the one right decision is, as it were, a position in legal ideology according to which the judge must seek this one right decision in every case. On the other hand, the opinion of the younger generation among the judges can no longer be interpreted so that a final decision of the Supreme Court and of the Supreme Administrative Court is, at the same time, considered to be the one right decision. The openly admitted fact that lower instances cannot be punished for breaking with a precedent where the case is ambiguous, and that the Supreme Court itself can (following a special procedure) break with its earlier position given in a similar case, both reflect the opposite view. The way in which the attitude towards the doctrine of the one right decision has changed over the past few years also reflects the significance that legal theory has in a small country. Up to the 1950s, the unanimous opinion in legal theory had been that the doctrine of the one right decision could not be justified at least in its traditional form. Gradually, for example as a consequence of teaching at the University, the doctrine has become accepted widely also in the court system.

When the Supreme Court or the Supreme Administrative Court is not agreed on the final decision, a vote is taken and the dissenting opinions are noted. In such a situation, one cannot say that the opinion of the majority is the one right decision.

As for the question: 'Who are the addressees of the justification for decisions?', this depends on one's point of view. According to the Constitution Act, the Supreme Court and the Supreme Administrative Court decide individual cases. From this point of view, the primary addressees of the justification are the parties in the case. Indeed, it is the specific intention of the two Supreme Courts to write the justification with the parties in mind. As we have seen, the Supreme Court has emphasized the nature of its decisions as precedents. In fact this means that the justification is written also for other judges, and the precedents are seen to guide their activity. In part, lawyers are in the same position, since it is their function to anticipate how a legal problem that they meet shall be decided. Legal science, in turn, is responsible not only for describing and explaining legal practice, but also for subjecting it to critical examination. Thus the justification for decisions also provides material for research.

On the basis of Finnish legal practice, it is not possible to draw an unambiguous picture of who the intended addressees of the two supreme courts are, and whether there is a conscious priority among the different addressees.

The nature of justifications for decisions reflects a felt need to legitimize the decisions taken. Also people are no longer (as had been the case, for example, in Finland as recently as before the Second World War) satisfied solely with the decision. The breakdown of unquestioning respect for authority is seen in the fact that people ask *why* a decision was made, and expect a justified answer. These expectations, in turn, are connected, for example, with the present and future state of democracy. The demands for openness and publicity in democracy can be met only when the exercise of power in society can be controlled through public justification.

X   INTERPRETATION WITH REGARD TO THE CHARACTER OF THE STATUTE

1   Apart from the fact that the different fields of substantive law also have substantive reasons of their own, there are certain rather typical tendencies present in legal reasoning.

In criminal law, one favours a *literal interpretation* that at least avoids any kind of extensive interpretation. One speaks about the prohibition of analogous interpretation 'in malam partem', that is, to the disadvantage of the accused. Even the most flagrant shortcomings of criminal law legislation are left to the legislator to abolish.

Procedural norms as well as all provisions on form have to be interpreted restrictively. For instance, no single formality may be added to the form of legal transactions; one must instead use *e contrario* inference. The same holds true as far as 'lex specialis' norms (special laws) are concerned.

In tax law there is a tendency to resort to literal interpretation, but this is often also the intention of the legislator. The decision makers in the first instance in tax cases are often non-lawyers. For this reason, one attempts to write the provisions in such a manner that conclusions *e contrario* are justified. For instance, if something is not explicitly exempt from tax, it is not exempt from tax at all. This method, however, competes with the principle of the neutrality of taxation: unless the facts are otherwise proven, one starts from the assumption that taxation does not intend to create economic inequality, but rather to level it. As a whole, it can be said that the Supreme Administrative Court pays relatively little attention to the underlying economic and political goals of the tax statutes, and starts instead from the text of the statute.

This attitude seems to be quite usual in administrative practice in general. Trusting, as they do, to literal interpretation, non-lawyers often tend to be more legalistic than professional lawyers. Hence the development in Finnish administration is paradoxical compared to the development in adjudication. The legalist tendency is slowly disappearing in judicial decision making but clearly increasing in administration.

2   Otherwise one cannot generally say that the characteristics of the addressees have or should have an impact upon the way in which the courts interpret a statute. This can be seen, for example, in the practice with the law of contracts. So-called 'error juris' has only marginal relevance in decision making. Professional technical terms, of course, are in most cases understood as a part of the professional language in question.

3   Finnish courts are accustomed to dealing with old and partially obsolete statutes, but in such cases the courts often *interpret their own practice* (often without explicitly referring to it) instead of the text. This is also the case with many general clauses. Slowly but surely a covering network of precedents is replacing the value-laden discretion conferred under the general terms of statutes. Thus, when a new type of situation does require the taking of a position on the applicability of the statute, one at least *begins* with a case-by-case comparison before exercising discretion.

In this way the interpretation of such general clauses as s. 33 of the Contracts Act or s. 56 of the Taxation Act is in fact interpretation of the pertinent judicial practice. In the former case, the statute speaks about circumstances under which a contract clause would be unconscionable; in the latter case, the tax authorities are entitled to take into account the substance of a contract (or the like) and not only its form (which does not correspond to the substance). Judicial decision making has yielded a body of *typical cases* that form the guiding standards for further interpretation.

4   In Finland legislation is drafted, on the one hand, by the Ministry of Justice and, on the other, by the different Ministries (of Finance, Agriculture, the Environment, and so on). The Ministry of Justice supervises the statutory texts drafted by the special Ministries, which may not have mastered the required legislative techniques. Quite often a bill is passed without sufficiently close scrutiny.

It is not part of the Finnish tradition for parliament to issue instructions on interpretation. The drafting of a law has been described as having a value as a source of law, but otherwise parliament does not authoritatively interpret laws that have already been signed into law. Not even so-called resolutions of parliament on what legislative measures should be undertaken in order to remedy a defect are relevant as sources of law in court.

XI   THE ROLE OF THE COURT

The principle of the tripartite division of powers, which is noted in the Constitution Act, establishes the independence of the courts from the legislative and the executive branches. This independence is strengthened by two facts: first, courts will not accept guidance on interpretation from any other bodies. For example, the Ministry of Justice may issue regulations on administrative matters, but it cannot interfere with judicial matters. Second, judges are 'unremovable', that is, a judge cannot be removed from office before the age of retirement other than through a court decision on the basis of an offence, or if permanently incapacitated by an illness. In practice, judges have almost never been removed from office. If such a measure were considered – which is very rare – the judge would resign voluntarily. A judge may not accept instructions from any person or any body, and must closely follow the law (Art. 52, s. 1 of the Constitution Act).

The court may interpret the meaning of a statute expansively or restrictively, and it has the power (with some exceptions) to fill gaps, for example, through analogy. In this way, the court may 'update' and 'revise' statutes to keep them from becoming obsolete.

As has been noted earlier, the court also has the right to use so-called free discretion in gap cases, where it is not a question of interpretation or of gap-filling through analogy, but rather of the free creation of law.

In particular, over the past 15 years, there has been a clear increase in the role of law in Finnish society typical of a welfare state: more and more aspects of life in society are becoming subject to norms. This has led not only to the strengthening of bureaucracy but also to the increase in the powers of general courts. On the other hand, this development has been affected by the creation of several special courts, which take over cases in particular from the general courts. The increase in the societal power of courts has been quite evident in the two following areas.

The Supreme Administrative Court has taken upon itself to decide cases which, in accordance with the true division of labour, should be decided by the executive branch. Examples include cases posing issues of community planning. According to the interpretation of the Supreme Court, questions of policy (that should ultimately be decided by the Government in cases of appeal; Supreme Administrative Court Act, s. 5) turn out to be questions of law, if a statute openly refers to expediency. In this way the Supreme Administrative Court has begun to exercise control over, for example, building permits.

The Supreme Court, in turn, has strengthened its position as a court of precedent. The Supreme Court itself construes the matter to be that it simply gives decisions on individual cases, as required by the Constitution. The concept of precedent and the concept of the guiding effect of precedents, however, necessarily mean that each (published) decision of the Supreme Court takes on the nature of a norm. The decision applies to every similar case. The precedent establishes a general norm.

XII STATUTORY PRESCRIPTIONS ON INTERPRETATION

There are no norms in the Finnish Constitution on this issue. (See sections III and V.) However one feature that is typical of Finnish legislative techniques is that an act of parliament may empower the President or the Government to issue binding decrees (of a lower level) on the interpretation and/or implementation of provisions left open in the texts of the act. This is a method of avoiding the need for judicial interpretation.

XIII   CONSTITUTIONAL LAW AND INTERPRETATION

As has been noted in sections VI and XI, there is no special constitutional court in Finland. Thus there are no problems in the application of law over whether or not it is unconstitutional. The law is taken as the basis in all cases, since its constitutionality has already been examined by the Constitutional Committee of parliament before it was adopted. A possible conflict between constitutional provisions (for example with civil rights) and the prima facie meaning of the provision to be applied is eliminated through interpretation. The law is brought, all things considered, into harmony with the manifest principles of the Constitution.

In some cases the justification for court decisions refers directly to constitutional norms, for example to the principle of equality expressed in Art. 5 of the Constitution Act. In such cases the reference to the Constitution is specifically an argument in interpretation, which gives substance to an alternative meaning of a statute. However in this form direct references to the Constitution are not common.

XIV   INTERPRETATION AND PRINCIPLES OF LAW

In case of gaps, but also in difficult cases requiring interpretation, a case is decided on the basis of general principles of law. Examples include 'pacta sunt servanda', 'nulla poena sine lege', 'good faith', 'loyalty in the law of contracts', 'the principle of protection of the weak' and so on. These types of principles and values (other than the constitutional principles and values referred to in section XIII) are not explicitly referred to in the justification (see section IX). In particular, political ideology, social values (democracy, equality and so on) or even the goals of statutes are not to be found in the justification given for decisions.

Also, when the judicial function is clearly exercised for political ends (as was the case following the 1918 civil war when dealing with the 'Reds' on the losing side, and during the 1920s and the 1930s against the outlawed extreme left), the justification for decisions referred to the provisions in the Penal Code on treason and high treason, which were in themselves abstract. Today this no longer happens, even though in cases involving espionage or blasphemy (which are very rare) and in certain libel cases with political overtones the courts must of necessity take certain ideological positions.

It has also been argued in the legal literature that the political opinions of judges appear in a latent form, for example, in cases that deal with labour contracts and collective bargains. This argument has been presented on the basis of the conclusions in such cases and by studying the assumed political values of those judges who have taken part in the hearings, not on the basis of the justifications in the decisions. However, in the light of research, this can be claimed only if judges are placed on a rough continuum running from 'right-wing' to 'left-wing'. In peacetime circumstances, there is no evidence in Finland that a certain political ideology or – even less – a party opinion would affect the view of judges. On the contrary, it appears that the social background of judges is irrelevant in respect of the overall decisions made. It appears that the ideology of judging is emphatically objective, and has an essentially greater impact on the world view of judges than does their political opinion.

In cases dealing with community planning and the protection of the environment, the courts (deliberately) *avoid making reference* to the values in community planning policy or environmental policy. The decisions are written as if they would follow directly from the law.

So-called alternative legal dogmatics (such as the critical legal studies movement) has been quite well represented in Finnish legal science, influenced by the 'uso alternativo del diritto' tendency in Italy – the view that decisions should support the value goals of the working class. However this doctrine has not been favourably received by the courts in Finland. It has remained a theoretical model that solely appears in legal science.

On the other hand, there is reason to emphasize that protection of the weaker party, which is characteristic of the welfare state, has begun to obtain a considerable foothold in civil law, for example in consumer protection issues and in insurance law (standardized insurance agreements). We can speak of a tendency towards social civil law.

XV   THE CHARACTER OF THE HIGHER COURT IN FINLAND

1   There are two types of general courts of first instance in Finland, the district courts in rural areas and the city courts in the larger towns (see Preliminary). The divisions of the city courts have a chairman and two other judges. They are appointed by a political body, the city council, but the Supreme Court may intervene in the appointment if there has been a formal error in the appointment procedure.

The district court judges and the circuit court judges who serve in the district courts are appointed by the Supreme

Court. The members of the courts of appeal as well as the members and the senior secretaries of the Supreme Court and the Supreme Administrative Court are appointed by the President of the Republic.

Regardless of what body has the power of appointment, in the great majority of cases the judges are appointed from the ranks of legally trained persons who have qualified for judicial office. It is true that, during the past few years, an attempt has been made to recruit members of the two supreme courts from outside those who have made their career in judicial office, for example from the Bar and the universities. It appears that the tendency is to recruit the members of the two supreme courts from a wider circle than before. In general, direct party politics do not appear to influence the appointment process.

2 The so-called appeal system is in force in Finland (see Preliminary). According to this system, the appellate level (the court of appeal and the Supreme Court, or correspondingly the county administrative court and the Supreme Administrative Court) decides both issues of fact and issues of law. If a procedural error has occurred in the case, the case can be returned to the lower court in question. Otherwise the appellate level itself deals with the case without transferring it to another instance.

3 According to the system of leave to appeal the appellant must first request leave to appeal from the Supreme Court, and only after leave is granted may he or she appeal the decision to the Supreme Court (see Preliminary). The system of leave to appeal in the Supreme Administrative Court applies only to a very few matters.

In many administrative fields, for example in tax law, the precedents of the Supreme Administrative Court have in practice strong binding effect, owing to the mass nature of the issues. (See also what has been said about the conservative attitude of the Supreme Administrative Court to changes in policy, section IX.)

4 The 'party' principle is in force in civil procedure, with some exceptions. According to this principle, the party has the right to determine whether he/she wants the protection of the law, and to what extent. In criminal procedure, on the other hand, the 'official' principle prevails. With the exception of some so-called complainant offences, the protection of the law is granted regardless of the will of the party concerned.

There is a difference between civil and criminal procedure in respect of the substantive conduct of the proceedings. The basic principle in civil procedure is that each party must demonstrate the facts on which that party relies. However the inquisitorial system is blended in the proceedings to the extent that the judge has the right, by conducting the proceedings, to guide the proof. Some Finnish court proceedings today suffer from a lack of preliminary preparations and poor conduct of proceedings. When this is combined with possible poor skills on the part of a few lawyers, the results have included delay and increased difficulty in determining the truth.

Traditional criminal procedure in Finland was inquisitorial and, even though the accusatorial principle (the active obligation of the prosecutor to prove the case) is the rule today, the court takes an active role in conducting the proceedings.

Since 1948, the theory of the free weighing of evidence has been followed in Finland in the consideration of evidence. According to this theory, it is for the court to assess on the basis of everything that has become evident in the case what is to be deemed proven.

Traditionally, parties and witnesses have been heard only before the courts of first instance in Finland. The superior courts rely only on the records prepared in the lower court. It is true that an oral hearing is in some cases obligatory and can always be arranged both before the court of appeal and the Supreme Court, but this possibility is used relatively rarely — in the courts of appeals, it is used in about one per cent of all cases. In the vast majority of the cases, therefore, consideration before the superior courts still depends on the lower court records.

XVI THE LEGISLATURE: STRUCTURE AND PROCEDURE

1   In normal cases the legislative process in Finland involves the following stages. After a political decision has been taken to initiate a legislative reform, a body is appointed to prepare the matter. A Ministry may appoint a commission or assign the matter to a civil servant or working group of civil servants in the Ministry. In the most important reforms, the Council of State appoints a committee, which either consists of expert members or is a so-called parliamentary

committee in which different political groups are represented. In practice, a parliamentary committee is appointed only when decisions have to be made on important issues of principle or when the mandate includes the formulation of the general outline of a reform that has just been initiated. Regardless of which body does the drafting, experts are usually heard, in addition to which the committees have expert members and a secretary or secretaries familiar with the field in question.

Following the preparatory work, the Government decides on whether a Government Bill shall be presented to parliament in the matter. If such a Bill is to be introduced, the Ministry in question is assigned the task of preparing it. Such Bills contain a general justification for the reform, its broad outlines and the proposed provisions, with more detailed justification for each of the provisions.

The Supreme Court can also be asked to submit its opinion on the quality of a draft Government Bill. In particular, before and immediately after the Second World War, the Supreme Court participated actively in the legislative process by issuing its opinions. With the increase in the backlog of cases during the 1960s and the 1970s, the resources of the Supreme Court have not made it possible to use this mechanism very often. Now the practice of seeking opinions is used all too rarely.

The Ministry of Justice also has civil servants who bear responsibility specifically for checking the language of the Bills. This checking of language is important in Finland, partly because Finland has two national languages. The Finnish and Swedish texts of the Bills must be identical, even though the Swedish translations of statutes have no binding force in interpretation.

After being submitted to parliament, the Government Bill is dealt with by the special committee of parliament established for the field in question. If the proposed statute is to be passed in accordance with a special procedure for adopting constitutional provisions, the Bill is considered by the Constitutional Committee.

The committee that deals with the Bill hears experts, for example academics, representatives of working life, economic life and interest groups, leading civil servants from the administrative field in question, judges and attorneys. The hearing of experts in connection with major reforms may last several months, and dozens of experts may be heard. The committee prepares a report on the Bill, in which it reviews the general justification, the proposed provisions and the justification for the detailed provisions. The committee may, and in practice often does, propose numerous amendments of the Government Bill.

Following certain intermediate stages, the Bill goes from the Committee to a plenary session of parliament, where a vote is taken on adoption or rejection. In practice, amendments are no longer made at this stage to the individual provisions.

2   Political negotiations may be involved at several stages:

- The first is when deciding on whether or not to initiate the process of reform. At this juncture, decisions may be taken on the general outline of the reform, the procedure and timetable to be followed, and so on.
- Political negotiations usually take place within the Government before deciding on the presentation of a Government Bill. At this stage the Government attempts to anticipate whether or not it is possible to get a sufficient majority in parliament to back the Bill. If needed, the Bill will be amended so that adoption by parliament is deemed probable.
- Political negotiations are carried out in the Committee stage of the legislative process in parliament, primarily on those technical details that reflect political differences of opinion. The Constitutional Committee is the most political of the committees, even though it also hears the best available experts.
- In certain situations the Government will withdraw a Bill that has already been submitted to parliament if it appears that this Bill will meet with excessive opposition in parliament. Either the reform is abandoned, or the Bill is amended in order to reflect the views of the majority. In this connection, it must be noted that the coalition governments in Finland have generally not even submitted a Bill to parliament if a compromise has not already been reached among the majority political parties represented in the Government. In general, when the Government has consisted of a coalition of both Socialist and non-Socialist parties, the absence of agreement has slowed down many legislative reforms, despite the fact that there is wide agreement on the importance and urgency of these reforms.

- In plenary sessions of parliament, the subject of political negotiations is the adoption or rejection of Bills.

3   Committee reports, Government Bills and the reports of the parliamentary committees are published. They are thus available to all interested parties, and this material is sent through official channels to the courts. Reports of commissions and working groups appointed by Ministries are not always published, and as a result limited use is made of them in courts, with the exception of the Supreme Court and the Supreme Administrative Court.

   In practice, the lower courts have relatively little access to the *travaux préparatoires*. The most important sources of information are the Statutes of Finland, precedents and the legal literature. The justices and senior secretaries of the two supreme courts, on the other hand, have access to all available *travaux préparatoires*.

4   In Finland the legislative machinery deals very slowly with defects in adjudication, and the process in itself is slow. Thus, to a large extent, it is the function of the courts to develop law up to the limit set by the need to guarantee due process.

XVII   FEATURES OF THE LEGAL CULTURE

1   The Finnish legal culture is formal and positivistic. In the foregoing, this fundamental feature and the ways in which it is manifested have been termed 'legalism' (see sections VI and IX). In addition, in administrative cases, the increasing influence of law has signified the increased role of law in decisions of policy otherwise primarily justified on material grounds and with value arguments.

2   The interpretive method followed by the courts is relatively uniform, although to some extent differences exist between different fields of law (see section X). One of the functions of the Supreme Court and the Supreme Administrative Court is to secure the uniformity of law. This primarily means uniformity of decisions in similar cases, although the exercise of the control has a unifying indirect influence also on the method applied.

3   In the justification of decisions, references to the *travaux préparatoires*, to precedents and to the legal literature are

today more common than, let us say, ten years ago. A slight change towards the Swedish model is thus going on in the Finnish practice. Yet at this moment (1990) it would be safer to speak about a tendency to change the style of justification than about a final and clearly identifiable move to a quite new 'culture' of justification.

4   The justices of the Supreme Court have not become specialized in the sense that one justice would decide only certain types of cases. However the Supreme Court may order one of its members to deal with cases requiring certain expert knowledge, and this member will be knowledgeable in the field in question. In some special cases, such as military law cases, the Supreme Court has expert justices. In the Supreme Administrative Court, on the other hand, expert members in fields such as taxation, community planning or general administrative law are used as short-term holders of vacant positions.

Specialization in the proper sense exists in specialized courts, such as the Labour Court, the Land Rights Courts and the Water Rights Courts, which have expert members, and in courts of arbitration, where the composition varies on a case-by-case basis. The courts of arbitration in particular have taken cases away from the general courts of first instance, since it is possible for the courts of arbitration to get specialized expert knowledge, and the procedure in such courts is substantially more rapid than in general courts. Examples of the types of cases dealt with by courts of arbitration include construction, international trade, general contract law and industrial rights.

REFERENCES

Aarnio, Aulis (1978), *The Rational as Reasonable*, Dordrecht: Kluwer Academic Publishers.

Aarnio, Aulis (1990), 'Taking Rules Seriously', in: *Law and the State in Modern Times* (ed. by Werner Maihofer and Gerhard Sprenger). ARSP Beiheft 42, 1990, pp. 180–92.

Brusiin, Otto (1958), *Tuommarin harkinta normin puuttuessa*, Helsinki 1938.

Constitution act and Parliamentary act of Finland (ed. by Ministry of Foreign Affairs), Helsinki: 1967.

Frände, Dan (1989), *Den straffrättsliga legalitetsprincipen*, Helsingfors.

Helin, Markku (1989), 'On the Evolution of Argumentation in Finnish Private Law Research, 1920–1960', in: *Scandinavian Studies in Law* (ed. by Anders Victorin), Vol. 33, pp. 137–66.

Hidén, Mikael (1974), *Säädösvalvonta Suomessa. I. Eduskuntalait*, Vammala (with English summary).

Kastari, Paavo (1969), 'Le systéme constitutionel de la Finlande et son devéloppement', Helsinki.

Kastari, Paavo (1963), 'The Historical Background of Finnish Constitutional Ideas', in: *Scandinavian Studies in Law* (ed. by Folke Schmidt), Vol. 7, 1963, pp. 61–77.

Klami, Hannu Tapani (1981), *The Legalists. Finnish Legal Science in the Period of Autonomy 1809–1917*, Helsinki.

Makkonen, Kaarle (1959), *Ajatuksia juridisen kielen loogisesta analyysista*, Lakimies, pp. 49–72.

Pöyhönen, Juha (1988), *Sopimusoikeuden järjestelmä ja sopimusten sovittelu*, Vammala (with English summary).

Takki, Tapio (1985), *Lainkäyttäjä lainsäätäjän*, Helsinki (with German summary).

The Supreme Administrative Court (1976), *The Supreme Administrative Court and the Finnish System of Application of Law*, Helsinki.

Pöyhönen, Juha (1988), *Sopimusoikeuden järjestelmä ja sopimusten sovittelu*, Vammala.

Takki, Tapio (1985), *Lainkäyttäjä lainsäätäjän työn jatkajana*, Helsinki.

Utriainen, Terttu (?), 'Näyttökysymys henkirikoksissa', *Juridica Lapponica*, 1, pp. 367–80.

6 Statutory Interpretation in France

MICHEL TROPER, *Paris*, CHRISTOPHE
GRZEGORCZYK, *Paris* AND JEAN-LOUIS
GARDIES, *Nantes*

PRELIMINARY

The French legal system is one of written law. It is centralized and, since the beginning of the nineteenth century, to a large extent codified. The three great codes (civil code of 1804, code of commerce of 1807 and criminal code of 1810) have been constantly revised since their enactment. The criminal code, for example, does not retain more than 5 per cent of its original provisions of 1810, all the others having been replaced by new rules. There are moreover other 'pseudo codes', like the code of social security or the code of tax law, which are in fact mere compilations of statutes enacted at different times and published in one volume in order to facilitate their use.

The system of courts shows one important characteristic: because of the special French concept of the separation of powers, there are two systems of courts, called 'jurisdictional orders': judiciary courts under the Cour de Cassation, and administrative courts under the Conseil d'Etat. One consequence is that before deciding a case the competent court must be determined. A special court was established in the nineteenth century, the *Tribunal des Conflits*, to make such determinations.

In both systems of courts, there are two levels. The Cour de Cassation is in principle not a third level but its function is to review the application of statutes by the lower courts. It is only a judge of the law and has no power to examine the facts. The Conseil d'Etat has a mixed role: in some cases it is a 'juge de

Cassation' like the Cour de Cassation and in other cases it acts as a court of appeal, examining both points of law and points of fact. For all kinds of reasons, the courts are overloaded, and the period of time before final decision on a case, examined first by the lower courts, then by the Cour de Cassation or the Conseil d'Etat, can be as much as several years.

A further important characteristic of the French legal system is that the courts have no power to review legislation and to invalidate an unconstitutional statute. This is the function of a special authority created by the Constitution of 1958, the Conseil Constitutionnel. Its jurisdiction can be invoked only by a limited number of political authorities and it can only examine proposed statutes before they have been enacted. For further comments on the court system, see section XV.

It should be noted that French judicial opinions are extremely concise, often not longer than a few lines. A comparative study of three decisions on the same subject in France, Germany and the USA revealed that the French decision had 300 words, the German 2 000 and the American 8 000 (not counting concurring and dissenting opinions) (Touffait and Tunc, 1974 (LXXII) 487). Only main arguments are discussed, or rather mentioned, in very short and elliptic formulas, very carefully styled, so that there is an important and difficult task for the scholar to interpret the texts of the decisions. However, in many cases, the work of a reporter judge is also available for that purpose.

I   THE GENERAL ORIGINS OF INTERPRETATIONAL ISSUES

In France the most important origin of interpretational issues is certainly the necessity of adapting statutes to transformations in the economy. Bear in mind that the initial drafting of the main French codes dates back to the first ten years of the nineteenth century; that is, it predates the industrial revolution. From that time the social situation changed so quickly that, on account of the inadequacy of the initial texts, legislation was inevitably behind in its evolution. Judges, professionally in constant contact with the facts, very often made indispensable adaptations while waiting for statutory modifications. This elaboration of a sort of customary law completing the statutes was exerted not only for lack of statutory rules (*praeter legem*), but sometimes also, according to some jurists, against them (*contra legem*).

It is usual to give the two following examples of this phenomenon, both related to the law of insurance. The authors of Art. 1119 of the Code Civil evidently were not in a position to predict that its prohibition of 'stipulations pour autrui' (stipulations for others) could be an obstacle to the future institution of life insurance. Already in the nineteenth century, judges knew how to infer from Art. 1119 contrary to what its author had clearly meant, that is the principle of the freedom of 'stipulations pour autrui', with only a few restrictions. In the same way, Arts 1382 et seq., requiring that *the victim* prove the personal fault of the actor, did not preclude the rules commonly applied to accident insurance. But increasing mechanization at the beginning of the twentieth century led judges to admit some presumptions of fault, the consequence of which was to abolish the important limitations contained in the Code Civil, without any modification of the legal text. The acceleration of economic development today increases even more this necessity of adapting statutes to social transformations by way of interpretation. There are many examples in which judges have anticipated a reform of the statutes which occurred later. They have even sometimes, by an interpretation *praeter legem* or *contra legem*, assumed the role of the law-giver to modify statutes, without textual adaptations, when they felt that they are clearly not adapted to new situations.

Sometimes the origin of interpretational issues is to be found in an ideological discordance between the court at the present time and the earlier legislature which originated the statute. Let us quote the *Dame Lamotte* decision of the Conseil d'Etat (17 February 1950): the legislator, in that case the Vichy government, had decided that against certain administrative acts there was 'no remedy, either administrative or judicial'; the Conseil d'Etat interpreted this phrase as though it did not exclude a remedy for abuse of discretion ('recours pour excès de pouvoir').

Next, after social transformations, the major origins of interpretational issues are antinomies in statutes. But one must bear in mind that antinomies themselves, to a great extent, result from these social transformations. The first source of antinomies in the legal text is that the legislator, while adopting new rules, does not always take pains explicitly to abrogate former ones. In such a case, it is usual, in the language of the courts, to speak of *implicit abrogation*: it is the duty of the judge to determine which of the anterior rules are implicitly abrogated by the more recent ones.

This source of antinomies which the judges later rectify derives partly from the modern tendency of the legislator to multiply statutes, considering them less as measures which would warrant a certain durability than as temporary devices which may cause confusions. Therefore it is up to the judge to determine which of two incompatible provisions is to take precedence over the other.

A major new source of statutory antinomies leading to difficult interpretational issues is the integration into French law of the law of the European Economic Community. In the absence of appropriate legal provisions, especially in the field of economic activities, French courts must interpret national statutes as compatible with the substance of the Treaty of Rome (and other international rules) in order to avoid censorship by the EEC Court or the International Court of Human Rights.

It is obvious that another important source of interpretational problems lies on the one hand in the incompleteness of statutory law, and on the other hand in the obligation to decide, even in the face of an actual gap in the law. (As will be seen, the French system adopts the fiction that there are no gaps.) Art. 4 of the Code Civil states: 'The judge who refuses to decide a case under the pretext of silence, obscurity or insufficiency of the Law can be prosecuted for déni de justice.' We postpone this question for now (see Sections II and III).

Antinomies and incompleteness, whether they originate in social transformations or not, seem to be the major sources of interpretational issues. In addition, some minor sources are still to be mentioned, such as overgenerality of a term that obliges the judge to introduce distinctions between subclasses of cases or, on the contrary, undergenerality that forces him to extend by analogy a solution explicitly given for some cases to others considered to be similar.

Ambiguity is also sometimes a source of interpretational issues. Ambiguity can be unintentional. For example, the statute concerning the *Commission Nationale de l'Informatique et des Libertés* (National Board of Information Processing and Liberties) gives to this Board the power to state norms as to the computerization of databases, but does not specify whether these norms are technical ones, to which the databases have to conform, or genuine juridical norms to be considered administrative rules. Ambiguity can also be intentional. For example, the legislator may be at a loss, and prefer to rely on the decision of a judge, because the political problem involved is too ticklish. Thus the law prescribing that the operating costs of private schools contracting with the State shall be provided for 'on the same conditions as for the public ones', that is by the communes, does not specify whether these communes are those where the schools are, or those where the pupils of these schools live, or if this obligation concerns only primary education or also kindergarten.

In the first period of the application of French codes, lack of definition was only exceptionally a source of interpretational issues, for a well-known historical reason: some of the authors of

the Code Civil (particularly Portalis) were convinced of the importance of definitions, and their view prevailed in the drafting. By
contrast, this problem seems nowadays to be one of the major
sources of interpretational issues. The quality of legislative drafting
being much less important in the eyes of the legislator, the courts
resolve definitional ambiguities by making constant interpretative
adjustments, and often generate entirely new judicial concepts. An
example of a juridical concept introduced without any definition
can be mentioned: it is that of *natural obligation* ('obligation natu-
relle') at Art. 1235.

Grants of administrative discretion have generated interpretational difficulties only in relatively recent times. There were such
difficulties earlier, but there were only specific statutes granting
administrative authorities discretionary powers, exercisable on
certain conditions. Administrative courts had merely to verify that
the conditions existed, but had only limited power to review
administrative discretion. In their opinion, a more extended review
would have concerned not only the legality but also the expediency of the administrative act. The function of interpretation was
then only to ensure the legal definition of facts. But in the last 15
years the distinction between legality and expediency has become
less clear and the Conseil d'Etat now seems to consider expediency
to be an element of legality; therefore, while interpreting statutory
rules, it enquires about the means necessary to the administration
in order to attain the objects the law has in view.

Generally speaking, the origins of interpretational issues relate
less to the meaning of the legal text than to the willingness of the
judge to extend his review to new categories of acts. The jurisprudence of the Conseil d'Etat provides many examples of this: thus it
has manifested its will to review decisions made in application of a
law adopted by referendum (19 October 1962, Canal), or some
decisions made by the President of the Republic in application of
Art. 16 of the Constitution. In connection with this last example, it
must be emphasized that interpretational issues sometimes depend
not only on the law in question, but also on the decision which the
judge intends to control.

II GAPS AND THEIR ORIGINS

One should stress that the word 'gap', in the mind of the authors
and of the first commentators of the Code Civil, could have two
radically different meanings.

1   If the word is used in reference to matters which are not

ruled by any provision, it is a presumption of French law that such gaps do not exist. We have already seen that, according to Art. 4 of the civil code, 'the judge who refuses to give a decision *under the pretext* of silence, obscurity or insufficiency of the Law can be prosecuted/or déni de justice' (emphasis added). Since it could be only a pretext, it is here implicitly claimed that there is in the law no real gap. The refusal to admit the possibility of such gaps is connected with the prohibition, stipulated by Art. 5, of any interpretation of general and regulatory provisions. In both cases, the intention of the authors of the Code Civil was to prevent the so-called 'arrêts de règlement' of the old monarchy. According to the principle of the separation of powers proclaimed by the French Revolution, a judge cannot act as a law-maker. Filling the gaps would be on this account a legislative function.

2   If, on the other hand, we use the word 'gap' to refer to the lack of particular provisions ruling a concrete case, arising from the fact that the law-maker cannot enter into all the details, the judge is not only permitted to fill such a gap, but Art. 4 puts him under such an obligation. Therefore we shall take the word 'gap' exclusively in this second sense in our answer to the present question.

We must make another remark: the obligation to fill a gap should not be confused with the creation of a new rule. A judge who nonsuits the plaintiff (or defendant) does not really fill any gap, but only decides that the gap does not exist (or that it is a 'false gap'). This remark leads us to distinguish between formal and substantive (or material) gaps. In the French traditional approach, there are no formal gaps: Art. 4 of the Code civil formally (that is, decisionally) closes the system. At the same time, for logical and practical reasons, the system is obviously open in the substantive sense, and does contain gaps in the sense we mentioned above.

From a modern point of view, French scholars are far from unanimous about the existence of gaps in the law (in the substantive sense). Even those who admit their existence are in general very cautious in their approach to the problem and they very often prefer to avoid the use of the notion of gap and replace it with such circumlocutions as 'new cases', 'new problems raised by judicial activity' or 'cases not foreseen by the legislator'.

The statement that 'a gap exists in law' is a kind of proposition *de lege ferenda*, including some value-statements and, as such, can be asserted only on the doctrinal level. In other words, the concept of 'gap' is typically theoretical and not judicial (except for the very evident technical gaps resulting from a lack of concrete legal acts foreseen by the statute and not yet settled by competent authority).

A majority of scholars seem to admit the distinction between interpretation and gap-filling (those who recognize that gaps do exist); interpretation is conceived as an intellectual conception of the correct understanding (and the application, if necessary) of legal provisions. Gap-filling is mere application itself, if it is done by the judge, and creation of the law on the part of the legislator.

An interpretation can be given by scholars, other authorities (executive authorities, for instance, in the case of international conventions) and even by private persons. Among them different *comités des sages*, with a consultative role, have a particular position. But gap-filling is an exclusive task of the legislator, and in some respects, of the courts. Interpretation is mainly text-oriented and intellectual (or cognitive), and thus prior to any application and to gap-filling. Properly speaking, the existence of a gap can be asserted only after interpretative operations, but not before.

If we now turn to the courts, and especially to the Cour de Cassation, we can observe that their theory is much more restrictive or dogmatic on this point. Judges do not use the concept of 'gap' at all. They follow a formal (decisionist) point of view. The first task of lawyers is — according to this view — to use all possible interpretative techniques and arguments in order to avoid the appearance of gaps in the law, even if there actually are some in particular texts. The general assumption of completeness can even be characterized as a main current of the (implicit) doctrine of the Cour de Cassation, especially in criminal matters (cf. Crim. 21 oct. 1942, D.A. 43.4; 10 nov. 1959, Bull. Crim. n°476; 12 mars 1984, Bull. Crim. n°102). In taking this line, the Cour de Cassation has obliged other courts to deny the existence of gaps.

Therefore, instead of drawing a distinction, French judges tend to disguise the filling of gaps as interpretation. One famous example is that of the right to strike. The Constitution of 1946 proclaimed this right and provided that it was to be exercised 'according to the statutes that regulate it'. The Constitution thus called for statutes, which were never adopted. In 1950, The Conseil d'Etat decided that, 'in the absence of such a regulation, the recognition of the right to strike cannot entail the absence of limitations, which must be applied to this right, as well as to every other right, in order to avoid an exercise of it that would be abusive or contrary to public order . . . it is the duty of the executive, responsible for the good functioning of the public service, to determine for itself, under the control of the judge, the nature and extent' of limitations that can be brought to that fundamental right (C.E., 7 juillet 1950, Dehaene, Rec. p. 426). Thus the absence of legislation is not a gap to be filled by the judge. According to the Conseil d'Etat, the Constitution and the statutes organizing the civil service gave the executive discretion to regulate.

If one does admit the existence of substantive gaps, these gaps proceed from the unintended underinclusiveness of a statute rather than from any deliberate intention of the legislator. The deep explanation is the general fact that, in French law, new social and economical developments are, as explained in our first part, ruled by ill-adapted and old-fashioned legal provisions. Judges are nowadays more and more often confronted with situations so radically new that there is no scope for mere speculation upon the (hypothetical) intention attributable to the historical authors of the legal texts. On the other hand, the sources of antinomies are also sources of gaps: the EEC legal integration, already mentioned, is an important source of gaps in every national system.

One should not neglect the recent evolution of the general functions of the State, and especially its tendency to assume the role of a 'welfare state' in particular in the field of health. The French system of health protection and its economic consequences raise more and more questions about its administration and its relations to the traditional functions of the State.

Although statutory activity is extensive, it is never sufficient to fill all possible, and quite real, gaps. The economy is partly controlled by way of statutes, especially for those companies belonging (partly or entirely) to the State. But the legislator is never able to keep up with the rapid development of economic forms in which the State is involved.

On the technical level, new scientific activities, especially in the field of biotechnology, are constant sources of gaps that cannot be easily filled without a wide social consensus on the moral principles underlying and/or resulting from these activities. Of course such a consensus does not exist.

In the criminal field, scientific developments generate new types of offences which are completely unknown in classical statutes, as for instance computer criminality. None of these phenomena can be grasped by statutes until they have been crystallized and then comprehended in general and abstract legal concepts.

III TYPES OF JUSTIFYING ARGUMENTS

1 French scholars generally reconstruct the practice of the courts, by drawing a distinction between, on the one hand principles of interpretational method, and on the other hand methods of interpretation or rules or techniques of interpretation, such as reasoning by analogy or *a contrario* or maxims of interpretation (Weil; Carbonnier).

The former is a set of general principles which inspire interpretation and on which techniques of interpretation are based. In this respect French scholars distinguish between the exegetical method and 'modern' methods (such as historical, teleological or 'libre-recherche scientifique'), considered to be of greater value. This distinction has been devised by followers of Gény, who wished to promote 'modern methods' and persuade courts to abandon the exegetical method. This classification is clearly ideological and, like 'libre-recherche', has not been followed by the courts.

2 Whatever the typology, the methods of interpretation all aim at a statement of the 'meaning' of a statute, but not every justification presupposes the same concept of 'meaning'. The 'meaning' can be the intention of the law-giver or the 'objective meaning', independent of any law-giver's intention.

When courts speak of the *law-maker's intention*, they can mean several things. With regard to the *law-maker*, there are several authorities that may be distinguished, from a temporal point of view or from the point of view of their participation in the enactment of the statute.

From a temporal point of view, the law-maker can be (a) the historical law-maker, as when the court refers to preparatory work (*travaux préparatoires*); or (b) the present law-maker, who can be either the present hypothetical law-maker (such as parliament in its present political composition) to whom an intention is ascribed, or a present fictive law-maker, one who would reasonably take account, if he were to change the statute, of political and social changes that have occurred since that statute was first enacted. Thus, according to the premier president of the Cour de Cassation, Ballot-Beaupré, in his speech for the hundredth anniversary of the civil code, one must not

> search obstinately for the ideas of the authors of the code, as they were a hundred years ago, when they wrote such and such provision; the judge must ask himself what those ideas would be if the same provisions were to be written by them today; he must tell himself that, on account of all the changes that, for a century, have occurred in ideas, in habits . . . Justice and Reason order us to adapt liberally, humanely, the text to reality and to the demands of modern life

Also 'An entirely rational legislator, who does not contradict himself, adapts means to ends, does not do anything without a purpose, etc. . . .' (F. Ost, in van de Kerchove, 1978, 97 ff).

From the point of view of participation in the enactment of statutes, the law-maker is not always the author of the statute in the sense of positive law. According to French public law, the author of the statute is that organ or those organs of the State that took part in a decisional way in the enactment of that statute; that is, those whose consent was indispensable, but not those who merely participated intellectually in the formulation of the text, for example, by giving advice, like experts. Thus in French public law, the actual law-makers are, according to the present constitution, the two houses of parliament, if they have both adopted the bill; or, in the case of a conflict between the two Houses, and if the cabinet has granted the National Assembly the last word, the law-makers are the cabinet, plus the National Assembly. Yet the courts will look for the intention not of that law-maker, in the legal sense, but for that of one of the political organs having a legislative function, selected either because its intention can be discovered more easily (for example, because debates have been recorded) or because it has exercised on other partial organs an influence considered to be decisive (as with the Conseil d'Etat and Bonaparte in the case of the civil code). The courts may also look for the intention of a body which is not at all one of the authors of the statute, in the legal sense, but which took part intellectually in the preparation of it and exercised an influence in favour of its adoption. Thus, in the process of interpreting the French Constitution, one does not refer to the intention of the French people, who adopted it, because that intention cannot be described precisely. One refers instead to the intention of the Comité Consultatif Constitutionnel, which was not the author of the Constitution in the legal sense, but undoubtedly exercised considerable influence.

By *intention* the courts may refer to the actual psychological state of mind of a certain number of men or, in the case of the rational law-giver, to an entirely hypothetical state of mind. In most cases, it is the conscious will of the law-maker, the will that he deliberately and clearly expressed in the course of preparatory work.

Sometimes the intention of the law-giver is expressed neither in the text, nor in preparatory work, but results from the very existence of the statute and can be formulated by assuming the rationality of the law-maker. Thus the Conseil d'Etat has decided that the provision of the constitutional preamble of 1946, 'the right to strike can be exercised in accordance with the statutes that regulate it', means that 'the Constituent Assembly intended to invite the law-maker to form a necessary reconciliation between the defence of professional interests, of which strike is but a modality and, on the other hand, the safeguarding of the general interest that striking could jeopardize' (7 July 1950, Dehaene, Rec. 426). The intention is not in that case an actual, but an entirely hypothetical state of mind. This is also true when the law-giver, whose intention is sought, is the present law-giver.

The courts sometimes refer to an *objective meaning* independent of any law-giver's intention. In some cases, such arguments as 'literal meaning' or 'objective purpose of the statute' are not used to discover any state of mind, whether actual or hypothetical, but as absolute presumptions of a meaning, which prevail over any sort of evidence regarding what the law-maker actually meant. This is the case when the courts wish to preserve important values or interests, with which the statute is not supposed to conflict. In a case already mentioned, a statute issued under the Vichy régime, giving wide discretionary powers to administrative authorities and stating that there was no remedy against a certain type of administrative decision, was interpreted, in a way considered by a vast majority of scholars to be *contra legem*, as not excluding a 'recours pour excès de pouvoir' (ultra vires), because that type of remedy had not been expressly excluded. Although the true intention of the law-giver was known to all, an argument drawn from an omission in the text enabled the court to find the 'objective' meaning of the statute (C.E. 17 fév. 1950, *Dame Lamotte*, Rec. 110).

Thus, in both these cases, whether meaning is conceived as an intention or, as an 'objective' meaning, it is determined by means of all the three types of arguments. For example, the intention of the original law-giver can be established by linguistic, historical or functional arguments. Similarly, the objective meaning can be established by linguistic or functional arguments. The criterion of choice between two meanings can therefore be treated as a meta-argument.

3   We may now classify types of arguments, leaving aside the classification of French scholars and distinguish between linguistic, systemic, functional and genetic types of arguments.

Linguistic arguments are based on the language in which the text is written. In case of a conflict between the meaning of a term in ordinary language and in the technical language of the law, in most cases the latter prevails. When courts use linguistic arguments, they sometimes speak of the 'literal meaning' of the statute, but by this expression they can refer to several entirely different things.

The meaning in 'natural' or 'normal' language is the meaning that any person knowing the language would understand. It must be stressed that courts usually refer to that meaning either because they intend to avoid justification or because they wish to give only a minimum justification. In the former case, they implicitly declare that the meaning is obvious and that any justification would be useless. For example, some court decisions consist only of the following sentence: 'it emerges from the text itself that . . . [statement of the rule]'. (Cf. van de Kerchove, 'La doctrine du sens clair', in van der Kerchove, 1978, p. 13). In the latter case, the courts wish to stick to that minimum justification which consists in declaring that they refer to the 'ordinary' or 'usual' or 'natural' meaning of the words in the statute, eventually citing the authority of a dictionary.

In addition there is the meaning of legal language when it differs from the usual meaning and the meaning resulting from definitions given in the statute itself.

By 'systemic interpretation' we use a loose concept of a system. A systemic interpretation simply assumes that the law is systematically structured, and that the meaning of a text results from its place within the system. French courts use systemic arguments in several ways: (1) a particular provision of a statute is interpreted in the light of the statute as a whole; (2) a particular statute is interpreted in the light of other statutes in the same field; (3) a particular statute is interpreted in the light of the law envisaged as a substantive system, considered to be coherent and complete (often a statute must be interpreted in order to determine whether conflicts arising from it fall under the jurisdiction of judicial or of administrative courts; for example, the French legal system gives competence to administrative courts for all cases in regard to a public service); (4) a particular statute is interpreted in the light of the law envisaged as a hierarchical system; for example, if a statute permits the Executive to enact general rules it is interpreted in such a way that it takes into account the supremacy of statutes over government regulations and of the constitution over statutes. Among systemic arguments we find logico-axiological arguments in their positive form (such as *per analogiam, a fortiori*) or their negative form (*ad absurdum*).

Functional or 'purposive' interpretation rests on the idea that any rule has a special purpose or function. The meaning of the rule is that which allows it to exercise its function. Functional arguments are related sometimes to the subjective function actually intended for the rule, sometimes to an objective function, economic or social. The subjective function derives from the will, express or implicit, of the law-maker himself. That is why functional arguments are often related to genetic arguments in interpretation. But, sometimes, the function is that which has been assigned to the statute by the maker of another rule, either one of a higher level (for example, the constitution-maker setting goals in a declaration of rights or a preamble) or one of the same level (this is the case of a law-maker who modifies certain rules but keeps in force the statute subject to interpretation, because he assigns to it a new function, different from that which had been assigned by the historic law-maker).

The objective function (sometimes called by French scholars 'social finality') is that which the rule fulfills independently of the original law-maker's intention. This is the type of argument most often used when courts wish to adapt ancient statutes.

Genetic or historical arguments are sometimes distinguished from the preceding ones in so far as they are aimed at discovering the meaning of the statute through the will of the law-maker, whenever that will cannot be known through linguistic interpretation, or appears to have been badly expressed in the text. French scholars use the term 'historic' – in a sense not synonymous with 'genetic'. 'Genetic' refers to historical conditions prior to the enactment or at the time of the enactment. 'Historic' refers to an interpretation taking into account all the historic developments that have taken place since the enactment. Nevertheless genetic interpretation is actually a variety of functional interpretation, since it aims at discovering the meaning of the statute by examining its function at the time of the enactment, especially the historical conditions that the law-maker intended to remedy. It should therefore not be treated separately.

Finally we find other modes of interpretation, which cannot be subsumed under 'systemic', 'linguistic' or 'functional'. For example, there are ideological arguments, such as the necessity to search for justice, or arguments that are used in a semi-clandestine way, never in the text of the decision, but sometimes in the 'conclusions' of a reporter-judge. Typical of this group are arguments based on the authority of scholarly opinions ('la doctrine').

IV TYPES OF GAP-FILLING ARGUMENTS

There are no specific types of arguments that are recognized only in the filling of gaps.

V THE MATERIALS OF INTERPRETATIVE ARGUMENTS

There are very few statutory rules regarding the construction of arguments. Rules on the justification of statutory interpretation can therefore only be found in the decisions of the supreme courts (Cour de Cassation and Conseil d'Etat) striking down decisions of lower courts because of the type of justification given.

The extreme conciseness of French decisions has already been mentioned. No form of justification is mandatory and, though there are some sources which must be mentioned (but not necessarily quoted) in the 'visas', there is no type of material other than the statute itself that a court must take into account. It is often the case that a court only states the meaning it has attributed to the statute without giving any justification. It is also often the case that a supreme court states that the lower court has interpreted 'correctly' the statute and that the justification of the interpretation was 'sufficient' (for example, Cass. Crim. 8 March 1930, D.P. 1930.1.101, quoted below). Therefore a court decision is never struck down because it did or did not take into account a particular element in the construction of the argument.

One further remark ought to be made. When a higher court examines the validity of the justification provided by a lower court, it is only in order to control the reasons for the interpretation. It is the real motivating reason for the interpretation that can be considered valid or invalid and not the ostensible justification. Thus, if there is no doubt that a court has based its interpretation on some reason it did not mention in the argument, the reason mentioned will be taken to be the real reason for the interpretation. Conversely, if the court has mentioned a material consideration, but without taking real account of it, the real rather than this ostensible reasoning will be sought. The higher court will in that case disregard the justification and review the real reasons. The higher court is only interested in justification to the extent that it helps reveal the motivating reasons.

It is therefore impossible to say that there is any particular kind of factor or material that must, should, may or may not be incorporated in the construction of arguments. But, as mentioned in points 8 and 10 below, some materials are forbidden in argumentation: prior judicial interpretation and scholarly opinions. None of those listed below must or should be taken into account by courts in the justification of their interpretation and none must be excluded. All listed below may be taken into account. It must be stressed that the court only has an obligation to discuss the grounds of the claim ('moyens') invoked by the parties, but not all the arguments that support these motives. There is not even an obligation to quote the statute subject to interpretation (for example, Cass. Crim. 8 March 1930, D.P. 1930.1.101, just mentions the statute by its date, without quoting its provisions and states that 'the lower court interpreted correctly the statute as meaning that . . .').

1   The courts refer to the historical knowledge of conditions the statute was intended to remedy in order to find the law-giver's intention, particularly in the case of recent statutes (cf. Rieg, 1980).

2   Legislative history of 'travaux préparatoires' are widely used. French scholars who address the use of *travaux préparatoires* as part of the exegetical method, and also in functional interpretation, are generally critical. They think either that preparatory works can provide no precise sign of the law-maker's real will and of the function he assigned to the

statute, because of the ambiguities and contradictions of parliamentary debates, or that preparatory works can actually lead to some knowledge of the law-maker's will, but that this knowledge is and should be considered irrelevant for purposes of interpretation.

The courts use *travaux préparatoires* mainly when the objective is finding the intention of the historic law-maker and when this material will provide a basis for linguistic or functional justification, because by way of arguments of the type *a contrario, a simile* and so on it is thought possible to discover the true state of mind of the legislator. This material is used preferably for the interpretation of recent statutes. Even in that case, courts refer to debates, but do not usually quote from them. Most often, legislative history is mentioned in extremely general terms, such as: 'it comes both from the terms of the statute and the preparatory works that . . .'.

3   Interpretation by addressees of the law may also be mentioned but may not be presented as the sole motive for the interpretation of a statute by a judge. Among addressees, particular mention must be made of administrators, even when they are not always direct addressees of the statute. Their role is multifold. First, some statutes are directed towards public administration. Secondly, the public administration has the duty to enforce a large number of statutes, not only materially (by appointing civil servants, building roads and so on) but by issuing orders necessary for the application of the statute and by adopting secondary legislation. In all these cases, the French Public Administration has the right to interpret the statutes. Ministerial interpretation is naturally subject to control by administrative courts, but at the same time, it may be used as material in the process of interpretation by the courts themselves. Thirdly, the cabinet has been in the last decades the intellectual author of 90 per cent of statutes: civil servants have prepared the bill, ministers presented it in parliament, defended it through the debates and finally induced the majority to vote for it. Therefore in all these capacities, administrators, especially ministers, contribute to interpretation of statutes.

Their interpretation is introduced in courts in two different forms: either as secondary legislation containing implicitly or explicitly such an interpretation or as answers to written questions addressed to ministers by members of parliament. These questions frequently deal with legal matters and the answers even have the character of legal advice, so that, in answering them, ministers frequently interpret statutes, either statutes which they have the duty to enforce or statutes which they helped to draft. These answers are often used by lawyers and sometimes by courts to justify their own interpretations, but, as in the previous case, they must not be used alone, so as to avoid transforming them into the sole motive and they are rarely present in the justification (cf. Oppetit, 1974). Interpretations by private persons are never mentioned.

4   The language and purposes of other statutes 'in pari materia' may be referred to when arguments of the types *a contrario*, *a fortiori* are used. If the statute to be interpreted makes an exception to another statute and if the court wished to use the principles 'exceptio est strictissimae interpretationis', then the latter statute is quoted.

It may also be the case that the meaning of a statute is determined by reference to another statute concerning a related matter. Thus a statute of 1884 gives power to the mayor to issue police regulations with the purpose of keeping public order. But the extent of the powers of the mayor to issue a regulation concerning religious funerals is determined by reference to a statute on religious freedom (C.E. 19.2.1909, abbé Olivier, Rec.181).

5   Mention of prior statutes that have been modified by the statute being interpreted is frequent. It is often the case in French legislation that the text of a statute ends with the words 'all prior texts are abrogated to the extent that they conflict with the present statute', but these conflicting texts are generally not listed, so that the meaning of the latter statute can only be determined by an interpretation of prior ones in order to decide which are conflicting and therefore abrogated.

6   Prior legal history of the language used in the statute may be used to justify interpretation of the law-giver's intention.

7   EEC Law and treaties deserve a special mention. According to Article 55 of the Constitution, 'Treaties and agreements that have been regularly ratified have, from the date of their publication, an authority superior to that of statutes, provided that for every agreement or treaty, it is enforced by the other party.' This provision has raised many difficulties, especially since the Conseil Constitutionnel refuses to declare unconstitutional a statute contrary to a prior treaty. (15 janvier 1975, Interruption volontaire de grossesse, Rec. p. 19, 'a statute contrary to a treaty is not for that reason contrary to the constitution'). While courts were not permit-

ted to nullify statutes, until recently, the only solution was for them to interpret statutes in such a way that they would appear to be in conformity with the treaties (Chapus, 1986).

Yet this practice has recently undergone very deep transformation. First, the Cour de Cassation has interpreted Article 55 of the Constitution and the Conseil Constitutionnel's decision as giving competence to the courts to review statutes and to decide therefore that a statute contrary to a prior treaty ought not to be enforced (Cass. Ch. mixte, 24 mai 1975, Administration des Douanes, c. société des cafés Jacques Vabre, Dalloz, p. 497, concl. Touffait; Ch. commerciale, 24 juin 1986, Mme Dumoussaud, Bull. n°134; 5 mai 1987, Soc. anonyme Auchan, n°109: ch. crimin. 5 déc. 1983, Jeanfra et Patrex, n°352: 3 juin 1988, Klaus Barbie, n°246). After some resistance, the Conseil d'Etat has followed the Cour de Cassation (20 octobre 1989, Nicolo, not yet published).

Therefore, from now on, an interpretation of a statute will often require taking into consideration a prior treaty, if one of the parties claims that there is a contradiction. In the Nicolo case, the 'commissaire du gouvernement' explicitly argued that this new practice will not take the courts too far, because the judge 'always enjoys the very useful resource of interpretation, which enables him to empty applicable texts of their contradiction (with treaties)'.

Secondly, directives of the EEC must be applied ('mises en œuvre') by way of domestic legislation. These directives may be cited, when the court wishes to justify a certain interpretation, by showing that only that interpretation can make the statute appear to be an application of a directive.

8   The citation of prior judicial interpretations by a court of the same degree, though not forbidden, is extremely rare and never used as the only or even as the main reason for an interpretation. The reason is that courts not only are not bound by precedent, but, further, that a decision grounded only on precedent would be considered illegal, because it would substitute the authority of the courts for that of the statute. Moreover the characteristic dualism of the French court system will normally prevent courts belonging to one jurisdictional order to mention decisions from a court belonging to the other order.

The main type of precedent that judges sometimes explicitly incorporate is an interpretation by a superior court of their own jurisdictional order, or their own previous interpretations. Thus, the Conseil d'Etat censured a decision of the Cour des Comptes, because the latter rested on an interpretation contrary to that of the Conseil d'Etat itself (C.E. 8.07.1904, Botta, Rec. 557).

Some materials, although not cited in the decision itself, influence the court and are thus taken into account. There is even one situation, albeit extremely rare, when one source must be taken into account: when the Cour de Cassation, having twice censured a decision by the court of appeal and given a sovereign interpretation of the statute, sends the case to a third court of appeal, which is under an obligation to apply this interpretation.

9   Reference to the teleological or normative nature of a phenomenon is frequent and carries great weight. The courts very often mention the 'legal nature' or 'legal character' of an institution to justify interpretation (for example, Cass. Civ. 23 nov. 1956, Trésor public. C. II. 407, in which the court interpreted article 1384 of the civil code to mean that the police do not possess the character of the guardian of a private house to which a doctor had been brought by an officer and where the doctor had been wounded by an explosion. The police therefore could not be liable on the basis of Article 1384).

10   Opinions of law professors, though used and sometimes quoted in the 'conclusions', are never mentioned in the decision itself. If such a material was used as the main justification, it would be considered illegal for the same reason as in 8 above.

11   Occasionally court decisions mention local traditions to justify the interpretation of statutes for a particular case. Thus, in a case we have already mentioned, the meaning of a statute concerning the powers of the mayor to issue police regulations on the matter of religious funerals can be determined only in the light of local tradition (C.E. 19.2.1909, abbé Olivier, Rec. 181).

VI   PRIORITIES AMONG CONFLICTING TYPES OF ARGUMENTS

1   Scholars generally agree in thinking that it is extremely hard to systematize the practice of the courts and that there is no general rule of priority. This can partly be explained by the duty of the judge to inquire into the law rather than rely on counsel. Most scholars would accept the idea that 'courts practise today a tactical eclecticism', meaning that one type

of argument may prevail in some instances and another in a different instance, according to the practical result courts want to achieve in a particular case (J. Carbonnier; Rieg, 1980).

On the other hand, courts do not in general openly recognize the existence of a conflict between arguments. For example, the courts do not oppose the intention of the law-giver to the literal meaning or the plain meaning of words in the statute. The latter is considered important as a means to discover the actual intention. Furthermore, as already mentioned, the most generally accepted principle is 'interpretatio cessat in claris' and courts stress that they do not really interpret but rather that the meaning springs obviously from the words of the statute. Thus a court sometimes expressly acknowledges that 'any search for the intention of the law-maker is forbidden to the judge whenever the meaning of the statute, as it appears from the text, is neither obscure, nor ambiguous and must therefore be treated as certain' (Trib. Seine, 24 avril 1952, Sem. Jur.II.7108; id Ci v. 22.11.1933, DH 1933.2).

2   An evolution in the French tradition has to be taken into account: (a) The so-called Ecole de l'Exégèse, in the first half of the nineteenth century, presupposed that the law was an expression of the will of the law-maker and that it was entirely incorporated in the texts of statutes. If interpretation was necessary, which could only be the case when the text was not clear, it ought to be a search for the intention of the law-maker and thus favoured a linguistic and eventually a genetic interpretation. The original French codes were still tolerably adapted to the social and economical situation. Therefore it was sufficient to seek what the law-maker had meant, by consulting the *travaux préparatoires* of the codes. Meaning of the statute and intention of the law-maker generally coincided. (b) From the second half of the nineteenth century, judges were confronted with social realities, which the authors of the initial texts could not have taken into consideration, and had to make room for a functional interpretation. Nevertheless, the semiotic and historic interpretation could not entirely disappear, particularly for recent statutes, for which it remains necessary to know what was exactly the will of the law-maker.

At the end of the nineteenth century, François Gény favoured a 'free scientific research' of social needs whenever any reference to the law-maker's intention would be arbitrary (Gény, 1899). On this view, the 'meaning' of the statute was different from literal meaning and different also from the intention of the law-maker. These ideas were influential among scholars, but never among judges, who always applied a compromise motto suggested by Saleilles: 'beyond the civil code, but by the civil code' (Preface to Gény's book), meaning that judges may go beyond the intention of the law-makers, as suggested by the words of the statute, and look for the actual intention or even disregard the intention itself and look for the purpose of the rule, but that they ought to find in any case support in the words of the code.

3   It is therefore possible to distinguish several situations. Whenever possible or desirable, and in practice whenever the statute is a recent one, the court will favour linguistic arguments in order to discover the intention of the law-maker. Linguistic arguments are especially important when the statute has a highly technical character. In that case, the court does not consider itself competent and will not use axiological arguments. On the contrary, the law-maker is presumed to be rational and well aware of the ends, so that linguistic arguments will only be supplemented by functional. If this is considered impossible, because linguistic interpretation will not yield the meaning, then one looks directly for the will of the empirical law-maker.

Without openly disregarding linguistic arguments, the court will supplement them with genetic, systemic or purposive interpretation. But even then, the court will not openly admit that the meaning is different from the intention of the law-maker. On the contrary, it will always try to find some way to show that, first, it only aims at discovering that intention and second, the interpretation finds some support in the words of the statute. Occasionally the literal interpretation is openly put aside. This is the case when the court wishes to establish an entirely new rule. One famous example is that of article 1384 of the civil code, which has been interpreted in a way generally thought to be *contra legem*. According to article 1384, 'one is liable not only for damages caused by one's own actions, but also by those caused by people for which one is responsible or by things of which one is the guardian'. This provision had been interpreted during the greater part of the nineteenth century as a special case of liability for torts: It created a presumption of tort, which could be waived by proving that no tort had been committed. But later, by interpreting the words 'choses que l'on a sous sa garde', the Cour de Cassation established a general presumption of liability, in the absence of any tort, the effect being that the victim has a claim without having to prove a tort of negligence. This presumption has been widely used to impose liability on the owner of an automobile in the case of an accident (Cass. Ch. réunies, 13.02.1930, D.P. 1930.1.57, note Ripert).

But systemic and purposive interpretations, even when they appear to be *contra legem*, almost always find some support in the text. The court will use, for example, an argument *a contrario* to infer from the text some socially and axiologically acceptable meaning. In a famous case, judges justified the new rule by declaring that the law-maker did not mention it in the statute and therefore did not explicitly reject it, so that his intention must have been to establish that rule implicitly. It is the Conseil d'Etat that uses this technique most often. It has for example decided that a statute forbidding the manufacturing of certain dairy products without mentioning any compensation for the manufacturer meant that the law-maker did *not* wish to leave on the manufacturer the financial burden that should rest on the national community: 'Nothing, either in the very text of the statute or in the travaux préparatoires or in the general circumstances of the case, can support the idea that the law-giver has intended to place on the plaintiff a burden which normally is not incumbent on him; this burden, established for the general interest, ought to be borne by the community' (C.E. 14 January 1938, La Fleurette, Rec. 25).

Sometimes, but very rarely, the court disregards the actual intention of the historical law-maker and bases the interpretation of the statute on functional and axiological arguments. (cf. C.E, 17.02.1950, *Dame Lamotte*, Rec. 110). Even then the court tries to show that the interpretation, if not based on the text, is at least not absolutely incompatible with it.

The court will therefore openly ignore linguistic arguments only extremely rarely and when this would obviously lead to undesirable results. This is the case when such arguments would lead to an obviously absurd meaning or when the statute contains incompatible sentences. One famous example of such an interpretation is that of a statute containing an error in wording: it forbade passengers of trains to get on or off when it was not moving (Cass. Crim. 8 March 1930, D.P. 1930.1.101). Otherwise any attempt to ignore or openly disregard both the text and the intention of the law-maker is considered an abuse of power.

4   The duality of jurisdictional systems has an important consequence, namely that some statutes have to be interpreted by the two supreme courts (Conseil d'Etat and Cour de Cassation), so that one of the arguments that has to be taken into consideration by a court belonging to one of the systems rests on the interpretation given by courts of the other system. That interpretation is not binding, but is weighed in the general process and can be helpful in case of a conflict between different types of arguments.

Moreover it has become the habit of the Conseil Constitutionnel, when reviewing the conformity of a statute to the constitution, to interpret that statute, stating, for example, that it is constitutional if and only if it is understood in a particular sense. Such an interpretation of course rests mainly on a teleological argument. In principle, it is binding on all jurisdictional authorities (Art. 62, al. 2 of the constitution), although there is no remedy in case of a conflicting interpretation of the same statute by one of the supreme courts. Since the Conseil Constitutionnel interprets before the statute has been promulgated, an argument resting on such an interpretation becomes, when it is weighed by one of the supreme courts, genetic and teleological.

Thus, if we consider the principles which govern statutory interpretation and the possible conflicts between the types of arguments, we can observe, among a diversity of principles, a weighing process that the judge must go through and that it is impossible to reduce this to a logical form. No categorical priority rule can be induced from the decisions given by the Cour de Cassation or the Conseil d'Etat; so that, although these courts review statutory interpretation by the lower judges, no systematic priority rule emerges from exercise of the power of review.

Scholars have often stressed that it is difficult to find in court decisions

> answers to the problem of the methods of interpretation and particularly of the choice between those numerous methods that are available. Why has this text been interpreted strictly and that text extensively? Why has jurisprudence changed, for one and the same provision, from one method to another? The scholar frequently wonders about these attitudes and instead of an answer finds only conjectures about the individual psychology of those who decide. (M Batiffol, 1972)

VII   THE CONFLICT OF STATUTES WITH OTHER LEGAL NORMS

1   A preliminary remark is necessary. French legal language has an expression, 'conflit de lois dans le temps', that covers the problem of effects of statutes in time, namely that of the possibility of retroactive statutes. We examine here a different problem, that of a conflict between two (or more) valid norms, the subject of which is identical. There is a general presumption of coherence of the legal system. Therefore all conflicts between two norms, both regarded as valid, are supposed to be merely apparent conflicts. If the court is confronted with such an apparent conflict, it can choose between two different attitudes: (a) interpret the two texts as incompatible and decide that one of the norms only is valid; or (b) interpret them in such a way that they do not conflict and thus decide that they are both valid. It ought to be stressed that interpretation takes place *before* the issue can be resolved, but when it has been resolved, principles of priority may have to come into play:

- a rule of higher level prevails over a lower one ('lex superior derogat inferiori');
- a more recent over a prior one ('lex posterior derogat priori');
- a specific over a general one ('lex specialis derogat generali').

2   Where two texts are incompatible and only one is a valid norm, the first principle is used ('lex superior derogat inferiori'), but its formulation, as fixed by the Latin maxim, actually covers two distinct rules, which eventually can come into conflict one with the other: (a) the principle that a rule emanating from a higher level source prevails over one emanating from a lower level source: for example, a statute voted by parliament prevails over provisions of a decree issued by the executive power: (b) the principle that certain eminent norms, particularly acknowledged (for example, those securing individual liberties) must in case of a conflict prevail over others considered less fundamental.

3   The two maxims ('lex posterior derogat priori' and 'lex specialis derogat generali') are not prescribed by legal provisions, but by legal tradition. A majority of statutes contain one provision stating that 'all statutes contrary to the present law are abrogated'. But, since there is never a list of those statutes that are abrogated, courts often have a choice of deciding either that an

older statute has been derogated by a more recent one or that it is more special and has therefore not been derogated by a more recent more general one 'lex specialis per generalem non abrogatur').

4   There is one situation when the court may not choose between 1(a) and (b) above, and that is when there is an apparent conflict between a statute and a provision of the constitution. It is an essential feature of the French legal system that courts have no power to review legislation. The existence of the Conseil Constitutionnel is no real exception to that rule, since its jurisdiction can only be invoked before the statute has been promulgated. Once it has been promulgated its validity cannot be questioned.

It follows that a court may not assert the existence of a conflict between a statute and the constitution, but must interpret the statute in such a way as will render it compatible. It will at the most justify one particular interpretation, by stressing that any other would make the statute conflict with the constitution or by showing that the statute is being interpreted in the light of the constitution. But these occasions are extremely rare, particularly because of the absence in the constitution *stricto sensu* of substantive provisions. These can be found only in the Preamble and in the Declaration of the Rights of Man, but neither of these texts was considered, until 1971, part of the constitution or, for that matter, part of positive law (Conseil Constitutionnel, 71–44 DC, Liberté d'association, du 16 juillet 1971, Rec. 29).

VIII   PRESUMPTIONS

Most authors agree that there are some presumptions, although these generally are not written down in legal texts but are indirectly connected to them.

1   There is a presumption, already mentioned, that the statutes in force conform to the Constitution and to the general principles of law.

2   Art. 6 of the 'Declaration des droits de l'homme et du citoyen' of 1789 mentions, at least implicitly, the presumption that parliament expresses the will of the nation represented by the legislative power. But this will is not necessarily identified with the intentions which the law-maker effectively had in adopting the law, and which it is generally difficult to know today. Scholars often mention a presumption that the will of the law-maker is that which is expressed by the text, if only the text is clear, 'even though it is probable that the wording does not correspond to

the genuine intention of the law-maker' (Riom, 21 October 1946, D.47.90). The judge often seems rather to refer to that which could be or should be the intention of the law-maker, if he were confronted with the present situation, which the real law-maker generally was not in a position to predict. We have already mentioned the case of insurance, which the law-makers at the beginning of the nineteenth century could not imagine. Similarly they could not think of future technical realities such as electric current, with its implications for the law governing sales and theft. Therefore a few scholars uphold the opinion according to which the judge, while interpreting, has to conform to the supposed will of the *present* law-maker.

3   The judge presumes that the legislature does not intend absurd consequences. This leads him to inquire into the law-maker's intention, 'if the application of the text would result in nonsense' (T.C. Seine, 24 April 1952).

4   It is sometimes the case, though the recourse to such a presumption is less systematical, that judges support their own interpretations by arguing that a different one would render provisions of the legal text redundant. But this presumption that the law-maker does not intend to be redundant is not consistently invoked.

5   Administrative judges presume that the law grants powers to the administration exclusively for the common interest, even when this is not expressly stated in the legal text.

6   There is a presumption that the function of the judicial power is not only to do justice, but also to create a rational and coherent body of law. Here two levels must be distinguished: Art. 5 of the Civil Code, while forbidding a judge to 'pronounce by way of general disposition', seems to restrict the role of judges to deciding 'the cases which are submitted to them': they cannot go further without exceeding their jurisdiction. But, since the interpretation of statutes by the judge is reviewable by the Cour de Cassation, it is through the work of this court, which is empowered to reject an interpretation which seems to it defective, that the law can become a coherent set of provisions. Therefore, all things considered, this is the judicial body presumed to be responsible for the coherence and consistency of the law.

7   There is a general presumption, established by Art. 2 of the Civil Code, that statutes are not retrospective. But Article 2 of the Civil Code is itself a statute and can therefore be derogated by a new statute. The presumption thus functions as a mere 'relative' or 'simple' presumption: the statute must be interpreted so as not to be retroactive unless it has itself explicitly stated otherwise. That presumption normally applies in other fields. It must be

stressed that, even if non-retroactivity can be defeated by express provisions in a formal statute, the same does not hold for government legislation (Carbonnier).

Criminal law is a special case. Here the presumption has been established neither by the code, nor by a statute, but by Art. 8 of the Declaration of Human Rights: 'No one can be punished save on the ground of a statute established and promulgated prior to the crime.' This principle has itself been interpreted by the courts: it applies only to harsher statutes, not to milder ones. The Conseil Constitutionnel has given this principle of retrospection of milder statutes or retrospection 'in mitius' a constitutional basis, so that it cannot be derogated by the legislature (19–20 January 1981, 127 DC, rec. 15; cf. Jacques-Henri Robert, 1988, 155 ff).

IX   THE STYLE OF STATUTORY INTERPRETATION

1   The general style of French court decisions is one of extreme conciseness. The justification of the decisions should, in principle, come out of their general form, which can be described in the following simplified way: every decision has three parts, visas, reasons given and 'dispositif' provisions.

The visas are a statement of various elements, such as the statutes and the different steps of the legal proceedings which the court has considered. The reasons given include a brief discussion of the facts and of the legal question involved. Here the court states that the facts are regulated by the statutes mentioned in the visas. The 'dispositif' is a very brief statement, divided in articles, of the decision proper.

2   The reasons given are thus the most important part of the decision. They will normally include the following: (a) a quotation from provisions of the statutes, previously mentioned in the visas, under which the facts can be subsumed; (b) sometimes an interpretation of those provisions. Because of the general presumption of completeness of the legal system, the court will not define an issue of gap-filling, nor, in most cases, an issue of interpretation. Courts will generally be content to assert that the words of the statute have this or that meaning and will justify this assertion with a short reference to the plain meaning or, less frequently, to the *travaux préparatoires* or the purpose of the statute; (c) a discussion of the facts to be subsumed. Here it is important to distinguish between two intellectual operations related to the facts: a judgement on their material existence, and a judgement about their legal qualification, that is, their charac-

terization as instantiating a text or not.

Concerning the material existence of the facts, a lower court must always state express findings of fact, but is under no obligation to justify that statement and it is well known that the Cour de Cassation cannot review this type of statement. The Conseil d'Etat can review it when deciding on an appeal, but, when rendering a decision by way of cassation, it can only review the validity of the statement in the light of elements already examined by the lower court, and may not consider any new element.

The most delicate problem is that of legal qualification (characterization) of the facts. Generally speaking, legal qualification of facts is considered an element of the legality of a decision. Therefore a court must necessarily state that a given fact possesses a certain legal character regulated by the statute. But it sometimes happens, for some courts and some types of cases, that judges are bound by qualifications given by other authorities. This is the case for example in two types of situations: if the legal qualification depends on a technical qualification or if a judgement is one of suitability instead of mere validity.

In those cases, one ought to distinguish between jurisdictional orders. Judiciary courts decide on the complete legal qualification of facts in cases subject to review by the Cour de Cassation and they must therefore justify the qualification of facts. Administrative courts are in a different position: technical qualifications are given by special tribunals, for example medical disciplinary tribunals, whose decisions can be brought before the Conseil d'Etat, but this can be done only in the form of a recourse in cassation and not of an appeal, the consequence being that the Conseil d'Etat cannot review the qualification. In those cases, therefore, qualification by the lower and special tribunal is supported by few if any justificatory arguments.

When qualification seems to possess the character of a judgement of suitability, administrative courts do not exercise any control of the qualification of facts given by executive agencies but only check the material existence of the facts and the external validity of the administrative decision. In that case again, justification is reduced to a minimum.

On the whole, it is only when the court is competent to pronounce on the legal qualification proper of the facts, and when its decision on this ground is subject to review, which is not always the case, that it is under an obligation to justify the legal qualification. Even then, justification will always be concise.

Last, with respect to the case of the supreme courts, Conseil d'Etat and Cour de Cassation, whenever they have to pronounce either on the material existence or on the legal qualification of the facts, they justify their decision on that point with the greatest conciseness. One famous and typical case is that of a statute allowing administration officials to refuse a building permit if a project should alter a 'monumental perspective'. The Conseil d'État was content to state that 'the place Beauvau cannot be regarded as a monumental perspective' (C.E. 4.04.1914, Gomel, Rec. p. 122).

3   It follows from this description that interpretation of statutes can be given by French courts in two distinct ways: (a) by determining the meaning of the statute *in abstracto*, or (b) by determining *in concreto* the facts that can be subsumed under the statute (qualification). For example, in the Gomel case, the Conseil d'Etat had a choice between two attitudes: interpret the words 'perspective monumentale' in the statute or decide that this or that perspective is 'monumentale'. The former allows the court to lay down a rule, not only for the particular case, but also for a whole class of future cases. The latter is often considered more convenient, because it does not require a complex intellectual construction and leaves a wide discretion for the future. This attitude has been labelled 'legal existentialism', and it leaves to the scholars the task of discovering the meaning of statutes through the motives of court decisions. The conciseness of court decisions makes this task difficult and scholars too often have to satisfy themselves with the making of lists of facts or types of facts that might fall under such and such legislative provisions.

4   It should be added that purely substantive reasons, if they play an important part, are not, and may not be, mentioned as such in the opinion, since that would be considered beyond the judicial function defined as the application of the law and more precisely the application of statutes.

5   Other characteristics of French decisions make the task of scholars more complex. There are no dissenting (or concurring) opinions, and decisions are not signed. Published court decisions are only a small proportion of the total. In the case of the Cour de Cassation or the Conseil d'Etat, those decisions that are considered of at least some legal interest (by the court itself) are printed in an official publication. But in the case of lower courts there is no official publication. Decisions are delivered to the parties and to no one else. Only a few are printed in Law Journals (E. Serverin, 1985).

6   These characteristics of opinions can be partly explained by the social function of the opinion in the French system. A distinction should be made between the function of an opinion by the lower court and that of an opinion by a supreme court. The former is of

course supposed to justify the decision, but also to allow thesupreme court to exercise what has been called its 'disciplinary' power over the lower courts. The latter seems to be at the same time a statement and a justification of a new rule.

7   One element of change ought to be noted. Probably under the influence of foreign decisions in constitutional matters, recent opinions by the Conseil Constitutionnel have a far greater length than was formerly the usual case.

X   INFLUENCE OF THE SUBSTANTIVE LAW FIELD

1   The substantive legal field of a statute has some bearing on its interpretation by the courts. To a large extent this can be explained by the principle that defence of individual rights and liberties possesses eminent value. Among other things, this implies a differentiation concerning the admissibility of analogical arguments in different fields of law. This is particularly so for *criminal law as opposed to civil law*. Art. 4 of the 1810 criminal code provides that 'no misdemeanour, no felony, can be punished by sanctions that have not been stipulated by the law before it was committed'. This principle is a restatement in statutory form, of Article 8 of the Declaration of Human Rights: 'No one can be punished save on the ground of a statute established and promulgated prior to the crime.' Binding on the law-maker, this principle is *a fortiori* binding on the interpreter. Not only does it oblige the judge to abstain from applying to the offence criminal provisions adopted before it was committed, but also it forbids him to extend these provisions by way of analogy beyond the cases for which they were explicitly adopted.

Thus such principles, inspired by the respect for fundamental liberties of the individual, involve a restrictive interpretation of statutes providing sanctions. *Criminal law*, as opposed to civil law, must be treated as a closed system or, as scholars put it, as a system of strict law; courts are not permitted to inflict a sanction on the basis of an analogy with similar behaviour actually punished by the law-maker. This is why judges must state precisely the reasons for their decisions — so there can be review of the application of the statute to the facts of the case (Cass. Crim. 13.01.1970, Bull. crim. n° 18). In the absence of an explicit provision, judges are under the obligation to deduce, *a contrario*, the most liberal consequences for the individual. On this matter, the principle that the law permits everything that it does not explicitly forbid has priority over all other principles.

Yet two ideas lead us to soften the opposition between interpretation of *criminal law* and interpretation of *civil law*. First, in criminal law, as well as in other branches, courts sometimes give emphasis to the intention of the law-maker or the spirit of the law over the literal meaning, and it happens that they extend certain criminal provisions to technically and economically new situations, by mentioning the spirit of the law and pretending thus not to use reasoning by analogy (P. Escande, 1980). Second, the judge's duty to interpret criminal law restrictively is imperfectly applicable in the case of what are sometimes called 'elastic' definitions of offences. It is probably in relation to economic crimes that one could find the most significant examples. This is why some scholars, drawing a distinction between 'analogia iuris' (the rule is deduced from the spirit of the legal system as a whole) and 'analogia legis' (the applicable rule is that which is applicable to a similar case), write that, while 'analogia iuris' remains forbidden, 'analogia legis' is frequently used although that expression is never mentioned. There are many examples, especially when it seems necessary to punish new crimes made possible through technological innovations (Robert, 1988).

Criminal law is not the only field for which the substantive subject matter of the statute affects some aspect of interpretational method. Perelman (1968) has underlined that an opposition similar to the one we have just mentioned between criminal and civil law can also be found between tax and commercial law: 'In so far as a constitutional provision stipulates that only a statute can establish a tax . . . the judge cannot serve as a substitute for the law-maker who has omitted to fix the rate of a tax . . .; he has in such a case to nonsuit the fiscal authority'; while in commercial law, 'if a contract stipulates that interest must be paid for delay, without indicating the rate, the judge has to give in equity the supplementary ruling which allows the filling of the gap in the law between the parties'.

This exclusion of analogical arguments from tax law seems to have the same justification as their exclusion from criminal law: that is, the protection of the individual, in this case the owner, against breach of his rights, by giving him the possibility of taking refuge behind the rules explicitly made by the law-maker. By contrast, there seems to be no possibility of making a distinction according to the nature of the addressees of the statute. There is a general presumption in French law that statutes are general. This presumption results implicitly from Article 4 of the Declaration of the Rights of Man, 'the law is the expression of the general will', which is usually interpreted in the light of Rousseau's 'the will is general in its object as well as in its source'. Therefore every man is the addressee of every statute, no matter how technical. This presumption is also one of the bases for the maxim 'nul n'est censé ignorer la loi' ('no one can be supposed to be ignorant of the law').

3   As we have stressed, the age of a statute has an effect on its interpretation. For older statutes, less importance is given to the law-maker's intention and therefore to such materials as *travaux préparatoires*.

4   When the statute is drafted in general terms, the latitude of the judge in interpreting is naturally very large. The law-giver uses precisely this technique in order to give judges a wide discretion. The civil code is full of examples: 'bonnes mœurs', 'bon père de famille', 'urgence', and so on (S. Rials, 1980).

5   The influence of the quality of the drafting is very difficult to evaluate. First it is hard to state that the drafting is poor or good, because courts do not usually express a value-judgement on the quality of the statute and, if such judgements can be found in the opinion of a judge, they will normally be expressed in order to support the idea that an interpretation is necessary, not that a particular method of interpretation ought to be adopted for the particular statute.

6   Two other features of statutes are taken into account. First, the technical character of the statute is considered. We mentioned previously the fact that, in administrative law, in fields that the judge considers to be of a highly technical character, he will normally rely on experts or on administrative authorities for interpretation of the statute. For example, in a statute limiting the sale of drugs in pharmacies when the use of these drugs can be dangerous, the interpretation of the word 'dangerous' is largely left to the administrative authorities in charge of implementing of the statute (C.E. 28.04.1967, Fédération Nationale des syndicats pharmaceutiques de France, Rec. 180). In such technical matters the judge will engage in interpretation only when he considers that a 'manifest error', perceptible by a lay person, has been committed.

Conversely, the judge will interpret by himself, without recourse to experts or administrative authorities, words and expressions of statutes in fields where he considers that no particular technical skill is required, for example, 'monumental perspective' (C.E. 14.04.1914, Gomel, Rec. 488), 'pornographic publication' (C.E. 5.12.1956, Thibault, Rec. 463).

Second, the courts consider the effects of the statute on individual rights and liberties: there is a general principle that provisions limiting liberties ought to be interpreted restrictively.

XI THE ROLE OF THE COURTS

The general role of the courts in the French system is unquestionably small, compared to what it is in the Common Law tradition, even if it is much larger than in the East European 'socialist' countries. This is mainly owing to the distrust of the 'Parlements' of the ancien régime, judges who exercised true legislative power. The first concern of the Revolution was to limit the role of the courts to a judicial function, understood in the strictest manner. Members of the constitutional assembly repeatedly referred to Montesquieu, who had written that judicial power is null and that the judge is no more than the mouth of the law. In effect, the conception of the judicial function during the French Revolution was that it consisted in expressing syllogisms, the major premiss being the statute, the minor the facts and the conclusion the decision itself. Since the statute is the expression of the general will and the facts are objective, the only role for the judge is to draw an automatic conclusion.

Thus, in the special French conception of the separation of powers, the courts were and still are not considered as a third power and the expression used in most constitutional provisions to designate them is 'judicial authority' rather than 'judicial power'. Indeed, in the traditional debate over the classification of State functions, it was often argued that there is no separate 'judicial function' and that the courts merely participate, following a special procedure, in the execution of the law (meaning the execution of statutes). According to that view there are only two great functions, the legislative and the executive and the latter, which is naturally subordinate, is divided into non-contentious (or administrative) and contentious (or judicial) functions. Therefore the independence of the judiciary only means (relative) independence from the executive and never independence from the legislative branch.

This conception has at least three consequences. First, judges can have no influence whatever on the creation of the law and cannot participate in the formation of statutes. They are therefore prohibited, under severe penalties, from invalidating statutes (loi des 16–24 août 1790, still in force) article 10: 'The courts shall not take any part directly or indirectly in the exercise of the legislative power, nor prevent or suspend the execution of the decrees of the Corps législatif, sanctioned by the King, under the penalty of *forfeiture*.'

Secondly, there is a very strict limitation on the power to interpret statutes. First of all, interpretation was conceived of as the remodelling of the law and the exercise of a legislative power. Interpretation *in abstracto* was therefore strictly prohibited (loi des 16–24 août 1790, article 12): 'They [the courts] will issue no general regulation, but will address the Corps législatif whenever they will think it necessary to interpret a statute or make a new one.' Interpretation was only permitted when it did not appear to be a creation or recreation of the law, thus only *in concreto*. Even then, the process of interpretation was mostly presented not as an interpretation of the statute, but as 'qualification' of the facts of the case. For example, when the Civil Code speaks of 'bonnes mœurs', or 'bon père de famille', the court will normally not ask what these words mean, but whether this or that concrete behaviour can be regarded as that of a 'bon père de famille' or in conformity with 'bonnes mœurs' (Ivainer, 1988).

Third, in a similar way, courts were forbidden at the beginning of the Revolution to interfere in any way with administrative bodies and, naturally, forbidden to review administrative actions (loi des 16–24 août 1790, article 13). It is generally considered that this prohibition also implied a prohibition against deciding cases involving some administrative body. It remains in force to this day. Nevertheless, and paradoxically, it is this prohibition that led to a great development in the powers of administrative courts.

Since the courts were forbidden to decide on administrative cases, these cases had to be brought before the King himself as the head of the administration (loi des 7 et 14 octobre 1790). In order to receive advice on these cases (and also on other matters), Napoleon established the Conseil d'Etat, which acting in the beginning not as a court, but as an administrative body and advisor to the chief of the executive, was in a position to exercise very large powers in reviewing administrative action. It retained and expanded these powers after it became a sovereign court in 1872. Since there was a very small amount of statutory legislation that could be applied in deciding on cases, the Conseil d'Etat and the administrative courts that were created subsequently were left to develop administrative law, which is today to a very large extent judge-made law. This development was made possible by the position of the Conseil d'Etat, which is still at the same time a court and an administrative body, and plays an important role in the process of law-making. This role however does not extend to the review of legislation for constitutional validity, and the Conseil d'Etat is under the same prohibition as judicial courts to invalidate statutes.

Nevertheless it must be noted that the Constitution of 1958 established a constitutional council with the capacity to review new statutes. There is presently an amending process aimed at expanding the council's capacity to review old statutes. Under the proposed provisions, litigants before any court, judicial or administrative, will be able to raise issues of unconstitutionality which the court, if it considers them well-founded, will transmit to the constitutional council.

XII STATUTORY PRESCRIPTIONS ON INTERPRETATION

Although the constitution defines what constitutes a statute, there is no constitutional or statutory law that specifically prescribes how statutes are to be interpreted. One finds however, some interpretative statutes, which do not prescribe specific methods of interpretation, but give an interpretation of a specific statute. Since these interpretative statutes aim at correcting some interpretation given by an administrative body or by the courts, they are retroactive. It sometimes happens that the legislator uses this technique to enact a retroactive statute (without doing so openly).

XIII and XIV CONSTITUTIONAL LAW AND INTERPRETATION

Two characteristics of the French legal system must be taken into consideration. They force us to answer globally this question and the next.

1   The distinction between constitutional and non-constitutional principles and values is far from clear, for two reasons. First, the preamble of the present constitution refers to the Declaration of Human Rights and to the preamble of the 1946 constitution. The latter text mentions 'fundamental principles recognized by the laws of the Republic'. By virtue of this, all general principles can be considered constitutional, even when they have been first established by an ordinary statute and when that statute does not explicitly so state. For example, freedom of association was established by a statute of 1901, but the constitutional council has decided that it is one of the fundamental principles recognized by the laws of the Republic. Thus, in spite of the fact that a new statute can ordinarily replace an existing one, an ordinary statute cannot limit freedom of association (16 juillet 1971, Liberté d'association, 44 DC, Rec. 29). Similarly the principle of independence of university professors has been considered by the Conseil Constitutionnel as a 'fundamental principle recognized by the laws of the Republic', although it has never been mentioned as such in any constitutional text or even in a statute, because it can be built up by generalization from several statutes concerning professors (20 janvier 1984,; Libertés universitaires, 165 DC, Rec. 30).

      Second, courts do use principles and values, which can be intellectually related to a constitutional text, such as the Declaration of Human Rights, but courts often do so without referring to the text. For example, the Conseil d'Etat in a decision already quoted (La Fleurette) interpreted a statute as imposing responsibility on the State in the light of a principle of equality of all citizens in respect of public pecuniary burdens. The statute could not have intended to place that burden on one citizen or category of citizens only. Therefore a statute which (a) inflicts a damage on one or a particular category of citizens and (b) which does not expressly exclude public compensation for this category is interpreted to mean that the burden should be carried by the state itself, which led to the general principle of liability of the State because no specific statute so provided.

This principle of equality of all citizens in respect of public pecuniary burdens could have been related by the Conseil d'Etat to the Declaration of Human Rights (Article 13: 'For the keeping of a public force and for public expenditures, a common contribution is indispensable: it must be equally divided among all citizens, with respect to their abilities.' But the Conseil d'Etat did not mention explicitly this provision. This principle therefore is not formally constitutional, yet it is materially so.

In any case, judicial reference to such a provision would not, before 1958, have affected the nature of the principle and its value, because the Declaration was not part of the constitution. Therefore, the parliament could always change or eventually suppress such a principle. It is only since 1958, when the Preamble came to be considered part of the Constitution, that a principle held to be covered by the Preamble has been formally constitutional and thus mandatory for the legislature and courts.

On the whole there are now two sets of principles and values used in statutory interpretation (but also in the control of legal acts): some are formally constitutional, some are not. The former are mandatory for the law-maker. They can be invoked by the Conseil Constitutionnel. The latter can always be derogated by the legislature. We deal here only with the former.

2   Above all, the courts have no power to invalidate statutes as contrary to the constitution. Therefore they are bound by constitutional principles only in so far as they exercise control over sub-statutory acts. But even in that case it may happen that such an act conflicts with some provision of the constitution or some unwritten constitutional principle, yet is in conformity with a statute that is in violation of the constitution. The statute is then considered as a 'screen' between the constitution and the sub-statutory act and the latter is valid.

In the process of interpretation the courts can use constitutional principles in two different ways. They can on the one hand interpret a statute as contrary to some constitutional principle. This implies that the law-maker has intended to derogate the principle. Naturally, since there is no judicial review of legislation, the statute remains valid and the principle does not apply. On the other hand, the court may also adopt the following reasoning: the law-maker cannot have openly disregarded a principle and therefore the statute must be interpreted restrictively in such a way that it does not conflict with the principle. The choice between the two attitudes depends on the importance attached to the principle.

These difficulties can be illustrated by an example drawn from the separation of powers. The general principle of separation of powers can be considered constitutional because it is to be found in the Declaration of the Rights of Man (Article 16). Yet it is used by the courts to forbid judicial courts from judging cases where the administration is involved. The latter principle is generally considered to have been established by the statute of 16–24 August 1790 as a consequence of the principle of separation of powers and the majority of scholars thought that it was therefore itself a constitutional principle. In 1987, the Constitutional Council decided that it does not possess constitutional value and therefore that the law-maker may derogate from it (23.01.1987, Conseil de la Concurrence, 86–224, Rec. 8). Nevertheless it has been used by some courts as a constitutional principle in order to interpret some statutes restrictively. For example, Article 136 of the code of criminal procedure gave judicial courts exclusive jurisdiction to judge liability claims against civil servants for infringement on civil rights. The Tribunal des Conflits has decided that, in spite of the words of the statute, it must be interpreted restrictively because it is an exception to the principle of separation of powers (T.C. 16 novembre 1990, Clément, Rec. 796).

XV THE CHARACTER OF THE HIGHER COURTS

The two sovereign courts, Cour de Cassation and Conseil d'Etat, have some common characteristics, notably that they may not invalidate statutes, may not provide general and abstract interpretations and may not issue positive regulations (*arrêts de règlement*). Otherwise they are different in many important respects: in their function, organization, composition, procedure, and in the substantive rules they apply.

1   All judges, except on labour courts, are civil servants. They are initially recruited by the State according to an administrative process and their status is basically similar to that of other civil servants. Although there are some particularities as far as judges are concerned, the executive still exercises wide discretion in the appointment process to the Cour de Cassation and the Conseil d'Etat. A distinction must be made between the 'judiciary order'

and the 'administrative order'.

In the judiciary order a further distinction is important: between sitting judges and standing judges. Sitting judges at the Cour de Cassation are appointed by the President of the Republic. The role of the President is not merely formal. It is true that the Constitution of 1958 has established a Conseil Supérieur de la Magistrature and that the President can only appoint to the Cour de Cassation judges whose names have been proposed by the Conseil Supérieur de la Magistrature, but the Conseil is presided over by the President himself and its nine members are appointed by him. Once appointed they are independent and cannot be removed. Standing judges are also appointed by the President of the Republic, having been proposed by the Minister of Justice, and without any intervention of the Conseil Supérieur de la Magistrature. The Minister is the superior of these judges. He is kept informed on important cases and can instruct them on how to deal with them (Vincent, Montagnier and Varinard, 1985).

Judges in the Conseil d'Etat are also civil servants, but their previous career and method of appointment is very different. Whereas judges in the Cour de Cassation have received a specific training after law school and have served as judges in lower courts, members of the Conseil d'Etat have received the same very general training as other high civil servants in the Ecole Nationale d'Administration and have generally not been judges on lower administrative courts. Two-thirds of the Conseillers d'Etat are recruited among younger members of the Conseil d'Etat (on the basis of seniority) and one-third are appointed at the wholly unfettered discretion of the Executive among outside persons. *All* judges retire at age 68.

2   In the system of litigation, the two courts have a very different position. The Cour de Cassation is not a superior court of appeal, which is stressed by the fact that a claim is not called an appeal but a 'pourvoi'. The accepted principle, dating back to the French Revolution, is that there are two degrees of courts and that one should only go to the Cour de Cassation when there has been a violation of the law, namely a misinterpretation of a statute. Its role is generally described as that of ensuring a unity in the interpretation of the law.

Therefore the Cour de Cassation does not enjoy the power to decide on the merits and does not judge the facts but only the legal aspects of the case. The court accepts the facts as they have been found by the lower courts and examines whether, on these facts, the law has been applied correctly. If it holds in the negative, it does not judge again, but sends the case back to a lower court of appeal. That the Cour de Cassation is prohibited from reviewing questions of fact contributes to greater abstraction in the interpretation process and is part of the general ideology of the neutrality of the law.

The Conseil d'Etat is, for the larger number of cases, in a different position. It can exercise a review over both the facts and the legal question, and never transfers the case to a lower court, as does the Cour de Cassation.

The two courts are also in a different position regarding the law they apply. The Cour de Cassation applies mostly statutory law that is to a large extent codified. The Conseil d'Etat applies administrative law, which, since there is no code and relatively few statutes, is for the most part judge-made law. A special character of the Conseil d'Etat is relevant here. It is not a court separate and distinct from other parts of the administration, but at the same time a court and an administrative agency. Most members of the Conseil d'Etat have, at one time in their careers, been members of an active branch of the administration or of the brains trust ('cabinet') of a minister, and in that capacity they played a great part in the drafting of statutes that they, as judges, have to interpret. On the other hand, the Conseil d'Etat is divided into several sections: five are administrative sections, the role of which is to advise the executive on bills and proposed regulations; one is a court ('section du contentieux'). The sections are distinct, but members are not specialized and pursue the same career indifferently in all. It is therefore understandable that the interpretation of recent statutes, which have been drafted by members of the Conseil d'Etat, is influenced by this former participation.

3   The highest courts are obliged to hear all appeals. The consequences are very similar to those stressed in the Italian report. The number of appeals is enormous (more than 20 000 a year at the Cour de Cassation, more than 10 000 at the Conseil d'Etat) and is greater than the number of decisions, so that the stock increases every year and the delay between the appeal and the decision can extend to several years.

4   The courts do not rely solely on adversarial arguments in interpretation. The court has the duty to raise an argument not mentioned by the parties if it touches upon 'public order', which includes correct interpretation.

Nevertheless it must be mentioned that there is a special body of attorneys who have a monopoly of making appeals and writing briefs to the Conseil d'Etat and the Cour de Cassation. There are 60 of them and they are among the most competent lawyers in the country, so that, in practice, the courts find in the

briefs most of the arguments that they take into consideration.
5   Although there is nothing similar to the Brandeis Brief, it is
possible, under some conditions, for people who are not parties
to the case to make an intervention in order to protect their
rights and interests. On the other hand, the attorney general at
the Cour de Cassation presents for every case his opinion about
what is the objective legal solution. At the Conseil d'Etat, the
'Commissaire du Gouvernement' has a similar function. In spite
of his title, he does not represent the government, but what is
considered the objective point of view of the law. His opinions
are very often followed by the courts and are used by scholars to
supplement the conciseness of the courts' justification.

XVI   LEGISLATIVE STRUCTURES AND PROCEDURES

The following only concerns the most recent period (since 1958).
France has lived under a great number of different constitutions (17
since the Revolution) with very different structures and procedures, so
that the statutes now in force have been adapted in various ways.

The French parliament is bicameral. Bills can be introduced either by
members of parliament or by the executive. In practice 90 per cent of all
enacted statutes are introduced by the executive. They are drafted by
one or several ministers with the help both of experts who are civil
servants in their departments and of members of the minister's brains
trust. The bill is then submitted to the Conseil d'Etat. It seems that
recently the executive has been seeking an informal opinion of
members of the Conseil Constitutionnel to make sure that the statute
will not be ultimately declared unconstitutional. After the drafting, the
proposed bill is adopted by the Council of Ministers, sent to one of the
houses of parliament and examined by a committee, before being
debated by the house. Members have the power to introduce amendments. Once the house has adopted the bill, it is sent to the other house.
In case of a disagreement, the cabinet has the power to give the
National Assembly the last word.

All parliamentary discussions are recorded and, when the statute is
published, they are also published in a manner that allows judges to
follow easily the various stages of the procedure in their search for
travaux préparatoires.

The participation of the executive has important effects on interpretation. First, some of the civil servants who participated in the drafting
can later be judges in the Conseil d'Etat or, in the case of civil servants
in the Ministry of Justice, in the Cour de Cassation. Secondly, the
executive will often give an interpretation of statutes in answers to
questions set forth by members of parliament, and this interpretation,

which is published, may be used by the courts, even though it is not binding. Thirdly, the attorney general in important cases develops an interpretation of the statute corresponding to the intention of the executive.

The legislature has the power to pass an interpretative statute to correct or simply to prevent a judicial misinterpretation. These statutes are retrospective to the date when the interpreted statute was enacted. Sometimes this technique is used to pass a retrospective statute, which the Constitution does not allow, by presenting it as an interpretative statute.

XVII FEATURES OF THE LEGAL CULTURE

Since the Revolution, French legal culture can be characterized as dominantly positivistic, formalistic and statute-centred in the sense that any administrative or judicial decision has not only validity but also political and moral authority if it can be shown that it is based on a statute. The main reason is that statutes are presumed to be the expression of the general will and that it is the sole privilege of elected representatives of the people (and those who take part in the enactment of statutes) to form value-judgements or express policy arguments.

Legal education contributes to this culture. In the nineteenth century, law was taught on the margin of the universities and the law schools were considered more as technical schools than as full scholarly faculties. For example, there was no teaching of jurisprudence. A more advanced form of legal education developed in the 'école nationale de la magistrature' or in the 'école nationale d'administration' (for administrative judges). Most scholarly writings belong to the tradition of legal dogmatics and, to the extent that they follow the same type of reasoning as the courts, without expressing value or policy arguments, their influence can be described as important.

REFERENCES

Batiffol, H. (1972), 'Questions de l'interprétation juridique', in *Archives de Philosophie du Droit*, **XVII**, *L'interprétation dans le droit*, pp. 15–16.
Carbonnier, J. (1979), *Droit civil*, Paris: PUF.
Chapus, R. (1986), *Droit administratif général*, p. 64, Paris: Montchrestien.
Escande, P. (1980), 'Rapport français sur le droit pénal', in *L'interprétation par le juge des règles écrites, Travaux de l'Association Henri Capitant*, p. 267, Paris: Economica.
Gény, F. (1899), *Méthode d'interprétation et sources en droit privé positif*, Paris.
Ivainer, Th. (1988), *L'interprétation des faits en droit*, Paris: LGDJ.
Oppetit, B. (1974), *Les réponses ministérielles aux questions écrites des parlementaires et l'interprétation des lois*, Chron. p. 107 ff, Paris: Dalloz.
Perelman, Ch. (1968), 'Le problème des lacunes en droit', *Travaux du Centre national de Recherches de Logique*, p. 543, Bruxelles: E. Bruylant.
Rials, S. (1980), *Le juge administratif français et la technique du standard*, Paris: LGDJ.

Rieg, A. (1980), 'L'article 5 ds. Jurisclasseur civil, art. 5, Rapport français sur le droit civil', in *L'interprétation par le juge des règles écrites, Travaux de l'Association Henri Capitant*, p. 82, Paris: Economica.

Robert, J.-H. (1988), *Droit pénal géneral*, Paris: PUF.

Serverin, E. (1985), *De la jurisprudence en droit privé; théorie d'une pratique*, Lyon: Presses Universitaires de Lyon.

Touffait, A. and Tunc, A. (1974), 'Pour une motivation plus explicite des décisions de justice, notamment celles de la Cour de Cassation', in *Revue Trimestrielle de Droit Civil*, **LXXII**, p. 487 ff.

Van de Kerchove, M. (ed.) (1978), *Interprétation en droit, sous la direction de Michel van der Kerchove*, p. 13, Bruxelles: Facultés universitaires Saint-Louis.

Vincent, J., Montagnier, G. and Varinard, A. (1985), *La justice et ses institutions*, 2nd edn., Paris: Dalloz.

Weil, A. (19..), *Droit civil*, Paris: Dalloz.

7 Statutory Interpretation in Italy

MASSIMO LA TORRE, *Bologna,*
ENRICO PATTARO, *Bologna,* **AND**
MICHELE TARUFFO, *Pavia**

PRELIMINARY

The Italian system is a unified system of civil law (that is, of codified statutory law). It is based upon a written Constitution, enacted in 1948, that encompasses the fundamental rules and principles of the legal–political system. The Constitution is 'rigid' (that is, it can be changed only through a special parliamentary proceeding). The sources of law are mainly written: there are several codes (civil, criminal, civil procedure, criminal procedure) and a very large number of statutes. Each year many statutes are enacted by parliament. Precedents are used, but they are not a real 'source' of law. Their force is only persuasive.

The judiciary is structured on a national basis, but it is divided into several branches. 'Ordinary courts' are vested with 'ordinary jurisdiction': they are 'civil', 'criminal' or both. There are also several 'special courts'. The most important ones are the 'special administrative courts': their task is to review the legitimacy of administrative provisions and acts.

The organization of higher courts is rather complex:

1   First of all, there is a Consitutional Court. It has 15 members (five are appointed by the President of the Republic; five are elected by the parliament; five are elected by the judiciary) whose term is nine years (the Chairman is elected by the

members of the Court). The main task of this Court is to check the constitutional legitimacy of statutes. If a statute is found to be in contrast with a constitutional rule, it is invalidated by a judgement of the Constitutional Court: this judgement has *erga omnes* effects (binding on whole world) and it is then a form of abrogation of the statute. Only the Constitutional Court is invested with the power of invalidating statutes. The Court decides nearly 200 cases per year. It always delivers a judgement with a justifying opinion. The opinion is approved by the Court before being delivered.

Issues can be submitted to the Court only when they arise in the course of a judicial proceeding, and only when the judge of the case finds that the issue is relevant in order to decide the case and that it is not clearly lacking in a legal basis. The Constitutional Court is placed outside the ordinary judiciary; it has an autonomous role in the system.

2   The Corte di Cassazione is the Supreme Court in the ordinary judicial system. It is placed at the top of the hierarchy of ordinary courts. Its members are now about 500. They are appointed by the Consiglio Superiore della Magistratura (a special body that deals with the organization and functioning of the judiciary) on the basis of bureaucratic conditions (age, or career inside the judiciary).

The Corte di Cassazione is now divided into five civil chambers and six criminal chambers. Each chamber may have several panels, composed according to internal regulations.

In civil matters, the Court decides nearly 12 000 cases per year. In criminal matters, the Court decides nearly 43 000 cases per year. In both branches the Court is heavily overloaded: each year the number of cases submitted to the Court is larger than the number of cases that are decided. Thus the time before a case is decided is very long (from three to five years) and it is constantly growing. Each case is decided by a judgement with a written opinion, delivered by a member of the chamber in the name of the Court. As a rule, the task of the Corte di Cassazione is to check and ensure that the substantive and procedural law is correctly applied in the several cases by inferior courts (both of first and appellate degree). It should also ensure that the law is interpreted in a 'uniform' way. The Court does not deal with the facts of the case: it is obliged to take the facts as they were established by the inferior courts. It must only review for correctness in the application of the law to such facts.

The case is submitted to the Court on the basis solely of a party's motion. There is no machinery for selecting cases to be submitted to the Court, nor has it any possibility of choosing the cases it deals with. On the contrary, a constitutional rule (Art. 111, al. 2) states that every judgement by an inferior court can be submitted to the Supreme Court's power of review.

3   The Consiglio di Stato is the top court in the special branch of administrative courts. In its judicial task (it also has consultative functions) it works through three chambers. Its main judicial function is to review in appellate and final degree the legitimacy of administrative acts and provisions. It delivers several thousand judgements per year. Each judgement has a justifying opinion, written by a member of the chamber in the name of the court.

A very difficult problem is to establish whether the Italian procedural system is 'adversarial' or not. On the one side, there are relevant differences between civil and criminal procedure and, especially in civil procedure, between rules and practice. In general, criminal procedure (earlier based on an inquisitorial system) has changed its fundamental character and become adversarial with the new code of criminal procedure (from October 1989). Hitherto the judge and the prosecutor have had the predominent roles; henceforth, defence counsel are to have equal standing with the prosecution, and the judge will be a sort of umpire in an adversarial framework. Civil procedure can be defined as 'mixed'. The court has some powers concerning the direction and management of the proceeding, and also the collection and taking of evidence. Nevertheless the actual functioning of the civil proceeding is largely dependent on parties, in so far as it concerns the content of the case, the submission of evidence, the timing of hearings and many other features such as motions, conciliation, appeals and so on.

I   THE GENERAL ORIGINS OF INTERPRETATIONAL ISSUES

1   Interpretational issues about statutes are to a considerable extent linguistic in nature. In other words, their origin is traceable to such kinds of doubts as the following: syntactic indeterminacy, semantic indeterminacy (open texture, fuzziness, vagueness, borderline cases and so on), use of evaluative rather than descriptive terms.

The language of statutes (statutory language) belongs to legal language. Legal language is the language used by legal agents or agencies such as legislatures (statutory legal language), courts (judicial legal language), legal scholars (doctrinal legal language). Legal language overlaps largely with natural language. Moreover legal language is largely prescriptive in kind, and statutory language in particular is very largely prescriptive in kind. Legal language is also largely normative in kind, and statutory language in particular is very largely normative in kind. Finally legal language frequently overlaps with moral language, and statutory legal language especially so. (See, on these definitions and distinctions, Pattaro, 1987, pp. 13–101.)

In the light of these distinctions one may distinguish linguistic interpretational issues proper to various kinds of languages (legal, natural, prescriptive, normative, moral) involved in the statutory language. One should also distinguish linguistic legal and/or normative and/or moral interpretational issues, on one side, from non-linguistic legal and/or normative and/or moral interpretational issues on the other.

2   Statutory language has and must have in the Western legal–political tradition two important features: abstractness and generality. Abstractness is (has to be) a character of the depiction of fact-situation. Generality is (has to be) a character of the reference to the addressees by the statute. Interpretation is necessary in order to apply abstract statutory depictions to actual, concrete cases as well as in order to apply statutory references to actual individual persons.

The very first linguistic origins of interpretational issues about statutes are then to be recognized in the abstractness and generality of statutory provisions. For instance, the abstract statutory depiction of theft as 'the taking away of other people's movable things' raised interpretational issues on whether electricity (which may well be taken away) is or is not a movable thing as well as on whether a petrol pump (which may also be taken away) is or is not a movable thing. This is an example of an interpretational puzzle arising originally on linguistic grounds, but eventually becoming a legal and perhaps moral issue.

3   An example to be referred to as an interpretational issue based on presumptions or background considerations is that peculiar type of 'axiological' lacuna which arises when a legislator intervenes to discipline with restrictive rules and in general terms a behaviour assumed to be harmful, without

taking account of those cases in which the restriction introduced either totally prevents an activity that there was no
intention to prevent, or causes other unforeseen consequences.

This is frequently the case with law relating to accounting
(especially public accounting), fiscal laws and laws relating
to the building industry. For instance, the duty for public
administration to choose among a number of offers of goods
or services those available at lower prices sometimes obliges
public administration to choose second-class goods or
services, which is against the 'best choice' principle to which
public administration is expected to conform.

4   Many interpretational issues also arise from the internal
structure of a statute. In Italy it is a commonplace that the
legislature has become less and less good at drafting statutes. Inconsistency within the statute, incoherence of the
statute and incompleteness of the statute because of inadequate drafting are frequent and are among the current
origins of interpretational issues.

Two aspects in particular deserve attention. Firstly, it is
common to preface laws with declarations of principle,
which, since they set out the intention of the legislator,
ought, in theory, to facilitate the interpretation of the texts
in question, whereas in practice they are a source of interpretative controversy. This is because they enable jurists to cast
doubt even on individual, clearly-stated provisions.
Secondly, the individual provisions of the law text, instead
of setting forth brief, simple, general and abstract norms, are
as wordy and as detailed as administrative regulations. At
the origins of both these aspects of the Italian statutes, lie,
among others, the following factors: (a) a decline in technical
ability and in the will to make use of technical ability in the
drafting of laws; (b) the fact that law texts are proposed by
coalition governments representing four or five political
parties, which means that the texts produced are almost
always the outcome of compromises (which at times are
only verbal).

As a result, in one and the same law text it is not
uncommon to discover the juxtaposition of conflicting language. Sometimes, moreover, the composite character of
law texts is further aggravated by amendments that the
opposition parties manage to have included, either in agreement with dissenting groups within the parliamentary
majority or as part of a deal whereby the opposition undertakes to eschew obstructionist tactics, thus allowing the bill

a relatively swift passage through parliament.

5   Conflicts of value are often at the origin of interpretational issues. The uniformity of the laws, in terms of their meaning and interpretation, depends on the degree of social and ideological cohesion. We have already referred to the plurality of political orientations that take part in Italy in the drafting of laws. The same plurality of divergent (broadly speaking) political orientations also exists in legal doctrine and in case-law.

The unconscious, conscious or intentional lack of social cohesion and/or of ideological uniformity is reflected both in the wording of the laws and in their interpretation. As far as their wording is concerned, this lack gives rise to ambiguities in the use of language by the legislators, which in itself is a source of interpretative differences. At the level of interpretation, in fact, this lack gives rise to interpretations that differ in accordance with the orientation of the interpreters.

II   GAPS AND THEIR ORIGINS

The distinction between interpretation and gap-filling is well established in legal dogmatics, as follows. In any instance of interpretation it is presupposed that the case to be decided is contemplated by a rule. In any instance of gap-filling it is presupposed that the case to be decided is not contemplated by any rule. The aim of interpretation as an activity (reasoning) is considered to be the establishment of the correct meaning of a rule.

The aim of gap-filling as a reasoning is considered to be the finding either of (i) a rule ('analogia legis') to be used to fill the gap in the case at issue − even if the rule does not apply directly to the case − or, when no rule, not even an indirectly applicable one, has been found, of (ii) a principle ('analogia iuris') to be applied to the case at issue. Interpretation as an activity may lead to the following three possible results.

1   Restrictive interpretation. The legislator said more than it was his intention to say ('plus dixit quam voluit'). The interpreter, via interpretation as an activity, arrives at an interpretation as result, which restricts the prima facie meaning of the rule by reducing it to the original intention of the legislator.

2   Declarative interpretation. The legislator said exactly what it was his intention to say ('idem dixit quam voluit'). The

interpreter arrives at an interpretation which confirms the prima facie meaning of the rule by declaring that it corresponds to the original intention of the legislator.

3   Extensive interpretation. The legislator said less than it was his intention to say ('minus dixit quam voluit'). The interpreter arrives at an interpretation which extends the prima facie meaning of the rule by expanding it to the original intention of the legislator.

When gap-filling occurs, there is a case C', and there is no rule in the legal system directly applicable to C'. This means that there is a gap in the legal system. C', however, is similar in relevant features to a fact situation C depicted by a rule R, which is then directly applicable to any case C. Since C' is similar in relevant features to C, and R is directly applicable to C, R is also indirectly (by analogy) applicable to C'. This is so on the ground that 'ubi eadem ratio ibi eadem juris dispositio', that is, when the reason for a given regulation is the same (because C' and C are similar in relevant features), the same must also be the legal provision to be applied.

In scholarly debate the most important gap-filling issues are (i) the difference between extensive interpretation and gap-filling and (ii) the nature of so-called general principles of law. The latter point is related to the so-called 'analogia iuris'. The former point concerning the difference between extensive interpretation and gap-filling is theoretically very clear.

Extensive interpretation always presupposes that the legal system includes a rule contemplating the case at issue (that is, a rule directly applicable to the said case), while gap-filling presupposes that such a rule does not exist within the legal system. From a practical point of view, however, the matter is not so easy. Judges very rarely declare that they are applying a rule by analogy (indirectly); they prefer to say that they are applying a rule directly even if through an extensive interpretation of the rule in question.

This is so especially when judges are dealing with criminal cases. Since there is in the Italian legal system a legal prohibition on the analogical application of any criminal rule and since there is not a similar prohibition about extensive interpretation of criminal rules, judges dealing with a criminal case never appeal to analogy; on the contrary, they also present those cases where they actually have applied a criminal statute by analogy as cases where they have at the most had recourse to extensive interpretation.

According to Italian law, analogy is prohibited not only with criminal statutes but also with statutes enacted for special purposes ('leggi speciali'). These two prohibitions give rise to a number of interpretational issues among judges and scholars. The problem at stake is mainly whether a given case is regulated by a certain statute (in this hypothesis one applies the quoted second-level criterion *ubi eadem ratio, ibi eadem juris dispositio*) or is not regulated at all (in this hypothesis one applies another second-level criterion, namely *ubicumque lex voluit dixit, ubi tacuit noluit*: whereof the legislator wished something thereof he spoke, when he was silent he did not wish anything). This second criterion is well known as *argumentum a contrario*.

III   THE TYPES OF INTERPRETATIVE ARGUMENT AND THEIR INTERACTION

In the first paragraph of Article 12 of the Preliminary Provisions of the Italian Civil Code (disp. prel. cod. civ.) we find three general interpretative arguments which are fixed by law: (i) a semantic argument (one cannot attribute to the statute any other significance than that manifested by the proper meaning of the words); (ii) a syntactic argument (one has to attribute significance to the statute not only by reference to the proper meaning of the words, but also according to the connection of such words); (iii) a general argument, which is improperly called 'logical' in Italian doctrine (one has to take into account the intention of the law-giver). Article 12 disp. prel. cod. civ. states not only the content of these three general arguments, but also the order in which they are to be used: the interpreter should first use the semantic argument, then the syntactic and finally the genetic (or psychological) – the so-called 'logical' argument.

In addition to these three arguments set by Art. 12 disp. prel. cod. civ., Italian legal doctrine and judicial practical generally acknowledge two other arguments: the systematic, and the historical. The *systematic* argument consists in interpreting the norm according to its place in the code or in the statute and its connection with other parts of the code or of the statute. As outcome of an argument of this kind we get what we could call the contextual meaning of the statute. As far as the interpretation of contracts is concerned, this argument or method of interpretation is imposed by positive law in the Italian Civil Code. In fact, Article 1363 of the Italian Civil Code enjoins that: 'Clauses in contracts are to be interpreted each by means of the others, by attributing to each of them the meaning which ensues from the whole of the contract.' This argument is a very old one in the jurisprudential tradition and is handed down in the Digest: 'incivile est nisi tota lege interpretari' (Dig. I, 14, 'It is contrary to civil law to interpret without reference to the whole statute.').

The *historical* argument is conceived in two main ways in Italian legal doctrine: (a) as the interpretation of the norm on the ground of pre-existing law or of legal tradition (for instance, in Italy many rules of private law are rooted in the ancient Roman law and therefore are more intelligible if considered and examined with reference to that ancient law); (b) as interpretation of the norm on the ground of the historical situation of the law at the moment when that norm was issued. In particular, judges normally look at the preparatory works of the codes (which are extensively published) in order better to understand the purport and the content of the norm which is to be applied (see, for example, Cass. 3266/ 1989).

A last (but not least) method of interpretative argument is, according to some legal theorists, that which takes into account the so-called 'nature of the thing' (*Natur der Sache* in German, *natura della cosa* in Italian). In order to be able to grasp the purport of a rule the interpreter has to consider also the 'nature' of the relationship regulated or of some material elements which are distinctive of such relationship. This consideration can be one of the paths through which the interpreter arrives at what Italian doctrine calls 'historico-progressive interpretation' (interpretazione storico-evolutiva). This is opposed to the so-called 'logical–formal interpretation' (interpretazione logico-formale) and is focused to make the rule fit the social and historical reality (conceived as continually in progress). In 'historical–progressive interpretation' the law is seen not as a formally fixed datum, but as something which is continually moving and changing in correlation with the changes which take place in society.

As for the locution 'literal meaning', this is understood in the Italian legal system not as the literal meaning of words each considered as independent from the other, but on the contrary as the meaning of the word seen in the context in which it is written (cf. Art. 12, first paragraph, Disp. prel. cod. civ; see also, for example, Cass. 5822/1988).

As for the purport of the locution 'intention of the legislature', Italian legal doctrine has singled out several possible meanings. In the first place, the intention of the legislature is understood as the concrete psychological will of the law-giver. Yet to justify some techniques of interpretation such as those of (a) 'historicist' argument, (b) *reductio ad absurdum*, (c) 'teleological' argument, or (d) 'economic' argument, Italian jurists have enlarged the purport of that phrase and considered the intention of the law-giver as *ratio legis*, an objective standpoint to which the law gives expression.

The *'historicist'* argument is that by which one has to attribute to a norm the meaning which was imputed to a former norm on the same matter. The ground for such argument is that the legislator, in law-making, is presumed to aim at preserving the former regulation of a certain matter (hypothesis or, better, presumption of a 'conservative' legislator).

The *reductio ad absurdum* argument is that according to which one has to exclude that meaning of a law which would bring about 'absurd' effects. The ground for such an argument is that the legislator is conceived as not willing any absurdity (presumption of the 'reasonable' or 'rational' law-giver).

According to the *'teleological'* argument, a normative statement is to be given that meaning which corresponds to the intrinsic goal of the rule expressed in the normative statement. This goal has nothing to do with the 'will' of the legislator, that is with his intention meant as a psychological fact. This goal of the law, according to the 'teleological argument', is rather the so-called *ratio legis*. One ground for appealing to this argument is the presumption that the law-giver aimed at giving to the law the intrinsic goal of being useful in any social and historical setting. The outcome of a teleological argument is what we could call 'purposive interpretation'.

According to the *'economic'* argument a normative statement cannot be imputed a sense which is proper to another normative statement, that is with respect to the former, either pre-existing or hierarchical superior or more general. One ground for such argument is the presumption of a 'non-redundant' legislator.

An important source for the interpretation of laws in the Italian legal system is the proceedings of parliament and of the commission of parliament which drafted and discussed the law which is to be interpreted. By means of such proceedings, which are extensively published, one can better understand the intention of the law-giver as psychological and historical fact. As for the arguments from the age or obsolescence of a statute, these mostly take the form of the 'historical–progressive' argument. We may nevertheless distinguish between a 'silent' abrogation and a 'progressive interpretation' of a statute. An important example of 'silent' abrogation in our system is that of the 'corporative law' which, under Fascism, regulated many labour relations. Rules of this 'corporative law' have never been explicitly abrogated, but are nevertheless held as obsolete and therefore are never applied by the courts. This is, for instance, the case of Articles 448 ff of the Italian code of civil procedure.

As Professor Gavazzi remarked some years ago, in the Italian legal literature we seldom find a list of the arguments actually used by lawyers and judges in their argumentation. There are anyway two remarkable exceptions, represented by works by Giorgio

Lazzaro and Giovanni Tarello.

Gavazzi (1972) sees three reasons why we do not find an inventory of arguments in the Italian legal culture: (1) because the topoi or loci, or types of arguments, are much more effective when they are not overtly revealed; (2) because many traditional arguments are now regulated by specific articles of the law; and (3) because a list of arguments based more or less on the authority of the scholar does not meet the needs of a dynamic society.

Tarello (1980, 345 ff) proposes firstly an inventory of arguments consisting of 12 topoi:

1   The *a contrario* argument.
2   The *a simili ad simile* (or analogical) argument.
3   The *a fortiori* argument.
4   The *a completitudine* argument.
5   The *a coherentia* argument.
6   The psychological argument.
7   The historical argument.
8   The apagogic (or *reductio ad absurdum*) argument.
9   The teleological argument.
10   The argument from authority (or *ab exemplo*).
11   The systemic argument.
12   The naturalist argument.

Tarello then adds two other topoi to this inventory:
13   The equity argument.
14   The recourse to general principles of law.

The 'equity' argument is that by which decisions are justified, which avoid consequences seen by the judge, and by the community of which he is a member, as inequitable. The use of this argument is actually possible only if we assume the existence of a set of values largely shared by the members of a given society, which is indeed difficult to find in modern pluralist societies.

The argument from general principles of law is probably the most discussed by legal theorists in the last years, thanks to a new development of law in industrial societies. We experience a growing process of materialization of the law; that is, the law is charged with many tasks which were previously taken on by other social institutions (such as the family) or which were not even perceived as 'tasks' (for example, the protection of natural environment). That means that the law is used less as a formal frame for actions carried on by individuals, and more as an instrument to achieve specific goals. It thus turns out that the discussion about law is increasingly not about 'forms', but about 'goals', 'policies', and so about the 'principles' according to which we prefer certain goals and policies and reject others.

A very crucial question is whether these principles are to be drawn from the valid rules of a system via 'induction' (if there are, for example, ten rules based on a certain principle, then we could affirm by a kind of inductive jump that that principle is a general principle of the system in question) or better via 'deduction' from some principles stated in important laws of the system, so that we could assume that they have the special and higher status of general principles.

To Tarello's inventory we might add another argument, which is very often used and is in a sense preliminary to all the others: the argument from the ordinary use of the language (see Lazzaro, 1981). According to this argument, a rule is to have ascribed to it the meaning which emerges from the linguistic rules of the natural language in which the rule is expressed. The 'literal meaning' of a rule is thus the result of the use of this argument. The 'ordinary language' argument may conflict with the 'conceptualist–systemic' argument, often grounded in technical legal language the meanings of which are sometimes different from those of ordinary language.

IV   TYPES OF GAP-FILLING ARGUMENT

As is well known, one of the most important assumptions of legal positivism is that a state legal order is a complete system; that is, that the state legal order is able to cope with any legally relevant problem arising from social life. Such a definition of legal order as complete is apparently circular. In fact, it presupposes what it tries to demonstrate. According to these theories a matter is legally relevant in so far as it is provided for by a legal rule. If we define a legal order (a system of legal rules) as providing for any legally relevant case, and at the same time we assume that a case is legally relevant when and only when it is the subject matter of a legal rule, we are affirming by definition that the latter is a complete system.

A way to avoid that kind of *petitio principii* has been the assumption of a 'general exclusionary norm'. According to this theory (held by Zitelmann in Germany and Donato Donati in Italy) every norm which regulates a state of affair or a behaviour 'includes' it among those regulated by the law. At the same time every particular norm presupposes a 'general exclusionary norm' which 'excludes' from legal regulation any other state of affairs or behaviour. According to Norberto Bobbio, we have in the Italian legal system an explicit 'general inclusionary norm', that is, Art. 12 Disp. prel. cod. civ., which provides for the way the judge has to decide in cases not expressly regulated by the law.

In any case the Italian legal system does not pretend to be complete. It recognizes expressly that there can be gaps in the law. In this respect, we have to read the second paragraph of Article 12 Disp. prel. cod. civ.: 'If a controversy cannot be decided by means of a determined provision, one has to take into account provisions which regulate similar cases or analogous matters; if the case still remains dubious, one decides according to the general principles of the state legal order'. Italian law therefore recognizes that a case might not be decided by means of a specific rule and consequently acknowledges the possibility of gaps in the law. In fact we have a gap whenever it is impossible to find a specific rule by means of which to decide a specific case.

In order to be able to find a rule for a case which is not provided for by a specific rule, we have – states Art. 12 par. II – to seek help from other legal rules which provide for similar cases or analogous matters. Here we find an important limitation to the use of analogy. The rule from which we take the desired provision must regulate an analogous case, similar to that which we are dealing with. To assess this similarity one has to take into account the *ratio legis*, namely the ratio of the rules from which we try to draw a provision for our unprovided case.

As regards recourse to analogia iuris, that is, to the principles of the legal order, Italian law sets two limitations: (1) there must be no rule which expressly provides for the case we are dealing with; (2) there must be no rule which we could apply to the case in question by way of 'analogia legis'. In so far as 'analogia iuris' means recourse to the principles ruling the legal system as a whole, we could infer a third limitation implicitly set by Art. 12 disp. prel. cod. civ: there must be no principle which directly or by way of analogy could be drawn from a specific rule to solve the case.

V   THE MATERIALS OF INTERPRETATIVE ARGUMENT

The practice of Italian courts is rather uniform in the use of argumentative materials. The main reasons are the high degree of homogeneity in the judiciary shaped by the model of the 'professional judge', the hierarchical organization of the court system and the prevalence of a model of opinion that conforms to the practice of the Supreme Court.

1   The historical knowledge of conditions the statute was intended to remedy may be referred to while interpreting a rule. However the meaning and the force of arguments

founded upon such a knowledge may be very different. When the interpretation deals with a statute recently enacted, these arguments are frequent, because they help in establishing the 'legislator's will' or the 'purposes' of the statute. In such cases, arguments founded upon the knowledge of such conditions should be used.

The case is very different when the statute is 'old', that is when around it there is a body of case-law and dogmatics. In such cases the historical knowledge of conditions the statute was intended to remedy is very seldom used, since establishing the 'original' purposes of the statute is usually not significant. When this argument is used, the aim of the judge is to show that the statute has been superseded by new historical situations.

2   The legislative history of a statute may be used in order to interpret its meaning. This is usual just after the enactment of a new statute, when neither a body of case-law nor a body of opinion by legal scholars exists about it. When the statute is no longer 'new' the use of legislative history decreases accordingly, because the 'systematic' interpretation prevails. When the statute is 'old', its legislative history may be used as a basis for an interpretative argument, but this very seldom happens. This can occur when a court is trying to change its interpretation by going back to the 'original' meaning of the statute.

3   Prior or current interpretations by addressees of the law may be used, in order to take into account the 'practice' in some fields (mainly commerce, contracts, administration). This reference is chiefly used to explain someone's behaviour or to appreciate it in the light of what usually happens. But it is very seldom used just to interpret a statute. By itself, the fact that a statutory rule is interpreted in a certain way by its addressees is not decisive for the interpretation made by courts. 'Other' interpretations are appreciated according to the interpretation given by the court: they can be referred to when they are *secundum legem*, but they are criticized and rejected when they are *praeter* or *contra legem*.

4   The language and purposes of statutes *in pari materia* may be and often actually are, used. There are two main ways to do it: in the case of argument by 'analogia legis', and when a statute in the same field or matter is taken as the basis for a 'systematic' argument. In the latter case, which is very frequent, the main factor is consistency among statutes dealing with the same or similar subjects.

5   Reference is usually made to the text of other laws that are

or can be superseded, modified or affected by the statute being interpreted. This reference should be incorporated in forms of arguments to justify the interpretation of the 'new' statute. But reference to this material may have different features. Sometimes it is used to stress some continuity between old laws and the new one: this may justify a 'conservative' interpretation. This means reducing the impact of the new law and searching for its 'consistency' with the pre-existing body of laws. But the same type of argument may be used also to stress the novelty of the statute being interpreted and to 'distinguish' it from other laws. This argument can justify a 'progressive' interpretation of the statute, increasing its impact on the legal system.

6   The prior legal history of the language and concepts adopted in a statute may be used as an argument for interpretation. Moreover this is the usual means to define the literal and conceptual meaning of a statute.

But some observations are needed concerning the kind of legal history that is taken into account. Usually what is taken into account is the history of language and concepts adopted in prior statutes and their interpretation. It is then the history of rules (in the widest meaning of the word) rather than the history of language and concepts. The statute being interpreted is, so to speak, connected with previous statutes dealing with the same matter; their interpretation is then used as a reference point to interpret the new statute. In most cases this argument is used to stress the continuity of the new statute in connection with prior ones. This gives a 'conservative' interpretation that aims at being consistent with the history of the legal regulation of the matter.

7   Rules of other legal systems are applied when necessary according to the principles of international law. Apart from this, these rules may affect the interpretation of 'internal' statutes when they are invoked as general principles or guarantees: for example, the European Declaration on Human Rights is sometimes referred to in the interpretation of Italian statutes. Reference to foreign legal systems (the 'comparative' argument) is very rare and has only minor importance.

8   Precedents should be used, and actually they are referred to very frequently, though in Italy there is no system of legally binding precedents. Very often they are the main or the only basis for the interpretation of a statute. In most cases, precedents are judgements of the supreme court. Very often

there is not 'one judgement', but a series of judgements about the same subject. Here the problem arises of the nature of the group of precedents that is significant for a case. When there is a consistent or uniform group of precedents, it has a strong influence upon the interpretation of a statute, though the court always has the possibility to 'overrule' precedents, or to 'distinguish' the particular case, or even just not to follow them (giving reasonable arguments for this). In most cases, however, where there is a uniform body of precedent it is followed and it is the main basis for the interpretation of the statute.

Quite often precedents are not consistent or are even conflicting. In such cases, referring to precedents implies a problem of interpretation that needs to be solved by adopting some precedents and rejecting the others, or even by not following any precedents. When a precedent, or a set of precedents, is overruled, or the case is distinguished, the precedent(s) should be quoted and discussed in order to justify the 'new' interpretation. The argument concerning the precedent(s) may be very weighty, since it has to show why the 'old' *ratio decidendi* is rejected in the 'new' case. Such an argument can be very important in justifying the need to seek a different interpretation of the relevant statute.

The 'precedents' are generally used in the form of the so-called 'massime'; that is, very short and abstract statements about the meaning of a statutory rule. These statements are usually framed, from the opinion supporting the judgement, by a special office of the Supreme Court (Ufficio del Massimario).

All this means that the 'precedent' is very seldom the *ratio decidendi* which was actually used to decide a case: it is only a general statement about a rule, taken without any reference to the merits of the concrete case. Sometimes such a statement was no more than an *obiter dictum* in that case.

9   The teleological argument is usually founded upon the purposes of a rule or of a statute. But the reference to the aims of a form of life or of other phenomena may also be used, and often is. Also the 'needs' connected with a standard social situation may be taken into account. The interpretation of a statute is expected to be consistent (or at least not to conflict) with the aims and needs that are supposed to be inherent in the 'nature' of something (human being, family, property, commerce, economy, administration; the same may happen with the 'nature' of legal phenomena or institutions).

10   Reference to law professors' opinion is forbidden by the law (Art. 118 disp. att., code civ. proc.). This traditional rule dates back to eighteenth-century ideas and reforms, when an important problem was to compel courts to judge according to the written law rather than on the basis of doctrinal opinions. It was adopted in nineteenth-century codes, and then in present ones, though its historical reasons are now completely superseded. Of course this does not mean that doctrinal ideas cannot be referred to; on the contrary, they are frequently used in the interpretation of statutes. The rule means only that authors cannot be quoted by name.

11   Reference to old laws (especially to Roman law) was rather frequent in the last century, but it is now very rare. When this happens it is usually made only *ad abundantiam*, that is, mainly to show the culture of the judge.

12   Courts have the possibility to refer to social, political and economic situations surrounding the facts in issue. Sometimes these situations are very important in relating the interpretation of a statute to the real meaning of the facts in issue, and sometimes they directly affect the meaning of a statutory rule. Nevertheless such situations are very seldom taken into account – sometimes in a labour case (for example, when something happens during a strike, or when an employer's behaviour is a part of an anti-union campaign) – but such cases are rare and they are usually criticized. The overwhelming opinion, and the prevailing practice of the courts, is that extra-legal factors, and situations surrounding the facts in issue, should not be considered. There are very few exceptions to this. The most important is probably the reference that is sometimes made to economic situations, mainly to inflation.

       Besides this, it must be underlined that there is a legal situation in which courts must take into account a wide range of extra-legal factors. This happens when the statutory rule contains a 'standard', that is when it refers expressly to extra-legal criteria. In these cases a reference to social, moral, economic or psychological criteria is necessary to define the meaning of the rule, mainly when it has to be applied to a case.

13   Among materials that may be incorporated into opinions in forms of arguments to justify an interpretation, two elements also deserve mention. The first consists of notions of so-called 'common experience' ('massime d'esperienza'; 'Erfahrungssätze'). These are standards, criteria, knowledge, 'rules' and 'regularities' that the judge is supposed to

know, not as a professional lawyer, but as an average man. These may refer to natural or scientific laws, or to notions concerning several fields (psychology, language, economy, social sciences) or even to mere generalizations drawn from everyday experience concerning, for example, the 'normal' behaviour in given situations, social standards and attitudes, widespread habits and 'common values', and so on. Anyway the basis of such notions is not science: it is only the average experience that the judge is supposed to have as a man living in a given society. These notions may have a twofold role: in the judgement of fact, when they are used as a basis of inferences from a fact to another fact, and in the interpretation of the law, when they are used in order to define the meaning of a rule according to the common experience of language or of life, nature, 'things of the world', human behaviour and society.

The second element consists of scientific knowledge as such. This is different from common experience notions, since the basis is science instead of everyday experience. Scientific data may be used as a basis for interpretative arguments, but this seldom happens, since the judge is not a scientist (though sometimes he is supposed to be something like one, when he plays the role of 'peritus peritorum').

The use of some materials has changed significantly in the history of the practice in Italian courts. Changes in the use of precedents are especially important. Till the end of the last century precedents were not quoted, probably because they were not supposed to be relevant in supporting the judgement. From the end of the century until about 1940 the Supreme Court did refer to its own precedents, but the prevailing way of doing it was very 'general': the Court referred to its own 'case-law' concerning the case in issue, but without quoting specific precedents. A practice of quoting specific precedents has grown up during the period since 1940: this probably derives from changes in the work of the Court (the office that frames the 'massime' was created in 1940) and also from the attitude of giving more importance to case-law in comparison with written law.

Another significant change concerns doctrinal materials prepared by scholars. Such material was very uncommon before the 1950s, but has grown since then, though always in an 'anonymous' form. This probably shows that judges have become more inclined to try to find 'outside' support for their interpretative choices.

VI PRIORITIES AMONG CONFLICTING ARGUMENTS

The Italian constitution imposes on judges a general obligation to justify their decisions. 'All jurisdictional acts,' says Article 111, first paragraph, 'must be justified.' As for the process of judicial interpretation, the Italian Civil Code prescribes — in its preliminary provisions (Disposizioni preliminari) — that the interpreter has firstly to consider the literal meaning of words and then to take into account the actual intention of the law-giver. This intention — as was said above — is seen either as the historical intention of the law-making organs or else as the ratio, the objective 'spirit' of the statute considered.

Italian law regulates not only some general interpretive arguments but also the order in which they are to be used. There are rules of priority for the use of the semantic, the syntactic and the psychological arguments (Art. 12, disp. prel. cod. civ.). The ranking prescribed in this Article, however, is only a criterion of chronological, not a matter of justificatory priority. That is, the judge has the obligation, in interpreting any statute, to consider first its literal meaning, then to proceed to take into account the intention of the law-giver or the *ratio legis* if the literal meaning of the statute is not clear enough (Cass. 2533/1970, Cass. 2000/1972). That does not mean that the literal meaning of the statute overrides its ratio or that in case of conflict between a literal and a psychological (or systematic, or whatever) interpretation of the statute, the former ought to prevail (see Guastini, 1989, p. 85). In a sense it is just the opposite. The judge, whenever not satisfied with a 'logical–formal' interpretation, is allowed to proceed to interpret according to the *ratio legis* criterion (Cass. 6907/1988) and then, whenever still not satisfied, according to other criteria. In any case the argument of *ratio legis* is seen by most judges as subsidiary with regard to the semantic argument (Cass. 4631/1984).

A problem of hierarchy may arise also from a conflict between the two concepts of intention of the law-giver which we have hinted at. We may consider either the actual historical intention of the law-giving organ or the aims or goals or whatever constitutes the *ratio legis*. If we opt for the first horn of the dilemma, we will probably use the *travaux préparatoires* as a source on which to make hypotheses about the historical intention of the legislator. If we choose the second possibility, we will have some systemic or teleological interpretation. Italian judges hold that *travaux préparatoires* should be used with much care, especially when they are used to interpret a law enacted in a social and historical context very far from the present (Cass. pen. 22 April 1980). Recourse to *travaux préparatoires* is considered a subsidiary and not decisive argument

(Corte Cost. 138/1972; Cass. 1955/1975; Cass. 1988/3550). In the Italian legal literature we do not find any reports of a possible scale of hierarchical criteria used to make one argument prevail over another. Nor are Italian judges much aware of the need for hierarchical criteria: they very seldom explicitly affirm a hierarchy of this sort. That might be due to the fact that in Italy the use of arguments is not in itself a justificatory ground for a decision: an argument is always a procedure to find a rule positively stated, which is then the ultimate basis for the decision.

Italian judicature is dominated by a formalist view of the role of the judge. The judge is seen as an organ which merely applies valid laws. That is the reason why the *a contrario* argument is one of the most used. In case of a conflict between a teleological argument and an *a contrario* one, the judge will probably prefer the latter.

We find, nevertheless, a kind of hierarchy among the above-mentioned arguments (see section III), which is due to the character of the different arguments. There are arguments which cannot be used independently without referring at least to another type of argument, and which therefore are hierarchically inferior with respect to those arguments.

Following the late Professor Tarello, among the 15 arguments mentioned above we might single out some which could be defined as 'incomplete' because, in order to lead to a decision, they need be accompanied by other arguments. These 'incomplete' arguments are the following: (1) the analogical argument; (2) the *a fortiori* one; (3) the argument of the 'completeness' of the legal system; and (4) that of 'coherence' of the system. All these four arguments are unable, by themselves alone, to give a substantive answer to the question of the interpretation of a law.

In the case of 'analogia legis' one has, first, to assume what are the relevant features according to which the two cases have to be seen as similar. To do that, of course, the analogical argument is not sufficient: we need other substantive criteria. In the case of the *a fortiori* argument, we have also to determine what are the relevant characters through which we build up the class of cases containing, or contained by, the other. Let us assume we have a law which forbids the use of wines in certain pubs or bars: we could then argue that, on the basis of that law, the use of marijuana also is forbidden in the same pubs or bars. That would be an example of *a minori ad maius* argument (from the lesser to the greater), assuming that marijuana has heavier consequences on the health or on morality than wine. But to apply the *a fortiori* argument in this case, we need the assumption that from the rationale of the law in question the prohibition of marijuana follows, because that rationale is the prohibition of unhealthy drugs, and wine and marijuana both pertain to that class. We can use the *a fortiori* argument in this case, because we have assumed that wine and marijuana pertain to a same wider class, that of drugs. The identification of a class as the relevant class with regard to the rationale of the law is also a matter of substantive criteria of valuation.

As regards the argument of 'completeness', we can conclude that the legal system as a whole offers a regulation also for a case which is not provided for by an apposite rule. It remains then to find, by other arguments, the rule which is applicable to this particular case. We could say that the argument of completeness is the basis on the one hand of a later use of an analogical argument, and then of a substantive argument, and on the other of *a contrario* argument.

Finally, as regards the *a coherentia* argument (argument from coherence) which is preceded by the assessment of an antinomy of at least two different rules, we need an argument by virtue of which to assess that antinomy. The coherence argument will serve then as a criterion of choice between competing substantive argument by making that argument prevail which does not give rise to an antinomy.

Among the various 'complete' or 'substantive' arguments, we can single out three main categories. (1) 'Legalist' arguments, which are connected with the assumption of statute as the main, or exclusive, source of law. These are the following five arguments: the *a contrario*, the psychological, the historical, the economic and the systematic. They are based on the idea that law is a value in itself, to be pursued as such. We might say that these five arguments are founded on a concept of rationality as correspondence to a certain formal standard. (2) The apagogic and the teleological are 'utilitarian' arguments founded on utilitarian considerations about the consequences of interpretive solutions. In a state ruled by the principle of legality, the utilitarian argument, whenever it conflicts with a legalist one, must fail. (3) We have then what could be labelled as ideological arguments, thus stressing their direct connection with a body of substantive values and policies: the 'naturalist' argument, the 'equity' one, and that of general principles of law. These three arguments are in a sense extra-legal, in so far as they make reference to standards which are not formally and explicitly stated by laws. In systems with a very developed process of materialization of the law, they can even be the highest in the hierarchy of arguments.

Outside our classification remains the 'authoritative' argument. This has been very important in ancient and pre-modern legal systems, but has lost much of its relevance since the law has been conceived in terms of statutes, that is, of formally enacted prescriptions issued by special law-giving agencies. The *opinio doctorum* (opinion of scholars) has therefore yielded the great influence it had in past times to the statute as a formal and authoritative document. The modern development of a non-authoritarian theory of knowledge has rendered the *ab exemplo* argument obsolete and a trifle suspicious also in the eyes of jurists, for whom authority is still a sacred word.

As far as the impact of arguments on the taking of the decision is concerned, the Italian system differs strikingly from the British system and from that of the USA. Common law systems have not codified, or otherwise legalized by a statute, the canons of interpretation. That means that these canons are presented and used as mere arguments and not as positive rules.

The question of priority among arguments is not even perceived by Continental and especially Italian lawyers and judges. In a codified legal order there is not much room left for arguments which are not embodied in some formal rule or statute, whereas in a common law order reference to precedent needs to be controlled in order not to be entropic or disruptive for the system. In short, whereas Continental systems maintain a control on the judicial decision according to the criterion of its strict correspondence to an enacted and binding legal norm, this control in common law systems is obtained through the criterion of rational argumentation. The latter, of course, requires a more detailed inventory or list of arguments accepted as rational, and criteria of priority among arguments which on the contrary are not needed in civil law countries. The major relevance of legal reasoning in a common law system explains also why it is precisely in those countries that we have a more developed debate on legal reasoning and rationality of legal argumentation.

VII   THE CONFLICT OF STATUTES WITH OTHER LEGAL NORMS

Rules of priority are established for the case of so-called antinomies, that is for the case where two different irreconcilable rules regulate the same matter. A first criterion, not explicitly stated by positive law but implicitly in the assumption of the supremacy of state rules over any others, is that of the membership of the rule in the legal system.

A second criterion is stated in Art. 134, 136, 117 Cost., Art. 4 and 8 disp. prel. cod. civ., Art. 1322, 1323 cod. civ., and Art. 360 cod. proc. civ. In the Italian system we find three main types of laws (statutes): (1) constitutional, (2) ordinary (state) and (3) regional laws. Constitutional laws prevail over ordinary ones (Art. 134, 136 Cost.), and ordinary laws prevail over regional ones (Art. 117 Cost.). Article 4 disp. prel. cod. civ. prescribes that a 'regolamento' (a regulation issued by the Administration) cannot contain rules contrary to those enacted in a statute, that is, a law issued by the parliament. And Art. 8 disp. prel. cod. civ. prescribes that a 'regolamento' prevails over customary rules (*usi*), in the sense that customary rules are binding only in so far as they are enshrined in a statute or in a regulation.

Article 1322 first paragraph and Article 1323 read as follows: (i) 'the parties may freely determine the contents of a contract inside the limits established by statutes'; (ii) 'All contracts, although not of any type especially regulated, are subordinated to the general norms provided for in this section.' The two rules imply that in case of incompatibility between a contract and a statute the latter must prevail. Article 360 cod. proc. civ. (the Italian code of civil procedural law) establishes that one of the reasons for the appeal to the Corte di Cassazione against a judicial decision is the violation or the incorrect application of a statute. This of course implies that statutes are ascribed a higher hierarchical status than judicial decision. We must also remember Article 113 cod. proc. civ., a very important rule which, in a sense, reproduces Article 4 of Code Napolù: 'In deciding about a case the judge must follow the norms of law unless he is given the power of deciding by equity.' Thus Art. 113 cod. proc. civ. establishes the rule that the judge is subordinated (thus) to the law. This rule is also in the Constitution, Art. 101, II paragraph: 'Judges are subject only to the law.' The above-mentioned second criterion for solving antinomies between norms is shortly but efficaciously expressed by the latin maxim 'lex superior derogat inferiori' (a rule hierarchically higher prevails over the rule which is hierarchically lower). A third criterion is that according to which 'lex posterior derogat priori' (that is a chronologically later rule prevails over a chronologically earlier rule). This criterion is established in Art. 15 disp. prel. cod. civ., the content of which is the following: 'Statutes are not abrogated save by means of later statutes, whether by an explicit declaration of the law-giver or by incompatibility between a later provision and an earlier one or because the later statute regulates the whole matter already regulated by the earlier one.'

A fourth criterion thought to solve antinomies between norms is the so-called 'speciality' criterion (specialità). According to this a special provision prevails over the general provision. This criterion is positively stated by Italian law in Article 15 of Italy's Penal Code. This prescribes as follows: 'Whenever several penal laws or several provisions of the same law regulate the same matter, the law or the provision of the law which is special derogates from the law or the provision of the law which is general, unless the law provides otherwise.' Among these four criteria, Italian jurists agree on considering the 'hierarchical criterion' 'stronger' than those of 'speciality' and 'time', and the criterion of 'speciality' 'stronger' than :hat of 'time'.

Italian legal doctrine has singled out at least two other forms or expressions of hierarchy between norms. On the one hand, we have the so-called 'structural' hierarchy, according to which norms on the interpretation, the application or the spatio-temporal scope of ordinary statutes or statutory provisions are said to prevail over the latter. We also have the so-called 'competence' hierarchy, according to which norms which enjoin the use of ordinary legislation, or prescribe criteria of substance for the content of a future norm, prevail over the norm whose enactment or substance is enjoined or prescribed. These two forms of hierarchy perhaps stem from a general presumption according to which a metanorm is given a higher status than the norm it deals with.

VIII   PRESUMPTIONS GUIDING INTERPRETATION

In the Italian Constitution and statutes there is no recognition of general presumptions or background considerations that should guide the judge in issues of interpretation. Nevertheless legal doctrine, by singling out some types of arguments which should guide interpretation, justifies these through some presumptions. As we have seen, these presumptions are particularly relevant as far as the interpretation of the intention of the legislator is concerned. We have considered the so-called presumptions of a conservative, a reasonable and a non-redundant legislator. By adopting one or another of these presumptions we may issue divergent interpretations and decisions of a case. Consider, for example, the contrast between the presumption of a conservative legislator and that according to which the law-giver aimed at attributing to the law the intrinsic goal of being useful in every historical situation. The adoption of one or other of these two presumptions is relevant in case of analogical interpretation, when we have to decide whether a law does or does not provide for a specific case. If we adopt the presumption of a conservative legislator, the statute considered will then cover a much less wide number of cases than will be the case if we adopt the presumption of a legislator who gives the law the purpose of being useful for as long a time as possible.

Background considerations are admitted so long as they take the form of a legal principle. We have at least two kinds of principles of law which are taken into account by Italian lawyers and judges: (1) the principles of the state legal order, inferable from a number of statutes or from the structure of legal statutes, and (2) the principles proclaimed in the Constitution. Nevertheless the legalistic tradition dominant in the ideology of lawyers and judges forbids justifying the legal decision on the ground of principles that are not enshrined in the Constitution and/or in statutes and that are not inferable (somehow) from the positive laws (Constitution included). Whenever referring to general principles such as those of equality, freedom, rule of law and so on, the Italian judges commonly cite specific articles of the Republican Constitution where those principles are expressly formulated. As regards the less general principles of law, as for example the principle of impersonality of administrative agencies, or that of *favor fisci* (favouring the public purse), they are often enshrined in a statute or in the Constitution as well. For instance, the principle of the impartiality of state administration can be deduced from Art. 97 Cost. I paragraph: 'State agencies are organized, according to legal provisions, so that the good order and the impartiality of the administration be assured.' When principles are not expressly formulated by a rule or are not inferable from a number of laws or from their structure, they are often deduced from the maxims which are held to govern the relevant legal field or subject matter.

IX   THE STYLE OF STATUTORY INTERPRETATION

The general style of written opinions in Italian courts has several features that can be sketched as follows: (1) prevalence of legal justification over fact justification; (2) length, often much beyond what is really necessary; (3) prevalence of some sort of logical (if not strictly deductive) mode of argument; (4) overwhelming use of legal language (or jargon); (5) little, if any, use of extra-legal arguments; (6) lack of explicit justification of value-judgements; (7) tendency to show that the final decision is the only one legally and logically possible in the given case; (8) tendency to present the judgement as an impersonal *Staatsakt*, rather than as a decision of a particular judge or court.

Nevertheless some distinctions need to be made inside this general style, according to the level and the role of courts. (a) In courts of first and second instance, there is more attention to the facts. This is especially true in first instance courts, where sometimes the factual judgement is the most important one, and the judgement on the law is less relevant (for example, because, once the facts are established, applying the law is easy or clear).

(b) The situation is different in the Supreme Court (the Corte di Cassazione), because it has no power to judge facts, and it can only review the decisions of the lower courts in respect of their legality (as distinct from factual soundness). The Supreme Court's judgements are then only judgements about the law. Therefore they embody at the maximum level the general style sketched above.

(c) To some extent, differences can be found in judgements delivered by the Constitutional Court (which judges only about the constitutional legitimacy of ordinary statutes). These judgements are shorter and sometimes they make room for value-judgements connected with the interpretation of constitutional rules and principles. The Constitutional Court never deals with the facts of a particular case; its role is to interpret the statute and to check if it is consistent with constitutional rules. So the core of the judgements is interpreting these rules, and this is the place in which value-judgements are made and sometimes justified in the Court's opinions.

(d) The style of opinions delivered by the Corte di Cassazione has changed significantly over time. In the nineteenth century Italian practice followed the French model: opinions were simple and strongly structured according to a deductive framework. Few arguments, very briefly developed, were deemed enough to justify the interpretation of the law; the statute was often simply quoted. Towards the end of the century and in the first half of the twentieth century the style changed a little under the influence of the German model. The tendency to respond to the parties' arguments came increasingly into use. The style was still neutral and detached, but the opinion became more complex and less clear.

An important change seemed to occur in the 1950s. The opinion now follows the model of a doctrinal paper; it is longer and it uses a complex and difficult legal language. There is often more than one argument on the same point; there are many *obiter dicta*; it is more and more difficult to understand the real *ratio decidendi*. Also the use of precedents and of doctrinal theories becomes wider. The opinion is therefore much longer and more complex; its style is conceptualist, neutral and difficult; the mode is technical and bureaucratic.

The Italian legal system contains several rules concerning opinions and their content: First of all, Art. 111 al. 1 of the Constitution states a general principle of guarantee, according to which every judgement must be justified by an opinion. According to code rules, the minimum content of the opinion is a 'brief statement of the factual and legal reasons of the decision' (see, for example, Art. 132 n. 4 code civ. proc., and Art. 474 n. 4 code crim. proc.).

This means 'stating the relevant facts of the case' and 'the legal reasons' for the judgement (see Art. 118 disp. att., code civ. proc.). It is also stated that the judgement is not valid when the opinion is 'lacking, not sufficient or contradictory' (Art. 360 n. 5 code civ. proc.; Art. 475 n. 3 code crim. proc.). In such cases the review of the opinion is made by the Supreme Court, on motion by the aggrieved party.

The interpretation of these rules raises several problems. The courts, and specially the Supreme Court, give them a restrictive meaning. They think, for example, that the opinion is contradictory only when the main arguments are in such an opposition that they destroy each other, but other forms of inconsistency are not taken into account. Therefore the actual criterion applied by the courts is that the opinion is sufficient when in some way one can understand whatever are the main points of the judgements.

The prevailing orientation of legal doctrine, based chiefly upon the constitutional guarantee stated in Art. 111 al. 1, is rather different, and the minimum opinion is defined in wider terms. It encompasses: (a) a reasoned justification of the judgement of fact, on the basis of proofs and their evaluation; (b) a reasoned justification on the interpretation of the rule of law governing the case; (c) the statement and a reasoned justification of the value-judgements underlying the decision about facts and law; (d) a reasonable consistency in the structure of the opinion as a whole. These points define what a minimum opinion *should be* but they do not describe what such a minimum actually *is* according to the practice of courts.

The judge is obliged by the law to specify the statutes and the 'legal principles' concerning the case (Art. 118 disp. att., code civ. proc.; Art. 474 n. 5 code crim. proc.). Thus courts always set forth the statute in question and define the issue of interpretation, but when the judge thinks that the law is 'clear', no issue of interpretation is defined. Usually opinions include a rather wide elaboration of the courts' reasons for choosing an interpretation of the statutory rule (exceptions are when the law is taken as clear). In most cases the opinion gives more than one argument to justify the interpretative choice: then it tends to be in the form of a 'legs of a chair' mode.

When the justification requires a many-step proceeding, each step is justified with reference to pertinent rules or principles and their interpretation. Some patterns can be identified in the organization of the average opinion. One of them is laid down by law; this concerns the contents of the judgement, which must include: (a) brief description of the proceeding before the court (and also before lower courts); (b) brief summary of the arguments submitted by the lawyers; (c) statement of facts, if any; (d) statement of the rule of law and inherent arguments; (e) final order.

Another pattern provided, perhaps the most important for the style of opinions, depends upon the role played by the judge. Usually this role is of one who responds to a question raised by the parties: the judge refers to the issues raised by parties, and gives answers to them. This is normal in the Supreme Court, since here the merits of the case are defined by specific reasons of appeal submitted by a party. The Court's approach to answering is by discussion of the several issues raised by the appellant (and also by the respondent, if any). The final judgement follows from the answers given to these issues, and then its main pattern is in the form of answers given to the parties' points of appeal.

In the Italian court practice there is a general justificatory style. Its main feature is a structuring of the opinion as a chain of steps organized in a logical–legal order; the aim is to show that the final decision is the only valid outcome of such reasoning. It is something different from a pure deductive or subsumptive mode: there is of course a subsumptive step concerning the connection between the (interpreted) rule and the (established) facts. But this is only a link, though a very important one, in the chain. The other links, and specially those which state reasons for the interpretation of a statutory rule, may have some deductive features (for example, when legal statement is drawn from a more general one) but pure deduction is not the fundamental pattern. The main pattern is the chain of steps, where each step is justified by means of several possible arguments. The general impression given is that the opinion is ordered, structured and going logically from given premises to a necessary conclusion. In such a context, little room is usually given to the weighing model. That model is, however, to be found in use when the law gives the judge a discretionary power to evaluate some circumstances (for example, interests of a party, character of a person, family relationships, value of the case). But this is not properly a weighing of conflicting solutions or conflicting arguments concerning an interpretational issue: it is weighing the relative importance of certain facts.

This overall style does not vary significantly in the Supreme Court's judgements. The only relevant exception is when the Sezioni Unite of the Supreme Court decide a conflict between judgements delivered by the ordinary chambers of the Court. In this case the Court must make a choice between conflicting interpretations of the same statute.

Some variations can be found in the practice of other courts. The most important one concerns the Constitutional Court. Here the merits of the case are normally focused only on a single issue, dealing with the constitutional validity of a statutory rule. Therefore the contents of the judgement are simpler. The opinion is usually very brief, with one or few arguments. The mode is highly technical, but value-judgements are frequent with reference to the interpretation of constitutional principles.

The proportion in which the opinion contains reasons which are moral, economic and so on is usually very small. Legal–technical arguments are clearly overwhelming. This is especially true in the Supreme Court's judgements, where there is no judgement of fact and the decision deals only with issues of law. But even when the interpretation of the law requires value-judgements, the style of the opinion is not openly evaluative. This does not mean, of course, that value-choices are not made, but only that they are not stated in express terms. The underlying structure of the justification is usually very clear. The structural patterns mentioned above are at the surface of the opinion: they are its structure: it is technical because the structure is founded upon legal and logical patterns, and because the opinion is a legal–logical answer to legal problems.

The Italian system is not based upon the legally binding precedent. Nevertheless the Supreme Court's judgements are often taken as *de facto* precedents for like cases. Moreover the Supreme Court's judgements are expected to be a sort of guideline in order to ensure uniformity in the case-law of lower courts as well as of the Supreme Court itself (Art. 65 judiciary law). According to the institutional situation the judgements of the Supreme Court should then work as (persuasive) precedents; therefore they should be written with this aim also. But the reality is quite different. The tremendous number of cases decided by the several chambers of the Court, and the fact that the Court is obliged to decide the same issue several times, have strongly affected the way in which the Court plays its role. This role is less and less one of stating general guidelines for the interpretation of statutory law, and more and more a matter of applying the law in the particular case. Moreover there are many fields or matters in which the Supreme Court's case-law is not fully consistent, or is even flatly conflicting, on the same issue.

: In such a situation attempts to lay down rules for other cases are useless. Nevertheless judgements of the Supreme Court are commonly used as precedents by the Court itself, by lower courts and by lawyers. The reason is that the judgement, though aimed at solving the concrete case, is made abstract when the maxims are drawn from the opinion. For the same reason, when the Supreme Court, other courts and lawyers use a precedent, they do not face the problem of establishing what is binding or not in the former judgement. Usually they do not consider the whole judgement:

they only use the *massime*, which are supposed to express the significant statement of law contained in the former decision. Only in a few cases is the whole judgement taken into account to be used as a precedent, but even in these cases a clear distinction between *ratio* and *obiter dicta* is not made.

In the Italian system dissenting opinions are not allowed. On the contrary, the rule is that decision making proceeds in secret, and that there has to be secrecy about positions taken by the members of the Court (Art. 276 code civ. proc.; Art. 473 code crim. proc.). The Supreme Court strongly adopts the 'one right answer' ideology. In part this depends on the fact that dissenting or concurring opinions are not allowed. But the most important reason is that the judgement is not presented as a choice among several possibilities; on the contrary, the opinion aims at showing that the final decision is the only right conclusion following from a set of given premisses.

The judgement is signed by the judges who delivered it. The Supreme Court's judgements are not published in full; many of them are not published at all. From about two-thirds of them, the *massime* are drawn out by the special office of the Supreme Court; the *massime* are published. Still, a significant number of judgements are published, sometimes in full but usually choosing the relevant parts of the opinion, by law journals. Often there are notes written by legal scholars. The Supreme Court's judgements are generally accessible: copies can be obtained by anybody from the office of the clerk of the Court. All the judgements of the Constitutional Court are published, in full, in the State Official Journal.

The main addressees of the opinion are the parties. But the style, the language and the structure of the opinion show clearly that judges speak to the lawyers rather than to the parties. They do not explain the substantial rightness of the judgement; they justify its legal correctness in the light of the issues raised by the lawyers, and by means of arguments that the lawyers only can appreciate. The audience presupposed by the reasoning process is, then, the class of professional lawyers. In any case this is the only class of people who have the technical knowledge needed to read and understand opinions. The main reason is that judges are professional lawyers and that they speak to other professional lawyers.

Courts do not speak to the legislature. Only occasionally does an opinion set forth observations about the opportunity to change a statute or to introduce new rules. This is mainly a way in which the judge apologizes for applying a statute that in his opinion is not fit for the case, rather than a question put to the law-giver. Some interesting exceptions can be found in the opinions of the Constitutional Court: sometimes it invalidates a statute and asks the legislature to make a new one; sometimes it saves a statute, but while suggesting that it needs to be changed, or even the Court says that the norm will be invalidated in the future if it is not changed.

The agreed general functions of the opinion are mainly the following: to justify the decision in the eyes of the parties (that is, of their lawyers); to show that the law has been applied when an appeal is admitted against the judgement, to help the aggrieved party to shape the appeal, and the appellate court to decide about it; to legitimize the role played by the court (opinion as auto-apology of the court); according to the prevailing legal doctrine, the opinion should set forth good rational reasons and arguments as a basis of the decision (but this function is very poorly implemented in current judicial practice); according to the prevailing interpretation of Art. 111 al. 1 of the Constitution, the opinion should allow a widespread supervision by the public upon the way in which courts use their power, as a fundamental principle in a democratic system. But this function is also very poorly implemeted.

X INTERPRETATION WITH REGARD TO THE CHARACTER OF THE STATUTE

The character of the statute affects the way courts interpret or fill gaps in it. This does not entail that courts use quite different interpretative methods, or have different attitudes according to the varying statutes they deal with. But this character is surely relevant at least because interpretative problems can be different when statutes are differently framed. A further problem arises concerning the age of the statutes involved.

1   The nature of the substantive law field of the statute can affect its interpretation in several ways. One of them is connected with the admission or exclusion of the argument by analogy: criminal statutes and also criminal rules included in other statutes cannot be analogically interpreted.

Another kind of influence is connected with the level of technicality that is required in some fields. While technicality is a general trend in modern law, it is not uniform. There are fields where the degree of technicality is especially high: one can take as examples tax law, statutes containing media regulations, and several parts of welfare legislation. A high degree of technicality in a statute can affect its interpretation: legal–technical means and arguments are preferred to commonsense ones; interpretational problems are more complex and sophisticated, and specialized knowledge is needed in order to solve them.

Further the substantive field usually affects the kind of statutory rules from the point of view of their being more closed or open to social, ethical or political values. Take, for instance, family law: although the legislature can try to enact precise rules, it almost unavoidably relies upon extra-legal values, such as for instance, children's welfare, family purposes and so on.

Sometimes a substantive field is characterized by special political features. This is the case of Labour Law, and was especially so in the 1960s and 1970s, when a trend existed towards establishing a number of legal guarantees for workers and unions.

2   The nature of the addressees of the statute can, in general, have some influence upon interpretative attitudes. In Italy this is a rather one-sided phenomenon, owing to the fact that almost no statute is actually addressed to the common people. The use of legal language and of technicalities is such that no statute can be considered as addressed to citizens. Even when statutes deal with very general issues, such as health, freedom, the environment and so on, they are not actually addressed to directly involved persons. The very addressees of statutes are professionals and technical people (doctors, civil servants and so on) who are trained either in the particular field or in law.

3   The age of a statute can affect its interpretation in several ways. It can happen, for instance, that a body of case-law is built upon a statute, so that its meaning is rather firmly established. Even openly stated rules can acquire an established meaning as time goes by. For instance, many interpretational problems concerning the statute of 1970 which gave guarantees to trade unions are now clearly solved. But it can also happen that a very old statute needs to be continuously adapted to changing situations which need to be regulated. For instance, some fundamental rules concerning the structure of the state administration in Italy date back to 1865, while many of them date back to the 1920s and 1930s. In the meanwhile the reality of administration has changed profoundly, compelling courts to interpret the old rules in new ways. The normal situation in the case of evident obsolescence of a statute is that it be set aside by tacitly avoiding to apply it. But courts cannot make holes in the legal system: therefore a statute can be set aside only

when the situation is actually changed, or when cases can be decided according to other statutes.

4   It is rather obvious that, when a statute is drafted in broad and general terms, and especially when it includes general clauses, its interpretation is 'free' and 'creative'; on the contrary, when a statute is drafted in specific and detailed terms, there is less room for evaluative interpretation.

In so far as this is true in general, it is so in the Italian legal system too. Therefore the interpretative practice in Italian courts tends to be rather different according to the way in which statutes are drafted. So literal and systematic arguments are typically used when a statute is technical and detailed, while evaluative or substantial arguments are typically used when the statute is broad and general. But looking at the Italian courts' practice one can remark that such a symmetrical relationship is not perfect. In fact, even when the statute should call for an evaluative and substantial interpretation, the prevailing attitude towards formalism and neutral interpretation affects the approach to the statute. Thus, even when the statute is framed in broad terms, formal and systematic arguments are preferred in so far as these are possible.

5   In Italy statutes are often poorly drafted. In most instances this is not owing to the lack of professional legal draftsmanship in the parliament or in the government, or to the intrinsic difficulty of some matter. The main reason is political; that is, the fact that the legislature does not reach a clear position about how to regulate complex or conflicting situations. The consequence is that statutes are often unclear, contradictory, inconsistent and ambiguous. Of course this means that a great deal of interpretative power is transferred to courts, since often the real choices are made by the judiciary rather than by the legislature.

XI   THE ROLE OF THE COURTS

In the Italian system the general role of courts, taken as a whole, is rather strong, though ordinary courts have no power to invalidate statutes (see Preliminary above). The strength of the judicial role derives on the one hand from the enormous number of statutes that must be applied, and from the consequent high number of cases that are submitted to courts. On the other hand, it has derived also in recent years from an ever more prevalent attitude in the legislature, which has led to a widespread tendency not to solve problems through precise and clear-cut statutory rules, though a lot of statutes are enacted each year about the most diverse matters. This gives the courts a wider and wider power to shape the rule that actually governs the case.

This situation is characterized as the supplementary role of the judiciary in the place of legislature, or also as an implicit delegation of powers from the legislature to the judiciary. The reasons for the development are mainly political: the legislature is called on to enact regulations concerning many features of social and economic life, but often there is no clear agreement about how to deal with the conflicts of interests involved. Then a statute is enacted, but its rules very often are vague, too general, ambiguous or even inconsistent or contradictory. The consequence is that it is up to courts to supply such rules with more specific meanings.

Only the Constitutional Court is vested with the power to invalidate statutes which are contrary to the Constitution. Ordinary courts of all levels (including the Supreme Court) have only the possibility of raising the issue of the constitutionality of a statute, submitting it to the Constitutional Court. But it is only the courts that have such a power, and only when the issue concerns a statute which is applicable in deciding a concrete case.

Courts usually exercise a rather wide power to expand and/or restrict the meaning of a statute in the name of interpretation. Of course this power is more widely exercised when statutes are, as often happens, stated in vague or general terms. Courts also exercise a rather wide power to fill gaps in statutes. They cannot formally revise a statute, but they are able to update them, by means of the so-called evolutionary interpretation. Theoretically courts are not allowed to make new law; at least, they cannot make wholly new law. Separation of powers forbids this. But courts actually make new law, on the basis of written statutes, by shaping, extending or updating the meaning of statutes in the name of interpretation.

A special branch of the judiciary (a special administrative jurisdiction) is vested with the power of reviewing acts issued by administrative agencies or officials. Every administrative act can be controlled, usually on motion of a private person, by these special courts. The review deals with the conformity of the administrative act to the law. It can concern only acts (orders, decrees and so on) formally issued, not the mere activity or general conduct of agencies and officials. The exercise of the discretionary powers vested in the administration by law is not subject to review by administrative courts, except when it produces illegal acts. Administrative law-making (for example, exercise of regulatory powers) is subject to the same control for conformity to the law, by the same special courts.

XII STATUTORY PRESCRIPTIONS ON INTERPRETATION

No constitutional rule prescribes how statutes must be interpreted and gaps filled. Prescriptions on that matter are stated by some rules contained in a group of rules (dealing with 'the application of the law in general') that form a sort of prologue to the civil code. In spite of this placing, these rules are created as very generally applicable: they have to be applied in every field of the legal system. Methods of interpretation and gap-filling are prescribed by Arts 12 and 14 of this prologue. Though these rules do not encompass a complete and systematic method of interpretation, they state general rules that must be applied in the interpretation of the law, and that are the outcome of a very general theory of interpretation (containing also a theory of gap-filling). They have been examined above, in sections III, IV and V.

XIII CONSTITUTIONAL LAW AND INTERPRETATION

It must be underlined that the Italian Constitution is a very wide catalogue of general rules and principles concerning fundamental rights and guarantees, as well as the several branches of the State organization. Such rules and principles often deal with several fields of the legal order, such as criminal law, private law, civil and criminal procedure, judicial review of administrative activity, citizens' fundamental rights, workers' and unions' guarantees and so on.

Since no rule deals with the interpretation of constitutional provisions, in the first years after the enactment of the Constitution a distinction was made, according to which many rules were considered as mere suggestions for the ordinary legislature (and therefore they were not applied by courts), while some rules only were considered as addressed to the courts also. This distinction is now almost completely out-of-date; the consequence is that every constitutional rule or principle can be used as a criterion for the interpretation of statutory laws. This does not happen only with rules that embody general principles or values (freedoms, equality, due process, rule of law, separation of power and so on) but also with rules stating more narrow directives concerning particular fields or matters (for example, tort liability of civil servants, workers' rights, private property and so on). Therefore there are no significant differences among constitutional provisions, from the point of view of their being used by courts as criteria for statutory interpretation.

When a court has to interpret an ordinary statutory rule, the need to take into account some constitutional principle is normal, since the Constitution covers a wide range of fields and matters. When a constitutional rule is relevant to the case in issue, the interpretative problem takes a rather peculiar form: the court can interpret the statute on the basis of the relevant constitutional principle (that is, giving it the meaning that is the most proper in the light of such a principle). If the court is less sensitive to the constitutional values, it can interpret the statute without using constitutional criteria (and sometimes this happens), but such an interpretation should not be in conflict with the Constitution. This sensitivity towards constitutional values is growing more and more: therefore the prevailing tendency is now to use such values as positive criteria rather than as negative limits on statutory interpretation.

When, on the contrary, a court finds that the prevailing or the only possible interpretation of a statute is in conflict with a constitutional rule, the only possibility is to raise the question and submit it to the Constitutional Court.

The difference between very general and more specific constitutional values (if and when it can be seen) is sometimes relevant from a different point of view: it may happen that more general rules are used to interpret less general ones, and the outcome is used as a criterion to interpret a statute. For example, some procedural rules are interpreted according to the due process clause (Art. 24 of the Constitution), but in its turn this clause is interpreted according to the equal treatment principle (Art. 3), which is a yet wider one.

XIV   INTERPRETATION AND PRINCIPLES OF LAW

The justificatory practice of Italian courts does not give evidence of any general or consistent set of basic values, if this means a system of general values connected with each other. Some basic values are sometimes referred to, in the relatively rare cases in which courts use evaluative arguments, but it cannot be said that they represent a set of values. For example, reference is made to equal treatment under the law, to the supremacy of the law, to the public interest, to the individual freedom of citizens, to the presumption of inno-cence, to the protection of workers' rights, to the protection of property, to the consistency of the legal system, to the hierarchy of legal rules, and so on. But such values cannot be considered as parts of a system, since each of them is invoked when this is necessary or useful for justificatory needs in the particular case.

In recent times, however, a set of values has begun to be used with increasing frequency, namely the Constitution, and especially those of its parts that concern the fundamental rights and guarantees of citizens. Constitutional principles are now widely used by ordinary courts also, as interpretative criteria applied to statutes. So, in so far as the Constitution can be considered as a consistent set of basic values, one can say that in the judicial practice there is a trend to use it as a reference system.

XV THE CHARACTER OF THE HIGHER COURTS

While considering the kind of interpretative activity usually carried out by the Italian supreme court (that is, the Corte di Cassazione), several features should be taken into account.

Some of them concern what the Corte di Cassazione is not. This means, on the one hand, that it is not the supreme court for the special administrative branch of the Italian judiciary. The main consequence is that the Corte di Cassazione is not enabled to review the action of administrative agencies and offices. Moreover this means that the court does not deal with the use of administrative discretionary powers, or with rules concerning administrative discretion.

On the other hand, one should remember that the Corte di Cassazione is not a constitutional court. Of course the court interprets and applies constitutional rules and principles whenever it is necessary or useful in order to interpret the statutory rules that are relevant to decide a case. But the court is not vested with the power to check the constitutional legitimacy of ordinary statutes: such a responsibility is exclusively conferred on the Corte Costituzionale. The Corte di Cassazione can refer to constitutional rules and principles as a means to interpret a statute in a specific case, but not in order to state a general evaluation concerning the constitutional legitimacy of a statutory rule.

Other features are directly connected with the institutional character of the Corte di Cassazione, and with the way in which it performs its task.

(a) A relevant feature is that its judges are career civil servants; they reach the court after a long career inside the judiciary in lower courts. The method of selection is thus typically bureaucratic: the time spent inside the judiciary is the main factor in the selection of a Supreme Court judge. Such a judge is thus a well-trained legal professional, whose experience has been gained completely in judicial functions.

(b) From the point of view of the system of litigation, the Corte di Cassazione is the court of last resort in civil and criminal cases. This means that it is the third court (after the trial court and the appellate court) dealing with the case. Unlike supreme courts in other systems, this court is not vested with the power to review the merits of the case. More properly, the courts cannot make judgements about the facts in issue. The role of the supreme court is to review the judgement of law concerning the case. This means mainly to check whether the lower court (usually the appellate court) has correctly interpreted and applied the relevant statute in deciding the case.

With reference to the concrete case under review, the Supreme Court can also (1) check whether procedural rules have been properly applied in the lower instance; if not, the judgement is invalidated and the process must be repeated; and (2) check whether the justification of the judgement stated in the lower court's opinion is sufficient and non-contradictory. This is a kind of check upon the logic of the lower judgement, that is, upon the justificatory force of the opinion.

Another function of the Corte di Cassazione is more general and deals with its role in the legal system, although it is performed on the occasion of the court's judgement in specific cases. Such a function is to ensure that the law is exactly observed (so-called function of protection of the law) and to ensure that the case-law is uniform (so-called function of case-law uniformity).

The actual meaning of both these functions is widely discussed; while the former is inherent in the role of the Supreme Court in controlling the equality of all lower court decisions, the latter is actually not performed since the court is unable even to ensure the uniformity of its own case-law. Nevertheless both can have some influence upon the way in which the court performs its interpretative task: in so far as it is able to take into account such general purposes connected with the interpretation of statutes, they can push the court towards a more abstract and formal interpretative attitude.

(c) A very important feature of the Italian Corte di Cassazione is that any case can be brought to the court, it being enough for a party to complain against the judgement of an appellate court. In other words, the appeal to the Supreme Court is an appeal as of right; no special prerequisite is needed and no selection of cases can be made. This system was traditional in the Italian Supreme Court, but now it is covered by a constitutional rule. Article 111 al. 2 of the constitution provides that every judgement can be appealed in the Supreme Court, and this rule is commonly viewed as quite a general guarantee of the legality of the judicial system.

Therefore, the court has no power at all in choosing or selecting the cases that must be decided. The rule is that every case must be decided on its merits by the court. If one considers, moreover, that the costs of an appeal to the Corte di Cassazione are rather low, one can understand why it is submerged by a flood of cases. All this raises a number of problems that cannot be discussed here, but two features need to be considered. The first one is that the great number of cases puts the court under great pressure to decide: this often means deciding a case at a low level of interpretative work, using formal and standardized interpretations of statutes.

The second feature concerns the kind of cases submitted to the court. Sometimes they are important cases with complex, interesting and doubtful questions concerning the interpretation of a statutory rule. But very often they are routine cases, where there is no real interpretative issue. In such cases the work of the court is routinized and standardized, being only the passive repetition of the same well-known interpretation of the statute.

(d) As a rule, the Supreme Court – as every Italian court – is sovereign and independent in establishing the correct interpretation of statutes. The general principle 'jura novit curia' (the court has full knowledge of the law) deals, of course, also with the knowledge and the choice of the right interpretation.

Moreover the judges of the supreme court make use of services aimed at giving them all the support they need in order to have 'knowledge' of the law. They can have, for instance, a bibliography or other materials concerning legal sources and authorities. Especially important is the *Ufficio del Massimario*, which supplies the judges with collections of statements drawn from the relevant precedents of the court itself. This relieves the court of the necessity to rely upon the parties' arguments and materials, in order to find the correct interpretation of a statute. Of course such arguments and materials can turn out to be useful as information concerning the interpretative issues; they can even be relevant in order to frame the issue which the court is expected to decide. Nevertheless one cannot properly say that the court relies upon the parties' arguments and materials in order to interpret the law.

(e) In the practice of the Italian Supreme Court, there is nothing similar to the Brandeis Brief of the American experience, nor is any form of *amicus curiae* intervention allowed. If and when (in a very rare case) the Court believes it needs some extra-legal data the judges themselves acquire them. The general rule is then that only the parties can argue and submit documents and materials, while the Court itself can get all that is needed in order to decide. But note that in the Supreme Court's procedure the Attorney General of the Court (the Procuratore Generale) is a sort of necessary party, for the sake of an impartial protection of the proper application of the law: therefore he is entitled to argue upon any case that is going to be decided by the court.

(f) One last feature of the Corte di Cassazione deserves mention here. It is the possibility that a 'full' panel of the Court (the so-called Sezioni Unite) will be entrusted with the decision of a case. This happens either when the Chief Chairman of the court believes that an especially difficult and complex interpretative issue must be decided, or when an interpretative issue has been decided in different and conflicting ways by the ordinary chambers of the court.

XVI   THE LEGISLATURE: STRUCTURE AND PROCEDURES

In Italy the structure and procedures of the legislature affect the interpretation of statute mainly because they directly affect the product of the legislative work, that is, the way in which statutes are framed.

1   This is, for instance, the case of the structure of the legislature, which is made of two chambers. A statute is enacted only when it has been separately approved by both chambers; if one chamber changes the text of a statute, the other chamber must re-examine it and approve it again. This procedure always takes a lot of time; moreover it often leads to statutory texts that are the outcome of bargains, adjustments and additions accomplished in the coming and going between the two chambers. Such problems have an important consequence concerning the relationship between the legislature and the executive: because of the poor functioning of parliament, a very large number of regulations are issued in the form of 'government decrees'.

2   Political bargaining usually has relevant and bad effects on the way statutes are drafted. This is not a consequence of political bargaining as such, since it is somewhat unavoidable in the legislative work, it is rather a consequence of a situation where political bargaining is a sort of never-ending story. It happens through the coming and going between the two chambers, inside each chamber, and the relationship between legislative and the executive power. It does not work as a means to reach clear political choices. On the

contrary, the outcome is that statutes are ambiguous, inconsistent or even contradictory. In the best case, they are very broadly framed or they try to establish a compromise between conflicting positions.

3   In general the drafting of statutes is in the hands of politicians rather than of professionals. Of course the government makes use of officials who sometimes can be considered as professionals in some fields; professionals in several fields are also to be found among members of parliament; experts can also be heard while a statute is examined. But all this remains in the background, while the political bargaining is the actual procedure for drafting statutes.

4   Exhaustive and complete records of legislative deliberations are kept in both parliamentary chambers, and are ordinarily accessible to the public, and also to courts. But it happens very seldom, if ever, that a court asks for such records in order to discover details of how a deliberation was made. Usually the legislature's purposes are drawn from an official text that justifies the statute (the so-called *Relazione*, that is a sort of introduction to the statute, and is normally written by its proponents) not from records of parliamentary debates. Usually such records are considered as a minor and unimportant source of data possibly concerning the interpretations of a statute.

5   The Italian legislature never acts to correct judicial misinterpretations. Even when misinterpretations are clear and dangerous, and when remedies are possible, one cannot reasonably expect quick and effective parliamentary action. Quite simply, it is impossible because of the workload, the delays and the substantial inefficiency of the legislature.

XVII   FEATURES OF THE LEGAL CULTURE

In general one can say that Italian judges are significantly affected by the prevailing legal culture; although they are a separate and autonomous branch of state bureaucracy, they are nevertheless inside the common legal experience and therefore they necessarily share in the legal culture. But some peculiar features of such influence deserve mention, in order to sketch the Italian situation.

1   If one speaks of the prevailing legal culture in Italy, then it appears to be formal and positivistic rather than substantive and open to value-arguments and policy-arguments. At

least, this is the side of the Italian legal culture that affects the courts. To put it in more specific terms: there are several trends in Italian legal culture that are directly based upon values and policies, in contrast with the traditional positivistic attitudes. They are characterized by anti-formalism, attention paid to consequences in the analysis of the law, sensitivity to social and ethical values, use of sociological methods and so on. These trends are very important in the academic legal culture, where they are the most advanced points of legal research; but they are not prevalent in the legal culture in general, including the culture of lawyers and judges.

Looking specifically at courts, one can observe that first instance courts are more open to value-arguments and substantive arguments, while this attitude decreases as one goes up through the judicial hierarchy. Its minimum is reached in the Supreme Court, where the culture of formalism is overwhelming. This is true not only in more formal fields, such as civil procedure, but also in less formal ones, such as criminal law or labour law.

The reasons for this are clear if one considers the hierarchical and bureaucratic structure of the Italian judiciary. Supreme Court judges are older and far from the facts, their role being only to check if a statute was correctly applied. No wonder, then, if the Supreme Court shares the traditional conservative attitude of Italian legal culture.

2   Something similar can be said for the legal methodology. Academic legal methodology is fragmented, disparate and conflicting, both in general perspectives and at the level of specific interpretational problems. In part this situation also affects the judges, but this does not significantly affect the interpretative practice, especially at the level of the Supreme Court. Some judges can individually share original perspectives of legal methodology, but when they act as Supreme Court judges they are absorbed by the prevailing attitude towards formalistic and positivistic methodology.

3   Judges are influenced by academic writings and legal dogmatics to a rather significant degree, and some features of this influence should be underlined. One feature is that traditional dogmatic writings are taken as ideal models when judges write their opinions for judgements. Thus the academic traditional style influences the judicial style in the way of framing issues and of structuring the justification of the decision.

Another important feature is that the academic legal

culture passes into the judiciary and influences the judges, but usually this takes rather a long time. Judges do not immediately absorb the outcomes of legal science. Therefore there is often a time lag between the level of scientific legal culture and that of the judiciary. Legal dogmatics and academic writings are many-sided, unclear and conflicting: in such cases courts do nothing more than choose what they prefer in the dogmatic emporium. From this point of view one cannot properly speak of an influence of dogmatics and legal writings upon judges; rather they supply judges with a great deal of inconsistent and confused material concerning the issue that must be decided. Rather often judges choose materials expressing old-fashioned and traditional ideas, only because they are in tune with the cultural outlook.

4   As a rule Italian lawyers and judges are generalists, and are expected to be well trained and skilful in every field of the law. Of course this cannot be. On the one hand, there are a large number of generalists among lawyers and judges, but often they are neither well trained nor skilful. On the other hand, a significant level of professional skill requires a certain degree of specialization. The main type is the distinction between civil law and criminal law: many lawyers and judges are specialized in one of the two fields. But this occurs by chance, and this kind of specialization has no formal consequences. So a civilist lawyer can deal with criminal cases, and vice versa, and a judge well trained in civil law can be sent to the criminal section of a court, or vice versa.

At higher levels of the legal profession and of the judiciary, a more advanced specialization can be found. Commercial law, tax law, family law, labour law, administrative law, international law and even narrower fields (for example, bankruptcy, patents, divorce, torts, leasing contracts, bank law) are fields of specialization for lawyers. It is partly the same for judges, although the image of the generalist judge is still prevalent.

In the Supreme Court specialization can have some influence, although only *de facto*. Sometimes parties use lawyers who are specialized in the field to which the case belongs. To a certain extent, the judge's specialization is also taken into account, and often the case is assigned to the chamber (and to the judge who prepares it) according to specialist criteria.

In so far as specialization has a significant influence, this is in the sense of increasing the technical level of the discussion and decision of the case. This probably increases the quality

of the final judgement. From the point of view of the way
interpretative devices are used, this means mainly relying
expecially upon technical arguments, using high-level technical language, giving the interpretative reasoning a more
sophisticated, logical and consistent structure. It is also
obvious that in such cases the main addressee of the judicial
argumentation is the specialized lawyer, rather than the
parties or public opinion at large.

REFERENCES

Gavazzi, Giacomo (1972), 'Topica giuridica', in *Novissimo digesto italiano*, **19**, Turin: U.T.E.T.
Gianformaggio, Letizia (1987), 'Analogia', in *Digesto*, 4th edn., **1**, Turin: U.T.E.T.
Guastini, Riccardo (1986), 'Problemi di analisi logica della motivazione', in *Contratto e impresa*, **2**, pp. 104–28.
Guastini, Riccardo (1989), *Produzione ed applicazione del diritto*, 2nd edn., Turin: Giappicchelli.
Jori, Mario and Pintore, Anna (1988), *Manuale di teoria generale del diritto*, Turin: Giappichelli.
Lazzaro, Giorgio (1981), *Diritto e linguaggio comune. Rivista trimestrale di diritto e procedura civile*, **35**, pp. 140–81.
Pattaro, Enrico (1987), *Introduzione al corso di filosofia del diritto*, **2**, Bologna: Clueb.
Tarello, Giovanni (1980), *L'interpretazione della legge*, Milan: Giuffry.
Taruffo, Michele (1975), *La motivazione della sentenza civile*, Padova: Cedam.

8 Statutory Interpretation in Poland

JERZY WRÓBLEWSKI, *Łódz**

PRELIMINARY

1   The Polish legal system is one of statutory law, rather than common law.

2   The courts are the organs of the administration of justice and have, thus, a special task among the other state institutions. (J. Wróblewski, 1987c). The administration of justice is organized on a two-instance basis matching the territorial administrative units in a unitary state. The competences of the several courts are determined by reference to territorial and substantive criteria. There are four higher courts: the Supreme Court, the Supreme Administrative Court, the Constitutional Tribunal and the Tribunal of State.

    The Supreme Court exercises control over the administration of justice, but in some cases functions also as a second instance court; it also has certain other competences (cf.ch.9(6)). The Supreme Court decides in benches of three judges, seven judges, the whole house, several houses or a whole assembly. The Supreme Administrative Court exercises control over the legality of administrative decisions. The Constitutional Tribunal exercises control over the constitutionality of statutes and sub-statutory acts, and the legality of sub-statutory acts in respect of their consistency and coherence with statutes. The Tribunal of State decides questions of the constitutional responsibility of the highest officials of the state when they are accused by the Sejm, that

*The reference system for judicial decisions cited is explained in a note at the end of the chapter.

is, by the Polish Parliament.

The Supreme Court is the most active of all the highest courts, and deals extensively with interpretational issues. The Supreme Administrative Court deals with a far more limited number of cases. The Constitutional Tribunal has only recently come into action and tries very few cases, about a dozen or so a year. The Tribunal of State has had only one case, and it was discontinued because of the amnesty.

In the following, our discussion of interpretation is based mostly on Supreme Court decisions, but reference will be made sometimes to decisions of the Supreme Administrative Court and the Constitutional Tribunal also.

3   Interpretation by courts is 'operative interpretation' when carried out with a view to deciding cases or answering legal questions posed in cases. (Ferrajoli, 1966; J. Wróblewski, 1959, chs V–VIII; 1983, A.11985 A).

I   THE GENERAL ORIGINS OF INTERPRETATIONAL ISSUES

1   Operative interpretation occurs when there are doubts concerning the meaning of norms relevant to deciding a case. There are two types of situation: Either 'lex clara est' ('the statute is clear' and a situation of isomorphy prevails) or there are some doubts concerning its meaning (a situation of interpretation exists) (J. Wróblewski, 1985a and b, 249 ff; 1987a, 35 ff).

(a) The difference between the two types of situation is determined by characteristics of the legal language in which statutory texts are formulated. Legal language is a fuzzy language, that is, there are cases to which legal texts refer without practical doubt (positive core reference), cases to which they plainly do not refer (negative core reference) and doubtful cases (penumbra) (J. Wróblewski, 1983b; 1985b, pp. 240, 243). The same text in various situations can be either clear or not. This is the most elementary form of fuzziness of legal language.

There are various factors which generate problems of the penumbra. This is so because doubt can be provoked not only by issues of purely linguistic reference, but also by other contextual elements affecting one's understanding of statutory norms. Their meaning is not only contextual in relation to the semantics of legal language, but also depends on the systemic context of statutory norms, that is, the context of the legal system this norm belongs to (section IV below) and on the functional context, that is, the sociocultural facts conditioning the origins and operation of statutory law (section V below).

Taking this into account, it is evident that the question whether 'lex clara est' in a concrete case depends on many factors and inevitably calls for interpretative choices. The concept of clarity is, thus, a pragmatic concept. Whether the text is clear or not depends on its use in a given situation, that is, according to the context in which it is used. This concept is known also in linguistic pragmatics, under the name of 'transparency'. (J. Wróblewski 1988 B, M. Dascal, J. Wróblewski 1988).

(b) To identify the situation of isomorphy expressed in the idea of clarity (*claritas*) therefore demands an evaluation. A choice exists between using the norm in its prima facie meaning and fixing the meaning by an act of interpretation. The prima facie meaning is determined by semantic rules of a legal language in the systemic and functional context. If the prima facie meaning of the text does not give rise to any linguistic doubts in the case, and there are no systemic and/ or functional factors disturbing this understanding, then one declares that 'lex clara est'.

Cases of lack of interpretative doubt are explicitly declared to be such by the courts, which then invoke the argument of the clarity of the texts applied. The Court states that one does not engage in interpretation of legal texts when '. . . they are so clear and precise, that in fact they do not require any interpretation' (SN 14.3.1950 KO 46/50 PP, 7, 1950). The same idea has been expressed by the Constitutional Tribunal, which, however, has spoken of 'direct interpretation' in the meaning of 'direct understanding of the clear text': '. . . in the situation where the normative text is clear, evident and does not stimulate any linguistic reservations, it should be interpreted directly, viz., according to the linguistic directives' (CT 3.3.1987 P 2/87 OTK 1988 P.2).

The existence of an 'evident meaning' (SC 21.9.1982 IV KR 178/82 OSPiKA 1983 K 126; SC 29.12.1987 VI KZP 35/87 OSPiKA 1988 K 147; SC 29.9.1987 VI KZP 27/87 OSPiKA 1988 K 107) or of an 'unambiguous meaning' of the provision cited (SC 18.10.1982 IV CZ 130/82 OSPiKA 198 1983 C 155) excludes doubt about it, and this also holds for constitutional provisions (CT 16.6.1986 U 3/86 OTK

1987/; CT 10.6.1987 P 1/87 OTK 1988 p. 1). One also finds an argument stating that there is 'lack of doubt' (CT 3.3.1987 P 2/87 OTK 1988 p. 2; CT 22.C4. 1987 K 1/87 OTK 1988 p. 3).

(c) A situation of interpretation occurs when there is no isomorphy. This situation is case-bound and context-bound. The same legal norm can, depending on the case, be clear or not clear for the same decision maker, even if the systemic and functional contexts are the same. *A fortiori* this holds when at least one of these contexts is changing in a manner relevant to interpretational issues. One should mention that there are some institutionally determined cases in which a situation of interpretation invariably occurs. This happens whenever a higher instance court decides a case which is presented before it because of an appeal against an interpretative decision of a lower instance. It occurs also where the institution exists whereby a higher instance court may be asked to interpret some norms concerning which a doubt has arisen during deliberation about the case in a lower instance. This institutional framework does not, however, change the pragmatic nature of doubts themselves, but only excludes the possibility of stating that 'lex clara est' in some situations.

2   The theoretical typology of doubts which stimulate statutory interpretation is based on the context which has a possible influence on the meaning of statutory norms or their parts. There are three types of context in question: linguistic, systemic and functional. It is convenient to single out the sources of doubt according to each of these contexts.

3   The linguistic context is that of the legal language in which statutory norms are formulated. (B. Wróblewski, 1948; J. Wróblewski, 1959, chap. V; T. Gizbert-Studnicki, 1986). This language is a type or 'register' of common language; it is a fuzzy language and the meaning of its terms, as a rule, is context-dependent. The characteristics of this context give rise to interpretative doubts because of vagueness, polysemy, evaluativeness and syntactic ambiguity (J. Wróblewski, 1985b).

(a) The links of legal language with common natural language are clearly recognized by the Supreme Court. For example, the meaning of the term 'group of persons' referred to in Art. 178 SS 1,2, c.p.p. determining a punishment for defamation of a 'group of persons' stimulated doubts of the district court which referred a question about it to the Supreme Court. The Supreme Court stated that the provision in question '. . . does not determine what one should understand by this expression' and added: 'In order to determine the content of the concept "group of persons" one ought to use a linguistic interpretation and determine the meaning of the term "group".' In the dictionaries of the Polish language by 'group' one understands several individuals gathered in a singled-out totality, the members of which are bound together by some links, or who are fulfilling some task (cf. *Dictionary of the Polish Language*, M. Szymczak (ed.), PWN 1978, p. 704, and W. Doroszewski, (ed.), *Wiedza Powszechna* 1960, vol.1.2 p. 1331). Taking this into account, the Supreme Court stated that the term in question used in the applicable provision '. . . designated a group of persons linked, even temporarily, by common purpose, interest, properties or by any link identifying them' (SC 18.9.1982 VI KZP 10/82 OSPiKA 1983 K 228). In a similar way a determination of the meaning of statutory terms has been made by reference to the *Dictionary of the Polish Language* for such terms as 'to produce' and 'to adapt' (SC 20.12.1985 VI KZP 41/85 OSPiKA 1987 K 90) 'cruelty' (SC 3.1.1986 Rw 1180/85 OSPiKA 1987 K 67) and 'to spill' SC 29.9.1987 VI KZP 24/87 OSPiKA 1988 K 36).

Sometimes no reference to the dictionary is made, common linguistic experience being deemed sufficient, as in the argument that the term 'peculiar' in common speech is a species of the term 'exceptional' or 'extraordinary' (SC 27.5.1986 IV KR 166/86 OSPiKA 1988 K 70).

The argument by reference to common language meanings appears when one uses the key-words of encyclopaedias. The Supreme Administrative Court has asserted its own competence in cases dealing with decisions about registrations in a register of legal advisors; this was done on the strength of Art. 196 S 2 p. 17 of the Code of Administrative Procedure. The decision includes the following reasoning. If the provision in question gives to the Court a competence of controlling decisions concerning

> . . . the right to participate in determined actions and occupations, then it gives to the court the competence to examine claims about decisions concerning professional activities. A profession is a sum of determined, singled out activities, performed permanently, or relatively permanently, within the social division of labour, for safeguarding the main source of an individual's maintenance. An enlarged definition of an occupation and a classification of occupations is contained in the *Great Universal PWN Encyclopedia*. (Warszawa, 1966, vol.

12. p. 665)' (SC 23.6.1983 II SA 475/83 OSPiKA 1984 AA 20).

(b) Fuzziness is typical of names and descriptions in legal language. In the area of penumbra there are doubts whether some object belongs or does not belong to the areas referred to as the positive or the negative core of meaning of this term (cf. 1(a) above). For example, the term 'near' is a typical fuzzy term. The administrative organ has given a licence for selling drinks having more than 4.5 per cent of alcohol in a place which is not 'near' schools or other places of education. There are doubts as to what the vague term 'near' in this context means. In one case the licensed shop was situated about 150m from the primary school and 500m from the nursery. The Supreme Administrative Court stated that '. . . the law-maker used the so-called fuzzy term "near" without defining it'. The Court stressed that this does not confer open discretion and singled out the following factors which should be taken into account: the distance between the shop and educational establishments; the surface and manner of construction; the relation of entrances and exits; and the facility of contacts between the customers and the school (SAC 25.2.1983 II SA 2075/82 OSPiKA 1983 AA 143).

It should be stressed that the fuzziness of a term in legal language could be evoked in a concrete case even if prima facie the meaning *in abstracto* seems clear, and this confirms our earlier general observations concerning the concept of clarity. For example, there are special provisions dealing with making an 'oral declaration of will' in testamentary acts by dumb, deaf, and dumb-and-deaf persons, and there is a question of whether and how to apply them. The Supreme Court stated that these persons can make a valid testament 'orally', if they have the necessary legal capacity and express their will in a sufficiently precise manner understood by the witnesses (SC 14.1.1982 III CRN 169/82 OSPiKA 1983 C 151).

Taking into account the dependence of the vagueness of legal terms on the concrete situations of their use, one should stress that there are cases of purposeful vagueness due to the style of statutory drafting, and the typical case of this is any use of so-called general clauses. The most typical example for the Polish, or any other socialist, system is a reference to the 'principles of social co-existence'. These principles determine the limits of using one's rights (Art. 5 c.code) in a manner known by analogous general clauses in other systems. (Leszczynski, 1987, and lit.cited therein). But there are many other general clauses of this type which demand in general legal usage a determination of their meaning in concrete cases (for example, SC 3.11.1986 IV CR 317/86 OSPiKA 1987 C 225). For example, 'evidently unjust temporary arrest' in Art. 487 S 4 Polish Code of Criminal Procedure (SC 24.4.1981 II KZ 67/81 OSPiKA 1983 K 200); a demand to change a name should be 'justified by important reasons' according to Art. 2/1 of the statute of 15.11.1956 (Dz.U. nr 59, poz. 328/SAC 26.5.1981 SA 974/81 OSPiKA 1982 AA 58); 'Interest of the Polish People's Republic (for example, SC 28.9.1982 II URN 136/82 OSPiKA 1984 P 18). Any use of such terms in statutory language is treated as leaving the implied evaluation 'to the competent organs' (SAC 24.2.1987 III SA 1152/86 OSPiKA 1987 AA 189).

Sometimes a statute explicitly refers to the features of concrete cases and calls for a more or less channelled evaluation. For example, in the statute concerning the administration of apartments (D.U. 1983 nr 11 pos. 55), Art. 41.1 refers to the cases '. . . justified by specific social and economic reasons'. This reference '. . . is a fuzzy expression for an application of this provision. It means that the proper evaluation should be made by a competent administrative organ in an individualized manner . . .' (SAC 1.3.1983 I SA 108/83 OSPiKA 1983 AA 216). Such 'evaluative–quantitative terms' as 'great quantity', 'great dimensions' and 'great damage' are not defined in the Polish penal code and their definition 'is not possible, or in any case exceptionally difficult. Their meaning ought to be in each situation determined by the court deciding the case' (SC 19.5.1987 VI KZP 46/86 OSPiKA K 13).

Even some prima facie descriptive terms call sometimes for this type of evaluation in a concrete case. For example, the term 'member of a family living in a common household' is vague in a situation when the person in question is taken care of by his family only during a period of sickness. Replying to the question about the meaning of the term in question the Supreme Court stated that 'It is not possible to enumerate in a sufficiently precise and complete way the factors which indicate the status of being in a common household because of the complexity of factual situations of life, which depend on many forms and conditions of milieux and features of a given occupation. The evaluation [in question] depends on the circumstances of a given case' (SC 11.8.1982 III UZP 18/22 OSPiKA 1983 P 75).

(c) Polysemy (or, in other words, 'semantic ambiguity') is defined as a situation in which a term has more than one meaning. Many legal language terms are polysemic at least when thought of in isolation from the context of their use. It is assumed, however, that the terms of legal language have the same meaning throughout the legal system. This argument has been used when dealing with the term 'worker' and 'person working in the labour relation' in the statute concerning trade unions, the labour code and the legal system as a whole (SC 21.2.1983 II PZP 72/82 OSPiKA 1983 P 69). Not always, however, is this assumption accepted; for example, the term 'employment' has different meanings even in the labour code (SC 1.3.1983 III AZP 11/82 OSPiKA 1984 C 1).

In legal language there are many evaluative terms, including those in general clauses. The identification of evaluative terms and their opposition to descriptive terms presupposes a linguistic or philosophical opposition of description and evaluation, which cannot be discussed here (cf. in general Zirk-Sadowski, 1984, J. Wróblewski, 1981).

(d) Syntactic ambiguity is not as frequent as semantic. An example, though, is provided by the use of the term 'or' both in the Polish natural language and in legal language as well. The issue is whether it means logically an alternative or a disjunction. There are no relevant differences between legal language and natural language in respect of syntactic rules. But faulty syntax in the formulation of norms can result in ambiguity of the norm, and hence syntax is a source of syntactic–semantical doubts. This is quite a common occurrence in natural language.

(e) From some arguments concerning linguistic sources of lack of clarity and a resultant need for interpretation, it seems that the source is a lack of legal definition of the unclear terms. If there is a statutory definition of terms then the provision containing it is referred to (for example, SC 19.12.1986 III CZP 89/86 OSPiKA 1987 C 168). But more often the lack of definition is stressed as if this were the source of the need for interpretation (for example, SC 30.12.1986 III PZP 42/86 OSPiKA 1988 P 185; SC 9.12.1986 III CZP 61/86 OSPiKA 1987 C 191; SC 21.10.1987 III CRN 286/87 OSPiKA 1988 C 141).

4   The systemic context of a legal norm is constituted by the legal system of which this norm is a member. The conception of a legal system is rather controversial.

(a) For our purposes it is sufficient to state that the following features of a legal statutory (civil) system are

presupposed in the interpretation of statutes: (i) A legal
system is an ordered set of valid enacted legal norms together
with valid rules inferred from them by accepted principles of
legal reasoning (J. Wróblewski, 1986a). (ii) Legal norms are
ordered hierarchially according to the hierarchy of law-
making agencies and to the substantive criteria of their
relevance (principles, ordinary norms) (Wronkowska, Zielinski and Ziembinski, 1974; J. Wróblewski, 1984a). (iii) A
legal system is thought of as a consistent and coherent set of
norms (MacCormick, 1978, chs VII, VIII, J. Wróblewski,
1986b, van der Kerchove and F. Ost, 1988, ch. III (1.2)). (iv) A
legal system is thought of as qualifying (characterizing) every
possible fact situation in terms of accepted legal concepts
(substantive completeness of law) or, if not, then this qualification is the task of some law-applying agency. (v) The systematization of normative acts (for example, division into titles,
parts, chapters, articles, paragraphs and so on) is relevant to
determining the meaning of norms.

(b) Interpretative doubts are connected with the enumerated features of a legal system. If the norm understood in its
prima facie meaning is inconsistent (incoherent) with any
other legal norm valid in the system in question, then there
is a doubt as to whether this prima facie meaning is correct.
Then one should either search for another meaning of the
norm in question or ask whether the norm with which the
applied norm is inconsistent (incoherent) is rightly understood. For example, elimination of interpretation because of
inconsistency (for example, SC 19.8.1982 III CZP 21/82
OSPiKA 1983 p. 76, SC 30.11.1986 III PZP 36/87 OSPiKA
1988/p. 81). Incoherence is constituted by a lack of harmonization between particular provisions, or between principles
and ordinary norms. An ordinary norm cannot be incoherent with principles, as norms of special relevance (for example, SC 19.4.1983 IV PR 65/82 OSPiKA 1984 P 103).
Sometimes one uses the argument of the general function of
the code, as a guiding principle of proper interpretation. See,
for example, the proper interpretation of a Decree of the
Council of Ministers according to the functions of the
Labour Code (SAC 21.1.1982 II SA 888/81 OSPiKA AA
75).

In the case of inconsistency and incoherence one takes
into account the hierarchal ordering of norms; the doubts are
stronger if a norm in its prima facie meaning is inconsistent
or incoherent with a norm hierarchically higher, than in the
opposite case. The formal hierarchy of norms based on the

hierarchy of law-making agencies usually is not problematic. A 'principle' is higher than ordinary norms, but there is a practical and theoretical problem as to how to identify principles.

(c) The prima facie meaning of a norm is treated as doubtful if one cannot qualify (characterize) the facts of the case in terms of legal concepts. In such a case, one is apt to speak of 'gaps' in the law (see section II).

(d) The systematization of normative acts appears as an element of the systemic context. The place of a norm within the structure of a whole enactment is thought of as significant for its understanding. If this place seems not to be adequate to its prima facie meaning then this is a source of doubt. On the other hand, this place also helps to determine the meaning in cases of doubt. For example, the titles of the parts of a statute are sometimes used as arguments (SC 12.8.1966 VI KZP 15/66 OSPiKA 1967 K 43; SC 10.2.1982 II CZP 62/81 OSPiKA 1983 C 116; SC 29.9.1987 VI KZP 5/87 OSPiKA 1988 K 206); and the division of articles into separate subsections is relevant for interpretation (SC 15.4.1982 VI KZP 2/82 OSPiKA 1983 K 7).

5   Last but not least, there is a rather complex functional context. This context contains all phenomena which influence the meaning of a norm, excluding the linguistic and systemic context. There are extra-legal norms functioning in social groups and in a whole society. There are evaluations of various phenomena including extra-legal rules and the law itself. These evaluations are ascribed to the law-making and law-applying agencies and are thought of either as alleged facts or as postulates. The former occurs if one tries to reconstruct them as an axiology of law making or an axiology of law; the latter if one expresses an ideology (or a normative theory) about the application and interpretation of law.

(a) Typical doubts concerning the prima facie meaning of a legal norm are linked with arguments stating that an application of a norm in this meaning would be contrary to its purposes. For example, there are the typical arguments: 'The law-maker's purpose was that . . .'; 'From the clearly expressed will of the law-maker . . .'; 'The law-maker was not interested in . . .'; 'There are no justified reasons to go against the will of the law-maker . . .' (SC 15.2.1983 III CZP 65/82 OSPiKA 1984 C 49). Also there is an argument that 'it is not possible to ascribe to the law-maker, that . . .' (SC 10.7.1982 I SA 2587/81 OSPiKA 1983 AA 138; SC

3.6.1982 III CRN M0182 OSPiKA; KA 1983 C153). There is quite common reference to the *ratio legis* (for example, SC 17.12.1981 III CZP 32/81 OSPiKA 1983 C 111; SC 3.6.1982 III CZP 24/82 OSPiKA 1983 C 117; SC 26.7. 1982 Rw 474/82 OSPiKA 1983 K 35).

The second type of arguments arising from functional context are those stating that the result would be evaluated as 'unjust', which is equivalent to 'unreasonable' or 'unacceptable', depending on the underlying theory of interpretation (see Aarnio, 1987, chap. IV). For example, social disapproval of cheating by the seller is taken into account in interpreting the adequacy of a penalty (SG 30.9.1982 Rw 843/82 OSPiKA 1983 K 232), strong provocation as a factor mitigating the penalty should be justified and this justification is based on accepted moral norms and principles of social coexistence (SC 19.11.1980 Rw 399/80 OSPiKA 1982 K S). It is a good argument for an interpretation that, besides certain stated legal reasons, it 'corresponds to the sense of justice and to the necessary stability of legal relations in family law' (SC 11.10.1982 III CZP 22/82 OSPiKA 1983 C 255).

(b) A special case of doubt concerning prima facie meaning within the functional context is a change in context which affects the 'proper' meaning of a statute. This is not the case where a change of the legal system gives rise to contradictions, that is, not a case of change in systemic context, but one of alteration in the functional context itself which makes the meaning in question 'obsolete' or 'inadequate'. Cases of this type were especially important when the Polish courts were applying statutes enacted during the pre-war period. There has been an essential change of sociopolitical context relevant for issues both of validity and of interpretation. The former is not discussed here, the latter consisted in the task of the court to state whether the 'old' statute had not changed its meaning in the new functional context (J. Wróblewski, 1959, ch. VI, S 4).

The problem whether a statute enacted in the inter-war period and not repealed is still in force should be solved by testing whether it is not in conflict with premises and principles of the Polish constitution of 1952 (SC 12.2.1955 'Panstwo i prawo', 7–8, 1955). The application of enacted provisions '. . . is demanded by revolutionary legality but not when the changes of constitution and of the principles of social coexistence, resulting from the change of the bourgeois state to the People's State, command that these provisions be treated as not corresponding to the changed social relations . . .' (SC 30.6.1951 C 649/50 *Panstwo i prawo*, 2, 1952). See, for example, the change of the meaning of the term 'strong provocation' according to the change from bourgeois to socialist morality (SC 16.4.1953 C 1985/55 '*Panstwo i prawo*', 1, 1954); the change of the meaning of the term 'important reasons' justifying the paying of a single lump-sum compensation instead of a pension according to Art. 164 S 1 of the Code of Obligations, because of the change of the economy, as a part of the functional context of law (SC 14.11.1950 C 229/50 '*Zbiór Orzecen*', IC 11, 1952). These interpretational issues were highly important in legal practice until the old statutes were replaced with new ones. After the 1960s, this special problem of interpretation lost its relevance in the practice of the Polish courts.

II   GAPS AND THEIR ORIGINS

1   The problem of gaps is rather controversial. There are some basic questions concerning gaps: What does 'a gap' mean? Can a gap be determined descriptively or does one only arise out of a legal evaluation? Is the filling of a gap an interpretation of existing law or the creation of a new rule? What is analogy in legal reasoning? What are the descriptive and/or evaluative presuppositions of using arguments from gaps or from analogy? (Cf. Nowacki, 1966).

2   If the existence of gaps is admitted, the task of the court is to fill them by using statutory provisions which regulate essentially similar problems or cases. The Supreme Court uses the term 'gap' but the difference between the 'filling of gaps' and 'interpretation' is not precise. The closest way of identifying them is the statement that there is no gap '. . . because the decision is made through interpretation or through reasoning from norm to norm . . . It should be accepted that the filling of a gap using an analogy should be restricted to the case of a gap of construction, when the use of analogy is not law-creating' (SC 5.2.1987 III CZP 97/86 OSPiKA 1988 C 29). The problem is when the gap in question exists. It is theoretically explained that, when one speaks about a gap, one must have made a value-judgement that something is not regulated which should be regulated. This is implied by the argument that some lack of regulation is not 'an oversight of the law-maker' (SC 27.3.1987 III AZP 1/87 OSPiKA 1987 C 222). Only if one accepts that this is not the case can

one assert the existence of a gap and use the technical means to fill it; for example, there is a lack of regulation on how to give leave to the court executive officer, and one applies by analogy the rules concerning the judge (SC 23.4.1987 III CZP 12/87 OSPiKA 1987 C 223).

III THE TYPES OF INTERPRETATIVE ARGUMENT AND THEIR INTERACTION

1   There are two approaches to the arguments used in statutory interpretation: (a) a typology singling out the types of interpretation as dealing with the groups of arguments; and (b) an enumeration of arguments which are especially relevant in all or in some types of interpretation. I will deal with both of them, calling (a) 'typology' and (b) 'enumeration'. Typology and enumeration deal with the same set of arguments, but the difference consists in the focus of research; the first is more theoretically orientated, the second more descriptively orientated.

2   There may be many typologies of interpretative arguments adapted to various purposes. Particularly common have been those linked with the typological traditions of the German historical school and with those of legal positivism. The Polish Supreme Court used such a typology too, but, step by step, the typology presented below has recently come into use. The typology presented here is based on the semantic approach to legal interpretation, and singles out the three types of argument corresponding to three types of context which influence meaning in operative interpretation. Accordingly, interpretation is either linguistic, systemic or functional (J. Wróblewski, 1959, chaps V–VII, 1985a, chap. 4, 1987a, chap. VII; S. Grzybowski, 1985, ch. V, S 20). This typology is a theoretical rationalization and/or reconstruction of the interpretative arguments actually used in practical judicial interpretation by the Polish Supreme Court and the Polish Constitutional Tribunal.

Each type of interpretation is defined by the interpretative directives it uses (J. Wróblewski, 1983, 1987a; Ost and van der Kerchove, 1989, part I, ch. V). The term 'directive' is used by convention and in this context could be treated as a synonym of 'guidelines', 'maxims', 'canons', 'principles' or 'reasons' used in a justification of interpretative decisions. There are two levels of these directives. The first level directives (DI1) determine how one ought to handle the semantically relevant contextual elements they refer to. The second level (DI2) are of two sorts: the DI2 of procedure determine the conditions and procedures for using one or more DI1; the DI2 of preference determine what meaning to prefer if there is a conflict between meanings ascribed to the interpreted text when using different DI1. The difference of DI1 and DI2 is sometimes explicitly referred to (CT 03.03.1987 P 2/87 TK 1988 p. 2).

3   Linguistic interpretation deals with the determination of a meaning of the interpreted provision taking into account the language in which the text is formulated. This *ex definitione* is a legal language, but, according to the presumptions dealing with linguistic interpretation and legislative technique, one takes into account also common language and legal terminology. Linguistic argumentation makes reference to the natural common language in general (SC 26.08.1986 III AZP 9/86 OSPiKA 1987 C 130; SC 27.05.1986 IV KR 166/86 OSPiKA 1988 K 70) or to the dictionaries of this language (cf. para 2 of the 'Preliminary' section of this chapter); syntactic arguments are also used, for example, the use of a comma and of the word 'or' in enumeration of premises is interpreted as indicating that any of them is a sufficient condition (SC 15.04.1982 VI KZP 2/82 OSPiKA 1983 K 7); the term 'or' between a description of situations denotes their alternativity (SC 25.02.1986 VI KZP 52/85 OSPiKA 1988 K 35).

Interpretation of this type is referred to in the Polish Supreme Court's decisions as 'linguistic interpretation' (for example, SC 17.11.1986 III PZP 64/86 OSPiKA 1987 P 102; SC 30.04.1986 II URM 3/86 OSPiKA 1987 P 79 CT 03.03.1987 P 2/87 OTK 1988 p. 2; CT 22.04.1987 K 1/87 OTK 1988 p. 3) or more traditionally as 'grammatical' (for example, 29.10.1987 III UZP 30/87 OSPiKA 1988 P 120 SC 11.03.1988 VI KZP 46/87 OSPiKA 1988 K 205; SC 06.11.1987 IV PR 282/87 OSPiKA 1988 195 SC 27.03.1986 I CZ 137/85 OSPiKA 1987 C 23); the two terms are explicitly treated as synonymous and the term 'grammatical (linguistic) interpretation' is used (SC 30.11.1987 III PZP 36/ 87 OSPiKA 1988 P P 81). Even the term 'semantic interpretation' appears (SC 22.09.1987 III CZP 46/87 OSPiKA 1988 C 128), which obviously means 'linguistic interpretation' too.

4   Systemic interpretation deals with the determination of meaning of the interpreted provisions taking into account the systemic context they belong to. Several features of the

legal system and the systematization of the statutory texts are presumed and are the basis for formulation of systemic DI1.

This type of interpretation is especially relevant in the activity of the Constitutional Tribunal which reviews issues of constitutionality and of legality, determining the relations between constitution, statutes and sub-statutory normative acts. This means that the hierarchical structure of the legal system is the basis for assessing the issues of validity that the Constitutional Tribunal is interested in, and this also implies resort to systemic interpretation, if needed (CT 05.11.1986 U 5/86 OTK 1987 p. 1; CT 28.05.1986 U 1/96 OTK 1987 P). Because of the systemic unity of the legal system, different interpretations of the same term in various legal normative acts have to be eliminated (SC 30.11.1987 III PZP 36/87 OSPiKA 1988 P 81).

Systemic interpretation takes into account not only the legal system and its main sub-divisions (the branches of law) but also the various parts systematically singled out in the legal normative act the interpreted rule or terms belong to, such as the chapter of the same normative act (SC 29.09.1987 VI KZP 5987 OSPiKA 1988 K 206). Systemic interpretation compares various sections of the same act (for example, SC 20.06.1986 VI KZP 7/86 OSPiKA 1987 K 197) or sub-sections in one provision (SC 15.04.1982 VI KZP 2/82 OSPiKA 1983 K 7). The Supreme Court sometimes uses the proper term 'systemic interpretation' (for example, SC 17.11.1986 III PZP 64/86 OSPiKA 1987 P 102; 30.11.1987 III PZP 36/87 OSPiKA 1988 P 81; SC 19.11.1988 III PZP 52/87 OSPiKA 1988 P 187 cf. CT 22.04.1988 K 1/87 OTK 1988 p. 3); sometimes, however, the old term 'systematic interpretation' is also used (for example, CT 03.03.1987 PZ/87 OTK 1988, p. 2).

5   Functional interpretation deals with a rather complicated functional context which includes various factors thought of as relevant for determining the meaning of interpreted statutory provisions. The ideologies of interpretation enumerate different sets of relevant factors and ascribe to them various weights. The following elements of the functional context are usually taken into account:

(a)   Sociopolitical facts and relations, their changes and their evaluation.
(b)   The purposes ascribed to law or to the law-maker.
(c)   The axiology of law and of its application.

(d)   The extra-legal rules and evaluations thought of as relevant to law and its application.

These factors are taken into account either from the time of the enactment of a statute or from the time of its application and/or interpretation. Various arguments are used in this type of interpretation, which appears traditionally as 'teleological interpretation' (for example, SC 27.03.1986 I CZ 137/85 OSPiKA 1987 C 123) or as reference to *ratio legis* (for example, SC 29.01.1987 III CRN 298/86 and III CRN 348/86 OSPiKA 1987 C 192) coupled with the reference to the will of the law-maker. There are, however, other arguments in this type of interpretation such as, for example, a reference to 'sound reasons' (CT 22.04.1987 K 1/87 OTK 1988 p. 3), to 'axiological reasons' (SC 20.06.1986 VI KZP 7/86 OSPiKA 1987 K 197), reference to sociopolitical facts, such as the fact of the repatriation of Poles after the Second World War (CT 20.10.1986 P 2/86 OTK 1987 p. 6), or to the political principles stated in the Constitution (CT 11.07.1986 K 1/86 OTK 1987 B); the functions of some institutions are discussed also; for example, the functions of 'price' in the Polish economy (SC 14.10.1987 I CR 216/87 OSPiKA 1988 C 203). All this justifies the use of the proposed term 'functional interpretation', which has been accepted in the Supreme Court terminology (for example, SC 30.11.1987 III PZP 36/87 OSPiKA 1988 P 81; SC 19.11.1988 III PZP 52/87 OSPiKA 1988 P 187; SC 30.04.1986 II URN 31/86 OSPiKA 1987 P 79) and by the Constitutional Tribunal too (CT 03.03.1987 P/87 OTK 1988 p. 2).

6   An interpretative decision is justified by reference to DI1 and to DI2 and to the evaluations needed for their choice and for their use (J. Wróblewski, 1983a, 82 ff, 1984b, 260 ff). Taking into account the various choices and uses of DI1 and DI2 it is not surprising that there exist various interpretations of the same statutory text, each of which could be properly justified. Hence there are some possible differences between the results of linguistic, systemic and functional interpretation, and in consequence the decision maker has to choose between them. From a theoretical point of view, the justification of interpretive decisions is made by reference to the directives of legal interpretation and to values. These directives and values are used in practice, but rather exceptionally stated explicitly, and mostly they are referred to as 'general directives of interpretation accepted in legal theory'

(SC 13.05.1987 III CZP 86/86 OSPiKA 1988 C 200) or referred to by the name of a particular type of interpretation, which implies these directives.

7 After presenting the typology of interpretation according to the semiotic approach, one can enumerate typically used arguments, which appear in any of these types although having different relevance. These arguments are used in all three types of interpretation singled out above, viz. linguistic, systemic and functional and, therefore, could be labelled 'transcategorical arguments'. There are two groups of these transcategorical arguments: (a) arguments dealing with the materials of argumentation, and (b) arguments especially relevant in comparative law, that is, those concerning 'literal meaning', 'intention of the law-maker' and 'reasonable sense'. The (a) arguments dealing with materials connect up with such kinds of interpretation as 'historical', 'comparative', 'genetic' and so on, depending on the materials used. The (b) arguments will be described below. What must be noted is that these are characteristically used in one or other of two contrasting ways: one deals with them in a static way, that is, in reference to the so-called historic law-maker's language, intention and reasons, or in a dynamic way, that is, with the present-day law-maker's language, intention and reasons. This dual perspective is inherent in any justificatory argument and is based on the opposition of static values (legal certainty, legal security, predictability and so on) and of dynamic values (such as the adequacy of law to the needs of life, the justice or equity of a concrete decision) (J. Wróblewski, 1959, ch. IV; 1983a, pp. 46–8, ff, 1987a, chs XI–XIV). Sometimes, however, justificatory arguments are not so clearly ascribed to this dual perspective. In the decisions of the Polish Supreme Court it would be rather difficult to determine a definite tendency to a primary emphasis on any of the three types of arguments in question.

8 'Literal meaning' as an argument in statutory interpretation is used at least in the following ways:

(a) 'Literal meaning' as the clear or plain meaning which does not need any interpretation. Thus, in this sense, the appeal is not strictly to an argument in interpretation but rather to the lack of any need for operative interpretation.

(b) 'Literal meaning' as a meaning of the interpreted text according to common language semantics. This meaning is referred to when one uses, for example, common dictionaries in legal interpretation. If, however, the interpreter thinks that the meaning in question is that of legal language or of its particular terminology, then this special meaning is used. The 'literal meaning' in this sense has been relativized to the common language, legal language or its terminology.

(c)   For 'literal meaning' also the terms 'grammatical' or 'linguistic meaning' are used in the sense that this is the meaning determined within semiotic interpretation, that is interpretation according to the linguistic context of the interpreted text.

9   The intention of the law-maker is a standard ground of argument in statutory interpretation. Theoretical analysis demonstrates that the law-maker in question (either a 'historical' or a 'present' one) is really a rational law-maker in the form of an ideal construct and not any concrete person or group of persons. Several features of the law-maker are identified: rationality, an adequate or perfect knowledge of the past, present and future expressed in a set of true and consistent propositions; adherence to a coherent and consistent set of accepted values; the proper use of correct rules of reasoning. All of these are implicitly presupposed by the arguments used in legal interpretation.

The argument from law-maker's intention is used in many theoretically identified ways, but these become blurred in common instances of argumentation (Nowak, 1973; J. Wróblewski, 1979b, 1985c, chs 8–14; Wronkowska, 1982, ch. V). First, the law-maker is the historical law-maker, or rather his theoretical construct. In this case, *travaux préparatoires* and data about the functional context are relevant materials of interpretation. Secondly, the law-maker is the present law-maker and his intention is expressed in the currently valid system of law and his preferences correlate with the actual functional context of the law. Then the whole body of the currently valid law is the proper material for interpretation. Thirdly, the law-maker has no determined place in time, and is referred to generally as the rational law-maker.

The law-maker's intention can be used as a positive or as a negative argument. In the former situation the intention is ascribed to the legislative materials and/or inferred from the text of statutory provisions. For example, the arguments referring to the will of the law-maker use the following formulations: 'The aim of the law-maker was . . .'; '. . . the evident will of the law-maker expressed in the first part of the provision . . .'; '. . . according to the will of the law-maker . . .' '. . . the law-maker was not interested in . . .'; '. . . there are no sufficient reasons to argue that the will of the law-maker was . . .' (SC 15.02.1983 II CZP 65/82 OSPiKA 1984 C 49; SC 17.12.1981 III CZP 32/81 OSPiKA 1983 C 111, SC 18.10.1982 IV CZ 130/82 OSPiKA 1983 C 153; 10.02.1983 III PZP 73/82 OSPiKA 1983 P 236). In the latter situation the will of the law-maker is used negatively for elimination of some meanings ascribed to the interpreted text and qualified as 'spurious' or 'wrong' interpretations. Such formulas as the following are used: 'the law-maker could not have intended . . .'; 'it would be contrary to the law-maker's intention, purpose or will, and so on (SC 10.07.1982 III UZP 19/82 OSPiKA 1983 P 175; SC 15.2.1983 II CZP 65/82 OSPiKA 1984 C 49). This negative use is supported by the presupposed features of the law-maker, such as rationality, consistency, coherence and so on, used in assessing the content or result of an interpretation which is eliminated.

The argument from the law-maker's intention seems to be the *façon de parler* instead of a reference to other arguments. It has a strong traditional background in legal thinking, and is supported by the assumptions concerning the rational law-making activity which results in interpreted legal rules. The rational law-maker is consistent and coherent in his actions, hence interpretation uses the argument of the 'tendency of the law-maker' (SC 18.10.1982 IV CZP 130/82 OSPiKA 1983 C 155) which corresponds with the 'uniformity of the legislation' (SC 17.12.1981 III CZP 32/81 OSPiKA 1983 C 111). As a rational actor the law-maker is interested in the actual working of the instruments created by him, and hence there is no merit in an interpretation which would result in the inoperability of the legal institutions created by him (SC 10.05.1982 III PZP 12/82 OSPiKA 1983 P 74). The law-maker has all relevant information concerning the functioning of law, and if he makes no legislative intervention it is inferred that he accepts — or at least tolerates — the reality, and this is an argument against an interpretation which would not take into account the silence of the law-maker (SC 04.03.1983 III CZP 6/93 OSPiKA 1983 C 190).

10   The argument of a 'reasonable sense' is rather rarely used explicitly as an independent argument like that of the 'literal meaning' or 'law-maker's intention'. Nevertheless interpre-

tative leeways do occur and then the interpreter should choose the most reasonable interpretation. This situation exists either when there are competing interpretations and the most reasonable has to be chosen, or when an unreasonable interpretation has to be eliminated. In Polish interpretational practice the term 'reasonable sense' is not used and its various functional correlates appear as 'sound', 'justified' and so on. For example, there may be a reference to the 'feeling of equity' (SC 11.10.1983 III 22/82 OSPiKA 1983 C 255) or to the 'principles of justice' (SC 24.04.1981 II RZ 67/81 OSPiKA 1983 K 200).

IV   TYPES OF GAP-FILLING ARGUMENT

1   The difference between the case of a doubt and the case of a gap is, as was said above, not easy to define. The prima facie meaning of a norm is treated as doubtful if one cannot characterize the facts of a case in terms of legal concepts. For example, there is difficulty in determining whether or not a seller in a socialized shop counts as a person performing a public function for the purposes of a particular criminal law protection (SC 14.12.1982 III KR 1982 OSPiKA 1983 K 224) or whether some text is 'a criticism' or 'a defamation' (SC 17.12.1965 VI KR 14/59 OSPiKA 1966 K 69). In this situation of difficulty either one seeks a solution by interpretation or one asserts the existence of a 'gap' (in one of the meanings of this metaphorical term) which is to be filled by reasoning from analogy. One can cite, for example, the gap about the effective date of a statute because of the lack of transitional provisions (SC 145 1982 IV CR 1970/82 OSPiKA 1983 C 28), or a gap in statutory implementation of a decision about the removal of a child from the custody of a parent (SC 25.11.1947, C. Prez. 6/47; OSPiKA IC 1/48). The difference between analogy and extensive interpretation thus seems to be dubious. There is an argument that, since in a case there is no gap, then one ought not to use any analogy (SC 9.10.1985 III CZP 53/85 OSPiKA 1987 C 193).

2   In Polish practice, the analogy issue is treated rather cautiously. Firstly, there is the accepted maxim 'exceptiones non sunt extendendae' ('exceptions are not to be extended') and extension could mean either extensive interpretation or resort to an analogy (for example, SC 10.2.1982 II CZP 62/81 OSPiKA 1983 C 116; SC 10.2.1983 III PZP 73/82 OSPiKA 1983 P 239) especially inappropriate in case of *leges*

speciales (SC 11.3.1988 VI KZP 46/87 OSPiKA 1988 K 205). In particular this makes reference to the provisions restricting the rights of the parties (SC 4.4.1986 V KRN 101/86 OSPiKA 1987 K 143) or of citizens (SAC 3.5.1985 II SA 112/85 OSPiKA 1987 AA 56). A quite unique case is that of the Supreme Court decision which used a 'cautious analogy' from exceptional provisions in spite of endorsing the referred-to maxim (SC 30.11.1987 III PZP 36/87 OSPiKA 1988 P 81).

3   There are some normative restrictions on analogy. In penal law, reasoning by analogy may not be used against the accused. Theoretically one can reconstruct the possible axiological reasons supporting analogical reasoning, such as the coherence of law and its completeness, the value of uniformity of judicial application of law and, perhaps, the value of formal justice. Against analogical reasoning there is the argument of legal security, of course. It is important to stress that the same values are relevant as the axiological background relevant for and against some sorts of extensive interpretation.

V   THE MATERIALS OF INTERPRETATIVE ARGUMENT

1   The materials of statutory interpretation used in the Supreme Court's decisions are grouped according to their use as:
(a) always used; (b) used depending on the circumstances; (c) not used. Taking into account a sufficiently large sample of decisions these three sorts of materials are an indication for classifying the materials into 'must-materials', 'may-materials' and 'may not-materials' available for justifying interpretative decisions.

2   Among material always used is obviously the text of the applicable statutory provision. The use of this material is determined by law; the applied provision is the 'legal basis' of a law-applying decision, and therefore is used *ex lege* in all decisions. This is a neccessary element of the justification of any judicial decision, but the 'rule' of decision, that is, the rule directly justifying it, is often 'legal material' supplemented by rules that the applied provision refers to, or by the interpretation of this provision (J. Wróblewski, 1971). In an interpretational decision, the basic 'legal material' is the text of the interpreted statutory provision. Legislative

material confirms the interpretation, the lack of it appears as an argument for elimination of this interpretation (SC 1.3.1983 III AZP 1/82 OSPiKA 1984 C1). Preambles are not often used in Polish legal texts, and will only exceptionally appear in an argument in legal interpretation (for example, NSA 15001. 1987 II SA 1829–1830/86 OSPiKA 1988 AA 256).

3   All other materials are used if needed, depending on the history of the case and its features as a hard case; usually the cases decided by the Supreme Court are hard cases. I propose only a hermeneutical typology singling out materials as 'used', 'exceptionally used' and 'not used'. 'Used' material is referred to usually when called for in application of relevant directives of interpretation, or relevant to evaluations. Material is 'exceptionally used' when it appears only in peculiar cases and cannot be counted among the standard practices of interpretation. The material 'not used' does not appear *rebus hic stantibus* even exceptionally in interpretative decisions, and is not thought of as relevant in a decision.

4   The enumeration of the materials is grouped in several types:

(a)   Historical knowledge of conditions the statute was intended to remedy is used in arguments referring to the purposes of the statute. This is the standard argument in functional interpretation.

(b)   Legislative history is used when dealing with the preparatory works of big codifications (SC 19.5.1987 VI KZP 46/86 OSPiKA 1988 K 13). The special case is that the Constitutional Tribunal when testing the validity of controlled normative acts has to verify the observance of obligatory procedures of law-making (CT 28.5.1986 U 1/86 OTK 1987, 2). The history of legislation prior to the enactment of the interpreted text is taken into account (SC 15.12.1987 VI KZP 43/87 OSPiKA 1988 K 204) and treated as 'comparative historical argument' (SC 29.9.1987 VI KZP 25/87 OSPiKA 1988 K 65).

The references to the legislative history are used in a 'positive way', that is, to give the background for interpretative decision. There is also a 'negative way' of using the history in question: the argument is that the meaning of the term has not been questioned or challenged in the history (CT 11.7.1986 K 1/86 OTK 1987). Also the argument that the statutory provision is not sufficiently adapted for definite demands is rejected by stating that were it so it would be impossible to justify why the provision in question remained unchanged over half a century in spite of many changes and amendments of the normative act, and why it has not stimulated any criticism in legal doctrine and legal practice (SC 26.6.1985 III CZP 27/85 OSPiKA 1987 C 190). Legislative history, including reference to other laws that may arguably have been superseded or modified or otherwise possibily affected by the statute being interpreted, is used exceptionally.

(c)   The prior legal history of the language and concepts actually adopted in the statute are used implicitly in historical arguments, but sometimes they are explicitly treated as an argument relating to the 'historical content' of a notion (SC 14.11.1985 III UZP 42/85 OSPiKA 1987 P 109).

(d)   The language and purposes of other statutes related in some way to the subject of the statutes being interpreted are used when the interpreted statute in question is not a code. The material in question is relevant to systemic and functional interpretation.

(e)   Laws of other legal systems are used very exceptionally as a comparative-law argument, and sometimes duly ratified international treaties are referred to (SC 26.3.1985 I CR 304/84 OSPiKA 1987 C 169, CF 3.8.1987 P 2/87 OTK 1988).

(f)   Prior judicial interpretations are extensively used as arguments supporting decisions. Widely used are arguments referring to well established lines of precedents. There are arguments referring to a fixed line of decisions (for example, SC 20.1.1983 II KR 347/82 OSPiKA 1984 K 57) or arguments stating that the Supreme Court has several times already explained the issue (SC 1.10.1982 IV KZ 104/82 OSPiKA 1983 K 162). Sometimes the argument of preceding interpretative decisions is illustrated by the citation of the list of the decisions in question ranging from several decisions (cf. the citation of seven in SC 29.7.1982 Rw 474/82 OSPiKA 1983 K 3) to one decision (SC 30.7.1983 IV KR 53/83 OSPiKA 1984 K 97). The institutional place of the Supreme Court in Poland makes for a rather wide review of previous decisions, but not in all cases does the deciding bench agree with the preceding one (for example, SC 30.11.1987 III PZP 36/87 OSPiKA 1988 P 81; SC 29.9.1987 III CZP 54/87 OSPiKA 1988 C 130; SC 26.9.1986 III UZP 37/86 OSPiKA 1987 P 53). The Constitutional Tribunal in Poland has been functioning only two years, but still it uses its own decisions as arguments (CT 22.4.1987 K 1/87 OTK 1988 p. 3; CT 13.10.1987 P 4/87 OTK 1988 p. 6). This Tribunal feels bound by its own precedent which stated the legality of a sub-statutory normative act (CT 20.10.1986 P 2.86 OTK 1986 P 6). There is in Poland no system of precedent and, therefore, 'overruling' is always possible. The role of the precedent decision is, however, very highly relevant for the uniformity of the judicial application of law, especially in lower courts (J. Wróblewski, 1983a, pp. 157–77).

(g)   Opinions of the law professors are used as the *communis opinio doctorum* (for example, SC 8.10.1982 I PR 90/82 OSPiKA 1983 P 243; SC 30.8.1983 IV KR 153/83 OSPiKA 1984 K 97; SC 11.10.1982 III CZP 22/82 OSPiKA 1983 C 255). This general reference to science is more frequent than the citation of named authors and their works. This type of use of scientific opinion is rather differentiated: the Constitutional Tribunal uses legal literature quite extensively and even calls professors as experts on legal issues, using their views explicitly as arguments (for example, CT 28.5.1986 U 1/86 OTK 1987 p. 1; CT 16.6.1986 U 3/86 OTK 1987 p. 4; CT 3.3.1987 P 2/87 OTK 1988 p. 2); it has once rejected opinions of one law professor called as an expert, while endorsing the contrary opinion of another (CT 10.6.1987 P 1/87 OTK 1988 p. 1). The Supreme Administration Court sometimes uses this kind of reference to individual authors and their works (for example, SAC 21.10.1983 II SA 1964/83 OSPiKA 1984 AA 48; SAC 17.12.1985 III SA 988/85 OSPiKA 1987 AA 116; SAC 30.4.1986 SA/Wr 137/86 OSPiKA 1987 AA 82; SAC 26.3.1987 II SA 1553–1554/86 OSPiKA 1988 AA 199). This type of reference is, however, quite exceptional in the Supreme Court and exceptions have only been made in the last two years (SC 29.5.1987 III CZP 25/87 OSPiKA 1988 C 4; SC 25.5.1987 WR

214/87 OSPiKA 1988 K 109). One may ask whether this is matter of style or of deeper reasons behind it.

(h)   There are arguments proper for each of the types of legal interpretation here identified, that is, the linguistic, the systemic and the functional. As special arguments one can mention: the reference to the 'directives of the administration of justice and judicial practice' which are formulated by the Supreme Court and *ex lege* binding other courts (for example, SC 17.11.1987 III KR 381/87 OSPiKA 1988 K 208; SC 5.2.1988 IV PR 15/88 OSPiKA 1988 P 197; SC 13.6.1984 III CZP 22/84 OSPiKA 1987 C 126). The preamble is only exceptionally used as an argument by the Supreme Court (SC 15.4.1982 VI KZP 2/82 OSPiKA 1983 K 7; SC 5.8.1987 III CZP 17/87 OSPiKA 1988 C 126) and this is also the case with the Supreme Administrative Court (SAC 15.1.1987 II SA 1829–1830/86 OSPiKA 1987 AA 166), which has summarized the role of this argument in rather a good way: 'The preamble is not a legal norm, it is however an explanation of the motives' which have stimulated the law-maker. 'The motives cannot have influence on the interpretation of the norms contained in the act in question' (SAC 6.8.1984 II SA 735/84 OSPiKA 1987 AA 80). The teleological or normative nature of relevant phenomena is exceptionally used and thought of as their teleological essence (for example, SC 19.8.1982 III UZP 21/82 OSPiKA 1983 P 76).

Among the arguments which are not used in the Polish Supreme Courts' decisions are prior or current interpretations by the addressees of the law.

VI PRIORITIES AMONG CONFLICTING ARGUMENT FORMS

1   In the process of interpretation the judge has to choose between various possible meanings of the interpreted provision (heuresis) and between conflicting DI1 and DI2 justifying the interpretative decision, as well as among the 'may-materials' of arguments. These choices, the choice of mate-

rials excepted, are justified by the DI and by evaluations, but are the result of weighing pros and cons when comparing the possible and/or already-made interpretations of a given text. Eventually the end of the chain of justificatory reasoning appears as an implicit choice between static and dynamic values coupled with the idea of the proper task of the interpreter as contrasted with that of the law-maker. But this fundamental issue is only exceptionally articulated in argumentation, although sometimes it is discussed in doctrinal glosses commenting critically on the interpretative decisions of the courts.

2   The typical conflict of arguments is presented on the level of fundamental values of legal interpretation and on the level of conflicting sorts of argumentation. The fundamental opposition of values is between static values and dynamic values. Static values are certainty, predictability, security and stability; these are thought of as values inherent in law-applying decisions and, therefore, as values of interpretative decision too. There are strict links between static values. The certainty that a decision will be made and what its content will be results in its predictability, which means for interested persons the position of legal security and stability of their status. These values are linked with the (formal) legality, formal justice and uniformity of decision-making. The theoretical corollary of these values is the idea of the unchanging meaning of statutory provisions, which is traditionally expressed in the metaphor of the will of the historical law-maker.

Dynamic values are adequacy of the law to the needs of life, or adaptability of law to the changing contexts of its functioning. With these values is linked also the preference of some values of judicial decision such as substantive justice and a right decision of individual cases.

3   Conflict of arguments on the level of the conflicting sorts of argumentation typically occurs when the result of a linguistic and/or systemic interpretation is contrasted with the result of a functional interpretation. In fact, this is an opposition between various DI1 giving rise to a choice to be solved according to different DI2; that is, either preferring the former or the latter (J. Wróblewski, 1985a, app. 52–5). The traditional metaphor is the opposition between 'the letter' and 'the spirit' (Ost and M. van de Kerchove, 1989) of law, which even terminologically is biased in favour of the latter. The solution of the conflict of arguments is also sometimes made by reference to transcategorical argu-

ments: the 'literal meaning' is opposed to the other meanings, the 'reasonable results' are opposed to other results, the reference to the contemporary law-maker is opposed to a reference to a historical law-maker or to an interpretation which does not take into account any law-maker at all, and so on.

To make some order of all current conflicts between various interpretations it is theoretically necessary to stress that the deep ground of these conflicts is the opposed values referred to above, and on the level of arguments the opposition between the meaning determined in the linguistic interpretation (linguistic meaning Ml), often combined with the meaning stated according to the directives of systemic interpretation (systemic Meaning Ms) on the one hand, and the meaning fixed with the help of functional directives (functional meaning Mf) on the other. The judicial interpretation has to solve: (a) how to use the first level DI1, that is, linguistic, systemic and functional directives; and (b) how to solve the conflicts between Ml, Ms and Mf, if any. These issues are linked together and theoretically described as the use of the second-level directives of interpretation DI2. The first issue is solved by procedural DI2 and the second by DI2 of preference.

4 No fixed procedural DI2 can be reconstructed from the Polish Supreme Court decisions where one finds various DI2 of this type.

(a) The DI2 of procedure is implied in the opinion that there is '[N]either need nor possibility of using either systemic or functional interpretation, when the result of the linguistic analysis is clear (*clara non sunt interpretanda*)' (SC 28.1.1987 III PZP 82/86, quoted in SC 30.11.1987 III PZP 36/87 OSPiKA 1988 P 81) (cf. J. Wróblewski, 1988b). That is the DI2 stating that the condition of the use of non-linguistic, viz., systemic and functional directives, is not needed if after linguistic interpretation the text is clear.

(b) The underlying conflict is patent when clarity, which is a static value, is opposed to some teleological, that is, functional and dynamic, arguments. This is clearly formulated by the Polish Constitutional Tribunal declaring that '. . . the analysed provisions of the Constitution are formulated unambiguously, and because of that one cannot use any extralinguistic directives of interpretation and suggest an actually convenient ratio legis good for the interpretation in a given situation' (CT 3.3.1987 P 2987 OTK 1988 p. 2). The corollary of this DI2 is formulated in the opinion that '. . . if the grammatical [that is, linguistic] interpretation . . . does not give any definitive reply to the doubts, then one ought to seek the functional and systemic interpretation, but excluding analogy' (SC 30.11.1987 III PZP 36/87 OSPiKA 1988 P 81).

(c)   The DI2 of procedure opposite to (a) and (b) states that in Ml meaning should be reconfirmed by the Ms and/or Mf meaning: 'Grammatical [that is, linguistic] interpretation is a deceptive method and results in unacceptable results from the legal and social point of view. Because of that one should use other methods of interpretation, and in particular systemic and functional interpretation' (SC 19.11.1988 III PZP 52/87 OSPiKA 1988 P 187). In other words, the result of linguistic interpretation should be confirmed by the other types of interpretation, and especially by functional interpretation (for example, SC 20.1.1982 VI KZP 14/81 OSPiKA 1983 K 59; SC 30.4.1986 II URN 31/86 OSPiKA 1987 P 79).

It seems that one can treat Art. 4 of the Polish Code of Civil Law (1964) as implying this sort of DI2 for civil law provisions: 'The provisions of the Civil Code should be interpreted and applied according to the principles of the constitution and purposes of the Polish People's Republic'. This directive could be extrapolated from the area of the civil law, and treated also as implying DI2 of preference too.

5   If, following the DI2 of procedure, the text is interpreted with the linguistic DI1, systemic DI1 and functional DI1, then there is a possibility of conflicting meanings determined by the use of each of them. One thus faces divergent Ml, Ms and Mf. The choice of one of them is necessary for any operative interpretation, because one cannot decide the case without applying a legal rule in one meaning or with consistent meanings. The DI2 of preference justify the choice and can also be used to make it (heuresis). There are no fixed DI2 of preference in the practice of the Polish highest courts.

(a)   Sometimes no interpretation could be accepted if it is in manifest contradiction to the content of the interpreted provision, which means the preference given to the M_1 (SC 4.12.1987 III PZP 85/86 OSPiKA 1988 P 191): 'There are no justified legal reasons to assert that art. 40 of the statute concerning the compensation for the work accident and accident and occupational diseases excludes any possibility to sue the work place for a disease connected with work which is not an occupational disease, because this would be in manifest contradiction with the content of the said provision ...' But, on the other hand, one rejects an interpretation based 'solely on the formulation of the provision' (SC 11.6.1982 III CRM 6/82 OSPiKA 1983 C 57). Also the Constitutional Tribunal criticized the Minister of Health and Social Care because he had used functional interpretation and accepted its results, whereas he should have preferred a linguistic interpretation because of the clarity of the text (CT 3.3.1987 P 2/87 OTK 1988 p. 2).

(b)   There is a repeated preference given to functional interpretation when it conflicts with linguistic interpretation (SC 27.3.1986 I CZ 137/85 OSPiKA 1987 C 123; 19.11.1987 III UZP 42/87 OSPiKA 1988 B 186). There is a similar case in the Constitutional Tribunal (CT 22.4.1987 K 1/87 OTK 1988 p. 3). The preference of functional argumentation could be treated as implied in Art. 4. Code Civil Law, quoted above (point 3).

(c)   The special case of DI2 of preference could be reconstructed as a postulate to prefer the meanings which are consistent with the interpretation of terms in various branches of the law in force. This preferential DI2 does not decide the choice substantively but only formally: it is for the uniformity of interpretation without deciding the issue in concrete cases of divergencies (SC 30.11.1987 III PZP 36/87 OSPiKA 1988 P 81).

(d)   It seems, therefore, that it is up to the court to choose between the competing DI2 of preference. The choice is among the relevant alternatives, which oscillate between the static and dynamic values referred to above. Within the former the Ml and Ms are preferred and, thus, one keeps to the 'letter of the law'. Within the latter the area of interpretative leeways is quite large and the conflicts between various interpretations are discussed using the qualificative terms *praeter legem* and *contra legem* (Wróblewski, 1961). This value-laden qualification is axiologically involved with the conceptual opposition between an operative interpretation as law-applying activity and law-making.

6   In the Polish practice the burden of argumentation in interpretation is not explicitly stated in Supreme Court decisions, but it can be determined in the directives of interpretation theoretically reconstructed from interpretative practice. (J. Wróblewski, 1987a, p. 49). These directives are based on some presumptions concerning the language in which interpreted legal rules are formulated:

(a)   One should not without sufficient reason ascribe to the interpreted terms any specific meaning different from the meaning these terms have in common natural language.

(b)   One should not without sufficient reason ascribe different meanings to the same terms used in legal provisions.

(c)   One should not without sufficient reason ascribe the same meaning to different terms.

VII   THE CONFLICT OF STATUTES WITH OTHER LEGAL NORMS

1   Issues of validity in statutory law (civilian) systems presuppose a systemic conception of validity (J. Wróblewski, 1986a). According to this conception, roughly speaking, a legal rule is valid in a system with determined spatio-temporal dimensions if it: (a) has been enacted according to rules valid in the system; (b) has not been repealed; (c) is consistent (coherent) with other rules valid in the system; or (d) if inconsistent (incoherent) with them, is not invalidated on the strength of the conflict of law rules, or interpreted in such a manner as to eliminate the inconsistency (incoherence) in question.

The assessment of validity of a rule is conceptually different from assessing its meaning, although there are some links between determining the validity and ascription of a meaning to a rule, and thus, in case of a doubt, with its interpretation. This is the case of the inconsistency of rules, because some uses of rules for resolving conflict between legal rules presuppose interpretation (substantive relation of *lex specialis* and *lex generalis*) and systemic interpretation is needed as a way of determining the meaning of the rule, which is inconsistent (incoherent) with other valid rules.

2   The hierarchical structure of the legal system is relevant for practical decisions concerning conflicts of validity and interpretation in three aspects:

(a)   In the aspect of validity, the higher rule is the basis of enacting the lower rule.

(b)   In the aspect of derogation, the derogating rule is hierarchically higher than a derogated rule (Pleszka, 1986).

(c)   Rules which are treated as principles are substantively higher than other rules.

Of these hierarchical relations, (a) and (b) are especially relevant in conflict of validity cases and (c) in systemic interpretation.

3   Conflicts of validity have both a procedural and a substantive dimension. An instance of the former is the situation where a rule's enactment is not in accordance with the governing procedural rules; of the latter, when the lower rule is not in accordance with the content of the higher. This type of conflict of validity is solved in the Polish system in two ways, depending on the institutions dealing with them.

The Constitutional Tribunal controls the constitutionality and legality of legal rules. The constitutionality control has two dimensions, viz., the relation of statutes to the constitution, and the relation of sub-statutory rules to the constitution. In the former situation of unconstitutionality, the Tribunal presents the case for the qualified vote of parliament, which either accepts the decision or, as a sovereign, rejects it. In the case of sub-statutory rules, these are nullified unless within three months they are changed by the law-maker in accordance with the Tribunal's decision so as to eliminate their unconstitutionality.

The legality control concerns the relation of sub-statutory rules with the statutes. Here the Tribunal, when it makes a finding of the illegality of the rule in question, annuls it unless the law-maker changes it according to the decision of the Tribunal in a three-months period in such a way as to eliminate the illegality. The Supreme Administration Court, when it makes a finding of the illegality of an act which has been the basis of the controlled administrative decision, does not apply it in the case in question. The same holds for ordinary courts, which have the duty to test the legality of sub-statutory acts relevant for the decision of a case. If such an act is held to be illegal, they ought not to apply it (CT 21.9.1987 P 3/87 OTK 1988 p. 5).

4   The texts of decisions dealing with conflicts of validity contain no explicit statement of the interpretative issues involved.

5   The hierarchical substantive structure of the legal system is highly relevant for systemic interpretation. The DI1 of this interpretation postulate such an ascription of the meaning of the interpreted rule as will be consistent with the meaning of the hierarchically higher rules. A DI2 states that among the possible meanings one has to choose the meaning in which the rule will be more consistent (coherent) with the higher rules. The standard case is when the higher rule is treated as principle in relation to the interpreted rule (for example, SC 6.12.1963 RN 28/63 OSPiKA K 168; SC 25.2.1978 III CZP 100/77 OSPiKA 1983 C 217). The term 'principle' is used, however, in many senses in legal language, whether in the juridical language of legal practice or in the juridical language of legal science. In one of those senses, a 'principle' is a legal rule of special substantive importance, and among the criteria of importance is the hierarchical place of the rule, and/or the special significance of the rule within the legal system or legal institution.

VIII   PRESUMPTIONS GUIDING INTERPRETATION

1   The 'general presumptions' of statutory interpretation are thought of here as reasons for formulation and/or acceptance of interpretative directives. It is a fair hypothesis that each directive or set of directives has such reasons, if it is not a directive authoritatively imposed and valid *ex auctoritate*. We reconstruct the presumptions in question for sets of interpretative directives, corresponding to the types of arguments we have singled out. These presumptions could also be treated as features ascribed to the (rational) lawmaker. The presumptions stated here are theoretical reconstructions; they are not explicitly formulated in the justifications of interpretative decisions.

2   Linguistic presumptions are proper to the linguistic context
of the provision interpreted. Such presumptions include:

(a)   Presumption of common language: the law-maker
does not without sufficient reason use common
language expressions with a special legal meaning
(J. Wróblewski, 1985a, p. 47). When a legal definition is lacking one should use a common language
meaning (SC 27.4.1982 II URM 74/82 OSPiKA
1983 C 1982) cf. Section III (3(a)) above. But the
term 'tort' has a different meaning in common
language than in civil law (SC 23.8.1968 II CR 318/
68 OSPiKA 1969 C 201).

(b)   Presumption of legal language: the law-maker does
not without sufficient reason use technical legal
expressions, save with their special terminological
meaning, proper to determined branches of law
and/or normative acts. (J. Wróblewski, 1985a, p.
47). But there are some exceptions, for example,
even the difference of the term 'statute' in civil law
and in criminal law (SC 16.3.1967 VI KZP 55/66
OSPiKA 1967 K 200). The special meaning of the
term 'statute' in civil law was relevant also in a case
before the Constitutional Tribunal (CT 28.5.1986 U
1/86 OTK 1987 p. 2).

(c)   Each term used by the law-maker has one determined concept as its meaning, and each concept in
use has one term expressing it (J. Wróblewski,
1985a, 47 ff; SC 21.10.1983 III CZP 48/82 OSPiKA
1984 C 82). This presumption expresses an ideal of
legal language which is, however, in contrast with
the fuzziness of actual legal language (cf. section I
(3(b)) above.

(d)   The legislature observes its own directives of interpretation, as one of the presumptions of its rationality (J. Wróblewski, 1985c, ch. 11).

3   Systemic presumptions are linked with the systemic context
of interpreted provisions.

(a)   The law-maker intends not to be redundant (J.
Wróblewski, 1985a, p. 48). One cannot interpret
the text as if one part of it were non-existent (SC
24.8.2965 III PO 31/65 OSPiKA 1966 U 82).

(b)   The law-maker does not enact contradictory provisions (J. Wróblewski, 1985a, 48 ff) (SC 26.2.1969 III CZP 131/68 OSPiKA 1969 C 231; SC 19.8.1982 III CZP 21/82 OSPiKA P 76).

(c)   The law-maker intends to be coherent, and gives more weight to principles than to 'ordinary rules' (cf. Section XIV, 5 below) and makes the system a coherent (harmonious) set of rules (J. Wróblewski, 1985a, p. 49). For example, rejection of an interpretation may occur because of inconsistency with the principles of criminal law (SC 6.12.1963; RNw 28/63 OSPiKA 1965 K 168) or with principles of civil procedure (SC 27.6.1969 III CZP 31/69 OSPiKA 1979 C 87).

(d)   The law-maker does not intend to create gaps in law.

(e)   The law-maker groups enacted provisions according to principles of proper logical division.

4   Functional presumptions are correlated with the functional context of interpreted provisions.

(a)   The law-maker's intention is that interpretation should support positively evaluated decisions (just, rational, sound, reasonable and so on) (J. Wróblewski, 1985a, 50 ff, 1973b, chaps VIII, IX).

(b)   According to the law-maker's intention, enacted laws have to be effective (J. Wróblewski, 1985a, p. 51; SC 11.8.1982 XII UZP 18/82 OSPiKA 1983 P 75); an interpretation is rejected if it makes a provision have no practical importance (SC 6.5.1966 VI KZP 62/65 OSPiKA 1967 K 11) or practical applicability (SC 10.5.1968 VI KZP 2/67 OSPiKA 1969 K 68).

(c)   The interpretation should be coherent and, therefore, it should follow the axiology the decision maker accepts. For an operative interpretation, for example, the DI2 is formulated that an interpretation has to be eliminated if it is '. . . in contradiction with the postulates of the certainty and stability of judicial decision, with their weight and with procedural expediency' (SC 18.12.1986 000 PZP 78/86 OSPiKA 1988 P 48).

5   I do not treat as presumptions of interpretation generally accepted directives making a part of our legal culture, such

as 'where the law makes no distinction, it is not for us to make one' — *lege non distinguente nec nostrum est distinguere* — (SC 29.1.1987 III CRN 298/86 III CRN 348/86 OSPiKA 1987 C 192) or 'law works not retrospectively' — *lex retro non agit* — (for example, CT 28.5.1986 OTK 1987 p. 2).

Such principles govern judicial application of law in all statutory (civil) law systems and have a general importance.

IX   THE STYLE OF STATUTORY INTERPRETATION

1   In Poland the highest courts' decisions are always collective decisions, and this means reaching a consensus of a majority of decision makers. The opinion of the court gives reasons for the decision. Not all decisions have a stated justification, but — according to the universal legal culture in contemporary administration of justice — all of them are justifiable. This means that they should be rational decisions, as opposed to arbitrary decisions. Justifiability means that for each decision one can formulate answers to two questions: (a) 'Why is decision D correct?' and (b) 'Why is decision D the unique decision which ought to be made?' (J. Wróblewski, 1978, p. 120). One finds an answer in the judicial opinions formulated in a determined form (surface justification) or in the theoretical analysis determining what arguments should support a decision in a hard case.

2   The Polish system imposes no duty to present a stated justification for each judicial decision. A justification (that is, a written statement of justifying reasons) has to be prepared in the following situations:

(a)   when a party demands it;
(b)   if a dissenting opinion has been stated;
(c)   if the final judicial opinion (or verdict) is attacked by a competent person; and
(d)   if the case raises especially important questions of a general kind.

These requirements as legally formulated apply to first instance courts. In any case these courts, when pronouncing final decisions, have the duty to present orally the main legal grounds and reasons for their decision. Decisions of second instance courts, and *a fortiori* of the highest courts, are always justified in a written opinion.

3   The law in force determines also the content of the minimum

judicial justification, singling out the following elements for all cases:

(a)   the determination of the factual basis of the decision;

(b)   indication of the accepted facts;

(c)   enumeration of the accepted evidence and the reasons for rejection of other evidence; and

(d)   the normative basis of the decision, that is, the valid rules applied.

These common elements are enlarged in case of a final decision of penal law, in which there must also be included the facts determining the features of penalty, measures of prevention, relations with civil proceedings, if any, and other important arguments.

4   The style of judicial opinions, in spite of all their diversity, has some common features:

(a)   The opinions are formulated in juridical operative language, which is closely related to the legal language in which the applied rules are formulated (J. Wróblewski, 1988c, 17–20). This gives the opinion its special style of argument-formulation.

(b)   The style is anchored in the legal regulation of the contents of the minimum legal opinion, which is especially relevant for decisions of the Supreme Court.

(c)   The style is based on the presupposition that the given decision is the unique right decision in the case. This is strictly linked with the underlying ideology of the judicial application of law, and is easily explicable, but not, in my opinion, theoretically supportable (J. Wróblewski, 1989a).

(d)   The style of argumentation, as a rule, stresses mostly the logical arguments, keeping out the underlying evaluative issues, which can be easily identified in a theoretical analysis, but which the court either conceals or at least only mentions without going into detail.

(e)   The arguments are formulated in an impersonal way, although the judges of the bench are named, not anonymous.

(f)   There are differences of style depending on the types of case decided in various highest-level courts, that is, in Poland by the Supreme Court (SC), Supreme Administrative Court (SAC), and Constitutional Tribunal (CT) (cf. Preliminary).

5   Supreme Court (SC) decisions deal with cases as a second instance court, or as the court deciding cases according to special procedural provisions after the case has been decided by a second instance, or as the court answering questions presented by the courts (including 'lower benches' of the same SC) for which a solution is required to essential problems of interpretation, or as an organ issuing binding guidelines for the administration of justice. The present chapter deals only with the style of SC opinions in decisions of concrete cases. In these cases the minimum legal justification is relevant, because the SC has to decide the legal consequences of the concrete proven facts according to the valid legal rules applicable in the case.

The position of the SC influences the style of decisions:

(a)   The prior history of the case is described, up to the point of the decision of the court below with its justification.

(b)   The grounds of attacking this decision and the content of criticism is referred to.

(c)   The fact-situation is described, and its legal qualification stated.

(d)   The applied rules are stated, along with their interpretation in any case of controversy.

(e)   The justification of the decision is expounded in relation to (a) and (d); this determines the further proceedings in any case where the decision of the court below is changed and the case has to be decided afresh.

The peculiarity of the style of SC decisions lies in the way in which these deal with the previous decision in the case. They cover the problems of validity and applicability, of interpretation, of evidence and of the choice of consequences, but all those issues depend on the case in question and on the arguments which are controlled because of its history. The grounds for reversing the prior decision are, of course, enumerated in the rules of procedure: the underlying model is a subsumptive model, but to justify the premises various arguments are used to make the SC's own opinion stronger. The use of precedents is quite extensive and appears in various forms (J. Wróblewski, 1983a, pp. 157–68). The reference to scientific opinion is rather scarce, and almost exclusively to the *communis opinio doctorum* (the general run of scholarly opinion), not to concrete persons or scientific monographs or commentaries.

6   The Supreme Administrative Court (SAC) decisions have a style determined by its competence, viz. the review of legality of administrative decisions. The observation of valid rules is controlled and, because of that, sometimes the correctness of their interpretation is discussed, together with issues of qualification (characterisation) of the facts of the case. The most significant element of style is an analysis of the validity of rules applied in reviewed administrative decisions – here the activity of the SAC has preceded the work of SC. The negative result of validity control results in declaration of the lack of a normative basis of the controlled decision. The scope of control excludes arguments dealing with policy factors, although various evaluative elements are used when the interpretational issues are discussed. The SAC sometimes refers to its own precedents, and also to those of the SC. It occasionally (but not often) refers to named scholarly works as arguments, besides making reference to *communis opinio doctorum*.

7   The Constitutional Tribunal (CT) has been at work scarcely more than two years now, and it is still shaping its own style.

X INTERPRETATION WITH REGARD TO THE CHARACTER OF THE STATUTE

1   Interpretative arguments are in the main independent of the subject matter of the statute interpreted. But there are exceptions. In some branches of law there are exclusionary directives of interpretation, such as that which prohibits argument by analogy against the accused in criminal matters. In others there are mandatory directives, such as that in Art. 4 civ. code, which directs that interpretation take into account social coexistence and the interest of the state; and in labour law, Art. 1 of the labour code directs that interpretation accord with the principles and purposes of the state, this being clearly a directive which requires preference for a functional interpretation of relevant legislation.

2   The age of a statute is also relevant in interpretation, for reasons indicated in the preliminary section above, namely

because of the problem of adapting prewar law to the functionally different context of the postwar political system. The present deep changes involved in the movement away from the socialist system is expressing itself in frenetic law-making which is intended to serve the new society by eliminating existing regulations. It is as yet (March 1990) too soon to explore the impact of this change on interpretational practice.

3   Legislative technique certainly has a bearing on legal interpretation. Particularly relevant is recourse to general clauses, which improve the elasticity of the legal text, opening it to various changing evaluations and individualizations of judicial decision, but at the same time creating interpretational leeways. General clauses concerning 'principles of social coexistence' or 'social danger of behaviour' occur in various Polish statutes, the latter invoking a concrete assessment of individual cases which is an essential prerequisite for an infraction of criminal law to count as a 'crime'.

4   Legislative procedure includes work by parliamentary commissions of plenary sessions of the House of Sejm and the House of Senate. Even the best draft is subjected to debate, with possible resultant amendments and compromises which make the final text ambiguous. Here there is a dilemma between democracy and 'scientism' in law-making. There is a draft 'statute on law-making' which might discipline legislative procedures and stimulate greater rationality in law-making; but it is not yet implemented (see J. Wróblewski 1982b, 1985f).

XI   THE ROLE OF THE COURTS

1   The constitution and some statutes define the place of the courts within the organization of the state machinery (J. Wróblewski, 1987c). The general principle is that the courts are the only organs of administration of justice, and that this task is performed by common courts, with historically diminishing exceptional jurisdictions (military courts, state economic arbitration, labour courts), and the two recent tribunals of special character, that is, the Tribunal of State and the Constitutional Tribunal. The constitutional principle of judicial independence states that the judges are subordinated only to statute law. The principle of independence is understood in a manner historically shaped by European legal culture and faces analogous problems as in other

statutory law systems (normative vs. factual independence; the nomination and advancement mechanism; the problem of relations between courts and politics and so on) (J. Wróblewski, 1987b). Judicial subordination to statute law defines the role of the courts in relation to the legislature and to the executive (cf. 2 and 3 below). In any case, this means that courts cannot change the statutes they are expected to apply, and this is thought of as an important feature defining legality (section XIV (3)).

2   The legislature plays a vital part in the administration of the courts through the Council of State, elected by the parliament from its members and functioning as the 'collective head of the State'. The Council of State nominates the judges. The First President of the Supreme Court presents the report on the functioning of the judiciary before this Council. The judges of the Tribunal of State and of the Constitutional Tribunal are elected by the parliament.

The principle of judicial subordination to statute law has some reservations only in the case of the judges of the Constitutional Tribunal, who control *inter alia* the constitutionality of statutes. This task of the Constitutional Tribunal has to be combined with the constitutional principle of the sovereignty of the parliament, and this is a common problem of all systems in which the controlling agency is not the parliament itself. The Polish solution is that the Tribunal's verdict of unconstitutionality of a statute has to be presented to the parliament, which must decide whether to change the statute according to the verdict, or to reject the verdict by the majority of three-quarters of deputies voting.

Notwithstanding the subordination of the judge to statute law, there is also a practice of giving the courts a decisional leeway as a result of a purposeful legislative technique. The paradigm example is the use of general clauses or evaluative terms referring to extra-legal evaluations, discussed in section X above (cf. Leszczynski, 1986, chs III and IV). Last, but not least, one should stress that the law-maker can always react to the practice of the courts, and especially to an interpretation considered wrong, by changing the law and thus making an authentic interpretation (J. Wróblewski, 1985e). This is the ultimate instrument of legislative control over the courts.

3   The relations of the courts with the executive depend on the role of the latter, namely whether the executive is a law-maker or is a decision maker in a concrete case. The execu-

tive is the law-maker which enacts rules of a sub-statutory level. The relations in question are expressed in the principle that the judge is subordinated only to the statute and is not subordinated to the sub-statutory rules. The common court or the Supreme Administrative Court when deciding a case can decide that a sub-statutory level rule is unconstitutional or illegal and then it has the duty not to apply it (CT 21.9.1987 P 3/87 OTK 1988 p. 5). For the common law court the sub-statutory rule could be relevant for an application of a statute and this is the occasion of not taking it into account if unconstitutional or illegal. The Supreme Administrative Court reviews the legality of decisions, necessarily reviewing also the sub-statutory rules if they constitute the normative basis of the decision in question. Here also non-application of the sub-statutory rule is the appropriate remedy in case of unconstitutionality or illegality. The competence of the Constitutional Tribunal in respect of sub-statutory rules is different. In the case of their unconstitutionality and/or illegality the Tribunal nullifies them if the law-maker does not change them according to the verdict in three months. This is not a case of non-application but of derogation, which gives, of course, a more clear and final solution.

4   The administration of justice in the common courts is hierarchically ordered in two levels (regional courts and district or 'wojewodship' courts) with the Supreme Court at the top. The Supreme Court has several Chambers, one of which reviews cases decided by military courts. There are two tribunals with special competence – the Tribunal of State and Constitutional Tribunal – and the Supreme Administrative Court is the agency of judicial control of the administration. There is no system of binding precedent. But the decisions of the higher courts do have an important functional impact on later decisions of the same or of lower courts (J. Wróblewski, 1983a, pp. 157–79). And there is a peculiarly Polish institution in the way of a rather developed system whereby binding directives of interpretation can be formulated by various benches of the Supreme Court.

XII   STATUTORY PRESCRIPTIONS ON INTERPRETATION

1   In Poland there is a rather well-developed system of legal regulation of statutory interpretation, whereby binding

directives of interpretation are formulated in an authoritative way. This depends on a rather complicated framework
within the State apparatus (cf. Wlodyka, 1971; Garlicki,
1984, chaps V–VIII). The basic forms of legal regulation of
statutory interpretation in Poland are as follows:

(a)   Statutory provisions containing directives of inter-
       pretation.
(b)   Authentic interpretation enacted by the law-maker.
(c)   Interpretation enacted by the Council of State.
(d)   Resolutions of the Supreme Court containing direc-
       tives of interpretation and application of law.
(e)   Interpretative principles voted by the Supreme
       Court.
(f)   Concrete interpretation of statutory provisions
       applied in a given case, binding the court of lower
       instance, and fixed by the court of higher instance in
       the case.

Not legally binding is interpretation in the form of commonly accepted directives which are elaborated in theory
and accepted in practice (J. Wróblewski, 1959, chap. VIII S 2,
1983a, 92 ff). There is in Poland no tendency towards
enactment of a general law on interpretation.

2   The closest instruments to a law on interpretation are the
interpretive directives contained in statutory provisions.
There is one provision of this type in Art. 4. civ. code: 'The
civil law provisions should be interpreted and applied in
conformity with the principles of the constitution and the
purposes of the Polish People's Republic.' Other forms of
generally binding interpretation are practically not so relevant. Authentic interpretation appears in the form of legal
definitions, whose legal nature is theoretically rather controversial (W. Gregorowicz, 1962; Nowak, 1969; Alchourrón
and E. Bulygin, 1983). The Council of State, is an emanation
of the Polish parliament. It has only twice exercised its
interpretational competence to fix the meaning of determined statutory provisions.

3   The important legal regulation of statutory interpretation
binding all the courts and the organs supervised by the
Supreme Court is contained in the 'directives of interpretation and judicial practice' issued by the courts. The statutory purpose of these directives is to engender uniformity of
decisional practice (cf. Art. 13, point 3, Statute of 20 September 1984 on the Supreme Court).

Other forms of legally binding interpretation from the point of view of their legal impact are not as relevant as those mentioned above. It should be stressed, however, that in practice the interpretations adopted by the Supreme Court, albeit not legally binding, are extensively used as arguments supporting interpretative decisions, a fact which pushes towards uniformity of legal interpretation (J. Wróblewski, 1973a, 1983a, pp. 157–79).

XIII CONSTITUTIONAL LAW AND INTERPRETATION

1   One should differentiate between interpretation of the constitution and the role of constitutional principles in interpretation of non-constitutional statutes.
2   Reference to constitutional norms and principles has been extremely rare in the decisions of the administration of justice in Poland at least until the last two years.

Analogy as a tool of interpretation has been used to expand the constitutional principle of protection of the family (Art. 79 sec. a 1 Polish Const.) to cover the protection of the children's rights (SC 30.11.1987 III PZP 36/87 OSPiKA 1988 P 81) and the constitution has been used to apply the principles governing the administration of social organizations to trade unions (SC 20.7.1987 I PRZ 6/87 OSPiKA P 85).

XIV INTERPRETATION AND PRINCIPLES OF LAW

1   The ideology of legal interpretation identifies the values which have to be implemented in it and/or the directives of interpretation which ought to be applied. The ideal elaboration of such an ideology would take the form of a normative theory of interpretation thought of as a set of values and directives which is consistent, coherent and complete, and which is adequate for any purposes of interpretation. In practice, however, we have to do usually with ideologies of legal interpretation which form neither coherent nor complete sets determining our interpretative activity (J. Wróblewski, 1972a, 1985a, chap. 6, 1987a, ch. 6). The values ascribed to or referred to in interpretative justifications can be classified through various typologies. The most simple

typology singles out:

(a)   values referred to in the applied rules;
(b)   values implied by the texts of the applied rules;
(c)   values accepted by the courts and expressed in justification of their decisions;
(d)   values implied by the justifications of the interpretative decision of the courts; and
(e)   values accepted in the body of doctrinal opinion (J. Wróblewski, 1973b, chap. II).

2   Values referred to in applied rules or implied by them (points (a) and (b) above) express the axiology of the law. According to the ideology of operative interpretation in the Polish Courts, it is expected that interpretation has to implement the axiology of law. There is no space here to enumerate these values or, in other words, to reconstruct the axiology of Polish law. It is worth mentioning that there are some values directly dealing with the administration of justice: the principle of legality and the values of social coexistence which should be implemented by it. The values 'transferred' from the axiology of applied law are referred to in justification, especially when the applied texts do refer to them. Values proper to judicial decision ((c) and (d) above) are proper to the ideology of the application of law (including its interpretation) or have a mixed character, that is, in part belong to the axiology of the applied law and in part to the values of the application of law. Among them there are legality, certainty, objectivity, justice, equity, uniformity, praxiological values (effectiveness, speed) (J. Wróblewski, 1973b chaps III–IX) and rationality of decision implied by its proper justifiability (J. Wróblewski, 1985a pp. 49–56; cf. Aarnio, Alexy and Peczenik, 1981, part II; Aarnio, 1987, chap. IV.2; Peczenik, 1983, ch. 4; Perelman, 1979, chap. 11; Zirk-Sadowski, 1984, chs 4–6).

3   Legality has a special place among the values (or principles) of judicial decision making, including interpretation. The courts are expected to apply law and not to make it and, hence, the essential issue in controlling legal interpretation is whether it is an assessment of the meaning of pragmatically doubtful rules or is surreptitious law-making. The value (principle) of legality is clearly stated in the constitutional and statutory regulation of the tasks of the courts. Moreover it is explicitly stated as an argument in justification in Supreme Court decisions. The Supreme Court has stated:

'The courts have the duty . . . to apply the valid provisions without taking into account whether these provisions – according to the bench – could be considered as more or less convincing and right' (SC 13.6.1959 3 CO 11/59 OSPiKA 1960 C 45); 'the courts have only to apply the law and to interpret it properly'.

4   The value of rationality is a theoretical reconstruction of the justifying reasons for the courts' duty to justify their decisions and of the background reasons for the institutions for review ('control') of judicial decisions (J. Wróblewski, 1983a, pp. 127–55).

5   Legal texts, legal practice and legal sciences all commonly refer to 'principles' instead of to 'values'. The term 'principles' is, however, used ambiguously in law and there is a problem of identifying the senses in which it is used in operative interpretation (Wronkowska and Zielinski 1972). We can distinguish the following senses (Wróblewski, 1984a), which are identified by conventional names and symbols: 'positive principles of law' (PPL), 'implicit principles of law' (IPL), 'extra-systemic principles of law' (EPL), 'name-principles of law' (NPL) and 'construction-principles of law' (CPL).

6   PPL are explicit legal provisions treated as more important than other 'ordinary' provisions. So some statutory provisions are labelled 'principles' or treated as expressing 'principles' of law. Such PPL are used in legal interpretation alongside other provisions, but carrying particular weight in systemic interpretation. 'Ordinary' provisions should be interpreted so as to be coherent with them. IPL are rules thought of as premises or consequences of valid legal provisions, and assumed to be so logically bound to enacted provisions that they are virtually valid legal rules themselves. IPL are usually more general than the provisions from which they are derived. Their function in legal interpretation is the same as that of PPL. EPL are sometimes used in response to explicit reference in the interpreted legal provisions, sometimes without such explicit reference. The standard case of the former is in the use of general clauses and/or evaluative terms in statutes.

7   NPL are names of essential features of legal institutions, such as principles of good faith, or liberty of contracts, of objective truth and so on. NPL are only exceptionally used as justifying arguments in statutory interpretation, but are widely used as arguments in interpretation of individual

normative acts such as contracts, and in the justification of decisions on evidence. CPL are used mostly as the underlying principles of several interpretative arguments. The principle of the rational law-maker is such a principle.

8   A peculiarity of interpretation in the Polish courts has been their extensive use of extra-systemic principles (EPL) in the form of 'principles of social coexistence in a socialist state', both when these are referred to in interpreted provisions and when they are not. On analysis, it can be seen that the EPL in question functions analogously to equity in other continental systems of law; it is usually treated theoretically as a part of socialist morality (J. Wróblewski, 1973b, ch. X).

XV   THE CHARACTER OF THE HIGHER COURTS

1   There are four higher courts in Poland: the Supreme Court, the Supreme Administrative Court, the Constitutional Tribunal and the Tribunal of State (cf. Preliminary). Each of them has special competences and faces different interpretative issues. Leaving aside the Tribunal of State which deals with the constitutional responsibility of the highest officials, the remaining courts have published records of their decisions, including interpretative issues. The most complicated scope of activities is that of the Supreme Court. Interpretation can be inherent in the performance of the following functions of this Court:

(a)   In decisions made by the court as a second instance court.

(b)   In decisions on extraordinary forms of appeal from decisions having the validity of law (*res iudicata*).

(c)   In resolutions of the court establishing guidelines for the application of law and of judicial practice.

(d)   In resolutions explaining rules which have given rise to doubts or whose application has resulted in conflicting judicial decisions.

(e)   In resolutions deciding legal issues which have caused serious doubts in concrete cases.

The interpretative activity of the Supreme Court occurs in most cases; that is, seven to ten thousand cases per year. Interpretation in decisions of (a) and (b) appears as judicial interpretation of substantially the same type as occurs in lower courts, but more developed. In resolutions of types (c) and (d), interpretation is not linked with concrete cases but rather with general issues and therefore is expressed in a different style and without case-bound arguments. Interpretation in cases of type (e) has mixed features.

The interpretation of the Supreme Administrative Court concerns the legality of administrative decisions. Its interpretative argumentation is rather similar to that of the Supreme Court but the interpreted texts are often enacted on a sub-statutory level. The scope of argumentation is in principle the same.

The Constitutional Tribunal deals with the constitutionality of statutes and sub-statutory acts. It deals extensively with constitutional interpretation which has several peculiarities because of the 'language of the constitution' (J. Wróblewski, 1985a, section 8), but also interprets statutes and other normative acts. The issues involved have impact on the style of the decisions. These make extensive use of doctrinal legal writings and academic experts for discussing *questiones iuris* (questions of law).

2   Judges of the highest courts in Poland exhibit different career patterns. The judges of the Supreme Court and Supreme Administrative Court are professional career judges. At present they are appointed by the President on the nomination of the Minister of Justice, who chooses among the candidates presented by self-governing judicial bodies. Judicial office is for life, this being aimed at safeguarding judicial independence. The normal judicial career requirements do not apply to law professors, who are treated as *ex officio* qualified. The judges of the Constitutional Tribunal and of the Tribunal of State are elected by parliament for fixed periods of time. The judges are thus not career judges, but do have to have judicial qualifications.

3   Cases in the highest courts are heard without any selectivity exercisable by the courts. Exceptions to this rule of non-selectivity are Supreme Court activities of types (c), (d) and (e) above; these depend on the Court's evaluation of a need for intervention by itself. Factual questions are dealt with by the Supreme Court, subject to certain procedurally stated limitations, whereas the Supreme Administrative Court deals in the main with legal issues alone and the Constitutional Tribunal exclusively analyses issues of constitutionality and of legality. The Tribunal of State acts like any court dealing with factual and legal questions and, if there are no special rules, follows the Code of Criminal Procedure.

XVI   THE LEGISLATURE: STRUCTURE AND PROCEDURES

1   Legislation is a rather complex process. Drafts are formally presented only by the agencies which have the legislative initiative, that is by government or groups of representatives in parliament. Government drafts, which in practice until now are the majority, are prepared by government agencies using their specialized administration units for drafting. During the preparation of drafts various opinions are used, especially the opinions of the Legislative Council as a body nominated by the Prime Minister and consisting of legal scholars and top practitioners. Opinions of other bodies are also given, depending on the subject-matter of statutory regulation, and during consultation with various organizations 'private' drafts are sometimes presented. The drafts are presented to the Sejm, which has the exclusive competence of statutory law-making. After the first reading and discussion, the draft is elaborated by commissions of the Sejm and, after the second reading, a vote on it is taken. After the vote, the draft goes to the Senate, the Second House, is discussed and either accepted or returned with proposals for change. These are discussed by the Sejm, which can either approve them or reject them by special vote. Parliamentary discussions are, of course, political because of the character of the legislature. Debate is ended by the vote, which is ordinarily by simple majority. Now political discussion runs as in other parliaments; the Senate–Sejm relations have no background in long-established practice, because the Senate is a new institution in the postwar system in Poland. Also the recent change from the formal three-party system, with the hegemony of the Communist Party, to the present political pluralism has had real impact on the discussion and voting patterns. The phenomena are, however, too new to allow for any generalizations.

2   In law-making there is an important conflict between the procedural values of democracy and the demands of 'scientific' law-making (J. Wróblewski, 1982a, 1985c, ch. 14). Parliament is a representative body and the degree of its democratic character depends on electoral law and electoral practices. The last elections (1989) were fully democratic for the Senate and had a predetermined proportion of places for the 'government' and 'opposition' in the Sejm according to the 'Round Table' agreements of 1989. The 'scientific' element in statutory law-making is in some degree assured for

government-presented drafts, but at a level lower than that postulated by legal science. Parliamentary commissions can call experts to advise them on legal issues. There are rather few lawyers serving as deputies in parliament.

3   All the materials of legislative history are easily accessible from plenary sessions of parliament, but this is not the case of the commissions' deliberations. The material most relevant to the 'will of the historical law-maker' is the official record of the parliamentry plenary session, but this is not used in argument about statutory interpretation.

4   The legislature has several opportunities to react to judicial interpretations of legislation. Interpretations can be accepted, or tolerated if deemed not too bad. If they are rejected, the legislature can give an 'authentic interpretation', or can change the law (J. Wróblewski, 1985e).

XVII   FEATURES OF THE LEGAL CULTURE

1   The very concept of legal culture is ambiguous and not easy to define. It seems that at least the following elements enter into any use of the term in discussions of the judiciary: (a) the epistemic and axiological attitudes of judges; (b) their dominant approach to law in terms of a 'formalistic' or 'anti-formalistic' attitude; (c) their legal skills, including their use of academic doctrine. Of these elements, (a) is the most basic and most difficult to grasp, but is discussed extensively in only one scholarly work (B. Wróblewski, 1934). Here the discussion focuses on (b) and (c).

2   By 'formalism' one may understand a stress on arguments of the linguistic and systemic types, linked with a commitment to the idea that interpretation ought to stick to determination of meaning and hold back from judicial creativity. Thus understood, it describes well the general climate of justification of operative interpretational decisions in Poland. It is linked with the ideology of legal and rational judicial decisions (J. Wróblewski, 1987b, pp. 28–31, 1988a, ch. XIV). But this formalism is upheld only so long as the pressure of functional arguments is not too strong.

Statutes quite often include general clauses which necessarily open the way to non-formalist modes of argument, for example, clauses about the principles of social coexistence, or the interest of the state, or the social destination of rights and so on. Again there are contexts in which the pressure of functional arguments is great; this occurs especially in interpretation of the 'old' rules. Here the preference given to functional directives of legal interpretation over linguistic and systemic ones could be treated as a symptom of anti-formalism.

There is an additional peculiar feature which is already noticeable and which will probably be rather significant in the future. Formerly, during the period of 'real socialism', the idea of the political character of the administration of justice was treated as self-evident (J. Wróblewski, 1987c, p. 87). Now, in the present great political changes, this idea is discarded. The apolitical character of the administration of justice is very strongly stressed, and with it is postulated the requirement that all political affiliation and activity of judges be suspended. This tendency could mean a stricter following of the law than the previous ideological climate allowed for.

3   The skills of judges in interpretation are, of course linked with their training. The standards of judicial training are set in legal doctrine both as this is involved in legal education and as it provides the independent critique of judicial practice through notes and glosses on judicial decisions, especially those of the highest courts.

REFERENCES

In referring to judicial decisions, I identify the Court: either Supreme Court (SC) or Supreme Administrative Court (SAC) or Constitutional Tribunal (CT) with the relevant date (written: day, month, year), the official identification of the case, and the source, which is usually *Orzecznictwo Sadów Polskich i Komisji Arbitrażowych* (OSPiKA) and the identification of the place of the cited decision by a letter (A, K, P, etc.) and a number. The letters indicate: A – the SAC, C – Civil and Administrative SC Chamber; K – Criminal SC Chamber; P – SC Chamber of Law and Social Insurance. For CT the publication is *Orzecznictwo Trybunalu Konstytucyj-nego'* (OTK).

For example, the Resolution of the Supreme Court of 15 March 1982 identified as III CZP 18/82 published in *Orzechnictwo Sadów Polskich i Komisji Arbitrazowych* of the 1983 year, under position CO-Number 44, is written: SC 15.3.1982 III CZP 18/82 OSPiKA 1983 C 44 (analogously for the SAC or CT).

Bibliography

Aarnio, A. (1983), *Philosophical Perspectives in Jurisprudence*, Helsinki.

Aarnio, A. (1987), *The Rational as Reasonable, A Treatise on Legal Justification*, Dordrecht/Boston/Lancaster/Tokyo.

Aarnio, A., Alexy, R. and Peczenik, A. (1981), 'The Foundation of Legal Reasoning', *Rechtstheorie* **12**.

Alchourron, C.E. and Bulygin, E. (1983), 'Definiciones y normas', in E. Bulygin *et al.*, (eds), *El Linguaje del derecho*, Buenos Aires.

Alexy, R. (1978), *Theorie der juristischen Argumentation*, Frankfurt am Main.
Borucka-Arctowa, M. (ed.) (1978), *Poglądy społeczeństwa polskiego na stosowanie prawa* (The Opinions of the Polish society concerning the Application of Law), Wroclaw.
Dascal, M. and Wróblewski, J. (1988), 'Transparency and Doubt: Understanding and Interpretation in Pragmatics and in Law', *Law and Philosophy* **7**.
Ferrajoli, L. (1966), 'Interpretazione dottrinale e interpretazione operativa', *Rivista internazionale di filosofia del diritto*.
Garlicki, L. *et al.* (1984), *Sąd Najwyzszy w PRL* (The Supreme Court in Poland), Wroclaw/W-wa/Kraków/Gdańsk/Łódz.
Gizbert-Studnicki, T. (1975), 'Koniunkcja w kodeksie karnym' (Conjunction in the Penal Code), *Studia Prawnicze* 1–2.
Gizbert-Studnicki, T. (1986), *Język prawny z perspektywy socjolingwistycznej* (Legal Language from the Sociolinguistic Perspective), Warszawa/Kraków.
Gregorowicz, J. (1982), *Definicje w prawie i w nauce prawa* (Definition in Law and in the Legal Sciences), Łódz.
Grzybowski, S. (1985), *System prawa cywilnego, Czcść ogólna* (System of the Civil Law. The General Part), Wroclaw/Warszawa/Krakòw/Gdańsk/Łódz.
van der Kerchove, M. (1978), 'La doctrine du sens clair et la jurisprudence de la Cour de cassation en Belgique', (in M. van de Kerchove (ed.), *L'interprétation en droit. Approche pluridisciplinaire*, Bruxelles.
van der Kerchove, M. (1986), 'La théorie des actes de langage et la théorie de l'interprétation juridique', in P. Amselek (ed.), *Théorie des actes de langage, d'éthique et de droit*, Paris.
van der Kerchove, M. and Ost, F. (1988), *Le Système juridique entre ordre et désordre*, Paris.
Kowalksi, J., Lamentowicz, W. and Winczorek, P. (1986), *Theorie państwa i prawa* (Theory of State and Law), Warszawa.
Lang, W., Wróblewski, J., and Zawadzki, S. (1986), *Teoria państwa i prawa* (Theory of State and Law), 3rd edn., Warszawa.
Leszczyński, L. (1986), *Klauzule generalne w stosowaniu prawa* (General Clauses in the Application of Law), Lublin.
MacCormick, N. (1978), *Legal Reasoning and Legal Theory*, Oxford.
Nowacki, J. (1966), *Analogia legis*, Warszawa.
Nowak, L. (1969), 'Spór o definicje legalne a sposób pojmowania prawodawcy', (The Controversy about Legal Definitions and the Ways of Conceiving the Legislator), *Państwo i prawo* **3**.
Nowak, L. (1973), *Interpretacja prawnicza* (Legal Interpretation), Warszawa.
Ost, F. and van der Kerchove, M. (1989), *Entre la lettre et l'esprit. Les directives de l'interprétation en droit*, Bruxelles.
Peczenik, A. (1983), *The Basis of Legal Justification*, Lund.
Peczenik, A. (1989), *On Law and Reason*, Dordrecht/Boston/London.
Perelman, Ch. (1979), *The New Rhetoric and the Humanities*, Dordrecht/Boston/London.
Płeszka, K. (1986), 'Niektóre wasności hierarchicznego uporzadkowania systemu prawa', (Some Features of the Hierarchical Ordering of the Legal System), *Studia prawnicze*, s. 3–4.
Stelmachowski, A. (1984), Wstęp do teorii prawa cywilnego (Introduction to the Theory of Civil Law), 2nd edn., Warszawa.
Tarello, G. (1980) *L'interpretazione della legge*, Milano.
Włodyka, S. (1971), *Wiążąca wykładnia sadowa* (The Binding Judicial Interpretation), Warszawa.
Wróblewski, B. (1934), *Studja z dzedzony prawa i etyki* (Studies in Law and Ethics), Warszawa.

Wróblewski, B. (1948), *Język prawny i prawniczy* (Legal Language and Juridical Language), Kraków.

Wróblewski, J. (1959), *Zagadnienia teori wytadni prawa ludowego* (Problems of Interpretation of the People's Law), Warszawa.

Wróblewski, J. (1961), 'Interpretation secundum, praeter et contra legem', *Państwo i prawo* 4–5.

Wróblewski, J. (1968), 'Décision judiciaire: l'application ou la création du droit', *Scientia*, 11–12.

Wróblewski, J. (1971), 'La règle de la décision dans l'application judiciaire du droit', in Ch. Perelman (ed.), *La règle de droit*, Bruxelles.

Wróblewski, J. (1972a), 'L'interprétation en droit: théorie et idéologie', *Archives de philosophie de droit XVII*.

Wróblewski, J. (1972b), 'Systems of Norms and Legal Systems', *Rivista internazionale di filosofia del diritto* 2.

Wróblewski, J. (1973a), 'The Concept and Function of Precedent in Statute Law Systems', *Archiuum Iuridicum Cracoviense*, 7.

Wróblewski, J. (1973b), *Wartości a decyzja sądowa* (Values and Judicial Decision), Wroclaw/Warszawa/Kraków/Gdańsk.

Wróblewski, J. (1978), 'La motivation de décision', in Ch. Perelman and P. Foriers (eds), *La motivation des décisions de justice*, Bruxelles.

Wróblewski, J. (1979), 'A Model of Rational Law-Making', *ARSP* 2.

Wróblewski, J. (1981), 'Evaluative Statements in Law. An analytical approach to legal axiology', *Rivista internazionale di filosofia del diritto* 4.

Wróblewski, J. (1982a), 'Democracy and Procedural Values of Law-Making', *Rechtstheorie Beiheft* 4.

Wróblewski, J. (1982b), 'Dilemmas of Gesetzgebungskontrolle' in O. Ballweg and T-H. Siebert (eds), *Rhetorische Rechtstheorie*, Freiburg/München/Berlin.

Wróblewski, J. (1983a), *Meaning and Truth in Judicial Decision*, 2 edn., Helsinki.

Wróblewski, J. (1983b), 'Fuzziness of Legal Systems', in *Essays in Legal Theory in Honour of K. Makkonen, XVI Oikeustiede Jurisprudentia*.

Wróblewski, J. (1984a), 'Le rôle des principes du droit dans la théorie et idéologie de l'interprétation juridique', *Archivum Iuridicum Cracoviense XVII*.

Wróblewski, J. (1984b), 'Paradigms of Justifying Legal Decisions', in A. Peczenik *et al.* (eds), *Theory of Legal Science*, Dordrecht Boston/Lancaster/Tokyo.

Wróblewski, J. (1985a), *Constitucion e teoria general de interpretacion juridica*, Madrid.

Wróblewski, J. (1985b), 'Legal Language and Legal Interpretation', *Law and Philosophy* 4.

Wróblewski, J. (1985c), *Teoria racjonalnego tworzenia prawa* (A Theory of Rational Law-Making), Wroclaw/Warszawa/Kraków/Gdańsk/Łódz.

Wróblewski, J. (1985d), 'Pre-suppositions of Legal Reasoning', in E. Bulygin *et al.* (eds), *Man, Law and Modern Forms of Life*, Dordrecht/Epston/Lancaster/Tokyo.

Wróblewski, J. (1985e), 'Rational Law-Maker and Interpretative Choices', *Rivista internazionale de filosofia del diritto* 1.

Wróblewski, J. (1985f), *Les principes de base des projets de la loi polonaise relative à la création du droit*, Warszawa.

Wróblewski, J. (1986a), 'Concept of Legal System and Conceptions of Validity', *Acta Universitatis Lodziensis, Folia Iuridica* 24.

Wróblewski, J. (1986b), 'Representation Models of Legal Systems and the Problem of their Computerization', in A. A. Martino and F. Socci Natali (eds), *Automated Analysis of Legal Texts*, North Holland.

Wróblewski, J. (1987a), 'An Outline of a General Theory of Legal Interpretation and Constitutional Interpretation', *Acta Universitatis Lodziensis, Folia Iuridica* 32.

Wróblewski, J. (1987b), 'Theoretical and Ideological Problems of Judicial Independence', in I. Igartua Salaverria (ed.), *Los Jueces in una sociedad democratica*, Onati,

Instituto Vasco de administration publica.

Wróblewski, J. (1987c), 'The Place of the Courts Among the Socialist State Institutions', in J. Igartua Salaverria (ed.) *Los Jueces*.

Wróblewski, J. (1987d), 'Uzasadnienie aktu prawnego' (Justification of Legislative Acts), *Panstwo i prawo*.

Wróblewski, J. (1988a), *Sadowe stosowanie prawa*, (Judicial Application of Law), PWN 2nd edn., Warszawa.

Wróblewski, J. (1988b), 'Pragmatyczna jasność prawy', (Pragmatic Clarity of Law), *Państwo i prawo* **4**.

Wróblewski, J. (1988c), 'Law and Socio-Economic Change: Introductory Observations', *European Yearbook in the Sociology of Law*.

Wróblewski, J. (1988d), 'Les standards juridiques: Problèmes théoriques de la législation et de l'application du droit', *Droit prospectif* **4**.

Wróblewski, J. (1989a), *Contemporary Models of the Legal Sciences*, Wroclaw/Warszawa/Krakow/Gdańsk/Łodz.

Wróblewski, J. (1989b), 'Problems Related to the One Right Answer Thesis', *Ration Juris* **3**.

Wróblewski, J. (1989c), 'Conceptions of Justification in Legal Discourse', *Rivista internazionale di filosofia del diritto* **4** 1989 (in print).

Wronkowska, S. (1982), *Problemy racjonalnego tworzenia prawa* (Problems of the Rational Law-Making), Poznan.

Wronkowska, S., Zieliński, M. and Ziembiński, Z. (1974), *Zasady prawa. Zagadnienia podstawowe* (Principles of Law. Basic Problems), Warszawa.

Zieliński, M. (1972), *Interpretacja jako proces dekodowanie teksta Prawnego*, (Interpretation as the Process of Decodification of a Legal Text), Poznań.

Ziembiński, Z. (1972), *Etyczne problemy prawoznawstwa* (Ethical Problems of the Legal Sciences), Wroclaw, Ossolineum.

Ziembińaki, Z. (1980), *Problemy podstwawoe prawostnawstwa* (Basic Problems of the Legal Sciences), Warsaw.

Zirk-Sadowski, M. (1980), 'Tak zwana prawotwórcza decyzja sadowego stosowania prawa', (The So-Called Law-Making Decision of the Judicial Application of Law), *Studia prawnicze* **1—2**.

Zirk-Sadowski, M. (1984), *Rozumienie ocen w języku prawnym* (Understanding of Evaluations in the Legal Language), Łódz.

9 Statutory Interpretation in Sweden

ALEKSANDER PECZENIK, *Lund* AND
GUNNAR BERGHOLZ, *Lund*

PRELIMINARY

The Swedish system has features both of civil law and of common law. Thus precedents play a more important role than they do in a clear-cut civil law or code system. Sweden has courts of first instance, six courts of appeal and a Supreme Court. Since Sweden is not a federal state, it has – apart from administrative courts and the like – only one court organization. We shall discuss mainly the practice of the Supreme Court, with occasional reference to one or other of the courts of appeal.

The Supreme Court report shows on the average about 130–160 cases per year with full written opinions and 160–180 cases of lesser importance with a very short or almost no opinion at all. The substance of the cases is mostly in fields of civil law, for example, contracts, criminal law and the law of procedure, and the court mainly handles questions of law, or mixed questions of fact and law, on a basis equivalent to the Anglo-American *certiorari*. It must be noted that all Swedish courts have the right to issue dissenting or concurring opinions and they make use of this right.

I THE GENERAL ORIGINS OF INTERPRETATIONAL ISSUES

It is difficult to generalize confidently about the origins of interpretational issues, because (1) Swedish judges and jurists tend to avoid general statements about juridical method; and (2) vast differences exist between different parts of the Swedish law. Keeping this in mind, one may distinguish between the following.

1   'Linguistic' sources of interpretational issues including vagueness ('open texture' and so on). Some fundamental norms of various parts of the law serve as a starting-point of reasoning but do not give detailed guidance for solution of cases. For example, Ch. 2, s. 1 of the Tort Damages Act stipulates that, if someone wilfully or negligently causes injury to a person or to property, he shall pay damages. The statute says nothing about the meaning of the words 'cause', 'negligence' and so on. The courts must interpret the provision creatively (cf., 1966, p. 210).

2   Inconsistency or incoherence between different statutory provisions can also be a source of interpretational problems. However this is not very common in Sweden.

3   Swedish courts are very frequently engaged in a mutual adaptation of interpretation of statutes and other sources of law, such as legislative history and precedents. Apparent inconsistency or incoherence of these sources is thus an important origin of interpretational issues.

4   Economic and other evaluations may contribute to indeterminacy. For example, s. 2, item 1 of the Silviculture Act stipulates that a 'forest estate' is a real estate which is appropriate for the production of timber provided that it is not used to a 'significant degree' for other purposes. A rather free interpretation is necessary to state precisely what degree is 'significant'.

5   One may also mention mutual adaptation of statutes and moral opinions. There may thus exist conflict of values between the wording of the statute and the moral opinion of the interpreter. One ought to interpret a statute so that it may be recognized as 'reasonable', which may often mean just and moral. The law is supposed to be just and, if its literal content is not, the judge corrects it by interpretation.

6   Social change may also necessitate an interpretation of the provision, or even its elimination as obsolete. The following special feature of the Swedish system is important. Mutual adaptation of interpretation of statutes and other sources of law, such as legislative history and precedents (cf. (3) above) is commonly regarded as the core of statutory interpretation in Sweden. This gives the Swedish doctrine of interpretation a special flavour. Deeper reasons for this situation are the following. First, Sweden is a highly organized society where the interpreter naturally looks for institutional advice as to

how to do his job. Secondly, the influence of Legal Realism on the Swedish practice some years ago exposed objections that interpretations express the interpreter's feelings, lack 'scientific' basis and so on. To follow institutional advice, given, for example, in *travaux préparatoires*, is an excellent way to avoid this objection.

II GAPS AND THEIR ORIGINS

Though the words 'gaps' and 'gap-filling' are commonly used in Swedish judicial practice, the distinction between interpretation and gap-filling is unclear. The following rational reconstruction of the use of the word 'gap' is, however, possible. A gap means that (1) the statute does not regulate a given case (an insufficiency gap); (2) the statute regulates the case in a vague or ambiguous manner (an indeterminacy gap); or (3) the statute regulates the case in a morally unacceptable way (an axiological gap). (Cf. Peczenik, 1989, 24 ff.)

1   *Insufficiency gaps* result, *inter alia*, from the fact that the literal text of the statute does not regulate a given case. A statute stipulates, for example, that a certain (lower) norm should be enacted or a legal action (such as the appointment of an official) should be performed. Such a norm can be enacted, or such an action performed, only if the law states precisely who may do it and how it may be done. The gap consists in the fact that the law leaves the question of competence and/or procedure entirely open.

Insufficiency gaps occur in Sweden, albeit not often. To fill them up, one may employ *travaux préparatoires*. For example, the statute of 1915 concerning installment purchase received in 1953 an amendment stipulating invalidity of a reservation making the buyer's right to the goods dependent on his fulfilling another obligation. The statute was then replaced by the Consumer Credit Act (1977:981) and the Commercial Installment Purchase Act (1978:599). Neither contains a corresponding provision. Section 15 para. 2, concerning *another* question is, however, accompanied by *travaux préparatoires* stating precisely that such a reservation is invalid.

Sometimes the legislator intentionally creates insufficiency gaps. For that reason, for example, the development of the law of torts 'in a number of central respects — such as negligence, causation, remoteness of damage, unlawfulness, and what is meant by damage . . . , must to a large extent fall to the courts' (CONRADI J. in case NJA, 1966, p. 210).

2   In some cases, especially as regards general clauses, one can speak about a gap resulting from *vagueness or ambiguity* of legal norms. As regards general clauses, such 'gaps' are intentionally created by the legislator. However vagueness and ambiguity (also in the case of general clauses) are generally regarded in Sweden as a matter requiring interpretation, not 'gap-filling'.

3   *Axiological* gaps occur when the law regulates a given case in a morally unacceptable way. Of course one cannot establish such gaps in a 'value-free' manner. To fill them up, one must rely upon (moral) value-judgements, either one's own or ones derived from, for example, *travaux préparatoires*.

       'Gap-filling' and interpretational issues have the same origins. The 'gap' terminology is used in a rhetorical manner, to emphasize need for interpretation.

III THE TYPES OF INTERPRETATIVE ARGUMENT AND THEIR INTERACTION

1 Linguistic Interpretation

This is often called 'interpretation following the words of the law' (Swed. *lagens ordalydelse*; the word *'ordalydelse'* corresponds to German *'Wortlaut'*). More abstract and general terms, such as 'semantic', occur seldom, mostly in theoretical contexts. No generally recognized abstract definition of *linguistic interpretation* exists in Swedish practice or literature, probably because Swedish jurists regard the term as self-explanatory and consider the problem of definition as too theoretical. In any case linguistic interpretation is a clarificatory description of the content of the statute in accordance with the ordinary, general or legal, linguistic usage.

There is a trend in Sweden towards making statutes understandable by the general public. In civil law this may even result in a lesser precision of statutes. Yet, on average, statutes are often written in a highly technical way. Consequently the argument from the evidence of a special technical meaning of the words of the statute is used frequently. Sometimes such a meaning is taken for granted without arguing. For example, taxation law is full of technical terms, hardly comprehensible to non-experts.

2 Systemic Interpretation

Systemic interpretation of statutes takes into account several features of the legal system. It includes *inter alia* the following arguments: (1) the use of a statutory provision for interpreting another such provision; (2) interpretation influenced by the systematics of the statute. Also the term 'systemic interpretation' may be extended to (3) interpretation influenced by another type of conceptual analysis; and (4) interpretation influenced by other legal–dogmatic theories (of professors). Such an extension is theoretically justifiable, although it does not correspond to current linguistic usage.

1   When interpreting a statutory provision one must pay attention to other provisions which (a) are necessary in order to make the answer to the considered legal question complete; (b) deal with cases relevantly resembling those the interpreted provision regulates; and (c) in any other way contribute to understanding of the interpreted provision.

Several examples elucidate this norm of reasoning. First, in order to apply a penal provision one must also pay regard to other statutory norms which answer the question as to how criminal responsibility is affected by, for example, mental illness or other grounds for diminished responsibility.

Second, an old statute is frequently interpreted in a way adapted to new enactments which regulate similar questions. In this manner the remaining rules in the Commercial Code of 1734 can by means of interpretation be adapted to the Contracts Act, Sale of Goods Act, and so on.

Third, various expressions in statutes often form a kind of hierarchy. See, for example, the following expressions from the Sale of Goods Act of 1905: 'immediately' (ss. 27, 32, 52); 'as soon as it can be done' (s. 6); 'without unreasonable delay' (ss. 26, 27, 31, 32, 40, 52, 60); and 'within a reasonable time' (ss. 26 and 31). Owing to the fact that these expressions are interpreted in connection with one another, we see for example that the expression 'within a reasonable time' refers to a longer period than the expression 'without unreasonable delay'.

Fourth, sometimes, a certain statutory provision, for example, Ch. 8, s. 13 of the Criminal Code, is applicable to certain cases (theft, larceny and so on). Another provision, for example, Ch. 9, s. 12 of the Criminal Code, states, however, that the first provision is also to be applied to other cases (such as deception or blackmail). In this way the first provision, in addition to its ordinary area of application, acquires another, secondary area.

2   When interpreting a statutory provision one may pay attention to (a) the title of the statute and (b) the membership of the

interpreted provision in a certain part of the law, a certain statute and a particular part of it. Thus Ch. 3, s. 9 of the Criminal Code reads as follows:

> If anyone through gross carelessness exposes another person to mortal danger or danger of severe bodily injury or serious illness, he shall be sentenced for causing danger to another person to a fine or to imprisonment for not more than two years.

In connection with this provision there arose the question whether for the responsibility to apply it must be required that a specified person or group of persons was exposed to danger. The question can be answered in the affirmative since in the Criminal Code the offence has been placed among offences *against individuals*. (A number of authors have, however, rejected this interpretation, proffering substantial reasons and analogies with other provisions).

3   When interpreting a statutory provision one may pay attention to conceptual analysis. See, for example, NJA, 1976, p. 458. NORDENSON J. performed an extensive and subtle analysis, making sophisticated distinctions between negligence, adequate causation and purpose of protection.

3   'Functional' Interpretation of Statutes

According to Wróblewski's well-known terminology, 'functional' interpretation takes into account social and political facts and relations relevant to the law; goals ascribed to the law or legislator; and moral ('axiological') values and norms related to the law. All this is common in Sweden, albeit the general concept 'functional' interpretation is not used.

1   *'Teleological interpretation'*, or goal interpretation, that is, interpretation of a statute in the light of its goal(s), plays a particularly important role.
     (a) The goals are often found in *travaux préparatoires* (cf. section V below). Also the so-called *subjective* or *historical interpretation* in Sweden is normally based on preparatory materials. This reflects the fact that interpretational issues are ordinarily viewed as a problem of harmonization of the statute and other materials. The latter are often regarded as sources of the law. *Travaux préparatoires* are a prominent source of this kind.
     (b) Instead of reliance on preparatory materials, Per Olof

Ekelöf proposed the 'radically teleological method' based on the objective reason and purpose of the statute (Ekelöf, 1958, 79 ff). It is not clear to what extent his views have affected the courts.

2   Interpretation adapted to various values is also common.

(a) Values are often indicated implicitly, by such formulations as 'the court finds is *reasonable* that . . .'. 'Reasonableness' in such contexts is always value-laden.

(b) Moreover, the method of *weighing and balancing of reasons* is clearly evaluative.

The case NJA, 1984, p. 693 may serve as an example. A foreigner, A, who had considerable ties to both Sweden and the Federal Republic of Germany, owned a car, registered in the latter country. He borrowed a sum of money, giving the right to the car as security (a so-called 'security transfer'). Later a person rented the car and visited Sweden. The Swedish authorities sequestered the car as security for A's unpaid taxes. The dispute concerned the question whether the German security transfer should prevent sequestration in Sweden. The Supreme Court overruled the sequestration and stated:

> The demand for order and simplicity of the system together with difficulties for the creditors in Sweden to judge the credit risks otherwise than according to Swedish rules constitute the main reason against ascribing security transfer according to foreign law an effect against the transferor's creditors here in Sweden . . . The interest of the creditors in Sweden to be able to assess their credit risks according to Swedish law competes with the interest of the foreign transferee/creditor not to risk a loss of his right because the property without his participation has been moved to Sweden . . . One should weigh the proffered reasons against each other and one must then pay attention to the development of the international trade and to more and more intense commercial cooperation between various countries.

(c) One may also mention some maxims whose function is to make the law coherent with some requirements of justice and equity. It is possible for one to regard the maxims of this kind as norms of customary law, moral norms or even logical propositions. Let us mention three of them. No one has a duty to do what is impossible; nobody can transfer more rights than he himself has; a statute cannot have effect in the past. The first maxim has been cited, for example, in the following connection. Section 21, para. 1 of the Sale of Goods Act reads: 'Where goods have not been delivered at the proper time, and this is not due to the buyer or to an event for which he bears the risk, it is open to him to decide whether he will demand the delivery of the goods or cancel the purchase.' Jan Hellner made the following comment:

> The Sale of Goods Act does not make any exception to the buyer's right to demand fulfilment of the contract even for the case where the purchase related to certain specific goods and these were already destroyed at the time of the contract or were destroyed later. If this is established, however, the buyer cannot obtain a judicial decision for the fulfilment of the purchase; this is usually justified by reference to the maxim 'impossibilium nulla est obligatio' ('No one can be under an obligation to do the impossible').

(d) Considerations concerning analogies, for example the so-called 'analogia legis' are important in the Swedish practice of interpretation. By virtue of 'analogia legis', a statute should be applied not only to the cases covered by its linguistic meaning but also to relevantly similar cases. When deciding not to reason by analogy, one can follow the *argumentum e contrario*. By virtue of (strong) *argumentum e contrario*, (similar) cases not covered by the linguistic application area of the statutory norm in question should not be treated in the way stipulated by the norm. The fact that one must make a *choice* between the use of analogy and *argumentum e contrario* shows that these concepts do not indicate the content of interpretation but are mere argument forms, each supported by a set of reasons which a judge has to weigh and balance. They enable the judge to reach the conclusion which is justifiable in the circumstances.

Some limitations of the use of analogy follow particularities of some parts of the law, such as criminal law. This problem will be discussed in section X below. On the other hand, analogy is particularly important in private law. This reflects the fact that, in private law, statutes do not always play the central role in the decision making. The situation varies, however, from one part of civil law to another. The use of statutory analogy demands, for example, a fairly detailed statutory regulation. When the statute is extremely vague, as in the case of general clauses (such as Section 36 of the Contracts Act, see section X below), no statutory analogy is feasible. In such cases one should follow preparatory materials and/or precedents, depending on how much information they convey.

The use of analogy depends on other circumstances as well. For example, one should not interpret provisions establishing time limits by analogy. Neither should one interpret them extensively, unless particularly strong reasons for assuming the opposite exist. When, for example, Ch. 9, s. 1 of the Parents and Children Code says that 'a person under eighteen years of age . . . is a minor' this means – without the least doubt – that people older than this are of full age. In this context it would be strange to reason extensively or analogically and to draw the conclusion that some 18-year-old people are minors because they resemble 17-year-olds.

Also one should not interpret provisions establishing sufficient conditions for not following a general norm extensively or by analogy, unless strong reasons for assuming the opposite exist. Thus, in the Real Property Code, Ch. 4, s. 3, it is laid down that a contractual provision concerning purchase of real-estate property, not included in the written purchase document, is invalid if it implies that (1) completion or existence of the acquisition is subject to conditions; (2) the vendor shall not carry such responsibility as is referred to in s. 21; (3) the buyer's right to transfer the real-estate property or to apply for a mortgage or to transfer a right in the property will be restricted. It seems strange to use analogy and draw the conclusion that such a provision will be invalid even in some cases not fulfilling the conditions (1)–(3).

Further, one should not interpret provisions constituting exceptions to a general norm extensively or by analogy, unless strong reasons for assuming the opposite exist. Also, only very strong reasons can justify a use of analogy leading to the conclusion that an error exists in the text of the statute. With regard to acquisition in good faith the Real Property Code distinguishes between three cases. *Case 1:* A unlawfully transfers ownership of a real estate to B, who is not acting in good faith and consequently also does not thereby acquire the property. B transfers the ownership to C, who is in good faith. C can maintain his acquisition in accordance with an explicit provision in Ch. 18, s. 1, para. 1 of the Code. *Case 2:* A unlawfully mortgages a real estate to B, who is not in good faith and thus does not acquire the mortgage. B transfers the claim with the mortgage to C who is in good faith. Under a provision in Ch. 18, s. 2 of the Code, C acquires the mortgage. *Case 3:* A unlawfully transfers ownership of a real estate to B, who is not acting in good faith and consequently does not acquire the property. B mortgages the real estate to C who is in good faith. Does C acquire the mortgage? N. Hessler (1970, p. 24) stated that no explicit provision regulated the question. Then he continued:

> One possibility is [thus] . . . to interpret the provision restrictively and not to admit any acquisition in good faith except in such cases where a clear and direct provision exists in support of this. The other possibility is to apply analogically to Case 3 the rules that apply to Cases 1 and 2 or for one of them . . . The second alternative would, however, in fact mean that there was an editorial error in the text of the statute. And normally this should not be taken into account unless every other possibility of interpretation is excluded. It would therefore seem desirable to assume — even if the result may be considered strange — that the possibility of acquisition in good faith in accordance with Ch. 18 does not exist in the case now under consideration.

Finally, a provision should be applied analogously to cases not covered by its literal content, if another provision states that they resemble the cases thus covered.

(e) *Argumentum a fortiori* is also well-known in the Swedish interpretation practice. In fact it is an amplified reasoning by analogy. One concludes that a case should be treated similarly to another one. The reason is not only that the cases are similar but also that the latter deserves this treatment in a still higher degree than the former. Despite its apparently formal character, *argumentum a fortiori* in most cases presupposes evaluations. Its formal application may lead to questionable results. For example, one can regard the publishing of secret information as 'something more' than revealing it to friends. But in Sweden, as a consequence of the Freedom of the Press Act (cf. Ch. 7, s. 3), an official publishing in some circumstances secret information in print is not criminally responsible; the same official, however, would be prosecuted for revealing the information to his friends (cf. Ch. 20, s. 3 para. 2 of the Criminal Code). The estimation of what is 'more' and what 'less' thus competes with other value-judgements. When weighing and balancing them, one takes into account considerations similar to those relevant as regards other types of reasoning by analogy.

In general, all internationally known classifications of arguments are applicable to Swedish practice. But statutory interpretation in Sweden has the following special properties. First, as mentioned above, interpretational issues are in Sweden ordinarily viewed as a problem of harmonization of the statute and other materials, often regarded as sources of law; for example, *travaux préparatoires*, precedents, standard contracts, collective labour agreements and juristic literature are prominent sources of this kind. It makes no sense in the Swedish context to pose the question whether these sources are used to *interpret* statutes, or merely to answer the question how to apply them. This fact reflects the general scepticism of Swedish lawyers about vague and abstract distinctions. Indeed, who knows where interpretation ends and application begins? And who knows when a material becomes a source of law? (See section 7 below.) This approach of Swedish lawyers to interpretation has been influenced by many factors. One of them is the conviction that the legal system must be presented as a coherent whole. The *meaning* of statutes must be such that it warrants coherence with other materials. Another factor is a common recognition that all meaning is contextual.

Second, the identification of the problems of interpretation, materials and sources reflects a Swedish disposition to avoid abstract distinctions in general, unless they have a clear meaning and direct practical relevance. In turn, this may reflect the influence of Scandinavian Realism.

Third, by reducing interpretation to harmonization of materials, a Swedish judge gives the impression that he can safely rely upon pronouncements of legislators, courts and various organizations. He is reluctant to take individual responsibility for his interpretation and prefers to refer to the authorities. This factor is attributed to a long Swedish tradition of the highly organized state. See Peczenik, 1989, ch. 7 (372 ff) for further references.

IV   TYPES OF GAP-FILLING ARGUMENT

The same kinds of argument are recognized in filling of gaps and in interpretation. The sole exception consists in purely logical and linguistic arguments, appropriate to the latter problem only.

One may perhaps consider such arguments as statutory analogy and hypothetical intention of legislature ('if the legislator had thought about the matter, he would have said this or that') to be especially appropriate for the filling of gaps. Certainly both kinds of arguments are used in Sweden (see section III above on analogy and section VIII below on presumptions concerning the legislator), but they are not systematically linked with the notion of gaps in the law.

V   THE MATERIALS OF INTERPRETATIVE ARGUMENT

1   Materials which 'Must' be Taken into Account

1   When performing statutory interpretation, one must, of course, use the very text of the statute interpreted. The very concept of 'statutory interpretation' justifies the 'must' character of this material.

2   Some *linguistic materials* must be taken into account, again because of the very concept of 'interpretation'. When establishing the linguistic meaning of the statute, one must study legal definitions and other explanations contained in the statute itself, regarding the meaning of words and expressions which occur in the text; one must also study stylistic qualities and peculiarities in the statutory text interpreted.

3   *A statute can* decide that some materials must also be applied within legal reasoning. This is a normative, not analytic, sense of the 'must': one has a duty to use the materials. Let us give some examples.

First, some forms of custom, such as commercial custom, must be thus applied. (Cf. s. 1 and s. 10, para. 2 of the Contracts Act; s. 1 of the Sale of Goods Act of 1905; s. 1 of the Commission Business Act; Ch. 5, s. 12 of the Marriage Code.) A body organized within the Chamber of Commerce publishes the content of commercial custom.

Second, contracts must be also thus applied (cf. s. 1 of the Contracts Act). Standard contracts play a particularly great role. Further, collective agreements are very important, especially for the practice of the Labour Court; see s. 1 of the statute, regulating the judicial procedure in labour disputes.

2   Materials which 'Should' be Taken into Account

Paying attention to other materials, though neither required by the concept of statutory interpretation nor commanded by binding law, is such that statutory interpretation becomes *incorrect* if they are ignored. These materials *should* be taken into account: precedents, if any, legislative preparatory materials (*travaux préparatoires*), if any are applicable, international conventions underlying the applicable national legislation, together with preparatory materials and other interpretatory data concerning these conventions, and some customs, well-established in the society, expressing general principles or accepted by previous decisions of the courts or authorities.

1   *Precedents* deserve much attention. Although not binding,

they are regularly followed by Swedish courts. The view that precedents are not binding has been officially expressed in Sweden. The Parliamentary Commissioner for the Judiciary (*Justitieombudsman*), in his annual report (1947), criticized a lower-court judge who had dealt with a legal question in conflict with a decision by the Supreme Court *in pleno*. In consequence of this, the parliament's First Standing Committee on Legislation declared that the lower instance is not bound by precedents and that 'only the weight of the reasons referred to by the Supreme Court in justification of its judgements should be determinative for the influence of the Supreme Court on the application of law in the lower instances'. This pronouncement provoked a discussion, in which Folke Schmidt (1955, p. 109) stated the following:

> The Swedish judge follows precedents precisely because they derive from the Supreme Court. He does this even where he believes that a different decision would in itself have been more suitable. Only if there are strong reasons indicating that he ought to adjudicate in the matter in a way different from that indicated by the precedent does the question arise of examining the weight of the reasons invoked by the Supreme Court.

The actual role of precedents in Swedish law is significant. A lower court decides contrary to a precedent, established by a higher one, in principle only when wishing to give the higher court the possibility to reconsider its practice, for example because the precedent conflicts with a statute, legislative materials or another precedent. If one ignores precedents, one does not know at all many important segments of such parts of the law as torts. Indeed the influence of precedents in Sweden is even greater than in England, where some rules state when a court is not bound by precedents. In Sweden, in the absence of such rules, precedents have a very strong influence.

It is also relevant to take into account the amendments of 1971 to the procedural law, and the corresponding rules of administrative law. According to Ch. 54, s. 10 of the Code of Judicial Procedure and s. 36 of the Code of Administrative Procedure, in principle the Supreme Court and the Supreme Administrative Court are only to give *certiorari* in cases in which (a) it is important that a general ruling be given by way of precedent for judicial practice or (b) special reasons exist, such as a grave mistake made by the lower court. The preparatory materials to these provisions support the conclusion that the law-givers intended to strengthen the role of these courts in creating precedents (cf. Government Bill 1971 no. 45 for amendment of the Code of Judicial Procedure and so on, especially p. 88). It is not certain whether the amendments caused the increase in the role of precedents (as, for example, Stig Strömholm claimed) or vice versa. A reasonable hypothesis is that of a feedback: the increased role of precedents caused the amendments, and then the latter amplified the former (cf. Bergholtz, 1987, 429 ff).

One may also take into account Ch. 3, s. 5 of the Code of Judicial Procedure, and s. 5 of the Administrative Courts' Act, according to which the Supreme Court and the Supreme Administrative Court may decide a case at a plenary sitting, if any of the divisions of the Court, when deliberating a decision, expressed an opinion diverging from a legal principle or statutory interpretation formerly adopted by this Court. It is impossible to read into these provisions a formal legal duty of these courts to follow their earlier decisions. But decisions rendered *in pleno* have a great influence.

2   Attention should also be given to *legislative preparatory materials*. The role of these in Sweden is greater than in other legal systems. A draft of a statute is often accompanied by legislative preparatory materials, explaining its meaning, reasons and purposes. In Sweden, one elaborates the *travaux préparatoires* at the following stages of the legislation process: (1) The government or the parliament takes the legislative initiative; the latter may demand that the government appoint a legislation committee. (2) The government appoints the legislation committee or, in some cases, an individual investigator. The responsible minister issues a pronouncement, containing directives for the committee or the investigator, prepared by the staff of the ministry. The directives are published in a series of 'Committee Directives' and in the Parliamentary Reports (*riksdagstrycket*). (3) The committee or the investigator prepares a report, published in the series 'Official Investigations of the State' (*Statens offentliga utredningar*, SOU). The government can instead let a ministry or a central administrative agency perform the investigation; the ministry publishes the resulting memorandum in a special series. The government can also appoint a *governmental* committee. (4) The ministry staff discusses the report. (5) Several persons and bodies are invited to present comments. (6) The report is again discussed within the ministry. (7) The Council on Legislation (*lagrådet*) may be asked to issue a pronouncement about the report. (8) The ministry prepares a Government Bill. It consists of a draft of the statute, a general justification, a

special justification, section by section, and a summary of the previously elaborated material. The Bill is published and included in the Parliamentary Reports. (9) The relevant parliamentary committee discusses the Bill. The result is published in the Parliamentary Reports. (10) The parliament *in pleno* discusses the Bill. (11) The parliament enacts the statute; the statute is promulgated and published in the official statute-book, *Svensk författningssamling. Nytt juridiskt arkiv (NJA)*, part II, contains a survey of important preparatory materials.

The following texts constitute the *travaux préparatoires* that *should* be considered in legal reasoning: the legislation committee reports, memoranda prepared by a ministry or a central administrative agency; statements by persons and bodies invited to present comments; pronouncements of the responsible minister; pronouncements of the Council on Legislation; bills of the members of the parliament and reports of the relevant parliamentary committee on the proposed bill. Consideration should be given, as a rule, only to materials published in printed form. Most important is the government bill, together with its justification. One may also consider the directives for the legislation committee and what is said during plenary debates in the parliament. This material is as a rule not respected very much, because it may contain things said for political advantage. Pronouncements in the preparatory materials relating to questions outside the scope of the legislation under consideration should, as a rule, not be taken into account. However the following exceptions must be noted: (a) A body drafting a number of statutes may in connection with one draft statute express its opinion about another draft. Such a pronouncement has an equal standing with other *travaux préparatoires*. (b) In the interpretation of an earlier statute one should pay attention to preparatory materials of new statutes which regulate an adjacent area. The antiquated but valid provision in Ch. 1, s. 5 of the Commercial Code of 1734 ('If one sells goods to two persons one shall pay damages and he who bought first shall keep the goods') has been commented upon in the light of an inquiry of 1965 (SOU, 1965:14, 37 ff).

The opinion that preparatory materials are as important as precedents was expressed by Folke Schmidt in 1955. Schmidt influenced the subsequent development of the practice and theory of statutory interpretation. In another work (1976, p. 262), Schmidt stated the following:

> The text of the statute served more and more a function of a headline to remember when one searches for what has been intended in detail. The pronouncement of the responsible minister states the main purposes, what alternative solutions have been refuted and what can be the more

precise content of the draft . . . , all this to govern the administration of justice.

Pronouncements in the preparatory materials should, however, *not* be taken into account if they introduce entirely new norms without support in the statute. In spite of this principle, a so-called 'legislation through preparatory materials' can occur. This takes place when (1) the *travaux préparatoires* claim priority before the wording of the statute; (2) they are relatively precise while the statute is very vague; or (3) they contain norms not supported at all by any statutory provision. Let us discuss some examples.

First, s. 3 of the MBL (the statute stipulating a right of the employee representatives to be consulted as regards the employer's policy) admits that a special provision contrary to the MBL is valid if included in a statute or a norm enacted on the basis of a statute. The Stock Corporation Act, Ch. 8, s. 11, contains such a provision. Yet the minister claimed in the *travaux préparatoires* to the MBL (Government Bill 1975/76:105, appendix 1) that, as regards collective agreements, the MBL has priority before this provision. To ensure that this pronouncement does not overrule the statutory provision itself, the new parliament, elected in 1976, had to complete the MBL with a new s. 32, confirming that s. 3 still was in force.

Second, s. 36 of the Contracts Act gives the courts the possibility to modify or set aside an undue contractual stipulation. Preparatory materials completed this general clause with more precise guidelines. See section X below concerning Government Bill 1975/76:81, 118 ff.

Third, the statute of 1915 concerning instalment purchase received in 1953 an amendment stipulating invalidity of a reservation making the buyer's right to the goods dependent on his fulfilling another obligation. The statute was then replaced by the Consumer Credit Act (1977:981) and the Commercial Instalment Purchase Act (1978:599). Neither contains a corresponding provision. Section 15, para. 2, concerning *another* question is, however, accompanied by the *travaux préparatoires* stating precisely that such a reservation is invalid.

The importance of the *travaux préparatoires* varies from one part of the law to another. It is greatest in the tax law and significant in private law. Criminal jurisdiction is less affected, since the so-called legality principle, 'nulla poena sine lege' implies high respect for the literal wording of the statutory text. Yet the *travaux préparatoires* may be important in criminal cases, too. In, for example, NJA, 1980, p. 94, the decision of the Supreme Court supported itself on the preparatory materials to the statute (1976:56), amending the provision of Ch. 11, s. 4 of the Criminal Code.

Age weakens the position of the *travaux préparatoires*. One may pay attention to them, but it is no longer the case that one should take them into account. Sometimes preparatory materials age rapidly. In Government Bill 1932:106, containing proposals for *inter alia* an act on mortgages on farming stock, the responsible minister made the following pronouncement: 'Only such property as belongs to the debtor is covered by the preference right in mortgaging. This right can thus not be applied to effects which have been purchased on instalments' (NJA, 1932, II, p. 223). Twenty years later (NJA, 1952, p. 195), however, the Supreme Court extended the preference right in mortgaging to effects which have been purchased on instalments. An influential minority of Swedish lawyers, led by Per Olof Ekelöf, protests against the great role of the preparatory materials. In some cases the Supreme Court decided to disregard some preparatory materials conflicting with the wording of the statute; see, for example, NJA, 1978, p. 581. In case NJA, 1972, p. 296, the Supreme Court dissociated itself from a series of statements by the responsible minister in the *travaux préparatoires* of the Liability for Damages Act (see NJA, 1977, p. 273 and 1976, p. 483). We should also mention NJA, 1976, p. 483. The Real Property Code, Ch. 4, s. 7, stipulates as follows:

> Purchase according to which a separate owner acquires some area in a real estate is valid only if a creation of a [new] real estate takes place according to this purchase through an official proceeding for which one applies at the latest six months after the purchase contract was drawn up and, if the proceeding is not finished within this time, it shall be executed in accordance with the purchase.

In the case at bar, the seller applied for a creation of the new real estate and later sold the area. The proceeding was not finished within six months. The buyer applied for an entry in the land register. The court registrar refused, since the contract was to be considered invalid, on the basis of clear preparatory materials to the quoted provision. The Supreme Court, however, refuted the preparatory materials and remanded the case to the court registrar. The decision was based on the literal text of the statute and its purpose to avoid prolonged uncertainty concerning validity of purchase. This purpose was not actual in the decided case, since no uncertainty would remain after the proceeding was finished. There follow ten reasons, recognized in Sweden, for taking legislative preparatory materials heavily into account.

1   When interpreting statutes, one should pay attention to their purpose (*ratio legis*). Though *ratio* is not the same as personal views of the individuals who participated in the legislative process, it may be rationally constructed on the basis of

travaux préparatoires.

2   The *travaux préparatoires* should be taken into account because they form a part of a democratic and rationally justifiable legislative procedure.

3   Provided that the preparatory materials fulfil high standards of quality, the following advantage occurs. By keeping the text of statutes short and leaving the details to the *travaux préparatoires*, the legislator brings more information and morally justifiable elasticity into the legal system. Different persons, whose pronouncements the preparatory materials contain, formulated different reasons. One can conceive the preparatory materials as a dialogue. The interpreter thus gains access to a many-sided 'store' of reasons to weigh and balance.

4   A rational interpretation uses as many reasons as possible. There is no reason to abstain from making use in statutory interpretation of all the aids which are available, including preparatory materials.

5   Regard for justice and legal certainty requires that statutes shall be interpreted uniformly. Uniformity is promoted if all interpreters take into account the same preparatory materials.

6   The high speed of legislation does not leave jurists time to elaborate commentaries, handbooks and other auxiliary means of interpretation. The interpreter thus needs all the help the *travaux préparatoires* might give him.

7   Rapid changes in society diminish the confidence of lawyers in customary law. This fact increases the need for help from preparatory materials.

8   Political stability, typical in Sweden, gives the judges a high degree of confidence in the civil servants and politicians who elaborate the legislative materials.

9   If the preparatory materials fulfil high standards of quality, one may also state that the authors of the *travaux préparatoires* were outstanding experts and used much time to prepare the pronouncements. One may expect their opinions to be well-founded.

10   The persons participating in the legislative process expect *travaux préparatoires* to be taken into account. In this context, one may say: (a) the statute is often formulated in a short, abstract and vague way, since the legislators expect that provisions which are found to be unclear will have been commented upon in the *travaux préparatoires*; (b) were the courts to show indifference towards preparatory materials, they would run the risk that the legislator might restrict the court's competence in the field of statutory interpretation.

3   Materials which 'May' be Taken into Account

When performing legal reasoning, one may use, *inter alia* the following materials:

1   General recommendations and advice, issued by various authorities and public, semi-public or even private institutions. Let us here mention the National Tax Board, Bookkeeping Board, Consumer Authority, Bank Inspection Authority, Swedish Banking Association, Press Ombudsman, Press Opinion Council, Radio Council, Trade and Industry Stock Exchange Committee, Sweden's Bar Association. The Supreme Court in some cases requests their opinion, as a kind of 'amici curiae'.

2   Professional legal literature (such as handbooks, monographs and so on).

3   Precedents and preparatory materials which do not directly touch upon the interpreted legal text but which give information on evaluations in adjacent areas of law.

4   Judicial and administrative decisions which are not reported in the leading law reports, NJA (and thus do not have the same standing as precedents published in NJA).

5   Draft statutes.

6   Repealed statutes, provided that they give relevant information.

7   Foreign law, unless it is incompatible with some overriding reasons, such as the so-called *ordre public*.

8   Other materials, revealing established evaluations, such as private pronouncements by members of legislation draft committees, members of parliament, ministers and so on.

9   Materials elucidating the linguistic meaning of the statute, for example dictionaries, results of linguistic research; the ways in which words and expressions occurring in the text have been used in other legal sources, in technical legal usage, in everyday speech and so on; stylistic qualities and peculiarities in other texts which have been written by people who have exerted great influence on the legislative work interpreted.

10   Historical knowledge of conditions the statute was intended to remedy.

11   History of the language and concepts.

12   The 'nature of things' subject to the statute and so on.

Of course it is difficult to make an exhaustive list of such reasons.

As regards foreign law, the following may be added. A conceptual *distinction* made in a foreign statute, a *question* asked in a foreign case and so on may influence interpretation of domestic law. *Substan-*

tive reasons proffered in foreign decisions, doctrine and so on are also applicable in Sweden. This is obvious, as regards empirical reasons, for example, concerning the nature of causation. Causality in Sweden cannot differ from causality abroad. Though the matter of *practical* reasons is more complex, one certainly may find moral reasoning performed by a foreign court right, just and so on. Finally, one may regard foreign law as a kind of *authority* reason. First of all, foreign law may gain authority in consequence of the following special circumstances:

1   Some domestic norms of so-called international private law, international criminal law and so on authorize an application of foreign norms in cases which in various manners have relationship to foreign countries.
2   Domestic norms may also be based on international law. As regards interpretation of rules based on international conventions, much importance is attached to foreign law which may have influenced the convention. NJA, 1983, p. 3 concerns the application of a Swedish statute on oil pollution. The statute was based on an international convention of 1969. The Court found that the rule under consideration had been introduced at the proposal of the British delegation to the conference at which the convention was adopted. Consequently the Court interpreted the convention in accordance with the English interpretation rules, especially the principle 'ejusdem generis'. The Court thus surveyed English cases starting with *Sandiman* v. *Breach* (1827); cf. Hellner, 1988, p. 54.
3   International legislative cooperation can lead to uniform legislation. Uniform statutory rules may be interpreted uniformly in the cooperating countries. In Sweden this occurs in particular in connection with Nordic cooperation.
4   Harmonization can take place even if legislation is not uniform. At the beginning of the 1970s, particularly in Sweden, some influential politicians opposed uniform legislation, since it slowed down their attempts to bring about reforms. In 1974, the Nordic Council recommended that efforts should be made to adapt statutes in the Nordic countries to one another, even if uniform legislation was not possible in some branches of the law. Ministers of justice of the Nordic countries established a net of relationships promoting harmonization of the law.
        Harmonization measures may lead to attempts to seek a mutual adjustment of statutory interpretation in the countries concerned. The interpretation of uniform Scandinavian laws

thus tends to be quite similar in particular countries (see Eckhoff, 1987, p. 256). A common Scandinavian case-law, however, has not evolved, except in maritime law (Sundberg, 1978, p. 188). The existence of harmonization of statutory rules and so on is not necessary for foreign statutes and their interpretation to gain influence as authority reasons. For example, a foreign decision may deserve attention not only because it has been well justified but also because it has been made by a respected court. In particular, statutory interpretation chosen in a foreign context may be proffered as a kind of support for a similar interpretation of a corresponding domestic statute.

4   Materials which May Not be Taken into Account

It is difficult to make a complete enumeration of materials that one may *not* use in legal reasoning. Certainly, within justification of *judicial* decisions, one may not use political opinions expressed by the parties or interest groups, such as trade unions or employers' organizations. This fact reflects the objectivity demanded of the courts and other legal authorities. This demand for objectivity is, however, difficult to state precisely. One certainly *may* use materials showing that a given group, say consumers, deserves special protection.

The Swedish courts may not use sociological evidence and the like (the Brandeis Brief). A district court once sentenced a drug dealer who had serious drug problems himself. A non-prison sentence was chosen, though the court stated explicitly that a long prison term would have been appropriate. The court stated that, as everybody knows from statistics and other research, the prisons are flooded with drugs; consequently the court could not sentence this man, who suffered from drug problems, to prison. The decision was criticized and the argument was considered as a most improper one. Another case, commonly considered as ridiculous, is the following: a non-prison sentence was chosen for a gypsy defendant, on the ground that, as everybody knows, gypsies love freedom more than anyone else.

On the other hand, the courts may, of course, rely upon common sense within the limits of the law. In general, one must repeat here the observation made in section III above. Interpretation issues are in Sweden ordinarily viewed as a problem of harmonization of the statute and other materials, often regarded as sources of law, such as, *travaux préparatoires*, precedents and juristic literature.

VI   PRIORITIES AMONG CONFLICTING TYPES OF ARGUMENTS

As a rule, a Swedish judge prefers to harmonize the results of different interpretative arguments, not to construct lexical orders of them. In this reconciliation, the weight of different arguments is difficult to determine generally. However the following may be said. *Contextual meaning* has generally a greater weight than literal meaning. Established *technical* meaning of the statute often has more weight than ordinary usage. Certainly one must not interpret words and expressions of the statute in conflict with ordinary usage unless strong reasons for such an interpretation exist. If, however, it has previously been established that a word or an expression has a technical meaning incompatible with everyday language, one should interpret that word or expression as having such a special meaning, without reference to everyday language.

Neither literal nor contextual meaning of the statute is followed if the consequences are absurd from any evaluative point of view. Taxation law is sometimes regarded as an exception, but recent decisions show that even there common sense takes priority over the letter of the law.

When the *purpose* of the statute apparently contradicts its (contextual) meaning, one re-reads everything relevant to the establishing of both the meaning and the purpose, and hopes to find that they are, after all, compatible. One thus tries to make deviation from the (contextual) meaning in favour of the purpose as small as possible, and vice versa. It is not correct to follow the meaning at the cost of a flagrant violation of the purpose, nor to do the opposite. It is even plausible to argue that the notion of the 'contextual meaning' of a statute *includes* its purpose. At least some evidence of the purpose is a part of the context of the statute. And a statute without a purpose is pointless, in a certain sense meaningless. A purpose of the statute, established according to objective teleological method, may be important, but it normally yields to clear *travaux préparatoires*.

The relative weight of arguments is different in different parts of the law. For example, in criminal law the primary emphasis is usually given to *contextual meaning* of the statute. Moreover the context is restricted: the contextual meaning is interpreted as fairly similar to the *literal* meaning. In taxation law the primary emphasis is usually given to the *intent of the legislature*, expressed in relatively new (not old!) legislative preparatory materials.

Only a small minority of Swedish lawyers would give *primary* emphasis to the *literal meaning of the statute* in all parts of the law. For instance, some critics of the objective teleological method pointed out that it might lead to undue diminishing of the role of the literal meaning; see, for example, Hult, 1952, 41 ff. The increased disposition of the court to interpret the taxation law relatively freely was also criticized (by a professor of law, Göran Grosskopf).

One may conclude as follows. Swedish judges, jurists and lawyers follow quite closely the wording of a clear and not too old statute, but once they recognize – under the impact of the factors mentioned above in section I – that this should not be done, they go over to interpretation influenced by the preparatory materials or (less frequently) by deliberations concerning the 'objective' reason and purpose of the statute. General priority rules, applicable to conflicts between different arguments, are impossible to formulate. The choice is always a matter of a contextual weighing of pros and cons in the case at bar.

In general one must pay attention to the pragmatic and contextual character of Swedish practice. If possible, one always prefers to harmonize the results of the use of different interpretative arguments. Whenever the use of different methods of statutory interpretation in a given situation results in an apparent incompatibility, one tries to reinterpret the provision in question in such a way that the different arguments no longer collide. If such a reconciliation is impossible, one rather attempts to weigh and balance the arguments in the concrete case, instead of attempting a construction of general priority rules.

VII   THE CONFLICT OF STATUTES WITH EACH OTHER AND WITH OTHER LEGAL NORMS

One must keep in mind that interpretational issues are in Sweden ordinarily viewed as a problem of harmonization of the statute and other materials, often regarded as sources of law, e.g., *travaux préparatoires*, precedents and juristic literature. Cf. section III above. The Swedish doctrine of the sources of law is very flexible and complicated. It thus differs, for example, from the view, defended by the French exegetical school of the nineteenth century, that all legal questions are to be answered by recourse to statutes. The sources are then divided into three categories, respectively those that *must*, those that *should* and those that *may* be taken into account in legal reasoning. This classification corresponds to, but is not identical with, the classification of materials. Consequently repetition here of some things already stated in section V above is unavoidable.

The differences are only two: first, purely linguistic materials, such as dictionaries, are not sources of law. Second, social facts and circumstances, such as historical events accompanying legislative process, history of the language and concepts, the so-called 'nature of things' subject to the statute and so on are perhaps 'materials', but are certainly not considered to be sources of law. We will now discuss some explicitly recognized or at least implicitly presupposed source-norms, concerning the sources of law and their collisions.

1   Sources of Law

1   When performing legal reasoning, one *must* use statutes and other regulations as formal reasons from authority, if any are applicable. All courts and authorities must thus use applicable statutes and other regulations in the justification of their decisions. The expression 'other regulations' refers to general norms issued by the government, subordinate authorities and municipalities. The government can issue regulations (a) on the basis of authorisation given by the parliament (cf. Ch. 8, ss. 6–12 of the *Regeringsformen*); (b) as regards enforcement of a statute (cf. Ch. 8, s. 13, para. 1, item 1 of the *Regeringsformen*); and (c) as regards matters that, according to the *Regeringsformen*, should not be regulated by the parliament; this is the so-called 'residual competence' of the government (cf. Ch. 8, s. 13, para. 1, item 2 of the *Regeringsformen*). Subordinate authorities can issue regulations on the basis of authorization, given by the government (cf. Ch. 8, s. 13, para 3 of the *Regeringsformen*) or by a statute. The National Tax Board has thus a statutory authorization to issue some norms that must be used as authority reasons; see, for example, s. 32, para. 3, item 2 of the Municipal Tax Act. The power of the municipalities to issue regulations is based on Ch. 1, s. 7, and Ch. 8, ss. 5, 9 and 11 of the *Regeringsformen*).

Source-norm 1 above does not exclude the fact that the courts and authorities may regard some statutes or regulations as obsolete or invalid on the basis of 'desuetutdo derogatoria' ('derogating contrary custom'). The duty to use statutes and other regulations in the justification of judicial decisions does not necessarily imply that a court must explicitly quote them. But it must be at least implicily clear what the statutory framework of the decision is. If a statute disregards some problems, such as the question of remoteness of damage, a court would often neglect to cite a specific provision of a statute. But if a statutory regulation is directly applicable, it would be a grave mistake not to follow it.

2   Sources which *should* be taken into account include the following: (a) precedents, if any are applicable; (b) legislative preparatory materials, if applicable; (c) international conven-

tions, underlying the applicable national legislation, together with preparatory materials and other interpretatory data concerning them; (d) customs, well established in the society, expressing general principles or accepted by previous decisions of the courts or authorities.

3   Sources which *may* be taken into account include, *inter alia,* the following: (a) general recommendations and advice, issued by various authorities and public, semi-public or even private institutions; (b) professional legal literature; (c) precedents and legislative preparatory materials which do not directly touch upon the interpreted legal text but which give information on evaluations in adjacent areas of law; (d) judicial and administrative decisions which are not reported in NJA; (e) draft statutes; (f) repealed statutes; (g) foreign law; (h) other materials, constituting evidence of well-established evaluations. See also section V above.

2   Collisions

The following norms, explicitly discussed, or at least tacitly presupposed in Swedish practice, regulate the collisions of the sources of law:

1   Whenever one discovers a collision of legal norms one should set it aside, either by reinterpreting (and thus reconciling, harmonizing) these norms, or by arranging a priority order between them.

2   Whenever one reinterprets or ranks norms which are colliding with each other, one should do so in a manner which one can repeatedly use when confronted with similar collisions between other norms. Strong reasons are required to justify a reinterpretation or a priority order applied *ad hoc,* that is, only in the case under consideration. This collision norm expresses an important idea of rationality, that is, universalizability.

3   One should interpret different sources of law, if possible, so that they are compatible. Interpretation of statutes, precedents, legislative preparatory materials and so on should thus affect each other. A reconciliation is thus often more important than arranging of priority orders.

4   If strong reasons militate against reconciliation, the 'must-sources' of law have prima facie priority over the 'should-sources', and these over the 'may-sources'. If one abandons this priority in an individual case, one should justify one's departure with strong reasons. One must thus proffer strong

reasons for, for example, giving precedents priority over a clear statute. On the other hand, no reasons are required to assign the latter a priority over the former. I case RÅ, 1974, Fi 850 the Supreme Administrative Court followed the *travaux préparatoires* instead of the wording of the statute. REUTERS WÄRDJ.claimedthataliteralinterpretationwouldbebothstrange and irrational. The case was criticized however, in the juristic literature.

Moreover legal consequences of disregarding the 'should-sources' are usually milder than in the case of 'must-sources'. For example, an official's or a judge's failure to take into account a statute may in some cases constitute a ground for criminal prosecution; his failure to use 'should-sources', however, has no such consequence. Legal consequence of disregarding 'should-sources' consists mainly of the risk of cancellation of the decision. The state may also be liable in tort, should its agent negligently disregard a 'should-source'.

5   When a higher norm is incompatible with a norm of a lower standing, one must apply the higher. Consider, for example, the following hierarchy of Swedish legal norms: (a) Constitution; (b) statutes; (c) 'other regulations' issued by the government (on the basis of a parliamentary authorization, as regards enforcement of a statute or as regards matters that, according to the Constitution, should not be regulated by the parliament); (d) 'other regulations' issued by subordinate authorities on the basis of authorization, given by the government or by a statute; (e) 'other regulations' issued by municipalities within the statutory framework. This list omits individual norms, such as judicial decisions.

Conflicts between statutes and the *Constitution* are regulated in Ch. 11, s. 14 of the *Regeringsformen*. This stipulates that, in the case under consideration, no court or authority may apply a regulation incompatible with the Constitution. But, if the parliament or the government had issued the regulation, the court or the authority may refuse to apply it only when incompatibility with the Constitution is 'obvious'. In practice, such a refusal is extremely rare. For that reason, there exists a considerable political pressure to establish in Sweden a special Constitutional Court, similar to, for example, the German Bundesverfassungsgericht. So far, there is no parliamentary majority in favour of this project.

6   Where an earlier norm is incompatible with a later one, one must apply the later.

7   One may apply a more general norm only in cases not covered by an incompatible less general norm. A person

making a false income tax return is thus responsible only for a tax offence, according to ss. 2–4 of the Tax Penal Act, but not for fraud, despite the fact that his action also fits Ch. 9, s. 1 of the Criminal Code (concerning fraud).

Which norm is more general and which is less general? The statute can explicitly answer this question through the use of such words as 'although', 'unless', 'apart from', 'in accordance with what is stated below', 'to a wider extent than' and similar expressions. The provision of Ch. 9, s. 3 of the Code on Parents and Children thus constitutes an exception from Ch. 9, s. 1. Sometimes the answer is obvious, even though no express term in a statute indicates this, above all in the cases where the area of application of one statute falls entirely within that of another. In this way the provision of Ch. 3, s. 3 of the Criminal Code, concerning 'a woman who kills her child at birth', is an exception from Ch. 3, s. 1, dealing more severely with 'anyone who deprives another person of his life'.

But many cases are uncertain and then one must rely on weighing and balancing of various reasons. Assume that an employer has deducted an amount from his employees' wages in order to pay tax, and that the employer's bankruptcy is impending. If he pays the amount to the authorities, he can be punished for partiality against creditors, under Ch. 11, s. 4 of the Criminal Code. If he does not pay, he can be punished in accordance with s. 81 of Tax Collection Ordinance. If the Ordinance is 'less general' in comparison with the provision of the Code, then he should pay, but there are also reasons for the opposite view.

8   If a later general norm is incompatible with an earlier but less general norm, one must apply the earlier and less general norm. The Bills of Exchange Act of 1932 is thus less general in relation to the Promissory Notes Act of 1936, since a bill is a kind of promissory note. The former statute must thus be regarded as an exception from the latter.

9   If it is not possible to reconcile different precedents, one should determine which are the most important. In so determining, the following is relevant: the decisions of the Supreme Court have greater authority than those of lower courts. Among the Supreme Court's decisions the most important are those reached in a plenary sitting. Old precedents which have not been confirmed by new ones have as a rule less authority than do new precedents. The value of a precedent decreases if the bench was markedly divided or if the precedent has been criticized. The authority of a prece-

dent increases if a strong need exists for a legal regulation in a given area, for example, one not covered by sufficiently clear legislation. Published cases have more authority than those which are not reported. Cases fully reported in the NJA have more authority than cases summarily reported. An established practice, based on several decisions, has greater importance than a single precedent.

10   If it is not possible to reconcile different pronouncements in the *travaux préparatoires*, one should apply the following priority order: (a) pronouncements of the responsible minister (the government bill with its justification); also reports of relevant parliamentary committees on the proposed bills; (b) other materials.

However incompatibility results in a decrease of authority of all the incompatible parts of the *travaux préparatoires*. A pronouncement in the preparatory materials has thus greatest authority if not questioned by other pronouncements. As regards interpretation of the collision norms themselves, one must consider the fact that they are very seldom explicitly enacted in binding statutes. Most of them are tacitly presupposed. That is, a scholar can rationally reconstruct the judicial practice in such a manner that it appears to follow them. In this situation, no literal interpretation of these norms is possible. Everything depends on weighing and balancing of various considerations determining whether the norm in question should be applied in the actual case. If not, one may always say that other reasons weigh more than the collision norm in question cf. Peczenik, 1989, 418 ff.

VIII   PRESUMPTIONS GUIDING INTERPRETATION

Many interpretation norms, well-known in Sweden, can be expressed as, or at least explained in terms of, presumptions concerning the intention of the legislature, such as (1) that the legislature intends that the law be kept up-to-date; (2) that the legislature generally uses statutory language carefully and does not intend to be redundant; (3) that the legislature generally intends no contradiction; (4) that the legislature does not intend absurd results; and (5) that the job of a judge is to do justice, and yet also to make a rational and coherent overall body of law.

Swedish practice commonly recognizes norms on interpretation that impose some demands for rationality on statutory language. *Inter alia*, the following norms belong to this category.

(a) One must not interpret the same words or expressions

occurring in different parts of the same statute in different ways unless strong reasons for such an interpretation exist. This idea of uniform interpretation was expressed, for example, in the pronouncement of the Council on Legislation on the concept 'business activities' in the Liability for Damages Act (cf. Government Bill 1972:5, p. 635). Sometimes, however, strong reasons justify a shifting interpretation: the penal-law term 'resistance', for example, was not interpreted uniformly even in the same statute. But the lawgiver found the shifting interpretation to be unsatisfactory. This fact affected the new formulation of Ch. 8, s. 5 of the Swedish Criminal Code.

(b) If different words or expressions are used in the same statute, one should assume that they relate to different situations, unless strong reasons for assuming the opposite exist. In fact, however, some statutes are not perfect from this point of view. In ss. 6 and 45 of the Insurance Contracts Act we find the words 'the occurrence of the insurance case or the extent of damage', whereas in a similar context, in s. 121 of the same statute, we find the words 'the occurence or extent of the insurance case'. There are strong reasons for assuming that this divergence is not relevant.

(c) One must not interpret a statutory provision in such a way that some parts of the provision prove to be unnecessary.

(d) One must not interpret words and expressions occurring in the statute in conflict with ordinary linguistic usage unless strong reasons for such an interpretation exist. If, however, it has previously been established that a word or an expression has a technical meaning incompatible with everyday langauge, one should interpret that word or expression as having such a special meaning, without reference to everyday language.

To be sure, such norms are coherent with the presumption that the legislature generally uses statutory language carefully and does not intend to be redundant. But one can also avoid mentioning such a presumption and derive these norms from the goal of legislation to direct human behaviour as efficiently as possible. If the statute is to be a perfect means of directing people it must not contain words whose interpretation shifts from one part of it to another. Nor may it be formulated in a misleading manner. Furthermore it must be intelligible and thus must deploy everyday language. And so on.

Still presumptions concerning the legislator are sometimes explicitly formulated in the juristic literature. Consider two examples. First, Jareborg, 1979, p. 64 wrote that: 'A basic principle for objective interpretation of statutes is that the interpreted text is regarded as *rationally formulated*. This means, *inter alia*, that one shall eliminate interpretational alternatives which imply that parts of the text are redundant, that words which are used many times change their meaning, that the text . . . contains logical contradictions.'

Second, according to Agge, 1969, p. 69, statutory analogy is justifiable only in cases in which 'strong reasons indicate that the legislator would, if he had been able to foresee these cases, have extended the enactment to cover them as well'. Of course, the word 'legislator' must mean here 'a rational legislator'. (Agge had no way of knowing what an irrational legislator would have done in a contrary-to-fact situation.)

The presumption that the legislature generally intends no contradiction is coherent with the so-called collision norms, commonly accepted in the Swedish practice (see above).

Swedish practice certainly avoids interpretations which would imply that a statute is absurd. Again one may justify this fact with the presumption that the legislature does not intend absurd results. On the other hand, one may simply say that it is a duty of a person interpreting the law to do it in a non-absurd manner, regardless of whatever the legislators thought or meant.

The rationality norms discussed in the answer to this question have the same character as other reasoning norms. They do not solve particularly 'hard' cases. The practice of their application differs from one part of the legal order to another. One can disregard them if important reasons for doing so exist. Yet they enhance the rationality of statutory interpretation. They thus constitute additional reasonable premises, necessary to present legal reasoning as a series of logically correct inferences. They constitute a kind of customary law or at least expressly established moral judgements. Finally, they are connected with the very meaning of such words as 'legal reasoning'; if one refutes a great number of them, one's reasoning is no longer 'legal'.

Of course one may justify such norms by recourse to the presumption (or fiction) that the law-maker generally intends rational legislation. We have heard many such expressions from both colleagues and students, but they are more rare in writing. Presumptions concerning the law-giver's rationality are hardly compatible with Olivecrona's 'non-voluntaristic' philosophy of law. As a true Legal Realist, Olivecrona condemned such things as fictions. For that reason, several generations of his pupils, working as superior judges, professors and so on, have not often explicitly expressed this kind of thinking. More frequently, these presumptions exist, so to speak, 'in the background', actually leading thought, if not explicit writing.

Every judge in Sweden recognizes that his job partly consists in a rational interpretation of statutes; see above, under items 2–4. Almost every judge also recognizes that he must do justice, albeit there are some exceptions. (We have heard a judge asserting that his job is only to execute political decisions.) In this context, one may also quote Ch. 1, s. 2 of the *Regeringsformen*, stipulating that public power shall be exercised with respect for the equality, freedom and dignity of human beings. This provision is directed to both judges and other persons of authority. The values it promotes are certainly connected with justice. As regards the possibility of overriding such norms or presumptions, everything depends again on an overall weighing and balancing of pros and cons. No exceptionless rules can be formulated.

IX   THE STYLE OF STATUTORY INTERPRETATION

1   According to the Code of Procedure, a judgement of a Swedish court has the following content:

- statement(s) of claim(s) and defence(s);
- the issue(s) as presented before the court;
- the reasons given by the court for its order or decree;
- the order or decree itself.

2   The Code of Procedure states briefly – without further specification – that the court must give its reasons for the decision. According to actual practice and doctrinal writings, this means that the court must state the 'ultimate facts' – those which directly constitute the legal conditions of the decision – and its legal reasoning. All Swedish jurists agree that the court should also state other relevant facts and credibility findings. On the other hand, a judgement with incomplete reasons is not void, voidable or appealable on this ground. Such reasons are merely not reviewable.

This general structure is – *mutatis mutandis* – the same in all kinds of cases.

3   Older Swedish decisions, until the first half of the twentieth century, were relatively brief.

(a) In some cases the courts gave extremely *brief* and *unclear* reasons for the decisions. In the decision it was written, for example, that the plaintiff or the respondent had or had not a certain right, without stating any exact ground for this statement. Often it was not possible to know at all which general rule the court had followed. One might call such opinions 'pseudo-justifications'. As an example one may cite NJA, 1947, p. 299. An association was held responsible for damage negligently caused by the supervisor of a shooting range owned by the association. The Supreme Court majority expressed itself so obscurely that it was not clear whether it considered the association liable because the supervisor's position was considered to be equivalent to one of management, or because his position was judged as connected with particular risk, or because a contract-like relation was considered to exist between the association and the injured person.

A decision might also be justified with the use of unclear expressions of the type 'must be assumed' and so on. For example, in the case NJA, 1954, p. 268 a person having a significant connection with Bulgaria made an application to collect an amount which had been deposited in Sweden for his account. The Bulgarian state contested his right to collect the amount personally and stated that the payment should take place through a Swedish–Bulgarian clearing account and be made to him in Bulgaria. The Supreme Court majority recognized the Bulgarian state's right to plead in the case but without giving any reason other than that the members of the majority 'found no hindrance to exist to the consideration of the Bulgarian state's plea', after which the case was decided in a way favourable to that state.

(b) The simple subsumption method was even older. The court presented the decision as a logical consequence of a general rule and some facts. It did this even in hard cases, in which the general rule was not contained in a statute but constituted the result of an evaluative interpretation, based on additional premisses which were not stated. The method dominated in Sweden at the end of the nineteenth century. In many cases the court forced the whole reasoning into one sentence with many subordinate clauses and the decision as a consequence ('since ... and since ... inasmuch as ... , then' and so on). Strömholm, 1989, p. 336 cites the following cases: NJA, 1875, p. 489; 1876, p. 458; 1877, p. 487 and 1877, p. 334.

Pseudo-justification and the simple subsumption method are due to the old tradition with its roots in the nineteenth century. In those days the Supreme Court often used two formulae after applying one of the above-mentioned methods when revising a decision of a lower court, that is either 'according to the law, we revise the decision as follows' (. . . prövar lagligt att . . .) or 'in order for justice to be done, we revise the decision as follows' (. . . prövar rättvist att . . .). Both formulae were used in interpretation and gap-filling cases.

The present trend, however, is to give discursive and thorough going justification (the sophisticted subsumption method and the dialogue method). Tradition is losing its grip and the higher courts are giving justifications more in line with American and English higher courts, although the Swedish courts do not overdetermine their judgements by giving more than sufficient reasons for decision. Also the Swedish courts seldom deliberately use the technique of giving dicta (see below, item 5).

4   The relevant statutory provisions must be indicated, explicitly or at least implicitly.

5   The following justificatory models dominate the recent practice of writing opinions.

(a) The *fact-stating method* is extensive but insufficiently general. In the decision there are statements concerning facts, but neither value-judgements nor norms. The interpreter must himself guess which statutory rules, norms for statutory interpretation, moral value-judgements and other premisses together with the proffered facts logically imply the conclusion. The method is often used in the lower courts and even in the courts of appeal, albeit there to a decreasing extent. See also NJA, 1952, p. 184 (the Supreme Court). The High Insurance Court uses this method frequently; see, for example, cases 1086/75:1, 872/79:8, 1498/81:3 and 1516/82:4.

(b) The *dialogue method*. The court proffers clearly both the reasons for and those against the decision, including facts, norms and − often general − value-judgements; then it concludes that the former weigh more in the case at bar. See NJA, 1984, p. 693, where the Supreme Court performed weighing and balancing of reasons for and against the principle that security transfer according to foreign law should have an effect against the. transferor's creditors in Sweden. The method is frequently used, for example, by the Housing Court. See, *inter alia*, case RBD, 1978 38:78, where the court completed an extensive reasoning with the following statement: 'A reasonable weighing and balancing of the reasons proffered above leads, according to the Housing Court, to the result that the tenancy-relation ought to expire, unless particular reasons tell against this conclusion.'

(c) The *sophisticated subsumption method* (or 'scientific' method). The court proffers clearly the reasons both for and against the decision, including facts, norms and value-judgements; then it modifies the reasons for the decision in such a way that the decision becomes a logical conclusion of them. The proffered norms and value-judgements are often general. *Inter alia*, one aims at formulating a clear precedent-norm. The method occurs especially in some courts of appeals. As regards the Supreme Court, see NJA, 1983, p. 487. (See also

Peczenik, 1989, 336 ff.

6   The use of purely substantive reasons (moral, economic, social, political and so on) is more and more common, especially in connection with the dialogue method. See *inter alia*, case RBD, 1978, 38:78 above.

7   The underlying structure of justification is more and more visible in the style of the opinion. Whereas complex reasoning in older cases was often concealed behind a brief façade, modern judges often feel obliged to present openly their real reasons.

8   The dialogue method and the sophisticated subsumption method of today may in some cases involve formulating general rules and principles. The traditional scepticism of Swedish courts with regard to general and abstract opinions is thus continually decreasing. The majority of the Supreme Court in case NJA, 1977, p. 176 thus expressed the following, both important and highly controversial, general principle of evidence.

> In torts, there is often a controversy about what caused the actual damage or injury . . . Many courses of events . . ., independently of one another, can constitute a possible cause . . . In such cases, full evidence . . . can scarcely be given . . . If thus, in the light of all the circumstances of the case, it is clearly more probable that the actual course of events was that which the plaintiff has pointed out than that . . . pointed out by the defendant, the statement of the plaintiff should form the basis for the decision.

In case NJA, 1976, p. 458, a bicycle pump was changed so that it could be used for shooting a cork. The owner of the pump, A, a 9-year-old, permitted B, a 6-year-old, to play with it. The cork got stuck. B asked D, a 9-year-old, to withdraw the cork. D tried to do it, accidentally 'shot' with the pump, and the cork hit B's eye. All instances ruled against B's claim for compensation from A. The majority of the Supreme Court denied A's negligence, since the risk of injury had been minimal. NORDENSON J. dissented and made several subtle conceptual distinctions, in a way unthinkable in the older Swedish practice, *inter alia* between the problems of negligence, remoteness of damage and the purpose of protection given by the law of torts. He also expressed a series of general principles (cf. NJA, 1981, p. 622). Concerning the practice of the Supreme Administrative Court (*Regeringsrätten*), see, for example, case RÅ, 1978, 1:19.

9   The 'one right answer' ideology is not adopted in Swedish

courts. On the contrary, the judges realize that many interpretations are plausible in hard cases. The Swedish courts frequently apply the system of dissenting opinions. The dissenting opinions can be long and discursive.

10   The opinions of the Supreme Court are published in *Nytt Juridiskt Arkiv* (NJA), the opinions of the Supreme Administrative Court in *Regeringsrättens Årsbok* (RÅ). The opinions of the highest special courts and *some* opinions of Courts of Appeal are also published. All these publications are easily accessible.

11   A special question concerns the adaptation of the style of justification to the institutionally prescribed addressees or at least expected readers of the decisions. As far as we know, no institutional prescriptions of this kind exist but the courts try to use as plain a language as possible. Lip-service is paid to the demand of comprehensibility of the decision to everybody, especially to the parties, yet highly technical justification is not rare at all.

12   The following functions of the opinions may be listed (cf. Bergholtz, 1987, 352 ff).

(a) The opinion should give satisfactory information to the parties. The modern society is no longer oriented towards obeying judgements merely supported by an uncontroversial authority, perhaps felt as reflecting God's or the king's will. The parties rather wish to have immediate access to general and extensive reasons, answering the question *why* the court has decided in a certain way. Moreover an extensive and general justification helps the parties to decide whether to appeal against the decision. It also increases their chance of obtaining a change of the decision, if such is justifiable.

(b) An important function is to legitimize the decision. Democracy requires that the courts sufficiently respect the statutes enacted by the representatives of the people. In hard cases, an extensive and general justification is a necessary condition for making it clear that the court has actually fulfilled this requirement. An extensively and generally justified decision directly fulfills the demand of intersubjective testability. In other words, one knows on which grounds one may criticize it.

The most distinctive characteristics of the modern Swedish style of writing opinions are (1) open reporting of the reasons, substantive as well as authoritative (including *travaux préparatoires*); (2) cautiousness as regards drawing general conclusions which would transcend the limit of the case; and (3) weighing and balancing of reasons in the particular case, rather than reliance upon abstract priority rules.

X   INTERPRETATION WITH REGARD TO THE CHARACTER OF THE STATUTE

1   The Nature of the Substantive Law Field

The following examples elucidate the influence of the nature of the substantive law field of the statute.

1   The so-called legality principle in penal law demands that no action should be regarded as a crime without statutory support and no penalty may be imposed without a statutory provision ('nullum crimen sine lege, nulla poena sine lege'). This is a classical requirement of legal certainty, eliminating unforeseeable punishment.

2   In taxation law, the principle 'nullum tributum sine lege' justifies the conclusion that one should apply analogy with restraint if it leads to increased taxation. Moreover the Swedish taxation law is usually interpreted fairly literally. This created some problems when a general clause was added to the tax law. Section 2 of the Tax Evasion Act of 1980 (changed in 1983) stipulates as follows:

> When making the tax assessment, one should not pay attention to a transaction performed by the taxpayer . . ., if 1. the transaction . . . is included in a procedure that gives the taxpayer a not irrelevant taxation advantage, 2. the advantage, in view of the circumstances, can be regarded as having been the main reason for the procedure and 3. the tax assessment based on this procedure would contradict the grounds of the legislation.

But what 'contradicts' the grounds of the legislation? Assume that A transferred a number of houses to a company he owned all by himself and then sold shares in this company to a third party. In this way, A obtained a taxation advantage in comparison with a hypothetical situation in which he sold the houses directly. This procedure was judged as not contradicting the grounds of the legislation (cf. case RÅ 83 1:35). On the other hand, the Supreme Administrative Court found that the following procedure did contradict these 'grounds': The estate of the deceased was divided in such a way that the widow received a farm. Then she sold it to the heirs who in this manner obtained a taxation advantage (cf. the case RÅ, 1984, 1:92). What support can the interpreter find for making such distinctions? He may pay attention to the *travaux préparatoires*, 'general structure of statutes' and 'their purpose' (Government Bill 1980/81:17, pp. 26 and 197; Government

Bill 1982/83:84, p. 19.) The *travaux préparatoires*, however, do not always give the required information. No wonder that the courts use this general clause very restrictively.

3   On the other hand, conclusion by analogy has priority before *argumentum e contrario* in private law; cf. section III above.

4   The role of preparatory legislative materials varies from one part of the law to another. Their greatest importance is in the tax law. Their role in private law is also significant. Criminal jurisdiction is less affected by the preparatory materials. This is a consequence of the so-called legality principle, 'nulla poena sine lege', implying high respect for the literal wording of the statutory text, yet the *travaux préparatoires* may be important in criminal cases, too. In, for example, case NJA, 1980, p. 94, the decision of the Supreme Court supported itself on the preparatory materials to the statute (1976:56), amending the provision of Ch. 11, s. 4 of the Criminal Code.

5   Some scholars, such as Per Olof Ekelöf, clearly wish to diminish the importance of preparatory materials in the law of procedure. It is not clear whether this view reflects some properties of this legal discipline itself, or merely follows from their theoretical views.

6   In public law in general one meets two phenomena, so to speak acting in opposite directions. Interpretation tends to be very loyal to the statute, especially to the intentions of its authors. On the other hand, the statutes themselves are often vague. The interpreter would guess what evaluations the authors of the statute had in mind, rather than openly perform independent evaluations. Another thing is that the guesses can be more or less consciously affected by the interpreter's own evaluations.

7   The role of the juristic literature varies also from one part of the law to another. In classical parts of civil law, juristic treatises and textbooks are very important for interpretation, *inter alia* because of their theoretical load. This is the case, for example, in torts and contracts, where it makes a great deal of difference what, for example, Professor Jan Hellner thinks. Legal writing has a great influence in international private law. In public international law it also has a clear position as a recognized source of the law; cf. s. 38 of the statute of the International Court of Justice. On the other hand, in administrative law, juristic literature often tends merely to systematize the decisions.

The following factors increase *de facto* the probability of a high position of modern doctrine.

- The greater respect the decision makers have for rational reasoning, the greater is the role of doctrine.
- The lower the speed of legislative change, the greater is the chance that jurists have sufficient time to produce elaborate commentaries, handbooks and other auxiliary means for statutory interpretation.
- The more numerous statutory provisions, precedents, pronouncements in *travaux préparatoires* and other sources of the law are, the greater is the need for their systematization and interpretation in legal writing.

2   The Nature of the Addressees

This certainly influences *legislation*. In principle, a statute addressed to professional lawyers is usually drafted in a technical manner, whereas a statute addressed to ordinary citizens is kept closer to ordinary language. Yet the nature of the matter may require a technical language even in the latter case, for example, as regards some details of the tax law.

Interpretation is another matter. Even a statute drafted in ordinary language and addressed to ordinary citizens may require a technical and complex interpretation in order to ensure justice and coherence. In such a case these values have priority over linguistic simplicity.

3   The Age or Possible Obsolescence of the Statute

This may be an important problem. For example, in Sweden in 1940 (and in Finland even later) the Criminal Code still contained Ch. 7 on the breaking of the Sabbath, increasing punishment for a crime committed during a Church holiday. In practice the chapter was tacitly ignored, without much talk about the intent of the legislature.

Another example is the following. Suppose that A produces sausages containing some controversial chemicals and does not ask proper authorities for approval according to the law. B buys a sausage. A zealous prosecutor accuses the buyer on the basis of Ch. 1, s. 10 of the Swedish Commercial Code of 1734. The provision stipulates as follows: 'The goods that *stadens vräkare* should behold and examine may not be taken by the buyer before that happened; or both buyer and seller are to be fined 10 dalers each.' Is this old provision applicable to modern cases? Logically it is possible. To be sure, no *stadens vräkare* exist any more. (This old Swedish word, hardly comprehensible today, designated more or less a 'municipal heaver'). Yet one could assume that present supervisory authorities correspond to them. In fact the provision is commonly regarded as obsolete.

A striking historical example is that s. 4 of the old *Regeringsformen*, derogated as late as 1969, stipulated that 'the King has the right to govern the realm alone'. Between 1969 and 1 January 1975, when the new Constitution came into force, the old *Regeringsformen* still proclaimed at the very beginning that 'the realm of Sweden shall be governed by a king' (s. 1). The actually applied norm was, instead, 'The *Government*, responsible to the Parliament, has the *executive* power.' To be sure, nobody wished to call these sections obsolete. Instead one regarded them as a main rule, whose application was very much limited by other laws. In the commentary to the old Constitution, one could thus read that 'of course, the King is bound in his execution of the power to govern [the realm] both as to form and as to content within the framework laid down by legislation' (Malmgren, 1971, p. 6). The same commentary calls the reform of 1969, *inter alia* the derogation of s. 4, 'writing into the Constitution the parliamentary form of government already developed in practice' (p. 5). One may certainly find this reasoning coherent with the presumption that the legislature intends that the law be kept up to date. On the other hand, the whole reasoning was based rather on the realistic recognition of norms embedded in practice than on a presumption concerning the intention of the law-giver.

4 The Terms in which the Statute is Drafted

The question whether the statute is drafted in relatively broad and general terms (such as but not limited to, statutes including general clauses) or is relatively specific and detailed is also important.

General clauses and so on require evaluative interpretation, presupposing weighing and balancing of various values. To make the job of the interpreter easier, the legislator may provide extensive preparatory materials. In due course a series of precedents provides additional help. For example, s. 36 of the Swedish Contracts Act stipulates that a contractual condition may be modified or disregarded by the court 'if it is undue (unreasonable) with regard to the content of the contract, circumstances of its origin, subsequent circumstances and other circumstances'; one must also pay particular attention to the need of protecting the person who, 'as a consumer or otherwise occupies an inferior position in the contractual relation'.

The pronouncement of the responsible minister in the preparatory materials provided more precise guidelines. One should set aside a contractual stipulation giving a party unilateral right to decide, especially if the stipulation is included in a standard contract prepared by the clearly stronger party. One should also set aside a contractual stipulation contradicting good business custom in a given branch; but one need not accept a stipulation which a certain branch considers to agree with good business custom and so on (Government Bill 1975/76:81, 118 ff).

The courts elaborated more detailed guidelines. Suppose, for example, that an inexperienced businessman enters into a contract with a big company, dominating the market. The contract permits the company to decide unilaterally whether future disputes are to be decided by a general court or arbitration. A dispute occurs. The businessman sues the company before a general court. The company claims that the case should be referred to arbitration. Is the arbitration clause 'undue'? A reason for this conclusion may be that it deprives the weaker party of the possibility of having his right examined (cf. NJA, 1979, p. 666).

5 Standards of Statutory Draftsmanship

As regards the question whether the statute is relatively well drafted or relatively poorly drafted, the following may be stated. A considerable juristic literature claims that the standard of legislation is continually decreasing, yet the courts seem to cope with the problem. Implicitly, poorly-drafted statutes permit a more free interpretation. The purpose is then more important than the wording. But this distinction is never made explicit. The courts do not openly criticize statutes as being poorly drafted. Poorly-drafted *travaux préparatoires* may be simply ignored. The purpose of the statute must be then established in an independent way.

XI THE ROLE OF THE COURTS

The Swedish courts play only a limited role when it comes to declaring a statute unconstitutional. Still less is their role as regards expanding or restricting the provisions of the Constitution itself. As stated in section VII above, Ch. 11, s. 14 of the *Regeringsformen* stipulates that, in a particular case, no court or authority may apply a regulation incompatible with the Constitution. But if the parliament or the government issued the regulation, refusal is possible only when incompatibility with the Constitution is 'obvious'. The role of the courts is thus limited by the requirement of 'obviousness' and by the fact that the review is not effective for future cases.

As regards the power to review administrative decisions made within the statutory limits, Sweden has three levels of administrative courts, similar to, those, for example, of the Federal Republic of Germany (*Verwaltungsgerichte*). As a signatory to the European Convention, Sweden also has to give full access to administrative courts for appeal against agency action. Yet in many kinds of cases concerning public-law claims of an economic kind, statutes establish an exclusive competence of the administration, with the result that a party cannot appeal to an administrative court (cf. Ch. 10, s. 17, para. 1, Code of Procedure; Strömberg, 1978, pp. 207–24). Swedish courts certainly exercise some power to restrict or expand the meaning of statutes by interpretation. On the other hand, the courts do not go so far as to make wholly new law without authorization by the legislature.

XII STATUTORY PRESCRIPTIONS ON INTERPRETATION

Explicit constitutional or statutory rules on statutory interpretation are both few in number and of little importance in Sweden. This is a result of the common conviction of the Swedish lawyers and politicians that such rules would themselves require interpretation. The resulting circularity is not attractive to the law-giver. From a theoretical point of view, one may add that statutory interpretation functions as a tool for adapting the written law to moral values. The latter cannot be written down completely, because of the role of weighing and balancing in moral reasoning. This means, again, that the rules of interpretation must themselves be interpreted.

The most striking example of an explicit interpretation rule has now a merely historical importance, yet it elucidates the problem very well. The interpretation norm, formulated in s. 84 of the old *Regeringsformen* of 1809, derogated as late as 1969, prescribed that 'Constitutional laws shall be interpreted according to their wording'. However this norm did not prevent a radical reinterpretation of many constitutional provisions; see, for example, section X above, *re* s. 4 of this *Regeringsformen*.

When Swedish law was codified in 1734, there were added to the code some general rules for judges, originally written down in 1540 by Olaus Petri. These rules are customarily reprinted each year, in any edition of the semi-official Swedish collection of statutes. But they do not have a character of statutory law, merely constituting a customary appendix to the collection of statutes. Some of the rules are relevant for statutory interpretation, for example: 'The judge has to pay attention . . . to what the intention was of him who made the statute, otherwise it will be abused and turned to another sense than the opinion of him who made the law.' This rule seems to stipulate subjective interpretation, according to the intention of the law-giver. No doubt the Swedish practice pays great attention to the intention of the law-maker. Olaus Petri's rules are, however, seldom quoted.

Chapter 2, s. 10, para. 1 of the *Regeringsformen* stipulates that no penalty or another penal sanction may be imposed for an action without a provision in a statute which was valid when the crime was committed. This is the so-called legality principle ('nullum crimen sine lege, nulla poena sine lege'). The Law on Introducing the Criminal Code, s. 5, para. 1 includes a similar norm. One may ask whether these provisions imply an interpretation-norm, forbidding the use of statutory analogy against the defendant. According to Ch. 8, s. 1 of the Criminal Code, a person should be sentenced for theft if he 'takes what belongs to another'. It is thus theft for one to come into possession of a valuable trade secret by unlawfully taking an already existing copy of a drawing. But to come into possession of the secret by copying the drawing, on the other hand, is no theft; copying is no 'taking'. One pays no regard to the fact that the difference between taking the existing copy, and the action of copying it, is not important for the victim.

Yet the opinion has been expressed in the literature in penal law that the quoted provision does *not* entail prohibition of the use of analogy to justify punishment. Punishment may be justifiable by the fact that (1) a statutory provision existed at the time when the crime was committed and (2) this provision could be extended *by analogy* to cover the action in question. In some cases the Supreme Court has applied criminal law analogically. The Tax Crime Act, s. 2, stipulates punishment for one who omits to declare his income and thus causes the fact that insufficient tax is imposed on him. In case NJA, 1978, p. 452, the Supreme Court applied this provision by analogy to convict a person who had omitted to declare his income with the consequence that no tax at all was imposed on him. The Court stated that the decision corresponded to the purpose of the statute and the *travaux préparatoires*.

In NJA, 1959, p. 254, two men left a radioactive isotope unguarded at their workplace. They were sentenced for 'causing general danger through spreading poison or . . . such like' (Ch. 19, s. 7 of the Penal Code then in force; cf. now, Ch. 13, s. 7 of the Criminal Code). To *leave* the stuff unguarded was judged as analogous to *spreading* it. In NJA, 1956 C, p. 187, a person threatened a cashier with a pistol that later turned out to be a toy and thus obtained some money. The Swedish Supreme Court decided that such an act constituted a robbery. The decision was based on analogy between a real danger and an action which the victim considers to constitute a danger.

In NJA, 1954, p. 464, a man who made a withdrawal from his

account was sentenced for unlawful disposal, since he realized that the amount had been credited to the account by mistake. This was judged as analogous to unlawful disposal of what one has in one's possession (Ch. 22, s. 4 of the Penal Code then in force; cf. now, Ch. 10, s. 4 of the Criminal Code). Literally, however, the defendant never has possession of the money.

The descriptions of offences in the Criminal Code are in general concerned with positive actions. They are also applied analogically to omission to act. According to Ch. 3, s. 1 of the Criminal Code, 'a person who deprives another person of his life' shall be convicted of murder. This enactment would, however, be applied analogically to certain omission cases. If a person having the task of pumping air to a diver underwater ceased pumping with intent to kill, and the diver was suffocated, he must be sentenced for murder.

XIII CONSTITUTIONAL LAW AND INTERPRETATION

The Swedish Constitution contains very few material principles which are supposed to generally bind statutory interpretation.

1   The following provisions of the *Regeringsformen* are considered as justifying (a) the requirement of statutory authorization for judicial practice and (b) the demand that statutory interpretation be kept close to the letter of the law and loyal to the intentions of the legislature. Thus Ch. 1, s. 1, para 3 provides, 'The public power should be executed under the law', and Ch. 11, s. 4, 'The questions of the duties of the courts in regard to administration of justice, their organization and legal process shall be written down in the law.'

2   Chapter 1, s. 2 of the *Regeringsformen* stipulates that 'the public power shall be exercised with respect for the equal value of all human beings and for each individual person's freedom and dignity'. These values are expected to affect interpretation of statutes.

3   As regards the division of powers, the following may be stated. Though the *Regeringsformen* (Ch. 1, ss. 4 and 6 and so on) in principle denies the division of power and regards parliament as a supreme representative of the sovereign people, it stipulates independence of the courts and, to a lesser extent, state bureaucracy. No one, not even parliament, may instruct the courts in how to interpret the law in a concrete case (Ch. 11, s. 2). It is, difficult to see however, how these provisions may affect statutory interpretation.

XIV   INTERPRETATION, LEGAL VALUES AND PRINCIPLES OF LAW

Many decisions explicitly refer to the demand of *rättssäkerhet* ('legal certainty'). The concept is vague but it implies that legal decisions must be predictable on the basis of statutes (legal certainty in the formal sense). In some cases this constitutes a reason for interpreting statutes literally. In other cases, however, legal certainty is understood in a material sense: the decisions must optimize the demands of predictability (based on the enacted law) and other demands of justice, moral acceptability and so on. Such demands may justify deviations from literal interpretation.

Another relevant value is democracy. The argument that a too-free interpretation of statutes would collide with democracy is well-known in Swedish political debate. The courts themselves do not proffer it explicitly. Implicitly, however, they are very loyal to the democratically elected legislative power. On the other hand, not even the most self-restraining court can avoid paying attention to ethical values and thus transcending the limits of literal interpretation.

Last, but not least, one must emphasize the value of reasonableness. The Swedish courts do everything to present the interpretation as reasonable.

XV   THE CHARACTER OF HIGHER COURTS IN SWEDEN

The appellate courts and the Supreme Court try all sorts of cases with the exception of cases under the jurisdiction of administrative law. For those, there are certain administrative courts.

1   The judges of the appellate courts are career judges and they normally reach those courts after 10–15 years inside the judiciary. On this level, there is no exchange among the legal professions. In the Supreme Court, the judges have a somewhat different background. Normally one of them has been a private attorney, one a prosecuting attorney, one or two a professor of law and a couple of them judges in trial courts and appellate courts. Several, and some say too many, have been high officials in the Ministry of Justice. This is a regular base for recruitment to the court. The Supreme Court judges are appointed by the government, usually after consultation with the Supreme Court itself. Other judicial candidates are recommended to the government by a council of judges and

lawyers, but the government is not bound to follow the recommendations, even if it mostly does.

2   The Supreme Court is a court of last resort. This means that it is the third court involved in the case, after the trial court and the appellate court. The court of appeal reviews cases on their merits in fact and law, with smaller limitations as to evidence. The Supreme Court, on the other hand, working with *certiorari*, tries, with some exceptions, mostly very important questions of law. But the court does review the merits of the case.

3   Both the appellate courts and the Supreme Court in civil cases rely only on the facts submitted by parties, but of course in a criminal case a convicted person can be acquitted with regard to a non-submitted fact. The principle or maxim 'iura novit curia' means in Sweden that all courts search for the interpretation of a statute without limitation of arguments invoked by parties. In Sweden the Brandeis Brief type of argument is unknown and may be considered improper.

4   If the Supreme Court wants to deviate from its own practice in a certain question, it may use the court *in pleno*, which means all of the 22 judges or 12 of them sitting on such a case, compared to an average sitting of five judges.

XVI   THE LEGISLATURE: STRUCTURE AND PROCEDURES

1   In Sweden statutes are nearly always drafted by highly-skilled lawyers, mostly judges on temporary leave from court, or sometimes law professors. They do the work in legislative committees, often together with politicians. Now and then, political concerns do interfere with the work, making the drafts difficult to read and interpret, but mostly a consensus is reached. The most important feature in Swedish law drafting is the high standing of preparatory materials, which is next in importance to the wording of the statute. This tradition, of course, affects the law drafts dramatically. Maybe Sweden uses *travaux préparatoires* in statutory interpretation most extensively of all the countries in the world, and laws are written with this peculiarity in mind. In any case the drafting of statutes is done by the best professional lawyers in the country. This way of doing things is not totally unknown even in the USA; one can cite, for example, the Uniform Commercial Code.

2   The report of the legislative committee, the governmental bill

with its extensive arguments and the debates of the parliament are all printed and, as said, much used in interpretation.

3   If the government or the parliament think the courts are
misinterpreting a statute, which happens from time to time,
speedy action is taken to change or amend the law.

XVII   FEATURES OF THE LEGAL CULTURE

1   Swedish legal culture may be characterized as *open to evaluations within a positivistic framework*. At the end of section IX
above, we stated that the most distinctive characteristics of
the modern Swedish style of writing opinions are (a) open
reporting of the reasons, substantive as well as authoritative
(including *travaux préparatoires*); (b) cautiousness as regards
drawing general conclusions which would transcend the limit
of the case; and (c) weighing and balancing of reasons in the
particular case, rather than reliance upon abstract priority
rules. This creates an impression of a relatively substantive
legal culture, open to value and policy arguments. On the
other hand, the courts keep this freedom to evaluate within
limits determined by their loyalty towards the legislature.
Natural law has no influence. The courts proffer value-judgements because they feel that the legislator gives them the
power to do this. Doing so, they often realize that another
judgement would be equally reasonable and justifiable.

2   Legal methodology of the *courts* is quite unified. Only some
special courts, such as the Labour Court, may show peculiarities, depending on their particular role. At the same time, the
legal methodology of academic jurists is disparate and conflicting. We have scholars following the tradition of legal
dogmatics, that is, the same method as the courts, albeit on a
higher level of abstraction. We also have some 'Legal Rea-
lists', sceptical towards all legal method, and some 'critical
legal students', sceptical towards our type of society, but
these have little influence on the courts.

3   Legal dogmatics, on the other hand, exerts considerable
influence on operative interpretation. Academic writings are
quoted in some cases and followed in most. Meanwhile the
judges increasingly regret that the lack of time, caused by
excessive burden of work, prevents their more profound
studies of legal literature. Scholars have this kind of problem,
too, since it is difficult to follow the rapidly changing legislation. This explains why *travaux préparatoires* are so popular.
They are the only kind of materials which are nearly always

accessible.
4   Most judges are 'generalists' but some are specialized, for
     example in taxation, economic crimes, company law, credit
     market, stock exchange and so on. Technical specialization
     may influence statutory interpretation. For example, intricate
     problems concerning so called 'insiders' are likely to be
     judged on the basis of economic knowledge rather than legal
     dogmatics.

NOTE

The authors express their gratitude to Jan Hellner who participated in this report at
its early and thus decisive stage.

ABBREVIATIONS

NJA (*Nytt Juridiskt Arkiv*). The leading law reports in Sweden. Cases are quoted by
    indicating the year and the first page of the report.
RÅ (*Regeringsrättens Årsbok*). Law reports of Supreme Administrative Court.
RBD (*Rättsfall från Bostadsdomstolen*). Law reports of the Housing Court.
Regeringsformen. (The Instrument of Government). The law which contains the most
    important part of the Swedish Constitution.

REFERENCES

Agge, Ivar (1969), *Huvundpunkten av den allmänne rättsläran*, 2 edn., Stockholm:
    Juridiska Föreningens Förlag.
Bergholtz, Gunnar (1987), *Ratio et Auctoritas*, Lund: Acta Societatis Juridicae Lunden-
    sis No. 88.
Eckhoff, Torstein (1987), *Rettskildelaere*, 2 edn., Oslo: Tano.
Ekelöf, Per Olof (1958), 'Teleological Construction of Statutes', 2 *Scandinavian
    Studies in Law*, Stockholm: Almvist & Wiksell.
Hellner, Jan. (1988), *Rättsteori*, Stockholm: Juristförlaget.
Hessler N. (1970), *Nya jordabalken*, Kap. 16 and 18, *Hävd och godtrosförvärn*, Uppsala:
    Juridiska Föreningen.
Hult, Ph. (1952), 'Lagens bokstav och lagens andemening', *Svensk juristtidning*,
    Stockholm: P.A. Norstedt & Söners Förlag.
Jareborg, Nils (1979), *Brotten I*, Stockholm: P.A. Norstedt & Söners Förlag.
Malmgren, R. (1971), *Sveriges grundlagan*, 2nd edn., Stockholm: P.A. Norstedt &
    Söners Förlag.
Peczenik, Aleksander (1989), *On Law and Reason*, London: Kluwer Academic
    Publishers.
Schmidt, Folke (1955), 'Domaren som lagtolkare', *Festskrift till Herlitz*, Stockholm:
    P.A. Norstedt & Söners Förlag. – 1976 *Facklig arbetsrätt*, Stockholm: P.A. Norstedt
    & Söners Förlag.
Strömberg, Håkn (1978), *Allman förvaltningsrätt*, 9 edn., Lund: Liberbärnmedel.
Strömholm, Stig (1989), *Rätt, rättskällor och rättstillämpning*, 3 edn., Stockholm: P. A.

Norstedt & Söners Förlag.
Sundberg, Jacob W.F. (1978), *Fran Edda til Ekelöf*, Lund: Studenlitteratur/Akademisk Förlag.

10 Statutory Interpretation in the United Kingdom

ZENON BANKOWSKI, *Edinburgh*, AND
D. NEIL MacCORMICK, *Edinburgh*

PRELIMINARY

The United Kingdom consists of three legal systems, to varying degrees distinct: those of Northern Ireland, England and Wales, and Scotland. They exist, for various historical, political and cultural reasons, within the context of a unitary state. We do not have a federal system. For all three systems the supreme civil court is the same, namely the Judicial Committee of the House of Lords. For Northern Ireland and England this is the supreme criminal court; but in Scotland the High Court of Justiciary, acting as a criminal appeal court, is the final instance in matters criminal. Where appeals to the House of Lords are competent, these are all by leave (that is, selective). The current annual case-load is about 70 cases per year.

There is a single legislative authority for all jurisdictions, viz., the United Kingdom Parliament. Statutes either apply to all jurisdictions or it is specifically noted to which jurisdiction they apply or which jurisdictions are excluded. Within each jurisdiction the system of *stare decisis* binds courts at inferior levels in the hierarchy but decisions at the same level are not binding. Though precedents outwith the jurisdiction but within the country are not binding they are persuasive and, because of the common supreme courts, there is a great deal of intermingling. In interpretation of statutes this is more so, since many of the statutes are common. Because of these factors, we believe that it is possible to construct a common interpretational practice across the jurisdictions; although England and Northern Ireland have pure common law systems while the

Scottish one is a mixed system, that is, one mixed as between civilian substantive law and (largely) common law methodology including methodology of statutory interpretation.

I   THE GENERAL ORIGINS OF INTERPRETATIONAL ISSUES

Problems of statutory interpretation have, most fundamentally, a pragmatic or processual origin. That is, they are problems generated by the very character of the legal process as essentially adversarial (in the UK, this is so even in the case of criminal processes), by the nature of statutory texts as bearers of norms regulating conduct and by problems generated from within the theory and practice of legal interpretation.

Within the legal process one party's ascription of meaning to a text is always open to challenge by another. In this state of controversy, what has to be decided is which interpretation ought to be accepted. In an adversarial process one sometimes wins by showing that the other side's case is unsatisfactory, sometimes by showing that one's own is the better, and often by showing that the other side's view is unsatisfactory because there is a better case for one's own.

But why can such controversies arise so often, or indeed at all? The basic answer has to be in part linguistic. Natural languages have some degree of vagueness and open texture in all their uses (see Hart, 1961; Waismann, 1951); they can also give rise both to semantic and to syntactic ambiguities. Such determinacy of meaning as linguistic utterances can achieve depends not merely upon the general semiotic (semantic and syntactical) conventions of the language in use, but on a common understanding of the whole context of the utterance and its relationship to that context. Certainly there can be cases where faulty syntax creates irremediable ambiguity, and there can be undue resort to terms which are extremely general or vague semantically. But sometimes extremely general terms give rise to largely uncontested meanings, as in the Scottish or English occupier's statutory duty to take 'reasonable care' for persons on the premises occupied; and sometimes very specific terms can be problematic, as with the quasi-mathematical formula for computing penalties in cases of unpaid taxes in the case of *Inland Revenue Commissioners* v. *Hinchy* ([1960] A.C. 748).

It is terms in systemic context which can prove problematic in interpretation, throwing up ambiguities which litigants conceive it potentially helpful to themselves to exploit. A good example of the judicial recognition of the importance of this is LORD SIMON OF GLAISDALE's remark in *Ealing L.B.C.* v. *Race Relations Board* [1972] A.C. 342 at p. 361 that a 'conspectus of the entire relevant body of law for the same purpose' may be essential to sound interpretation of legislation.

The content of all statute law is necessarily legal–political, for statutes emerge from politics and operate in law. Further, in their operation they have human and social impact. Hence the final reasons for interpretive conflicts are evaluative and teleological. Within the ranges of ambiguity left open by language in context, rival views as to the principled rightness which law does and should manifest, as to the values and disvalues of states of affairs constituted by the statute-as-implemented given one or other rival interpretation, must be what animate opinions as to the preferability or correctness of one against another interpretation. Since evaluative and teleological questions are deeply disputable (whether or not in the last resort rationally resoluble), it follows that the nature of the legal context guarantees a plenitude of interpretational problems whatever care is taken in statutory drafting. Good drafting can minimize and focus the range of disputes. But that is the most it can ever do. Certainly the modern standard of statutory draftsmanship in the UK is high, even if the style tends to be detailed and technical (see Bennion, 1980, p. 92). In our view, although certain grounds of argument are special to the solution of problems about statutory interpretation, there is no radical discontinuity between the modes of reasoning appropriate to problems of statutory interpretation and those appropriate to other problems in common-law reasoning. Reasoning about statutes in their common-law setting is a mode of common-law reasoning and thus a part of the special practical reason appropriate to resolving legal disputes.

Finally one must remark that the drafting and interpretation of statutes involves, or should involve, a dialogue which extends beyond legislators, draftsmen and judges. This point is well taken in the joint report of the Law Commission (for England and Wales) and the Scottish Law Commission of 1969:

> The intelligibility of statutes from the point of view of citizens and their advisors cannot in fact be dissociated from the rules of interpretation followed by the courts, for the ability to understand a statute depends in the ultimate analysis on intelligent anticipation of the way in which it would be interpreted by the courts. We have constantly in mind these rules being workable rules of communication between the legislator and the legislative audience as a whole.

II   GAPS AND THEIR ORIGINS

In so far as a distinction is drawn by judges between interpreting statutes and filling gaps in them, this is normally done with a view to denying the legitimacy of the latter. The classical statement of this view was by VISCOUNT SIMSONDS. On appeal from a decision in which DENNING LJ had argued in the English Court of Appeal that:

> We sit here to find out the intention of Ministers and of Parliament and carry it out, and we do this better by filling in the gaps and mak- ing sense of the enactment than by opening it up to destructive analysis . . .,

VISCOUNT SIMSONDS said:

> [This] appears to me to be a naked usurpation of the legislative function under the thin disguise of interpretation . . . If a gap is disclosed, the remedy lies in an amending Act. (*Magor & St. Mellons RDC* v. *Newport Corporation* and [1952] A.C. 189 at p. 191)

The general line to be drawn appears to be between those cases in which an interpretation of a text, even a somewhat strained one, is treated as legitimately preferable because by it a gap is avoided, and a decision which would amount to judicial law-making to fill in a defect within a statutory scheme. The former, 'interpretative gap-filling' as we shall call it, is acceptable. The latter, 'substantive gap-filling', is not. Since only the former is legitimaté, there is strictly speaking no such thing as gap-filling apart from interpretation in the British systems; but the difference between interpretative and substantive gap-filling is itself a matter of interpretative contro- versy.

The case of *F* v. *Kennedy* (1988 SLT 404) concerned the possibi- lity of intervention by public authorities in a family in which a young girl had allegedly been subjected to indecent assaults by her father, viz. by tickling her private parts. Intervention under the statute was provided for only in case of 'any . . . offence involving bodily injury to a child under the age of 17 years'. The court decided that 'the tickling or touching of the child [in this way] could not, on any proper reading of the words, constitute an offence involving bodily injury to the child' (p. 408). Although this interpretation left a gap in the law, in the sense that a sensible child-protection law would protect children from this interference, the Act was so generally defective in this and related ways as to exclude any merely interpretative rectification of the defect.

This approach reflects the absence of general codification in the UK, hence an absence of any doctrine of the omnicomprehensiveness of statute law. It is a separate question whether novel remedies for novel ills can in appropriate cases be developed out of common-law principles. If so, this is a part of the ordinary process of the common law, not a matter of filling in gaps or lacunae in a code or statute. But there are limits even to this, since the existence of a statutory scheme may preclude recourse to common law. (See *B v. Forsey* 1988 SLT 572: a carefully designed statutory scheme regulated detention by hospital authorities of persons suffering from mental illness and apt to be dangerous to themselves or others. A patient who had partially recovered during an initial period of detention, but then suffered a severe relapse, fell into a category unregulated by law. Hospital authorities which detained the patient to save extreme danger to his family had no statutory authority to do so under any conceivable interpretation, but the statute had abrogated any common-law power of detention.)

As this suggests, the concept of a 'gap' or 'lacuna' in law requires explanation in the context of the relation between common law and statute law in the UK systems. There is a general conception in the British legal systems of statute law as ultimately superimposed upon a common-law substructure.

It must be acknowledged, however, that there are many departments of modern law which depend fundamentally on legislation (and case-law only as interpreting the legislation and thus auxiliary thereto) of a comprehensive and quasi-codifying sort; not infrequently such legislation and its underlying principles represent a derogation from common law, as in the case of Mental Health Legislation, or Children's Law, or Rent Restriction Acts, or Town and Country Planning Law, or Licensing Law.

Where one is dealing with such a domain of essentially statutory law, the presumption is that the whole of the law in question is exclusively that contained in the text(s) of the relevant Act(s); where statute is silent, the law does not extend, and it is generally not legitimate to fall back on superseded common law where the statute fails to make some seemingly desirable provision. In such settings, interpretative gap-filling comes into its own, since an argument about gap-avoidance may be an available technique of interpretation. It can really be taken to be a special form of the argument from necessary implication (see section III, below).

A convenient illustration may be given in respect of the Rent Restrictions Acts, which were originally passed during the First World War to protect poorer tenants of houses from the risks of eviction or exploitative rent increases in circumstances of wartime shortage of accommodation. These Acts conferred upon any tenant of a relevant dwelling house a 'statutory tenancy' of the let property from the moment of the expiry of the contractual tenancy, but the statutory tenancy continued only so long as the tenant remained in possession and fulfilled all the obligations of the prior contractual tenancy. On the face of it this involved a contradiction, since one of the obligations of a contractual tenancy is to give up possession of the subjects on the expiry thereof. Therefore, to make the Acts effective, the courts read in a qualification not explicit in the Acts, to the effect that the tenant had to fulfil all the obligations of the contractual tenancy which were also consistent with a statutory tenancy. This qualification they (rightly) considered to be necessarily implied in the Acts, since without it their provisions would be self-defeating.

To the above general conclusion there is one narrow but important exception, applying only in Scotland. In virtue of its so-called *nobile officium*, the Court of Session in Scotland has a power (of restricted range in modern times) to grant special remedies where these are demanded for the sake of equity and justice. This may involve provision of remedies in the context of statutory arrangements which are manifestly defective (though it does not allow of the substitution of remedies for those actually provided in Acts of Parliament). See *Roberts, petitioner* ((1901) 3 F. 779) where the court granted a discharge from bankruptcy in the case of a petitioner who had become of unsound mind since going bankrupt, dispensing with the statutory requirement of an oath. Within its rather narrow ambit, this equitable power is clearly one which may be used to fill gaps in statutory schemes. A like power, similarly restricted in ambit, is exercised by the High Court of Justiciary in criminal matters.

III   THE TYPES OF INTERPRETATIVE ARGUMENT AND THEIR INTERACTION

Given the fundamentally pragmatic character and setting of interpretational problems, interpretative arguments can be appreciated for what they are only through reflection upon their pragmatic setting and deployment. Here we assign such arguments to one or other of three types. They deal with (1) the meaning of the words in the text considered in their linguistic setting but without explicit regard to the legal context of their use; or (2) their meaning as clarified by explicit reference to the legal context of their statutory utterance; or (3) the meaning preferably to be ascribed to them given certain value-judgements about the consequences of implementing them in their functional context. The several types of argument can thus be considered as 'linguistic', 'systemic' or 'teleological/evaluative' in accordance with the common typology announced in Chapter 1 of the present volume.

1   Linguistic Arguments

Either or both of syntactic and semantic arguments are always available, and in problematic cases must always feature in justification. For arguments must be given to the effect that a particular proposed reading of a statute is possible on a reasonable understanding of the terms used in the given context, taken as being terms in everyday speech, except if there are grounds for taking them as specialist terminology, in which case, specialist usage should be considered (and will normally prevail). This argument from possible meaning is essential in every case and is at least implicitly present in any legal decision upon a point of interpretation. It must be possible to say that the particular interpretation that has been chosen falls within the range of possible meanings of the provision in view. This is subject to only one exception, viz., where all the linguistically possible meanings result in an 'absurdity' (see below), and where the Court is called upon in effect to rewrite the Act, supplying missing words or eliminating surplus ones.

Linguistic arguments in interpretative reasoning are commonly signalled by resort to such expressions as the literal (passim) or ordinary (Cross, 1976) or obvious (MacCormick, 1978) or 'plain' meaning of statutory words and provisions. Implementation of 'literal' or 'plain' meaning is often justified in terms of fulfilling legislative intention, 'the intention of parliament', which is in turn represented as being the fundamentally relevant test for soundness of interpretation. As was stated in *A.-G. for Canada* v. *Hallet and Carey Ltd.* ([1957] A.C. 427 at p. 449), 'There are many so-called rules of construction . . . but the paramount rule remains that every statute is to be expounded according to its manifest and expressed intention.'

This conception of the 'manifest and expressed intention' of the statute is used by many to justify the relatively high priority always given by English and Scottish judges to the types of linguistic argument we have been reviewing. There are different varieties of linguistic argument, as follows:

1   A strong version is one where arguments are given to show that the preferred reading is, upon due reflection, the only possible reading of the text in context, and thus must prevail as the 'plain' or 'obvious' meaning of the statute. We may call this the 'argument from the only possible meaning'.

2   Arguments may be given to show that the preferred reading
        is the only obvious, or the more obvious, among a range of
        linguistically possible readings, the circumstances being
        such that no sufficient reason obtains for displacing the
        presumption in favour of the more 'plain meaning' or the
        more 'obvious meaning'. We call this the 'argument from
        undisplaced obvious meaning', and observe that this argu-
        ment defeats a rival interpretation which is admittedly
        possible (that is, where there is a genuine ambiguity in the
        text read fairly) on the ground that no sufficient reason has
        been shown for preferring the rival possibility.
3   The argument from logical absurdity may be deployed to
        show that the statutory text contains a self-contradiction,
        which no possible (and otherwise acceptable) reading of the
        text can evade. Such an absurdity arises from the very words
        used, and is not to be confused with various forms of
        evaluative absurdity (see p. 373). But all the forms of
        argument from absurdity have it in common that they
        permit an overriding of the argument from possible mean-
        ing. These arguments may lead on to 'arguments from
        necessary implication' or to 'interpretative gap-filling argu-
        ments'.

2   Systemic Arguments

Ascription of meaning can never be carried out as an absolutely
abstract exercise. There is always reference to some assumed
context, some understood background beyond the purely linguistic context. Sometimes this is simply taken for granted. But often it
is necessary to resolve ambiguity by examining the context of a
text and its interpretation in closer detail, rather than passing over
it in silence as a merely presupposed background to a straightforward discovery of meaning in text. Hence linguistic arguments are
always liable to, and often require, supplementation by recourse to
other arguments. In the case of legal interpretation, these other
arguments are concerned with matching the interpreted text to the
legal context, that is the whole context of the legal system.
Whenever the systemic context can be shown to be relevant for
understanding the linguistic sense of a provision, the argument
from 'ordinary meaning' is understood as referring to ordinary
meaning in that context (*Att. Gen.* v. *Prince Ernst Augustus of
Hanover* [1957] A.C. 436).
     These arguments locate the text under dispute in its setting
within the legal system, first, as against the other parts of the same

Act, secondly as against other pieces of legislation (if any) which, together with the present Act, form a single statutory scheme, and finally in the general relation of the relevant whole to the bodies of statutory and/or common law which make up 'branches' of law such as 'family law', 'landlord and tenant', 'property', 'succession', or the like. (If, as a matter of family law, a wife has a right to reside in her husband's house, then, even after his desertion of her, her continuing occupancy of a house may count as his 'retaining possession' of it for the purposes of the Rent Acts – see *Old Gate Estates Ltd.* v. *Alexander* [1949] 2 All E.R. 822). Arguments (1) and (2) below stress the diachronic aspect, the origins and historical evolution of legislation, while the others emphasize more the synchronic qualities of law existing as putatively coherent order at any moment of time.

1   Genetic arguments deal with the origins of the Act and the presumed or disclosed purposes for which it was enacted. Such arguments are often expressed as seeking to establish the 'mischief', or 'defect' in less archaic terms, of the preceding law for which the Act in view was or is supposed to supply a remedy. Ascription of such intentions is a matter of trying to capture the actual intention of those who were historically responsible for enacting the law in question. Indeed, if we can establish or reasonably surmise the aims in the sense of social effects which the legislator meant to achieve by enacting the law, we can correct or adjust our ascription of intentionality in the sense used above. We may find that the legislature used somewhat inexact or misleading expressions, given the object exactly in view.

     The force of resort to 'genetic arguments' is to contend that the actual intention ought to prevail as a guide to interpretation over some alternative meaning which is supposedly or arguably more obvious in purely linguistic terms. We can see this in so-called 'Mischief Rule', the rule in Heydon's case (1584) Co Rep 7a at 7b:

> And it was resolved by them that . . . the office of all the judges is always to make such construction [of a statute] as shall suppress the mischief, and advance the remedy . . . according to the true intent of the makers of the Act, pro bono publico.

2   Historical arguments indicate both the relationship of the Act to the prior state of the law in the light of political and social history, and the part which the Act (or whole relevant body of legislation) has come to play in the general fabric of the law as a whole. For example, although the British Rent

Restriction Acts originated in legislation rushed through parliament in the wartime circumstances of 1915, it has been judicially noted that, 'There is no doubt that these Acts, which started out as a moratorium on rents, have developed into something of the nature of a social housing code' (*Temple* v. *Mitchell* 1956 S.C. p. 267 at 272).

3   The argument from Necessary Implication is concerned with establishing some provision as necessarily implied in an Act to give it practical effect in the light of its overall scheme and purpose. See, in the case of the Rent Acts, *Barton* v. *Fincham* [1921] All E.R. Rep. 87 at p. 90: 'The qualification was not contained in the Act . . . but was held . . . to be necessarily implied, as without it, the whole subsection would be meaningless' (this concerns the point discussed at pp. 363–4 above).

4   Interpretative gap-filling arguments were discussed in full in section II above. These are closely related to arguments from necessary implication.

5   'Term of Art' arguments can be used in two senses. In general, technical legal terms are interpreted in their technical sense. They come into play when a statute uses some such term as 'possession' (see the Rent Act cases cited above and below) or 'offer for sale' (see *Fisher* v. *Bell* [1961] 1 Q.B. 394; a shopkeeper displaying a flick-knife in the shop window does not thereby 'offer [it] for sale', but merely issues an invitation to treat, and hence is not guilty of the statutory offence of 'offering for sale' a prohibited article). Further, where an Act contains an interpretation section supplying definitions of terms, or where a term is used for which a definition is supplied in the Interpretation Act 1978, the relevant statutory definition governs. 'Term of Art' arguments in the second sense apply in the case of statutes addressed to particular trades, professions and the like, in respect of which it may be presumed that terms which have a technical sense as terms of art in the relevant trade or profession are used in this technical sense in an Act regulating the trade or profession.

6   Arguments from binding precedent apply where the doctrine of *stare decisis* makes a higher or coordinate court's interpretation of a statutory provision binding for later interpreters. Where the very word, phrase or provision under consideration in a given case has already been subjected to prior judicial interpretation in relation to the same act in a prior case, such a precedent is binding, depending on the hierarchy of the courts. But only an express ruling on the

specific provision comes directly within the narrower doctrine of precedent; that apart, precedents play their more
normal role as a source of arguments by analogy.

7   Arguments from analogy. A problematic word or phrase
used in one statute may be identical to or similar to a word
or phrase used in another statute dealing with similar subject-matter. The meaning ascribed through precedent or
present interpretation to the word or phrase in the latter
statute may be applied by analogy to argue for a solution to
the present problem. Thus where the question is whether in
a statute dealing with arson the phrase 'any person' may be
read as meaning any person other than the accused, the
point may be argued on the analogy of the proper (or the
established and unchallenged) interpretation of the same
terms in relation to offences against the person, where
criminal harm must be harm to a person other than the
accused. (See *R. v. Arthur* [1968] 1 Q.B. 810.)

Where the problem is whether or not to qualify a problematic phenomenon as instantiating some statutory term or
another, analogy to less problematic instances covered by
prior decisions is relevant (see, for example, *Imperial Tobacco,
v. A.-G* [1979] Q.B. 555 – is a 'Spot Cash' scheme more like a
lottery or a competition?).

8   Comparativist arguments in effect use comparable other
systems as sources of persuasive analogy for interpretations
of statutes. In the UK, reference is still quite regularly made
to Commonwealth precedents on statutory interpretation
and also, if less frequently, to the USA. Most frequent are
comparativist arguments internal to the UK. Judicial efforts
are directed towards securing common interpretations of
common or closely analogous bodies of statute law; but the
interaction with systemic arguments always has also to be
considered. Thus, because of disanalogies in family law, the
Scottish courts found it impossible to follow the English
judges in interpreting the Rent Acts in favour of a deserted
wife whose husband was the statutory tenant but has
deserted home and family with no evident intention to
return: *Temple v. Mitchell* 1956 S.C. 267.

9   The argument from Legal Principles is an important type of
systemic argument. Legal principles are those general norms
that we frame with a view to capturing the rational coherence of the various branches of the law separately and in
combination. In the case of statutes, principles like that
whereby the Rent Acts are construed as essentially concerned to protect the family homes of poorer people play an

important part in interpretation. Nor can one sensibly approach the interpretation of statutes in criminal law without regard to those basic principles of civil liberty which in part define the 'Rule of Law'.

Singly or (all the more persuasively) in cumulative sets, such systemic arguments may provide a necessary basis for the sound deployment (perhaps one should even say 'completion') of any of the first three of the linguistic arguments. At the least, such arguments can help to satisfy the test of the 'argument from possible meaning', as when in *R*. v. *Arthur* the defence's argument about the meaning of 'any person being [in the house the accused had set on fire]' was accepted as semantically possible only in virtue of the analogy with a statute prohibiting the malicious wounding (and so on) of 'any person' [that is, somebody other than the accused]. At the most, systemic arguments can go so far as to permit deployment of what we call 'the argument from the only possible meaning' as when the majority in *Temple* v. *Mitchell* concluded that the only possible meaning of 'retains possession' in the Rent Acts viewed contextually was one which excluded the case of a permanently departed tenant, even when his deserted wife continued in occupancy by his presumed wish. Most commonly, they supply reasons, of contextually greater or less weight, for choosing which among rival possible interpretations is more or less obvious once the question is located clearly in its legal setting.

At this stage, however, competing interpretations may remain in play as possible ones, and victory does not always go to that which is simply the relatively more obvious in the light of ordinary language or of systemic considerations. Our third main type of interpretative arguments must also be taken into account.

3   Teleological/Evaluative Arguments

These arguments deal with values expressed in or purposes pursued through the text that is to be interpreted, rival possible interpretations often being tested in the light of the probable consequences of their adoption. Such arguments can operate either as first-order interpretative arguments or as elements in second-order arguments. On the one hand, they can provide simply a third set of considerations for or against one or other of a rival set of possible interpretations of a disputed text or term. For example: 'I have no doubt that a truck is a machine and its engine is machinery, but I think the full width of the words "any machinery" in section 14 of the Factories Act, 1937, must be controlled by consideration of the scope and objects of the Act' (*Cherry* v. *International Alloys* [1961] 1 K.B. 136 at 148, per DEVLIN LJ). Here the function or purpose of the act is simply a further element of context relevant to interpretation of the terms used in an Act. Purpose helps to establish possible meaning, or to support the idea that one meaning is contextually more obvious than another.

On the other hand, there are evidently many cases in which more than one interpretation can be supported by good arguments of the first order. Then we face the problem of conflict or competition between prima facie justifiable interpretations, and the problem is that of making and justifying a priority choice between or among intrinsically acceptable arguments. Teleological and evaluative arguments figure largely at this level of priority choices among rival interpretations. These two uses of such interpretative arguments are not, in practice, easily separable. We defer to section VI below the attempt to account for the teleological/evaluative elements in second-order argumentation (concerning priorities between rival interpretations). At this stage, we merely enumerate some main subtypes of teleological/evaluative argument.

1   The Purpose of the Act: apart from 'genetic' arguments aimed at establishing the original legislator's intention, we can consider statutes in terms of objective purpose, the rational ends or values they can be considered as serving or having.

(a) Arguments from Justice express a concern for the purpose of a text as supposedly aimed at realizing justice in the light of what Ronald Dworkin (1986) calls the 'integrity' of the legal system. Although integrity is a systemic virtue, the argument from integrity transcends the merely systemic and goes beyond the scope of pure *ius positivum*, becoming axiological in a broader way. It is a matter of controversy how far this gets one beyond merely expressing, in a summary way, an appeal to straightforwardly legal principles and values. *Pace* Dworkin, such arguments seem relatively rare, and perhaps properly so given the separation of powers; but it is sometimes possible to argue that an Act on one interpretation would be so unjust in its effects that parliament cannot be presumed to have intended such an interpretation, however seemingly obvious the interpretation in merely linguistic terms.

(b) Policy Arguments: the empirical consequences of an

interpretation can be scrutinized in order to see which are
the more consonant with realizing some standing elements
of public policy as the presumed policy of the Act. (See *R*. v.
Registrar General ex parte Smith [1990] 2 All E.R. 170, where
'public policy' in favour of protecting life justified interpreting the statutory right of adopted persons to information
about the true circumstances of their birth as being subject
to exceptions in the case of dangerously insane persons. The
argument from 'public policy' concerns some aspect of good
order or some matter of supposed public moral concern or
economic good, which parliament is deemed not to trench
upon save when this is done by express and unambiguous
provision.)

2   Legal Principles as a basis of evaluation also play an important part. To some extent, of course, this harks back to
systemic argumentation, and to the discovery and elaboration of the principles which enable us to give coherence to
the various branches of the law separately and in combination. But it is an important part of the legal and constitutional tradition to acknowledge as fundamental the values
expressed by some such principles, for example those
favouring freedom of the individual, or freedom of speech or
of association, or favouring 'natural justice' and fairness in
legal proceedings of all sorts, or favouring the right to
compensation for harm carelessly inflicted, or favouring the
upholding of bargains freely made, subject to protection of
the weak from economic oppression, or requiring that guilty
intent be proved against anyone charged with serious crime,
or, compendiously, the set of values commonly referred to
as comprising the 'Rule of Law'. Where one interpretation
rather than another will more steadfastly uphold some such
value, this is a weighty argument for such an interpretation,
often justified on the ground that parliament must be
deemed to intend the preservation of such values, and only
to abrogate them by express provision. Where legislation
deliberately invokes new principles, as in the relatively
recent growth of Race Relations legislation, the relative
priority of the new principle (or legislative purpose) as
against traditional ones has to be determined, an often
controversial matter. (See, for example, *Charter* v. *Race
Relations Board* [1973] A.C. 868, 889.) LORD MORRIS said of
the Race Relations Acts 1965 and 1968:

> Parliament [has] introduced into the law . . . a new guiding
> principle of fundamental and far-reaching importance. [D]is-

crimination against a person on the ground of colour, race or ethnic or national origins has become unlawful . . .

3   Arguments from Common Sense, concerning what is practically workable in a legal setting, are frequently to be found, and carry great weight both as justifying rejection of narrowly literalistic interpretations of statutory texts (a law requiring pharmacists' shops to be closed at 11 p.m. cannot reasonably be interpreted as permitting them to reopen five minutes later and to remain open all night and through the following day) and as justifying the adoption of provisions considered to be 'necessarily implied' in the statutory scheme to give it proper effect (see the discussion of *Barton v. Fincham* under 'the Argument from Necessary Implication' above).

4   Arguments from Absurdity: apart from strict logical absurdity (self-contradiction), courts sometimes reject proposed interpretations of Acts as 'absurd', even when on the face of it the proposed interpretation seems to satisfy the 'plain meaning' test. This is no more than a strong way of expressing a negative evaluation of the Act so interpreted; the significance of the strength of the negative is that it justifies departure from the normal priority in favour of a more obvious over a less obvious meaning. See *McMonagle* v. *Westminster City Council* [1990] 1 All E.R. 993 at 997: '[W]e should be giving effect to the true intention of the legislature if we could avoid this absurdity by treating the phrase "which is not unlawful" . . . as mere surplusage.' Further consideration of this is deferred to section VI below.

The above ordering, typology and nomenclature is new and is the present authors' own analysis, aided substantially by the intention to match as far as possible our European colleagues' approaches. Nevertheless we believe that in substance it is accurate, and re-names and re-orders materials discussed in established texts such as those of Cross and of Bennion on statutory interpretation, rather than importing a quite idiosyncratic view of interpretative arguments.

IV   TYPES OF GAP-FILLING ARGUMENT

As has been explained, only 'interpretative gap-fillling', not 'substantive gap-filling', is considered permissible in the systems of the UK (with the exception of the *nobile officium* of the higher courts in Scotland). Thus a gap-filling argument is itself a type of interpretative argument, aimed at supporting a particular interpretation of a provision on the ground that rival interpretations would leave a gap in the statutory scheme.

V   THE MATERIALS OF INTERPRETATIVE ARGUMENT

This section explains the types of material which must be, should be, may be, or may not be cited or adduced in constructing arguments of the types described in section III. It deals, that is to say, with the kinds of material available for making up interpretative arguments, and with the evidentiary status of this material — whether as mandatory, as persuasive, as merely admissible, or as inadmissible — for the purpose of giving content to arguments of the stated types. The general principle (but with important exceptions) is that any material relevant to building a sound justificatory argument is admissible. We shall therefore try to indicate the way in which different kinds of material may be relevant to different argument-types. We shall deal with categories of evidentiary material under the headings of 'mandatory', 'persuasive/admissible' and 'inadmissible', in each case explaining the sense of the terms used.

1   Mandatory Material

This is material which must be taken into account in the course of interpretative argument. The decision of a court upon a point in issue reached without regard to such material would be binding upon the parties (and would count as *res judicata*) but would be liable to be summarily set aside and corrected on appeal. From the point of view of the doctrine of precedent, the decision would be considered as one reached *per incuriam* and hence lacking in authority, even if it were a decision by an appellate tribunal, including the ultimate tribunal (see *Young* v. *Bristol Aeroplane Co. Ltd* [1944] K.B. 718).

A peculiarity of the British systems of law is the high degree of reliance which courts place upon counsel to ensure that all relevant legal materials are brought to the attention of any court deciding any question of law. In this light, one might further explain the category of mandatory material as that which it is the duty of counsel to adduce in argument before the court, whether the material be on the face of it favourable or unfavourable to the case argued. This duty of counsel to draw all relevant and mandatory materials to the court's attention is a highly important one.

Most generally one may define as mandatory materials those whose absence from consideration renders an act of interpretation legally inept as such, as distinct from merely diminishing the strength and persuasive force of a competent argument. Such materials are as follows.

1   The text of the Act which is supposed to govern the case. The unit of construction is the Act read as a whole. In *Dixon v. British Broadcasting Corporation* [1979] 2 All E.R. it was held that an interpretation of a particular paragraph of an Act in a previous case was in error, as the court had then overlooked the effect of the preceding sections of the Act on the section in question. This illustrates the point about a decision's being *per incuriam*. For this purpose, however, it has been stated on high authority (LORD REID in *Chandler* v. *D.P.P.* [1964] A.C. at p. 791) that the short title, side-notes and headings of an Act are not intrinsic parts of it for interpretational purposes.

2   The text of any directly relevant delegated legislation made under the authority of an Act of Parliament; also of any binding materials issued by the executive under prerogative powers, as, for example, the materials formerly governing the Criminal Injuries Compensation Scheme in the UK.

3   Treaties binding in the UK in virtue of enabling Acts of Parliament giving the treaty in question the force of law domestically. For the contemporary UK, the leading instance is supplied by the European Communities' Treaties (given statutory force by the European Communities Act 1972, which also confers statutory force upon all 'community obligations' determined by the Treaties or by the exercise of powers thereunder by organs of the European Communities). These texts in turn carry with them interpretational practices suitable to their style and juridical setting.

4   Judicial precedents directly bearing upon the interpretation of the text to be applied or other relevant parts of the same statute must be taken into account by the court. It is the duty of counsel to be meticulous in citing relevant precedents and, if the report of a case showed that some crucial precedent had not been cited, the decision would to that extent count as one reached *per incuriam*, and hence as itself not a binding precedent upon the relevant point of interpretation. Of course arguments may also be made to show that particular precedents should be distinguished, overruled, or simply not followed (though in *Jones* v. *Secretary of State for*

the Social Services [1972] A.C. 944 it was declared that the power of the House of Lords to depart from its own precedents should be used very sparingly with regard to prior interpretations of a given statutory text).

The special quality of these four types of mandatory material is that they supply the concrete subject-matter for interpretation, the authoritative texts which have to be interpreted. But where attention is focused on the interpretation of one word or phrase or sentence in, or one section of, an Act, the rest of that Act, and other statutes and relevant precedents, are vital for grasping the systemic as well as the linguistic context of the interpretational question in issue.

2   Persuasive/Admissible Material

This is material which ought to be considered by (and cited to) the court where it appears strongly relevant to the issue in hand (highly persuasive material) or which counsel at any rate may adduce as giving some further weight to an argument. The degree of persuasiveness being context-dependent, there is no clear cut-off point between the persuasive (the 'should-material') and the simply admissible (the 'may-material'). The court's use of such material in its own justification of the interpretation finally given is at its discretion, the value of the material being to indicate the weight or relative weight of the arguments for the favoured interpretation. In general such material is of value chiefly for its contribution to 'systemic arguments' (see section III). But they may also on occasion contribute to establishing the statutory purpose or to confirming fundamental principles as elements in evaluative/teleological arguments. Examples of such persuasive/admissible material follow.

1   Other parts of the same statute. Where the text appears ambiguous, even when read in the light of its other intrinsically governing parts, side-notes and the like can be brought into the argument. As this may suggest, problems arise because one has to see what is to be counted as extrinsic and what as intrinsic to the statute. Thus, if the doubt in the interpretation arises because the words of the statute become unclear when considered in the light of the Act's title, preamble, heading or side-notes, then these latter must be disregarded as being for this purpose extrinsic to the unit of text under interpretation. If, however, the grounds of

doubt are independent of such items, other rules apply. LORD UPJOHN in *DPP* v. *Schildkamp* [1971] A.C. 1 p. 28 puts the general point thus:

> When the court construing the Act is reading it through to understand it, it must read the cross-heading as well as the body of the Act and that will always be a useful pointer to the intention of Parliament in enacting the immediately following sections. Whether the cross-heading is no more than a pointer or label, or is helpful in assisting to construe, or even in some cases to control, the meaning or ambit of those sections must necessarily depend on the circumstances of each case and I do not think that it is possible to lay down any rules.

2 Statutes *in pari materia*. Earlier statutes dealing with similar matters will be treated as part of the context of the statute and may thus furnish aids to interpreting it. (See *Jennings* v. *US Government* [1982] 3 All E.R. 104, where it was held that the court could consider the entire legislative history of road traffic offences.) They are not now, however, to be treated as one statute, as was implied in *R.* v. *Loxdale* (1785) 1 Burr 445. Consolidating acts and the like are to be treated as not designed to change the law. Hence earlier interpretations of the Acts brought into the consolidation continue to prevail.

3 Governmental guides to good conduct in some context. The most significant and well-known example of this category is the *Highway Code*, which is a booklet published by the Ministry of Transport in many editions since its publication was first authorized by the Road Traffic Act, 1930, s. 45. It gives guidance on the proper conduct of persons using the roads as motorists, cyclists, horse-riders, pedestrians and so on. The provisions of the Code are not binding in themselves, but are by statute given strongly persuasive weight in interpretation.

4 The prior legal history of language and concepts in the statute. Where a conceptual expression has a previous legal history, even if borrowed from different legislation, it will be relevant in the instant case (*Welham* v. *DPP* [1961] A.C. 103). The question will be whether parliament intended this meaning, but in the absence of some contrary indication this will be presumed.

5 Treaties and the like. The UK sometimes subjects itself to treaty obligations without at the same time adopting the treaty into domestic law by enabling legislation. It is then a question whether the treaty is admissible for the purposes of supporting an interpretation of any relevant legislation.

Here the rule as laid down in *Ellerman Lines* v. *Murray* [1931] A.C. 126 is that, if a statute is clear and unambiguous, then an International Convention to which it refers cannot change that clear meaning. Where there is a doubt, however, it may be resolved by recourse to the presumption that parliament does not intend to act in breach of international law. (*Salomon* v. *Commissioners of Customs and Excise* [1967] 2 Q.B. 116.) Numerous references to the European Human Rights Convention are to like effect. In interpreting a treaty the court is entitled to look to materials not normally permitted when interpreting UK statutes, such as *travaux préparatoires*.

6   Precedents. Previous judicial interpretations of given words in one Act are not binding as to interpretation of the same words in a different Act, for though one can arrive at general rules through the cases one cannot overextend their applicability since the *ratio* of such a case will always be specific to the Act interpreted. Thus the cases might offer a welter of rules and principles but nothing that can constitute a binding precedent when interpreting another, similar, statute (see *Carter* v. *Bradbeer* [1975] 3 All E.R. 158 at p. 61). In general, precedents not in point and precedents from other jurisdictions may be cited for whatever weight they may bring to comparativist arguments, arguments from analogy and arguments establishing legal principles.

7   Historical knowledge of conditions the statute was intended to remedy. This has to be invoked in building either a genetic or a historical argument (see section III). In *Chandler* v. *DPP* [1964] A.C. at p. 791, LORD REID invoked the historical conditions of the passing of the Official Secrets Act, 1911 in support of his interpretation of that Act. In *B.* v. *Forsey* (see section II) the judge argued to the effect that the legislative history of the Mental Health (Scotland) Act 1984 precluded its being interpreted to allow of successive resorts to emergency detention of dangerous patients.

8   Legislative history. See 'Inadmissible Material' below. This is only very restrictedly admissible for citation by counsel or adduction by judges in their opinions in the UK. Where legislation has followed upon the report of a Committee or Commission, and has given effect to its recommendations, such a pre-parliamentary report is admissible as evidence of the mischief the Act was aimed at curing (that is, it is admissible as helping to establish the statutory purpose) but not as evidence about the meaning of the words of the act in the case before the court (*Fothergill* v. *Monarch Airlines Ltd*

[1980] 2 All E.R. 696). In the parliamentary process, when standing committees make amendments to bills at the committee stage, these amendments are reported to the relevant House without statements of reasons; hence a source of useful *travaux préparatoires* in other systems is missing in the UK.

9   Prior or current interpretations by addressees of the law. There are two problems here: first, the courts recognize that in many cases administrators have to form a view of a doubtful enactment before, if ever, the matter is litigated. Their rulings are communicated to those whom the law concerns and their advisors and other administrators and the courts in interpreting an Act have to take this into account. In *Wicks* v. *Firth (Inspector of Taxes)* [1983] 1 All E.R. 151 the House of Lords considered a press release issued by the Inland Revenue indicating how they would construe some enactments concerning the tax position of children holding certain scholarships. LORD BRIDGE said of the press release that it 'was not a decisive consideration', but one which could properly be taken into account between competing interpretations. But a government department, since it has no power to legislate, cannot of its own accord change the true meaning of a statute. (See *Vestey* v. *IRC* [1979] 3 All E.R. 976 pp. 984–6.)

10   Scholarly writings and academic opinion. None of the legal traditions of the UK at present attaches strong persuasive force to the juristic writings of living authors. It is still sometimes said that an author cannot become an authority until he/she is dead. Conversely, great weight attaches, especially in Scotland, to the great institutional writings of the past, such as those of Stair, Erskine and Bell, with whom Blackstone in England is perhaps comparable. Some later textbooks are treated with great authority by virtue of their many editions and great standing. Reports by law-reforming bodies such as the Law Commissions are also particularly persuasive. There is at present a growing tendency among English judges to cite in their opinions articles in learned journals, monographs and so on. Scots judges, however, remain somewhat less willing than their English counterparts to take any express account of the views of living writers, however learned and distinguished. Arguments from scholarly sources may be and not infrequently are adopted and deployed without ascription of authority to their original authors.

11   The teleological or normative nature of the phenomenon in

question is hardly to be considered as material or 'information' in the same sense as most of the foregoing, though it is clear that appeal to this may take place in systemic arguments and legal–conceptual arguments. As distinct from a regard to the legislator's purpose, one may seek to interpret an Act in terms of the proper ends or intrinsic principles of some institution. The family, especially in its connection with procreation as a goal, is an obvious example. So, in *Corbett* v. *Corbett* [1970] 2 All E.R. 33, it was held that a man could not validly marry a male transsexual who had undergone a sex-change operation. Conversely, in *Maclennan* v. *Maclennan* 1958 S.C. 105, a wife's being pregnant through artificial insemination by donor was held not to partake of the essential normative quality of adultery.

12   Linguistic material has an obvious and important relevance. Much such material is admissible, such as dictionaries and technical lexicons for elucidating terms of art; also grammatical (syntactical) rules and conventions of punctuation; also 'rules of language' or 'canons of construction' such as the *noscitur a sociis* rule, according to which the interpretation of one word in a group is to be taken in the light of others grouped with it by the legislature, or the *eiusdem generis* rule, according to which general words are to be taken only as alluding to other things of the same class as that constituted by the more particular terms to which the general ones are subjoined.

3   Inadmissible Material

This includes, obviously and uninterestingly, any such material as would be irrelevant or of no weight for the purposes of building an interpretative argument. More interestingly, it includes at least two types of relevant and weighty material which may not be cited by counsel to courts in the UK and which judges will only very exceptionally adduce as an explicit ground of interpretative justification. These are as follows.

1   Legislative history in the way of citation of parliamentary debates for the purpose of genetic arguments aimed to establish the historic legislature's intentions in enacting some statutory provision. The ban on citation of parliamentary materials is supposed to be absolute, making them inadmissible for any purpose whatever (*South Eastern Railway Co.* v. *Railway Commissioners* (1881) 50 L.J.Q.B. 201).

However this is no longer so certain and some such materials have been admitted in some circumstances. (Cf. *Sagnata Investments* v. *Norwich Corporation* [1971] 2 Q.B. 614; *Beswick* v. *Beswick* [1968] A.C. 58 and *Warner* v. *Metropolitan Police Commissioner* [1969] 2 A.C. 256. See Cross (1976) pp. 129–41 and Bennion (1984) pp. 513–65). According to the Law Commissions, one serious difficulty about a practice whereby counsel could or *a fortiori* were expected to cite in court parliamentary materials is the increased research time and research costs counsel and thus their clients would face. Lawyers' libraries would become weighted down with parliamentary reports, without any noticeable gain in clarity of interpretation in most cases. This consideration again reflects the British practice of relying upon counsel to do the legal research on which decisions of the courts are based. In other traditions, this objection would seem merely quaint. Other objections focus more on constitutional issues, concerning the separation of powers. Since most legislation is promoted by the government, it is a check on excessive executive power to insist that the law be found in Acts as enacted, not as supplemented by ministerial statements in parliament during the passage of a bill.

In fact it is increasingly disputed how far the restriction on reference to parliamentary materials remains valid. Recent decisions have chipped away at its edges, and some judges admit freely to doing some research of their own. As LORD HAILSHAM has said:

> I always look at Hansard [the official parliamentary record of debates], I always look at the Blue Books [reports of parliamentary Committees], I always look at everything I can in order to see what is meant . . . The idea that [the Law Lords] do not read these is quite rubbish . . . (1981 HL Rep (5th series) col. 1346)

Even if the main rule stands as stated, it has come to admit of exceptions. There can be no reference to material extrinsic to the enactment to justify an interpretation which is other than the obvious or plain meaning of the statute itself, when it has one. But what if it has not?

> If the words of the Act are capable of one meaning we must give them that meaning, no matter how they got there. But if they are capable of having more than one meaning, we are, in my view, well entitled to see how they got there. For purely practical reasons we do not permit debates in either House to be cited: it would add greatly to the time and expense

involved in preparing cases involving the construction of a statute if counsel were expected to read all the debates in Hansard . . . But I can see no objection to investigating in the present case the antecedents of s. 56. (*Beswick* v. *Beswick* [1968] A.C. 58 at pp. 73–4 (LORD REID))

2   The 'Brandeis Brief'. Given the clear importance of evaluative/teleological arguments as frequently the decisive element in interpretative (and other sorts of) legal reasoning and argumentation, it would obviously be relevant and weighty if counsel could cite to the court carefully established sociological and economic studies estimating probable effects of this or that interpretation of a statutory text. Such materials are at least sometimes admissible in the USA for the purposes of backing a contested interpretation of, for example, a constitutional text. But no recourse has ever been made to such material in the UK, and it seems clear that the courts would treat it as inadmissible if ever adduced. The reason again seems to be one of legal economy.

VI   PRIORITIES AMONG CONFLICTING ARGUMENTS

The classical British statement of the ordinary order of argumentative priorities in interpretation is the 'Golden Rule'. The following are its terms as enunciated by LORD BLACKBURN in *River Wear Commissioners* v. *Adamson* (1887) 2 App. Cas. 743 at pp. 764–5, viz., the rule:

. . . that we are to take the whole statute together, and construe it all together giving the words their ordinary signification, unless when so applied they produce an inconsistency, or an absurdity or inconvenience, so great as to convince the Court that the intention could not have been to use them in their ordinary signification.

As this shows, a strong prima facie priority is accorded in the UK to the 'ordinary signification' ('plain meaning', 'obvious meaning' and so on) of terms in statutes. This suggests a preference, if all things are equal, for simple linguistic arguments as sufficient to deal with points of interpretation. This approach has quite frequently been commended in terms of the politico-legal values it serves. As a matter of constitutional theory, the interpretative preference can be commended as that which upholds the Rule of Law and the Separation of Powers. This has been expressed in many judicial dicta. In *Stock* v. *Frank Jones (Tipton) Ltd* ([1978] ICR 347 at 354) LORD SIMON OF GLAISDALE put the point in the following terms:

In a society living under the rule of law citizens are entitled to regulate their conduct according to what a statute has said, rather than by what it was meant to say or by what it would otherwise have said if a newly considered situation had been envisaged.

On the other hand, regard must be paid to the democratic notion that the judiciary should not impede the implementation of the express decisions of an elected legislature. A relatively plain statement of this point is LORD DIPLOCK's in *Duport Steel Ltd* v. *Sirs* [1980] 1 All E.R. 529 at 541:

When Parliament legislates to remedy what the majority of its members at the time perceive to be a defect or lacuna in the existing law . . ., the role of the judiciary is confined to ascertaining from the words that Parliament has approved as expressing its intention what the intention was, and giving effect to it.

LORD BLACKBURN's above-cited statement of the golden rule, however, itself indicates the defeasible quality of the priority accorded to the 'ordinary signification' of the words of an Act of Parliament. In the first place, we have to note that the 'ordinary signification' of legal terms may well be ascertainable only in the light of systemic arguments establishing the meaning of terms in their legal context. This applies particularly in the case of the more technical branches of law, for example, property law or commercial law; in criminal law, by contrast, it may be deemed important for the ordinary citizen to be able to understand criminal prohibitions of a general sort in the light of ordinary linguistic competence, rather than with a view to legal technicality (though sometimes a technical sense of words may be preferred when this favours the defence, as where it was held that the accused did not 'offer for sale' offensive weapons merely by exposing them in the shop window, for that is technically only an 'invitation to treat': *Fisher* v. *Bell* [1961] 1 Q.B. 394). 'Term of Art' arguments can have decisive force in the case of the usages of specialized trades and professions where legislation specifically concerns these.

Further weightings for 'systemic' interpretations arise from the considerable force of the doctrine of precedent in the UK systems. An interpretation given in a binding precedent prevails wherever it applies, and the House of Lords has indicated that the power it has to reconsider its own precedents should not be used in the case of previously determined interpretations of recently enacted statutes. Where precedents constitute only analogical grounds of interpretation, however, rather than specifically speaking to the sense of the statutory section under consideration, they have of course less weight against other considerations. Statutes which have been in force for a long period and have come to be understood as constituting a kind of codification of a particular branch of the law are particularly susceptible to what we called the 'historical argument', where the sense and purpose of the whole scheme comes to be dominant in interpretation; here also arguments from analogy and comparativist arguments may have considerable force. The 'genetic' argument can be particularly significant in relation to 'consolidating legislation', that is, legislation passed by a specially simplified parliamentary procedure, being legislation which brings together in an orderly form statutory elements gathered from a plurality of previously enacted (and often themselves reforming) Acts. Here the rule is to avoid reading the consolidating enactment as if its purport was to change the law from that settled in the consolidated statutes. For this purpose, precedents concerning the consolidated Acts remain in point, whereas, in the case of reforming legislation, there is no presumption that precedents which determined the prior law remain of any considerable force, even persuasive force.

Consideration of the various systemic arguments thus further underlines the slippery quality of LORD BLACKBURN's notion of ordinary signification. The truth is that systemic arguments are not so much rivals to linguistic ones as arguments which, when relevant, complete the linguistic picture. Rather than displacing obvious meanings, they may either confirm or lead us to revise our sense of what is obvious, given that legal enactments have to be read in legal settings, and given that the context of the statutory text within the legal system is essential to determining what it plainly means.

It remains the case, however, that the arguments which rank first in order of normal application are the simple linguistic ones: a statute can only be interpreted in terms of some possible, even if strained, meaning which its words can bear; and a statute should be interpreted in favour of its most obvious or 'plain' meaning unless some reason is shown which displaces that interpretation. But a judgement as to what is prima facie obvious can be challenged and corrected in the light of one or more of the systemic arguments; and, moreover, there may be less obvious interpretations or less plain meanings which can be shown to make better sense in the legal context of the enactment. Where this is so, the alternative interpretation is properly to be preferred. Systemic arguments, however, have to be specifically deployed on the basis of appropriate information, and can have force only when so deployed.

Finally, all proposed interpretations are subject to challenge by teleological/evaluative arguments where their adoption will generate unacceptable consequences. These can scarcely ever be deemed to justify a complete overriding of the words of the act in any possible linguistic meaning, however strained; but, subject to the (sometimes quite loose) constraints of the argument from possible meaning, consequentialist arguments and the values they deploy are properly accepted as the finally justifying arguments in cases which transcend legal technicality and engage the fundamental values of the legal order.

This last element of the discussion focuses in effect on the qualification stated by LORD BLACKBURN — take words in their ordinary signification unless when so taken 'they produce an inconsistency, or an absurdity or inconvenience'. So far as this concerns an outright logical or linguistic inconsistency, this does not itself take us outside the sphere of linguistic arguments, though the resolution of such points will usually involve recourse to the (teleological/evaluative) argument from common sense. If 'absurdity' or 'inconvenience' can be taken in a wider sense than this (and sometimes they are, see *McMonagle*), this involves evaluation in terms of some substantive values. In this case the evaluative argument operates both at the first level as arguing in itself for a particular interpretation, and then it exercises a second influence in outweighing the normal preference for a more obvious over a less obvious meaning. The values deployed in such a case will usually involve an appeal to values enshrined in important legal principles, though one or all of justice, common sense and policy may also be in issue. Hence it can be seen that such argumentation may draw force from its systemic as well as its evaluative quality. The normal understanding is that the cumulative force of such arguments must be considerable if the argument from obvious meaning is to be displaced. After all, the inconvenience or absurdity must be 'so great' that one cannot suppose them to have been intended.

Given the general prioritization derivable from the Golden Rule, the choice between different arguments comes down to one of balancing and weighing. This cannot be well captured by statements of rules or maxims, since each decision will have its unique concatenation of circumstances, and differing considerations have differing weight in different branches of law. For the values and systemic features present in any given case are largely field-dependent. For example, the priority between individual justice and statutory policy is different as between criminal law and administrative law. The systemic completeness and overall coherence of property law may matter much more greatly than the same qualities in some other branches of law, such as trade union law.

As all this acknowledges, the teleological/evaluative element bulks large in prioritization. In cases of radical ambiguity or where two possible interpretations conflict, the rival consequences of one or the other interpretation or style of interpretation may be the only rational ground available to support a choice one way or the other. Hence the appeal to consequences or purposes always tends not merely to show why one interpretation is a good one but also to show why it is better than its rivals: it is better than them because it favours or promotes more important values than they do. However, as was said above, there are reasons of substance not only in favour of expressly teleological/evaluative arguments, but also in favour of linguistic and systemic arguments. We have shown how 'plain meaning' justifications can be taken to uphold constitutionalist or democratic values, or systemic ones versions of the value of 'integrity'. We repeat that there is not in our view any single reconstructable rule or set of rules to determine the proper choice among rival values implicit in different interpretational approaches. These choices ought to be and are treated as field-dependent. In so far as there is a rule of priority, it is that the operative values of the different branches of law ought to be upheld, subject to such variation as is from time to time introduced by parliament through clearly phrased legislation discernibly related to changing social and popular values.

Thus this review of priorities requires consideration also of the section below on the character of statutes (section X). It might also be said that the highest-order duty of judges is to keep all the values of the law in proper overall balance, that is, to sustain law's integrity in the grandest sense of the term. Neither Dworkin nor his critics would think this to be any ordinary sort of a 'rule' — and they would be right not to. But there is perhaps here a genuine if elusive and perennially controversial ultimate justifying ground of ultimate priority choices.

A Note on 'Legislative Intent'

We have not hitherto treated 'the intention of the legislature' either as the basis of a special type of argument, or as itself a ground for priority choices among different interpretations or types of inter-pretative argument. Yet it will have been noted that, in our citations of judicial opinions, there is frequent allusion to the intention or intent of the legislature. The trouble about judicial appeals to legislative intention, however, is that they appear to be highly ambiguous, as follows.

Sometimes the reference is to 'manifest and expressed intention' (see, for example, *A.-G. for Canada* v. *Hallet and Carey Ltd* [1957] A.C. 427 at 449) in the sense of the legislative intention imputable on the basis of the plain meaning of the terms enacted, read in

their whole linguistic and systemic context; sometimes the reference is to the end or purpose rationally imputable to the legislature
given that it has enacted a statute endowed with this plain
meaning, understood as aforesaid; sometimes, but rather rarely in
the UK, the reference is to an actual historically formed aim or
purpose of the legislators, discoverable from sources other than or
additional to the text of the statute itself. The first of these is really
the linguistic argument, coupled possibly with systemic arguments, reinterpreted as disclosing an 'objective' intention ascribable to the legislature as an ideal rational legislator; the second is an
evaluative/teleological argument based on the statutory text and
its systemic context, yielding an argument from purpose conceived
as the objectively imputable intention of the legislature; the third is
a version of what we called the 'genetic argument', where the
historical genesis of legislation is taken to justify imputing to the
legislature as a legal institution the actual subjective motivation of
leading legislators, or draftsmen, or participants in the preparation
of legislative proposals or in legislative debate.

This range of ambiguity indicates why it is not possible to treat
'legislative intent' as a single argument type or a special ground of
priority in interpretative argument. Nevertheless the phrase is not
an empty one. The separation of powers doctrine gives a strong
ground for the thesis that it ought to be the laws as made and
meant by the legislator, not the laws as the judges would prefer
them to be, that are decisively binding upon the citizen. Democratic theory also requires non-elected judges to acknowledge
the authority of decisions taken by the majority's representatives
in parliament.

VII   THE CONFLICT OF STATUTES WITH OTHER LEGAL NORMS

Our answers so far may be taken as suggesting that the differences
between statutory interpretation and common law reasoning are
less than is sometimes supposed. Such is in fact our view, though
this is by no means uncontroversial. It is certainly true that
statutory interpretation works always with a text in 'fixed verbal
form' and is a deliberate statement of what the law is to be (see
Twining and Miers, 1982, pp. 30–37). Common-law materials, on
the other hand, are more flexible. They are primarily judgements in
particular cases with the reasoning that leads to that judgement set
out in rather discursive form (see section IX). This does make a
difference. But many of the elements here identified in the reasoning relevant to interpreting statutes can be found in a similar mix in

common law reasoning (see MacCormick, 1978).

To say, however, that the mode of argument and its ordering of priorities is similar is not to suggest that the relationship between the statute law and the common law is unproblematic. Since statutes and case-law are distinct sources of law in our jurisdictions, we must look to the relations between them. The main priority rule would seem to be implied in one of the fundamental doctrines of the British Constitution, namely that statutes duly enacted by parliament override all and any prior rules and principles whatever. It is not quite as simple as that, though. The forum in which these priority claims occur will be the common law courts. Thus both the statutes and the priority rule (the constitution is unwritten) will at least be within the grid of the common law. The most important question here then is how far common law and statute law are kept distinct. Sir Rupert Cross (1968) suggested that judges have received statutes fully into the body of the law to be reasoned from by analogy in the same way as in cases. He also suggested that in some cases they were treating statute law as a superior source of analogy. He thus implies that the law should be looked at as one and that there is no clear distinction between the two sources. Patrick Atiyah (1985) doubts this view. Our tendency is to support it but to see the question as one of weight or gravitational force. Many of the constitutional provisions (see section XIII) will be unwritten and thus be elucidated within the cases by the courts and thus statutes will be interpreted in the light of these principles. The doctrine of the supremacy of parliament will ensure that statutory texts will be more strictly interpreted than the more discursive common law texts. In terms of direct conflict too, the statutory text will prevail but this does not mean that it will necessarily be extended far into the common law. Thus in some cases the courts will treat legislation that reverses a judgement as not undermining the underlying principles of these judgements (see *Derry* v. *Peek* 1889 14 App. Cas. 337 and *Dunlop* v. *Selfidge* [1915] A.C. 847), whereas in other cases the abolition of the rule also implies the abandonment of the principle upon which the common law rule is based (*Davies* v. *Swan Motor Co.* [1949] 2 K.B. 291. In *Shiloh Spinners* v. *Harding* [1973] A.C. 691 at 725 we read:

> In my opinion where the courts have established a general principle of law or equity, and the legislature steps in with particular legislation in a particular area, it must, unless showing a contrary intention, be taken to have left the cases outside that area where they were under the influence of the general law.

On the other hand, in certain areas, where the law is mainly statutory, the judges will be reluctant to admit common-law principles. Thus in planning law LORD SCARMAN refused to extend to it principles drawn from 'the private law' (*Pioneer Aggregates (U.K.) Ltd* v. *Secretary of State for the Environment* [1985] A.C. 132). The fact that the legislature has taken the matter in hand will often act as a disincentive to judicial action.

Declaratory Acts which might be taken to set out the common law on the matter are perhaps a different matter. In the *Ashington Piggeries* case LORD DIPLOCK said that the Act:

> ought not to be construed so narrowly as to force on parties to contracts for the sale of goods promises and consequences different from what they must reasonably have intended. They should be treated rather as illustrations of the application of simple types of contract of general principles for ascertaining the common intentions of the parties as to their mutual promises and their consequences, which ought to be applied by analogy in cases arising out of contracts which do not appear to have been within the immediate contemplation of the draftsman of the Act in 1893.

The interrelations between the common and statute law are perhaps more complicated than Cross had supposed and cases can be found both ways. It seems to us, however, that there is a cross-fertilization between the two sources, the degree of it being a matter of weight which is generally achieved interpretively. Thus it will be the way judges take the constitutional principles of the rule of law and parliamentary supremacy which will determine how they see their role and therefore the degree of cross-fertilization. These interpretations will not be literal or formal but will, as we have stressed throughout, depend on substantive considerations as well, indeed the whole mix of reasoning that we have outlined in previous sections. One can say, however, that interpretation in the statutes will be characterized by more formality than the common law. See section II above for an account of the relations between gaps in statutes and the common law.

We deal with the role of unwritten principles of the constitution in section XIII. In certain instances however, provisions of the constitution could be seen as taking written form. In this case the problems of conflict will be ones of statutes conflicting with other statutes. We deal with the latter case first before passing on to the more complicated constitutional cases. In a straightforward conflict with other statutes the maxim 'leges posteriores priores contrarias abrogant' holds but this is subject to the maxim 'generalia specialibus non derogant'. It is also, with the advent of more skilful drafting, subject to the presumption that parliament does not intend an implied repeal. Thus in *Jennings* v. *United States Government* [1982] 3 All E.R. 104 it was held that the common-law offence of 'motor manslaughter' had not been abrogated by section 1 of the Road Traffic Act 1972: 'A person who causes the death of another person by driving a motor vehicle on a road recklessly shall be guilty of an offence.' Earlier cases had to be applied with caution because 'statutes were not drafted with the same skill as today'. In the main, however, the establishing of conflict rests on deciding whether 'repugnancy', 'absurdity' or 'inconsistency' exists and that rests on prior interpretive decisions (see section III).

Though the doctrine of Parliamentary Supremacy is sometimes said to imply the impossibility of a written constitution like, say, the American one, it has also been argued that the Articles of Union (or 'Treaty of Union') which were put into legal effect in 1707 by Acts of the former Scottish and English Parliaments, thereby for the first time establishing Great Britain as a single state, a single United Kingdom, must be seen as an original written constitution for the UK. It has been argued that, since the UK was a new kingdom formed from the amalgamation of two older ones, the treaty must be seen as fundamental law for the new kingdom and that governmental acts contrary to its terms could not be valid. At the very least, legislation is to be interpreted as not conflicting with the fundamental provisions in the Union preserving Scottish legal institutions save where such an interpretation is unavoidable. This argument was brought forward in *MacCormick* v. *Lord Advocate* 1953 S.C. 396, where it was argued that the Royal Style and Titles Act 1953, if it authorized Her Majesty to be called 'Elizabeth II' in Scotland, was invalid by reason of article 1 of the Treaty of Union. The case was dismissed on the grounds that the petitioners had no title to sue but LORD PRESIDENT COOPER said, 'the principle of the unlimited sovereignty of Parliament is a distinctively English principle which has no counterpart in Scottish constitutional law'. He argued that the treaty should be seen as fundamental law. The same goes for treaties establishing the EEC and enabling British accession thereto.

In *R.* v. *Secretary of State for Transport ex p. Factortame Ltd* [1989] 2 C.M.L. 353 the EEC issue was confronted specifically:

> Where the law of the Community is clear . . ., the duty of the national court is to give effect to it in all circumstances. Any rule of domestic law which prevented the court from, or inhibited it in, giving effect to directly enforceable rights established in Community law would be bad. To that extent a United Kingdom statute is no longer inviolable as it once was. (per BINGHAM L. J. 403–4)

VIII PRESUMPTIONS GUIDING INTERPRETATION

Presumptions afford a prima facie indication as to the interpretation of the Act; that is, as to readings which are to be preferred unless a contrary intention is expressed. When looking at presumptions which should guide the judge in the interpretative purpose, one has also to look to the principles and rules that are to guide statutory interpretation, for it will be a presumption that they apply in the interpretative process. In the most general sense, there will be presumptions which are coextensive in content with the matters of general principle discussed in sections XII and XIV below. For parliament is presumed not to trespass upon fundamental principles, even if it is able to do so by provisions enacted in unequivocally clear terms. The implication here is that these principles are so embedded in the law that they will be taken for granted and will be presumed to apply even where there is no question of linguistic ambiguity. They are, so to speak, part of the text. They can thus be seen to operate in a quasi-constitutional way, expressing fundamental rights and liberties of citizens and regulating the relations between parliament, the executive and the courts. Among the presumptions here we may note that parliament is presumed to act justly and reasonably;

> In general if it is alleged that a statutory provision brings about a result which is so startling, one looks for some other [possible] meaning of the statute which will avoid such a result, because there is some presumption that Parliament does not intend its legislation to produce highly inequitable results. (per LORD REID in *Coutts & Co.* v. *IRC* 1953 A.C. 281)

Powers exercised under statutes are subject to the duty to act fairly (*Payne* v. *Lord Harris of Greenwich* [1981] 2 All E.R. 842 at 145). The principle that legislation ought not to be retrospective becomes (under our doctrine of parliamentary sovereignty) a presumption that legislation applies only prospectively; but this would be rebuttable by a clear and unambiguous legislative provision to the contrary effect (see WRIGHT J. in *Re Athlumney* [1892] 2 QB 547 at 551). Other presumptions, though they might be seen as embodying principles, can be seen more as aids to resolving ambiguity. Thus the presumption that the legislator's words are intended to secure some reasonable purpose, and not to generate absurd or illogical results; the presumption that pre-existing law continues in force until effectually superseded. (On all this, see Bennion (1984) sections 300–42. See also sections III and V of this chapter.)

Linguistic rules of interpretation are sometimes stated in the form of presumptions, and in so far as they are it could be argued that they are principles without which one could not understand English texts, rather than aids to resolving ambiguity. Further, the Interpretation Act 1978 includes some more technical, but highly useful, word-saving presumptions; for example:

> [s.6]   In any act, unless the contrary intention appears:
> (a) words importing the masculine gender include the feminine;
> (b) words importing the feminine gender include the masculine;
> (c) words in the singular include the plural and words in the plural include the singular.

IX   THE STYLE OF STATUTORY INTERPRETATION

In terms of surface structure, British judicial opinions on questions of interpretation (as on other questions) tend to be long and discursive, containing substantial narrative elements. They will usually start by indicating briefly the factual background and nature of the claim in issue, will always quote verbatim the statutory text(s) to be considered and applied, and will then proceed to sift the facts of the case in their bearing on the law, and to expound and evaluate discursively the various interpretative arguments raised by the parties, structuring the account of the arguments in such a way as to show their persuasive or even conclusive force in favour of the interpretative conclusion reached. The interpretative conclusion is then applied to the facts and the issues of the case, and judgement pronounced accordingly.

This discursive style stands in marked constrast to, for example, the terse and quasi-syllogistic statement of 'visas' and 'motifs' in the 'arrêt' of a French civil court. Recourse to anything like a formal–logical or syllogistic structure of presentation is extremely rare. Still what is involved is a reflective account of the reasons which favour a certain interpretation of the major premiss of a hypothetical argument in *modus ponens*, coupled with the reasons favouring a matching characterization ('qualification') of the facts which constitute the necessary minor premiss. The reasoning for the interpretation and the qualification is not deductive but discursive, yet the discursive reasoning is in effect the necessary prelude to a deductively statable conclusion. It is sometimes contested (see Gottlieb 1968; Wilson, 1982) whether or not such a logical (deductive) characterization of the deep structure of reasoning from statute law is accurate; but for a convincing rejoinder to all the doubters, see R. E. Susskind (1987).

The discursive and narrative style of exposition can make for difficulties in identifying clearly the specific *ratio decidendi* of the case as distinct from more general observations or *obiter dicta* which do not, in the theory of precedent, have binding force. Nevertheless, since a decision upon a point of statutory interpretation must always proceed by way of a ruling either that the text does (or does not) bear the interpretation argued for by a party, or at least that the facts in issue do (or do not) count as an instance of the operative facts required for application of the statutory norm, the determination of the ratio of an interpretative judgement is usually somewhat easier than in the case of a judgement of pure common law.

In appellate courts there will frequently be more than one opinion stated, and this can add further complications. Though judges might agree as to the result, their analyses of the facts and arguments might produce widely differing grounds of decision. Furthermore dissenting opinions are also issued and some of these can have great influence later. In the House of Lords there seems to be evolving a practice whereby only a single majority opinion is normally presented. This will be by one law lord, after consultation with the others of the majority opinion. Such a practice could over time influence the style of decisions by reducing the degree of explicitness of presentation and weighing of interpretative arguments, while at the same time perhaps promoting increased superficial clarity of decision making.

The institutionally prescribed addressees of the judgement are (technically) the parties to the judgement, though it must be remembered that the judgements of the highest civil appellate tribunal are cast in the form of speeches to the House of Lords (the second legislative chamber), as the court is the appellate committee of that House. However, whoever the addressees are technically, the judges in the highest courts see the most important addressees of their judgements to be first of all their fellow judges, and then secondarily the barristers who practise in the high courts as important participants in the arguments leading up to the making of the judgement. These factors cannot but help to influence the style of judgements (see Paterson, 1982, for a sociological account of all of these factors).

X INTERPRETATION WITH REGARD TO THE CHARACTER OF THE STATUTE

Judicial approaches to statutory interpretation vary noticeably from one branch of law to another. They do so because of the difference of systemic and teleological/evaluative context which arises from a difference of underlying principles in different branches of law. As this suggests, it is not the structure or the method of reasoning which differs, but the content, so far as this relates to underlying principles of law in establishing the context of the enactment, or evaluating the consequences of a proposed interpretation of it.

In section III, attention was drawn to the crucial role of fundamental principles in statutory interpretation (as a vital element in systemic arguments and as furnishing grounds for critical evaluation of rival interpretations and their consequences). These principles of course are different in respect of different branches of law. The principles of 'nulla poena sine lege' and of 'mens rea' as a requirement for criminal liability in the case of serious charges apply specifically to criminal law. That requiring a fair hearing of any question affecting a person's interests has special importance for public law, though also bearing on criminal procedure and on the private law of membership of voluntary associations. It is always possible to ascribe to an ideal legislator the intention to legislate compatibly with the demands of these principles in any case of statutes bearing on criminal law, public law or (for example) trade union law, and it is usually proper to ascribe an appropriate relevant intention to the historic legislature. This justifies a special stringency against extensive or analogical applications of criminal statutes; it justifies reading into criminal statutes requirements of 'mens rea' even where the legislature has omitted to provide expressly for this; it justifies reading administrative decision-making powers as being subject to the requirements of natural justice, and so on.

Generally interpretation of statutes dealing with criminal offences or with taxation tends to be much more strict, and the rectification of perceived mistakes and strained interpretations (interpretative gap-filling) are here less readily than elsewhere accepted in the name of the 'intention of parliament'. It should now, however, be added that the recent case of *Ramsay* v. *IRC* [1981] 1 All E.R. 865 has somewhat diluted the prior principle stated in *IRC* v. *Westminster* ([1936] A.C. 1 at p. 19.) that 'every man is entitled if he can to arrange his affairs so that the tax attaching under the appropriate Acts is less than it otherwise would be'.

Where statutes are envisaged as addressed directly to lay persons, their 'ordinary' or 'obvious' meaning is usually favoured; this has a significant bearing on criminal statutes, but nowadays tax statutes are probably considered as addressing specialist advisers directly, and citizens only indirectly. All the more so, in spheres such as conveyancing (that is, transfers of immoveable property) the understanding ascribed to technical professionals has greater authority than that of laypersons, and the technical meaning of terms will normally be taken as prevailing.

Ancient statutes, when still in force, either directly or by incorporation in later enactments, have often over the years attracted a great accretion of interpretative overlays, so that their contemporary meaning depends as much on case-law and customary understanding as on any approximation to 'ordinary meaning' – the ordinary meaning has become that enshrined in customary legal understanding. Classical examples are the (English) Statute of Frauds (1677), or the Charitable Gifts Act of 1601, the preamble of which still defines the legal concept of charity. Both these acts are now intelligible only through the case-law, not by reference to their express words alone. Older statutes which are not encrusted into case-law doctrines are normally subjected to rather broad interpretation to avoid clash with contemporary common sense. In all such cases the 'historical argument' has an obvious importance. The modern process of highly professional statutory drafting being a twentieth-century phenomenon, older statutes are sometimes more open to criticism for quality of drafting, and this can also make a difference.

Statutes such as the Occupiers Liability Act, 1957, or the similar Scottish Act of 1960, which prescribe in general terms a 'duty of care' in connection with the occupancy of premises, and other similar private law legislation adapting and adjusting general common law rules, are read much less narrowly and literalistically than more detailed and technical statutes. See, for example, *McGlone* v. *British Railways Board* (1966 S.C. (HL) 1), interpreting the statutory duty to take 'such care as in all the circumstances of the case is reasonable to see that [a] person will not suffer injury or damage' in the case of a boy trespasser climbing on an electricity pylon by an electrified railway line.

XI   THE ROLE OF THE COURTS

No court in the United Kingdom has power comparable with that of the US Supreme Court or the Federal German Bundesverfassungsgericht. That is, there is no court with the role of policing the constitutionality of legislation against tests of form and substance prescribed in a comprehensive constitutional code. Human rights protection in the UK is either a matter of common law and parliamentary tradition or a question of international law cognizable by the European Commission on Human Rights under the

European Convention. British courts may seek to interpret legislation so as to fulfil the international obligations of the state in
respect of human rights, but the constitutional doctrine of parliamentary sovereignty leaves them powerless in the case of clear and
express parliamentary trespasses against human rights. The thesis
that the Articles of Union of 1706–7, which founded the UK as a
unitary state, ought to be judicially sustainable (at least in the Scots
courts) against contrary legislation has considerable intellectual
weight, but has never been judicially acted upon or unequivocally
endorsed (see Preliminary, VII, XIII, XIV). Only in the case of
'community obligations' as defined in the European Communities
Act 1972, can British courts reject British Acts of Parliament as (in
effect) ultra vires; and then they do so under the supervision of the
Court of Justice of the European Communities.

Perhaps because of this relatively weak position of the judicial as
against the legislative branch of government, the courts have
always tended to show a jealous concern for fundamental rights
and liberties enshrined in common law according to a traditional
view of the liberties of the subject in Britain. Conversely they have
been strict in their construction of the powers conferred by statutes
upon the executive and administrative officials of the state, and on
public authorities generally. Indeed, since parliament has unres-
tricted legislative power, normally exercised through the party
system at the initiative of the government of the day, and since the
government has at its disposal the services of a corps of highly
trained draftsmen, the courts have traditionally sought to protect
and preserve a constitutional balance of powers by generally
taking a relatively restrictive approach to statutory interpretation.
This is expressible in terms of the strong prima facie weight
attaching to the rule of law as a value. The leading doctrines of
administrative law clearly exemplify this view of the courts' role
and position in the division of constitutional powers.

A high point of this tendency is the 1969 case of *Anisminic v.
Foreign Compensation Commission* ([1969] A.C. 147). The Commission was set up under statute with certain decision-making powers
over claims by British nationals for compensation for certain sorts
of losses occasioned by foreign powers. It was expressly provided
that 'A determination by the Commission [of claims submitted
under the Act] shall not be called in question in any court of law.'
Yet, when one particular decision was challenged on the ground
that it had been reached on the basis of irrelevant considerations,
the House of Lords held both that such a defect rendered any
purported determination a mere nullity in law, and that the clause
excluding the courts' jurisdiction was not effective to prevent them
exercising jurisdiction to review null 'determinations' and to

declare them such.

Decisions such as this doubtless give rise to a certain annoyance on the part of the executive branch of government. In the case of recent legislation having a controversial party political character, there can be vociferous complaints in parliament about judicial interference in statutory schemes. It is sometimes argued that judges may be particularly ready to take an extremely narrow view of the pet legislation of Labour governments, and that the common law rights most vigorously defended tend to be those most congenial to political individualism (see Griffith, 1977). Yet on the whole the independence of the judiciary is acknowledged and respected.

XII STATUTORY PRESCRIPTIONS ON INTERPRETATION

The UK has never legislated in any form for any prescription about method in statutory or constitutional interpretation. In 1969, the possible desirability of such measures was considered in a joint report of the two Law Commissions (Law Com 1969, Scot Law Com 1969). They suggested that legislation might assist in broadening the scope of materials available as aids to interpretation, in strengthening judicial readiness to discover and pursue legislative purposes, in ensuring interpretations favourable to the upholding of international obligations, in elucidating the provision of civil remedies for breaches of statutory duties and in encouraging greater uses of explanatory materials in statutes. But they also acknowledge the inevitable weakness of legislation about method, which has to be interpreted itself. No general legislation was undertaken, the Report itself having been considered sufficient to encourage a modification of judicial interpretative practice. This strategy of inaction has worked, for there has been a certain tendency in the judiciary towards more purposive and less formalistic styles of interpretation in the UK since 1969.

In certain specific pieces of legislation there has been a growing tendency to legislate in terms of non-exclusive lists of examples of conduct fulfilling some statutory value-condition. For example, in the Unfair Contract Terms Act 1977, examples are given of cases in which exclusions of liability may be upheld as 'reasonable'; but it will be for the judiciary to develop the concept of reasonableness so exemplified in cases going beyond the statutory examples, but analogous to them.

There is an Interpretation Act (of 1978, re-enacting and consolidating a series of prior measures) and this is of great help for some interpretational purposes. But this Act is primarily a word-saving rather than a general-interpretation-guiding measure. It is more lexicographical than methodological.

XIII   CONSTITUTIONAL LAW AND INTERPRETATION

Traditionally the fundamental doctrine of British Constitutional Law was that of parliamentary sovereignty: the doctrine that statutes duly enacted by parliament override all and any prior rules and principles whatsoever. An important corollary was that parliament could not bind its successors, this amounting to the only recognized exception to the perpetual momentary sovereignty of parliament. Since the United Kingdom was first established in 1707 by a treaty between the former Parliaments of England and of Scotland, it has been argued that the provisions entrenched in the treaty in favour of the continuing independence of Scots law, Scots Courts and the Scots Church constitute a further exception, but English commentators have denied this (although in fact the provisions in favour of Scottish institutions have been largely respected).

In any event it now seems clear that British accession to the European Communities (achieved, from the point of view of UK law through the European Communities Act 1972) has radically altered the standing of parliamentary sovereignty, since by that Act parliament has in effect bound its successors, so long as the UK remains a member of the EC (and leaving seems economically and politically inconceivable). Now all UK legislation must be interpreted to avoid conflict with Community law (on its proper interpretation) and, in the event of irreducible conflict, it is Community law which must prevail. Since questions raising problems of Community law ought to be the subject of a reference to the Court of Justice of the European Communities, the requirement of compatibility of UK with EC law is subject to external checks as well as internal ones, and the interpretative approach of the European Court (hitherto a markedly purposive one) must become ever more influential domestically. Since the European Court has held that respect for the European Convention on Human Rights is an implicit requirement of Community law, it is even arguable that by this process the UK has impliedly acquired a justiciable and entrenched bill of rights in respect of those areas of life and work which fall within the scope of Community law.

Hitherto there have been doubts about the possibility of entrenching human rights in the domestic constitution in view of the parliamentary sovereignty doctrine. But the degree to which fundamental rights are already deeply embedded in the flexible constitution should not be underestimated. A. V. Dicey's classic statement of the 'Rule of Law' expresses this in terms of basic common law rights upheld by ordinary courts. Most modern work since W. I. Jennings's (1952) has radically revised Dicey's thesis as to the Rule of Law, and some even dismiss it as empty rhetoric. Yet certain basic principles of procedural fairness – for example against retrospective law-making, in favour of fairness to accused persons and all persons whose rights are affected by official decision making, against the interpretation of discretions as entailing arbitrary power or the right to act unreasonably – are widely regarded as fundamental. See Wade (1982); Finnis (1980, ch. 12); Raz (1979, ch. 11). Constitutional principles such as those clustered under the Rule of Law ideal do clearly guide and constrain judicial interpretations and effectively operate as presumptive but not completely irrebuttable constraints on any unbridled exercise of parliamentary power. We discuss the way they appear in the form of presumptions in section VIII above. This ties in with our general point, made throughout the chapter, as to the absence of discontinuity between statutory and common law reasoning.

XIV INTERPRETATION AND PRINCIPLES OF LAW

It seems impossible to conceive of any approach to legal interpretation which does not presuppose a background understanding of general principles of law. The very idea even of a 'literal' interpretation of legislation aimed at applying the 'plain' or 'obvious' meaning of a statutory text seems to require some regard to considerations of principle. Thus MacCormick (1978, p. 205), backed by Bennion (1986, p. 668) suggests that

> . . . the 'obviousness' of an interpretation of enacted words may, perhaps must, depend on an understanding of the principle or principles which are supposed to inform the enactment.

Certain principles such as those in favour of fair hearings to be accorded to interested parties by public decision makers, or in favour of a requirement of 'mens rea' as a prerequisite of guilt under any statutorily created criminal offence, implicating some real stigma, that is not of a purely 'regulatory' character (see *Sweet* v. *Parsley* [1976] A.C. 132, where LORD DIPLOCK said that statutory words describing prohibited conduct are 'to be read as subject to the implication' that a certain mental element is necessary) or that requiring public authorities to exercise powers reasonably and with regard only to relevant considerations, or that requiring fair compensation in any case of confiscation of property for public good (see *Burmah Oil Co. v. Lord Advocate* [1980] A.C. 1090) are principles which will qualify the interpretation of Acts. Since parliament is presumed not to intend invasion of such principles save when the contrary is made clear beyond doubt, the legally plain meaning of legislation may be narrower (or broader) than would appear to a lay reader unaware of relevant principles. For a listing and discussion of some highly important 'Principles derived from Legal Policy', see Bennion (1984) sections 126–34 and our section III above.

No doubt these (legislators') principles may on occasion be incompatible with certain principles of common law. For example, the principles favouring freedom from incitement to racial hatred which inform the Race Relations Acts cut into the common law principle favouring freedom of speech. But even then, the intelligibility of the statute as implementing this novel principle requires a view of the way in which the novel principle is supposed to fit in with an existing background body of legal principles.

What we have seen about principles mirrors Ronald Dworkin's distinction between rules and principles, in that they do not operate in the on/off mode but rather weigh the decision in a certain direction. It does not follow from this, however, that we have to accept his views as to their origin and the (im)possibility of their subsumption under a master rule of recognition.

XV THE CHARACTER OF THE HIGHER COURTS

The higher judiciary in the UK are invariably appointed from the ranks of very senior legal practitioners, hitherto always advocates or barristers rather than solicitors. Some of them will have had experience at some time as academic lawyers, even in quite senior posts, but this is not in itself a qualification; it is undoubtedly a lawyer's standing in practice at the senior bar which is decisive for judicial appointment.

The UK has no tradition of having a Ministry of Justice. The provision of legal advice to government, and the conduct of many tasks in public and criminal law, and the oversight of (in Scotland, ministerial control of) criminal prosecutions rests with the 'law officers of the Crown', the Attorney General and Solicitor General for England and Wales and for Northern Ireland, and the Lord Advocate and Solicitor General for Scotland. It is common (though no longer invariable) for former law officers to be appointed judges, a practice which ensures awareness of political and parliamentary practice among the judiciary. The head of the judiciary in England and Wales, and the person who presides over the House of Lords both in its legislative and in its judicial capacity is the Lord Chancellor, who is also a Cabinet minister (and thus in his – never yet her – own person a living denial of any perfect separation of powers in the UK). The other judges in the House of Lords (the highest judicial tribunal), the Lords of Appeal in Ordinary, are also members of the House of Lords in its legislative functions; while by convention they must avoid participating in debate upon matters of party political controversy, they can and do intervene weightily in matters of technical law reform.

Judicial appointments are absolutely different from civil service appointments. Judicial appointments are made by the monarch as head of state on the advice of ministers (variously, the Prime Minister, the Law Officers, the Lord Chancellor, the Secretary of State for Scotland). The most important formative element of the judicial character is the experience of practice at the bar.

Litigation both civil and criminal is always in the main adversarial in the UK. Jury trial is the rule for all serious crimes, but civil juries are now relatively rare. There is a strong degree of trust in the honesty and honour of members of the bar, and stringent professional discipline in matters of ethics. Judges do not have large personal staffs or clerks in the American model and have by most standards even rather rudimentary office facilities. It is an important feature of this sytem that the courts rely on members of the bar to inform them fully and fairly of all legal authorities (statute or case-law) bearing on a point in issue between parties; the court has no duty to decide any matters not in issue, or to inform itself independently about the law governing them. Under a fairly strict doctrine of precedent, one of the few ways of challenging the authority of a precedent is if it can be shown to have been decided *per incuriam*, that is, without citation of all relevant statutes or other authorities. Conversely, where a court is of the view that some points not argued by counsel might be decisive in a case, these points ought to be put to counsel for the purposes of hearing argument upon them before any decision is reached.

Legal debate before the courts is still largely oral argument, with a comparatively small part played by any forms of written argument or 'brief', as distinct from written pleadings and written records of evidence and of prior phases of judicial decision in a case.

As a generalization, litigants and accused persons have (except in minor and summary matters) an appeal to a first appellate level as of right – in England, to the Court of Appeal, in Scotland, to the Inner House of the Court of Session or the High Court of Justiciary in its appellate function. Beyond this, the final level of appeal to the

House of Lords is only by leave, that is, only where either the court below or the House of Lords (acting through a sub-committee) is satisfied that there is a point of general legal importance requiring determination. That is, the final level of appeal is always subject to judicial permission, and the appellate function of the House of Lords is directed towards final determination of points of general legal significance. There is no appeal at all to the House of Lords from Scotland in criminal matters.

XVI THE LEGISLATURE: STRUCTURE AND PROCEDURES

The parliament of the United Kingdom is bicameral. The House of Commons, now the dominant element in parliament, has 650 members, each selected by and for a distinct constituency by a simple majority system of voting (no element of proportional representation of parties is allowed for). Although there are about a dozen political parties which have been represented in the Commons over the past 20 years and although in recent elections the popular vote has been so distributed as to leave the largest party well short of an overall majority of the votes cast, it has been usual for one of the two main parties (Conservative or Labour) to achieve an overall Commons majority. The leader of the Commons majority party is appointed by the Queen as Prime Minister, and the rest of the government is formed on her or his advice, by appointment of ministers to the cabinet and to non-cabinet office. Except in times of national emergency, it has been usual for the government to be a single party government; and, in the Commons, fairly strict party discipline prevails, securing that the government of the day can normally keep a voting majority for any policies (including legislative policies) it deems important.

The second chamber is the House of Lords, still partly hereditary from the old (and the more recent) nobility, but now largely appointive, through the presence of a substantial number of life peers. On the whole, there is a Conservative majority, but by convention this is rarely used to block legislation passed by the Commons when the majority is Labour; in any event, the Lords have only a delaying power, effectively for a year or something less in the case of general legislation other than 'money bills', after which an act may be passed without their support. The real value of the House of Lords in legislation is as a revising chamber composed of members with considerable seniority and political or other expertise and standing. The House makes considerable improvements to legislation by way of detailed amendments to bills, without on the whole obstructing the principles of legislation for which there is a majority in the lower house.

The legislative process in each House involves a first reading, whereby a bill is formally introduced, a second reading at which the proposals are debated in principle and either rejected or accepted as a whole, a committee stage when the details arc scrutinized and amendments considered, a report stage at which the amendments (but no printed statement of the reasons for them) are reported to and considered by the House as a whole, and finally a third reading at which the whole bill as amended is accepted or rejected. Once a bill has been adopted in the same terms by both houses, it is sent for the royal assent, and formal enactment is completed upon signification of the royal assent. By convention, the monarch as head of state is not free to withhold consent, save in very exceptional cases involving the integrity of the constitution.

The legislative process is thus largely controlled by the government of the day. Most legislation is introduced by ministers on behalf of the government, and the little which is not so introduced can pass into law only with the active support of government in securing adequate parliamentary time. There is scope for political bargaining and compromise, not least within the governing party; and the strength of opposition criticism, especially on technical points, can lead to amendment.

Full records (known as Hansard, after the original publisher) are kept of parliamentary debates, and these include legislative deliberations. Relevant committee reports are also kept. But the whole volume of material is so forbiddingly large that the rule has prevailed that legislative materials are ordinarily excluded from interpretative debate in the courts (see section V).

There is an expert corps of professional legislative draftsmen who draft legislation on behalf of government departments. They do so in the knowledge of judicial interpretational practice. Further, government departments can and do monitor the use made of 'their' legislation, and can seek to bring forward amending legislation (subject to pressure of competition for parliamentary time) if the course of interpretation cuts sharply against government policy. This happens not infrequently.

Given the existence of well-recognized canons of statutory construction and of standard types and styles of interpretative argument, and given a standing set of judicial attitudes to the areas in which relatively restrictive and literalistic interpretations are to be preferred (criminal law, tax law, administrative law), it is possible to envisage the whole process of legislation and interpretation as a kind of running dialogue or conversation between courts and parliament, with the parliamentary draftsmen acting as interpreters and go-betweens. Since each side acts with a relatively clear awareness of the way the other does, the system works acceptably.

XVII   FEATURES OF THE LEGAL CULTURE

Though the British judiciary is independent and not part of the state bureaucracy the judges are, of course, shaped by and shape the legal culture in which they find themselves. The prevailing legal culture is formalistic in the sense that the 'Rule of Law' is so understood as to prevent legislation from infringing basic common-law rights through vague or general phrases, while preserving the power of the democratically elected legislature to change any part of the law in sufficiently clearly expressed terms. This means that, though value and policy arguments are used, the culture is in general less open to them than to arguments which focus on the 'plain and literal meaning' of the statute. The structure of the legal profession in Britain makes this easier. In Britain the legal profession is divided into two: barristers (or advocates in Scotland), who have hitherto had the sole right to appear before the High Courts, and solicitors. It is from this former group that judges are by and large selected. This is a small group, as compared to solicitors, and very homogeneous in class and cultural terms and this makes it easier to construct taken-for-granted norms of 'obvious' and 'plain' meaning than would be the case with a more fragmented group. To some extent this situation is beginning to change and one can detect the beginnings of a more 'open' legal culture and methodology. It is likely that the present proposals for the reform of the legal profession, including the abolition of monopoly rights of audience of barristers and advocates, will have far-reaching effects.

Judges are influenced by legal writing and dogmatics. Though technically it might be said that academic texts are not authority (except for the 'institutional' writers in Scotland), modern texts are now used in legal argument in the courts and, especially in criminal and administrative law, frequently cited by judges in their opinions. Even if they are not used as authority they are often very important source material for judges and barristers. This, to some extent, determines the cases cited as well, since often the cases cited will be those culled from academic writing which will already have been pre-selected. In this way the academy exercises an influence on the interpretational practice of the courts. Judges also reflect the way that they were taught and the methodologies that they learnt. Legal scholarship has expanded and is now established more firmly in the universities, and this has also had a great influence on what is now virtually an all-graduate profession. The law schools now exhibit many and various paradigms of the study and methodology of law and some of these more 'open' variants are filtering down to judicial practice. There is something of a 'time lag' in these matters.

REFERENCES

Atiyah, P.S. (1985), 'Common Law and Statute Law' in *Modern Law Review* **48**, pp. 1–28.
Bell, G.J. (1899), *Principles of the Law of Scotland*, 10th edn., Edinburgh: T&T Clark.
Bennion, F.R. (1980), *Statute Law*, London: Butterworths.
Bennion, F.R. (1984), *Statutory Interpretation*, London: Butterworths.
Blackstone, Sir W. (1829), *Commentaries on the Laws of England*, 18th edn., London: S. Sweet.
Cross, R. (1968), *Precedent in English Law*, Oxford: Oxford University Press.
Cross, R. (1976), *Statutory Interpretation* (2nd edn., by Bell, J. and Engle, G.), London: Butterworths.
Dias, R.W.M. (1976), *Jurisprudence*, 4th edn., London: Butterworths.
Driedger, E. (1976), *The Construction of Statutes*, Toronto: Butterworths.
Dworkin, R. (1986), *Law's Empire*, London: Fontana Press.
Erskine, J. (1812), *An Institute of the Law of Scotland*, 5th edn., Edinburgh: Bell and Bradfute.
Finnis, J. (1980), *Natural Law and Natural Right*, Oxford: Oxford University Press.
Gottlieb, G. (1968), *The Logic of Choice*, London: George Allen and Unwin.
Griffith, J. (1977), *The Politics of the Judiciary*, London: Fontana Press.
Hart, H.L.A. (1961), *Concept of Law*, Oxford: Oxford University Press.
Jamieson, N.J. (1976), 'Towards a Systematic Statute Law', *Otago L.R.*, **568**.
Jennings, W.I. (1952), *Law and the Constitution*, 4th edn., London: University of London Press.
MacCormick, D.N. (1978), *Legal Reasoning and Legal Theory*, Oxford: Oxford University Press.
Paterson, A.A. (1982), *The Law Lords*, London: Macmillan.
Raz, J. (1979), *The Authority of Law*, Oxford: Oxford University Press.
Stair, James Viscount (1981), *The Institutions of the Laws of Scotland*, 6th edn., Edinburgh: Edinburgh University Press.
Susskind, R.E. (1987), *Expert Systems in Law*, Oxford: Oxford University Press.
Twining, W. and Miers, D., *How to do Things with Rules*, 2nd edn., London: Weidenfeld.
Wade, H.W.R. (1982), *Administrative Law*, 4th edn., Oxford: Oxford University Press.
Wade, E.C.S. and Phillips, G.C. (1977), *Constitutional Law*, (10th edn., by A. Bradley and St. J. Bates), London: Longman.
Waismann, F. (1951), 'Verifiability', in A.G.N. Flew ed., *Essays in Logic and Language*, Oxford: Basil Blackwell.
Wilson, A. (1982), 'The Nature of Legal Reasoning: a Commentary with respect to Professor MacCormick's Theory' in *Legal Studies* **2**, pp. 269–85.

References to Cases

In this chapter, cases have been referred to from several series of law reports.

For England, Wales and Northern Ireland

The Law Reports, in several series:

Appeal Cases, cited as '[1990] AC 378'.
Queen's Bench Division reports, cited as '[1990] 1 Q.B. 378'.
Chancery Division reports, cited as '[1990] Ch 378' Family Division reports cited as '[1990] F 378'.

Note that the year, in square brackets, serves also as the volume number, save that sometimes a given series runs to more than one volume per year, as with '1 Q.B.', '2 Q.B.' etc.

During the reign of a king, the relevant series is for the King's Bench Division, cited as 'K.B.'. The Appeal Cases report only decisions by the House of Lords and the Judicial Committee of the Privy Council.

The All England Reports are a privately published series, cited by year, in square brackets, volume number within that year (1, 2, or 3) and page number, thus: '[1990] 2 All ER 378'.

For Scotland

The Session Cases is the official series of reports of Scots cases decided in the House of Lords, the Court of Session and the High Court of Justiciary; it is cited by year, without any bracketing, and page number, thus: '1990 SC 378'; House of Lords cases are cited as '1990 SC (HL) 27'.

The Scots Law Times is a privately published series, cited as '1990 SLT 378' etc.

In all these series, save the Appeal Cases, decisions are published only selectively, the decision to publish being determined by the significance of the legal point of any given decision.

11 Statutory Interpretation in the United States

ROBERT S. SUMMERS, *Ithaca*

PRELIMINARY

The United States is a complex legal order comprised of 50 different states within a single superimposed nationwide federal system having superior power under the federal constitution over limited yet very important subject-matter areas. The states are supreme within their own subject-matter areas under the federal constitution. There is not any highest legislative, judicial or administrative body that exerts final control over all statutory interpretational practices of all courts within all fields. The United States Supreme Court, the highest federal court, has final judicial authority only in regard to the interpretation of federal statutes. The appellate judicial authority of the federal Supreme Court extends, among other things, to cases interpreting federal statutes decided by the various federal courts of appeal, and to cases interpreting federal statutes decided by state supreme courts. The appellate judicial authority of the federal Supreme Court does not extend to the interpretational practices of state supreme courts with respect to state statutes, that is, statutes passed by a state legislature rather than by the federal Congress. In regard to statutes passed by the state legislatures, the state supreme courts have final authority.

The totality of cases posing issues of statutory interpretation decided by the 50 state supreme courts vastly exceeds the number of such cases decided by the US Supreme Court. In this chapter, however, I have chosen to focus on the interpretational practices of the federal Supreme Court during the decade 1980–90. For the purposes of our comparative study, this choice of court seemed more defensible than any other. The US Supreme Court is the

407

highest court in all federal matters, and its approach to interpretation is not less 'representative' than that of any other 'higher court'. Moreover the number of cases involved is not unmanageable. It must be borne in mind, however, that the federal Supreme Court decides relatively few genuine 'private law' cases. Moreover the US Supreme Court is not always consistent in its general approach (but the same is true of state supreme courts). Inevitably some of the generalizations to be set forth here are subject to qualification. Not all of the cases I refer to here are US Supreme Court cases, nor are all of them post 1980 decisions. But the overwhelming majority are, on both counts.

The Supreme Court decides about 5000 cases a year and writes about 150 opinions a year. Most of the Court's case-load consists of cases in which the Court reviews statutes or official action for unconstitutionality. About 80–90 of the Court's cases in recent years are decided partly on the basis of statutory interpretation. The Court has almost total discretion to choose the cases it will hear.

The US system is not a Code-law system, but a common-law system. In most fields, however, statutes are rapidly becoming the dominant source of law in the USA as well. This has significance for interpretation in several ways, most of which I will identify in the pages ahead.

I ORIGINS OF INTERPRETATIONAL ISSUES

Most statutory interpretation issues arise from the following sources.

1   Linguistic and related sources. Issues of interpretation may be traceable to ambiguity of ordinary words or sentences, to whether the words are used in accord with one of several standard ordinary meanings or in accord with a standard technical meaning (legal or non legal) or some special (non standard) meaning, to vagueness of the words used, to the generality of the words, and to the use of evaluative words. The above are the main linguistic sources of issues. Some further remarks on ambiguity and vagueness now follow.

In the American system, a leading authority has said that the most common linguistic source of issues of interpretation is syntactical ambiguity — the kind that arises from uncertainty of modification or reference on the face of the particular statute. (See Dickerson, 1975, p. 46). There are also semantic ambiguities as where a word used in a statute is a word with two or more standard ordinary meanings, and where a word might have a technical or a special meaning (neither ordinary nor technical). It is always possible to prove or show a technical meaning even of an otherwise unambiguous ordinary word. But that an ordinary or technical word with an otherwise unambiguous standard meaning may have a special meaning is a source of ambiguity only if the legal system allows the party so claiming to show as much. This showing might be made from other parts of the statute, or statutes *in pari materia*, or other similarly 'facial evidence'. But what if the only such evidence lies outside statutory language and other facial sources altogether, and is to be found only in legislative history? Here there will be no ambiguity and thus no such source of interpretational issues unless the court resorts to such evidence. Frequently, however, judges of the US Supreme Court do resort to such evidence, at least to establish that there is an interpretational issue.

Vagueness is another major linguistic source of issues of interpretation. For example, the word 'vehicles' is vague in the now famous hypothetical statute: 'No vehicles may be taken into the park.' Borderline cases can easily be imagined here: a military jeep no longer in running condition which is placed on a pedestal in the park as a war memorial; a toy airplane with a motor for flight subject to remote control from the ground; a motorized wheelchair; a horse; roller skates; a pram.

2   'Background' general principles as sources of issues. A statute may be clear in general terms. Thus, for example, it may say that 'the property of a dead person shall pass to his heirs at law'. What if the heir murdered the dead person to get the property? As to such an heir, the statute is literally overinclusive. But the legislature cannot spell everything out. It may also be that the legislature took for granted the continued applicability, when adopting the statute, of a widely recognized general principle such as that 'no person may profit from his own wrong'. At the least, the court might say that a presumption arises that the legislature did take this for granted. Thus, if the murdering heir cannot rebut this presumption with specific evidence to the contrary, the heir loses. But, win or lose, the issue has arisen, and it does not arise solely from a linguistic source but from what one might call a 'background' principle – here a principle generating a presumption. For a famous example, see *Riggs* v. *Palmer*, 115 N.Y. 506, 22 N.E. 188 (1889) (New York's highest court).

3   Internal structural issues within the statute. Many issues arise distinctively from the internal structure of a statute, that is, from asymmetries, inconsistencies, internal incoherence and so on. A common example is where different words are used in two otherwise parallel and functionally similar provisions of the same statute. The issue then arises whether this indicates a difference of meaning.

4   'Relations' between the statute and other statutes or between the statute and prior law as sources of issues. The uncertain 'mesh' between two statutes can generate an issue. So too can asymmetries, inconsistencies and the like between two otherwise parallel statutes. When a statute carries over terminology from prior law, is that terminology to be given the same meaning as in prior law? What if the statute does not use the same terminology as prior law? Does this necessarily signify a change?

5   Inadequate design as a source of issues. Doubts about the meaning of a statute may arise because of such factors as (a) legislative misunderstanding and statutory miscategorization of the problem; (b) faulty statutory ends, including indeterminacies of statutory ends; (c) mistaken assumptions about means; (d) inappositeness of means; and (e) bad drafting as such.

6   'Conflicts of value' sources. A statute may incorporate a term or concept that merely restates, reformulates, or introduces into the law a value controversy in the society at large. For example, a statute may require something like 'equality of employment practices', language which merely restates the controversial issue of whether it is enough for the employer to treat existing employees equally or whether the employer must engage in some form of affirmative action to increase the proportion of a certain class of employees who in the past have been subjected to discrimination.

7   'Change' sources of issues. Some change in knowledge, in technology, in circumstances or in general values bearing on the statute, or in the way officials or private persons have come to administer the statute since its adoption may give rise to issues of interpretation.

8   General 'methodological' sources of issues. Within a given system, a general method of interpretation may prevail. For example, if the general method of statutory interpretation emphasizes literal or plain meaning, this can give rise to issues about the very meaning of 'literal' or 'plain'. Or if the general method of statutory interpretation emphasizes

9 'purpose', this can give rise to issues about the very meaning of 'purpose'. Indeed, purpose can be ambiguous or vague.
'Special' features of the case as sources of issues. The facts may be somewhat in doubt, or the way they should be characterized may be in doubt, and this may give rise to an issue. Also exceptionally strong equitable considerations may arise on the particular facts and this may pose an issue of interpretation. Or the entire set of facts that has arisen may be quite unusual and pose an issue of whether the statute could ever have been intended to reach such facts.

10 Other sources of issues. There are various other sources. One common one in the American system is that prima facie a statute may seem to conflict with a constitutional provision. This may lead the court to take a special step and interpret the statute to remove the conflict. Another source of issues is the punctuation of a statute. Still another is the inherent indefiniteness of the subject-matter of the statute. As Aristotle said, 'When the thing is indefinite, the rule also is indefinite.' See Aristotle, *Nicomachean Ethics*, V 10.1137b.

II INTERPRETATION AND GAP-FILLING

In the US system there is no generally accepted way of distinguishing between interpretation and gap-filling. One way to draw this distinction is to say that interpretation is concerned with the essentially cognitive function of ascertaining the meaning of the express words of a statute in regard to matters within the scope of these words; all else in relation to the statute is gap-filling. It might be said that *any* creative element in regard to a statute should really be viewed as gap-filling. A sharp distinction between interpretation and gap-filling cannot be drawn.

It is, however, possible to formulate a general typology of gaps. A gap in a statutory scheme may be said to exist when a statute includes a general clause or other terms which grant discretion to courts or administrators, when the implementing language of a statute is undergeneral in relation to its purpose, when an integral part of a statute is omitted, when a statutory scheme is left in fragmentary form, left unspecified, or left implicit in some respect, and when the relation between subsections or sections is left unspecified.

There is little systematic scholarly analysis of the nature and varieties of gaps and gap-filling. Nor have the courts adopted a uniform typology. Yet American courts regularly engage in filling gaps such as the above, though they usually refer to this process as interpretation. Of course interpretation may also be necessary to determine if a gap exists. An example is *Mobil Oil Corp.* v. *Higginbotham*, 436 U.S. 618 (1978) (no gap in the Death on High Seas Act sufficient to allow recovery of award sought).

The origins of gap-filling issues vary to some extent with the nature of the issue. Where the gap arises because the legislature has delegated open-ended power to courts or administrators to fill the gap by adjudication or by rule-making, it may be said simply that the origin of the gap is intentional or deliberate.

The undergenerality of the implementative language of a statute in relation to its purpose may also be deliberate. If so, then the statutory scheme should *not* be viewed as having a gap in it to be filled. If the undergenerality is not deliberate, but is attributable, for example, to mistake or lack of foresight, then a genuine gap-filling issue arises.

Gaps in the form of the omission of integral parts of statutory schemes also arise from oversight or mistake. The same is true of gaps as to the essential relations between two statutory subsections, or between two different statutes.

III   TYPES OF INTERPRETATIONAL ARGUMENT

Once an issue of interpretation has arisen, various types of argument may become relevant to resolution of this issue. Complex questions can arise as to what qualifies as a distinct and autonomous type of argument. In order to maximize the potential range of conflicts between types of argument and thus pose for Topic VI as many 'conflict settling' issues as possible, I have tended to individuate rather than to aggregate the argumentational phenomena. However I have not split the phenomena into more types of argument than are actually recognized, explicitly or implicitly, by the courts.

The main types of argument *frequently* invoked by the courts are:

1   The argument from a standard ordinary meaning of the words in issue. Here 'standard ordinary meaning' means a recognized common, that is, non-technical usage of the words. Evidence of this usage may be marshalled from dictionaries, other standard literary reference works, relevant judicial pronouncements on the ordinary meaning of such words, prior legal history, including evolution of the statute, and other sources. See, for example, *Ernst and Ernst* v. *Hochfelder*, 425 U.S. 185, 199 (1976); *Pittston Coal Group* v.

Sebben, 109 S. Ct. 414, 420 (1988). Understandings of grammar, syntax, punctuation and the like may also play a role in an argument of this type. See, for example, *U.S. v. Ron Pair Enters. Inc.,* 109 S.Ct. 1026, 1030–31 (1989). A word or phrase may have more than one standard meaning. Here, the general context of use in the statute will usually indicate the appropriate meaning.

2   The argument from a standard technical meaning of the words in issue. This technical meaning may be a standard legal meaning that the words have in the law, or a standard meaning that the words have in a particular branch of knowledge or technology, or a special trade, or the like. Various forms of evidence, including prior legal history and expert trade usage testimony may be utilized to prove as much. See, for example, *Kungys v. U.S.,* 485 U.S. 759, 770 (1988); *La. Pub. Serv. Comm. v. F.C.C.,* 476 U.S. 355 (1986).

3   The argument from the meaning indicated by contextual-harmonization. Various elements of statutory context may either confirm a standard ordinary or technical meaning or, instead, support a special meaning. Such elements include the following:

(a)   how the words in issue fit with the rest of the sentence in which the words appear (see, for example, *Mills Music v. Snyder,* 469 U.S. 153, 167–68 (1985));

(b)   how the sentence in which the words in issue appear fits with the rest of the specific paragraph or specific section involved, (see, for example, *Shell Oil Co. v. Iowa Dept. Revenue,* 109 S.Ct. 278, 281 n.6 (1988)) (' "Words are not pebbles in alien juxtaposition; they have only a communal existence; and not only does the meaning of each interpenetrate the other, but all in their aggregate take their purport from the setting in which they are used. . .' "). (quoting *NLRB v. Federbush Co.,* 121 F. 2d 954, 957 (2nd Cir. 1941));

(c)   how the same words as the words in issue are used elsewhere in the statute (see, for example, *Mohasco Corp. v. Silver,* 447 U.S. 807, 818, 826 (1980));

(d)   how far a proposed meaning of the words in issue affirmatively harmonizes with other sub-sections of the same section of the statute and with other sections of the same statute, and with related sections of closely related statutes (see, for example, *Public Employees Retirement System of Ohio v. Betts,* 109 S.Ct. 2854, 2868 (1989); *American Textile Manufacturers Institute v.*

Donovan, 452 U.S. 490 (1981) and *Dickerson* v. *New Banner Institute, Inc.*, 460 U.S. 103, 115–116 (1983));

(e)   the fact that a proposed meaning of the words in issue would or would not render part of the statute redundant (see, for example, *Mountain States Tel. and Tel.* v. *Pueblo of Santa Ana*, 472 U.S. 237, 249 (1985));

(f)   any other relevant internal elements, such as titles and section headings, and the bearing of such notions as 'words grouped in a list should be given related meaning' (see, for example, *Schreiber* v. *Burlington Northern, Inc.*, 472 U.S. 1, 8 (1985)).

4   The argument from precedent. This argument in its simplest form proceeds by way of citation of a prior decision interpreting the provision in question.

5   The argument from statutory analogy. One form of this argument is that a word should be interpreted in a given way because this will treat similar cases similarly under related statutory provisions. See, for example, *Moragne* v. *States Marine Lines, Inc.*, 398 U.S. 375, 392 (1970) wrongful death statutes apply by analogy in maritime law).

6   The argument from coherence with a general legal concept operative within the branch of law concerned. This type of argument draws on the 'logic' of a general concept, for example contract, or corporation, as the concept appears in the statutory scheme. In the absence of special circumstances, the general concept should be given a consistent application.

7   The argument from congruence with relevant and authoritative public policy operative within the field in which the statute falls. This type of argument brings generally authoritative policy in the area to bear. The policy and its authoritativeness are explicit or implicit in the language of the general statutory scheme.

8   The argument from general legal principles that bear upon the issue of meaning that has arisen. Here are two examples of such principles: (1) the principle that no person shall profit from his own wrong is presumed to remain in force if the legislature merely adopts a general statute allowing heirs to inherit; (2) the principle of 'mens rea' or mental culpability is presumed to remain in force if the legislature merely adopts a general penal statute.

Principles sometimes appear in the clothing of 'presumptions' of legislative intention. The force of such a presumption depends partly on the force of the principle and the extent of its acceptance. The force is all the stronger where any departure from the principle would raise a question whether the legislature had constitutional power to so depart.

9 The argument from the historically evolved meaning that the statutory words have come to have within the system. Statutes at the hands of courts can take on a life of their own somewhat different from what they were originally designed or formulated to do. When courts so interpret a statute they engage in what Europeans call 'historical' interpretation. A prominent example of this type of interpretation in the USA is the Supreme Court's construal of the Sherman Act as merely ruling out unreasonable rather than all restraints of trade, although the word 'unreasonable' does not appear in the Act.

10 The argument from the ultimate purpose of the statute. The ultimate purpose of a statute may be explicit or it may be implicit from a reading of the statute as a whole. An example of explicit ultimate purposes as defined here is as follows. Imagine a statute with an explicit ultimate purpose section and an implementive section:

Section One. The ultimate purpose of this statute is to promote quiet and safety in the park.
Section Two. No vehicle may be taken into the park.

Now let us suppose a person rides a shod horse on the sidewalks in the park. A court might justify classifying the horse as a vehicle. After all, to so define the meaning of the vague implementing language of the statute would serve its ultimate purpose, even though it might conflict with or strain an ordinary meaning of 'vehicle'.

The ultimate purpose of a statute may appear in sources outside the statute, such as legislative history. Thus Section One, above, might not even exist, but the legislative history might reveal an unanimous intention that the prohibition against vehicles promote quiet and safety in the park.

Arguments that favour one choice of meaning over another because the one better serves the ultimate purposes are 'evaluative' in an important though attenuated sense. That is, they provide a basis for the comparative evaluation of alternative readings of the statute as more or less suitable means to statutory ends. Important factors limit the availability of this mode of argument. The ultimate purpose may not be clear, or may rest on dubious evidence. The facts may be unclear as to which meaning better serves the purpose. Precisely how generally the intended purpose should be formulated is often controversial. Frequently the implementive language of the statute is less general than the ultimate purpose. It would be objectionable for a court automatically to expand the meaning of the implementive language in all such cases. (See pp. 435–6.)

Arguments appealing to the ultimate purpose of the statute perhaps have most independent significance now in US Supreme Court cases where the implementing language of the statute is ambiguous or vague. See, for example, *Mills Music, Inc.* v. *Snyder*, 469 U.S. 153, 185 (1985).

An ultimate purpose of a statute can be an object of actual legislative intention (manifest in legislative history or on the face of the statute). When this is so, ultimate purpose arguments are also often characterized as arguments from legislative intention. But there are other kinds of 'intention' arguments that are not characterizable as appeals to ultimate purpose. See immediately below.

11   The argument from legislative intention. This argument presupposes an object of intention relevant to interpretation, and the argument itself may be subjective, that is, based on evidence of actual subjective intention of real legislators, or it may be more objective. Most often, it purports to be subjective, and derives from various forms of legislative history ranging from committee reports to floor debates, to prior drafts of the bill and so on. Many examples from cases will be cited later in this chapter.

In 10, above, we saw that, among many other things, the ultimate purpose of a statute may itself be an object of actual legislative intention manifest in legislative history. But purposes are not the only possible objects of legislative intention. For example, evidence of actual legislative intention in materials of legislative history may show a specific denotative intent as to the meaning of the statute. Suppose, for example, that the implementive language of our statute said: 'No vehicles and other self-propelled conveyances may be taken into the park.' Does the statute cover skateboards? By ordinary usage of the word 'vehicle', the answer would seem to be affirmative, but the wording of the statute (the phrase beginning with 'and other') suggests that the drafters may have meant the word 'vehicle' only to cover self-propelled vehicles. But even in the absence of any basis for a general argument from ultimate purpose, legislative history might reveal evidence indicating that the word 'vehicle' covered skateboards. For example, the evidence might clearly show that the legislature intended to prohibit skateboards specifically (a 'denotative' intent). Or the evidence might indicate a clear intent to use the word 'vehicle' in a sufficiently *generic* way to include skateboards, even though there was no mention of them as such in legislative deliberations (connotative intent).

Increasingly in recent years arguments from subjective legislative intention based solely on legislative history must be very strong to count for much in the US Supreme Court, except where the language of the statute on its face is ambiguous or vague.

Several presumptions of legislative intention also figure in interpretational argument. Among these are presumptions that:

(a) the legislature intended to enact a constitutionally valid statute;

(b) the legislature intended the statute to be prospective rather than retroactive;

(c) the legislature did not intend an absurd or manifestly unjust result;

(d) the legislature intended to use ordinary English words in their ordinary senses.

12 The argument from deference to interpretation of the statute by an administrative agency entrusted with applying it. This complex argument takes a number of different forms and can have decisive force. The Court may decide to defer to an agency interpretation even though this is not the interpretation the Court itself would have given the statute.

13 The argument from choice of a meaning that avoids a constitutional issue. See, for example, *Gomez v. U.S.*, 109 S.Ct. 2237, 2241 (1989) ('settled policy to avoid an interpretation . . . that engenders constitutional issues').

14 The argument from substantive reasons. Most of these arguments invoke moral, political, economic or other considerations. These arguments fall into two broad categories: (1) arguments to the effect that a given result is best because it best accords with a moral norm of rightness applicable to the circumstances; and (2) arguments to the effect that a given result is best because it can be predicted to have consequences in the future that serve a good social goal. See, for example, *Massachusetts v. Morash*, 109 S.Ct. 1668, 1675 (1989). See generally, Summers, 'Two Types of Substantive

Reasons: The Core of a Theory of Common-Law Justification', *Cornell Law Review*, 63, p. 707 (1978).

The argument from substantive reasons commonly occurs in Supreme Court opinions. Often it is invoked to reinforce other arguments, including arguments from ordinary or technical meaning, purpose or intent arguments, and arguments deferring to agency interpretations. But the argument from substantive reasons probably has greatest importance when the statute is ambiguous or vague. See, for example, *C.I.R.* v. *Asphalt Products Inc.*, 107 S.Ct. 2275, 2277 (1987).

This mode of argument does not require that the substantive reason be previously authenticated, that is derive from an authoritative source of law, such as a statute, or case or legal principle. The force of the argument depends primarily or exclusively on its intrinsic weight.

15   The argument from the normative nature of the phenomena to which the statute is addressed. The statute may be addressed to a public park, or to the family or to banks or to other generic yet variant normative phenomena. When this is so, the precise nature of the phenomena may render one interpretation more appropriate than another. For example, 'vehicle' might mean one thing if the park is an amusement park, and another if it is supposed to be a place of relaxation and rest.

16   The argument from 'rule of law' values. A number of major 'rule of law' values figure in interpretational argument. The desirability of clear general rules is one. See, for example, the dissent in *Jeff. Co. Pharmaceutical Ass'n.* v. *Abbott Labs.*, 460 U.S. 150, 174 (1983). The desirability of protecting citizen reliance on statutory language is still another.

17   The argument from recognized canons of construction. Various so-called canons of construction play a role. These include 'ejusdem generis' ('of the same kind'), 'noscitur a sociis' ('a thing known by its associates') and 'expressio unius exclusio alterius' ('mention of one excludes another'). This latter canon, in particular, seems to be taking on a new life. See, for example, *Chan* v. *Korean Air Lines, Ltd.*, 109 S.Ct. 1676, 1683 (1989).

18   The argument from recognized legal authorities such as law professors. In many branches of the law, the Supreme Court cites and relies on the opinions of experts in the field, especially where the statute is indeterminate.

19   The argument from hypothetical cases. The Supreme Court frequently deploys hypothetical cases in argumentation, and

not merely in the *reductio ad absurdum* argument. See, for example, *Bob Jones University* v. *United States*, 461 U.S. 574, 618–621 (1983) and *T.V.A.* v. *Hill*, 437 U.S. 153, 203 (1978).

20   The argument from legislative acquiescence in prior administrative or judicial interpretations of the statute. This is often a controversial type of argument, but it is frequently made by counsel, and appears with some regularity in opinions.

21   The argument from statutory obsolescence or the age of the statute. See, for example, *Markham* v. *Cabell*, 326 U.S. 404 (1945).

22   The argument from logical forms. Various standard forms of logical argument regularly appear in interpretational reasoning. These include *a fortiori, reductio ad absurdum*, analogy and so on.

IV   TYPES OF GAP-FILLING ARGUMENT

The Supreme Court does not distinguish sharply between interpretation and gap-filling, and there is no general jurisprudence specifically addressed to gap-filling. The types of argument actually used vary somewhat with the nature of the gap. Although there is no accepted typology of gaps, the account that follows reflects the typology sketched earlier at pp. 411–12.

1   Delegations

This topic is exceedingly complex and many-sided, and need not be treated in detail here. Where the gap arises from an express delegation of power by the legislature, the grant may include statutory guidelines. If it does, the court will make an effort to follow those guidelines. If the grant includes little by way of guidelines, the court will still seek to take due account of any general purposes, policies or principles on the face of the statute or appropriately attributable to it. The court will also look to legislative history.

Sometimes the court will find that the Congress has *impliedly* delegated power to the courts to fill a gap. See, for example, *North Dakota* v. *United States*, 460 U.S. 300 (1983) (denying North Dakota right of revocation once consent granted is necessary gap-filler implied from statutory purpose).

The Supreme Court itself will defer to a reasonable effort by an administrative agency to fill a gap in a statutory scheme which it is the agency's responsibility to administer. See, for example, *Chevron U.S.A.* v. *Natural Resources Defense Council, Inc.*, 467 U.S. 837, 844 (1984) ('court may not substitute its own construction . . . for reasonable interpretation made . . . by an agency').

2   Undergeneral Statutes

Many statutes include implementing language that is undergeneral in relation to its purpose. Where undergenerality is seen to be the result of a lack of foresight or mistake, the court may choose to fill such a gap. If it does, it will usually attempt to do so in the light of the ultimate purpose and the specific implementive approach embodied in the undergeneral statute itself. Often this will call for little more than characterization and reclassification of instances otherwise outside the statute. See, for example, *Rodriguez* v. *United States*, 480 U.S. 522 (1987) (statute requiring mandatory two-year sentence reclassified as falling under prior statute giving judge discretion to suspend sentence).

3   Omission of an Integral Part of a Statute

This can only be the result of mistake or oversight. Sometimes the statute will be patterned upon a uniform act, a model act, or a state act with a federal prototype. Here courts sometimes turn to the relevant uniform or model act or prototype and insert the missing segments accordingly.

Where 'mens rea' or a mental state is omitted from a penal statute, a court may invoke a presumption and supply what it considers to be an appropriate mental element, given the nature and purpose of the statute. See, for example, *Morissette* v. *United States*, 342 U.S. 246 (1952).

4   The Unprovided Case ('Casus Omissus')

Sometimes a statute will purport to treat a topic exhaustively but an 'unprovided case' will arise. Here the court may treat this case analogously to the way in which 'provided' cases are treated in the statute. This may require, as a first step, the deployment of interpretational arguments of the kind canvassed at pp. 412–19 above, to determine how the 'provided' cases would be treated. Sometimes the court will engage in a hypothetical analysis in which the court argues somewhat as follows: 'If the legislators had thought about the matter, then here is what they would have said, given our interpretation of what they did say.' One court has said that where an issue arises within a general area covered by statute but for which the legislature has not made specific provision:

> The court must discern the applicable legislative intent by what is necessarily an act of projection — starting from the areas where the legislative intent is readily discernible, and projecting to fair and reasonable corollaries of that intent for the specific issue before us.

See *Montana Power Co.* v. *Federal Power Commission*, 445 F.2d 739, 746 (D.C. App. 1970).

Sometimes the Court will fill the gap by looking at the way an analogous statute provided for the matter. See, for example, *Firestone Tire and Rubber Co.* v. *Bruch*, 109 S.Ct. 948, 949 (1989) (*de novo* standard of review adopted in ERISA cases on analogy with trust law).

5   Partial Intrusion upon Common Law

Sometimes the legislature adopts a statute that alters the common law of, say, tort or contract or property. This statute will incorporate an authoritative policy or principle and the question may later arise whether the common law courts should extend that policy or principle beyond the scope of the language of the particular statute in which it originated. Strictly speaking, this may not pose an issue of gap-filling. But if the legislature invoked the principle or policy in one area to change the common law, a court may be asked to decide whether that principle or policy should be carried even farther — should be invoked to 'fill the gap' in the remaining area of the common law to which it was not, but might have been, expressly applied by legislation more comprehensive in scope. Here there are at least two ways American judges act, not one uniform way.

Some judges pay little or no attention to the statutory principles or policies as such, and merely proceed to apply or develop the common law as if the statute had not been written, given that, by its precise terms, the statute itself does not apply. This might be called, simply, common law argumentation, and it involves no recognition of anything resembling a gap. See, for example, *Norfolk Redevelopment and Housing Authority* v. *Chesapeake and Potomac Telephone Co.*, 464 U.S. 30 (1983) (court refused to extend statute, holding instead that long-established common-law rule governed). Other judges will regard the statute as an authoritative source of policy or principle higher than the common law and will extend this policy or principle by analogy or the like to renovate or substitute for the common law. This process might be thought of as similar to gap-filling. That is, we could say that, prior to the extension, there was an area or gap to which the statutory policy or principle was applicable but the legislature had not yet expressly so extended it. (See, for example, *Moragne* v. *States Marine Lines, Inc.,* 398 U.S. 375, 392 (1970)).

6   Gaps Arising from Unclear Relation between Two Statutes

Such gaps are common. Courts turn heavily to legislative history for guidance. See, for example, *Green* v. *Bock Laundry Machine Co.,* 109 S.Ct. 1981 (1989).

V   THE MATERIALS OF INTERPRETATIVE AND GAP-FILLING ARGUMENT

Below, the main types of materials that may figure in one or more of the basic types of argument referred to in Sections III and IV are treated in terms of whether the courts *must*, or merely *should*, or *may* or *may not*, incorporate such materials into a type of argument, when such materials are available. As to some types of materials, the line between what courts (1) *must* take into account and (2) only *should* take into account, is very difficult to draw because there are no settled conventions. I have tried to draw this line mainly in terms of the severity of the criticism I believe the court would receive if it were to treat material merely as 'should' rather than 'must' material.

1   Materials Courts *Must* Consider

1   Not only the language of the statutory text in question, but also of other sub-sections of the same statute, of titles and subheads and the like. The courts *must* address such material. As one lower court recently said, 'meaning will be given to one section ... only after due consideration of the other sections so as to give effect to each provision and to produce a harmonious and consistent result' (*Ram Broadcasting of Michigan, Inc.* v *Michigan Public Service Commission,* 113 Mich. App. 79, 317 N.W.2d 295, 298 (1982)).

2   Dictionaries, standard literary reference works such as grammar books and manuals of punctuation or style relevant to the ordinary meaning of words in the statutory text. Many cases cite and rely on dictionaries. If authentic, relevant, and put before them, courts *must* consider them.

3   Any relevant evidence of technical meanings of words in the statutory text. Technical usages may be legal or non-legal. Courts *must* consider relevant prior statutes and prior common or other law also using the language of the statute being interpreted. Frequently such materials will be highly persuasive. For example, 'courts generally interpret words and phrases that are defined in the common law according to their common law meaning unless they are defined by the statute in which they appear'. *In re Diana P.*, 120 N.H. 791, 424 A.2d 178 (1980) (interpreting a child custody statute, the court used the common law definition of 'in loco parentis').

   As for non-legal technical terms and as for trade usages possibly incorporated in the statute, courts generally receive expert witness evidence of technical or trade usage as well as written industrial or trade lexicons or codes to determine statutory meaning when it is claimed that the statute incorporates technical or trade usage. See, for example, *U.S.* v. *Sanders*, 893 F.2d 133, 139 (7th Cir. 1990).

4   The text of closely-related statutes. Generally, the courts *must* consider the text of closely related statutes. This is especially true where the related statutes comprise part of a general code or compilation. There are countless examples. See, for example, *Cargill, Inc.* v. *American Pork Producers, Inc.*, 415 F.Supp. 876, 878 (1976) (chapters of South Dakota statutory law on corporations 'should be read as an integrated body of law not as fragments').

5   Superseded or modified prior law. Courts *must* also consider superseded or modified prior law when interpreting a new statute. To interpret a new statute, it is usually helpful to determine the meaning of the prior law and then compare the new statute with that prior law in detail. This process will often generate specific interpretational arguments that would not occur to the interpreter if the interpreter were only to review and analyse the new statute alone. This technique of generating interpretational arguments has long been recognized in the American system (see Sutherland, 1985, ch. 50).

6   Formal legislative history of the statute. Here there is a major difference between interpreting federal statutes and

interpreting most state statutes. In appropriate circumstances, as when the statute is unclear on its face, courts interpreting federal statutes *must* consider evidence of the history of the statute as it moved through the legislature and became law. Courts interpreting the statutes of all but a few state legislatures cannot rely on such legislative history simply because no official records thereof are kept.

In the federal system, courts have made extensive use of legislative history in formulating interpretational arguments especially when the statute is unclear (see Sutherland, 1985, ch. 48. Often such arguments are entitled to little weight. The US Supreme Court sets the standards in this area and, of late, they are becoming much more stringent. There are many varieties of legislative history and their weight varies greatly. For example, the weight of an official committee report is generally greater than the weight of a speech by a legislator interested in the bill. Some judges regard such reports as the most persuasive evidence of legislative purpose. See, for example, *Mills* v. *United States*, 713 F.2d 1249 (7th Cir. 1983). See generally, Dickerson, 'Statutory Interpretation: Dipping into Legislative History', *Hofstra Law Review*, 11, p. 1125 (1983). Occasionally the materials of legislative history generate arguments that are very weighty. It may be that an amendment defeated on the floor where the amendment was addressed to reasonably clear text to the contrary should have greatest weight of all.

Cases purporting to set standards for use of legislative history in statutory interpretation have not, until recently, been at all numerous. Below are set forth a number of general propositions applicable to the use of legislative history in the Supreme Court.

(a) Intrinsic quality of the evidence. Evidence that is 'planted', ambiguous, vague or very general is usually given little or no weight. Thus, in one case, the Supreme Court said: 'Legislative history here as usual is more vague than the statute we are called upon to interpret': *United States* v. *Publ. Util. Comm. of Calif.*, 345 U.S. 295 (1953); and see *Regan* v. *Wald*, 468 U.S. 222, 237 (1984), where the Court pointed out that statements of legislators during the evolution of a proposed statute often lack sufficient precision to have much bearing. The Court also warned against 'planned undermining of the language actually voted on' through the manufacture of legislative history.

(b) Reasonable availability to addressees. Legislative history materials not reasonably available to the intended audience of the statute should not be considered. See Dickerson (1975) pp. 147–54.

(c) Extent taken into account by legislators in the legislative process. A statement of a witness or of a legislator may be too early or too late. If it was made prior to the bill being put into final form in the relevant respect, this will usually be 'too early' to bear on the precise meaning of the final version of the law. See *Regan* v. *Wald*, 468 U.S. 222, 237 (1984). If the statement or other material was not yet available at the time the legislature acted, this will usually be too late. See *Nat. Ass'n of Greeting Card Pub.* v. *U.S. Postal Service*, 462 U.S. 810, 832 n.28 (1983).

(d) Authoritativeness of the statement or document. The Supreme Court has said that a conference committee report is quite authoritative. (A conference committee is a body consisting of representatives from both houses who negotiate a compromise between a bill passed by one chamber and a different bill on the same subject passed by the other chamber.) See, for example, *Commissioner of Internal Revenue* v. *Acker*, 361 U.S. 87 (1959). In addition to Conference Committee Reports, the Supreme Court may consult reports of Standing Committees, House reports and Senate reports. See, for example, *Thornburg* v. *Gingles*, 478 U.S. 30, 43–44 nn.7–8 (1986). The Court may also consult reports of committee hearings on the nature of the problem the bill addressed. See, for example, *Baker* v. *General Motors Corp.*, 478 U.S. 621 (1986).

(e) Nature of author, speaker or witness. Generally statements by non-members of Congress, or statements by members not included in the Senate, House, Conference or other official body above, are given little, if any, weight. See, for example, *Kelly* v. *Robinson*, 479 U.S. 36, 51 n.13 (1986). Statements by legislators sponsoring the bill and managing its progress through the legislature are generally entitled to more weight than isolated remarks of an individual legislator. Compare, for example, *Otero* v. *New York City Housing Authority*, 354 F.Supp. 941 (1973) (court stressed chief sponsor's statements) with *Weinberger* v. *Rossi*, 456 U.S. 25, 35 n.15 (1982) (isolated remark of single senator entitled to no real weight). See also *Brock* v. *Pierce County*, 476 U.S. 253, 263, (1986).

Shared understandings of competing interest groups affected by the statute, if in reliable evidentiary form, are consulted. See, for example, *Community for Creative Non-Violence* v. *Reid*, 109 S.Ct. 2166, 2176 n.12 (1989) (joint memo of publishers and artists under Copyright Act); *Chicago & N.W. Ry.* v. *United Transp. Union*, 402 U.S. 570, 576, 580 n.13 (1971) (labour and management under Railway Labor Act).

The views of official administrators who 'participated in drafting and directly made their views known to Congress in committee hearings' are entitled to 'great weight'. See *United States* v. *Vogel Fertilizer Co.*, 455 U.S. 16, 31 (1982). See also *Zuber* v. *Allen*, 396 U.S. 168, 192 (1969). A presidential message may also be considered. See, for example, *McDonald* v. *Santa Fe Trail Transp. Co.*, 427 U.S. 273, 295 n.26 (1976). So, too, the opinions or views of US Attorneys General or other Department of Justice officials. See, for example, *U.S.* v. *Bd. of Comm'rs.*, 435 U.S. 110, 131–32 (1978).

But it cannot be said that the Supreme Court is wholly consistent in the standards it applies to legislative history. Moreover there is a major recent development. Where the argument from ordinary meaning or from technical meaning has real force, or a special meaning arising from contextual harmonization of the statute as a whole has real force, the Supreme Court is increasingly reluctant to use legislative history to override such arguments (see Section VI below). Where the statute is ambiguous or otherwise unclear, the Court is much more willing to swim in legislative history.

7   Historical conditions the statute was intended to remedy as evidence of ultimate legislative intent or purpose. At least courts interpreting federal statutes must consider such social facts and related material when it is relevant, reliable and of sufficient weight. Some such material will take the form of ordinary legislative history. Other such material may take the form of studies, articles, books and the like which preceded the enactment of the statute and which may or may not have been entered into the formal record of legislative history. See, for example, *American Federation of Musicians* v. *Wittstein*, 379 U.S. 171, 177 (1964) (court asserts that Labor-Management Reporting and Disclosure Act was intended to remedy problems discovered by McClellan Committee). See also Sutherland (1985) at 48.03.

Mainly in federal courts, but occasionally in state courts, the lawyer will file a so-called 'Brandeis Brief' setting forth the social conditions behind the adoption of a statute. The first major American case in which this was done was *Muller* v. *Oregon*, 208 U.S. 412 (1908) (facts and statistics showing bad effects of long working hours on women). Usually such historical evidence is introduced to show that the statute has a valid constitutional base, but frequently the evidence bears on the interpretation of the statute too.

8   General legal facts about the extent or degree of general legal acceptance of a principle or policy that might be presumed to remain in force despite enactment of a generally worded statute not specifically taking account of the principle or policy. The legal acceptance here is to be found in other statutes, in cases, and even in constitutional materials. There is nothing problematic about introducing such material to show wide acceptance of a principle such as that of 'mens rea' as a condition to penal liability, or wide acceptance of a policy such as that administrative agencies are rarely granted *discretion* to take private property. See generally, R. Dworkin (1977) ch. 2. In the light of such facts the Court may then cut down the scope of the overgeneral statute.

9   Prior decisions of higher courts or the same court interpreting the statute. Courts must consider such precedents; if directly applicable, their force is *binding*; otherwise they may still be persuasive to some degree. See, for example, *Patterson* v. *McLean Credit Union*, 109 S.Ct. 2363, 2370 (1989).

10   Prior interpretations of the statute by officials charged with its administration. Courts must consider such official interpretations (often embodied in official regulations). In *Power Reactor Development Co.* v. *Int'l Union of Electrical Radio and Machine Workers*, 367 U.S. 396, 408 (1961), the Supreme Court said:

> We see no reason why we should not accord to the [official's] interpretation of its own regulation and governing statute . . . respect. . . . Particularly is this respect due when the administrative practice at stake 'involves a contemporaneous construction of a statute by men charged with the responsibility of setting its machinery in motion, of making the parts work efficiently and smoothly while they are yet untried and new'.

2   Materials Courts Merely *Should* Consider

11   Prior interpretations by private parties to whom the statute is addressed. Courts *should* consider such material, especially where the private addressees have not unreasonably relied on their interpretation after taking advice of counsel. Thus:

> A practical construction given a statute by the public generally as indicated by a uniform course of conduct over a considerable period of time, and acquiesced in and approved by a public official charged with the duty of enforcing the act, is entitled to

great weight in the interpretation which should be given it, in
case there is any ambiguity in its meaning serious enough to
raise a reasonable doubt in any fair mind. (*Hennessey* v. *Personal
Finance Corp.*, 176 Misc. 201, 26 N.Y.S. 2d 1012 (1941)).

12   Prior judicial interpretations of the same or quite similar
statutes in other jurisdictions. The materials discussed here
are of most relevance in cases arising in state supreme
courts. Not uncommonly a state legislature will adopt a
'mini' version of a *federal* statute. A prominent example is the
'little Norris-LaGuardia Act' regulating labour relations in
the private sector adopted by many states. Another related
example consists of the wholesale adoption by many state
legislatures of federal statutory language and concepts when
developing statutory frameworks for the regulation of
public sector labour relations on the state level. See, for
example, Wellington and Winter (1971); see also N.Y. Civil
Service Law s. 200 (McKinney, 1983); R. S. Summers (1976).
    Occasionally the United States Congress will adopt lan-
guage and concepts derived from state statutory schemes. A
prominent source of examples consists of federal criminal
statutes applicable only within federal jurisdiction. See also
Potomac Electric Power Co. v. *Director OWCP*, 449 U.S. 268,
275n. 13 (1980) ('The schedule adopted by Congress in the
LHWCA was substantially identical to the New York schedule of 1922').
    It is also very common for one American state legislature
to adopt a statute previously adopted in other American
states. For example, in the USA, the Commissioners on
Uniform State Laws have drafted Uniform and Model Acts.
These in turn have often been adopted in many states.
Courts regularly interpret uniform laws in the light of
interpretations that courts have already given those laws in
other states. See, for example, the discussions of such cases
in White and Summers (1988).
    In all of the foregoing types of legislative 'borrowings' it
is natural for courts of the borrowing jurisdiction to consider
and (frequently) to adopt interpretations already given by
courts to the statute or type of statute being borrowed. See,
especially, Sutherland (1985) ch. 52. An example is *Krystad*
v. *David Lau*, 65 Wash 2d. 827 (1965) in which the Washington State Supreme Court construed a state statute
modelled upon a federal statute to *add* a basic provision to
the state statute not found there, yet found in the federal
law. Many such borrowings occur in the American system in

the name of 'interpretation'. Of course such action is only partly interpretative.

13   Evidence of the essential nature of, or the normative character of, the form of life or other phenomena to which the statute applies. Courts *should* take into account the nature of, and the intrinsic demands of, the phenomena, such as a park, or the family, or a banking system, to which a statute applies. Here the arguments favouring one interpretation over another may be said to arise from or be generated by the extent to which the proposed interpretations respect the essential nature of, or normative character of, the phenomena or institution involved. In a sense, the 'nature' of such an institution then becomes a factor affecting interpretation. For example, a statute providing that 'No vehicles shall be taken into the park' should be interpreted in the light of the *kind of park* involved. If the park is for rest and relaxation, some vehicles (such as toy airplanes that run on petrol) would be excluded that would not be excluded if the park were an amusement park. This type of evidence is commonly considered relevant. For examples, see McKinney's *Consolidated Laws of New York, Statutes,* sections 341, 342, 343.

14   Opinions of law professors. In many fields of law, the opinions of law professors as to the proper interpretation of statutes are widely cited and even regarded as authoritative, especially in the absence of prior judicial interpretations. Numerous cases cite Wright (1983), R. Gorman (1976) and White and Summers (1988) — cited about 1 000 times by federal and state courts between July 1983 and July 1990.

3   Materials Courts May *Not* Consider

15   Testimony of a legislator in court as to the intent or purpose of a statute the legislator voted for. Post-enactment testimony of a legislator is either subjective testimony of personal motive or is objective testimony reiterating the discussion and events surrounding the enactment process. See *Rich* v. *State Board of Optometry,* 235 Cal.App.2d 591, 603 (1965). Testimony about personal motives is of no use in determining legislative intent. Each legislator has personal motives for supporting legislation and there is no guaranty that any view testified to is shared by anyone other than the testifying individual. In contrast, testimony reiterating the process has the facial appearance of a valuable source of

legislative history, but it is in actuality of negligible worth. The frailty of human memory, combined with a tendency for greater recollection of events and statements in support of one's own current position make such testimony highly suspect. See, for example, *Mohasco Co. v. Silver*, 447 U.S. 807, 823 n.42 (1980). See generally, 'Note, Statutory Interpretation in California: Individual Testimony as an Extrinsic Aid', *U.S.F. Law Review*, 15, p. 241 (1981).

16   Documentary 'substitutes' for authoritative legislative history. Where the state legislature of the state involved has no official legislative history, courts generally may not consult letters, memoranda, diaries, books, newspapers, or any other such material when interpreting a statute, at least in so far as such material purports to report the actual legislative history of the statute.

See also 'Materials Courts Must Consider', item 6, above.

VI   RESOLUTION OF CONFLICTS BETWEEN ARGUMENTS

In Section III, I set forth the main types of arguments encountered in statutory interpretation cases in the US Supreme Court. Frequently, two or more of these arguments will be in conflict. But it is possible to imagine an idealized case in which that is not so. Thus, in the best possible overall justification for an interpretation, all significant types of arguments would converge to support only that *one* interpretation. For example, a 'no vehicles in the park' statute would clearly be interpreted to prohibit a sports car being driven at high speed through the park on a leisure outing. We might easily imagine that this interpretation could be supported (1) by the ordinary meaning of the word 'vehicle'; (2) by contextual harmonization analysis in light of related statutory materials; (3) by reference to applicable general principles of law; (4) by congruence with general authoritative policy in the area; (5) by the ultimate statutory purpose; (6) by extrinsic evidence from legislative history showing specific intent of the legislature to rule out sports cars; (7) by substantive reasons favouring this result; (8) by prior interpretational precedent; (9) by prior official administrative interpretations; (10) by prior general 'citizen' interpretations; (11) by reference to rule of law values; (12) by the essential character of this type of park; (13) by reference to legislative acquiescence in prior such interpretations; (14) by professional writings, and more.

But it is rare that a case so clear ever arises for courts to decide. This is so largely because of three factors. First, seldom does any party have the incentive to litigate such clear cases. Second, in the cases that do arise, many of the above types of arguments are simply unavailable because the information, or social facts, or other ingredients required for the material content of such arguments is not available. Thus, for example, the language of the statute may be so unclear that no credible argument from ordinary meaning arises. Or, for example, the materials may be insufficient to generate an argument based on the ultimate legislative purpose of the statute. For one thing, the evidence of such purpose may be ambivalent. Other types of arguments may simply be unavailable. Thus there may be no prior judicial interpretations of the statute, or no prior administrative interpretation, and so on. Third, when the materials for a range of arguments are available, they often generate conflicting arguments.

Of course cases do arise in the Supreme Court in which there are no *major* arguments in conflict. In such cases one or two arguments robustly emerge on one side and any argument or arguments on the other side prove to be only of slight force, usually because they are only marginally available in the first place. In these cases it is not appropriate to characterize the court's mode of resolution as one in which the court resolves a conflict between arguments, for it cannot be said that there is a genuine or significant conflict in the first place. Examples of such cases are: *Perrin v. United States*, 444 U.S. 37 (1979) (ordinary meaning of term 'bribery' indisputable); *Rubin v. United States*, 449 U.S. 424 (1981); *Consumer Product Safety Commission v. GTE Sylvania, Inc.*, 447 U.S. 102 (1980) (no weight given to contention that disclosure under Freedom of Information Act not 'public disclosure'); *Potomac Electric Power Co. v. Director of Workers' Compensation Programs*, U.S. Dept. of Labor, 449 U.S. 268, 280 (1980) (respondent's arguments have 'insufficient force to overcome plain language of statute itself'). It is perhaps not surprising that the court was unanimous in three of these cases. In the fourth there was a single weak dissent.

But in the usual litigated interpretation case in the Supreme Court, significant competing arguments are available on each side. This leads us to a central problem in the subject of statutory interpretation: how does the court settle such conflicts? The resolution of such conflicts in the US Supreme Court is far from 'free'. In the Supreme Court there is now a lot of case-law on *how* statutes are to be interpreted. The Court regularly cites and purports to follow this case-law. This is not to say that the Supreme Court is always consistent. And, in a particular case, much scope for judgement may remain.

A fundamental distinction should be drawn between two types of statutes: (a) statutes which generate a sufficiently credible argument from ordinary meaning or technical meaning, and thus are not *so* silent, ambiguous, vague or general, or otherwise so unclear as to exclude any such arguments, and a conflict arises between such ordinary or technical meaning argument and one or more other types of arguments; and (b) statutes which are so silent, ambiguous, vague or general, or otherwise so unclear that they cannot generate a credible argument from ordinary or technical meaning, yet conflicts arise between the other types of arguments that are available.

No sharp line can be drawn between (a) and (b): 'Of course, there is no errorless test for identifying or recognizing plain or unambiguous language' (*United States* v. *Turkette*, 452 U.S. 576, 580 (1981)). And whether there is a credible argument from ordinary or technical meaning may itself be sharply contested. See, for example, *Bankamerica Corp.* v. *United States*, 462 U.S. 122 (1983). Sometimes the language of a section unambiguous on its face may be shown to be ambiguous or otherwise unclear by reference to materials of legislative history.

But the major importance of the foregoing distinction is this: the arguments from ordinary and from technical meaning are far more frequently available than any other types of argument. Moreover, when the statute generates one or the other of these arguments, and it has its *normal force*, it will be decisive more frequently than any competing type of argument. (These facts can be readily explained.)

Of course, sometimes arguments from ordinary or technical meaning will lack normal force, that is, they will not really be available, or sufficiently so, and for this reason not be decisive. Various factors may diminish or impair the normal force of such arguments, including the inapplicability of linguistic conventions as to meaning, and poor drafting.

Of course, sometimes the argument from a standard ordinary meaning arising from the language of the statutory section in issue comes into conflict with the argument from a standard technical meaning. If sufficient evidence of the technical meaning is shown, the effect of this will not be that it 'outweighs' the argument from ordinary meaning, but that it 'cancels' or 'nullifies' that meaning, that is, saps or deprives it even of its normal force. This may be called Cancellative Maxim No. 1. Such a technical meaning may be (a) an established industrial or trade meaning; (b) a meaning drawn from some particular branch of knowledge or technology; (c) a legal meaning for the word or words in issue; or (d) some other term of art. Cases on the cancellative effect of technical meaning include *La. Public Serv. Comm.* v. *F. C. C.*, 476 U.S. 355 (1986) ('charges' in the industry has a trade meaning which includes depreciation); *Bob Jones Univ.* v. *United States,* 461 U.S. 574 (1983) ('charitable' has a legal meaning such that it does not apply to a non-profit organization acting contrary to public policy).

The decisiveness of the argument from a standard technical meaning in such cases can be readily explained. When the argument is truly made out, any contrary argument from a standard ordinary meaning of the words in issue loses its force, that is, it is cancelled, for the legislature in fact expressed itself in terms of a technical rather than an ordinary meaning of the words in question. The ultimate value served here, then, is legislative supremacy.

In addition to the cancelling effect of the technical meaning argument, the argument from contextual harmonization in support of a *special* meaning may also cancel or nullify a standard ordinary meaning otherwise determinative. This may be called Cancellative Maxim No. 2. It will be recalled that the argument from contextual harmonization arises from the rest of the statutory section involved, or the statutory scheme as a whole, or closely related statutes. Such an argument may, of course, show that a technical meaning controls. But here I stress that such an argument may show that a special meaning of an ordinary word or words controls, not a standard ordinary meaning. Again this mode of conflict resolution is not a matter of weighing and balancing, but of cancellation. Cases in which this mode of resolution is recognized, explicitly or implicitly, include: *Watt* v. *Alaska,* 451 U.S. 259, 266 (1981) ('Congress did not intend words of common meaning to have their literal effect'); *Massachusetts* v. *Morash,* 109 S.Ct. 1668, 1673 (1989) ('vacation benefits' has special meaning); *Mountain States Tel. & Tel.* v. *Pueblo of Santa Ana,* 472 U.S. 237, 249–50 (1985) (ordinary meaning not true meaning because this would render an additional portion of the statute meaningless).

Again the cancelling effect of such contextual harmonization arguments can be explained on the basis that, when applicable they show that the legislature was not really using the words in the ordinary way. Thus legislative supremacy and democratic values are served.

1   Statutes Generating a Sufficiently Credible Argument from Ordinary or Technical Meaning

By a sufficiently 'credible' argument from ordinary meaning, I mean an argument in which the ordinary meaning or technical meaning has normal force, as explained above, and in the circumstances is 'reasonably plain', as the Supreme Court has put it. (See *Griffin* v. *Oceanic Contractors, Inc.,* 458 U.S. 564, 570 (1982).) If there are two closely competing ordinary meaning arguments, then neither is alone reasonably plain and neither has normal force. The same is true of competing technical meanings.

We have already seen how the Supreme Court generally resolves any conflicts between the ordinary meaning argument and the technical or special meaning argument. I now turn mainly to the resolution of conflicts between the ordinary meaning argument and other arguments that are *not* resolved *either* by showing that the ordinary meaning argument is, on closer analysis unavailable, that is, lacks normal force, *or* by showing that the ordinary meaning argument is displaced, that is, cancelled by a showing that a technical meaning controls, or a special meaning in light of contextual harmonization or the like governs. Rather, here the general tendency is for the court to settle the conflicts in accord with what I will call general maxims of priority.

1.1   *Priority Maxim One*

In criminal cases, when a sufficiently credible argument from a standard ordinary meaning of ordinary words favours a defendant, it will usually override any competing arguments. See, for example, *Dowling* v. *United States*, 473 U.S. 207, 213–214 (1985) (ordinary meaning of 'stolen, converted, or taken by fraud' is limited to physical property and does not include copyright infringement).

1.2   *Priority Maxim Two*

In civil (non-criminal) cases, a credible argument from a standard ordinary meaning of ordinary words generally prevails over all other competing arguments (other than, as seen above, the arguments from technical meaning and from contextual harmonization supporting a special meaning) except the argument from very *clear indicia or evidence*, deriving from materials of legislative history, showing an intention (or purpose) to the contrary. See 'Priority Maxim Three' below. Priority Maxim Two, as thus qualified, is generally applied today even though two or more *other* types of argument to the contrary are available, including, for example, the general argument from more effective implementation of an authoritative public policy in the field involved, the argument from deference to an official agency interpretation, the argument from statutory analogy, the argument from a general legal principle, the argument from the substantive reasons favouring the substantively best result, the argument from recognized canons of construction, and more.

Support for Priority Maxim Two, as qualified above, is to be found in many cases. See, for example, *Griffin* v. *Oceanic Contractors, Inc.*, 458 U.S. 564, 570 (1982) (language 'shall pay . . . for each and every day' leaves the Court no room for discretion in assessing penalties); *TVA* v. *Hill*, 437 U.S. 153, 173 (1978) (statute plainly bans agency actions which 'jeopardize the continued existence' of, or 'result in the destruction or modification of habitat' of an endangered species); *United States* v. *Locke*, 471 U.S. 84, 93 (1985) (language 'prior to December 31' cannot be read as 'on or before December 31'); *Commissioner of Internal Revenue* v. *Asphalt Products Co., Inc.*, 482 U.S. 117, 120 (1987) (statutory language 'the underpayment' imposes a penalty on the entire underpayment not just portion due to negligence).

As the foregoing qualification on 'Priority Maxim Two' indicates, however, very clear legislative intention or purpose to the contrary may defeat the argument from ordinary meaning. I take this up in 'Priority Maxim 3', below. Beyond this, there are also several *exceptional situations* in which a credible argument from a standard ordinary meaning may not govern. I will now take up these exceptions.

First, the ordinary meaning will not govern if it produces a 'manifestly absurd or unjust result'. This is an extremely narrow exception, and the Supreme Court has seldom applied it within the last ten years. A case which applies the exception is *Jackson* v. *Lykes Brothers Steamship Co.*, 386 U.S. 731 (1967) (literal reading of statute unjust as it would call for smaller recovery when plaintiff is employed by shipowner than when employed by third party operating ship). See also *Green* v. *Bock Laundary*, 109 S.Ct. 1981 (1989) (literal reading of 'defendant' absurdly treats civil plaintiffs and defendants differently). The applicability of the exception (or something quite like it) has been urged upon the court without success in a number of recent cases. See, for example, *Griffin* v. *Oceanic Contractors, Inc.*, 458 U.S. 564, 570 (1982); *TVA* v. *Hill*, 437 U.S. 153, 173 (1978); *Potomac Electric Power Co.* v. *Director, Office of Workers' Compensation Programs, U.S. Dept. of Labor*, 449 U.S. 268 (1980).

Second, generally authoritative and widely accepted principles or policies are presumed, unless rebutted, to remain in force and thus cut down facially overgeneral or unqualified ordinary meaning. See *National Railroad Passenger Corp.* v. *Atchison, Topeka Co.*, 470 U.S. 451 (1985) (presumption against construing legislation to create contractual rights against government), and the now famous 'Dworkin' case: *Riggs* v. *Palmer*, 115 N.Y. 506, 22 N.E. 188 (1889) (presumption that wrongdoer shall not be allowed to benefit from own wrong).

Third, and similarly, where the implementing language of a

statute is overgeneral in relation to its ultimate purpose, and there is strong evidence of this more restricted ultimate purpose, the court will usually cut the ordinary meaning of the implementing language back consonant with the purpose. See, for example, *United States* v. *Kirby*, 74 U.S. (Wall) 482 (1868) (language restricted so as not to exempt mail carriers from arrest on felony charges); *Church of the Holy Trinity* v. *United States*, 143 U.S. 457 (1892) (purpose of broadly-worded statute did not include restricting immigration of church pastors); *United States* v. *American Trucking Associations*, 310 U.S. 534 (1940) (statute limited in accordance with legislative purpose that ICC's power to regulate working hours was to extend only over workers who affect safety). The facts of this exception arise only in 'rare and exceptional circumstances'. *Crooks* v. *Harrelson*, 282 U.S. 55, 60 (1930). See also *Howe* v. *Smith*, 452 U.S. 473, 483 (1981) and *Rubin* v. *United States*, 449 U.S. 424, 430 (1981).

Fourth, in certain legislation dealing with matters of racial or sexual discrimination, the argument from ordinary meaning may be overridden. (This is a very difficult exception to formulate.) See, for example, *United Steel Workers of America* v. *Weber*, 443 U.S. 193 (1979); *Co. of Washington* v. *Gunther*, 452 U.S. 161, 184–88 (1981); *Bob Jones University* v. *U.S.*, 461 U.S. 574, 586 (1983); *North Haven Bd. of Ed.* v. *Bell*, 456 U.S. 512, 541–42 (1982).

Fifth, very occasionally a strong argument from statutory obsolescence will take priority over ordinary meaning. See, for example, *Cabell* v. *Markham*, 148 F.2d 737, aff'd 326 U.S. 404 (1945) (statute of limitation provisions of Trading With Enemy Acts is specific to WWI and obsolete with regard to WWII).

As can be seen, most of the foregoing exceptions are seldom in play, and none except the fourth is very wide. As a result, the exceptions do not cut down the original basic priorital proposition as to the primacy of ordinary meaning as much as might appear from their mere enumeration. We can see that the argument from a credible ordinary meaning is very powerful. Indeed it is generally the most decisive type of argument.

Why is this so? The materials for its construction are always to some extent available, and are frequently available when other arguments are not. It is also commonly decisive when in conflict with other arguments. What are the general rationales or values behind this high decisiveness? First, the argument usually serves legislative supremacy and democratic values. It is the text of the statute that the elected legislature adopts. See, for example, *U.S.* v. *Locke*, 471 U.S. 84, 95 (1985) ('Congressmen typically vote on the language of a bill'). The legislature can be assumed to know and understand the English language and the ordinary usage of English words. Indeed the legislature necessarily relies on such linguistic conventions. Moreover the very words of the statute and their ordinary meanings in English are not merely linguistic phenomena, but usually also authoritatively convey the intent and purpose of the sovereign legislature. The Supreme Court has regularly stressed that 'Congress . . . is assumed to have intended what it enacted': *U.S. R.R. Retirement Board* v. *Fritz*, 449 U.S. 166, 179 (1980). The Court has also said, 'There is, of course, no more persuasive evidence of the purpose of a statute than the words by which the legislature undertook to give expression to its wishes. Often these words are sufficient in and of themselves to determine the purpose of the legislation' (*U.S.* v. *American Trucking Assn's.*, 310 U.S. 534, 543 (1940)).

Second, the argument from ordinary usage of the words in issue is regularly reinforced by the contextual harmonization argument, thereby vastly strengthening the immediately preceding point. See, for example, *Bankamerica Corp.* v. *United States*, 462 U.S. 122, 128–30 (1983) (non-ordinary usage of phrase 'other than Banks' would be incongruous with contextual meaning from surrounding text).

Third, when the Court follows the dictates of the argument from ordinary usage of the statutory words, the Court avoids the necessity of making its own legislative judgements about the reasonableness of ultimate purposes and about the suitability of means. See, for example, *TVA* v. *Hill*, 437 U.S. 153, 187 (1978) (by following ordinary language the Court avoids a utility-based choice between huge public monetary loss and preservation of endangered species).

Fourth, the Court's emphasis on ordinary usage restricts the scope for judges and administrators to substitute their own personal political views as to what the law should be in place of the legislature's view. See, for example, *C.I.R.* v. *Asphalt Products Co., Inc.*, 482 U.S. 117, 121 (1987). For examples of such substitution, see *United Steel Workers* v. *Weber*, 443 U.S. 193 (1979), and *Sullivan* v. *Hudson*, 109 S.Ct. 2248 (1989). Both cases evoked strong dissents on this ground.

Fifth, the Court's stress on ordinary usage encourages the legislature to legislate explicitly and carefully and thus discourages hidden legislation which could not gain assent if more explicit language had been used. *U.S.* v. *Taylor*, 108 S.Ct. 2413, 2424 (1988).

Sixth, the Court's resort to the ordinary usage of the statutory words confines the statute to that formulation which the legislature and the executive are most likely to have agreed upon at the time of enactment, in contradistinction to materials of legislative history and the like, which most members of the legislature never see, and which the executive does not sign into law. See, for example, *U.S. v. Taylor*, 108 S.Ct. 2413, 2424 (1988) and *Wallace v. Christensen*, 802 F.2D 1539, 1559–60 (9th Cir. 1986).

Seventh, in invoking the ordinary meaning of the statutory words, the Court protects the interests of those who relied on such meanings and does not, after the fact, spring on them legislative history or other material supporting a contrary meaning. See, e.g., *BankAmerica Corp. v. U.S.*, 462 U.S. 122, 131–33 (1983). The Court also enables citizens to save additional costs of legal advice required if lawyers must track down legislative history in advance. These points have special force where the legislative history or other material is not reasonably available to relying parties.

Eighth, judicial emphasis on the ordinary meaning of the statutory words encourages careful legislative drafting. Among other things, the drafter will know that, if there is to be any departure from ordinary word meanings, this should be made clear in the final draft of the statute. See, for example, *Watt v. Alaska*, 451 U.S. 259, 285–86, 101 St.Ct. 1673, 1687 (1981) (where a literal reading of the statute would have, by implication, repealed an earlier statute).

At this juncture it is appropriate to remind the reader that the technical meaning argument cancels the ordinary meaning argument, and is second only to the ordinary meaning argument in overall decisiveness. It is only because the technical meaning argument is rather less often in play than the ordinary meaning argument that it is not here ranked as most decisive. How are we to explain the very high decisiveness of the technical meaning argument when it is in play? The answer is that nearly all eight of the foregoing rationales for the high decisiveness of the argument from ordinary meaning also apply, *mutatis mutandis*, to the argument from technical meaning. Several of these arguments similarly apply, *mutatis mutandis*, to a third type of argument of high decisiveness when in play, that is, the argument from contextual harmonization.)

1.3   Priority Maxim Three

Very clear indicia or evidence from legislative history, of legislative intent (which may include legislative purpose) that is contrary to a credible argument from ordinary meaning will *sometimes* take priority over such ordinary meaning. See, for example, *Public Citizen v. U.S. Dept. of Justice*, 109 S.Ct. 2558 (1989) (ordinary meaning of 'utilize' would expand statute beyond intended purpose of legislature as found in legislative history. It is also

possible to cite here some of the cases supporting the proposition
that, where the implementive language of a statute is *overgeneral* in
relation to its intended purpose, and there is very strong indicia or
evidence of this more restrictive purpose, the court will cut the
implementing language back consonant with the intended purpose
(see p. 435–6).

But 'Priority Maxim Three' favouring very strong evidence in
legislative history of legislative intent or purpose over credible
ordinary meaning to the contrary is a maxim the Court more often
states or quotes than applies. Indeed, in recent years the Court has
seldom allowed such evidence deriveing merely from legislative
history to override a credible ordinary meaning argument. The
Court has said: 'General statements of overall purpose contained in
legislative reports cannot defeat the specific and clear wording of
the statute: *St. Martin Evangelical Lutheran Church* v. *South Dakota,*
451 U.S. 772, 786 n.19 (1981) (statement in legislative history that
tax statute covers all wage earners did not override explicit
exemption). See also *U.S.* v. *Ron Pair Enterprises,* 109 S.Ct. 1026,
1031 (1989) (plain meaning 'conclusive except in rare cases'), and
Rubin v. *U.S.,* 449 U.S. 424, 430 (1980).

The Court also regularly finds legislative history of intent or
purpose not 'clear enough' to override ordinary meaning. See, for
example, *Regan* v. *Wald,* 468 U.S. 222, 228–29 (1984) (legislative
history not clear enough to support severe restriction of Executive
Power under International Emergency Economic Powers Act). See
also *U.S.* v. *Ron Pair Enterprises, Inc.,* 109 S.Ct. 1026 (1989), and
Hallstrom v. *Tillamook County,* 110 S.Ct. 304 (1989).

Moreover, in a large number of recent cases, the Court has
declined to give serious consideration to arguments from legislative intent or purpose based on legislative history. See, for example, *Public Employees Retirement System of Ohio* v. *Betts,* 109 S.Ct.
2854, 2863–64 (1989); *Mackey* v. *Lanier Collection Agency and Serv.,*
486 U.S. 825, 840 (1988).

Further, where the implementing words of the statute are
undergeneral in relation to the allegedly intended ultimate purpose
of the legislature as found in legislative history (or on the face of
the statute), the Court is today not generally disposed to extend
the statute contrary to its ordinary meaning. Quotations from two
cases aptly express the rationale for this:

> But no legislature pursues its purposes at all costs. Deciding what
> competing values will or will not be sacrificed to the achievement of a
> particular objective is the very essence of legislative choice – and it
> frustrates rather than effectuates legislative intent simplistically to
> assume that whatever furthers the statute's primary objective must be

the law. (*Rodriguez* v. *United States*, 107 S.Ct. 1391, 1393 (1987)

Application of 'broad purposes' of legislation at the expense of specific provisions ignores the complexity of problems Congress is called upon to address and the dynamics of legislative action. Congress may be unanimous in its intent to stamp out some vague social or economic evil; however, because its members may differ sharply on the means for effectuating that intent, the final language of the legislation may reflect hard fought compromises. Invocation of the 'plain purpose' of the legislation at the expense of the terms of the statute itself takes no account of the process of compromise, and, in the end, prevents the effectuation of Congressional intent. (*Board of Governors of Ed. Reserve* v. *Dimension Fin. Corp.*, 106 S.Ct. 681 (1986)).

See also *Patterson* v. *McLean Credit Union*, 109 S.Ct. 2363 (1989) and *Amoco Production Co.* v. *Village of Gambell, Alaska*, 480 U.S. 531 (1987). To spell all this out with a concrete example, a 'no vehicles in the park' statute with an ultimate purpose of park quiet and safety still does not in terms ('vehicle') apply to raucous rock bands in the park. It certainly cannot be assumed that the legislature simply lacked foresight as to the cause of noise, or made a mistake. Moreover there are, as the above quotations indicate, good reasons why a legislature may fail to implement an ultimate purpose fully. This might unduly encroach on other ends (for example, the desires of those who like rock music). The need to have certain and administrable rules may also call for a bright line short of full implementation. The goal of cost minimization may further explain why a statute does not implement fully its ultimate purpose.

It must be acknowledged that there is the occasional Supreme Court case where a credible ordinary meaning is displaced or overridden by a special meaning supported by the argument from purpose as found in legislative history or on the face of the statute. Such cases are, for the most part, cases in which the implementive language of the statute is overgeneral in relation to purpose, and the Court cuts down the scope of the statute. See the cases cited at pp. 435–6.

1.4   *Priority Maxim Four*

Where a credible argument from ordinary meaning (or technical meaning for that matter) is significantly reinforced by the argument from contextual harmonization (that is, from coherence with the wording of the rest of the statute or closely related statutes), these two arguments combined almost always overrride even very clear evidence of contrary legislative intent (or purpose) found in legislative history.

I have found no Supreme Court case in recent years contrary to this maxim. Numerous cases appear to support the maxim. See, for example, *C.I.R.* v. *Asphalt Products Co., Inc.,* 482 U.S. 117 (1990). An articulate Court of Appeals case is *In re Sinclair,* 870 F.2d 1340 (7th Cir. 1989).

2 Statutes so Silent, Ambiguous, Vague or General, or Otherwise so Unclear that they Cannot Generate Ordinary or Technical Meaning Arguments that are Dispositive

Where the statute is criminal and is ambiguous or vague, the Court will usually try to give it a narrow meaning (if it does not invalidate it.) See, for example, *Williams* v. *United States,* 458 U.S. 279, 290 (1982) (court refuses to read statute prohibiting the overvaluing of securities as broad enough to cover the writing of bad cheques) and *Crandon* v. *U.S.,* 110 S.Ct. 997 (1990). Where the statute is criminal, and is silent about 'mens rea', the Court will usually read in such a requirement. See, for example, *Morrisette* v. *U.S.,* 342 U.S. 246 (1952).

I turn now to civil statutes. The main types of arguments most prominent in the decision of cases under unclear statutes generating no sufficiently credible ordinary or technical meaning arguments will now be set forth, roughly in the order of their relative importance. It must be borne in mind that such arguments must still support what is at least a plausible meaning of the imperfect statutory language. Frequently these arguments conflict, and the Court adopts that interpretation supported by the arguments on one side having superior weight.

2.1 *The Argument from Contextual Harmonization*

Where the words in issue are themselves ambiguous or otherwise unclear, the Court may adopt that meaning which best harmonizes the various parts of the statute or the statute and related statutes into a coherent scheme. See, for example, *Pauelic and Le Florc* v. *Marvel Entertainment Group,* 110 S.Ct. 456 (1989). *C.I.R.* v. *Engle,* 464 U.S. 206, 217 (1984); *United Savs. Ass'n. of Texas* v. *Timbers of Inwood Forest Assocs.,* 484 U.S. 365, 371 (1988).

2.2 *The Argument from Implementation of the Intended Ultimate Purpose*

The Court accepts the 'principle' of statutory construction that an ambiguous statute should be interpreted in light of the statutory purpose: *Mills Music, Inc.* v. *Snyder,* 469 U.S. 153, 185 (1985). See also *C.I.R.,* v. *Engle,* 464 U.S. 206, 217 (1984) (where there are different possible interpretations, 'our duty is to find that interpretation which can most fairly be said to be imbedded in the statute, in the sense of being most harmonious with its scheme and with the general purposes that Congress manifested'). See also *Sony Corp.* v. *Universal City Studios, Inc.*, 464 U.S. 417, 431–32 (1984); *First Nat'l Maintenance Corp.* v. *N.L.R.B.*, 452 U.S. 666 (1981); *United States* v. *Bacto-Unidisk*, 394 U.S. 784, 799 (1969). Where the statute is vague, the argument from ultimate purpose may receive special emphasis in resolving the borderline case. See, for example, *N. Haven Bd. of Education* v. *Bell*, 456 U.S. 512, 521 (1981).

2.3   The Argument from Evidence of Legislative Intention Manifest in Legislative History

The Court utilizes various forms of legislative history to guide it with respect to the meaning attributable to an unclear statute. See, for example, *Green* v. *Bock Laundry Mach. Co.*, 109 S.Ct. 1981 (1989) (likely drafting error); *Bowsher* v. *Merck & Co.*, 460 U.S. 824 (1983) and *First Nat'l. Maint. Corp.* v. *N.L.R.B.*, 452 U.S. 666 (1981).

2.4   The Argument from Prior Judicial or Administrative Interpretation Plus Legislative Acquiescence

A prior court or an administrative agency may have assigned a meaning to an unclear or very general or vague statute, with the legislature thereafter clearly acquiescing in this interpretation. Any such combination is, of course, a very powerful argument, one with established standing in the Supreme Court. See, for example, *Bob Jones Univ.* v. *United States*, 461 U.S. 574 (1983). Compare *Motor Vehicle Mfrs. Ass'n.* v. *State Farm Mut.*, 463 U.S. 29 (1983).

2.5   The Argument from Prior Judicial or Administrative Interpretation Alone

In many cases, the Supreme Court defers to an agency interpretation of an ambiguous, general or vague statute. See, for example, *Chevron, U.S.A. Inc.* v. *Natural Resources Defense Council*, 467 U.S. 837, 843 (1984); *E.E.O.C.* v. *Commercial Office Products, Co.*, 486 U.S. 107 (1988); *K Mart Corp.* v. *Cartier, Inc.*, 486 U.S. 281 (1988); *Dept. of Treasury I.R.S.* v. *Federal Labor Relations Authority*, 110 S. Ct. 1623 (1990).

2.6   The Argument from the Substantially Best or Fairest Result or Policy

Sometimes the Court will focus frontally on what would be the best or fairest result or policy. See, for example, *Aaron* v. *S.E.C.*,

446 U.S. 680, 701 (1980).

2.7 *The Argument from Recognized Legal Authorities such as Law Professors*

The US Supreme Court often cites the writings of law professors on issues of interpretation, especially where the statute is ambiguous, vague or otherwise unclear.

Of course, when the statute is ambiguous or otherwise unclear on its face, and the problem at hand was unforeseen, some types of arguments will not, in the nature of things, be available. In these circumstances, for example, no instances of intended application can appear in legislative history.

Concluding Caveat

This account of conflicts between arguments and their mode of resolution does not purport to cover all possible conflicts. It addresses several basic conflicts, and provides a framework for analysis of those not considered.

VII   THE CONFLICT OF STATUTES WITH OTHER NORMS

I will only briefly discuss these questions in terms of four different types of conflicts.

1   Statute in Conflict with Constitution

In the American system there is a flat rule of hierarchical priority that the constitution prevails over a conflicting statute. However the Supreme Court generally attempts to interpret the statute when it can so that it does not conflict with the Constitution. This is done partly on the theory that the legislature did not intend an invalid statute. It is also done partly on the theory that it is wise to avoid deciding constitutional issues if it is possible to resolve a matter merely on the basis of a statutory interpretation. Frequently, when the potential conflict is between a substantive content-oriented constitutional standard on the one hand, and a statute on the other, the only way the statute can escape invalidation is by interpreting it to include the required substantive content, or to be free of whatever substantive content is proscribed. The Supreme Court and lower courts, when given the opportunity, may from time to time thus enhance the actual substantive quality of a statute by 'interpreting' it to include constitutionally non-offensive content. See, for example, *Ellis* v. *Brotherhood Ry. et al.*, 466 U.S. 435 (1984). It follows that in the American system the rule of hierarchical priority of constitution over statute is not applied in a wholly formal way but is applied to some extent in substantive fashion.

Once part of a statute has been declared unconstitutional, a gap in the statute may have to be filled before it can be operational. A court may be called upon to fill this gap. See, for example, Ginsburg, 'Judicial Authority to Repair Unconstitutional Legislation', *Cleveland St. Law Review*, 28, 301 (1979).

2   Statute in Conflict with Statute

The so-called supremacy clause of the US Constitution has been interpreted to mean that a state statute in conflict with a federal statute is invalid. See the Supreme Court decision in *McDermott* v. *Wisconsin*, 228 U.S. 115, 132 (1913). But a state statute need not be on its face contradictory to a federal statute to be in actual conflict therewith and so invalid. The court may *interpret* the state statute to be in substance or spirit in conflict and so invalid. See, for example, *Hines* v. *Davidowitz*, 312 U.S. 52, 67 (1941). It therefore follows that this, too, is not merely a formal or mechanical approach to the application of a rule of hierarchical priority.

What if two statutes of the same federal or state legislature conflict? There are several rules here. Probably the most wide-ranging rule is that the subsequent statute repeals an inconsistent earlier statute. But again this rule of priority is frequently not applied in a formal or mechanical fashion. The Court applies a presumption against 'implied' repeal and strives somehow to reconcile the conflicting statute. See, for example, *TVA* v. *Hill*, 437 U.S. 153 (1978).

3   Statute in Conflict with Administrative Regulation

Here, of course, the statute controls over contrary regulation. But a court must decide this question, and the court may first interpret the statute and decide that the regulation either is or is not invalid. Thus, again, it would be misleading to say that a hierarchical rule of priority is applied in a purely formal fashion. See generally, Davis (1978) sec. 17.13 at 62–63 and 17.14 at 68–69.

4   Statute in Conflict with Common Law

Again there is a rule of hierarchical priority. The statute controls. But it must usually be interpreted in order to determine *how far* it controls (see Dickerson, 1975, pp. 206–8. This process of interpretation may also raise a question analogous to a gap-filling question. See section V above.

VIII   'PRESUMPTIONS'

I have chosen to identify and discuss two examples of such presumptions (or 'background' principles) in Section III at item 8. There I have conceptualized them as arguments from general principles. Also, in section III at item 11, I have identified a number of presumptions of legislative intent. These presumptions apply both to interpretation and to gap-filling.

IX   THE STYLE OF STATUTORY INTERPRETATION

There is, by convention, a minimal essential content of the usual written opinion of the highest federal and state courts. The opinion must set forth a statement of facts, the issue or issues, the resolution of those issues, reasons for the resolution, and a procedural order. The opinion may be quite lengthy, and will usually report the facts of the case rather fully. The opinion usually sets forth the statute in question and explicitly defines the issue in statutory terms.

The opinion is usually rather elaborate in its reasoning and seeks to supply the justificatory steps between the general statutory language and resolution of the concrete issue in relation to the facts. The opinion usually includes references to the statute or other law to support major steps in the reasoning. In sum, the opinion is rather self-contained, and experts can judge its legal correctness without recourse to further documents or materials and from any applicable law missed by the court and parties.

The opinion is usually divided up in the order indicated in my opening paragraph, above. The general justificatory model is not a deductive or subsumptive one. Rather, the key conflicting arguments are set forth, the values behind them are frequently explored to some extent (see section VI above) and prior case authorities may be cited for various rough maxims of priority between the competing arguments. Also factors bearing on the particular force or weight of these arguments are discussed, and a choice made, either in accord with any cancellative effects, or any rough rule of priority, or any particular weightings as appropriate. Sometimes, in regard to a given argument type, a kind of burden of persuasion is imposed on one party to the case. For example, it now seems safe to generalize that the Supreme Court imposes a relatively heavy burden of persuasion on the party who claims that legislative history demonstrates an actual legislative intent or purpose requiring a result different from that otherwise required by the ordinary meaning of the statute. See p. 439.

The opinion will frequently contain some purely substantive reasoning. That is, the court may explicitly analyse and discuss the bearing not only of the general substantive values or rationales behind each main type of argument and the substantive policies and principles informing the content of the statute itself, but also invoke independent substantive reasons of principle and policy favouring the result. Thus one frequently finds, particularly in Supreme Court opinions, various rightness reasons and goal reasons that the Court believes support the interpretation adopted. Sometimes the Court will also link these reasons somehow to the statute so that they can be viewed as having, in at least some degree, the authority of the legislature behind them.

Many opinions are dialogic in character, with the Court answering arguments of dissenting judges, opposing counsel, lower court judges and so on (though not necessarily by name).

On one level, the Supreme Court practice is inconsistent with a one-right-answer ideology. Dissenting opinions are common. In the US Supreme Court they are the rule rather than the exception. Indeed, sometimes there will be as many as five or six opinions in the same case. This may pose problems for lawyers and citizens in deciding what the law is. Dissents are sometimes quite vigorous and occasionally reveal some anger.

The opinions are signed, published and generally accessible to lawyers. A limited number of copies are distributed immediately upon the rendering of a decision to interested people waiting at the Supreme Court. The opinions are also distributed to computer database services, who make the opinions available within 24 hours. Unofficial services have printed opinions in loose-leaf form within one to two weeks, but official versions are often not available for many months or even years.

In substantive terms, the Court's audiences vary greatly depending on the nature of the issue and the author of the opinion. An opinion about the scope of a criminal statute may be more or less addressed to police chiefs. An opinion about a regulatory statute may be addressed primarily to the agency charged with its administration. An opinion about a tax statute may be addressed mainly to the Internal Revenue Service. An opinion about a statute dealing with employment discrimination may be addressed mainly to employers. And so on. I do not mean by this that the addressees, above, will be formally identified as such. I mean only that the opinion may so read, in substance. Of course, some opinions will, in effect, be addressed to the Congress or a state legislature. Many opinions are also written with an eye to the legal profession advising the general public, too.

The general functions of the opinion are the obvious ones: to report the result to the parties, the profession and the public, to make the result available to the legislature that enacted the statute, to show how the result is grounded in law and, perhaps, to show how substantive reasoning supports the results. Sometimes the court may be especially concerned to justify its own role as interpreter in a controversial case, so as to legitimate that role.

X   INTERPRETATION IN THE LIGHT OF THE CHARACTER OF THE STATUTE

The character of the statute certainly affects the way the Supreme Court interprets it or fills gaps in it. The nature of the substantive law field involved can make a difference in various ways. The field may affect the type of argument that is acceptable. For example, the analogical extension of criminal statutes to interpret or to fill gaps is not permitted. This is usually said to be an aspect of the doctrine 'nulla poena sine lege'. See *U.S.* v. *Wiltberger*, 18 U.S. (5 Wheat.) 76 (1820). However a statute may be narrowed to favour a criminal defendant, as where the court reads into a statute a 'mens rea' requirement. See, for example, *U.S.* v. *Morissette*, 342 U.S. 246 (1952).

The nature of the substantive law field may be one in which broad or open-ended drafting is appropriate. Such drafting invites resort to the substantive arguments that have status in the field. Family law statutes, labour law statutes and certain regulatory statutes are examples. See, for example, *N.L.R.B.* v. *Curtin Matheson Scientific, Inc.*, 110 S.Ct. 1542 (1990) (goal-oriented policy arguments adopted in deciding employer's duty to bargain under NLRA).

The nature of the substantive law field may, on the other hand, be one where very precise and detailed drafting is appropriate. Here arguments arising from technical and special meanings of words are more prominent. This is true in such fields as tax law, social security law, and in some branches of regulatory law. A famous view about tax statutes is this:

> In the interpretation of statutes levying taxes it is the established rule not to extend their provisions, by implication, beyond the clear import of the language used, or to enlarge their operation so as to embrace matters not specifically pointed out. In case of doubt they are construed most strongly against the government, and in favor of the citizen. (*Gould* v. *Gould*, 245 U.S. 151 (1917))

The nature of the substantive law field may affect the interpretational approach in another way. Some statutes are not 'run' through the legislature in the ordinary way. Rather they represent compromises largely worked out by competing interests outside the legislature, compromises which the legislature thereafter more or less endorses. This may affect the very availability of arguments from legislative history as to intention and purpose, or at least affect the kinds of materials from which such arguments are constructed. See Litman, 'Copyright, Compromise and Legislative History', *Cornell Law Review*, 72, p. 857, 860–61 (1987) (statute drafted not by members of Congress or staff but by negotiation among authors, publishers and others).

The substantive law field also affects the rough general priority accorded to types of arguments. Thus, in the criminal law, the argument from the ordinary meaning of the statute generally has especially strong overriding force. See *U.S.* v. *Wiltberger*, 18 U.S. (5 Wheat.) 76 (1820) and *Winters* v. *New York*, 333 U.S. 507 (1948). In the tax field, arguments from technical meaning and arguments in support of special meaning arising from considerations of contextual harmonization have cancellative or overriding force. See Zelenak, 'Thinking About Nonliteral Interpretations of the Internal Revenue Code', *N.C. Law Review*, 64, p. 623 (1986). The same is true in regard to statutes in the field of property law, including security interests in personal property. The same is also true of commercial statutes regulating the rights of parties to negotiable instruments. See generally, White and Summers (1988).

Very few American statutes are addressed to private citizens. Usually it is expected that lawyers will interpret statutes. But regulations may be prepared under a statute by an agency, and these may purport to interpret the statute in terms meaningful to the laity. When this is so, the court will generally uphold the regulation if it is not contrary to the statute, especially where there is an argument that lay citizens have justifiably relied on the agency's interpretation. See, for example, *BankAmerica Corp.* v. *U.S.*, 462 U.S. 122, 132 (1983).

The age of a statute may affect its interpretation. A precisely worded statute may become obsolete and a court may, within limits, 'revise' it somewhat. Sometimes technology renders a statute somewhat obsolete, as where the wire transfer of funds rendered some of the Uniform Commercial Code on notes and cheques obsolete. Here the court may seek to 'revise' the statute a bit, or it may say the statute does not apply, and develop new law outside the statute. See, for example, *Delbrueck & Co.* v. *Mfrs. Hanover Trust Co.*, 609 F.2d 1047 (2nd Cir. 1979).

A statute that is open-textured may, over time, be filled out with judicial interpretations and then new developments may occur which require that the statute's open-textured concepts be reinterpreted. Many examples of judicial interpretation affected by the age of the statute appear in Calabresi (1982).

When a statute is relatively well drafted and is precise, this means that arguments from ordinary meaning or from contextual or technical meaning will be specially influential. But when the statute is poorly drafted, the courts will more often turn to arguments from legislative history, from general intention and purpose, from substantive reasons of policy and principle, and the like. See pp. 441–3.

XI　THE ROLE OF COURTS

The Supreme Court of the United States exercises *much* power to invalidate statutes as contrary to the federal constitution and, in the course of this, exercises much power to create constitutional case-law. The American Supreme Court has final authority in the federal system to interpret statutes. The Supreme Court exercises considerable power to fill gaps in statutes, expecially in public law fields. (See my answer in section V.) The Supreme Court has limited power to 'update' or otherwise revise statutes to keep them from becoming obsolete. This is especially true where technological change renders the precise language of a statute under- or over-inclusive. But there are other examples, too (see Calebresi, 1981).

The Supreme Court generally does not exercise power to make common law without specific constitutional or legislative authorization. But the state supreme courts do exercise much power to make common law. See Atiyah and Summers, (1987) ch. 5; *Kaiser Aluminum & Chemical Corp.* v. *Bonjorio,* 110 S.Ct. 1570, 1587 (1990) (SCALIA J. concurring).

The Supreme Court exercises *much* power to control law-making by administrative officials and agencies. This means the courts ultimately have a large collaborative role in making the law that administrative officials and agencies in the first instance have power to make. See Atiyah and Summers (1987) ch. 3.

In general, then, it may be said that the overall law-creating and law-declaring role of the Supreme Court (and of higher courts generally) in the American system is a very large one. This probably inclines the Supreme Court (and other higher courts) to invoke substantive reasoning more readily when interpreting statutes, and to take more 'liberties' with statutory language than seems true in some of the countries where the overall law-creating and law-declaring role of courts is much smaller or at least is said to be so.

XII   LEGAL NORMS ON INTERPRETATION

Constitutional Law

First, constitutional law in effect prescribes what can constitute a statute in the first place, thereby identifying and demarcating the very *subject-matter* that is to be interpreted. The federal and state constitutions in the USA in effect provide that statutes consist only of those laws duly adopted in accord with lawful power and appropriate procedures. (See Article 1, section 7 of the federal Constitution.)

Many state constitutions explicitly provide that 'no law may be enacted except by bill'. See, for example *Calif. Const'n.*, Art. IV, s. 8(b). See generally Sutherland, (1985) sec. 1.02; E. Crawford (1940) pp. 58–9. A number of important consequences follow from the foregoing proposition. The courts are not to interpret a statute in a fashion that the language of the statute will not bear (in the absence of a mistake or the like by the legislature). Moreover informal resolutions or 'open letters' to the public simply cannot qualify as statute law. Further, no matter how formal in nature, documents of legislative history cannot, in themselves, qualify as statute law. Although on some occasions courts have seemed to treat a document of legislative history as a kind of 'rival' to the duly adopted statutory text, this is not now common in the Supreme Court, and is widely acknowledged to be improper.

Second, constitutional law provides that, in matters of valid legislation, the legislature is supreme. That is, the legislature's meaning is supposed to control, not the substantive political views of the judiciary. This principle of legislative supremacy is expressly or implicitly embedded in the federal and state constitutions. See U.S. Const., Article I, sec. 1; see also Crawford, (1940) pp. 10–14 and Dickerson (1975) pp. 7–9. It follows that courts should not, in the guise of interpretation, substitute their own policy views for the views enacted by the legislature. Even more fundamentally, it follows also that the courts ought to see their own interpretational task *primarily as a cognitive rather than a creative one.* That is, when interpreting a statute, courts should seek so far as possible to ascertain as a matter of fact how the statute actually disposes of the issue that has arisen. This, of course, will require that the court engage in reasoning, but, in regard to the usual interpretational issue arising under the vast majority of statutes, this will not call for creative law-making. (In the case of gap-filling, there is obviously more scope for judicial creativity.) Of course the foregoing are constitutional norms and they are not always honoured. The Supreme Court of the United States decides some cases every year which are widely criticized for departing from the above norms. But it can no longer be said that the proportion of such cases is high.

Third, it of course remains true that the federal Constitution (and, as applicable, the state constitution) takes priority over *contrary* statutes. At the same time, the courts presume that the Congress intended to enact a valid statute. As a result, the courts will, so far as reasonably possible, try to interpret a statute (within limits) so that it does not conflict with the constitution. See Sutherland, sec. 45.11 (1985). See also my earlier discussion of this in section VII.

Statute Law

The Congress of the United States has not adopted a general statute prescribing modes of interpretation. However, many American states have adopted general statutes specifying how statutes of those states must be interpreted. See, for example, Model Statutory Construction Act (14 Uniform Laws Ann. 513) adopted in Colorado, Iowa and Wisconsin. Sections 13, 14, and 15 of this law provide:

s.13   *Intentions in the Enactment of Statutes*
In enacting a statute, it is presumed that
(1) compliance with constitutions of the state and of the United States is intended;
(2) the entire statute is intended to be effective;
(3) a just and reasonable result is intended;
(4) a result feasible of execution is intended; and
(5) public interest is favored over any private interest.

s.14   *Statutes Presumed Prospective*
A statute is presumed to be prospective in its operation unless expressly made retrospective.

s.15   *Aids in Construction of Ambiguous Statutes*
If a statute is ambiguous, the court, in determining the intention of the legislature, may consider among other matters:

(1) the object sought to be attained;
(2) the circumstances under which the statute was enacted;
(3) the legislative history;
(4) the common law or former statutory provisions, including laws upon the same or similar subjects;
(5) the consequences of a particular construction;
(6) the administrative construction of the statute; and
(7) the preamble.

For an authoritative general discussion of state statutes prescribing interpretational method, Dickerson (1975) ch. 14.

Many American statutes include statements of preferred general approaches to their own interpretation. For example, the Uniform Commercial Code in section 1-102(1) provides 'This Act shall be liberally construed and applied to promote its underlying purposes and policies.' Such purposes and policies are often further specified in subsequent Code sections.

Also some statutes incorporate specific canons of statutory interpretation. The extent to which a court takes these canons seriously varies and it is not possible to generalize usefully. One scholar once argued that almost all such specific norms have 'counter-norms' that point in the opposite direction. See Llewellyn, 'Remarks on the Theory of Appellate Decision and the Rules or Canons About How Statutes Are to be Construed', *Vand. Law Review*, **3**, p. 395 (1950). A former professor, now federal judge, Richard Posner, has recently taken a more sympathetic position with respect to certain of the specific canons of statutory interpretation. See Posner, 'Statutory Interpretation – in the Classroom and in the Courtroom', *University of Chicago Law Review*, 50, p. 800 (1983).

XIII   CONSTITUTIONAL LAW AND INTERPRETATION

In the American system, fundamental constitutional principles and values such as separation of powers, equal protection of the law, freedom of expression and the rule of law directly and indirectly influence courts to interpret particular statutes so that they do not conflict with such principles and values and are therefore not invalid. See my earlier discussion in section VII.

Some very general constitutional principles or values may be reflected in presumptions or background considerations, so that, unless rebutted, these principles or values are taken to qualify otherwise categorical statutory language (even though that language would probably be constitutional). See my earlier discussion of general principles in section III, above.

Although the federal and most state constitutions do not use the expression 'the rule of law', important aspects of the rule of law are nevertheless embodied in state and federal constitutions. Thus, for example, a statute must be reasonably available and 'knowable'. In particular, a criminal statute that is too vague will be invalid under the federal Constitution. See, for example, *Kolendar* v. *Lawson*, 461 U.S. 352 (1983) (statute requiring a loiterer to provide 'credible and reliable identification' too vague). As another example, courts must interpret at least criminal statutes in a fashion that is closely congruent with the statutory text. See *U.S.* v. *Wiltberger*, 18 U.S. (5 Wheat.) 76 (1820). A general legal *requirement* of interpretational congruence with the statutory text is widely recognized as a desideratum of the rule of law. See, for example, L. Fuller (1969) pp. 81–91.

XIV   SPECIAL SOCIAL VALUES AND INTERPRETATION

In the American system, legislative supremacy and democratic values are themselves constitutional in nature. The higher courts – and here I refer particularly to the US Supreme Court – do not characteristically appeal to any *one* single set of values when interpreting statutes or filling gaps. Instead there are different sets of values that may support different 'rough rules of priority' or 'weightings' as between conflicting types of arguments. For example, legislative supremacy resting on democratic and other principles justifies giving preference to a technical meaning of a statute over an ordinary meaning where appropriate. It is important to note that such sets of values supporting certain very general rules of priority or weightings may not be the same values that actually inform the content of the legislation itself. See section VI above.

XV   THE CHARACTER OF COURTS AND COURT PROCEDURE

The character of the US Supreme Court and other courts, and their procedures, affect the way the judges interpret statutes or fill gaps in them. Judges in the American system are not career civil servants and as a result do not have a bureaucratic mentality. They are selected by political and semi-political processes, and this generally leads them to be rather independent and, in a few cases, even rather bold. See Abraham (1985) pp. 24–28; H. Chase (1972). The Justices of the US Supreme Court and of all the federal courts are appointed by the President of the United States, U.S. Const., Art. II, s. 2, with the advice and consent of the Senate, and nominees are sometimes highly controversial and may not be confirmed by the US Senate. See R. Bork (1990). The nominees usually have had distinguished careers in legal practice (or in academic law) or in public service, or as judges in a lower court. The prestige of Supreme Court justices is probably higher than that of all American office holders, except perhaps the President of the USA.

Although the justices of the US Supreme Court, the federal court of appeals judges and the federal trial court judges are all appointed by the President with the advice and consent of the Senate, the judges of the state supreme courts are selected in a variety of ways. Some are appointed by a process similar to that in the federal system. In some states, such as California, even the highest judges are publicly elected at extended intervals, and usually even 'run' for judicial office on political party slates.

The Supreme Court of the United States is the premier constitutional court in the United States, as well as the court with final authority over the interpretation of *all* federal statutes. This means that the Supreme Court also reviews decisions of federal administrative agencies, which have interpreted statutes, but only after these decisions have been reviewed by a federal court lower in the hierarchy.

The Supreme Court consists of nine judges, and does not sit in panels. It sits only *en banc*, that is, as a whole bench. The Justices each have about 20 full 'majority opinions' to write annually.

The Supreme Court is the court of last resort in all cases it hears, civil and criminal. This means it is usually the third court in the hierarchy although, in a few cases, the Supreme Court even has original jurisdiction. See U.S. Const., Art. III, s. 2; 28 U.S.C. s. 1251 (1988). The most common federal pattern is for there to be a decision in a trial court appealed to an intermediate appellate court and then appealed to the Supreme Court. Where the appeal is from a federal court decision reviewing a decision of an administrative agency, there may be no trial court decision at all. Where the trial court is a state court, there may be an appeal to a state intermediate level court, then the State Supreme Court, and then, where there is a question of federal law, to the US Supreme Court. Normally the US Supreme Court reviews only issues of law and does not find facts. For a discussion of the Supreme Court's appellate jurisdiction and its relationship to state and lower federal courts, see Wright (1983) pp. 725–63.

Normally the Supreme Court either affirms or reverses the judgement appealed from. Here the Court will set forth what it considers to be the proper statutory interpretation, even if there is to be a new trial. In this way, guidance is provided for the court below.

Very few cases can be appealed to the Supreme Court by litigants as a matter of right. That is, nearly all the cases now reach the Court via a process of discretionary selection in which the justices of the Court select the cases to be heard (see Gunther, 1985). A major basis on which cases are selected to be heard in the Supreme Court is that there is a conflict between federal appellate courts as to the proper interpretation of a federal statute. The Court also selects cases where the issue involved is likely to recur frequently. This means that the Court hears only statutory interpretation cases of substantial importance.

The Supreme Court relies heavily on the litigating parties to provide relevant arguments and authorities. In major constitutional cases, and occasionally in statutory interpretation cases, the parties will present 'legislative facts' to the Court through variations on the so-called 'Brandeis Brief'. The Court also has law clerks and staff to do legal research, and relies heavily on these as well. Each Supreme Court justice has four law clerks who are recent honour graduates of leading law schools. A major part of the work of such clerks is to do relevant legal research supplementing that of the litigants. On law clerks see, generally, J. Oakley and R. Thompson, 1980.

In cases involving the government, the Solicitor General plays a large role. In cases where the government has lost in a lower court, the Solicitor General may appeal the case on behalf of the government. Where the Solicitor General believes that an administrative agency has misinterpreted a statute, he may seek to have the ruling overturned even if the government was not involved in the dispute. The Solicitor General may also intervene as *amicus curiae* in cases where the government was not a party. Because the Solicitor General is charged with acting in the public interest, the Supreme Court may give special weight to the Solicitor General's arguments. See, generally, Griswold, 'The Office of the Solicitor General – Representing the Interests of the United States Before the Supreme Court', *Mo. Law Review*, 34, p. 527 (1969).

XVI   LEGISLATIVE STRUCTURES AND PROCEDURES

The structure and procedures of the federal Congress affect the interpretation of statutes and the filling of gaps in a number of important ways. As already indicated, Congress is a bicameral legislature. The Executive must also approve a bill (unless the Congress votes by a two-thirds majority to override a veto). This means the process yields many statutes that are essentially the result of two- and three-sided bargains or compromises. This, in turn, poses *more* problems of interpretation and gap-filling than would be true if the legislative draftsmen did not have to serve so many masters. It also affects the nature of those problems. The legislature is sometimes forced to adopt legislation that includes vague or highly general terms, thereby merely passing the problem off to the courts or to administrative agencies to decide. For such cases, 'legislative intention' as to the meaning of the terms used is essentially non-existent – the only intention is to pass the issue to the courts. See Atiyah and Summers (1987) pp. 318–22.

Most legislative drafting in the Congress is done by professionals and the quality of the drafting in technical fields such as taxation, some forms of business regulation and commercial statutes is quite high. But sometimes members of Congress who are also lawyers inject themselves into the drafting process and this can have distorting effects. The quality of state legislative drafting is quite uneven. See, generally, Dickerson, 'Legislative Drafting: American and British Practices Compared', *A.B.A.J.*, 44, p. 865 (1958).

Extensive records are kept of legislative proceedings. These are now generally accessible to the public and to courts. The history of any bill introduced into either House of Congress, from its introduction to its ultimate disposition, can be found in the Congressional Record. The Congressional Record also includes edited statements of remarks made by members of Congress concerning a bill. Both the official *United States at Large* and the unofficial *US Code Congressional and Administrative News* also make reference to the histories of major legislation. Furthermore many periodicals, such as *Congressional Quarterly Weekly*, also contain reports and analyses of Congressional action. Litigants frequently present such history to the courts as relevant to the interpretation of statutes.

The Congress has no general power to correct specific judicial misinterpretations as they immediately affect the parties at hand, but it can amend a statute or pass a new statute and thus alter the law for the future. In fact, where Congress does *not* 'correct' judicial interpretations by enacting subsequent legislation, courts may defer more fully to such prior interpretations. It should be added that the US Congress and the state legislatures seldom 'revisit' and revise statutes.

XVII FEATURES OF THE LEGAL CULTURE

Many features of the American legal culture affect the interpretation of statutes and the filling of gaps in them. The American legal culture is much more receptive to substantive reasoning and more open to value and policy judgements than the systems of the UK, for example. See, generally, Atiyah and Summers (1987).

The substantive and open nature of the American legal order can be explained partly on the basis of traditions of legal theory and legal education. An instrumentalist concept of law and a 'realist' view of the judge as a major participant in law-making were and continue to be major tenets of America's dominant philosophy of law, a philosophy born in the law schools at the turn of the century and vigorously advocated by many academics since. See, generally, R. Summers (1982). This openness is especially evident in the approach of most Supreme Court justices and many other American judges to issues of interpretation and gap-filling. They are, to begin with, more inclined to concur with counsel that issues of interpretation and gap-filling do exist in the first place and, in this, they do not confine themselves to the face of the statute. In the end the judges may conclude, however, that the argument from ordinary or technical meaning prevails nonetheless. If the judges were more uncomfortable with value and policy choices, they would acknowledge and take up fewer interpretational issues in the first place.

Until the 1980s, the Supreme Court of the United States was for many years rather inclined to rely less on arguments from ordinary language and considerations of contextual harmonization, and somewhat more on substantive arguments of principle and policy and on evidence of legislative intention (including purpose) found in legislative history. Even in the Supreme Court of today a few interpretation cases are decided each year largely by reference to substantive argumentation.

It is accepted that the Supreme Court justices are also relatively forthright and candid when writing opinions. That is, in major cases they tend to write full opinions discussing all the considerations they consider relevant. The opinions also purport to include all of the relevant facts. As a result, an opinion stands on its own, and its correctness under the statute (which is quoted) can usually be independently determined by an outside expert without further materials.

Today the approach to interpretation in the American federal system, particularly in the Supreme Court, increasingly accords primacy to arguments from ordinary or technical meaning and from special meaning in the light of considerations of contextual harmonization (other parts of the statute, and the like). There is less emphasis on legislative history. The opinions of SCALIA J. are expecially noteworthy here. See, for example, *Department of Treasury, I.R.S.* v. *Federal Labor Relations Authority*, 110 S.Ct. 1623,

458 *Interpreting Statutes*

1627 (1990); *Pavelic & LeFlore* v. *Marvel Entertainment Group*, 110 S. Ct. 456, 458 (1989); *Thompson* v. *Thompson*, 484 U.S. 174, 187 (1988) (concurring) and *Immigration and Naturalization Service* v. *Cardoza-Fonseca*, 480 U.S. 421, 450–51 (1987). Where the statute does not generate credible arguments from ordinary or technical meaning, nor credible arguments favouring a special meaning, the Supreme Court is usually ready to resort openly to full-fledged substantive argumentation.

There are some issues on which the court divides sharply as to methodology. Thus, in matters of race and gender, for example, the Court's approach to statutory interpretation is radically disparate and conflicting. See, for example, *United Steelworkers of America* v. *Weber*, 443 U.S. 193 (1979).

In many fields, academic writings have major influence. This is true in administrative law, in commercial law and the law of procedure, for example. Frequently treatise writers will have anticipated the very interpretational problem that has arisen and will have proposed solutions which the Court then adopts, with citations to the treatise (or essay).

But with regard to general methods of interpretation, the academic legal culture is generally highly substantive and constantly invites and even implores the justices to rely on values and moral argument, even when interpreting statutes. A growing body of academic writings on interpretation itself is overtly political, with certain professors (or ex-professors) favouring a quite limited role for courts in the interpretative process; see, for example, Easterbrook, 'Statutes' Domains,' *University of Chicago Law Review*, 50, p. 533 (1983) while other more 'liberal' professors advocate activistic interpretation to serve their own view of proper social ends. See, for example, Sunstein, 'Interpreting Statutes in the Regulatory State', *Harvard Law Review*, 103, p. 407 (1989).

Professors regularly publish specific criticisms of interpretational decisions of courts, and this has some effect on judicial practice. As noted earlier, the Supreme Court justices also each have four law clerks. These are recent graduates of top law schools, who bring to the Court a certain range of the most recent academic thinking with respect to interpretational method and substantive issues of interpretation.

The Supreme Court, the federal appellate courts, and the state appellate courts do not generally assign opinion writing to judges with prior specialization in particular areas. Of course many lawyers are highly specialized, and when the issue of interpretation is a technical one in a specialized field, the court is supplied with arguments that are often very sophisticated and technical. This, in turn, is usually revealed in the Court's opinion.

REFERENCES

Abraham, H. (1985), *Justices and Presidents: A Political History of Appointments to the Supreme Court*, 2nd edn., New York: Oxford University Press.

Aristotle, *Nichomachean Ethics*.

Atiyah, P. and Summers, R. (1987), *Form and Substance in Anglo American Law*, Oxford: Oxford University Press.

Bork, R. (1990), *The Tempting of America: The Political Seduction of the Law*, New York: Free Press.

Calabresi, G. (1982), *A Common Law for the Age of Statutes*, Cambridge: Harvard University Press.

Chase, H. (1972), *Federal Judges: The Appointing Process*, Minneapolis: University of Minnesota Press.

Crawford, E. (1940), *The Construction of Statutes*, St. Louis: Thomas Law Bk Co.

Davis, K. (1978), *Administrative Law Treatise*, 2nd edn., St. Paul: West Pub. Co.

Dickerson, R. (1975), *The Interpretation and Application of Statutes*, Boston: Little Brown.

Dworkin, R. (1977), *Taking Rights Seriously*, London: Duckworth.

Easterbrook (1983), 'Statutes' Domains', *University of Chicago Law Review*, **50**, p. 533.

Fuller, L. (1969), *The Morality of Law*, rev. edn., New Haven: Yale University Press.

Gorman, R. (1976), *Labor Law: Unionization and Collective Bargaining*, St. Paul: West Pub. Co.

Griswold (1969), 'The Office of the Solicitor General – Representing the Interests of the United States Before the Supreme Court', *Mo. Law Review*, **34**, p. 527.

Gunther, G. (1985), *Constitutional Law*, pp. 63–9, New York: Foundation Press, Inc.

Oakley, J. and Thompson, R. (1980), *Law Clerks and the Judicial Process*, Berkely: University of California Press.

Summers, R. (1976), *Collective Bargaining and Public Benefit Conferral*, Ithaca: Cornell University Press.

Summers, R. (1982), *Instrumentalism and American Legal Theory*, Ithaca: Cornell University Press.

Sunstein (1989), 'Interpreting Statutes in the Regulatory State', *Harvard Law Review*, **103**, p. 407.

Sutherland, J.G. (1985), *Statutes and Statutory Construction*, 4th edn.

Wellington, H. and Winter, R. (1971), *The Unions and the Cities*.

White, J. and Summers, R. (1988), *The Uniform Commercial Code*, 3rd edn., St. Paul: West Pub. Co.

Wright, C. (1983), *The Law of Federal Courts*, 4th edn., St. Paul: West Pub. Co.

12 Interpretation and Comparative Analysis

ROBERT S. SUMMERS, *Ithaca* **AND**
MICHELE TARUFFO, *Pavia**

I INTRODUCTION

In this chapter we seek to advance understanding by comparing
the major justificatory features of opinions of higher courts interpreting statutes in the various countries. We identify significant
similarities and differences in the arguments, in patterns of justification, in modes of settling conflicts between arguments, and in the
structure and style of these opinions as a whole. Increased understanding through comparison has practical value, and is worth
pursuing for its own sake. Further, a reader interested in justificatory practices in the interpretation of statutes in any particular
system can come to understand that system better by studying
what it is *not*; that is, how it differs from the various systems treated
here.

Another major aim of this chapter is to suggest explanations for
the similarities and differences. Explanations are not only of theoretical and practical interest in their own right; they also advance
understanding.

This chapter builds mainly on Chapters 3–11, in which justificatory practices in nine countries are set forth. The different authors
of each of these chapters have prepared them in accord with a
common plan, but neither with the intention nor the effect of
achieving identity of approach on all points. Most of our generalizations in the present chapter are based on material in Chapters 3–

*Dr Geoffrey Marshall of The Queen's College, Oxford and Professor John Bell of
Leeds University both read two prior drafts of this chapter and made many helpful
suggestions, for which the authors and project members are most grateful.

11, but in some instances they are based partly on 'minutes' of our formal roundtable discussions held once a year over the last seven years.

This chapter does not purport to provide a comprehensive analysis of all features of justificatory practice reported in Chapters 3–11. It is deliberately selective, and focuses only on several of the most significant points of comparison between systems that are of special justificatory interest.

Throughout this chapter and the next, we concentrate on the nature and quality of the published justifications of higher courts, and *not* on the actual historical processes, psychological or other, whereby those justifications and the decisions they support are arrived at. Our rationale for this delimitation is set forth in Chapter 2.

II   MAIN THESES

Our first main thesis is 'universalist' in tenor. This thesis is that basic features of justificatory practice appearing in the published opinions of the higher courts in the nine countries within our study share important similarities. These similarities consist mainly of: (1) a set of major types of arguments that figure in the opinions; (2) the materials incorporated into the content of such of arguments; (3) the main patterns of justification involved; (4) the modes of settling conflicts between types of arguments; and (5) the role of precedents interpreting statutes.

The similarities in these features reveal a shared general conception of good reasons for the resolution of interpretational issues. This shared conception is, we think, of profound significance, not least because it is anti-relativist in spirit. It (along with the rational explicability of any significant differences) implies a deep common rationality rooted in shared values, a topic we treat in detail at the close of the final chapter. This common general conception also implies the possibility and feasibility of constructing an elaborate normative model for the justified interpretation of statutes generally, and in the next chapter we take some initial steps in that direction. (Any such model, of course, would have to be adjusted to some extent for 'system-fit'.) On a less theoretical plane, the common general conception we discern from our study has positive implications for major contemporary experiments in the legal unification of diverse and highly developed national systems, as in the case of the European Community.

Our first thesis then, is what we call our 'universality thesis' and we seek to substantiate it here. Accordingly, we will identify and discuss shared similarities at length, and will suggest general explanations for each.* But we have also found significant differences, too. Our second main thesis is that these differences appear to be rationally explicable. At the least, we think they are consistent with the hypothesis that they are both explained by *and* rationally grounded in such factors as:

1   differences of political theory, for example with regard to the relative roles of courts and legislatures;
2   differences of institutional structure;
3   differences of legal culture, including legal theory;
4   differences of conceptual frameworks; and
5   differences of personnel (including training and background).

The identification of possible rational explanations for significant differences not only deepens understanding, but also reveals how these differences need not conflict with the common rationality we discern. Further, the overall analysis indicates in concrete terms how the interpretational practices of national judges may vary, depending on the political, institutional, cultural and other factors that operate in the various possible legal worlds that different judges may inhabit. It may also be that some major features of justification may be accounted for within each system in terms of a mosaic of interlocking and reinforcing factors rather than in terms of linear causality.

The explanation of differences in justificatory practice is ultimately an empirical enterprise. In the course of our project, we have drawn together a body of relatively well-known general facts with respect to the political, institutional, cultural and other explanatory factors operative within each system. We have done this with a view merely to formulating hypotheses as to how these factors might account for the differences in justificatory practices. We also acknowledge that Chapters 3–11 on the various systems are necessarily highly selective, given (1) the level of generality that any such study requires; (2) the variety of possible approaches to theoretical description; and (3) the vast quantities of primary source material available in each system over lengthy time spans. Accordingly our hypotheses are certainly subject to challenge in

*The expressions, 'UK', 'Poland' and so on used throughout this chapter refer to the specific higher courts reported on in the relevant chapters. The introductions to those chapters must, accordingly, be consulted to determine the court practices referred to. Thus, in the case of the United States, all references hereafter to the practice in the 'United States', or the 'USA', or 'America' refer primarily to the relevant justificatory practices of the US Supreme Court, particularly in the period 1980 to 1990.

the light of further study and research, and we hope that this first effort will bring still others to the task.

III   SIMILARITIES AND DIFFERENCES – ARGUMENTS

Of most fundamental interest are the types of argument that judges of the higher courts set forth in their opinions. Such arguments appear in three quite different roles. They are sometimes used to raise issues of interpretation. They are sometimes deployed to attack or undermine other arguments. Finally, and most often, they are invoked in opinions as reasons to justify the decisions reached. Arguments, as reasons for decision, are the most basic ingredients of justification, and will be our central focus throughout.

Perhaps the most important similarity between the systems in our study is that the higher courts in all systems appear to rely extensively on what might be called a 'common core' of *at least* 11 basic types of argument. These types of arguments may be summarized as follows:

1   Arguments from a standard *ordinary meaning* of ordinary words used in the specific section of the statutory text being interpreted. Where there is more than one standard ordinary meaning of an ordinary word used in the text, as is often the case, the general context of use in the section of the statute involved can usually be taken to indicate which meaning is linguistically appropriate.

2   Arguments from a standard *technical meaning* of ordinary words or of technical words, legal or non-legal. Whether an ordinary word or phrase is used with a standard technical legal meaning can frequently be readily determined from the general context of use in the section of the statute involved, from relevant history of the use of such words previously in the law, or from other evidence. A technical legal word or phrase with a standard meaning is usually recognizable as such by persons who are legally trained, but relevant history of the word or phrase in the law can be conclusive here, too. The appropriate meaning of non-legal technical words may or may not be readily apparent, and if not, may require resort to some form of factual proof.

3   Contextual-harmonization arguments. Further elements of context beyond the general context of use in the text of the statutory section being interpreted may confirm a standard ordinary ((1) above) or a standard technical meaning ((2)

above), such further elements of context consisting mainly of other parts of the same section of the statute, any related section of the same statute, and any closely related statute. Such elements are here conceptualized as the sources of a distinct type of argument here designated 'contextual-harmonization' argument. Instead of confirming a standard ordinary meaning of ordinary words or a standard technical meaning of ordinary or technical words, a contextual-harmonization argument may also support a contrary *special* meaning of the words in issue.

Not only a contextual-harmonization argument but nearly all of the remaining types of argument numbered 4–11 below may (a) confirm a standard ordinary meaning of ordinary words or a standard technical meaning of ordinary or technical words; or (b) support a contrary special meaning in place of a standard meaning of ordinary words or a standard technical meaning of ordinary or technical words; or (c) clarify and thus determine the statutory meaning where there is no determinative ordinary or technical meaning because of syntactic ambiguity, vagueness, evaluative openness or the like.

4   Arguments invoking precedents already interpreting the statute at hand.
5   Arguments based on statutory analogies.
6   Arguments of a logical–conceptual type in which implications are drawn from recognized general legal concepts (which may or may not be doctrinally elaborated).
7   Arguments appealing to general legal principles potentially or actually operative within the field in which the interpretational issue arises.
8   Arguments from any special history of the reception and evolution of the statute. Such arguments presuppose that the statute has come to stand for something rather different from what it was originally designed for.
9   Arguments from statutory purpose to the effect that a given possible meaning of the statute best serves that *purpose*.
10 Arguments consisting of substantive reasons the weight or force of which is not essentially dependent on any authoritativeness that the reasons may also have.
11 Arguments to the effect that the legislature *intended* that the words have a given meaning.

In a given case only one type of argument may be available as a robust and full-fledged argument, yet it may alone be decisive and justificatorily sufficient. In most cases, instances of two or more of the 11 types of argument will be available. When this is so, they may support the same result, that is, be cumulative in their force, or they may support differing outcomes.

All types of argument are potentially available in a substantial range of cases. The linguistic arguments from ordinary or technical meaning are the most widely available. The materials required for the availability of these arguments consist mainly of the section of the statutory text being interpreted, and applicable conventions of usage or other relevant linguistic background.

We will now provide somewhat more detailed analysis of each of the 11 types of argument, beginning with the first two, that is, with arguments which appeal essentially to an ordinary meaning of ordinary words, or to a technical meaning of ordinary or technical words, legal and non-legal. All systems in our study recognize the relative decisiveness and wide-ranging nature of these two types of argument. This is not difficult to explain. A statutory text consists of a set of words, and we must resort to these words if we are to interpret the text at all. Moreover statutes just are written in ordinary or in technical words (or a mix of both). It is entirely expectable that interpreters of statutes so written will invoke the linguistic conventions governing the standard meanings of those words. Generally, it can be assumed that the legislature was guided by these conventions in choosing those very words in the first place. Of course conventions may change over time. This may itself be one means of legal adaptation and evolution, with ordinary or technical meaning changing as conventions change.

There are intrinsic limits on the argument from ordinary meaning and the argument from technical meaning. In a particular case these limits may operate to weaken their force or foreclose them altogether. We return to this topic later.

The third basic type of argument recognized in all systems is the contextual-harmonization argument. Such an argument arises not only from the part of the statutory section in which the words in issue appear, but from usage in other parts of that section, in related sections of the same statute, and in sections of closely related statutes. As indicated, such an argument may (a) confirm a standard ordinary or standard technical meaning, or (b) support a contrary special meaning, or (c) clarify and assign meaning. Contextual-harmonization arguments are frequently available. Seldom does a statute consist only of a sentence or two. Also, today the entirely isolated statute is increasingly uncommon. So, too, the single section statute. The relative decisiveness of such arguments, when they are in play, can also be readily accounted for. Three factors appear to be at work. Some elements of context are strong evidence of meaning. This is true, for example, of uses of the same words in other parts of the same section of the same statute. In addition, it is reasonable for the interpreter to postulate a rational legislator striving for systemic coherence and unity, especially where diverse yet highly authoritative sources are being harmonized, as with statutes *in pari materia*. Thus the force of such arguments derives from evidence of intended meaning, from the desirability of unity and coherence and from the highly authoritative nature of the contextual elements themselves.

A more or less intrinsic limit on the availability of contextual-harmonization arguments is simply that the relevant elements of statutory context may conflict. For example, one section of the statute may suggest a given meaning while still another indicates a contrary meaning. Another limit is that part or all of the statute or statutory scheme may itself not be well drafted.

We now turn to argument types 4–11, all of which either (a) support or oppose one or more linguistic arguments of types 1–3 just considered, or (b) clarify and assign meaning when such linguistic arguments are indeterminate.

The fourth basic argument type consists of the argument from a precedent interpreting the statute. The argument from precedent is widely influential in Code systems, just as it is in the USA and in the UK, where it is sometimes said that a binding prior interpretation even becomes 'part of the statute'. Because of its special interest we treat the argument from precedent in detail in Section VI.

A fifth major type of argument is the argument from statutory analogy. For example, when a case is not provided for or is only at best dimly provided for in the statute, the case is to be treated in the same fashion that closely analogous cases are treated in the statute. Or one statute may be construed on analogy to the way another statute is construed. This type of argument is in fact recognized to some degree in all countries within our study. Its relatively universal appeal is presumably rooted not only in considerations of coherence and unity but also in the ideal of equality before law.

A sixth type of argument is the argument from the logical implications of a recognized general legal concept that appears expressly or impliedly in the statute being interpreted. Examples of such concepts are 'contract' or 'corporation'. The thrust of these 'logical–conceptual' arguments is simply that the concepts involved should, in the absence of special circumstances, receive consistent application within the system.

The argument from that meaning which coheres best with a general principle or principles of substantive or procedural law operative within the field in which the case falls is a seventh highly influential type of argument in all countries. This, too, can be readily explained. The argument from an accepted general principle derives its force not only from its essentially authoritative character, but also from systemic considerations of substantive (or procedural) coherence and harmony.

At least three senses of 'principles of law' must be distinguished: (1) substantive moral norms previously invoked by judges when interpreting statutes or otherwise (independently or as presumptions of legislative intention: for example, no person shall profit from his own wrong); (2) general propositions of substantive law widely applicable within a particular branch of law: for example, in some systems the principle of 'first in time, first in right' in personal property security law, 'nulla poena sine lege' in criminal law, 'no liability without fault' in tort law, and good faith in contract law; and (3) general propositions of law, substantive and procedural, widely applicable throughout the entire legal system. Examples of general procedural principles are those requiring fair notice and a fair hearing before an official may take adverse action against a citizen. Examples of such substantive principles are those protecting the rights to freedom of association and speech and to freedom from discrimination on racial or religious grounds, and the right to free movement.

Of course the precise content of all three of the above types of general legal principles varies from system to system. So, too, does their legal authoritativeness. The legal character of such principles may be grounded in the constitution, or in general statutory law, in non-constitutional case-law, or in a pervasive legal tradition. Where case-law is the legal basis, the precedents involved may not be precisely in point, yet still support the authoritative status of the principle in question for the matter at hand.

There are major variations between countries in the way coherence arguments based on substantive general principles arise or operate. We will cite two examples. In the Federal Republic of Germany, the higher courts systematically interpret statutes in ways that harmonize substantively with the broad implications of general constitutional principles. This is because the constitution lays down broad substantive principles to which all statutes are required affirmatively to conform in their content. These principles therefore cast an influential shadow across the surface of many statutes.

A second example of a major variation here is that, in the USA, the courts regularly invoke, as a coherence argument, the congruence of a proposed interpretation with a substantive legislative policy generally prevailing in the statutory field within which the issue arises (for example, the taxation and social security fields).

Given that, as we shall see, substantive policy reasoning is widely recognized in the USA, it is not at all surprising that American courts invoke general policies of the legislature in this way.

The European Community treaties are now in process of generating wide-ranging substantive coherence arguments in the various affected countries. In this, the practice of the Court of Justice of the European Community is at least as influential as the terms of the treaties.

An eighth basic type of argument is what we have called historical argumentation. Such an argument does not derive its force from language, or contextual harmonization, or substantive coherence or the like. Rather, its force derives from the fact that, as a matter of historical evolution, the statute has come to stand for something rather different from what its language facially indicates or its original design indicates. This occurs importantly in all systems. Two examples will suffice. The British Rent Restriction Acts originated in the First World War as a temporary 'moratorium' on rent rises, but then developed into a kind of 'social housing code'. Similarly the American anti-trust statute prohibited restraints of trade categorically, but was early 'interpreted' to prohibit only unreasonable restraints, and continues to be so construed today. Historical argumentation in common law systems tends to be 'pocketed', that is, specific to a particular statute or group of related statutes, and therefore not very wide-ranging, yet highly important where it is operative. But in codified systems, historical argumentation has a wide effect by way of the evolved understanding of the codes, or major parts of them.

The ninth basic type of widely recognized argument is teleological in nature, and is to the effect that one of the alternative interpretations best serves the ultimate purpose of the statute. The force of this type of argument derives mostly from the fact that the argument conceives of the legislature as an instrumentalist body seeking to serve ends through apt means.

The argument from statutory purpose is not identically constructed in all systems. Thus the 'purpose' may consist of the actual historic purpose of the statute as revealed on its face or the actual historic purpose as revealed in *travaux préparatoires* (the form and content of which vary considerably from system to system), or the purpose may consist of something else again, namely a purpose attributable to a rational or objective legislator (in the view of the court).

The tenth basic type of argument consists of direct invocation of substantive reasons, that is, moral, political, economic or other social considerations. This type of argument, as defined here, depends for its essential force or weight on the intrinsic strength of the substantive argumentation and not on the happenstance that a court, for example, has given such reasons in the past. Substantive reasoning occurs much less in some systems than in others but is important in all. (See further, section VIII of this chapter.) Such argumentation is most frequent where (1) the other types of argument, especially linguistic arguments, are not available (or only limitedly available) because of ambiguity, vagueness or the like; (2) general clauses or other evaluative phrases must be filled out; or (3) conflicts between arguments must be resolved. Two varieties of substantive reasons might be distinguished: particular ones informing the content of, or relevant to the immediate interpretation of, a statute; general ones stating the rationales for institutions and processes such as democratic values, fair process and the rule of law. (See Chapter 13, section V.)

Interpretative arguments appealing to the 'intention of the legislature' comprise the final eleventh basic type. It is perhaps enough to explain general recognition of this type of argument on the elemental ground that implementation of the legislative intent is a high value accepted in all systems. But arguments from legislative intention are conceptualized and constructed in variant ways within all systems. In the UK, the only system in our study generally proscribing the use of *travaux préparatoires*, the argument from legislative intention seems most frequently to be used to reinforce the argument from the ordinary meaning or the technical meaning of the words used. That is, the court assumes that ordinary or technical meaning is the best indication of the legislature's intention. This is essentially a linguistically oriented and thus objective concept of legislative intention, in contrast to actual subjective legislative intention based on *travaux préparatoires*. In the UK this linguistically oriented conception may be reinforced by evidence in the form of prior legislative changes in the text of the statute being interpreted, as well as by contrast with prior superseded law generally. The linguistically oriented concept of legislative intention differs from other concepts of 'objective' legislative intention, including an intent or purpose attributable to a rational legislature, for example, one which (as in the UK and elsewhere) is presumed not to intend violation of fundamental legal principles.

Germany, like the UK favours an objective conception of legislative intention, but with less emphasis on the purely linguistic conception. In all other systems some regard is had to subjective intention. In the case of Sweden, actual subjective intention is overwhelmingly dominant. (We are informed that the Finnish Supreme Court increasingly relies on *travaux préparatoires* for actual legislative intention, though this frequently does not show up in the opinions). In some systems, such as the US, very clear evidence of actual subjective intention must now be found before this version of the argument will be given much credence. In recent times, the US Supreme Court has frequently stressed that the statutory words are the best evidence of intention, that is, objective intention in its linguistic aspect. The UK and Argentine courts frequently make the same point.

The higher courts of all countries also invoke certain 'presumptions' as to legislative intention. Among such presumptions are: (1) that the legislature knows the national language and uses ordinary words or technical words accordingly; (2) that the legislature intends its enactments to be constitutionally valid; (3) that the legislature does not intend absurd or manifestly unjust outcomes; (4) that the legislature does not intend a statute to have retroactive effect; (5) that every penal (non-regulatory) statute requires 'mens rea'; and (6) that treaties are not to be infringed. In the UK and the USA, most such presumptions are rebutted only by very clear contrary statutory language.

There are certain types of argument that are widely influential in one or more systems, but not so widely influential in some of the other systems. We will now identify several of the more important of these. Though they are generally exaggerated, there are differences in the way precedent is treated in the various countries. Because of its special interest, we devote a special section of this chapter to precedent in general. See pp. 487–90 below.

It is apparent that systemic arguments based on general legal principles (substantive harmonization) are deployed very extensively and, indeed, developed to a high art in all countries except for the UK and the USA. The casuistic nature of the common law tradition is probably a major factor accounting for the less abstract and non-generalizing approach to statute law in Britain and America; but the significance of common law principles in statutory interpretation should not be overlooked.

Arguments from statutory analogies are widely deployed in Argentina, France, Germany, Sweden, Finland, Poland and Italy. These arguments are far less influential in the UK and the USA, a fact that scholars of comparative law have often noted. In the UK and the USA, if a statute is not by its terms applicable, courts frequently assume that any prior law continues to control, or that the matter is left for common law decision making, and refuse to apply the statute by analogy. The traditional explanation for this difference is that most continental systems view statutory law as the exclusive source of law. Thus the courts take the statute as the only law, and have to find legal solutions in that law, directly, by analogy or otherwise. In Anglo-American systems, on the other hand, the legislature often superimposes statutes on a vast background of common law, a type of law which the courts can fall back on to fill gaps.

But today the foregoing contrast is far less sharp than it once was. In code countries, at least new statutes can be viewed in some areas merely as superimposed upon codes in the background, with the result that the codes, whose meaning is now quite largely fixed in case-law, can and sometimes do have a function similar to that of the common law in the UK and USA.

Several basic limitations on the argument from statutory analogy do appear to be recognized in all countries, albeit in varying degrees. In general, this mode of argument may not be deployed to extend a criminal prohibition, or to extend a statute imposing a tax. Nor may it be used to expand an explicit statutory exception.

It also appears that in the USA there is significantly less logical–conceptual argumentation than in all of the other countries. Arguments by way of implication from general legal concepts, though they now occur in the USA more often than is generally acknowledged, fell victim to the anti-formalist legal culture that emerged there in the first half of this century, and have not yet regained their rightful place.

The argument from ultimate purpose is today most often invoked in the USA when there is no credible argument from ordinary or technical meaning or when the argument from ultimate purpose merely reinforces the argument from ordinary or technical meaning; in other countries, such as Germany and Italy, the argument is invoked rather more widely. On this spectrum, the UK appears to fall midway between the USA and Germany and Italy. The explanation for the declining repute of purposive argumentation in the USA, and for its relatively limited reception in the UK, is simply that it is often seen to conflict with arguments from ordinary or technical meaning which are taken to be the best evidence of purpose anyway.

In some systems the argument from a statutory purpose plays a different role depending on whether it is invoked to cut down or to extend a statutory provision. For example, the US Supreme Court is much more willing in the name of purpose to do the former than the latter, and this is not difficult to explain. For one thing, extension can involve costs, including the sacrifice of other goals, that the implementive language was deliberately drafted restrictively to avoid.

Arguments from actual (subjective) legislative intention are far less frequently encountered in the UK than in any other country. This, of course, is linked to the UK prohibitions against the use of committee reports and records of parliamentary debates. These prohibitions, in turn, can be rationally justified on democratic and rule of law grounds; but different conceptions of democracy and the rule of law may pull in different direction here.

Appeals in judicial opinions to substantive reasons of policy authoritatively influential in a given branch of law to resolve specific issues arising in that area do not often appear in Finland, Sweden, France, Italy, Germany or Poland. Such reasons are, however, frequently given by the US Supreme Court, and less frequently by the higher courts of the UK and Argentina.

Appeals to *independent* substantive reasons – reasons arising from moral norms or from policy ideas not more or less specifically connected to a specific formal source of law – are quite influential in the highest courts of Argentina and the USA, especially when the language of the statute generates no, or only a weak, argument from ordinary or technical meaning because of ambiguity, vagueness, the use of evaluative terms or the like. Such 'free floating' substantive reasons are found in opinions of other courts in our study less frequently. One explanation may be that, compared to all other countries, the highest Argentinean and American courts have, in effect, more extensive law-making power of their own, a fact long acknowledged in the USA and more recently in the case of Argentina. In the UK the courts do not invoke such free-floating arguments nearly so often, and while British judges make common law, they take a much more limited view of their law-making power than the higher American or Argentine (of late) courts.

A type of argument (though not one of the common 11 types) that is quite forceful in one or more countries but not nearly so forceful or indeed not recognized at all in other countries is the argument that, where an administrative agency has been charged by the legislature with administering a statutory scheme, an interpretation by the agency should be upheld by the court when it qualifies as one possible reasonable interpretation, even though it may not be the interpretation that the reviewing court would have given the statute if it were interpreting it *de novo*. (The treatment of regulations is another matter and we do not address it here.) Versions of this general doctrine of judicial deference to administrative agency interpretations are widely followed in the USA and to a lesser degree in France. The doctrine has less weight in the UK, and is not generally followed in Italy, nor in most other countries considered here. In the USA special institutional history is one factor that accounts for this doctrine of judicial deference. There, administrative regulatory agencies are not merely branches of the executive as in most other countries. In the USA they are also, in substance, arms of the legislature. This is especially so in the federal system. Indeed the Congress may have set up an agency in the first place and assigned it the specific job of developing regulatory policy under a broad grant of statutory power, subject to statutory policy guidelines. In these circumstances it is understandable that the courts tend to defer to agency 'interpretations' of the statute, as above.

Arguments appealing to the authority of legal dogmatics and to treatises of scholars and other commentators generally have considerable force in Argentina, in Germany, in the USA, in Sweden and in France in private law. The authors are not always cited, however. In Italy scholarly works have influence, but it is legally forbidden for judges to cite them. In the UK the courts regularly refer to dead scholars, but in most areas of law seldom cite living ones. Only recently have scholarly works come to be cited in Finland.

In actual opinions, the judges in the USA and in the UK make frequent use of arguments based on hypothetical cases. In most other systems, this occurs much less often.

In closing this section, we stress that the types of arguments invoked, the manner of their deployment, and how and when they triumph over other arguments is affected in all countries in our study by the general nature of the statute involved. For example, a statute that merely symbolizes a value commitment must be treated differently from one that incorporates a general principle. And both of these should be interpreted differently from a statute that states an exclusive rule. Also a statute that breaks sharply from the past should be read differently from one that merely tinkers with settled law. Further, an isolated statute must be treated differently from a statute that is to be fitted into an already existing statutory framework, for isolated statutes can generate fewer contextual harmonization arguments. An old statute may have to be interpreted differently from a recent one. Variations in the nature of statutes obviously extend to subject-matter, and we have seen from all the country reports, for example with regard to constitutionally sensitive statutes, criminal statutes and tax statutes, that certain special interpretive approaches or doctrines may apply. Variations in the nature of statutes extend as well to the essential processes by which they are made. For example, some statutes are the consequence of compromises that largely take place outside the legislature, as with certain labour-management law, and this may limit the utility of *travaux préparatoires* in support of arguments from the 'actual intention' of the legislature. An entire essay could be written on the general ways in which the nature of the statute might rationally affect how it is interpreted.

IV SIMILARITIES AND DIFFERENCES – MATERIALS OF ARGUMENT

Plainly, some material must necessarily figure in the content of an interpretational argument. Without material content, an argument can have no reality. Thus, for example, the argument from ordinary meaning simply has no reality until it is instantiated with content, that is, formulated in terms of the words of a particular statute as understood by the interpreter in the light of relevant linguistic conventions. Before that, it is no more than an abstract type of argument. Similarly the argument here called the argument from the actual subjective intention of the legislature can have no reality until it is instantiated with content, that is, is formulated in terms of specific evidence of actual legislative intent.

The materials that logically may figure in one or more types of argument may be classified under two very broad headings: authoritative and non-authoritative. The first category may be subdivided into binding and non-binding materials. Binding authoritative materials include the statutory text being interpreted, related statutory texts, any relevant constitutional provision, treaty, precedent, general principle of law, customary law, or the like. A distinctive feature of statutory interpretation is that the text of the statute in question incorporates the very words of the law which have authoritativeness. The text of other forms of law such as precedent may be subjected to relatively liberal readings aimed at extracting (and even reformulating) the *ratio decidendi*, or the principle of the decision, which is then regarded as authoritative. But, where a statute is involved, particular regard must be had to the exact words used. The fixed verbal formulae of the statute, then are, in a particular way, always essential 'material' on which 'interpretation' does its work.

Other authoritative material, current or superseded, yet not binding on the court, includes official regulations or interpretations, similar statutes in other related jurisdictions and interpretations thereof, prior versions of the very statute being interpreted, other statutes or common law superseded by the statute being interpreted, other law in which the words of the statute being interpreted originated, and the like.

Non-authoritative materials that logically may figure in instantiations of one or more types of argument include: (1) dictionaries, grammars, texts of technical terms and so on; (2) *travaux préparatoires*, that is, documents, records, and other materials relating to the legislative process by which the statute was enacted; (3) historical conditions the statute was adopted to 'remedy' not included in *travaux préparatoires*; (4) social facts including facts about the existence and bearing of moral norms, and facts about the 'policy' effects of alternative interpretations of the statute; (5) facts and maxims of common experience that, among other things, bear on the practicability of alternative interpretations; (6) the intrinsic nature of any normative or teleological phenomena to which the statute is addressed (for example, the family, a public park, a bank collection process and so on); (7) interpretations of the statute by citizens to which it was addressed; and (8) various other relevant materials.

In all systems in our study, judges of the highest courts *must*, of course, take due account of authoritative materials when formulating arguments. For example, judges quote statutes, quote prior interpretations of statutes, quote prior law including the same or similar language, and the like. This is perhaps the most obvious similarity between systems with regard to materials of argument, and it is hardly difficult to explain. It just is part of the meaning of the authoritativeness of legal materials that these materials must figure in any arguments the content of which is affected by such materials. The content of all the 11 leading types of argument, except for the argument from substantive reasons, requires the incorporation of authoritative materials.

The second basic similarity between systems relates to non-authoritative materials. All systems impose no, or very few, restrictions on the admissibility or use of such materials in constructing arguments. In general all materials that are logically relevant can be incorporated into any interpretational argument. Thus the highest courts of all countries generally exercise very wide discretion in choosing materials and in incorporating them into arguments.

Only two major variations between systems here will be discussed. First, there is the oft-noted fact that, in the UK, counsel are not allowed to refer to *travaux préparatoires*. This is a major limitation, for such materials may figure in at least five leading types of argument: arguments from ordinary or technical meaning (at least as indicating which of several usages is appropriate), arguments from considerations of contextual-harmonization (as reinforcing the ordinary or technical meaning, or indicating a special meaning), arguments from legislative intent (as indicating what meaning was in fact intended, ordinary, technical, or special), and in arguments from statutory purpose (as evidence of the purpose of the statute).

But although *travaux préparatoires* are fertile materials for the construction of a wide array of arguments, the intrinsic weight and force of such materials can vary greatly, depending on their documentary form, the circumstances of presentation (debate, hearing and so on), the official status of the legislator or committee speaking or writing, and so forth. Moreover, in a particular system, such materials may be relatively inaccessible, and thus costly to identify and present to the court. In the UK and in the USA (unlike the situation in France or Sweden) no basic document exists which more or less draws together all such materials relevant to a statute. Also it is argued that citizens ought not to be bound by 'law' they cannot readily find. Then, too, such materials may, in some systems, not reveal the intent of essential institutional participants in the law-making process such as the executive.

As already indicated, courts in the UK have developed a doctrine against allowing counsel to cite to them any records of debates, parliamentary committee reports and the like in argument. There are now a few signs that this general restriction is being relaxed a little. Moreover, in the UK, it has long been permissible to cite official reports of any relevant governmental commissions or committees of inquiry preceding enactment in order to establish legislative intent or purpose.

All other systems generally allow counsel and courts to make generous use of *travaux préparatoires*, though references thereto seldom appear in the opinions in some systems, such as Finland and Italy. One system, Sweden, accords very great weight and force to such materials. An eminent Swedish scholar, Professor Folke Schmidt, once characterized the Swedish statute as a mere 'headline', with the primary material of the law consisting of the *travaux préparatoires* behind this headline. In Sweden the legislative strategy is frequently to keep the statutory text short and abstract, and to create elaborate *travaux préparatoires* which are then embodied in an official document. The courts then may make much fuller use of this document than of the statutory text itself. Swedish observers extol several virtues of this. They argue that it allows for more democratically faithful law-making because the legislature can embody more of relevance in official *travaux préparatoires* than in the canonical confines of a stylized statutory text. Relatedly it is said that such materials can reveal more fully the legislature's intent and also the actual purpose of the statute itself. Such materials are also said to be more 'flexible and elastic', and thus applicable to a wider range of circumstances.

One observation on the current American scene may be added. For many decades the US Supreme Court imposed very few restrictions on the admissibility of *travaux préparatoires*, although great variations in weight have long been recognized. Recently a debate has broken out within the Court, with one of the judges, Antonin Scalia, taking a vigorous general stand against the use of such materials at least where there is a credible argument from ordinary or technical meaning. It is too early to say whether his view will prevail, but even before he became a member of the Court, in 1987, the Court had been according less weight to such materials.

Beyond *travaux préparatoires*, another significant area of divergence relates to what might be called independent social facts, that is, evidence of social facts not appearing in *travaux préparatoires*. One category of such facts concerns the existence and bearing of moral norms. Another concerns the policy effects (consequences) of alternative interpretations of a statute. Where substantive reasoning from moral norms or social policies is a permissible type of argument, social facts are obviously relevant to support or refute such argumentation. Of course the category of 'social facts' includes much besides evidence of moral norms or social policies, for example inflation, strikes, war, changing customs and so on. Of the various country reports addressing the issue, it appears that Sweden does not allow independent social facts to be presented. In Italy and Germany this is not forbidden but it seldom occurs. In the UK such evidence certainly could not be presented orally. Of course doctrines of 'judicial notice' in both the UK and the USA may allow the court to have recourse to some well-known social facts.

Another category of independent social facts (which may not be included in *travaux préparatoires*) consists of materials explaining the purpose of the statute. Here there is again a split along the lines indicated in the preceding paragraph, except that in the UK the material is usable if it appears in official reports of commissions and boards of inquiry that were before parliament when it adopted the statute.

In the Federal Republic of Germany, and in certain other countries, a specific category of materials is recognized that might be summed up as 'the teleological or normative nature of the phenomena' subject to statutory regulation. In German this is called 'Natur der Sache'. Under this general umbrella materials may be presented to the court as to, for example, the nature of the family, of public parks, of banks or other phenomena to which a statute is addressed. Though the UK and USA do not recognize this terminological umbrella, much similar material is used there by judges via doctrines of judicial notice.

In closing this section, we merely note an important type of material that two of the country reports (UK and Italy) refer to but which have so far received no systematic treatment in studies of statutory interpretation. This material consists of facts or maxims of common experience bearing on the practicality of alternative interpretations of a statute. This kind of material can be of major importance in some cases, and merits systematic study.*

V SIMILARITIES AND DIFFERENCES – PATTERNS OF JUSTIFICATION AND MODES OF SETTING CONFLICTS BETWEEN ARGUMENTS

In all systems the higher courts write opinions in which most of the same basic patterns of justification in cases of statutory interpretation recur. Here we will merely identify these patterns and will treat their justificatory features in more depth in the next chapter.

In the simplest pattern, the court marshals and deploys a single major argument as the only or the primary reason for the decision, and the court omits further arguments or views them largely as 'make-weights'. In this simplest pattern, the basic type of argument in all systems that most often generates the single decisive reason consists of linguistic arguments based either on a standard ordinary or standard technical meaning of ordinary words, or a standard technical meaning of technical words, legal or non-legal, as these words appear in the statute. In its most abbreviated form, the argument may consist of no more than the citation of the statute itself. As we have noted, statutes just are written in ordinary or technical language, and interpreters bring to the problem of interpretation their conventional understanding of these words. Where the words are legal words or non-legal technical words, the interpreter also turns to conventions, and non-legal technical words may require proof by way of expert evidence. Also of great importance, once a judge is satisfied that, in terms of ordinary or technical language, a statute is prima facie quite clear in meaning, in most systems this usually shifts the burden onto others to show that this prima facie ordinary or technical meaning is *not* controlling.

Beyond this simplest, 'single-argument' pattern of justification, there are two more complex patterns which often appear in published opinions. The first we shall call 'cumulative'. Here several different arguments of significance figure in the court's opinion, but all of them in the final analysis point in varying degrees to the same interpretational conclusion. Judicial resort to cumulative argument is motivated by such factors as doubt about the justificatory force of any single argument, the social importance of the issue or issues being resolved, a desire to relieve possible concern that the court might be exceeding its proper role, a felt need to provide a justification commensurate with a substantial burden being

*Its role is treated in an admirable recent book on the common law: M., Eisenberg, *The Common Law* (1988).

imposed on the losing party, a felt need to take account of arguments of counsel, and foreclosure of appeals.

The cumulative pattern of justification usually appears in one of two basic forms. In the first, an argument from ordinary or technical meaning is often reinforced by instances of one or more of the following arguments: contextual-harmonization, analogy, congruence with precedent or general legal principle, actual intention, and purpose. Indeed it is possible (though quite rare) that *all* major types of arguments may support a given interpretation.

In the second basic form of the cumulative pattern no really viable argument from the ordinary or technical language appears. Instead other types of arguments are marshalled to clarify and thus specify the statutory meaning of ambiguous, vague, evaluative or otherwise indeterminate language. In both basic cumulative patterns, judges strive to construe all available materials so that they generate several arguments that converge to support one interpretation. The cumulative pattern is recognized in all systems. In France, however, opinions tend to be quite brief, so that courts make much less use of 'cumulative modes'.

The remaining justificatory pattern might be called 'conflict settling', and is the most complex of all. It presupposes that conflicting arguments are cumulated on each side, discussed and the conflict resolved in the opinion. In settling the conflict, the court may deploy one or more of several distinct modes of resolution, only one of which consists of 'weighing and balancing'. Thus, when two or more arguments come into conflict, one argument may rationally prevail because (1) the other argument proves to be, on close analysis, unavailable inasmuch as the very conditions required for it to exist simply are not present; (2) the other argument (or arguments) is deprived of all or most of its prima facie force by the prevailing argument, a process we call cancellation; (3) the other argument (or arguments) is mandatorily subordinated pursuant to a general rule or maxim of priority; or (4) the other argument (or arguments) is simply outweighed.

Unavailability exists when, for example, it is shown that an ordinary meaning argument has no force because the presupposed linguistic convention does not exist. Cancellation occurs when, for example, the ordinary meaning argument is deprived of its prima facie normal force by a contextual-harmonization argument that makes clear that the legislature was using the words in a special rather than in their ordinary sense. An argument is mandatorily subordinated when the legal system has adopted a general rule or maxim of priority that such conflicts shall be so resolved. (Such rules or maxims are sometimes defeasible.) An argument is outweighed when the reasons behind that argument or the evidence in support of it are not as strong as those behind or supporting a competing argument. (This process may or may not involve invoking another type of argument, or further values at a second level.)

A striking difference between systems in patterns of justification emerges here. In Argentina, Sweden, the UK and the USA, and to a lesser extent Germany, the higher courts regularly publish opinions that more or less fully acknowledge the existence of opposing arguments and explicitly undertake to justify the resolution of conflicts between them. But in Finland, France, Italy and Poland, such robust conflicts of arguments are, in general, not acknowledged, and only the main arguments supporting the outcome are presented. This is both a matter of justificatory practice and a matter of style, and we seek to explain it in section IX on style.

In those systems that do frontally address conflicts between arguments as a regular matter, it appears that the arguments having greatest overall decisiveness in relation to the entire range of interpretation cases that arise are the ordinary and the technical meaning arguments with normal force. It appears that there are two quite different explanations for this. First, these types of arguments require for their construction the least by way of materials. They require mainly the statutory text being interpreted and the necessary linguistic background in ordinary or technical usage. Such arguments are therefore potentially available in a far wider range of cases than all the other major types of argument. This is so because these other types all depend for their construction on materials much less often available than merely the statute itself and its relevant linguistic background. As a result, and in the final analysis, the ordinary and technical meaning arguments are frequently in play without serious competitors, and therefore decisive. The argument from contextual-harmonization might be thought to be a serious rival here, but in its most powerful forms it requires other sections of the same statute or sections of closely related statutes that are appropriately worded, and such materials frequently do not exist. Precedents and close statutory analogues often do not exist. It might also be thought that the independent argument from statutory purpose is a close rival, but, again, this is not so. Independent evidence of statutory purpose frequently resides only in dubious legislative history. Also the implementive language will frequently not bear the proposed purposive reading without undue strain.

The second basic factor that explains why arguments from ordinary and from technical meaning are relatively more decisive than other arguments is that, when competing with other arguments, the linguistic arguments are relatively more difficult to cancel, or relatively less often subordinated pursuant to a mandatory rule or maxim of priority, or relatively more difficult to outweigh, than other arguments. Their superior comparative force is presumably attributable mainly to the great weight of the substantive rationales behind them, including democratic legitimacy of the legislature. (On this, see Chapter 13, section V.) Because of the force of such rationales, linguistic arguments also get the benefit here of a favourable allocation of the burden of proof. As indicated earlier, that burden is on the party who would show that another type of argument prevails over a credible linguistic argument. But, even if linguistic arguments were usually to lose out to serious competitors when those exist, linguistic arguments would, because of their wide-ranging availability, still very likely be the most decisive overall.

We have alluded to the 'normal force' of ordinary and of technical meaning arguments, and will now offer a tentative general sketch of this complex concept. The normal force of such arguments is *less* than the force they would have if the ordinary or technical meaning were 'reinforced' by instances of other types of argument such as those of context and system, or intent or purpose, yet such normal force is always more than 'weak' or 'slight'. Here what is called for is at least an account of *intrinsic* factors that may weaken the normal force of linguistic arguments. With such a general account we might then negatively define normal force as the force that such arguments would have in the absence of any significant weakening factors. Intrinsic 'weakening' factors appear to include the following: (1) any degree of indeterminateness of the background conventional meaning of the words used in the statute in the first place, including ambiguity; (2) any feature of the use of the words in the statute that casts any doubt on the appropriateness of the meaning that such words have in generally similar sentences in ordinary life, apart from the statute; (3) in the case of old statutes, the degree to which the background linguistic conventions at time of enactment have become irrelevant or obsolete; (4) any relevant vague or evaluative aspect of the words used; (5) any generality or abstractness of the words that renders their meaning indeterminate for disposal of the concrete case; and (6) looseness or awkwardness of draftsmanship of the statute overall. All of these factors diminish the normal force of arguments from ordinary or technical meaning. It follows that such arguments may vary in force. Such force may be low (as where weakening factors are operative), normal (as where such factors are not operative) or high (as where such factors are not operative and the ordinary or technical meaning is reinforced by instances of *other* argument forms).

Equally important, arguments from ordinary or from technical meaning may lack normal force – indeed lose their entire normal force because of what we call 'extrinsic' factors, too. The principal such factor, to be treated below, is simply that a sufficiently strong contrary argument *of an appropriate type* may deprive or sap ordinary and technical meaning arguments of their entire normal force and thus, as we have seen, cancel them, as when a contextual-harmonization argument establishes a special meaning that displaces the ordinary meaning.

But, even so, ordinary or technical meaning arguments in the final analysis often have their normal force and, because of their wide range, such arguments are commonly in play when other arguments are not, and are more often decisive. Again we stress that in our view even if ordinary and technical meaning arguments were regularly to lose out to any competing arguments, such arguments would still be decisive of most interpretational issues, overall, given their wide-ranging availability.

We will now consider further how several significant types of conflicts between arguments in fact appear to be resolved. Even though the higher courts of some systems do not overtly resolve conflicts between opposing arguments in their published opinions, it is still sometimes possible to infer which arguments generally prevail. What now follows is based not only on Chapters 3–11 but also on various formal roundtable discussions of project members. It is not possible, from the materials available, to attempt a comprehensive analysis.

When a standard ordinary meaning conflicts with a standard technical meaning of the same word, and the evidence indicates that the technical meaning applies, it generally cancels or displaces the ordinary meaning in all systems.

Another major type of conflict is that between a standard ordinary or technical meaning, and various contextual-harmonization arguments that favour a special meaning. Such an argument arises from the rest of the section, from related sections of the same statute, from related statutes, and so on. When the language of a contextual-harmonization argument is sufficiently 'close' to the words of the statute being interpreted, and when the statute is precisely drafted so that the special meaning it supports is strongly indicated, most countries in our study appear to hold that the contextual-harmonization argument supporting a *special* meaning in effect cancels or displaces the ordinary or technical meaning (rather than takes priority over or outweighs that meaning). Observe that the prevailing interpretation is not really *contra legem* because the authoritative meaning turns out not to be the prima facie ordinary or technical meaning but rather the special meaning with cancellative effect. (Any such special meaning thereafter becomes, then, a technical legal meaning.) On the other hand, where the materials of a contextual-harmonization argument are more remote, as, for example, when such an argument is based merely on another statute *in pari materia*, and when the statutory scheme overall is not carefully put together, the court is more likely to hold that the ordinary or generally accepted technical meaning prevails. The inherent force of contextual-harmonization arguments simply declines with the increasing remoteness and imprecision of the materials figuring in such arguments.

Now let us suppose there is a conflict essentially between a standard ordinary or technical meaning and *very strong evidence* of actual legislative intention in *travaux préparatoires* supporting a contrary *special* meaning. Here the systems in our study appear to split about evenly. Countries that generally seem to uphold the ordinary and technical meaning include the Federal Republic of Germany, Italy and, of course, the UK (for it generally does not allow reference to *travaux préparatoires* in the first place). Argentina, Sweden and the USA have generally followed the clear subjective legislative intent (though in the USA there is now a recent and powerful trend away from this). Our study does not appear to reveal what Finland and Poland generally do in such circumstances. As for those countries that accord primacy to the subjective intention, it is not entirely clear whether this is on a theory of cancellation and displacement or some other theory. As a matter of rational argument, however, it can be said that, when there is very clear evidence of contrary legislative intention strongly supporting a special rather than the ordinary or generally accepted technical meaning, and the courts opt for the special meaning, the prima facie ordinary or technical meaning is simply cancelled and displaced by the 'speaker's subjective intention' that the special meaning should prevail. That is, the standard meaning is not overridden via a priority rule. Except where addressees of the statutory language have relied on its ordinary or technical meaning excusably in ignorance of contrary *travaux préparatoires*, the implementation of clear legislative intention in a democratic order may also be thought to *outweigh* any residual force that the ordinary or technical meaning arguments may be thought to have.

We turn now to conflicts between standard ordinary or technical meaning arguments, on the one hand, and that meaning which would best serve the ultimate purpose of the statute, on the other. We will assume that the argument from ultimate purpose is strong. That is, we will assume that the purpose is either explicit or plainly implicit on the face of the statute or very clear from *travaux préparatoires*, and that the statutory purpose could be served through the implementive language without undue strain. A wide variety of cases can arise here, including cases in which the ordinary or technical meaning of the express implementive language of the statute does not go far enough fully to implement the purpose, and cases in which such meaning would include more than that required to implement the purpose. Purposive interpretation in the former type of case calls for extension of meaning, but in the latter for restrictive or 'reductive' interpretation. In most systems — Argentina, Finland, the Federal Republic of Germany, France, Italy, Sweden, the UK and the USA, the higher courts generally restrict or reduce the scope of the ordinary or technical meaning of implementing words to comport with purpose, at least if that purpose is evident on the face of the statute. It is not possible to say whether this triumph of purpose occurs on a cancellation, a priority or a weighing theory, but there is a strong case, again along the same line as above, that the correct analysis is one of cancellation.

It is not possible to say from the country reports whether most systems will extend the scope of ordinary or technical meaning to serve an evident purpose more fully. The highest courts of some countries, such as Italy, the UK and the USA, are not generally inclined to do so.

The argument from a precedent of a highest court relevantly interpreting the statute has substantial weight in all systems when in conflict with any type of argument, and in the USA and the UK may even enjoy priorital status. (See the next section of this chapter.)

So far we have not considered how the substantive *content* of arguments competing with the ordinary or technical meaning argument might make a difference to the outcome. We will only remark on two such conflicts here, both of which are well known. The first of these involves a conflict between an argument from ordinary or technical meaning, on the one hand, and the argument that this meaning leads to an absurd or manifestly unjust result, on the other. This latter argument is recognized in virtually every system in our study, though not always in the same form. It is sometimes formulated in the UK in terms of a presumption to the effect that the legislature does not intend absurd or manifestly unjust outcomes. In Germany and in Italy such an argument is typically constitutionalized, and thus formulated as an argument that invalidates the absurd or manifestly unjust result. In the USA the argument may also be constitutionalized, but it has an independent life in the realm of statutory interpretation as well. In recent years in the USA this independent argument has seldom been invoked and has prevailed even less often. Of course, where the manifest injustice argument is constitutionalized, its prevalence is priorital rather than cancellative or a matter of superior weight.

A second major category directly implicating substantive content arises when the argument from ordinary or from technical meaning conflicts with the argument from the datedness or obsolescence of the statute in question. Datedness or obsolescence implicates substantive content, and can pose acute problems, especially in countries with very old statutes or old codes. Within limits, the higher courts of all countries in our study *adjust* the ordinary or technical meaning of a statute to take due account of its datedness or obsolescence. The theory would appear to be that the force or weight of any 'old' meaning is outweighed. This general subject, however, is complex and requires extended treatment beyond what we can give it here.

Still another category of conflict concerning subject-matter arises when the ordinary or technical meaning does not *clearly* reach an allegedly criminal act. Here, as a matter of general priority, all systems generally tend to favour the accused even though in terms of substantive reasoning the accused has clearly behaved anti-socially and even dangerously.

Then there are the not infrequent cases in which there is ultimately no viable argument from ordinary or technical meaning whatsoever. The failure of the argument even to get started in a credible way may be attributable to syntactical or semantic ambiguity, to extreme vagueness, to resort to overgeneral clauses, to very sloppy drafting, or some other vice. Here the ordinary or technical meaning argument is simply inapplicable. That is, on close analysis, it does not arise. Here, in most countries, if there is a contextual-harmonization argument that supports a special meaning, or a credible version of an intention or purpose argument, these will prevail. In Argentina, Germany and in Italy the objective purpose argument, that is, the meaning that best serves the purpose attributable to the statute on objective rational grounds, plays a major role. In Sweden the actual subjective intent of the legislature is dominant, and in Finland this also plays a major role (through *travaux préparatoires*). In the US Supreme Court, emphasis in such cases is placed not only on contextual-harmonization, but on purposive argumentation, on subjective legislative intent when clearly discernible, and on robust substantive reasoning.

Of course a conflict may arise between ordinary or technical meaning on the one hand and *two* or more other types of arguments on the other. An exhaustive analysis would also address other conflicts in detail. It is not possible to pursue these matters further here; we must rest with having suggested a general approach (to which a substantial essay could be devoted for each country in our study).

VI SIMILARITIES AND DIFFERENCES – PRECEDENTS INTERPRETING THE STATUTE

Nearly all systems rely on any precedents already interpreting the statute. The only exception is France. The French Cour de Cassation generally does not *cite* precedent. Yet there is a very large number of articles of the Code Civil whose basic meaning was settled a century ago and which have been accepted ever since. The general French practice of not citing precedents can be explained by reference to the French doctrine that statutes do not need interpretation and the words of the law speak for themselves, so that the judge does not need anything further to apply the statute. Also the French separation of powers helps account for the practice: only the 'law', and not judgements of courts, can determine a decision.

Together with the statute applied in order to decide the case, precedents are the most frequently used materials in judicial opinions. This is true not only where precedents *must* be used because they are a source of law and have binding force (as in UK and USA), but also in the European systems which have no formal rule of *stare decisis*.

A very important remark must now be made: if one looks at the actual use of precedents in the opinions of the higher courts in the several countries, it can be observed that there are no great differences in their use between the so-called common law and civil law systems. It is true that, in the UK and USA, precedents must be used and that they have (under given conditions) a binding effect, while this is not so in other countries. But these other countries (with the exception of France) nonetheless make heavy use of precedent. Indeed in Argentina, Germany and Sweden precedents must be invoked when relevant for the case in issue (it being an error not to do so). In other countries, like Italy, Poland and Finland, the use of precedents is not something that must be done, yet it is quite common and, in the normal case, expected.

Even though in the UK and USA precedents of the higher courts are binding, this effect may be overcome or bypassed in several ways, for example, through distinguishing, overruling or simply not following the precedents, according to the rules of *stare decisis* in those two systems. It is of course true that civil law systems generally ascribe only a *persuasive* or *de facto* effect (that is, not formally binding) to precedents. But again this persuasive force is often very strong. It can probably be said that the substantial force of precedents is similar in systems of both kinds, notwithstanding differences in the theories of precedent. Also common to all systems is the fact that precedents of the supreme courts carry great weight with lower courts, and also with the higher court itself, so that good reasons have to be given for deciding differently.

The use of precedents and their binding force in the UK and USA does not require explanation, as it is a very well-known feature of these systems. More interesting is the widespread and important use of precedents in civil law countries. An explanation may be found in the fact that statutory law in nearly all of these countries is no longer considered sufficient in itself to support judgements. Formal reference to the text of the law can alone be a sufficient justification only in France. All the other systems have come to adopt more articulate justificatory reasoning in support of decisions. Thus the fact that the same case was decided in the same way in other circumstances can provide significant support, in terms of equality of treatment, of coherence of the legal system, and of consistency in the role played by courts.

Of course this complex and important phenomenon marks the emergence of new legal authorities in civil law countries. Beside the legislators, the higher courts now define themselves as authorities vested with power to deliver judgements that should be followed as rules in future cases. Probably all this reveals a shift in the allocation of powers inside civil law systems. The growing role of higher courts implies a less absolute role for statutes, and thus a somewhat less important role of the legislature. An obvious but relevant feature of this change is that the courts themselves brought it about through their adoption of a new approach to precedent.

Inside the foregoing general trend to a wide use of precedents in civil law systems one can discern some significant differences. First, what can be used as a precedent varies in the several countries. On the one hand there are countries, such as the UK and USA, where the precedent is the whole previous judgement: the *ratio decidendi* is identified by analysing the previous decision against the background of the full facts of the case. Indeed, under some statutes, the use of a precedent to decide the case in issue may depend on a close similarity between the facts of this case and the facts of the precedent. This is not true in some civil law systems, where the 'precedent' consists only of the very general and concise statement of the rule of law applied in the former case. In Finland, for instance, this statement is expressed at the beginning of the judgement, while in Italy it is stated by a special office of the *Corte di Cassazione*. In Italy the court never scrutinizes the facts of the precedent to decide whether they are sufficiently similar to the facts of the case in issue. What is taken as precedent is not properly the *ratio decidendi* of an individual case, but a general statement that is very similar – in its form – to a statutory rule. Moreover what is used as a *ratio* to decide the case is not an outcome of an analysis made by the court itself: this sort of rule (a 'massimo') is stated by someone else, and it is used merely to support the decision. Thus the common law idea of *ratio decidendi* is not appropriate.

Another important difference concerns the number of precedents used. In some countries the precedents cited are relatively few. For example, although in the UK the case-law is rich and complex, only one or a few precedents may be directly in point for each contested issue. The situation is very different in systems such as Italy and Poland. There, many previous judgements (sometimes dozens in a limited period of time) may have been delivered on the same issue. Then precedent takes the form of a *line* or a *series* of cited judgements. In these circumstances a rule obliging the court, as in the UK, to cite all relevant precedents would be absurd and impossible to apply, since the court could cite dozens or even hundreds. As a result, not all precedents are cited, but only some, these being chosen at random or among the most recent ones. In fact, sometimes there will be a precedent available to support all positions on an issue.

The obvious consequence is that the justificatory force of a *single* precedent is completely different in the two types of systems. When few precedents are cited, each has strong force: it is legally binding (if not distinguished or overruled) as in the UK and USA, or it is strongly persuasive, as in Sweden and Finland. But when many precedents are cited, as in some of the other countries such as Italy, each precedent may alone be very weak, and a whole series of precedents required to have persuasive force. Moreover, when many precedents exist on the same issue, the probability of conflicts and inconsistencies inside the case-law grows. This affords the court a wide range of discretionary choice and often means that the court must discuss conflicting lines of precedent.

A special factor here is this: if the deciding court includes many and diverse members, it may be more difficult to achieve a viable system of precedent. In the French Cour de Cassation there are 200 judges. In the House of Lords there are ten.

We may now turn to the explanatory potential of certain institutional features of courts in the various systems. The general trend now is to vest the highest courts with discretionary power to select the cases they want to decide on the merits. The traditional examples are the House of Lords in the UK and the Supreme Court of the USA, but Sweden, Finland and Argentina are now very important, since a system similar to American *certiorari* has recently been introduced in those countries.

Generally the power to select is the power to decide when a precedent should be set in order to confirm an old and debatable precedent, or to overrule an old one and state a new one, or to set a precedent in a case of first impression under the statute. Therefore many cases are chosen simply in order to set a precedent. The consequence is not only that the number of cases decided on their merits is very low, but also that the force of a single precedent is considerable.

But, when a highest court has no power to select cases (or has only limited powers of selection), so that it is obliged to decide every case or most cases submitted by the parties on the merits (as in Italy and Germany), it is obvious that the number of precedents will be higher and, consequentialy, their relative force lower.

These structural features reflect different ideas about the role of a highest court inside the legal system. On the one hand, the court can be conceived as an agency with power to set precedents and power to supervise legal doctrine. Such a court may set few and relatively strong precedents. On the other hand, the Supreme Court may be viewed as an ultimate agency for the correction of legal error in the individual case. When this is so, the selection of cases is not allowed or is reduced, and the setting of precedents is a kind of by-product of the court's activity.

An interesting comparison is between Italy and France. They share the same fundamental model of the supreme court (that Italy borrowed from France), but the practices of the two courts are now very different. The French Cour de Cassation maintains rigidly the principle of the supremacy of statutes and does not cite precedents, while the Italian Corte di Cassazione cites a lot of precedents.

VII   SIMILARITIES AND DIFFERENCES – STRUCTURE AND 'LOGIC' OF OPINION AS A WHOLE

By 'structure', we refer to the main justificatory elements of the opinion and to the way these elements are arrayed and interrelated. These elements consist of the facts, the statutory text and other materials used in constructing arguments, the issue or issues, the reasons given for their resolution and the conclusion or conclusions. The procedural posture of the case may also be of justificatory relevance.

In all systems there is, by specific law or by virtue of generally accepted conventions, a minimum essential content of the opinion of the higher courts. One criterion for evaluating the adequacy of this minimum is the extent to which it enables a law-trained party otherwise unfamiliar with the case to evaluate the legal correctness of the decision without having to go outside the opinion for essential justificatory elements. Several countries do not require even that the statute be quoted in the opinion (though all require citation to the statute). Several do not require that all the relevant facts of the case be set out either. These things hamper the independent critic.

In some cases, as in the USA and in the UK, conventions deeply rooted in the practices of highest courts govern minimum content. In civil law systems, Finland apart, there are specific statutory provisions on what a judgement must contain. This content usually includes several things not directly relevant here (identification of the court, names of parties and lawyers, and so on) but also much that is relevant to the justificatory structure of opinions: (a) a narration of procedural history of the case; (b) a concise summary of the submissions made by the parties and of their arguments; (c) a statement of the facts of the case; (d) a reference to the statutory rules applied; (e) the reasons supporting the decision; and (f) the final judgement of the court containing decision. This list holds more or less; for instance, an explicit reference to statutes is not always required and something else can be required (for example, evidence and evaluation of it in Poland).

The most problematic is (e), namely the reasons justifying the decision. The statutory requirement of 'reasons' may consist of no more than a statement of the relevant facts and a mere reference to the relevant legal rules, without any real justificatory effort by way of intermediate steps connecting the result to the statute in the light of specific interpretational arguments. This is true in France, where the judges generally presume that the law is clear. In other countries something more is taken to be required.

Fortunately the actual practice of courts is very different, and goes far beyond what is formally required by law. To state this in few words: what purport to be effective justifications are usually delivered by most of the higher courts in our study, especially supreme courts, even when not formally required.

The opinions actually delivered in practice, then, better serve both the internal and the external purposes of judicial opinions. In general, opinions in practice adequately serve the internal purposes of appeals and review. External purposes are not so well served. The opinion gives some idea of what the decision is and of reasons for it, but the degree to which the functions of justificatory opinions are fulfilled differs in the several systems (see Section VIII).

The largely prevailing practice, with the only exception being

France, is to write lengthy opinions in order to justify interpretations of statutes. Most justifications tend to be complex rather than simple, and to include several arguments rather than one or two. Sometimes one finds a baroque and redundant set of arguments, but the general tendency is to justify – by reference to the law or to some other element – each step of the reasoning.

Inside this generally prevailing practice there are significant differences as to the degree of richness and complexity, and also in the macro-structures or 'logic' of the justificatory reasoning. These differences can be sketched as follows:

(a) There is a *simple subsumptive* model in which the justification is reduced to the skeleton of a judicial syllogism. The court states only the legal rule, the relevant facts and their conclusion. Many French opinions approach this model, and the whole judgement is often phrased in what amounts to a single, very long, grammatical sentence. This structure has two main variations. One is when not all the elements of the syllogism are expressly stated (for instance when only the facts are stated and the statute is only implicitly referred to, as sometimes happens today in France, and earlier in Finland and Sweden). The other is when something more than a basic syllogism is stated, as where premisses are more than two.

(b) The court may deliver longer and more elaborated justifications, and in so doing adopt some version of the model of *complex* or *sophisticated subsumption*. Here the final decision is presented as a deductive consequence logically drawn from given premisses, but the statement of premisses is complex and elaborated because these premisses are, in their turn, justified by 'sub premisses'. This model prevails widely in such civil law systems as Germany, Italy, Finland and Poland. It takes two fundamental forms, although they seldom appear in 'pure' versions; mixtures are much more frequent. One version is that of complex but linear reasoning, step by step in a series of *cascaded* inferential passages. Deduction is the main logical form; the justification consists of a chain of deductive passages, and each of them is justified by the previous step. The other version, much more frequent, follows the 'legs of a chair' model of justification: its most important feature is that each conclusion (and mainly the final decision) is supported by several arguments.

An interesting mixed version occurs when there are several steps in the reasoning, and each is justified in the 'legs of a chair' mode, that is, using several converging arguments. Then we can have (as for instance in Poland and Italy) the *legs-of-a-chair syllogism*, where the premisses are each justified by several arguments.

Various cultural and institutional factors probably explain the resort to these complex forms of subsumptive justification. These forms reflect a transition from an authoritative to a more dialogic approach, according to which the opinion is viewed as an answer to arguments submitted by the parties. Another factor is procedural. In some systems the appeal to the Supreme Court is framed in terms of 'reasons of attack' pursuant to specific procedural law, so that the court must examine and decide several precisely defined issues. A third factor is that the legal culture is becoming less and less formal and more open to divergences, evolutionary changes and a plurality of viewpoints. A final factor is the shift to adversarial instead of inquisitorial procedure, in general and in the higher courts also.

(c) There is also a basic model of *discursive alternative justification* in which the final decision is not presented as a logical consequence of given premises but as the outcome of judicial choices made according to arguments and priority rules. Here the main feature is that on each interpretative issue the conflicting arguments are stated and discussed, the possible alternative choices identified, then open choices made, and for stated reasons. Not infrequently some substantive reasoning or discussion of values will appear. This model is followed in Argentina, in the USA and in the UK (though with less by way of substantive reasoning and values). This difference in justificatory structures between civil law and common law systems is one of the few differences of justificatory practice between countries in our project that largely tracks the traditional 'civil law – common law' divide. The difference cries out for explanation. Perhaps one factor is that judges in the UK and the USA were themselves once lawyers who practised law in the 'discursive' or dialogic style. Also the British and American judiciaries have traditionally played larger roles in their systems than most of the other judiciaries in their systems. Perhaps, then, those judiciaries feel less need to proceed by way of deductive subsumption than do judges whose legitimacy has been more in doubt and only relatively recently fully won. Confirmation of this is perhaps indicated by the style of judging in 'mixed' systems like those of Scotland or Louisiana, where an originally civilian body of law has been administered by judges whose methodology is essentially a case-law or common law-oriented one.

There are still other differences. A very important one concerns dissenting (and also concurring) opinions. These are widely utilized in common law systems, although in the UK the House of Lords tends now to deliver only one opinion. The tradition in continental countries, however, has been to have only one opinion of the court. But dissents now occur in all civil countries in our study except for France and Italy. Within the civil law countries allowing dissents, there are important variations. Argentina, Finland and

Sweden now have dissenting opinions (often long) so that their practice is now very near to that of the US Supreme Court. In Germany, however, dissents generally occur only in the Constitutional Court.

Three main factors seem to affect traditions with respect to dissent. One is the different degree to which systems adhere to a democratic model of the administration of justice. When this adherence is great, secret voting by judges is unknown, or is set aside in favour of 'openness'. It is also thought to be democratic to allow the judge the right to disagree openly with a majority decision and to state publicly the reasons for dissent. On the continent there may be a significant residue of authoritarian ideology in those systems that utilize secrecy of voting as a means of reinforcing the 'authority' of judicial decisions. The single opinion for the whole court is thought to strengthen the authority of the court and the overall force of its judgements.

Another important factor is the personal, moral and political responsibility of judges for the roles they actually play in making the decision. In some systems judges are ready to assume openly their own personal responsibility and they make use of the right to do so and to justify openly their own position. In other systems, where the judiciary is much more bureaucratic, some judges shun individual responsibility and seem to prefer to play out their role in the environment of secret deliberation. They purport to act as organs rather than as persons, and organs have no individual opinions.

A third factor is a special view of legal truth which does not allow for the possibility of dissent. This view prevails in French legal culture, among other places. It may be influenced partly by religious traditions.

In Germany the Constitutional Court issues dissents. But this court is thought to be very special and, moreover, the members of this court are chosen partly from outside the civil service judiciary. When the political features of adjudication are specially relevant, as in constitutional cases, it is thought that judges should have the possibility to express their own dissent from a majority opinion. Of course this reasoning applies more widely to courts with constitutional jurisdiction in other countries too.

In concluding this section, we would observe that there appears to be some trend away from deductive demonstration to discursive justification; from 'closed' to more 'open' forms of reasoning; from apodictic authority to dialectic choice between acknowledged alternatives. Of course this is occurring within the forms and institutions in each tradition and legal culture. The shift is taking place by small steps instead of sudden and complete changes. Yet we think it plainly perceptible.

VIII   SIMILARITIES AND DIFFERENCES – ADDRESSEES AND FUNCTIONS OF OPINIONS

Judicial opinions are directly and primarily addressed to the parties in the cases. In a sense the judgement is in fact a resolution of the issues and arguments raised by parties. Consequently an important function of the opinion is to show the losing party that the judgement is legal. The opinion should reveal that the judgement is no longer viewed merely as an act of state authority, but rather as a reasoned answer given by the court to the citizen who sought justice.

Do judicial opinions actually fulfil the functions of explaining to the parties and to the public how such decisions are legal and just? This question cannot be empirically answered here. Nevertheless an inference may be drawn from what we said earlier about the structure and logic of justificatory opinions. This inference is that, the more the opinions are technical, formal and deductive, the less are they capable of being read and understood by ordinary people lacking any legal training. Thus it can be argued that, in most systems where this model prevails, the function of persuading the parties of the soundness of the judgement is rather poorly fulfilled (if at all), except in so far as lawyers undertake to explain the result to the client. The same holds for the function of enabling the public at large to review the decision for legality and justice.

Lawyers are therefore by far the most important addressees of judicial opinions. Sometimes the role of legal academicians is also prominent (as in Germany). In other cases (as in the UK) the main addressees include other high-ranked judges as well as the barristers or advocates.

Supreme Courts, then, tend to shape their opinions for an audience of professional lawyers, to whom they speak on the basis and by means of a common technical culture. The judge writes as a professional lawyer for those who share the legal culture. Since the legal culture is a culture of experts, we have here a dialogue among experts.

Usually the function of demonstrating how the decision is consistent with the law can only be fulfilled through resort to formal and technical legal concepts. This kind of legitimization must occur inside the legal culture, rather than before the society as a whole. The legitimating audience, then, is the class of lawyers, not the body of citizens.

A related function of the opinion is to demonstrate that the court (and in its name the single judge who writes the opinion) is actually a competent expert panel, appropriately trained in the resolution of such legal cases. When this occurs it is the court itself (as well as the decision) which is legitimated and this is always within the framework of the legal culture.

Another important function of the opinion is of special significance where the Supreme Court plays the primary role of establishing precedents rather than correcting error. (See section VI.) In all the systems considered, except Italy, one function of the opinion is to set forth facts of the case of relevance to its use as a precedent. The opinion thus provides the very basis on which the precedent can control future decisions. It should be added that in France, although the facts are set forth, they are not set forth in much detail.

In this perspective other addressees of opinions besides the legally-trained can emerge, depending on the legal matter involved. An opinion can be addressed mainly to police officers when it deals with criminal matters, to tax agencies when it deals with tax law, to employers, employees and unions when it deals with labour matters, and so on. From this point of view, the justification in the opinion can be said to perform an 'explanatory' function; it states a rule to be followed as a precedent, and provides items of information and justification that enable people to understand the real meaning of a rule that governs part of their activity.

IX   SIMILARITIES AND DIFFERENCES – JUSTIFICATORY STYLE OF OPINION AS A WHOLE

Here we draw together several major features of justificatory style: (1) how openly the court acknowledges in the opinion the existence of issues of interpretation, that is, genuinely alternative readings of the statute; (2) how far the court assumes that there is only a single right answer; (3) the extent to which the court expresses itself in legal and technical, rather than ordinary language; (4) the extent to which the opinion is abstract rather than concrete, is generalizing rather than casuistic; (5) the degree of elaborateness of the opinion; (6) how far the model of rationality implicitly adopted in the opinion is one of logical deduction from authoritative premises as opposed to one of discursive rationality; (7) the proportion of formal as opposed to substantive reasons appearing in the opinion; (8) the extent to which the court not merely concerns itself with the cognitive ascertainment of existing statute law and the due application of that law to fact, but also openly confronts gaps and any other needs for additional law, evaluates alternatives and creates such law as required; and (9) how far the overall style is magisterial rather than argumentative. There are major differences between systems here, and some of them may again be explained in terms of special institutional, political, cultural and other factors at work. In the treatment of differences that follows, the countries that represent the polar opposites in regard to each attribute of style will usually be the French and the US systems.

Opinions of the higher courts differ greatly in the degree to which they acknowledge the existence of issues of interpretation. In some countries, most notably France, the opinions generally do not openly acknowledge the necessity for judges to choose between genuine alternative readings of the statute. Rather, French judges generally proceed as if there is only one possible answer to the question – indeed they generally refuse to acknowledge the necessity for any *interpretation* as such (and *a fortiori*, gap filling). In the United States, on the other hand, the necessity for interpretation is taken for granted, and issues of interpretation readily and openly acknowledged. The American judges set out the different alternative readings of the statute, and then openly choose between them on the basis of the statutory language and other arguments. Here the Italian, German, Polish and perhaps the Finnish systems are more like the French. The UK, Argentina and Sweden are more like the American.

The medium of expression adopted by the court is another feature of style. In France, judicial opinions of the highest courts are generally written in legalistic, technical and bureaucratic language, so that the proportion of ordinary, lay language is low. In the USA, on the other hand, while it cannot be said that the proportion of legalistic and technical language is low, it is still not as high as in French opinions, except in such technical fields as taxation, commercial law and economic regulation. Moreover, in many non-technical fields, the American opinions include a relatively low proportion of legalistic and technical expressions. Germany, Poland and Italy are more like France here than like the USA. But Argentina, the UK and, in recent times, both Scandinavian countries – Sweden and Finland, appear to be more like the USA.

Another stylistic attribute is the extent to which the opinion is abstract and general in tenor, rather than concrete and casuistic. Swedish opinions concentrate almost entirely on the concrete facts and the resolution of the issue arising therefrom. French opinions are extremely diverse. Some merely classify the facts as 'in' or 'out' of a general legal category itself taken for granted. Other French opinions are exceedingly abstract and general, with little or no applicational reasoning. The UK and US opinions often display both attributes at the same time. They state general rules and principles yet also apply them very particularly to the facts.

A further feature of justificatory style is the degree of elaborateness of the opinion. Here again, the opinions of the highest courts in France are in a class by themselves. They tend to be extremely brief and abstract — with their essence often running to no more than a few lines or a paragraph or two. The higher courts of the USA and of the UK both represent the opposite polarity. Their opinions usually include elaborate and extended discussion of the issues. The same is true in Argentina, Italy, Germany and Poland. It is also true of Sweden and Finland, although only very recently so. Overall there is a major trend toward the elaborate and lengthy judicial opinion.

Implicit in the style of any opinion that purports to be justificatory is some concept or model of rational justification itself. In France, and also in Germany, Italy, Poland and, to some extent, Finland, the generally prevailing concept or model of rational justification is that of logical deduction or syllogistic subsumption. As we saw in the preceding section, the opinions in these countries are generally set up so that they appear to proceed deductively from authoritative premisses to binding conclusions. Indeed there may even be a special effort to present the conclusion as the *necessary* consequence of accepting the premisses. The basic model, then, is more like the 'links of a chain' than the 'legs of a chair', though the premisses themselves may be supported by specific reasons on a 'legs of a chair' model. In Argentina, the UK, USA and Sweden, the concept or model of rationality generally implicit in the opinions is what we have called 'discursive'. According to this model, the conclusion to be justified consists of an acknowledged choice between alternative interpretations supported by one or more arguments in the fashion of legs supporting the seat of a chair (or in the fashion of strands in a rope). The court makes no effort to present the chosen conclusion as a necessary consequence of accepted premisses. The court's conclusion is simply the consequence of there being good and sufficient reasons for adopting it rather than any alternative.

We also find generally different proportions of formal and substantive reasons in the opinions. For this purpose, formal reasons are ones that arise essentially from authoritative sources of law including the statute itself and related statutes, any constitution, any precedent on the meaning of the statute, any precedent on interpretational method, any relevant regulations or official interpretations, any general principles of law, the logic of relevant legal concepts, any authoritative policies in the area, and official *travaux préparatoires*. Independent substantive reasons, on the other hand, are reasons of essentially moral, economic, political and social content the force of which depends more or less on their weight and not on whether they happen to be linked to some authoritative source or sources. Substantive reasons include rightness reasons arising under moral norms, goal reasons arising from possible social policy goals, and various institutional reasons arising from features of legal institutions and processes. Substantive reasons may inform the content of an interpretation at the first-order level or, at the second level, play a conflict-settling role as between competing reasons.

The proportion of formal reasons to substantive is, of course, very high in the interpretative opinions of the highest courts in all systems. Indeed, in the French system, formal reasons are almost always the only reasons. In the opinions in the Italian and Polish systems there is relatively little substantive argumentation not immediately traceable to a formal source of law. The same is true of the Finnish system. And in the UK substantive reasoning must be linked more or less to an authoritative source. On the other hand, purely substantive reasons are becoming more common in the Swedish system, are common in the Argentine system, and have long been frequent elements in opinions of the US Supreme Court in cases of statutory interpretation, especially when there is no, or only a weak, argument from ordinary or from technical meaning.

There is this important qualification: when the highest court of a system acts both as a constitutional court and as an ordinary supreme court, the style tends to be more substantive than otherwise. This signifies, for example, that the US Supreme Court opinions, even in statutory interpretation cases, tend to be more substantive than they otherwise would be. There is more independent substantive reasoning as well as more substantive reasoning linked to authorities or sources of law. Also, when a court with constitutional adjudicative power interprets statutes in the course of deciding on constitutionality, its interpretational reasoning also tends to be more substantive. One might state a kind of axiom: constitutional adjudication influences a court to adopt a more substantive style, even in statutory interpretation.

Style may also be compared in terms of how far courts concern themselves merely with cognitive ascertainment and application of law rather than the evaluation of alternatives and the creation of new law to fill gaps or meet other perceived needs for new law. The French courts almost never acknowledge, in the case being decided, any evaluative or creative element. In France the higher courts frequently appear to believe that judging is always merely a matter of cognition — of ascertaining and applying the law that exists. Relatedly the French courts frequently prefer not to narrate or expound meaning, but merely to classify the facts as 'in' or 'out' of the statute. This is perhaps an extreme manifestation of what one might call a cognitive style, and has been characterized as 'legal existentialism'.

At the other polarity, the US Supreme Court, which has a rather different history and functions under a different theory of separation of powers, adopts a general style in which the court acknowledges that some statutes may require the exercise of evaluative and creative judgement very different from the mere cognitive ascertainment and application of the law that exists.

In not openly recognizing an evaluative and creative judicial role, the Finnish, Italian and Polish courts are closer to the French here than to the American. Again the UK and Sweden here are closer to the USA. The German system is in the middle.

Finally the systems also differ dramatically in a further dimension, and this is most pronounced in the problematic cases. One may differentiate between a relatively magisterial style and what might be called a relatively argumentative and dialogic style. In the magisterial style, the court's opinion is presented as an impersonal, authoritative, unsigned, imperial 'Staatsakt', whereas in the argumentative style the opinion is more personalized, is duly signed by the author, and bears at least some recognizable stylistic traits of the author. Further, in the magisterial style, the court proceeds as if there is only one possible answer — the court's answer — to the issue of interpretation, whereas in the argumentative style the court assumes that more than one answer might be possible, rehearses the arguments for and against, and seeks to show by argument why the answer given is the most justified one. Additionally, in the argumentative style, the court enters into what might be construed as a dialogue with its various addressees. That is, some or all of the opinion can often be construed as a dialogic response to arguments of losing counsel, or to arguments of a lower court judge, or to arguments of a concurring or dissenting judge of the same court.

The French, Finnish, German, Italian and Polish styles tend to be relatively magisterial. The Argentine, Swedish, UK and US styles are less magisterial and more argumentative.

We have now identified a number of traits of justificatory style to be found in the opinions of the higher courts in our study. We believe that these traits display some affinities. Thus, one might categorize them into two columns of cognates as follows:

A	B
(1) genuine issues of interpretation not openly acknowledged	(1) open acknowledgement of alternative readings of statute
(2) only one answer possible	(2) more than one possible answer
(3) high proportion of legalistic, technical and bureaucratic language in the opinion	(3) lower proportion of legalistic and technical language in opinion
(4) abbreviated and terse opinion	(4) extended and elaborate opinion
(5) implicit model of rationality is logico-deductive, i.e., syllogistic subsumption	(5) implicit model of rationality is not deductive but discursive — open choice supported by arguments
(6) high proportion of formal rather than substantive reasons	(6) lower proportion of formal rather than substantive reasons
(7) evaluative and creative role not recognized; decisional process viewed as essentially one of cognitive ascertainment and application of the law that 'is'	(7) acknowledgement of some evaluative and creative role
(8) magisterial and authoritative	(8) argumentative and dialogic

Nearly all the items in each column above tend to go together, that is, have affinities. For example, if issues of interpretation are not openly acknowledged (A1), one would expect that the courts would not acknowledge any creative or evaluative element (A7) as well. Similarly, if the implicit model of rationality is one of syllogistic subsumption (A5) one would also expect to find a very high preponderance of formal over substantive reasons (A6). And so on.

But the 'cognates' thus identified are not logical relations. Thus, for example, the dialogic aspect of the argumentative style (B8) is also to be found in some opinions implicitly adopting the rational model of syllogistic subsumption (A5). There is nothing that is, strictly speaking, inconsistent in this. Similarly, lengthy and elaborate opinions (B4) could quite obviously include a high proportion of formal reasons (A6), or even be magisterial in tenor (A8).

Further, while most of the opposing pairs in each column represent opposite poles along a spectrum, some are perhaps more felicitously conceptualized as dichotomies. This is true of A1 and

B1 and (less so) of A5 and B5.

In the light of the foregoing, it would be most faithful to the facts to treat each of the countries included in our study *individually* in relation to the polar cases *on each continuum*. In so doing we would avoid lumping most systems in undifferentiated ways as 'intermediate cases' between France and the USA. It is important to see, for example, that, while the UK in regard to the acknowledgement of any creative and evaluative role for judges is 'intermediate' between the USA and France, it is nonetheless closer to the USA overall. Similarly, while Germany and Italy, in their frequency of resort to formal reasons over substantive ones are 'far' from the USA, they are even farther from France. Indeed France now seems relatively isolated overall.

Our general mode of analysis here also does not make any special place for trends. Yet overall there has been a dramatic movement away from the French polarity, on which more later.

It will be recalled that the higher French courts (Cour de Cassation and Conseil d'Etat) commonly refuse to acknowledge the existence of genuine issues of interpretation. These courts also appear to believe that there is only one correct answer, express themselves largely in technical and legal language, render quite terse opinions, adopt the model of rationality here called syllogistic subsumption, rely almost exclusively on formal reasons, disavow evaluative and creative elements in interpretation and generally adopt a magisterial approach with virtually no dialogue.

The opinions in the French system, then, answer in considerable measure to virtually all of A(1)–(8) above. We cannot offer final explanations for this, but we can suggest hypotheses that are more or less consistent with these attributes of French opinions. Moreover we can test these hypotheses in a limited way by considering their inapplicability to the most consistent opposite polarity – that of the USA. In so doing, we will draw mainly on institutional–political differences, differences of legal culture and legal theory, and differences of academic traditions. Basic facts about all of these are generally known.

The higher French courts certainly wish to *appear* to have only a relatively passive role, whereas the US Supreme Court (and most other higher US courts) can be seen to be much more active in comparison. The US Supreme Court openly acknowledges interpretational issues – indeed sometimes leans forward and identifies them entirely on its own. The French courts, on the other hand, generally disclaim any genuine interpretive role that would carry them beyond the statutory text. The French courts do not openly recognize any gaps in legislation either. But the US Supreme Court, at least until quite recently, has been ready to go beyond, or even in some cases to revise, the legislative text, and the Court openly undertakes to fill gaps, and thus 'make law'. The French courts disclaim any legislative role.

Many scholars agree that the efforts of French courts to cultivate an impression of judicial passivity may be in part attributable to the influence of the French Revolution. The pre-Revolutionary courts were highly activist, and were viewed as an official arm of the oppressive Ancien Régime. Judges today seek to disassociate themselves from this role. Relatedly, the post-revolutionary conception of separation of powers (Montesquieu, strictly construed) formally allows the French courts only a subordinate and passive role in which there is not even to be interpretation in the process of applying law. French judges thus purport to leave law-making entirely to the legislature, on the ground that the legislature is the democratically elected organ of the people. The French Executive, it should be stressed, has vast 'inherent' power on its own to make further implementive law ('decrees') to carry out statutory mandates. Some of this law does not require 'umbrella' legislation, particularly within public law fields. Thus the French courts can in effect say, mainly to the legislature: 'You do it.'

At the same time the Conseil d'Etat and the Cour de Cassation have no power to review statutes for constitutional validity. The Conseil d'Etat does, however, actively review administrative action for constitutional and legal validity. The only realm in which the Cour de Cassation acknowledges that it can 'make' anything analogous to common law is by way of evolving the Code Civil in private law fields such as contract and tort. Here the law of torts is a major field of private law in which there has been active judicial development. It must be added that the Cour de Cassation may, in its annual report, be somewhat more candid about areas in which it has undertaken a more creative role.

Thus the *official* and publicly cultivated impression is that the French higher courts have a largely passive role in most matters, including statutory interpretation. Moreover this is congenial to French legal culture and legal theory. For a very long while, this body of culture and theory has, in regard to judicial role, been essentially formal and positivist, rather than substantive and instrumentalist.

To determine whether French courts not merely appear but in fact are passive would require far more study than we have been able to carry out. But one thing is certain. The US Supreme Court is, by comparison, activist rather than passive and has, in matters of interpretation, undertaken a relatively creative and evaluative role. Several opposing institutional and cultural factors may be at work here. Before turning to these, it should be said that, if the French conception of democracy were transplanted to the USA, the US Supreme Court would behave differently, and would not be nearly so activist in matters of interpretation. Some French theorists view the activism of the higher American courts as undemocratic or perhaps even anti-democratic.

But apart from the possibility of differing conceptions of democracy here (Madisonian v. Rousseauian) the higher American courts also function under a different conception of the separation of powers and against a different historical background. Compared to the French, the American courts are a coordinate rather than a subordinate branch of government and have vast *de facto* law-making power. Thus the US Supreme Court is at the pinnacle of the judicial system and creates vast bodies of constitutional case-law against which it tests the validity even of acts of Congress. (As we have seen, neither the Cour de Cassation nor the Conseil d'Etat has such jurisdiction.) It also creates vast bodies of administrative–regulatory case-law doctrine pursuant to statutes that grant regulatory power to agencies and officials whose acts the Court may ultimately review for legality.

Elements of the American legal culture also suggest explanations. The highly influential instrumentalist revolution in American legal thought conceived of judges as 'social engineers' and, beginning in the 1920s, the 'realist' wing of this revolution exposed the very substantial degree to which American judges had been making (and continue to make) law in the guise of interpretation and otherwise. In all these respects, the French system is very different.

We now turn away from the active–passive issue to matters more intimately justificatory. It is sometimes suggested that the usual judicial opinion of a French higher court interpreting a statute is not really justificatory at all. Such opinions are, so it is said, essentially conclusory. Now it is true that most of these opinions are extremely brief and often purport to state answers rather than justify. But it does not follow that they are not justificatory at all. It is simply that they are not robustly so. That is, they seldom provide elaborate and extended argumentation, unlike their American counterparts. Again differing political, institutional and cultural factors are at work, some of which we have already explored. The French, perhaps, can be forgiven for thinking that robust and elaborate judicial argumentation, and not only when it invokes substantive reasoning and evaluative analysis, infringes upon the monopoly of legislative power shared by democratic legislatures and politically accountable executives.

Most American judges at the highest levels have not seen matters this way, and thus frequently write long and elaborate opinions filled with argument, including some open discussion of values. But it must be said that the opinions of the higher French courts considered here are *not* the only places where justifying reasons for decisions may be found. They may also be found in the 'conclusions' of the Avocat-Général or in official documents of the Commissaire du Gouvernement. Thus French judges may be excused if they also think that they need not discharge the entire justificatory burden in an opinion of the court. But the American higher judiciary has no such excuse, and must say what it has to say in its own opinions.

Another institutional factor is very likely this: in the higher French courts, the decision-making process does not countenance dissenting opinions, and this exerts its own pressure for brevity. No such factor operates in the American system, where dissents are common.

Differences of legal culture and legal theory doubtless apply here, too. The abbreviated and terse French opinions are consistent with their formal and positivist legal culture, while again the robust justificatory argumentation found in American opinions is consistent with the substantive and instrumentalist conception of the judge as 'social engineer'. Moreover, and as part of this, the American legal professoriat generally insists on robust justification and judicial candour in the matter of reason giving. The same is not true in France.

Finally we may also characterize French justificatory practice as essentially based on appeals to authority – to formal reasons. Thus the French higher courts generally adhere very closely to the written statutory text, often recite one or two other formal arguments of a systemic nature and commonly adopt a logico-deductive model of rational justification in which conclusions are presented as following from authoritative premisses. In contrast, the American justificatory style regularly invokes substantive reasons and is openly creative and evolutional. The American higher courts adopt a discursive 'good reasons' approach not confined to appeals to authority.

These differences can also be viewed as flowing from institutional, political and cultural differences of the kind already treated. Thus the authority that the courts appeal to in France is largely that of the democratic legislature. The judiciary is supposed to be a subordinate organ of that body carrying out the legislative will (or the will of the democratically accountable executive, as the case may be).

But, as we have seen, the higher American judiciary is viewed not as a subservient organ of other branches but as a coordinate body carrying out an independent judicial function that requires open and acknowledged interpretation, gap-filling, and even involves some modification and adjustment of statutes at point of application. After all, legislatures and other executive law-making bodies cannot draft statutes perfectly, do not have perfect fore-sight, and do not have the special benefit of those forms of insight into problems available at point of application. On this view it is natural that a judiciary would not confine itself merely to formal reasons of authority but would invoke substantive appeals to moral, economic, political and other social considerations emer-gent at point of application. It is also natural on such a view that judges would fulfil a somewhat creative role and even find them-selves from time to time engaged in robust evaluative reasoning.

Again the different legal cultures and legal theories in the two countries reinforce the differing orientations. The French practice is reinforced here by its formal and positivistic tradition; the Ameri-can practice by its substantive and instrumentalist tradition. The American judges can also be seen as responding to a legal profes-soriat that insists on a 'good reasons' approach to justification and regularly subjects judicial opinions to close scrutiny not merely in technical or formal terms.

Certain other countries in our study might, in the foregoing fashion, be plotted on a spectrum between the French and the US systems, and similar explanatory accounts could be provided in terms of varying institutional, political and other cultural factors. Moreover still further major factors, such as the Continental 'civil service' tradition of staffing the judiciary, should figure in the explanatory analysis, too. So also should styles of legislative drafting, just to name two more factors.

In closing, we wish to stress that the French case represents a sort of 'pure' polarity that is today alone in the European pano-rama. Moreover, while the other systems might be plotted as 'intermediate' cases between France and the USA, most of them are not merely 'scattered' between France and the USA. Indeed such systems as Italy, West Germany and perhaps Poland and even Finland reveal a clear *tendency* to what might be called a 'third style' or 'model', in which: (1) the evaluative and creative is generally not openly recognized (as in France), but the judges know they create law; (2) a high proportion of technical language appears (as in France); (3) complex structures of argument appear (as in USA); (4) the opinions are extended and elaborate (as in USA); (5) a high proportion of formal reasons appears (as in France); (6) the magis-terial style is adopted (as in France); and (7) substantive consti-tutional and other general legal principles play a major role in some interpretation cases (as in USA).

In the systems that typify the emergent third style or model, the

higher courts are relatively passive, yet heavily involved in interpretative problems. It may be that their courts are revealing a
deeper sensitivity to the social and political problems involved in
the administration of justice. Although creative choice is generally
not openly recognized, there are major exceptions. These courts do
tend to confront gaps directly, and to recognize that statutes and
codes may, because of age, require updating. These courts are not
so 'free-wheeling' as many American Supreme Court judges have,
until quite recently, seemed to be. They try to solve interpretative
problems by resort to legal sources and materials 'inside the
system'. They utilize tools of classical positivistic legal culture,
especially linguistic and systemic argumentation, and also appeals
to authoritative deductive methods as well as to authoritative
purposes and legal dogmatics.

This emerging third model or style differs significantly from
both the French style and the US style, and merits far more analysis
and exploration than we can provide in this chapter.

It is certain that basic similarities between all systems, though
profound in terms of the common core of accepted types of leading
arguments and in terms of most justificatory patterns (single,
cumulative and so on), do not also extend to the structure and style
of justifications. This important finding of our study also merits
much more attention than we can give it here. It might be that
there are factors that affect types of arguments and patterns of
justification: that is, substance, but not structure and style. Almost
all systems require, as a matter of positive law, that judges state
specific reasons for their decisions, and this may be a major factor
accounting for substantive similarities in types of arguments and
patterns of justification. Certain common underlying values (discussed in Chapter 13) may help account for such similarities, too,
yet have little or no bearing on style and structure.

The impact of style and structure on the types of arguments in
play is itself a topic worthy of extended study. But, presumably,
some factors may affect structure and style, yet have little or no
impact on substance, that is, types of argument and patterns of
justification. For example, formal and positivistic academic 'legal
science' provides models that affect style and structure particularly
for bureaucratic judiciaries in Italy and Germany, yet these models
may have little or no affect on the core types of arguments used.
Similarly, the casuistic and non-deductive nature of common law
judicial thinking in which all American lawyers and judges are
immersed may affect the style and structure of judicial opinions,
but have little bearing on the nature of argument types or patterns
of justification.

Finally the distinction drawn here between style and structure, on the one hand, and substance, on the other, allows for the possibility that systems with a formal style in which judicial creativity and evaluation are not, in general, openly recognized, as in the case of France and also those systems adhering to the third model, might still be systems in which the judges are in fact quite active and creative. We do not know if this is true of France, for example, but it might be. As we have indicated, an elaborate (and different) study would be required to confirm as much. But some scholars have even hypothesized that the higher French judges might in fact be even more active and creative in some respects than their most free-wheeling American counterparts. See Dawson (1968).

X   SOME POINTS OF CONTACT BETWEEN THIS PROJECT AND THE CURRENT STATE OF 'COMPARATIVE' LAW SCHOLARSHIP

Comparativists, in studying solutions to substantive problems, have often emphasized differences between the so-called common law and civil law systems, although some scholarship does play down this distinction. Our conclusion here is that much of what we believe we have found does not justify the traditional emphasis on this distinction, as applied to the subject of statutory interpretation. (Nor do our findings generally support the view that the common law and civil law systems are now 'coming together'.)

On the one hand, there are major similarities between the common law and civil law systems, similarities that may have existed for a very long while. These similarities encompass the common core of types of arguments and similarities in basic justificatory patterns – single, cumulative and so forth.

Furthermore, as section VI makes clear, precedent in the interpretation of statutes is now of great importance in nearly all of the systems in our study. This, of course, comparativists have increasingly recognized, and our study fully confirms it.

On the other hand, our study indicates that many important differences do not follow the traditional distinction between common law and civil law countries. Thus some largely civil law systems such as Sweden and Argentina appear to be more similar in matters of interpretation to the so-called common law systems than to Continental systems. This is true with regard to one feature of truly major justificatory significance. These systems join the common law systems as ones in which judicial opinions canvass opposing reasons and seek to justify the choice between them, rather than merely set forth the prevailing reasons. It may be that

Germany, too, is increasingly more like the common law systems in this respect. Moreover, in matters of style and structure in particular, the so-called civil law systems are themselves now far less homogeneous than they once were. As we have seen, there is an emerging third justificatory style or model in Germany, Italy and, to some extent, Poland and Finland, that differs in major ways from the traditional French style, on the one hand, and the 'common law' style, on the other. It is therefore now impossible to define a 'civil law' style as such. Nor can it be said that the newly emerging third style is one that, overall, is moving closer to the common law style. In some respects the two appear to be moving apart.

In this chapter we have considered, not solutions to concrete substantive problems of tort, contract or the like, as is customary in most comparative law studies, but rather how judges justify decisions applying statute law – a matter of method. Our emphasis has not been on the elusive psychological processes by which judges arrive at decisions but on what actually appears in their published public justifications (see Chapter 2). Even so, it may be that relevant comparability is somewhat harder to achieve in a study such as ours, that there is greater scope for differences between systems in matters of interpretation, and that a wider range of relevant variables may account for differences in general method. But from this it hardly follows that comparative analysis can yield no insight.

We hope that our efforts here will lead theorists and comparativists alike to undertake further work of the general kind we have done, and stimulate them to do it better than it has been possible for us to do through our joint project. In particular, we think it would be useful to have a number of studies in which the justificatory features of interpretative practices in only two countries are compared in detail.

REFERENCES

Atiyah, P. and Summers, R. (1987), *Form and Substance in Anglo-American Law*, Oxford: Oxford University Press.

Bridges, J. (1981), 'National Legal Tradition and Community Law: Legislative Drafting and Judicial Interpretation in England and the European Community', *J. Common Market Studies*, **XIX**, June, Oxford.

Dawson, J. (1968), *The Oracles of the Law*, Ann Arbor: University of Michigan.

Goutal, J. (1976), 'Characteristics of Judicial Style in France, Britain and the U.S.A.', *Am. J. Comp. L.*, **24**, p. 43.

Kötz, H. (1987), 'Taking Civil Codes Less Seriously', *Mod. L. Rev.* **50**, p. 1.

Lawson, F.H. (1977), *The Comparison*, New York: North Holland Pub. Co.

Markesinus, B. (1986), 'Conceptualism, Pragmatism and Courage: A Common

Lawyer Looks at Judgments of the German Federal Court', *Am. J. Comp. L.*, **34**, p. 349.

Rudden, B. (1974), 'Courts and Codes in England, France, and Soviet Russia', *Tul. L. Rev.*, **48**, p. 1010.

Wetter, J.G. (1960), *The Style of Appellate Judicial Decisions*, Leyden: A.W. Sijthoff Press.

Zweigert, K. and Puttfarken, H. (1970), 'Statutory Interpretation – Civilian Style', *Tulane L. Rev.*, **44**, p. 704.

Zweigert, K. and Kötz, H. (1987), *Introduction to Comparative Law* (Trans. J.A. Weir), Oxford: Oxford University Press.

13 Interpretation and Justification

D. NEIL MacCORMICK, *Edinburgh* AND
ROBERT S. SUMMERS, *Ithaca*

I INTRODUCTION

In this chapter we draw on the country-by-country chapters, on the insights of the chapter on comparative analysis, and on studies of legal reasoning generally to try to further a theory of interpretative arguments. We seek a theory of them as elements of rational justification within practical reasoning about issues of law. Everywhere there are huge volumes of statute law, everywhere this law has to be interpreted for the purpose of applying it to life in general and in legal dispute-resolution (our topic), and everywhere it is a matter of argument what is the best interpretation in each particular case, and what might be the right approach to interpretation in general in any case that arises. The connection with justification is clear: one's interpretation of a statute justifies the way one applies it in a case, and one's interpretation itself has therefore to be justified.

Hitherto we have assumed that one justifies interpretations by appropriate arguments, and that the arguments are classifiable into different types. To test this assumption we must — and shall here — ultimately look into the question of what lies behind or below the types of argument and particular instances of them: what underlying something accounts for their justificatory force?

In pursuit of this, we shall consider here the types of argument identified in Chapter 12 as the most pervasive throughout the countries of our study. We shall consider them in two main aspects. First, we shall look at what makes them 'fire', then in due course we shall see how to account for their 'fire-power' — their justificatory force. That is, we shall first set forth the governing idea of each type of argument, thus to clarify and to show how one might specify the general circumstances in which an instance of that argument is available and so becomes deployable to back up an interpretation of a statutory provision; and, following that, we shall seek to account for more complex modes of deployment where arguments may cumulate with others and have reinforcing effect, or may conflict, and some may be found inapplicable, or may be cancelled, or may take priority over others, or may weigh for or against each other, some outweighing others in the final result of a case. Then we shall seek the ultimate justificatory basis of each type of argument, to show why arguments of that type do have justificatory force at all. We shall locate this justificatory force, this 'fire-power', in certain pervasive underlying values of great importance to contemporary legal systems. But, before we come finally to these underlying values, we find it necessary to consider a rather simple and general model of the interactions among arguments, grouped under the very general typology we established in our opening chapters. Of course, this has to be very broad and general, since there are so many variables between and within legal systems. The model is, however, suggestive for ways in which the analysis of interpretational conflicts and their resolution might be pursued in later studies in a more rigorous and thoroughgoing way than ever hitherto in legal theory or in the particular jurisprudence of legal systems.

Finally we inquire into criteria of soundness in interpretation-as-justification. Can we now say anything useful about the way in which interpretation ought to be carried out? Have we any constructive suggestions of more or less universal relevance to make about better interpretative practice? We think so; but are well aware of the audacity of this claim. It certainly will, and should, be subjected to critical scrutiny. In any event, we are fully conscious that much work remains.

II   THE ELEVEN ARGUMENT TYPES

The previous chapter identified 11 major types of argument, all of which (subject of course to variations of terminology and of detail in the formulation) seem to play an important part in the interpretational reasoning of the courts in the various countries we have reviewed. Here we subsume the 11 under our standard categories, and restate each of them in terms of what we regard as its governing idea.

1   Linguistic Arguments

1   The argument from ordinary meaning: the governing idea here is that if a statutory provision is intelligible in the context of

ordinary language, it ought, without more, to be interpreted in accordance with the meaning an ordinary speaker of the language would ascribe to it as its obvious meaning, unless there is sufficient reason for a different interpretation; if ordinary meaning allows of more than one interpretation, the more obvious ought prima facie to be preferred.

2   The argument from technical meaning: the governing idea here is that, if a statutory provision is one that concerns a special activity with a technical language of its own, it ought to be interpreted so as to give technical terms and phrases their technical sense (not their ordinary meaning). ('Technical terms' here include technical legal terms, as well as the technical terms of other specialized activities.)

2   Systemic Arguments

3   The argument from contextual-harmonization: the governing idea here is that, if a statutory provision belongs within a larger scheme, whether a single statute or a set of related statutes, it ought to be interpreted in the light of the whole statute in which it appears, or more particularly in the light of closely related provisions of the statute or other statutes *in pari materia*, and that what is a more or less obvious 'ordinary' or respectively 'technical' meaning ought to be interpreted in that light, with the result that even a special meaning (different from ordinary or technical meaning) may be appropriate.

4   The argument from precedent: the governing idea here is that, if a statutory provision has previously been subjected to judicial interpretation, it ought to be interpreted in conformity with the interpretation given to it by other courts. (Where there is a strict doctrine of precedent based on a hierarchy of courts, lower courts must conform; where particular weight is given to a *jurisprudence constante* of the higher courts, this would also affect the exact application of this form of argument in the system under view; in general, the argument has to be constructed appropriately to the doctrine of judicial precedent prevalent in the legal system under consideration.)

5   The argument from analogy: the governing idea here is that, if a statutory provision is significantly analogous with similar provisions of other statutes, or a code, or another part of the code in which it appears, then, even if this involves a significant extension of or departure from ordinary meaning, it may properly be interpreted so as to secure similarity of sense with the analogous provisions *either* considered in themselves *or* considered in the light

of prior judicial interpretations of them. (The argument from analogy appears to be stronger on the second hypothesis, where it incorporates a version of the argument from precedent.)

6   Logical–conceptual argument: the governing idea here is that, if any recognized and doctrinally elaborated general legal concept is used in the formulation of a statutory provision, it ought to be interpreted so as to maintain a consistent use of the concept throughout the system as a whole, or relevant branch or branches of it.

7   The argument from general principles of law: the governing idea here is that, if any general principle or principles of law are applicable to the subject matter of a statutory provision, one ought to favour that interpretation of the statutory provision which is most in conformity with the general principle or principles, giving appropriate weight to the principle(s) in the light of their degree of importance both generally and in the field of law in question.

8   The argument from history: the governing idea here is that, if a statute or group of statutes has over time come to be interpreted in accordance with an historically evolved understanding of the point and purpose of the statute or group of statutes taken as a whole, or an historically evolved understanding of the conception of rightness it embodies, then any provision of the statute or group of statutes ought to be interpreted so that its application in concrete cases is compatible with this historically evolved understanding of point and purpose or of rightness.

3   Teleological/Evaluative Arguments

9   The argument from purpose: the governing idea here is that, if a general point and purpose are ascribable to a particular statutory provision or to the whole statute of which it forms part, the statutory provision ought, within limits, to be interpreted so that its application in concrete cases is compatible with the postulated point and purpose. Point and purpose are evaluational at least in the sense that they provide a ground for evaluating one interpretation as better than another.

10   The argument from substantive reasons: the governing idea here is that, if there is some goal or state of affairs considered to be of value or some conception of rightness which is considered fundamentally important to the legal order, and if this can be promoted by one rather than another interpretation of a given statutory provision, then the statute ought to be interpreted so that its application is compatible with (or favourable to) securing

that goal or upholding that state of affairs or conception of rightness.

4 'Transcategorical' – Argument From Intention

11 The argument from intention: the governing idea here is that, if a relevant legislative intention about a particular statutory provision can be identified, a statutory provision ought to be interpreted so as to secure conformity with that intention of the legislature (a) in accordance with some appropriate sense of intention and (b) in respect of some element which serves as the object of intention, that is, any core element of any of the 11 argument types such as an ordinary meaning, or a general principle, or a purpose.

Each of the eleven types of argument is common in all the systems we have reviewed.

We regularly find statutes being interpreted in terms of 'ordinary meaning' or 'analogy' or 'general principle' or 'legislative intention' or the like, though there are variations in the way some of these arguments are constructed system by system, and variations in terminology and nomenclature. But how are we to understand the justificatory force of these arguments? Why do they give acceptable justifications for the conclusions they generate, and on what basis? We postpone the question about the sources of 'firepower' till later, with a mere reminder that the answer depends on underlying values. For the moment, we deal only with the conditions under which 'firing' of the arguments can happen. Under what conditions are they to be deployed? That is, where are they available? The answer to this question can be developed out of the particular way in which we have just formulated the 'governing idea' of each argument form.

For each the governing idea appears to be expressible in terms of a manner of interpretation which ought to be adopted if certain circumstances obtain. To generalize, each is formulable in the terms: 'if interpretative conditions c exist, then statutory provision p ought to be interpreted in manner m'. This involves application of an insight of Jerzy Wróblewski (see Chapter 8 above), that interpretation is an activity which itself involves guidance by normative standards of its own, what he called 'directives of interpretation'. We have some unease about his terminology, since, among other things, a 'directive' may be thought to presuppose some 'director' who issues it; but no such implication was intended by Wróblewski, who adopted the term 'directive' from Alf Ross simply as the most general and colourless expression available to refer generically to every sort of norm, rule, principle, maxim, guiding standard, presumption and the like. Subject to this caveat, we here adopt his concept. Accordingly the governing idea of each type of argument can be captured by, or expressed as, a presupposed 'directive of interpretation'. As the above illustrations make clear, such directives may be rationally reconstructed through reflection on justificatory practice in legal systems. They do not necessarily consist of some kind of already-articulated rule of positive law.

III   THE LINGUISTIC, SYSTEMIC, TELEOLOGICAL–EVALUATIVE AND INTENTIONAL VARIETIES

1   About Linguistic Arguments

Each of our directives stipulates particular interpretative conditions. The satisfaction of these conditions depends, of course, on the facts of given cases. Where the conditions do not exist, the relevant directive lacks application, that is, it is simply not available, and therefore contributes nothing to justifying the interpretation given. In very general terms, the interpretative condition for the 'ordinary meaning' type of argument is that a statutory provision must be intelligible in the context of ordinary language; in that case the ordinary person's ordinary understanding of the most obvious meaning of the terms falls to be applied 'unless there is sufficient reason for a different interpretation'. Of course, many factors may operate to weaken such an argument, or even render it unavailable. When this is so, it may be said that the 'interpretative condition' for such an argument is not present. What this involves, in the case of the ordinary meaning argument, is complex and multifaceted. Thus the background linguistic conventions from which the words in the statute must draw their meaning may not wholly exclude all alternative meanings. For example, the particular words used may *to some degree* remain syntactically ambiguous or semantically ambiguous. Further, the way the words are used in the statute may cast substantial doubt on the appropriateness of the meaning that such words have in similar sentences in ordinary life. Moreover, where the statutory term is vague, the argument merely from ordinary or even from technical meaning may be relatively weak. This argument may also be weak where the statute is old, and background linguistic conventions irrelevant or obsolete. The same is true where the words used consist of evaluative terms often found in general clauses such as 'reasonable', 'dangerous', 'good faith' or the like. Even where background conventions are relatively clear (and this is by no means always the case), and even where the words are not vague or evaluative in nature, the statute (or Code!) may be drafted in rather general and abstract terms without much detail, so that the ordinary meaning is indeterminate for disposal of the particular concrete case. Even where technical language is being used, the syntactic or semantic conventions of the technical terminology may not be clear. The overall draftsmanship of the statute may also be relatively loose, thereby weakening the force of any argument from ordinary or technical meaning. Plainly a substantial essay could be written on the interpretative conditions required for viable linguistic arguments.

It is worth remarking that, whenever these issues arise in legal argumentation, it is the lawyer's understanding of what is intelligible in ordinary language or in technical language that governs the issue – in this sense, 'ordinary meaning' is as much a construct of the law as is 'legal principle'. Nothing in our account turns on the thesis or claim that there just are ordinary meanings quite apart from legal interpretational practices, or some other interpretational practices. But what is true, and is important, is that within legal interpretational practice the argument from ordinary meaning and the argument from technical meaning have in many settings perfectly clear conditions and consequences of application for resolving interpretational problems in law.

2   About Systemic Arguments

A problem, however, is that all meaning is at the deepest level dependent on the whole context of the utterance or reading of the text in view, and the degree to which the whole context is explicitly considered in reflecting on issues of meaning can have an effect on the depth of one's understanding of meaning, and thus also on the content of that understanding. But the legal system as a complex totality is a massive and crucial part of the whole context of any statute. This is reflected in the importance which attaches in law to systemic arguments (types 3–8: contextual-harmonization, precedent, analogy, logical-conceptual, general principles, history) where the particular point of the arguments is to check one's reading of a statutory provision in particular for its relation to, and for the sense it makes alongside, other relevant elements of the legal system. Here the effect of an argument reconciling a favoured interpretation of a statutory provision with its particular statutory context, or with precedent or with analogy or the standard understanding of a legal concept, or with legal principle may simply be to confirm one's reading of the most obvious understanding of 'ordinary meaning', and to strengthen the judgement that the interpretative reasoning in which one is engaged fits appropriately with its legal setting.

On the other hand, one's pursuit of the search for a sound interpretation into the whole range of systemic arguments may lead to a rejection of the interpretation which initially seems most obvious as a matter of ordinary meaning; this will lead either to the conclusion that the expression giving rise to interpretative doubt has to be taken as after all having a technical legal meaning (so a technical meaning argument comes into play), or to the conclusion that in the particular legal setting one ought to favour a meaning less obvious at first sight than that which would be generated by the unsupplemented argument from ordinary meaning — here statutory terms are given a special, albeit not a technical, sense.

It is also possible, of course, that arguments from precedent and from principle and the logic of concepts or history, or from statutory context or analogy may prima facie justify mutually inconsistent conclusions. The relative priority or strength of these reasons is then essential to justifying the interpretative conclusion to be reached. Here there will be significant system-based variables. For example, the British systems have stronger doctrines of binding precedent than most others, and these still (despite recent relaxations) apply to highest-level interpretative decisions; the French system gives special weight to arguments from general principle; in Germany, logical–conceptual arguments still appear to be regarded with more favour than elsewhere, particularly in the USA; both this and the contextual-harmonization argument, looking at one part of a statute in the light of its other parts, will be considerably affected as to weight by the quality and expertise of statutory drafting, and in the USA this appears still to be rather uneven from state to state; the argument from analogy is everywhere permissive rather than mandatory — it makes a perhaps less than obvious interpretation allowable, but not even prima facie mandatory.

3   About Teleological/Evaluative Arguments

Another important aspect of the whole context in which a statutory provision has to be read to give a fully justified interpretation of it is that which concerns the values to be realized through implementing it. Relevant arguments are arguments of value in a wide way, and they include legal consequentialist arguments of all sorts. The question here, in effect, is what the statute is for, and how interpretation of it can avoid a self-defeating quality. Such reasoning, in one of its types, is essentially teleological in a way which can be relatively neutral as to the aims and objectives favoured by the interpreter. This is the argument from purpose, 'purpose' being understood in the light of certain assumptions or presuppositions. The enactment of a statute as a deliberate act in the political arena is one which members of the legislature are assumed to put forward on the ground of its necessity for the pursuit of some aspect of justice or of public good. Regardless of any private or partisan motivation, some such publicly directed and publicly avowable end has to be presupposed as that which justifies resort by legislators to the enactment of a statute. Such an actual or imputed end is what we mean by 'the purpose' of the statute. The purpose of the statute so understood forms an evaluational ground for considering possible interpretations of its provisions, for in their concrete application such interpretations may be judged as favourable or unfavourable to realization of the postulated purpose.

A hotly disputed question in some systems concerns the proper factual basis (or interpretative conditions) for these purpose-based arguments. The issue is whose purposes should govern, and what evidence should be consulted as to purpose. It can be claimed that the only way to act with constitutionally appropriate deference to the authority of the legislature is to seek to implement as nearly as possible the exact politically justifying ends that were advocated by the real live legislators in the deliberations leading to the passing of the act. One important key to this, no doubt, is a careful reading of the statute as a whole for the light its design, structure and express provisions cast on the purpose of the enactment. But, if the real purposes of real legislatures matter greatly, there will surely also be the strongest of reasons for consulting as fully as possible the legislative *travaux préparatoires*.

On this, however, a radically different view is possible. It can be counter-claimed that the legislature is an ideal legal institution not identical with any actual human being or party or pressure group active in it, and hence the only decisions imputable to the legislature itself are those contained in acts of legislation. The purposes of statutes are to be gathered by reflecting on the rational ends attributable to an ideal legislator who in that historical and political conjuncture enacted this whole act with the provisions it makes and the design and structure it has. On this view, while *travaux préparatoires* will have some evidentiary value in elucidating the relevant historical and political background, they will have less compelling evidentiary value than in the former case. Careful study of the whole act may be more to the point – though sometimes this may reveal a legislative attempt to pre-empt the issue by including in the statute express provisions as to its purpose. A celebrated instance of this is to be found in section 1–102 of the Uniform Commercial Code in the USA.

Almost any participant in these debates will find highly tendentious any label attached to the rival views about resort to legislative purpose in interpretative argument. Following the German usage, we shall here call 'subjective purpose' that which is conceived as being the very purpose or end actually embraced by members of the legislature in the processes of legislation. 'Objective purpose' is, by contrast, that purpose imputed to the legislature as an ideally rational legislator responsible for enacting that set of provisions in those historical and political circumstances. The 'point and purpose' ascribed to a statute on the basis of the historical argument are, obviously, a special form of 'objective' purpose. Arguments can similarly be called 'subjectively teleological' or 'objectively teleological' on the basis of the same contrast.

We must repeat the caveat that some readers will find this well-established terminology rather tendentious, on just this ground: it can be contended that argument types which justify giving strong evidentiary force to *travaux préparatoires* are highly controlled and stylized; but in the USA, for example, they often themselves contain so many conflicting statements of purpose as to open again a broad range of judicial choice. Provided all this is borne in mind, it will not be objectionable or misleading to adhere to the traditional, but rather tendentious, differentiation of subjective and objective in the senses mentioned.

Earlier in this chapter we provided an illustrative sketch of the circumstantial factors figuring in what we called the 'interpretative condition' for the availability of one type of argument, that is, the argument from ordinary meaning. Though we do not purport to provide the same for each of the 11 types of argument here, perhaps one further illustrative sketch is in order. This one will be in terms of the circumstances present when one major version of the argument from the purpose of the statute is most plainly available. The argument from the purpose of the statute is most plainly available where (1) the evidence of ultimate purpose is unambiguous; (2) this purpose is clear from the face of the statute (either explicitly or implicitly); (3) there is no convincing evidence that the legislature deliberately selected implementive language that would be less than fully effective to serve the statutory purpose; and (4) the language is more consistent with the chosen interpretation (mean) than with any other interpretation. (All of this could be expanded considerably.)

Often, where there is significant doubt about the ordinary or technical meaning of the statute, one or more of the elements of the foregoing model of purposive argument will also be missing, so that there is no really forceful purposive argument. On the other hand, where there is a credible argument from ordinary or technical meaning, it is frequently also difficult if not impossible to differentiate the elements of that argument from the elements of a purposive argument. Indeed courts often remark that the ordinary or technical meaning just is the best evidence of the purposive meaning.

The argument we listed as the tenth above, that is, the argument from substantive reasons, is the one which engages most plainly and clearly the value-commitments of the interpreter. For, in this case, the weight attached to an interpretation on the ground that it favours some goal or upholds some state of affairs or concept of rightness is dependent wholly on the degree of value attached to the relevant goal or state of affairs or concept of rightness from the standpoint of economics, or political or moral principle. As noted in the previous chapter, these substantive reasons do not have to be conceived or represented as system-independent (indeed, it appears that only in the USA is there much of a practice of appeal to substantive reasons at large, independently of their location within or anchoring to the rules or principles or institutions of the legal system and, even there, as elsewhere, they are much more commonly authenticated by reference to statutes, or constitution, or governmental or other public backing). But the point is that substantive reasons carry a weight dependent on general practical reasoning or on the considered judgement of the interpreter, from the point of view of economics, politics or ethics, or all three in combination. A legal–constitutional order which, like that of Federal Germany, defers specially to arguments from natural law in certain spheres, also plainly allows a considerable place to such reasoning in its politico-ethical form even in matters of private law, commercial law or criminal law not expressly raising constitutional questions.

Wherever such argumentation occurs, and this is most often where there is no credible argument from ordinary or technical meaning, it entrusts much to the wisdom and judgement of the interpreter; whether this amounts to opening a dangerously wide door to subjective judgement by the judiciary, or simply entrusts to their judgement the resolution of fundamental and objective issues in philosophy of law and moral philosophy, is of course a question which would take us deep into metaethics. Such an inquiry lies well beyond the scope of this book.

4   About Arguments from Intention: Why 'Transcategorical'?

Finally we need to reflect upon arguments from legislative intention. A significant finding of the present project taken as a whole is that *there is no single type of interpretative argument which is exclusively determinable as the argument from intention*, though there may be a relatively predominant line of recourse to intention in any particular system at a given time. We can now readily account for this. Just as in the case of purpose so, in the case of intention, one can differentiate 'subjective' and 'objective' conceptions, depending on whether or not one ascribes to the legislature some actual subjective motivational state belonging to some individual legislator or official or group of legislators or officials. The alternative is to ascribe an intention to the legislature as a supposedly ideally rational agent uttering this statutory text with legislative intent in that historical, legal and political setting.

Further, even once the subjective/objective differentiation is made, the appeal to legislative intention in interpretative argument can then range over the whole possible range of contents of each of the other argument types we have considered; hence the 'transcategorical' quality we attach to arguments from intention. All of the following 'objects' might figure in an intention argument: that the legislature did or did not intend an ordinary meaning, or a technical meaning; did or did not intend the sense of one statutory provision to be affected by the terms of another part of the statutory text; did or did not intend to use an established legal concept in its established sense; did or did not intend to uphold or derogate from some principle of law; did or did not intend to confirm some precedent or analogy as decisive for present interpretational purposes; did or did not intend to confirm the historically evolved understanding of a certain body of law; did or did not intend the pursuit of certain purposes as purposes of the statute; did or did not intend to uphold or subvert justice or the public good according to some determinate conception. Especially where subjective intentions are involved and *travaux préparatoires* by way of legislative history are in use, evidence of actual denotative or connotative intentions of legislatures may be cited as strongly relevant. Thus, if some case or cases have been legislatively cited as paradigmatic examples of things the statute is supposed to deal with, these particular denotative intentions may be specially useful for constructing a more abstractly connotative sense of the statute's intended meaning. But again, this argument from subjective intention is one which locks onto, and supports or confirms, some one or more linguistic or systemic or teleological–evaluative types of argument.

Also the standard opposition of subjective and objective intention can also range across the subject-matters of all arguments of all the main types we have investigated. There may however be tendencies to use the appeal to intention differently in different aspects of justification.

1   In arguments of the linguistic types it is very common to find appeal made to the intention of the legislature in an objective sense: the legislature is presumed to intend what an ideally competent speaker, or an ideally rational legislator, would understand by the expressions used in the context of the given natural language. The intention of the legislature is imputed on the basis of an interpretation of the ordinary meaning of the words, rather than discovered aliunde as an independent test of their meaning. But an alternative possible argument at this level would rest upon the use of evidence, for example, from *travaux préparatoires*, that the 'ordinary meaning' was actually intended by some person or group whose actual intention is considered imputable to the institutional legislature. The appeal to 'denotative' intentions as noted above may also have particular force where subjective intentions are admitted at all.

2   In the systemic argument types, the reconciliation of a statutory provision with its systemic context can, in broad terms, be done in two ways: either by reading the legal context as having primacy, so that the best reading of the statute is that which makes the best overall sense of the system with this added element; or by reading the statute as having primacy or, more likely, something approaching coordinate standing with the rest of the system, so that the best reading of the sense of the system is that which reconciles it with the form and substance of the statute. The former style of reading is characteristic of 'objective' ascriptions of intention or purpose to the legislature, the latter with 'subjective'. In parallel, the types of systemic reason appealed to as objects of intention arguments will differ: arguments based on established principles of law commonly include allusion to the claim that the legislature cannot be presumed to intend subversion of such principles in the absence of express words to that effect; arguments based on the historical genesis of legislation in the setting of a given policy programme will impute to the legislature an actual intention to implement that programme through the enacted provision, and interpret it accordingly.

3   In the 'teleological–evaluative' types of argument (9 and 10), the same applies. The values here may be ones which are considered to belong objectively to the legal order (and such 'belonging' can be understood either in terms of natural law theory

or in terms of conventionalist, but not voluntarist, legal positivism) and hence to justify interpretations and decisions which impute to the legislature the intention to uphold fundamental values because of their fundamental character. Reasoning of this kind can be cast in terms of legislative intention or purpose — but such intentions or purposes are necessarily 'objective' ones. Alternatively arguments of value can be based on an attempt to discover actual value-commitments of real people as imputable to the legislature. These may take the form of purposes. Then any decision based on realization or promotion of such values can be presented as justifiable on the ground that the legislative intent ('subjective' intention) is thereby respected.

What all this shows is not that argument from intention is worthless, but that it is highly variable in content, indeterminate in itself and has a weight to be determined in the light of highly contentious issues in legal and linguistic theory, political philosophy and the philosophy of mind. The content of these arguments depends not only on the object of the intention involved, for example, an ordinary meaning, or a purpose and so on, but also depends upon the determination by an individual interpreter or a whole legal system in favour of or against the objective or the subjective conception of intention, either holus-bolus or on a topic-relative basis. Some systems do seem mainly committed to one or the other — Germany and the UK seem mainly wedded to objective, Sweden and the USA mainly to subjective conceptions; but, both ways, appearances may be somewhat deceptive and we suspect that disagreement about the right way to understand intention, and thus to see how it supplements or underpins other arguments, may well be endemic in all legal systems on account of the powerful appeal which each conception can exercise both in given case-contexts and at the most abstract levels of philosophical argumentation.

The weight of arguments from intention would seem, however, to be rationally affected by the objective/subjective distinction. For it is only in the case of subjective intentions that one must appeal to a ground of argument (some interpretative conditions) independent of the interpretative conditions postulated by other argument types. A subjective-intention argument for (let us say) a special rather than a more obvious ordinary language interpretation of a statute adduces some evidence of legislative intent other than the simple facts of the legal system itself. But the objective-intention argument for such a reading of the statute relies simply on the objective systemic grounding (or whatever) and thus postulates exactly the same interpretative conditions as the systemic arguments postulate. It seems as though such an argument cannot have weight independent of the systemic arguments (or relevant other arguments) onto which it is locked. On the other hand, if the objective-intention argument is taken to be the sound one, it will in its context simply cancel the force of any attempted (indeed even a well-grounded) invocation of an argument from a rival subjective-intention. As will be explained shortly, cancellation should not be confused with outweighing. Objective-intention arguments might lack independent weight, but that might leave them quite capable of cancelling certain other arguments, and thus buttressing the force of the arguments onto which they are locked.

IV   DEPLOYING THE ARGUMENTS – FROM SIMPLE TO COMPLEX FORMS

We have suggested that each argument type is such that an instance of that type is deployable whenever certain conditions ('interpretative conditions') obtain. This is also expressible in Wróblewskian terms as dependent on relevant directives of interpretation. Whatever the justificatory force of an argument belonging to a given type, it exerts that force only when the interpretative conditions of its governing idea are satisfied.

The case, however, is very often more complex than that in which the conditions for but one type of argument are realized. Arguments of more than one type can easily come into play in any situation of interpretation. We need, therefore, to consider both the possibility of a simple form or pattern of overall argument in which essentially only one argument of one type is deployed in the court's opinion and the possibility of different forms or patterns of complex argumentation where the court brings to bear a plurality of arguments on a single problem of interpretation. Chapter 12 has already drawn attention to the variety such complex forms to be found in the justifications offered for interpretative decisions. Here we commence again with the simplest case.

1   The Single-argument Form

This is the form or pattern of argumentation in which an interpreter advances a single argument as sufficient for justifying an interpretation of a given statutory provision and thus for justifying the decision of a case where that provision applies. For this to be an acceptable form of argument, it must of course be the case that the relevant interpretative conditions exist. But that will not entail that they exist uniquely. It could be that the conditions exist for other arguments of other types to be deployed, but that the court takes no explicit (or even implicit) account of this. If ever the single-argument form is to be found in the accepted practice of a legal system, then it seems this licenses interpreters to ignore the possibility of invoking arguments of different types, so long as an acceptable interpretation based on a single argument can be given.

It must at once be added that Chapter 12 in fact not merely reveals widespread acceptance of recourse to this single-argument form, but also reveals that it is in fact very common, in particular in respect of interpretative arguments of the linguistic type. The concept which seems best suited to accounting for this is perhaps that of the 'permissive sufficiency' of the argument-types in question. (We are not sure if only linguistic arguments are subject to permissive sufficiency; perhaps the argument from precedent, and maybe others as well, can in some systems also be treated as permissively sufficient.) The point is simply that the system permits recourse to a single argument as justificatorily sufficient, without requiring any inquiry into possibilities of conflicting relevant arguments and perhaps allowing any weak conflicting arguments (that is, ones which do not rise above some rather low implicit threshold of persuasiveness) to be dismissed without express rebuttal.

This is not, however, the only possibility. Even where it is permissible to treat one argument as sufficient, others may be added; and sometimes, where arguments conflict, it is not acceptable to ignore this. More complex argument forms have now to be considered.

2   The Cumulative-arguments Form

This is the first complex form to consider. In legal justification, arguments are not always, and certainly should not always be, deployed singly. It is common that more than one is applicable in a single situation. This might on occasion be no more than a case of coinciding arguments, where a variety of mutually independent arguments all separately justify the same conclusion. But it can be, and often is, the case that arguments cumulate rather than merely coincide. Where this happens the force of the whole may be transformed into something much greater than the mere sum of coinciding parts. Context-harmonization, precedent, analogy and legal principle, for example, might all operate as favouring a particular interpretation, for example in respect of a question whether social security legislation should be interpreted as requiring (or even allowing) the payment of a widow's pension to the widow who has murdered her late husband, or killed him by some lesser form of homicide. Such arguments might in turn cumulate with (or − see below − conflict with) either of the linguistic arguments. Further there might be arguments from statutory purpose or from substantive values or conceptions of rightness, which in addition cumulatively reinforce the case for the favoured interpretation (or, respectively, conflict with it). Moreover, either in the subjective or in the objective form, an argument from legislative intention might back up (or conflict with) a conclusion from any of the other argument types. As we saw, though, an intention argument can probably be regarded as cumulating with others only when deployed as a matter of subjective intention. What should be obvious is that a genuine cumulation of arguments enhances the weight of the case for the interpretation favoured in a manner quite absent from cases of merely coinciding arguments. This cumulation thus cannot be (as it were) a merely additive matter; the mere number of arguments for or against a given interpretation is not decisive in itself.

Even in cases where all the serious arguments lead to the same conclusion, there may be reason to state all the arguments in full to show their full cumulative strength, or with acknowledgement that they are merely coinciding. This may be for institutional reasons (for example, discouraging an appeal) or for political/constitutional ones, where courts wish to make clear that their decisions are based not on partisan preference but on strong legal grounds; or it may be for other reasons of style or of legal rhetoric, or to make clear to defeated parties the full weight of the case against their interpretation of the law.

3   The Conflict-setting Forms

It is very common that a plurality of arguments can be deployed, yet these justify rival interpretations. Here the situation is one of conflicting 'first-order' interpretations and arguments. The question how such conflict is to be settled belongs clearly to a 'second level' or order of argumentation (involving Wróblewskian second-level directives of interpretation). *It is an important finding of the present project that more than one form of argument is involved at this level.* As was said in Chapter 12 above any argument may be shown to be inapplicable (unavailable) or cancelled or overridden or outweighed. To explain: (a) Inapplicability − an argument is *rebutted* if it can be shown that, despite first appearances, the relevant interpretative conditions do not exist; for example, a phrase initially represented as intelligible and unambiguous in its ordinary meaning can be shown to be radically ambiguous either on syntactic or on semantic grounds. (b) Cancellation — an argument is *cancelled* if, despite its interpretative conditions being fulfilled, another applicable argument wholly nullifies its justificatory force; a special case of this, already noted, is where an 'objective intention' argument cancels a relevant subjective intention argument different in effect, and another illustration is that of an interpretation in favour of the most obvious ordinary meaning which is cancelled by a systemic argument which shows that a special, or a technical, meaning is in play. (c) Overriding and priorities — an argument can be *overridden* when some other argument takes priority over it under a priority-rule or (-canon or — maxim or -directive) established within the system; for example, a system with a strong doctrine of precedent may have a rule that an interpretation laid down in a binding precedent must be preferred to one supported by any other argument, or by certain other arguments. (d) Outweighing — an argument can be *outweighed* when, although its interpretative conditions are satisfied, its force is not cancelled, and it is not overridden by virtue of a priority-rule, there is nevertheless a counter-argument leading to a different interpretation which counts as a weightier argument in the prevailing circumstances; for example, it may be the case that an ordinary meaning argument, even one linked with a contextual-harmonization argument, leads to a different interpretation than one supported by an argument from general legal principle, and the argument from principle carries the greater weight (for example, cases involving statutory requirements for legal validity of wills, where ordinary meaning requires implementation of the will even in favour of the testator's murderer, but respect for the principle that wrongdoers may not profit from wrongdoing justifies interpreting the statute as subject to a tacit exception in such a case). The whole topic of conflict-settling, especially in the weighing mode, requires much further work. We can only stress here that what really carries the weight may not be so much the arguments themselves as the values which underlie them; again, of this more later.

It seems clear that, in cases of conflicting arguments, at any rate where the issue is one of the relative weight of arguments, as where we consider a question of outweighing (but not one of cancellation or of priority-governed overriding), the cumulation of arguments may be of considerable importance. For the relative weight of one interpretation in preference to another is conditioned by the weight, or cumulative weight, of the arguments supporting it. In systems in which conflicts of arguments are acknowledged, and the conflicts are explicitly resolved by the judges, it is to be expected that any cumulation of arguments either way will be quite explicitly considered, and the reason for the preference given to one interpretation over another in the light of the cumulative arguments will be made clear. (Of course, this does not always occur in such systems, desirable though it be.) Sometimes it may be that a statement of cumulative arguments for one side only, without explicit statement of rival arguments, amounts to a tacit recognition of the fact that there were strong arguments the other way, even though the reason for considering them outweighed is left unstated.

In a work of this kind it is clearly impossible to produce any standard set of second-order criteria by way of conflict-settling argument forms valid across all legal systems. Differences of approach to the relative weight of ordinary meaning arguments have been noted, different doctrines of precedent, different approaches to analogy, different conceptions of purpose and of intention ('objective' versus 'subjective' in both cases). So one cannot construct or reconstruct any general scheme of priorities in the case of overriding, or any general principles either of cumulation of weights of argument, or of conditions of outweighing. But we have significantly established that what is in issue is by no means always a simple issue of the relative weights of rival arguments. Sometimes the case is one of showing interpretative conditions to be unfulfilled (rebuttal), sometimes it is a matter of cancellation, sometimes of priority-governed overriding. Even where it is a matter of relative weight, weighing does not proceed simply at large, but only with due regard to the cumulative weight of different arguments in their whole context.

Wróblewski's theory of 'directives of interpretation', which we mentioned above, suggests that there has to be at least a second level or order of such directives. While each of the directives formulated earlier as expressing the governing idea of each argument type generates in itself a justifying argument for a corresponding interpretation in a concrete case, none has of itself anything to say about cancellation, or overriding, or cumulative or relative weight. To construct (or rationally reconstruct) a complete picture of interpretation as justification one would require to work out a set of second-order directives of interpretation prescribing the conditions in which: any argument is cancelled by another which does not otherwise contribute to justifying the finally chosen interpretation; any argument which is material to justifying the chosen interpretation takes priority over any specified or all other arguments; a weight is ascribable to a given argument in itself, and in cumulation with other arguments. Clearly this would be a complex task for any system, and there would be significant variations at least of detail between different legal systems. The different country-by-country chapters suggest that no system has yet succeeded in establishing any very clearly articulated picture of the law at this level, though the USA chapter goes further in setting out directives or maxims about cancellation, overriding priorities and relative weights (including cumulative weights) than any other. Here we indicate the general nature of the problem as a basic second-order problem of justification and leave it to future efforts of ourselves or others to take the matter further.

V   A GENERAL MODEL OF THE INTERACTION OF INTERPRETATIVE ARGUMENTS

The conclusion of the last section was inevitably a cautious one. But that does not preclude our proceeding to construct at least a relatively simple and perhaps sketchy general model of the interaction of interpretative arguments. The model we propose here exploits the general distinction of argument types into the four broad categories of linguistic, systemic, teleological-evaluative and transcategorical. The model also leads us towards inquiring about the values which underlie each of these broad categories. As is shown in the next section, this gives essential insights into the justificatory force of arguments of the various types, insights which would be essential to any more substantial attempts at building a more detailed model of priorities and preferences among different arguments of different types.

In this model, the first three of our categories form the ground for a *prima facie* ordering of arguments. When the interpretative conditions for linguistic arguments are satisfied, these arguments should be tried out prior to consideration of any other arguments; one should move to considering systemic arguments only after a preliminary scrutiny of the output of linguistic ones, and only if there is some reason to doubt the satisfactoriness of the linguistically derived interpretation; likewise, one should move to the teleological-evaluative arguments (if at all) only after scrutiny of the former two. The transcategorical argument(s), as the name suggests, range variably over this ordering. Resort to arguments from intention should take the form of a cumulation with some other argument, either to confirm the *prima facie* ordering of arguments, or (depending on the cumulative effect of regard to intention in a given case) to show a particular reason for departing from it.

This *prima facie* ordering seems to follow intelligibly from a

principle of economy of interpretative effort. If linguistic considerations (considerations of ordinary language or, respectively, technical language) do support one clear interpretation of a statutory
provision, it is justifiable to apply the provision in that interpretation, unless some reason is evident for proceeding to a more
complex mode of argumentation. Again, if for adequate reasons
one does proceed to the systemic level of argumentation, and this
generates a clearer or more satisfactory interpretation, that can
justifiably be applied as an operative interpretation without special
inquiry as to purposes or values. In some systems, it is indeed
rather rare for argumentation to proceed explicitly to consideration of purposes or values (except, perhaps, where 'intention'
arguments based on *travaux préparatoires* introduce a purposive
element). Where purpose or value is invoked, the point is usually to
justify a cancellation or outweighing of a *prima facie* acceptable
interpretative argument based either on purely linguistic grounds,
or some combination or cumulation of linguistic and systemic;
proceeding to this level of argumentation is not appropriate save
where considerable weight is ascribed to the purposes or values at
stake.

The relevance of arguments from intention to this model is that
they provide, as noted, one significant element in the considerations that can be brought to bear for departing from the *prima facie*
ordering here stated. One way to justify departing from the normal
order would be if that were done in order to fulfil a clear legislative
intention, either 'subjective' or 'objective' depending on the
accepted theory of the best construction of legislator's intention.

The model is, then, an agreeably simple one; it can be expressed
thus:

(a) In interpreting a statutory provision, consider the types of
argument in the following order:

(i)   linguistic arguments;
(ii)   systemic arguments;
(iii)   teleological-evaluative arguments;

(b) Accept as *prima facie* justified a clear interpretation at level (i)
unless there is some reason to proceed to level (ii); where level (ii)
has for sufficient reason been invoked, accept as *prima facie* justified
a clear interpretation at level (ii) unless there is some reason to
move to level (iii); in the event of proceeding to level (iii), accept as
justified only the interpretation best supported by the whole range
of applicable arguments.

(c) Take account of arguments from intention and other transcategorical arguments (if any) as grounds which may be relevant

for departing from the above *prima facie* ordering.

This model is of course very simple and (even if acceptable so far as it goes) leaves open many key questions about priorities and relative weights in interpretative argument, both as between the categories, and as between different types within them. The model may be considered as embodying three Wróblewskian directives of interpretation, (a), (b), and (c). They are clearly second order directives, giving guidance about the proper application of the first order directives, or of the aguments they guide. As such, they are what Wróblewski calls 'procedural' directives, for they provide *prima facie* guidance about the order in which one should apply first order arguments, not about the weight (etcetera) that one should ascribe to them. Even so, the model does establish a *prima facie* preference to the extent that it authorises the interpreter to take no account of certain sorts of argument when those earlier in line for consideration generate a clear interpretation, unless some sufficient reason appears to disturb that order. So we can establish at least the beginnings of a rational schema for interpretative arguments as justifications for practical legal decisions.

Still obscure, however, are the grounds for the claim that interpretation functions *as justification* in the legal setting. Does it? Why does it? Our suggestion is that arguments of all the types and categories we have considered rest upon and implement values of special significance in legal order. To explore these values is to see why interpretative arguments belong within the class of justifying arguments. It is also to discover the outlines at least of the grounds for the ordering in this model, and, more generally, for ascribing different relative weight to different arguments of the various types in particular concrete legal settings, or for according to some standing priority over others.

VI   UNDERLYING VALUES

This section must vindicate the concluding claim of the last one, that values form the ultimate level of justification of interpretative arguments and of their underlying directives of interpretation. Our claim is that interpretative arguments have genuine justificatory force to the extent that they are grounded in values, particularly the underpinning values of legal and constitutional order. These are of course controversial at least in detail. Yet in the preceding chapter we have seen that there is a good deal of similarity among systems belonging to significantly different legal, constitutional and political traditions, similarity sufficient to make plausible the simple model sketched above. So it may be that there is after all a measure of consensus across systems about the general underlying values of legal order as such.

The first step towards making out this case requires consideration of the linguistic types of argument. Why is it that legislation just as written down ought to be applied, simply on the basis of what it seems most obviously to mean in ordinary, or respectively technical, language? The answer seems obvious for any contemporary legal system, indeed for any system that acknowledges legislation at all.

In all the systems studied here, the linguistic aspect of interpretative justification has greatest prominence in the sense of nearly always coming first in order of consideration. Linguistic arguments are everywhere regarded as having extremely strong *prima facie* force in justification. Sometimes, no doubt, they can be resorted to in a conclusory way, rather than as expressing an argument carefully weighed against possible grounds of doubt – in effect, in such cases, the court refuses to enter fully into interpretative argument as an element in justification, but retreats behind the thesis that interpretation is after all unproblematic, or into an illegitimate use of the single-argument form. There are some grounds for supposing that the magisterial style of justificatory reasoning may particularly facilitate this evasion of arguments; but it need not do so even when that style prevails, and no system can perhaps be wholly acquitted of occasional resort to such rhetorical evasion. Anyway, the linguistic arguments are by no means in themselves evasive – there is every reason why statutes should be read simply in the context of an informed understanding of the natural language (or the technical language) in which they are written, and applied or not applied in that sense, unless some justificatory argument of the systemic or teleological-evaluative types can be shown to override an applicable linguistic argument rather than to complement it.

There is an obvious reason for all this. Legislation is, by definition, an authoritative enactment of explicitly stated rules (or 'norms'), applicable within a reasonably determinate scope of authority. The authority of the legislature is thus analytically a reason for its being obligatory upon judges (as other holders of public offices) to implement the rules enacted by it. To show that one is implementing a rule in the most appropriate interpretation of it for a given situation is to show that one is fulfilling this obligation, and hence to justify one's decision which implements the rule.

A question which might in turn be posed is what justifies the ascription of authority to the legislature. Here, in proceeding beyond the formal reason of the legislature's authority to the substantive question of the reason for that authority, one inevitably enters a realm of deliberation which might on the one hand be dubbed 'ideological', or might on the other be considered a sphere of rational practical discourse, concerning normative questions in the sphere of moral and political philosophy.

For all the systems considered in the present work, the current standard common answer to the question why the legislature's authority ought to be acknowledged seems to have three main points: (i) that the legislature is the supreme democratic body, whose decisions ought to be accepted as expressing the will of at least a majority of the people; (ii) that judicial respect for the decisions of the legislature is a necessary element in the 'separation of powers', a doctrine which requires that the lawmaker be kept distinct from the applier of the law once it is made, and that the law-applier apply the law as the lawmaker has made it, not as the law-applier might have wished to make it in his/her own right; and (iii) that the 'Rule of Law' requires clear advance determination and publication of laws before these may be applied onerously to citizens, hence a clear allocation of authority to some legislative body or bodies is essential. So democracy, the separation of powers, and the Rule of Law constitute underpinning values for simple linguistic argumentation at the level of statutory interpretation.

In this context, it should be stressed that the appeal to democracy as a standard underpinning reason that justifies the legislature's authority is always tendentious and contestable, since there are several rival conceptions of democracy, in particular as between socialist and liberal visions (and there are also differing rival versions of democracy within socialism and liberalism); it should also be stressed that it is of relatively recent provenance. The French Codes, after all, go back to Napoleon's Empire; the Swedish code even farther antedates democracy; the Finnish and the Polish originate from externally imposed systems; the German and the Italian contain elements deriving from the periods of Fascism and National Socialism respectively; the British Parliament and the US Congress have the same constitutional identity (though different internal composition) as in times when they were not in fact democratic, and when prevailing ideologies viewed the very concept of democracy with distaste and suspicion. The ideologies which underpin legislative legitimacy can change over time, while the formal authority of the legislature within the system remains the same and unimpaired through such changes. Still, the change has happened, and in the world since 1945, all the more since 1989, a sincere commitment to democratic order sustains the law now in force, whatever its past. The force of 'transcategorical' appeals to legislative intention also depends on this democratic commitment. But the whole going controversy between subjective and objective conceptions of 'intention' reflects controversy about conceptions of democracy, and about the value of democracy set against other values implicit in legal and constitutional order (or *Rechtsstaat, Etat de droit, Stato di diritto* and like ideas).

Similarly, while it may well be true that the separation of powers and the Rule of Law have relatively long histories as legitimating grounds for legislative authority, in different systems and at different times they have been subject to competing and even conflicting interpretations and degrees of acceptance − notoriously, the UK exhibits at best an imperfect form of separation of powers as against France or the USA; and in France, separation of powers is held to preclude any possibility of post-enactment judicial review of legislation, while in America a different understanding of the same doctrine is held to be a part of what mandates judicial review.

A further important feature to note is that the Rule of Law is an internally complex doctrine, which is far from giving unqualified endorsement to an unfettered legislative supremacy. As well as stressing the necessity for clear ex ante legislation regulating the use of coercive power, the Rule of Law is commonly understood as setting conditions for the proper exercise of legislative power, for example banning or restricting retrospection, and stipulating reasonable generality, clarity and constancy in the law. It also sets strict conditions on the legitimacy of coercion under criminal or penal law. In general terms, respect for the Rule of Law is expressed or expressible in terms of the postulate that a legal system must exhibit, and be interpreted as exhibiting, a relatively high degree of coherence as a normative system.

In relation to statutory interpretation, the implications of such a respect for legal coherence are obvious, and are considerable. In effect, the 'systemic' aspects of interpretative or justificatory reasoning have their ground in this ideal of coherence. For a system cannot exhibit normative coherence over time unless each of its provisions is so read as to be compatible (so far as possible) with relevant others. System-coherence is the vital underpinning value of the systemic arguments. A corollary of great importance is the value of overall intelligibility of law to a rational and reasonably well-informed citizen. This is a matter on which no contemporary system of law has anything on which to congratulate itself. Even well-informed lawyers now have to be specialists, and general understanding of law risks becoming more and more attenuated.

Even so, the importance of system-coherence is brought home by the part played in interpretation by systemic arguments. No system appears to or could operate without common recourse to systemic argumentation, either to resolve persistent doubt at the level of ordinary or technical meaning, or to generate such doubt and to resolve it in favour of some systemically more appropriate meaning. It would be inept, even if it were possible, to refrain from reading legal texts in the context of the legal ordering to which they belong; even the 'ordinary meaning' argument has this context behind it, for it is the legal context that sometimes makes it particularly appropriate to refrain from importing legal technicality into legal interpretation, while at other times making exactly this further recourse necessary or desirable. What are variable, however, are the priorities or relative weights attaching to the types of systemic arguments or legal rules, maxims, directives or canons of interpretation to which appeal may be made, and the relative weighting accorded to them. Here we have found considerable variation between systems, and indeed within systems, where there has been variation over time, and variation as between different legal subject matters. But in all, a very high regard is evidently paid to the need for coherence in the law as interpreted.

On some analyses of coherence, the appeal to coherence requires an identification of the deeper values embodied in the rules and principles in force within the system. Coherence is exhibited precisely in the interpretation and maintenance of the system so that it secures a relatively ordered and structured scheme of political, social and human values. Over and above this perhaps necessary reference to fundamental system-values in any discussion of coherence, it is also arguable that the justificatory power of law depends on a commitment of the system as implemented by its officials to substantive human values fundamental in character. Modern German law, at least in the Federal Republic, has expressed a rather strong commitment to fundamental values derivable from theories of natural law. The German *Grundgesetz* incorporates six basic principles the substantive content of which radiates through the interpretative process to inform the reading of all statutes. The natural rights tradition detectable in American constitutional jurisprudence is susceptible of a not dissimilar reading; and it may be that the *Droits de l'Homme et du Citoyen* in France, and perhaps more pallidly, the European Human Rights Convention elsewhere, have similar effects. A common law tradition of jealous regard for individual rights may again be weaker, but is not to be overlooked. The paper guarantees of the socialist countries have since the revolutions of 1989 shown a capability to become system-values with a real cutting edge, as the Polish report in this book suggests. Similar progress has been witnessed in the re-emergence of democratic government in Argentina.

In any event, whether interpreted as systemic values bearing on coherence in law, or as transcendental values shaping the legal and constitutional order from without, basic human values both play a part in underpinning the commitment to implementing statute law and yet at the same time place constraints on acceptable interpretations thereof. If there are statutes which cannot be, or simply are not, interpreted so as to exhibit consistency with values considered fundamental for the law, its legitimacy and justificatory power are thereby weakened.

Hence it is not surprising that we are able to identify, alongside the linguistic, the systemic, and the transcategorical, a teleological/ evaluative set among the arguments which can justify decisions through interpretation of statutes. To read a statute, even in a somewhat strained way, so as to save or even advance some legislative purpose or some fundamental value, is clearly to sustain the justificatory force of the statute itself, given, of course, the relevant interpretation and relative weighting of the relevant purpose or value.

Admittedly, the greatest variation between systems is in this aspect, concerning (at least) the degree of explicitness with which teleological or evaluative arguments are stated in judicial opinions as grounds for interpretative conclusions, and thus for the decision authorised by the favoured interpretation in any given case. At one end of a spectrum of explicitness in this, we find the French system (least explicit), with that of the USA at the other (most explicit). A further difference concerns the readiness of courts to treat substantive reasons deployed in arguments as independent fundamental grounds of argumentation, or as grounds which are dependent upon explicit or implicit principles of the system, or rooted in the lawgiver's intention or otherwise significantly system-dependent.

The importance attached to explicit system-dependency seems to be least in the USA, with the UK not far behind. (In the famous *Holy Trinity* case, a US statute prohibiting and penalising employment contracts with aliens to bring them to work in the USA was held not to apply to a church congregation contracting with an alien to come and be their minister; this was justified partly on the ground of the special value of religion in the American way of life – though presumably not in the constitution, where religious establishment is prohibited.) Anyway, in both Britain and the USA we should recall that a case law tradition (or traditions) itself contains (or even constitutes) a background of recognised non-statutory system values. Here, what is in play is not necessarily a value system quite independent of positive law. In the USA this is further buttressed by a congeries of values such as equality and due process enshrined in the constitutional tradition and in the jurisprudence of the Bill of Rights. Even in France, which again lies at the other end of this spectrum, the laconic quality of *motifs* does not always conceal the importance of argument from values, for example, in the Conseil d'Etat decisions reported in Chapter 6 above concerning the equality of burdens to be borne by citizens under the imposition of restrictions on particular business activities for the general good.

Again, it should not be thought surprising that in all systems, there is some appeal to purposive or evaluative considerations in interpretation. For it may often be the case that a plurality of rival interpretations can be credibly supported by linguistic or systemic arguments. And sometimes, there may be an unease about the value attaching to a seemingly plain or systemically unproblematic interpretation in view of its concrete results or generic consequences. Here, doubt can lead to re-interpretation and even, in some systems and in extreme cases, to what is admitted to be *contra legem* interpretation. There can be no finally justified resolution of value-laden or value generated doubt than by express resort to relevant evaluation, that is, either purposive or more strongly evaluative argumentation.

However, no one should be led into misunderstanding by the fact that values are openly and directly deployed only in arguments of the teleological/evaluative type. It does not follow that these are the only types of argument to which important values are relevant. As we have shown, the justificatory force of all the argument types depends on fundamental legal-constitutional and political values. That there are underlying values of linguistic argumentation, systemic argumentation and argument from intention (however conceived) is absolutely plain. That these are as fundamental as any invoked in teleological/evaluative argumentation is just as clear. So any satisfactory scheme of criteria to operate in complex deployments of interpretative arguments (that is, of second-level directives) must exhibit a reflective equilibrium among fundamental values. An interpretative practice will be fully satisfactory only if it expresses such an equilibrium.

Statutory interpretation is often treated by lawyers, and all the more by philosophers of law, as a forbiddingly dry and purely formal subject. The error in this view is now plain. Interpretation is through and through a matter implicating fundamental values of the law. It can be well done only by those who study to achieve a reflective and balanced overall conception of the full set of inter-subjectively acknowledged values of the law. To say that it is in this way value-laden is the opposite of advocating a freewheeling and highly subjective approach to momentarily appealing values in interpretation; but it does acknowledge that at the deepest level there are perennially controversial issues of balancing values on which reasonable persons can and do differ. A respectable theory of interpretation presupposes a coherently thought-out view of legal values.

VII   SOUNDNESS AND UNSOUNDNESS IN INTERPRETATIVE REASONING

Our model-building is still at a relatively primitive generalized stage. Even so, we are now in a better position than before to at least sketch a general line on the soundness of interpretative reasoning in law, and hence to lay down some warnings against unsound reasoning. The soundness of interpretative reasoning depends on due regard for the underlying values of the legal order and on a consistent approach to their relative weight in themselves and in a topic-relative way. A mark of this will be a properly discriminating recourse to the types of argument, without undue neglect or inept use, either of arguments singly, or of arguments in cumulation and in conflict. The soundness of interpretative argumentation, first-level and second-level, is a vast topic which our discussions of Bielefeld in 1988, 1989 and 1990 have exposed to us in full view. But, for now, we can focus only on various vices of interpretation rather than provide a positive account of the virtues of sound interpretation in general. We turn forthwith to some of the leading vices.

1   Arguments Underused or Misused

It is a fault of interpretation to omit due consideration of an argument where its conditions of application exist, and its applicability is not cancelled by sufficient reasons. A particular illustration of this occurs when a judge ignores the argument from ordinary meaning in favour of an argument from substantive reasons, without even offering to consider the sufficiency of grounds for bypassing ordinary meaning. The values at risk here are democratic legislative supremacy and separation of powers. Due respect for linguistic arguments, especially as supplemented by systemic ones, is also required if the judiciary is not to become highly politicized.

It does not derogate from this point at all if one adds that the judiciary may as easily misuse linguistic arguments as underuse them. The vices of 'literalism' or of a 'wooden' approach to interpretation are indices of this. A judge may fail to take seriously the possibility that there can be sufficient reason to depart from ordinary meaning, or to use a special (less obvious) or technical meaning, even when this could be well grounded in systemic or teleological/evaluative considerations. Such a judge is apt to apply statutes in an overly literal and wooden way. 'Conceptualism' is the closely related vice of adhering to traditional legal–conceptual definitions and ideas (cumulating linguistic and systemic arguments) without due regard to other considerations such as those of principle and purpose. Judges may also invoke ordinary meaning interpretations in a 'conclusory' way, that is, as though the mere fact that the conditions for their application are satisfied necessarily justifies a refusal to take serious account of alternative interpretations supportable by serious counter-arguments. A conclusory approach to interpretation may be a concomitant of an unthinking 'one right answer' ideology, and one to which the magisterial style of argumentation is particularly liable. Sometimes all these related vices are lumped together as vices of 'formalism'.

There are also vices more or less peculiar to systemic argumentation. One could mention excessive preoccupation with mere consistency, over-zealous analogizing and one-sided principle-pushing (ignoring the possibility of countervailing principles bearing on a statutory scheme) as examples. In common-law countries, the scourge of unreflective retreat behind distinguishable, or only persuasive, precedents may not be what it once was in the UK, but there are warnings to be gathered from not-too-distant pasts. As for underuse, there is always a risk of reading operative sections of a statute without any sustained effort to grasp and master the whole statutory scheme of which the statute is a part. As a result contextual-harmonization arguments may be culpably overlooked or underdone.

So far as concerns teleological/evaluative arguments, the literalist and the conceptualist are almost by definition culpable under-users. It is indeed by no means necessary in every interpretational situation to go deeply into purposes or values of substance. But a general failure to regard these matters, however pressingly relevant in particular cases, is both formalistic and also objectionable for its potential effects. Legislative draftsmen can be driven by it to an excessively detailed legislative style, seeking to cover every eventuality in such a way as to compensate for judicial refusal to go an inch beyond the very words of the act taken at their most obvious. The result is a severe loss of intelligibility of statutes to the general public, and thus detriment to the Rule of Law. (The UK Law Commissions' report of 1969 on the interpretation of statutes makes this point with great force and lucidity.) Of course a different and serious infraction of the Rule of Law follows from a free-wheeling judicial attitude to statutory purpose or substantive value cut from the whole cloth of unrestrained judicial initiative and activism.

So far as concerns arguments from intention, we have noted how these lock onto other arguments of other types. An unjustifiably conclusory resort to 'intent' is one which fails to specify adequately the relevant objects of intention as these are revealed by core elements of other argument types. Another misuse, to which proponents of objective intention may be more given, is that of treating an argument from legislative intention as though it were genuinely cumulative with one from (say) ordinary meaning, when in truth the only evidence used as to intention consists of no more than the very words of the act. Subjectivists, on the contrary, may be apt to misuse extraneous evidentiary sources to establish intention, taking liberties with the leeways in *travaux préparatoires* even where the statute can be read straightforwardly in terms of ordinary meaning. This particular vice may be characterized as that of looking to the words of the act only when the *travaux préparatoires* are obscure or insufficient!

In all these matters the traditional Aristotelian counsel in favour of the middle way remains sound. Any argument type is open to over- or underuse. Virtue lies in the middle way. But how is that judged or achieved? We return to a need for reflection about and a reflective equilibrium with respect to the law's deeper underlying values. It is necessary to cultivate a thoughtful and well-balanced view of the values of democracy, separation of powers and the rule of law, together with the human values of the fundamental rights tradition. Such a balanced view would express itself in steadiness on the *via media* between under- and over-resort to some argument types without proper attention to others.

2 Faults of Complex Deployment

These occur in defective cumulation of arguments and in mishandling argumentative conflicts. So far as concerns cumulation, it is worth repeating that the force of arguments is not additive. For example, merely stringing together a disparate set of individually weak systemic arguments does not it itself amount to making a powerful cumulative case for the interpretation proffered. Concealing a weak case behind a battery of ill-assorted arguments, though perhaps preferable to the conclusory presentation of a single, or a couple of, arguments, can also evidence a failure to think through the relative weight of arguments.

Faults in the resolution of interpretational conflicts are closely related and not infrequent. We have seen the need to differentiate rebuttal of arguments, cancellation of an argument, overriding an argument on account of a priority criterion and the outweighing of an argument or cumulation of arguments. Yet it may sometimes be the case (perhaps rather commonly in the USA) that a conflict of considerations for and against an interpretation is erroneously treated as though it were a matter of simple 'weighing' of considerations. This can debase the 'weighing' metaphor, and may cloak judicial subjectivity and radical unpredictability of judgement. These abuses may go along with, or even be responsible for, underuse of linguistic arguments, which in most systems ought to be applied whenever not cancelled, or underuse of precedents in systems which attach priority to them in argument, not just some persuasive weight.

3   Presentational Faults

As the term suggests, these go more to the style of argumentation than to its substance; but the one can be the mask of the other. A lack of candour in acknowledging, or openly dealing with, the complexity of interpretational issues is one problem. Reliance on fallacious theories of language is another related source of difficulty.

The French revolutionary (or elsewhere actually Benthamite) mistrust of judiciary law-making and the connected impulse to codification generated an attitude to the possibility of clarity of statute law which has cast a long shadow. As Chapter 6 indicates, it remains a part of the official ideology of adjudication in France that the judge applies the law, but does not interpret it (though problems of the qualification or characterization of facts may abound). Other code systems appear to have been at times more or less infected with this attitude (the converse common-law vice seems to be that of overuse of 'weighing' rhetoric). Although no reader of the best French judgements can fail to be impressed with the economy and yet subtlety and detail of analysis that can be built into the ostensibly deductive and fact-classificatory, highly impersonal style of judgement, it remains to be regretted that the problems of interpretation addressed thereby are largely unacknowledged as such.

It is no defect of a code or a statute that it must be interpreted, and no vice of the judiciary that interpretation of the laws is its inexorable lot when application of written law is in hand. One of the strongest messages of the present book is that, since interpretational problems are omnipresent and all-pervasive in modern law, lawyers ought to face them openly, and to seek to be as articulate and self-critical as possible in the way they handle them. The relatively recent changes in Sweden and Finland towards fuller and fuller elaboration of reasons is a welcome sign of increasing openness in judicial attitudes. The best response to the critique that judicial justification is but façade legitimation is to falsify it with unfailing candour in the statement of reasons for decisions. It follows that, where there are truly conflicts of reasons in matters of interpretation, these are best openly acknowledged. Since the resolution of such conflicts in a sound and justifiable way is of the essence of actual justification of decisions, and since judicial decision making is fully checkable only when its grounds are openly stated, there is everything to be said, in all our systems, for a full, though not an interminably prolix (prolixity is another special common-law vice) statement of arguments, including those that resolve interpretational conflicts. Everybody knows that law-yers and judges have to argue all sides, to weigh and to evaluate. While open access to every judicial debate or squabble would be in no one's interest, there is nothing to be said in today's democratic world for a judicial attitude of *pas devant les citoyens*!

4   Reforms?

If we are even broadly right about the vices in argumentation that we have here sketched, it does not seem that any contemporary legal system enjoys a fully sound approach to interpretation, and that the vices prevalent in the various systems will tend to be rather characteristic of the system in question, correlating with institutional, cultural and other particularities noted in Chapter 12. The question which thus remains open is: what should be done about this state of affairs?

One course which might seem tempting is that of the enactment of statutes prescribing methods of interpretation and argumen-tation. This would not be a particular novelty, since many systems have tried various versions of this – see section XII of Chapters 3–11. On the other hand, there is little evidence that the existing instances of interpretative directives enacted into positive law have had very positive effects. In general it seems more probable that a widespread and critical debate involving all branches of the legal profession – and not excluding other experts, or politicians or ordinary citizens – would prove more fruitful. On the other hand, it may be that some particular practices have become so inveterate locally that change may require at least the permissive intervention of statute law. Could French courts be released from the ban on acknowledgement that laws require interpretation without some

544   Interpreting Statutes

adjustment in the opening articles of the Code Civil? Could British courts be freed to have a more open view of *travaux préparatoires* without enabling legislation? (If so, the law reform would be wise to examine most closely the Swedish practice, which organizes and controls the quantity, quality and accessibility of the preparatory materials available to the judiciary.)

However that may be, this is hardly the time or the place to be advocating particular legislation for particular places. Everywhere it is mainly understanding and attitude that matters. Openness, fairness and impartiality have been said to be the special virtues of judicial tribunals. When coupled with a deeply reflective and reflectively balanced view of the ultimate values of the legal order, they are also ideal characteristics for operative interpretation of law.

Appendix: *Final* Version of the Questions, Comparative Statutory Interpretation Project 1 November 1989

Note:

> The following is the finally agreed list of the questions formulated for each author or authorial team to answer in the relevant 'country' chapter. Each of chapters 3-11 of the present book is an attempt at explaining statutory interpretation in the relevant country by answering these questions in this order. The main sections of the Chapters are numbered accordingly.

QUESTION ZERO

Treat exactly which higher court or courts you are reporting on, the nature of the court's workload, and the rough number of cases it decides each year, including the number of opinions it writes, whether the legal system is a Code system or a Common Law system, and whether it is federal or not. This material is all preliminary background material for each of the country chapters.

ORIGINS OF ISSUES

1   What are the most important general origins of interpretational issues? (Before answering, see questions 2 and 3 below to avoid overlap.)
2   Is there a distinction between interpretation and gap-filling? If there is such a distinction, explain it in general terms. Insofar as the filling of 'gaps' is discussed within

your system, what are the most important general origins of gap-filling issues?

3   What different types of general justifying arguments in the interpretation of statutes are recognized in your system? Define any key terms such as 'literal meaning', 'contextual meaning', 'intention of legislature' (several senses, if so used) and 'purposive interpretation'.

4   What different types of general justifying arguments, if any (see no. 2 above), are recognized in the filling of gaps?

5   What are the relevant types of texts, information, social facts and other materials that are always or sometimes used (when available) by judges to give content to the types of arguments in 3 and 4 above? Can one differentiate in terms of admissibility and or persuasiveness between types of materials which the judges of the country's higher courts (a) must, (b) should, (c) may, or (d) may not, incorporate into the content of such particular arguments? Consider here such possibilities as *travaux préparatoires*, judicial precedents, foreign legal materials, academic writings, historical context, social or biological facts or other information or data, etc. But do not treat the formal sources of law here, as such. The question here is about the materials that go into the content of argument-forms.

Insofar as it is possible to generalize, indicate how common the use of each type of material is, and its general weight or significance.

6   In what general and systematic ways, if any, are conflicts between instances of different arguments (see 3 and 4 above) resolved by the judges of the country's highest courts? What patterns, if any, are there here? In choosing between conflicting arguments, do the highest courts commonly give primary emphasis to what they assume to be the *literal or ordinary meaning* of words in the statute? Or to *'contextual meaning'* (if this is different)? Or to fulfilling the *intention* of the legislator? (If so, in what sense?) Or to fulfilling the *reasonable sense* of the statute in light of its *purpose*? Or to something else? Also, consider here any rules of priority between arguments; also any use of burden of proof in choosing between arguments; also ad hoc weighing of pros and cons, and the like. Be sure to discuss any *insights* into the weighing process that the judges of the highest courts have found helpful in making decisions. In adopting general rules of priority, or in

making priority choices (weighing) do the higher courts purportedly associate any of the above approaches with a distinctive set of values or rationales? (For example, do the higher courts associate 'literal' or 'ordinary' meaning with a distinctive set of values such as protecting the interests of those who have relied on such meaning where legislative history suggesting a different meaning is not generally available, or such as confining excessive discretion of lower judges and officials? Before answering this question, read Question 7 below to avoid overlap in regard to it. Question 7 might be viewed as a special sub-class of Question 6.)

7 What *special* issues arise when statutes come into conflict with each other, or with constitutional law, or with other types of legal norms? Is resolution of these issues considered to be a matter of interpretation or gap-filling or of something else again? How are such issues generally resolved by the highest courts? In particular, if hierarchical rules of priority are applied (e.g., statute takes priority over precedent), are they interpreted and applied only literally (formally) or are they interpreted and applied also in light of the substantive considerations or rationales reflected in the conflicting statutes or norms or emergent in the circumstances? Also, do the highest courts seek to interpret statutes so to avoid conflicts with the constitution? If so, how does this affect the interpretation of statutes?

8 In the constitution, in statutes or in judicial decisions of the higher courts is there any recognition of general presumptions or background considerations that should guide judges in resolving issues of interpretation? In gap-filling? If so, give examples of the most important ones and explain how, in a particular case, the presumptions or background considerations may affect a decision importantly. Also explain how the presumption or background consideration may be rebutted or overriden. Any general factors that may affect the weight or force of such presumptions or background considerations should also be explained.

9 What is the general style and structure in which judges of the higher courts *write* opinions in cases interpreting statutes? In gap-filling? Have there been stylistic changes over time which should be commented on? If so, identify any basic changes and comment on them.

INSTITUTIONAL AND THE LIKE

10   Does the 'character' of the statute affect how courts interpret it or fill gaps in it? The concept of 'character' includes
the following topics:

a   the nature of the substantive law field of the statute,
e.g., criminal law, tax law, family law, labour law;

b   the nature of the addressees of the statute, e.g., lay
persons vs. professionals or technical persons;

c   the age and possible obsolescence of the statute;

d   whether the statute is drafted in relatively broad and
general terms (such as, but not limited to, statutes
including general clauses), or is relatively specific and
detailed;

e   whether the statute is relatively well drafted or relatively poorly drafted;

f   any other important features of the essential character
of the statute.

11   Is the general role of the courts in the system a relatively
limited role, as compared to other institutions, or a relatively expanded role? Thus, do the courts have power to
invalidate statutes as contrary to the constitution? (Not
have such power?) Does the legislature grant, or acquiesce
in large interpretational, gap-filling, and collaborative law-
making roles of courts? Small? Do courts exercise large
power to review administrative action under statutes?
Small?

12   What, if any, constitutional or statutory law is there that
specifically prescribes how statutes are to be interpreted or
gaps in them filled? (This question relates to general
method, not statutory definitions. Before answering this
question, read Questions 13 and 14 here to avoid overlap.)

13   What, if any, role do constitutional principles and values
play in interpretation or gap-filling in the higher courts?
For example, do such fundamental constitutional principles
or values as the separation of powers and the rule of law
affect interpretation and gap-filling? If so, how?

14   Does justificatory practice in the interpretation and gap-
filling decision-making of courts characteristically make
appeal to any general principles and values other than
constitutional principles and values? (For example, do
courts appeal to democratic principles and values to justify
legislative supremacy over judicial interpretation? Unlimi-
tedly,

or subject to what limits? With what bearing on interpretational practices? As a second example, is there a body of opinion that judges should, when possible, 'serve the interests of the working class'?

15   Does the 'character' of the higher courts and of their procedures affect how the judges interpret statutes or fill gaps in them? The concept of character of a court and its procedures includes:

a   whether the judges are career civil servants or are selected by political or other processes;

b   the role and function of the highest courts in the system of litigation;

c   whether the highest courts are obliged to hear all appeals, or may choose the cases to be heard;

d   whether the court relies solely upon adversarial arguments and materials submitted by the parties and their lawyers or is an autonomous body independently searching for the correct interpretation;

e   any other features of the essential character of the highest courts and their procedures.

16   How do the structure and procedures of the legislature affect the interpretation of statutes and the filling of gaps in them? Consider:

a   the effects of the structure of the legislative body and its relation to the executive on how the statute is drafted;

b   effects of political bargaining on how the statute is drafted;

c   extent of professionalism in the drafting of statutes;

d   what records of legislative deliberation are kept and are accessible to courts;

e   extent to which the legislature acts to correct judicial misinterpretations;

f   others.

17   How do features of the prevailing legal culture affect the interpretation of statutes and the filling of gaps in them? Consider:

a   the degree the culture may be characterized as formal and positivistic rather than relatively substantive and open to value and policy arguments;

b   the degree to which the legal methodology of the culture is relatively unified or, instead, fragmented, disparate or conflicting;

c   the degree the judges are influenced by academic

writings and legal dogmatics;

d   the degree of technical specialization of lawyers and judges in the various fields of law;

e   other important features of the prevailing legal culture.

COMPARATIVE

18   Are there striking or salient similarities and differences or variations in interpretational approach as between your own legal system and the other systems as reported in the papers presented by the rest of the group? (If you wish to combine your answer to this question with your answer to Question 19, you should do so.)

19   In the light of such salient similarities or differences, what *explanatory, justificatory* or *critical* comment would you offer on the interpretational approach of your own system? In particular, consider the bearing of your own answers to Questions 10–17 here. (Perhaps one merely illustrative example will be helpful here. English courts generally give more weight to interpretive arguments based on the ordinary or literal meanings of the statutory words than do American courts. The American courts tend to rely more on arguments explicitly based on what the courts consider to be the substantive purposes or rationales of the statute. Usually this involves trying to reconstruct the substantive reasoning and the reconciliation of conflicting considerations that went into the legislative judgment expressed in the statute. This does not necessarily mean that either the English or the American emphasis on ordinary meaning or the American emphasis on purpose is unjustified. Thus, the English emphasis on ordinary meaning may be justified, given such institutional factors in England (not present to the same degree in the USA) as (1) more highly professional drafting (2) executive control over statutory texts so that they embody fewer ambiguities traceable to the necessity for compromise and (3) active legislation to correct judicial misinterpretation. Such differences are all institutional.)

Of course, we must be sure we have found genuine variations between systems, before we turn to explanations for, or justifications for, or criticisms of those variations.

PATHOLOGY AND CRITICISM

20   What features of the interpretational justificatory practices
     of the judges in your country do you consider to be
     pathological? Highly subject to criticism? For example, do
     judges manipulate statutory language? Do they conceal
     value choices? Do they make bad arguments of a given
     type? What else? How common are these?

ADDENDUM

Several project members have suggested a 'problem-solution'
exercise to go into the Appendix to our book. We will discuss this
proposal at Bielefeld III.

About the Authors

Aulis Aarnio is Professor of Law at the University of Helsinki, Finland. He was educated at the University of Helsinki. His books include: *Perspectives in Jurisprudence* (Helsinki, Acta Philosophica Fennica 1983), *The Rational as Reasonable* (Dordrecht, Reidel, 1987)

Robert Alexy is Professor of Public Law and Legal Philosophy at the University of Kiel, Germany. He received his degrees from the University of Göttingen, and is the author of *A Theory of Legal Argumentation* (Oxford, Oxford University Press, 1989) a translation of: Theorie der juristischen Argumentation (Frankfurt/M., Suhrkamp, 1978/1991), and author of *Theorie der Grundrechte*, Baden-Baden 1985: Nomos (Frankfurt/M., Suhrkamp, 1986).

Zenon Bankowski is Reader in Jurisprudence at the University of Edinburgh. He was educated at Dundee and Glasgow universities. His books include: (as co-author) *Lay Justice?* (Edinburgh, T. & T. Clark, 1987) and (as editor) *Revolutions in Law and Legal Thought* (Aberdeen, Aberdeen University Press, 1991).

Gunnar Bergholz is Professor of Procedural Law at the University of Lund, Sweden. He is a former district court judge and justice of appeal. He is author of *Ratio and Auctoritas*, (Lund, 1987) and other works in the field of procedural law.

Ralf Dreier is Professor of General Legal Theory at the University of Göttingen. He was educated at the universities of Hamburg, Freiburg/Br. and Münster. His books include: *Zum Begriff der Nature der Sache* (Berlin, 1965) and *Recht-Moral-Ideologie* (Frankfurt, Suhrkamp, 1981).

Christophe Grzegorczyk is Professor of Law at the University of Paris X (Nanterre), and Professor of Legal Theory and Philosophy at two Swiss Universities: Neuchâtel and Fribourg. He was educated at the Jagellonian University of Cracow (Poland), and he received his degrees from the University of Paris II. He is the author of *Théorie générale des valeurs et le droit* (LGDJ, Paris, 1982) and the co-author of *Positivisme juridique* (Economica, 1990).

Massimo La Torre is Researcher in Legal Philosophy at the University of Bologna. He was educated at the University of Messina, and received a LL.D. degree from the European University Institute in Florence. He is the author of *La 'lotta contro il diritto soggettivo'* (Milan, Giuffrè, 1988), and the editor of N. MacCormick and O. Weinberger, *Il diritto come istituzione* (Milan, Giuffrè, 1990). He is also Assistant Editor of 'Ratio Juris. An International Journal of Jurisprudence and Philosophy of Law' published by Basil Blackwell, Oxford, Cambridge (MA).

D. Neil MacCormick is Regius Professor of Public Law, the law of Nature and Nations at the University of Edinburgh. He was educated at Glasgow and Oxford universities and holds an honorary doctorate of the University of Uppsala. His books include: *Legal Reasoning and Legal Theory* (Oxford, Oxford University Press, 1978) and (as co-author with Ota Weinberger) *An Institutional Theory of Law* (Dordrecht, D. Reidel, 1986).

Enrico Pattaro is Professor of Philosophy of Law and General Jurisprudence at the University of Bologna. He is also Founder and Editor-in-Chief of 'Ratio Juris. An International Journal of Jurisprudence and Philosophy of Law' published by Basil Blackwell, Oxford–Cambridge (MA). He was educated at the University of Bologna. His books include: *Lineamenti per una teoria del diritto* (Bologna, CLUEB, 1991), and *Introduzione al corso di filosofia del diritto*, two vols (Bologna, CLUEB: vol. 1, 2nd edn, 1991; vol. 2, 1st edn, 1987).

Aleksander Peczenik is Professor of Legal Theory at the University of Lund. He was educated in Poland and in Sweden. His books include: *The Basis of Legal Justification* (Lund, University Press, 1983) and *On Law and Reason* (Dordrecht/Boston/London, Kluver, 1989).

Robert S. Summers is McRoberts Research Professor of Law, Cornell University, and during 1991–92, Arthur L. Goodhart Visiting Professor of Legal Science, University of Cambridge. He was educated at the University of Oregon and Harvard Law School and holds an honorary degree from the University of Helsinki. His books include: *Form and Substance in Anglo-American Law* (with P.S. Atiyah) (Oxford, Oxford U. Press, 1987) and *Instrumentalism and American Legal Theory* (Ithaca, Cornell U. Press, 1982).

Michele Taruffo is Professor of Law at the University of Pavia. He was educated at the University of Pavia. His books include: *Civil Justice in Italy since 1700* (Bologna, Il Mulino, 1980) and *Adversary Civil Procedure in the American Experience* (Padova, Cedam, 1979).

Michel Troper is Professor of Law at the University of Paris X (Nanterre). He received diplomas or degrees from the Institute of Political Studies in Paris and from the University of Paris. His books include: *The Separation of Powers in French Constitutional History* (LGDJ, 2nd edn, Paris, 1980) and the co-author of *Legal Positivism* (LGDJ, Paris, 1991).

Jerzy Wróblewski was Professor of the Theory of Law and State at the University of Łódz, in which he also served terms of office as Dean of the Law Faculty, and as the Rector of the University. He took his doctorate in law at the Jagiellonian University of Kraków in 1949. His books include: *Meaning and Truth in Judicial Decision* (2nd edn, ed. Aulis Aarnio, Juridica, Helsinki, 1983) and *Sadowe Stosowanie Prawa* (2nd edn, PWN, Warsaw, 1988; English translation *The Judicial Application of Law*, eds Z. Bankowski and D. N. MacCormick, Klewer, Dordrecht, 1991 forthcoming).

Enrique Zuleta-Puceiro is Professor of Law at the University of Buenos Aires. He was educated at Mendoza and Madrid Universities. His books include: *Dogmatic Paradigm and Legal Science* (Madrid, Editorial Revista de Derecho Prwado, 1981) and *Legal Theory, A Critical Introduction* (Buenos Aires, Depalma, 1987).

Index